D1757690

WITHDRAWN
FROM
UNIVERSITY OF PLYMOUTH
LIBRARY SERVICES

The art of persuasion

University of Plymouth Library

Subject to status this item may be renewed
via your Voyager account

http://voyager.plymouth.ac.uk

Exeter tel: (01392) 475049
Exmouth tel: (01395) 255331
Plymouth tel: (01752) 232323

MANCHESTER
UNIVERSITY PRESS

90 0532610 1

P.

The art of persuasion

Political communication in Italy from 1945 to the 1990s

edited by

Luciano Cheles and Lucio Sponza

Manchester University Press
Manchester and New York

distributed exclusively in the USA by Palgrave

Copyright © Manchester University Press 2001

While copyright in the volume as a whole is vested in Manchester University Press, copyright in individual chapters belongs to their respective authors, and no chapter may be reproduced wholly or in part without the express permission in writing of both author and publisher.

Published by Manchester University Press
Oxford Road, Manchester M13 9NR, UK
and Room 400, 175 Fifth Avenue, New York, NY 10010, USA
http://www.manchesteruniversitypress.co.uk

Distributed exclusively in the USA by
Palgrave, 175 Fifth Avenue, New York, NY 10010, USA

Distributed exclusively in Canada by
UBC Press, University of British Columbia, 2029 West Mall, Vancouver, BC, Canada V6T 1Z2

British Library Cataloguing-in-Publication Data
A catalogue record for this book is available from the British Library

Library of Congress Cataloging-in-Publication Data

The art of persuasion : political communication in Italy from 1945 to the 1990s / edited by Luciano Cheles and Lucio Sponza.
p. cm.
Includes bibliographical references and index.
ISBN 0-7190-4169-4. – ISBN 0-7190-4170-8 (pbk.)
1. Communication in politics–Italy–History–20th century.
I. Cheles, Luciano. II. Sponza. Lucio.
JA85.2.I8A78 1999
303.3′75′0945–dc21 99-43346

ISBN 0 7190 4169 4 *hardback*
0 7190 4170 8 *paperback*

First published 2001

08 07 06 05 04 03 02 01 10 9 8 7 6 5 4 3 2 1

Typeset in 9.5/12.5pt FF Scala
by Graphicraft Limited, Hong Kong
Printed in Great Britain
by Biddles Ltd, Guildford and King's Lynn

UNIVERSITY OF PLYMOUTH
LIBRARY SERVICES
Item No. 9005326077
Class No. 303.370945/ART
Contl No. 0719041694

Contents

PART II Persuasion through symbolism and spectacle

Illustrations

Unless otherwise indicated, pictures 1 to 76 were taken by the author of the chapter or provided by the parties in question

Contributors

Mino Argentieri teaches history of cinema at the Istituto Universitario Orientale in Naples. His publications include: *La censura nel cinema italiano* (Editori Riuniti, 1974), *L'occhio del regime. Informazione e propaganda nel cinema del Fascismo* (Vallecchi, 1979), *L'asse cinematografico Roma-Berlino* (Libreria Sapere, Naples, 1986), *Il cinema di guerra. Arte, comunicazione e propaganda in Italia, 1940–44* (Editori Riuniti, 1998), and the edited volume *Schermi di guerra. Cinema italiano 1939–45* (Bulzoni, 1995).

Luciano Cheles is Professor of Italian Studies at the University of Poitiers. His research has focused on visual propaganda in Renaissance and twentieth-century Italy and he has curated various exhibitions on this subject. He has published *The Studiolo of Urbino. An Iconographic Investigation* (Pennsylvania State University Press, 1986), and *Grafica Utile. L'affiche d'utilité publique en Italie, 1975–1996* (Université de Lyon, 1997), and co-edited (with R. G. Ferguson and M. Vaughan) *The Far Right in Western and Eastern Europe* (Longman, 1995).

Umberto Eco is Professor of Semiotics in the Department of Communication of the University of Bologna. His recent publications include: *The Island of the Day Before* (Secker & Warburg, 1995), *The Search for the Perfect Language* (Blackwell, 1997), *Serendipities. Language and Lunacy* (Weidenfeld & Nicolson, 1998), *Kant and the Platypus* (Secker & Warburg, 1999) and *Baudolino* (Secker & Warburg, in press).

David W. Ellwood teaches in the Department of Politics, Institutions and History of the University of Bologna. He is the author of *Rebuilding Europe. The United States and the Reconstruction of Western Europe, 1945–55* (Longman, 1992), and editor of *Hollywood in Europe. Experiences of a Cultural Hegemony* (Free University Press, Amsterdam, 1994). He is currently working on the cultural dimensions of the American–European relationship in the twentieth century.

Maria Adelaide Frabotta is Chief Librarian at the Italian Prime Minister's Office. She is the author of *Gobetti editore giovane* (Il Mulino, 1988) and *Il governo filma e'Italia* (Bulzoni, 2001), which deals with government newsreels. She has published several articles on the subject in cinema, contemporary history and mass-media journals.

Pier Paolo Giglioli is Professor of Sociology of Culture in the Department of Communication of the University of Bologna. His publications include: *Rituale, interazione, vita quotidiana* (CLUEB, 1990) and *Rituali di degradazione. Anatomia del processo Cusani*, co-authored with S. Cavicchioli and G. Fele (Il Mulino, 1997). He is currently working on symbolism in political life.

Cristina Giorgetti teaches Costume and Fashion Studies at the University of Florence and the Academy of Fine Arts of Carrara. Her publications include: *Manuale di storia del costume* *e della moda* (Cantini, 1992), *Il corpo esibito. Cent'anni di sport e moda* (Arnaud, 1992) and (with E. Colarullo) *La moda maschile dal 1600 al 1990* (Octavo, 1994). Her book *Il simbolismo nell'abbigliamento. Colore, forma, decorazione* is forthcoming.

Mario Isnenghi is Professor of History at the University of Venice. His books include: *Le guerre degli Italiani. Parole immagini ricordi, 1848–45* (Mondadori, 1989), *L'Italia in piazza. I luoghi della vita pubblica dal 1848 ai giorni nostri* (Mondadori, 1994), *L'Italia del Fascio* (Giunti, 1996), *Breve storia dell'Italia unita all'uso dei perplessi* (Rizzoli, 1998), *La tragedia necessaria, da Caporetto all'8 settembre* (Il Mulino, 1999), and *La grande guerra 1914–1918*, co-authored with G. Rochat (La Nuova Italia, 2000). He edited the three-volume series *I luoghi della memoria* (Laterza, 1996–97).

David I. Kertzer is Paul Dupee University Professor of Social Science at Brown University, Providence, RI, where he is also Professor of Anthropology and History. Among his recent books are: *Sacrificed for Honor. Italian Infant Abandonment and the Politics of Reproductive Control* (Beacon, 1993), *Politics and Symbols. The Italian Communist Party and the Fall of Communism* (Yale University Press, 1996) and *The Kidnapping of Edgardo Mortara* (Knopf/ Picador, 1997).

Robert Lumley is Reader in Italian Cultural History at University College London. He has edited *The Museum Time-Machine. Putting Cultures on Display* (Routledge, 1988), and co-edited (with Z. Barański) *Culture and Conflict in Postwar Italy* (Macmillan, 1990), (with D. Forgacs) *Italian Cultural Studies* (Oxford University Press, 1996) and (with J. Morris) *The New History of the Italian South* (University of Exeter Press, 1997). He is the author of *States of Emergency. Cultures of Revolt in Italy, 1968–78* (Verso, 1990). He is currently engaged in research on Arte Povera and experimental art in Italy.

Patrick McCarthy was born in Wales of an Irish family. He studied at Oxford and Harvard. At present he is Professor of European Studies at the Bologna Center of the Johns Hopkins University, Baltimore, MD. His most recent book is *The Crisis of the Italian State* (Macmillan, 1997). He has also edited *Italy since 1945* (Oxford University Press, 2000).

David Moss teaches Italian and European Studies at Griffith University, Brisbane. He has published widely on contemporary Italy, including studies of pastoralism in Sardinia, poverty and inequality, political violence, and social and political responses to HIV/AIDS. He is currently working on an analysis of Italian society in transnational perspective and a comparison of political transformations in Italy and Poland since 1989.

Isabella Pezzini teaches Semiotics at the University of Rome-La Sapienza. She is the editor of *Semiotica delle passioni* (Esculapio, 1991) and *Semiotic Efficacy and the Effectiveness of the Text. From Effects to Affects* (Brepols Turhout, 2001), co-author (with S. Cavicchioli) of *La TV-verità. Da finestra sul mondo a panopticon* (ERI-RAI, 1993), and author of *Le passioni del lettore. Saggi di semiotica del testo* (Bompiani, 1997), *La TV delle parole. Grammatica del Talk Show* (ERI-RAI, 1999) and *Lo spot elettorale* (Meltemi, 2001). She co-edits *Versus. Quaderni di studi semiotici.*

Alessandro Portelli teaches American literature at the University of Rome–La Sapienza. His recent publications include: *The Death of Luigi Trastulli and other Stories. Form and Meaning in Oral History* (State University of New York Press, 1991), *The Text and the Voice. Speaking, Writing and Democracy in American Literature* (Columbia University Press, 1994), *The Battle of Valle Giulia. Oral History and the Art of Dialogue* (University of Wisconsin Press, 1997) and *L'ordine è già stato eseguito. Roma, le Fosse Ardeatine, la memoria* (Donzelli, 1999).

Maria Pia Pozzato teaches Textual Semiotics in the Department of Communication of the University of Bologna. She has researched on television, fashion, political discourse and popular literature. Her recent publications include: *Lo spettatore senza qualità. Competenze e modelli di pubblico rappresentati in TV* (Nuova Eri, 1995), *L'homo sapiens in TV. Riflessioni sulla trasmissione 'Numero Uno'* (Nuova Eri, 1997) and *Scrivili ancora, Sam* (Meltemi, 1999). She has edited *Estetica e vita quotidiana in Europa* (Lupetti, 1995).

Jeff C. Pratt lectures in the School of European Studies of the University of Sussex. He has worked on rural transformations and issues in economic anthropology, and published *The Rationality of Rural Life. Economic and Social Change in Tuscany* (Harwood Academic Press, 1994). He has contributed to D. Forgacs and R. Lumley (eds), *Italian Cultural Studies* (Oxford University Press, 1996) with an article on Italian Catholic culture. He is currently working on class, ethnic and regional politics in a comparative perspective.

Lucio Sponza is Professor of Italian Studies at the University of Westminster, London. His publications include: *Italian Immigrants in Nineteenth-Century Britain: Realities and Images* (Leicester University Press, 1988), *Italy. World Bibliographical Series* (Clio Press, 1995), co-authored with D. Zancani, and *Divided Loyalties. Italians in Britain in the Second World War* (Peter Lang, 2000).

Abbreviations

AC Azione Cattolica (Catholic Action)
ACLI Associazioni Cristiane Lavoratori Italiani (Christian Association of Italian Workers)
AD Alleanza Democratica (Democratic Alliance)
AN Alleanza Nazionale (National Alliance)
ANPA Associazione Nazionale per la Protezione dell'Ambiente (National Association for the Protection of the Environment)
ANPI Associazione Nazionale dei Partigiani d'Italia (National Association of Italian Partisans)
ANSA Agenzia Nazionale Stampa Associata (National Associated Press Agency)
BR Brigate Rosse (Red Brigades)
CAF Craxi–Andreotti–Forlani
CCD Centro Cristiano Democratico (Christian Democratic Centre)
CDU Cristiano-Democratici Uniti (United Christian Democrats)
CEI Conferenza Episcopale Italiana (Italian Bishops' Conference)
CGIL Confederazione Generale Italiana del Lavoro (Italian General Labour Confederation)
CGT Confédération Générale du Travail (General Confederation of Labour [France])
CIA Central Intelligence Agency
CISL Confederazione Italiana Sindacati Lavoratori (Italian Confederation of Workers' Unions)
CISNAL Confederazione Italiana Sindacati Nazionali Lavoratori (Italian Confederation of National Unions of Workers)
CLN Comitato di Liberazione Nazionale (National Liberation Committee)
CNRD Comitato Nazionale Referendum Divorzio (National Committee for the Referendum on Divorce)
COBAS Comitati di base (Rank and File Committees)
DC Democrazia Cristiana (Christian Democratic Party)
DEFA Deutsche Film Aktiengesellschaft (German Film Company)
DIA Direzione Investigativa Antimafia (Anti-Mafia Investigative Bureau)
DP Democrazia Proletaria (Proletarian Democracy)
DS Democratici di Sinistra (Left-wing Democrats)
ECA European Co-operation Administration
ECSC European Coal and Steel Community
EEC European Economic Community
EMS European Monetary System
EMU European Monetary Union

ENI	Ente Nazionale Idrocarburi (National Hydrocarbon Agency)
ERP	European Recovery Programme
EU	European Union
FGCI	Federazione Giovanile Comunista Italiana (Italian Young Communist Federation)
FUORI!	Fronte Unitario Omosessuale Rivoluzionario Italiano (Italian Unitarian Revolutionary Front for Homosexuals). The acronym also means 'Out!'.
IMF	International Monetary Fund
INCOM	Industria Nazionale Cortometraggi (National Short Film Industry)
IRI	Istituto per la Ricostruzione Industriale (Institute of Industrial Reconstruction)
LUCE	L'Unione Cinematografica Educativa (Educational Film Association)
MINCULPOP	Ministero della Cultura Popolare (Ministry of Popular Culture)
MSI	Movimento Sociale Italiano (Italian Social Movement)
NATO	North Atlantic Treaty Organization
NSC	National Security Council
P2	Propaganda 2 (Masonic Lodge)
PCI	Partito Comunista Italiano (Italian Communist Party)
PDS	Partito Democratico della Sinistra (Democratic Party of the Left)
PdUP	Partito di Unità Proletaria (Proletarian Unity Party)
PLI	Partito Liberale Italiano (Italian Liberal Party)
PMLI	Partito Marxista-Leninista Italiano (Italian Marxist-Leninist Party)
PPI	Partito Popolare Italiano (Italian Popular Party)
PRI	Partito Repubblicano Italiano (Italian Republican Party)
PSDI	Partito Social Democratico Italiano (Italian Social Democratic Party)
PSI	Partito Socialista Italiano (Italian Socialist Party)
PSIUP	Partito Socialista Italiano di Unità Proletaria (Italian Socialist Party of Proletarian Unity)
PSLI	Partito Socialista dei Lavoratori Italiani (Socialist Party of Italian Workers)
PSU	Partito Socialista Unificato (Unified Socialist Party)
RAI	Radio Audizioni Italiane (Italian Radio [and Television Corporation])
RSI	Repubblica Sociale Italiana (Italian Social Republic)
RSU	Rappresentanze Sindacali Unitarie (United [Workers'] Unions)
SAM	Squadre d'Azione Mussolini (Mussolini Action Squads)
SIFAR	Servizio Informazioni Forze Armate (Armed Forces Information Services)
Sin.Pa.	Sindacato Padania (Padania Union)
SISDE	Servizio per l'informazione e la sicurezza democratica (Democratic Information and Security Service)
SISMI	Servizio per l'informazione e la sicurezza militari (Military Information and Security Service)
SPES	Studi di Propaganda e Stampa (Propaganda and Press Studies)
UDI	Unione Donne Italiane (Italian Women's Association)
UDR	Unione Democratica per la Repubblica (Democratic Union for the Republic)
UIL	Unione Italiana del Lavoro (National Labour Union)
UQ	Uomo Qualunque (Man-in-the-Street [Party])
USIS	United States Information Services

Acknowledgements

We are grateful to Robert Lumley for his advice at the early stages of the book's conception, and to Donatella Pallotti, Fausto Sacchelli, Maurice Slawinski, and the librarians and archivists of the Istituto Gramsci of Bologna and the Archivio Audiovisivo del Movimento Operaio e Democratico, Rome, for answering numerous queries. Thanks are also due to the private individuals, institutions and photographic agencies for their kind permission to reproduce the illustrations, details of which are given on pp. vii–ix. Matthew Frost at Manchester University Press has been a supportive editor who responded sympathetically to our request that the book's original scope be expanded to cover a much wider range of forms of political communication. We are much indebted to Hélène Bellofatto for the care with which she translated the Italian chapters into English, and to David Forgacs for his helpful comments on the edited manuscript.

The book is published with the financial support of the Universities of Lancaster, Poitiers (Maison des Sciences de l'Homme et de la Société) and Westminster.

L.C.

L.S.

1

Introduction: national identities and avenues of persuasion

Luciano Cheles and Lucio Sponza

When the political unification of the Peninsula was achieved in the middle of the nineteenth century under the Savoy household, one of the protagonists, Massimo D'Azeglio, was famously alleged to have said: 'We have made Italy; now we must make the Italians.' In his memoirs, which appeared posthumously in 1867, he had actually written: 'Unfortunately we have made Italy, but we have not created the Italians.'[1] Significantly, the spurious exhortative sentence was formulated in 1896, a time of national identity crisis following the defeat of the colonial army at Adowa in Abyssinia. (Never before had Africans defeated a European 'power'.) The attributed determination to 'make the Italians' was, therefore, merely an attempt at persuasion – and self-persuasion.

As a reaction to the Adowa humiliation, nationalism was relaunched in a more aggressive style in the quest for the international recognition of Italy as a major power. It is no coincidence that this occurred at a time of acute social tensions, when the narrowly based ruling class felt threatened by the growing strength of Socialism and the entry of Roman Catholicism into the political arena as an organised force.

The transition from elitist to mass politics was rendered more difficult by the deep-rooted economic and cultural cleavages which reflected a highly fragmented society. In post-unification Italy, when government was regarded by many as a hostile agency which imposed heavy taxation and lengthy conscription upon a largely illiterate and disenfranchised population, social control was secured through the strong arm of the law. Efforts were made to instil a sense of nationhood through education, but this could yield effective results only in the long term; in the meantime, the short cut was to be provided by the rhetoric of the Risorgimento, with the emphasis on Giuseppe Garibaldi as the unassailable folk hero, on Camillo Cavour as the intelligent and wise strategist, and on Vittorio Emanuele II as the generous and brave father of a grateful nation.[2] Later, and with some hesitation because of his republicanism, Giuseppe Mazzini was added to this triumvirate as the visionary apostle of Italian nationalism. Streets and squares were promptly named after him in virtually every city and town, where statues and monuments were also erected to remind Italians who their national saviours were.[3]

Two more waves of place-naming (and renaming) occurred in the inter-war period and in the period that immediately followed the Second World War. The inter-war period may in turn be divided into two parts, roughly corresponding to the 1920s and 1930s. The names that prevailed in the earlier decade were those of places where battles had been fought in 1915–18 (e.g. the rivers Isonzo and Piave, Mount Grappa and Mount Sabotino, and the town of Vittorio Veneto – though not the town of Caporetto, where the Italian front line had collapsed in October 1917), and of military leaders and martyrs (e.g. Armando Diaz, Francesco Baracca, Cesare Battisti and Enrico Toti). In the 1930s, some military mementos of the previous decade were given Fascist and imperial names such as Corso Littorio (the *Littori* were the Fasces), Via dei Fori Imperiali and Riva dell'Impero. The toponymical revision that occurred after the Second World War was smaller in scale but ideologically more divisive: streets and squares were named after anti-Fascist leaders (e.g. Antonio Gramsci, Piero Gobetti, Giacomo Matteotti, Giovanni Amendola and Carlo Rosselli), partisans and Resistance values in general ('Libertà', 'Liberazione').[4]

To return to the less controversial figures of the Risorgimento, Garibaldi was the quintessential popular hero for all seasons. His image was initially especially cherished by the patriotic middle classes, but his was an adaptable icon, if only because the red of his famous shirt later became the symbolic colour of the workers' revolutionary movement (and of the Communist partisans, who in 1943–45 were organised into 'Garibaldi Brigades').[5] Cavour inspired admiration rather than enthusiasm; his liberalism found few followers when it needed to be converted from an elitist world-view into modern political ideology. As for the royal household, its reactionary role soon became apparent and contributed to feed the burgeoning republicanism of a substantial proportion of the population, although the country was genuinely perturbed when Umberto I, Vittorio Emanuele's son and successor, was killed by an anarchist in July 1900. This event was the dramatic culmination of a couple of years of widespread social unrest, and the point when the tide of 'the politics of repression gave way to the new exercise in conciliation and consensus'.[6] The period in question was marked by the outstanding personality of Giovanni Giolitti (Prime Minister in 1903–05, 1906–09 and 1911–14); it reached its highest point in 1912 with the granting of the so-called 'universal suffrage' (women were actually excluded; they were not given the right to vote until 1946).

Although the Giolitti years of consensual politics reduced the scope of coercive measures to secure law and order, the traditional ways of manipulating the opposition through patronage in order to obtain its support (what became known as 'transformism') were not abandoned.

This practice may have been justified by the need to secure strong leadership in the face of a factious Parliament and a heterogeneous society, but it undermined the liberal system. The latter took a further battering early in 1915 when a right-of-centre government with the support of the monarch, Vittorio Emanuele III, forced Parliament to launch Italy into war. When, by the end of 1918, the war was over and Italy was victorious, the liberal state quickly collapsed, for it was unable to cope with the exacerbated social and ideological conflict that the war years had compressed and (almost) silenced, but which thereafter spread fast throughout the country.

The electoral successes of the Socialist Party and of the newly established Popular (Catholic) Party might have provided the opportunity for a broad-based government; however, even if these parties had had such a plan (which they did not, as they were paralysed by their mutual antagonism and prejudices), they would not have succeeded. Against the 'danger' of any such political revolution, a holy alliance of the agrarian and industrial bourgeoisie, together with the urban lower middle classes and the small farmers, was bound to be formed around whomever appeared to be determined to oppose radical change – even with the use of brutal force. Mussolini and his Blackshirts duly obliged.

Fascism was not invented for that purpose, but that was the logical outcome for a movement which saw itself as the vindicator of Italy's pride, that pride which had been allegedly offended both by the 'anti-national' internal enemies (the Socialists and, to a large extent, the Catholics, who had opposed the country's entry into the war and had only half-heartedly supported the war effort), and by the 'ungrateful' former international allies (who, acting on a script written by the nationalists, would not accede to the demands for territorial expansion made by the Italian government). In any case, Giolitti himself – the doyen of liberal Italy and master of tactical persuasion – supported Mussolini, believing that the brutality of the Blackshirts was only a temporary measure, unpleasant but necessary, to save the state from the Socialist and Catholic perils.

It would be wrong to assume that under Fascism the individual and social life of Italians was dominated by coercion and brainwashing orchestrated by the propaganda Ministry, the Ministero della Cultura Popolare (irreverently nicknamed MINCULPOP) – although the extent to which the masses supported the regime remains a controversial question.[7] Suffice it to say that only since the mid-1970s, with the loosening of the rhetoric of the Resistance, has Fascism ceased to be interpreted exclusively as a repressive system imposed on a people who longed to be freed from its yoke.[8]

Whatever view one takes on this matter, there is no doubt that Fascism attempted to persuade Italians that they formed one solid and uniform nation, with undiluted genetic characteristics going back to the ancient Romans. Consensus appears to have been strengthened by the Vatican's official endorsement of the regime: Pope Pius XI notably dubbed Mussolini 'the man of Providence'. Diversity expressed through opposing political parties was regarded as the terminal disease of parliamentary democracies. A one-way dialogue with people, reinforced by the use of the radio and other media, became a mere ritual of plebiscitary assent. Economics and politics became obsolete concepts, replaced by the notions of 'corporatism' and the 'ethical state', respectively. The former was to provide the framework for economic harmony; the latter simply meant that civil society was subsumed under the state, now magnified by that awesome title.

With the military and political defeat of Fascism, the unrealistic project of forging the nation into a uniform bloc also fell apart. It then became obvious that the attempt to equate Fascism with nation was in itself a divisive construct, as the civil war of 1943–45 had demonstrated. Indeed, Fascism and anti-Fascism turned out to be a persistent ideological battleground after the end of the war, with the equally unrealistic attempts made by the anti-Fascists to have the very concept of Fascism expunged from the spirit of the nation.[9]

But even before the Republican Constitution of 1948, the most important product of anti-Fascism, was in place, the ideological and policy differences within the early post-war governments had resulted in the split between the left (the Communist Party, PCI, and the Socialist Party, PSI) and the centre-right (the Christian Democrat party, DC, and the Liberal Party). Inevitably, the confrontation could not be confined to strictly national terms of reference. Behind the left-wing parties were the values of the Resistance, the myth of the Soviet Union and the utopian dream of a classless society. The Vatican threw all its formidable weight behind the DC, which also enjoyed the no less effective support of the United States in what turned out to be the beginning of the Cold War.

The climax of political propaganda was reached in early 1948, several months after the exclusion of the PCI and the PSI from government. The first post-war parliamentary election was to be held in April that year, and nothing was spared by either side to vilify its opponent. Indeed, both sides concentrated on raising fears as to the consequences of the enemy's victory, rather than fostering the hope of a better future. Italians knew that the only material help could come from the United States, but the economic prospects were not the main concern of the election campaign. What was at stake was not only people's material well-being but their very identity. For the left, 'real' Italians were anti-Fascist and internationalists; for the centre-right, 'real' Italians were anti-Communists and Roman Catholics. The religious expression of 'patriotism' became, arguably, the most persistent battle front, if only because, with over half the electorate represented by women, it was an obvious chord to strike.

The entire parish-based Roman Catholic network was mobilised, together with *ad hoc* task forces, such as the *Comitati Civici* (Civic Committees) led by Luigi Gedda.[10] 'Italians' had to be protected from the 'alien' forces of evil personified by the allegedly atheist Communists and Socialists: 'Either Rome or Moscow!' was their rallying cry.

Three weeks before polling day, Pius XII warned Rome's inhabitants that 'the solemn hour of Christian conscience [had] sounded'. No means were spared by the Conference of Italian Bishops (CEI) to persuade voters: it was simply and solemnly stated that it was a mortal sin not to vote, or to vote 'for lists and candidates who [did] not give sufficient assurances of respecting the rights of God, the Church and mankind'.[11] Parish priests in their Sunday sermons were more explicit and named the DC candidates for whom the faithful should cast their votes. The illiterate were taken care of by Gedda's Committees, which instructed them what to do once inside the polling booth. Meanwhile, miraculous crying Madonnas were sighted throughout Italy; this was widely reported as being the sign of trepidation on the part of the best-loved icon of Catholic faith.[12]

Interestingly, only a few weeks before polling day a new series of postage stamps was launched to commemorate the 600th anniversary of the birth of St Catherine of Siena, Italy's co-patron saint, together with St Francis of Assisi. It is worth adding that the engraver, Carlo Mezzana, was a famous artist who had built his reputation by designing religious images for the Vatican, as well as Fascist iconography (mostly reproduced on stamps) for the regime.[13] Continuity between Fascism and Christian Democratic Italy was not confined to iconography. Suffice it to note that the penal and civil codes, and the regulations concerning law and order, were all retained (with minor adjustments).

The roots of the post-war ideological division, heightened by Cold War tensions, were deeply entrenched in the main subcultural strands which had emerged at the turn of the century and gathered strength in the aftermath of the First World War: the Socialist-Communist strand (against which Fascism had found its *raison d'être*) and the Catholic strand (with which Fascism had reached a mutually advantageous compromise). These two subcultures had a distinct geographical dimension, as well as a socio-cultural connotation: the Christian Democrats dominated in the north-eastern regions (Veneto, Trentino-Alto Adige, Friuli-Venezia Giulia) and were also strong in the other major northern regions (Lombardy, Piedmont and Liguria); the Socialist-Communists dominated the central regions (Emilia-Romagna and Tuscany) and were strong in the neighbouring ones of Umbria and the Marches. In Latium, the southern regions and the islands of Sicily and Sardinia conservatism prevailed, under whatever banner – be it Monarchist, neo-Fascist or Christian Democrat. Thus, when several episodes suggested that left-wing mobilisation was spreading in some districts of the southern regions and in Sicily (where, incidentally, the danger was aggravated by the actions of a separatist movement), the DC complemented its anti-Communist appeal and the use of force to quell peasant agitations with mass patronage, in order to secure continuing political support.

This particular strategy of persuasion began in 1950, when the Cassa per il Mezzogiorno (Southern Development Fund) was set up. It was to characterise the subsequent decades, even though, despite the gargantuan sums channelled through the Cassa, the government failed to stimulate a self-sustaining process of economic development in the South.[14] Indeed, it can be argued that the southern regions became more dependent upon resource transfers from the central government. The Christian Democrats (and later their Socialist partners in government) succeeded in turning the South into their power base when, in the mid-1950s, they placed their own men at the heart of virtually all the economic bodies – from banks to state holding companies. Thus patronage was institutionalised on a national scale. It became, as Patrick McCarthy has remarked, 'less a matter of individual morality than a pillar of the post-war order'.[15]

As for the industrial work force in the North, a major blow was the split of their unitary trade union, so that, in addition to the left-wing labour confederation (CGIL), a Catholic union (CISL) and a Social Democratic union (UIL) were set up; these were effectively promoted by the Vatican and the United States respectively. In extreme cases of mounting social conflict, with strikes and demonstrations, the government did not hesitate to intervene with armed police. Several workers lost their lives in various clashes.[16] A less dramatic but more effective form of dissuasion, one that avoided class confrontation, occurred in workplaces, where employers systematically victimised left-wing 'agitators'. In this they were supported not only by the Italian government, but also by the American representatives in Italy – after all, the prospective benefits of the Marshall Plan had been a persuasive factor in many electors' minds in April 1948. Decisions as to how the resources made available under the plan should be employed were left to the Italian government. However, in the mid-1950s, when the US ambassador in Rome was the enterprising Clare Boothe Luce, the Americans' attention escalated to assiduous interference.[17]

The ideological assault through the apocalyptic imagery of the late 1940s persisted into the early 1950s, when it overlapped with, and was eventually superseded by, political manipulation, and the control and distribution of economic resources in order to secure uninterrupted power.

The rapid and unbridled economic growth which occurred in the North during the 1950s and 1960s had major consequences throughout the country, as it involved profound changes in the values and attitudes which had until then sustained social and economic life. Large-scale internal migration and urbanisation (mostly from the southern towns and villages to the main cities and to the industrial North), together with the emergence of widespread consumerism, threatened to undermine the traditional values which were an important element of the Christian Democrats' conservative ideology and which had equated 'Italianness' with Catholicism. Nor did the Communist opposition fare better with the myth of the Soviet Union once the drama of the immediate post-war years gave way to the 'years of improvement'. In the mid-1950s, when the crisis of the Communist world became obvious (especially at the time of the official denunciation of Stalin, soon to be followed by the repression of the Hungarian uprising), Italy's 'economic miracle' began to materialise. As Donald Sassoon has put it:

> Images cannot be constructed in a vacuum; the strategy of the Italian Communist Party, like that of much of the Western European Left at the time, was based on the twin concept of democracy and modernity, and the USSR had failed on both counts.[18]

On the other hand, it was no coincidence that, while the Catholic Church met the challenge of world-wide secularisation by initiating a process of reform through the Second Ecumenical Council, at the level of national politics the DC opened the door of government to the PSI (1963), in an attempt to secure a parliamentary majority that might make it possible to launch a programme of bold reforms. High on the agenda were the issues of poverty in the South, the outdated educational system, and the troublesome relationship between state and citizens.

The reformist programme of the centre-left government foundered against the opposition of conservative sections of the DC. The *Contestazione*, or students' and workers' unrest, which started in the late 1960s, and degenerated into left-wing and right-wing terrorism in the 1970s, was a reaction to this failure. Thus, paradoxically, one result of the anti-authoritarian protest of the late 1960s was violence – in itself a form of persuasion through authoritarianism.

The years of the *Contestazione* coincided with the end of the post-war cycle of world economic expansion. In Italy, economic problems added to social tensions: industrial restructuring (with a shift to small firms) contributed to growing structural unemployment, which weakened the unions and the left in general. This happened just when the PCI, under Enrico Berlinguer, was offering what might have been a plausible alternative to the exhausted DC: the proposal for an alliance between the two main parties, the so-called *compromesso storico* (historic compromise). However, the Cold War had not yet come to an end, and the political situation was one of paralysis, with the PCI withdrawing into sterile isolation and the DC buttressed by the ambitious PSI led by Bettino Craxi.

At the start of the 1980s, the social movements became disoriented after the ideological intoxication of the previous decade, and turned to counter-cultural expressions which emphasised the 'private' over the 'public' sphere of human action, and concerned themselves with the environment rather than with labour issues. This political impasse and cultural shift eroded the long-held assumptions which underpinned the Catholic and Communist systems of dogmatic belief – the two dominant subcultures in post-war Italy.[19]

Lacking any vision, the party leaders in government maintained that 'governability' was their main purpose. With pragmatic credentials and demagogic ability, Craxi became the successful symbol of the 1980s. However, in order to satisfy his ambitious aim of turning the relatively small PSI into the main party of the left, to the detriment of the respected PCI, and of challenging the inanimate but still predominant DC, he launched his party on a vigorous drive to share with his senior partners in government their well-tried policy of mass patronage and extensive corruption. The budget deficit accumulated into an uncontrollable public debt, met by the Italians' high propensity to save.

Then the political and economic scenario dramatically changed. At the end of the 1980s, a decade in which the loosening of ideological differences appeared to have led to a 'near-consensus on basic principles of [Italy's] social and political system',[20] the public became more alienated as a result of the widespread political corruption. In the North, anti-system regional movements began to develop first in the Veneto region, then in Lombardy, where they were more successful, not least because of the strongly demagogic personality of Umberto Bossi. With the end of the Cold War and the transformation of the PCI into the Partito Democratico della Sinistra (PDS, later renamed Democratici di Sinistra, DS), the role of the DC as the bulwark against Communism collapsed. The degeneration of patronage into systemic corruption could no longer be accepted as the price to be paid for political stability. Furthermore, the commitment to the Maastricht blueprint for a united Europe required a severe reduction of the public debt, and triggered the monetary crisis of September 1992, when the lira (and the pound sterling) had to leave the European Monetary System – which it re-entered in November 1996.

By the early 1990s, therefore, Italy was engulfed in a political and economic storm. This was the background to Silvio Berlusconi's extraordinary success in 1994 as tycoon-turned-political saviour and leader of a new conservative movement, Forza Italia.

Berlusconi's electoral fortunes have been attributed to a number of factors: his plain and commonsensical language; his confident message that the way out of the crisis was easy and painless; his skill in forging an unlikely partnership with Alleanza Nazionale (AN) (the party born from the ashes of the neo-Fascist Movimento Sociale Italiano, MSI) and the federalist Lega Nord; the adoption of marketing techniques; and the use of his own television channels to promote his candidature in variety shows as well as political broadcasts.[21]

But none of this would have been possible without a deep feeling of frustration and anger on the part of many Italians against the 'old' system, to which the broad left also belonged. Paradoxically, that 'old' system had its origins in the anti-Fascist commitment of the post-war years. This could not be comfortably put aside, and the sudden acceptance by AN of democratic principles, without apparently experiencing any of the torment suffered by the Communists in their transformation, was viewed by many as unconvincing.

Doubts about the democratic credentials of AN have led some to question the extent to which democracy has been interiorised by Italians, given that so many of them are so easily persuaded to support people and parties which more or less overtly praise authoritarianism and intolerance.

Indeed, the very concept of national identity has been called into question, as a result of the collapse of ideological world-views and of the cry for secession by the populist leader of the Lega Nord. In retrospect, at the close of the twentieth century, it became more apparent that the causes of failed attempts to 'make the Italians', first under the post-Risorgimento liberal governments, and then under the nationalist Fascist regime, were not effectively investigated at the end of the Second World War. For the next thirty years or so, the meta-national ideologies embodied in the two juxtaposed political fronts led by the DC and the PCI dominated the public discourse. To paraphrase Giulio Bollati,[22] we can say that persuasion-oriented communication in Italy, from the mid-nineteenth century to the 1990s, has tended to consider real Italians as abstract entities, while imagining an abstract idea of Italians as real.

The present volume examines the different means through which political information has been vehicled in Italy from the early post-war period to the 1990s. It consists of two parts. The first deals with party-led forms of persuasion, while the second considers the communicative approaches of movements, organisations and institutions outside the party system.

This division is not, however, clear-cut, since parties also make their influence felt in a mediated form. Moreover, some of the chapters discuss the use of a specific medium by parties and non-parties alike. Maria Pia Pozzato's chapter on the relation between politics and fashion in the last two decades features in the second section, despite the fact that it deals almost exclusively with the dress style of professional politicians, because chronologically and thematically it cannot be separated from Cristina Giorgetti's chapter, which mostly discusses the political significance of garments worn by activists from the late 1960s to the end of the 1970s.

Chapter 2 considers the propaganda onslaught that accompanied the Marshall Plan – a propaganda promoting American values, in opposition to Communist ones, that was legitimised by a clause, signed by all the European countries involved, allowing the dissemination of 'information and news' on the functioning of the aid scheme. David Ellwood surveys the many means that were used, drawing attention to the organisers' determination to reach the widest range of target groups. He dwells especially on cinema, a very popular form of entertainment in the early post-war years, which was rightly believed to be of far greater persuasive potential than the press, the illiteracy rate being high, or the radio, given that only half of all families owned a set.

The value of cinema as a form of propaganda was also recognised by the Christian Democrat leader and Prime Minister Alcide De Gasperi, as Maria Adelaide Frabotta shows in her chapter, which deals with the newsreels and documentaries produced by the government in the 1950s for screening in cinemas before feature films. She argues that, not unlike the Fascist Luce films, with which elements of continuity can be traced, the documentaries were the expression of a centralised and paternalistic state that handed down its values from above, instead of actively involving citizens in institutional action.

Lucio Sponza discusses the Catholic Church's attempt to fill the vacuum left in the collective identity of Italian immigrants' community in Britain after the collapse of Fascism and the dissolution of the monarchy. He focuses on the role played by the periodical *La Voce degli Italiani* (first published on the eve of the crucial elections of 1948), which, though professing itself apolitical, promoted religious and ethical values, and a political stance close to those of the Italian government.

Mino Argentieri deals with the Communist Party's use of cinema for propaganda purposes. From the late 1940s to the early 1950s, despite being harassed by censorship laws, the party's film division managed to produce a handful of feature films and several documentaries. The latter were an attempt to compete with the documentaries and newsreels made by the government and by 'independent' (in actual fact mostly pro-government) companies such as INCOM. Unlike these films, however, the Communist documentaries addressed themselves to a circumscribed public: the activists and sympathisers who frequented the *case del popolo* (Communist social and cultural centres), the party branches and the *Feste dell'Unità*, where they were screened. The aim of these films was to reinforce convictions and train militants to proselytise, rather than to convert.

The production of the documentaries owed much to the personal support of Giancarlo Pajetta, who was head of the Press and Propaganda Department of the PCI from 1948 to 1957. As Carlo Lizzani has remarked, other party cadres were less convinced of their political usefulness. In the 1950s they pressed for the party to devote its energies to trying to carve a niche for itself in the nascent state television, which would have enabled it to speak to the public at large.[23]

Nevertheless, film production did not cease altogether. Documentaries continued to be made, mostly for electoral purposes,[24] and to record and commemorate special events. In the past decade the practice of showing films to public audiences has been replaced by that of making them available on video, for private use.[25]

Jeff Pratt's chapter examines the different ways in which political identities found expression in everyday life in the 1970s – a period when people's political allegiances were stable. Taking as a case study the Tuscan town of Montepulciano, he shows how judgements (e.g. comments on the aesthetics of a building or on the celebration of a wedding) and practices (the attendance of a meeting or the display of a party paper) had a ritualistic function and acted as codes that signalled one's political 'distinctiveness'. He also considers the more discreet and circumspect forms of communication that take place in the culture of clientelism, where the political identities of 'clients' are necessarily more volatile, resting as they do not on class, social position, ideology or collective interests, but on the identification of power holders who have access to specific resources.

David Kertzer also discusses the importance assumed by symbolism in political life. He focuses largely on the process that led to the transformation of the PCI into the PDS at the turn of the 1980s to draw attention to the crisis brought about by the decision to shed some of the rituals which had contributed to the identity of the party, and to the latter's attempt to create new rites in order to prevent the faction opposed to the transformation from filling the vacuum. His examination of the rituals enacted at the 1995 congress of the MSI, which was to sanction the party's conversion into AN, an allegedly modern and moderate party of the right, points to strong analogies with the PCI experience.

Mario Isnenghi's overview of the Italian press deals both with the so-called 'independent papers' (all of which, as he notes, are politically slanted, being controlled by their owners) as well as with the official papers of the main political groups.

While the exercise of political influence through papers professing independence of parties, and thus impartiality, is far from being a uniquely Italian phenomenon, the existence of a multitude of party dailies has few parallels elsewhere in Europe. It is worth remarking that these papers are not merely the reflection of a crowded political spectrum; they have proliferated as a result of a generous funding system which supports virtually any movement represented in Parliament.[26]

Luciano Cheles examines the poster as a medium of political mobilisation. He discusses the reasons for its continuing appeal, and traces its evolution in terms of style, subject matter and function from the referendum on the monarchy and the elections for the Constituent Assembly of 1946 to the parliamentary elections of 1996, dwelling on the recurrent phenomenon of 'camouflage', namely the adoption by some parties of the visual codes of ideological traditions different from, and even opposed to, their own for strategic reasons.

Isabella Pezzini reviews the changes that have occurred in the realm of televised political communication, concentrating especially on the party election broadcast, which was first introduced in 1983. She discusses the role which commercial television stations have played in the establishment of this genre, and the extent to which the 'mediatisation' of politics has led to both spectacularisation and personalisation – phenomena which reached their peak during the 1994 elections. A semiotic analysis of election broadcasts enables her to identify the distinguishing features of the persuasive approaches pursued by the main parties.

Patrick McCarthy considers the language used by the main protagonists of the Italian political scene in the post-war period. He questions the traditional view that the discourse of the 'old' regime was vacuously arcane, arguing that the vagueness and obscurity often had precise communicative purposes. He equally disagrees with the notion that the idioms of the 'new' political leaders are factual, and shows that the simplicity and directness of Bossi's and Berlusconi's populist discourses, for instance, are, in fact, shrewdly calculated and allusive.

Umberto Eco examines a cultural phenomenon of the 1970s which he calls 'meeting-mania'. After its widespread use by students and workers in the highly politicised atmosphere of 1968, the open meeting was adopted in the 1970s by a wide range of categories of people, acquiring different forms. Eco analyses the language used in the different types of meeting, and gives a tongue-in-cheek account of their workings, and of the tactics and ploys associated with them. Written in the style of a user manual aimed at the non-initiated, the chapter is a subtle denunciation of the degeneration of a political act intended for the greater participation of the public, at the hands of 'political professionals' often bent on exploiting it for their own ends.

David Moss considers the rationality of seemingly senseless acts of terrorism. He reviews the attacks that occurred from 1969, when a bomb exploded in the Piazza Fontana in Milan killing sixteen people, to the early 1980s, to interpret them as messages aimed at specific audiences (the general public, the public of a politically opposed tendency, a social and professional group, or the victims and potential victims). Backed by textual documentation (the letters and communiqués which accompanied the terrorists' actions), his survey is an original way of tracing the characteristics and evolution of right- and left-wing violence.

Robert Lumley deals with satire as vehicle of dissident values. He takes as an example the hugely successful weekly *Cuore*, which originally featured as a satirical supplement to *L'Unità* in 1989, and began to appear independently in 1991. His analysis, covering the first five years of *Cuore*'s existence, a period that was also one of the most eventful in recent Italian history, centres on the magazine's treatment of the political crisis, on its frequent use of coarse bodily humour, on its relationship with the readers, and on the general problems which satirical publications face. *Cuore* closed down in November 1996, after languishing for two years: its satire had become monotonously predictable and clichéd, often bordering on *goliardismo* (rag magazine humour). It was reborn in January 1999, under a different editorial board; however, it failed to rekindle the enthusiasm of the public and folded two years later.

Alessandro Portelli's political history of Italian songs in the post-war period – an area which has received virtually no attention from English-speaking scholars – reveals the existence of a wealth of traditions and experimentation. As well as dealing with musical expressions with an overt political content (e.g. the parodies of popular songs by Communist activists and the 'new left' revolutionaries of the

Movimento del '77; the neo-Fascist protest songs performed by skinhead bands, and the aggressive rap played at the *Centri sociali* run by collectives of young people), the author investigates the political significance of cultural phenomena such as the televised karaoke spectacles that were all the rage in the mid-1990s, and the ever popular San Remo song festival.

Cristina Giorgetti shows how the radicalisation of political strife in the years of the *contestazione* led young activists to use their appearance as signs emphasising their ideological identities. The ostentation of political commitment contrasted with the earlier attitude of treating politics as a private matter of conscience, and, as such, of keeping it from public view. The rejection of fashion, which was regarded by left-wing students as the embodiment of consumerism and wealth, led them to adopt working-class garments, with the ultimate aim of distancing themselves from the middle classes from which most of them originated.[27]

The political disenchantment and apathy that set in in the late 1970s brought the protest mode of dressing to a close. As Maria Pia Pozzato explains in her chapter, in the last two decades the quest for sartorial distinctiveness has shifted from ordinary people to professional politicians. The aims have changed too: clothes are no longer used to convey ideological allegiance but to project a specific image, one that is usually unrelated to the actual qualities of the wearer, and whose sole function is to enhance his/her electoral appeal.[28] In such a context, it is hardly surprising that when fashion conflates with political ideologies today, it is for entirely frivolous ends. In July 1994, for instance, a fashion show by the Rome designer Raniero Gattimoni featured on the catwalk models in black blouses and skirts and military-style jackets to 'reflect' the presence of the 'post-Fascists' in Berlusconi's government.[29]

It is worth adding, parenthetically, that it is not only garments that are used for political ends, but the body *tout court*. This is no recent development. Suffice it to recall the centrality of Mussolini's physical appearance in Fascist propaganda,[30] and the rituals that were enacted on his corpse by anti-Fascists and Fascists alike.[31]

In recent years, it is the naked or near-naked body that has increasingly been used for political purposes. The trend started with the 1987 parliamentary elections, when the Partito Radicale fielded the candidature of the porn star Cicciolina (her campaign included impromptu strip-teases) to draw attention to the bigotry and sexual conservatism of the mainstream parties.[32] In 1995 eight leading members of the same party, including two deputies and a senator, appeared in the nude in front of an invited audience of journalists, in a Rome theatre, in order to protest against the media's silence over the Partito Radicale's proposal for twenty referenda. Their leader, Marco Pannella, who kept his clothes on, read out a communiqué explaining that they represented 'the naked truth' and the party's 'bare' (i.e. unadorned and plain-speaking) politics. The aim was achieved, since the happening, and with it the motive of the protest, was amply reported by the press and television.[33]

This type of protest has since spread to other parties, including AN, albeit in a more restrained form. In 1996 about fifty young 'post-Fascists' stripped to their boxer shorts before the Parliament building to express their view that the financial measures introduced by Prime Minister Romano Prodi were so harsh that they would deprive them of everything but the bare essentials.[34] The articulation of ideological messages through the medium of the body may be interpreted in the light of an allegorical tradition that derives from classical antiquity, and from the Church's long-standing practice of using representations of the human figure, often unclad and sensuous, to inspire devotion, to edify and to warn.[35]

In the last chapter Pier Paolo Giglioli analyses the trials of the businessman Sergio Cusani and the prominent political figures involved in the *Tangentopoli* investigations which were broadcast from December 1993 to April 1994 on the state-owned RAI 3 channel attracting large audiences. Unlike US President Clinton's interrogations of September 1998 over the Monica Lewinsky affair, the hearings were intended to be broadcast on prime-time television right from the start (they were either recorded for subsequent broadcasting or, as in the case of the Socialist leader Bettino Craxi, screened live). The author focuses on the ways in which television altered the nature of the trial to show that what was really at issue was not the legal question as to whether the defendants were guilty or innocent, but the enactment of a ritual of degradation intended to morally destroy the old political class in order to prevent it from returning to power. This study concludes the volume because the trial was also an attempt to lay to rest the corrupt communicative practices perfected during the 'First Republic'.

Clearly, the present survey is far from exhaustive. It is worth discussing briefly other media which are used for purposes of political communication and persuasion.

Stamps (briefly mentioned earlier in this introduction), on account of their everyday use by all sections of the population and the tendency to perceive them as ideologically innocent (they are produced by a would-be neutral state, and fulfil a practical function), are a subtle, and thus more insidious, form of propaganda. The extent to which their iconography can embody government views, values and policies was shown by the late Federico Zeri in his well-known study covering the period 1850 to 1948.[36] While waiting for its sequel to be written, it is worth mentioning one recent, albeit extreme, example of philatelic indoctrination. In late 1994, to commemorate the fiftieth anniversary of the end of the Second World War, the AN Minister of Postal Services, Pinuccio Tatarella, commissioned a series of nine stamps which caused national outrage when they were issued in March 1995 (by which time Lamberto Dini's 'technocratic' government had taken over from Berlusconi's) because of the absence of any mention of the Resistance or the Liberation. The stamps featured war episodes (some represented in the heroic naturalism style dear to the graphic artists of the last few years of Fascism) that occurred before 1944.[37]

As for more overt forms of party communication, the illustrated membership cards are especially worthy of study. Though their intended persuasive function may be limited (they address themselves to the converted), they are of interest because each embodies, in condensed form, an idea or value which the party deems worth stressing in a given year. Perusal of the cards used by a party over a period of time enables one to note the evolution of the image it wishes to project. Even the most cursory examination of the cards of the MSI, for instance, reveals the dramatic aesthetic and thematic shift that occurred after 1971, when the traditional Fascist motifs gave way to abstract and even high-tech imagery – a shift that reflected the (largely cosmetic) modernisation of the party undertaken by Giorgio Almirante shortly after his election as leader in 1969.[38]

The elaborate sets devised for congresses are another rich source of information on how parties wish to be perceived – by their supporters as well as the general public, since these events are televised. The spectacular designs created by Filippo Panseca in the late 1970s and in the 1980s for the Socialist Party's convention-like congresses were intended to contribute to the mythologisation of Bettino Craxi as the aggressively modern American-style leader of a party set to break the mould of Italian politics.[39]

Political merchandising – T-shirts, pens, scarves, keyholders, etc. – also play a role in a party's propaganda efforts: such mementoes help reinforce sympathisers' identification with the party and, since they are displayed for sale at events such as *feste* and rallies that are not attended exclusively by supporters, they contribute to the dissemination of its 'corporate image'. Merchandising also provides parties with a welcome source of revenue.

A case apart is the merchandising of the Lega Nord. In keeping with the party's style of campaigning,[40] it is designed to provoke, with the ultimate aim of attracting media attention. As well as the more conventional items, the Lega in fact sells bogus passports, identity cards, stamps, banknotes and coins bearing the name and insignia of Bossi's federalist and, later, independent Northern state.

The means of communication of oppositional forces at grass-roots level (students, workers, civil rights organisations, etc.) include the sit-in, the demonstration, graffiti, leaflet distribution, murals, and unauthorised posters – forms of 'invasion' of the public space *par excellence*, the street, used to draw people's attention to the very views which the authorities have tried to ignore or even suppress.[41]

In recent years two high-tech media have increasingly been adopted for political mobilisation purposes: the fax and the Internet. After providing students all over Italy in 1990 with a fast and effective means of co-ordinating their protest campaign against controversial proposals for university reform, faxing has been used by the general public to voice their outraged reaction to political events. The thousands of faxed messages and satirical drawings that flooded newspaper editorial offices, town halls and party headquarters in 1994 to protest against a decree that would have curbed the magistrates' power of arrest in corruption cases (July), Berlusconi's attacks on the *Mani Pulite* operations (October), and the resignation of the magistrate who led the legal onslaught, Antonio Di Pietro (December), functioned as a tumultuous virtual demonstration in a piazza which the media duly reported (and indeed sometimes encouraged by providing *ad hoc* fax numbers).[42]

As for the Internet, as well as being used by parties to provide official information on their own organisation, views and activities, it is exploited by political groups to communicate with one another instantly in order to exchange information, compare experiences, work out common strategies and activities (such as a 'net strike'),[43] and even instigate, in a macabre game, the 'virtual assassination' of right-wing politicians.[44]

What surprises one about Italian political campaigning is its intensity and the variety of media used. An important factor accounting for this has been the presence of so many parties and movements, all seeking to attract attention, assert their point of view and differentiate themselves from one another. The strongly polarised nature of political conflict (the traditional opposition between the Communist and anti-Communist forces, and, more recently, the confrontation between the centre-right and the left/centre-left alliances) has added considerable virulence to the propaganda battles.

Another factor is the electoral immobility that typified Italian politics particularly up to the early 1980s, an immobility resulting largely from the existence of strong subcultures (which produced 'loyalty votes') and from the clientelist practices of the government coalition parties (which delivered large blocs of 'exchange votes'): to attempt to defy such constraints vast propaganda arsenals needed to be deployed by the parties – although, with regard to the DC and the PSI, one might take a more cynical view and argue that their showy campaigns were frequently designed not so much to win over votes from other territories as to conceal the corrupt practices that were the pillars of their power systems.[45]

The quantity and range of propaganda produced would not of course have been possible without the availability of substantial funding – both legal and illegal.[46] It is worth remarking that the successive laws on party finance that were passed after the electoral system was reformed on a largely majoritarian basis to foster political alliances (laws No. 515 of 10 December 1993, No. 2 of 2 January 1997 and No. 157 of 3 June 1999), like the earlier ones, provided for funds to be allocated in proportion to the number of votes received at election times. Thus parties have continued to be encouraged to devise propaganda promoting their individual viewpoints and interests, and to compete with one another.

It should also be noted that, despite the fact that in the referendum of 19 April 1993 over 90 per cent of votes cast were in favour of the abolition of public financing of parties for both campaigns and organisations, parties have not ceased to be well funded by the state.[47] The latest law is particularly munificent: it apportions for the parliamentary and regional elections a 'reimbursement' of 4,000 lire for each voter, actual and potential alike (the sum fixed by the 1993 law, on which the 1999 law is largely modelled, was 1,600 lire), and for the European elections the sum of 3,400 lire (instead of 800 lire).[48] It remains to be seen whether this bonanza will be spent by parties to improve communication with the subjects and widen the latter's participation in public life, or mostly to bolster their own image in the interests of self-preservation and the advancement of their political agendas.

NOTES

1 S. Soldani and G. Turi (eds), *Fare gli italiani. Scuola e cultura nell'Italia contemporanea* (Bologna, Il Mulino, 1993), vol. I, p. 17 of the editors' introduction. See also the perceptive observations by G. Galasso in *Italia. Nazione difficile* (Florence, Le Monnier, 1994), chapter 1.

2 C. Pirovano (ed.), *Modern Italy. Images and History of a National Identity* (Milan, Electa, 1982), vol. I, chapter 1, 'Risorgimento Myth and the Exaltation of Unity', with contributions by various authors.

3 See B. Tobia, *Una patria per gli italiani. Spazi, itinerari, monumenti nell'Italia unita, 1800–1900* (Bari and Rome, Laterza, 1991), especially chapter II.

4 S. Raffaelli, 'I nomi delle vie', in M. Isnenghi (ed.), *I luoghi della memoria. Simboli e miti dell'Italia unita* (Bari and Rome, Laterza, 1996), pp. 215–42.

5 On the many interpretations put upon the figure of Garibaldi see M. Isnenghi, 'Garibaldi', in *id.* (ed.), *I luoghi della memoria. Personaggi e date dell'Italia unita* (Bari and Rome, Laterza, 1997), pp. 25–45. Garibaldi was even appropriated by the Fascists: see C. Fogu, 'Fascism and "Historic Representation". The 1932 Garibaldian Celebrations', *Journal of Contemporary History*, special issue *The Aesthetics of Fascism*, 31:2 (1996), pp. 317–45.

6 J. A. Davis, *Conflict and Control. Law and Order in Nineteenth Century Italy* (Basingstoke, Macmillan, 1988), pp. 343–4.

7 The idea of consensus under Fascism was forcefully argued by R. De Felice in *Mussolini il Duce. Gli anni del consenso, 1919–36* (Turin, Einaudi, 1974). The publication of the volume was followed by an acrimonious debate, at the end of which a comprehensive and balanced argument was provided by G. Quazza, *Resistenza e storia d'Italia* (Milan, Feltrinelli, 1976). See also G. Belardelli, 'Il "consenso"', in *id. et al.*, *Miti e storia dell'Italia unita* (Bologna, Il Mulino, 1999), pp. 133–41.

8 The weakening of the rhetoric of anti-Fascism and the Resistance was brought about by the experience of terrorism in the 1970s (and the consequent rejection of violence as a means to achieve political ends), the concurrent general crisis of the left (the PCI in particular) and the irritation of the younger generation at the obsequiousness of official commemorations. See G. De Luna and M. Revelli, *Fascismo/Antifascismo. Le idee, le identità* (Florence, La Nuova Italia, 1995), p. 155; C. Pavone, *Alle origini della Repubblica. Scritti su Fascismo, antifascimo e continuità dello Stato* (Turin, Bollati Boringhieri, 1995), pp. 189–90; C. Dellavalle, 'Resistenza', in B. Bongiovanni and N. Tranfaglia (eds), *Dizionario storico dell'Italia unita* (Bari and Rome, Laterza, 1996), pp. 778–83.

9 In actual fact a firm proposition was eluded from the onset. Though clause XII of the 'Transitory and final provisions' contained in the constitution of 1948 prohibited the 'reorganisation of the former Fascist Party under any form whatsoever', when, at the end of 1946, the blatantly neo-Fascist Movimento Sociale Italiano was founded, no serious attempt was made to outlaw it, nor was it done later. This was probably wise, as an aura of illegality might have strengthened the party, instead of weakening it; however, the conflict between reality and legality was evident.

10 P. Hebblethwaite, 'Pope Pius XII. Chaplain of the Atlantic Alliance?', in C. Duggan and C. Wagstaff (eds), *Italy in the Cold War. Politics, Culture and Society, 1948–58* (Oxford, Berg, 1995), pp. 72–5. For a first-hand account of the campaign of the Civic Committees see L. Gedda, *18 aprile 1948. Memorie inedite dell'artefice della sconfitta del Fronte Popolare* (Milan, Mondadori, 1998). Gedda was also the leader of *Azione Cattolica* (Catholic Action), an umbrella organisation co-ordinating several Catholic associations, whose aim was (and is) the promotion of Catholic values in society and institutions.

11 Both quotations are drawn from P. Ginsborg, *A History of Contemporary Italy. Society and Politics, 1943–88* (Harmondsworth, Penguin, 1990), p. 117.

12 C. Ginzburg, 'Folklore, magia, religione', in *Storia d'Italia*, vol. I, *I caratteri originali* (Turin, Einaudi, 1972), pp. 672–3.

13 F. Zeri, *I francobolli italiani. Grafica e ideologia, dalle origini al 1948* (Genoa, Il Melangolo, 1993), pp. 71–5, 78, 80–1.

14 J. Chubb, *Patronage, Power, and Poverty in Southern Italy. A Tale of Two Cities* (Cambridge University Press, 1982), pp. 28–54.

15 P. McCarthy, *The Crisis of the Italian State. From the Origins of the Cold War to the Fall of Berlusconi and Beyond* (Basingstoke, Macmillan, 1997), pp. 174–5.

16 The people killed included: a rice weeder who was taking part in a strike at Molinella, near Bologna – May 1949; five farm labourers who were demonstrating in support of land reform at Melissa (Calabria), at Torremaggiore (Apulia), and at Montescaglioso (Basilicata) – October–December 1949; six industrial workers who were attending a trade

union demonstration in Modena – January 1950; and four villagers who were protesting against the higher prices they were being charged for the poor water supply at Mussomeli, in Sicily – February 1954.

17 M. G. Rossi, 'Una democrazia a rischio', *Storia dell'Italia repubblicana*, vol. I, *La costruzione della democrazia*, ed. F. Barbagallo (Turin, Einaudi, 1994), pp. 979–80.

18 D. Sassoon, 'Italian Images of Russia, 1945–56', in Duggan and Wagstaff (eds), *Italy in the Cold War*, p. 190.

19 Stephen Gundle has argued that in post-war Italy four, rather than two, subcultures have prevailed: to the two with clear-cut and diametrically opposed ideological objectives he adds 'American culture', with its promise of social mobility and prosperity, and the 'culture of rebellion, pride, honour, self-assertion and invention'. See 'Sophia Loren, Italian Icon', *Historical Journal of Film, Radio and Television*, 15:3 (1995), pp. 367–85.

20 D. Hine, *Governing Italy. The Politics of Bargained Pluralism* (Oxford, Clarendon Press, 1993), p. 81.

21 See A. Lyttelton, 'Italy. The Triumph of TV', *New York Review of Books*, 11 August 1994, pp. 25–9.

22 Commenting on Vincenzo Gioberti's celebrated work *Del primato morale e civile degli Italiani* (first published in 1843), Bollati has written that, ever since, there has been a tendency 'to consider real Italians as abstract entities, and an abstract idea of Italy as real'. See 'L'italiano', in *Storia d'Italia*, vol. I, *I caratteri originali* (Turin, Einaudi, 1972), p. 960. Bollati's fine essay has been reprinted, in revised form, as a separate volume: *L'italiano. Il carattere nazionale come storia e come invenzione* (Turin, Einaudi, 1983; new edn 1998). On the question of the national identity (or identities) of Italians see also: G. E. Rusconi, *Se cessiamo di essere una nazione* (Bologna, Il Mulino, 1993); W. Brierly and L. Giacometti, 'Italian National Identity and the Failure of Regionalism', in B. Jenkins and S. A. Sofos (eds), *Nation and Identity in Contemporary Europe* (London, Routledge, 1996), chapter 8; J. Dickie, 'Imagined Italies', in D. Forgacs and R. Lumley (eds), *Italian Cultural Studies. An Introduction* (Oxford University Press, 1996), pp. 19–33; A. Schiavone, *Italiani senza Italia* (Turin, Einaudi, 1998); G. Calcagno (ed.), *L'identità degli italiani* (Bari and Rome, Laterza, 1998); E. Galli della Loggia, *L'identità italiana* (Bologna, Il Mulino, 1998); and F. Tarozzi and G. Vecchio (eds), *Gli italiani e il Tricolore* (Bologna, Il Mulino, 1999).

23 C. Lizzani, 'I film per il "Partito Nuovo"', in N. Tranfaglia (ed.), *Il 1948 in Italia. La storia e i film* (Florence, La Nuova Italia, 1991), pp. 100–1. See also M. Mida, 'Perchè sono morte le cooperative', in G. Aristarco (ed.), *Sciolti dal giuramento. Il dibattito critico ideologico sul cinema negli anni Cinquanta* (Bari, Dedalo, 1981), pp. 110–13.

24 For instance, as late as 1980, in preparation for the local elections, the PCI commissioned three short films from Ugo Gregoretti, Ettore Scola and Francesco Rosi on the theme of the city. See E. Rasy, 'Ballo, canto e, forse, voto', *Panorama*, 26 May 1980, pp. 182–7.

25 *Ciao, Enrico*, for instance, a documentary commemorating the tenth anniversary of the death of the leader Enrico Berlinguer, made with material shot by various directors (including Roberto Benigni, Bernardo Bertolucci, Gillo Pontecorvo and Ettore Scola), was released as a supplement to *L'Unità* on 11 June 1994. *Viaggio in Italia*, a video produced by a less distinguished team, which documented Romano Prodi's 1996 election campaign, was put on sale by the PDS and the other parties that made up the Olive Tree alliance just after their victory. Videos are now produced and sold by parties and movements across the full political spectrum. It should be noted that the public screening of propaganda films, which in the 1980s and 1990s tended to be treated as an obsolete form of political persuasion, was briefly revived in 1994, at the initiative of a group of politically committed directors led by Nanni Moretti. An anti-Berlusconi short entitled *L'unico paese al mondo* (The Only Country in the World), consisting of sketches directed by Francesca Archibugi, Marco Tullio Giordana, Daniele Luchetti, Mario Martone, Carlo Mazzacurati, Nanni Moretti, Marco Risi and Stefano Rulli, was in fact shown in a number of cinemas across Italy during the last week of the campaign for the parliamentary elections. See A. Samueli, 'L'unique pays au monde', *Cahiers du cinéma*, 479–80 (1994), pp. 66–7.

26 See M. Teodori, *Soldi e partiti. Quanto costa la democrazia in Italia?* (Florence, Ponte alle Grazie, 1999), pp. 129–35, 263–4. From 1994 to 1999, the papers attached to parliamentary groups received subsidies totalling around 300 billion lire (£98 million). To qualify, the papers must appear at least 240 times a year. The state's contributions are calculated on the basis of production costs and declared circulation figures. It should be noted that, despite these subsidies, in the past few years most papers have found themselves in serious financial difficulty, for the parties' undermined credibility and the weakening of political activism have had a dramatic impact on sales. Some papers (e.g. *Avanti!*) have been appearing intermittently. *La Voce Repubblicana* folded in May 1999. *L'Unità* was forced into privatisation in August 1998, but failed to be revitalised; for several months the newspaper ceased to appear on the news-stands. It was relaunched in April 2001 under the editorship of Furio Colombo, a distinguished writer and MP (Democratici di Sinistra).

27 See R. Lumley, *States of Emergency. Cultures of Revolt in Italy from 1968 to 1978* (London, Verso, 1990), p. 71.

28 The politicians' preoccupation with their image has led to the rise of a new profession, that of the 'personal photographer'. Appointed by leading politicians (especially Prime Ministers and aspiring Prime Ministers), these photographers escort them on a variety of public occasions, such as important meetings and official visits, to take pictures that present them in the most favourable light – pictures which, after the endorsement of the personalities concerned, are distributed to the press. Bettino Craxi was a forerunner in this respect: he called on the services of a personal photographer to promote his image well before he became Prime Minister – when he was still merely the leader of the PSI. Berlusconi had two photographers on his staff, as well as a personal cameraman, and a spin doctor (Mity Simonetto) who advised him on the clothes to wear and other matters concerning his appearance. Romano Prodi, too, had a personal photographer during his period as Prime Minister – the same one who had accompanied him on the 1996 campaign trail. Massimo D'Alema was only too happy to follow the trend shortly after becoming head of government in October 1998. See G. Quaranta, 'Il fotografo del potere. Sì, il Palazzo è tutto un click', *L'Espresso*, 28 January 1999, p. 60. The phenomenon in question disconcertingly reminds one of the control exerted by the Fascist regime over press photographs. See P. V. Cannistraro, *La fabbrica del consenso. Fascismo e mass media* (Bari and Rome, Laterza, 1975), pp. 195–6; *Fototeca*, 2:3 (1988), special issue on Mussolini's directives to the press; and A. Jaubert, *Making People Disappear. An Amazing Chronicle of Photographic Deception* (Washington, DC, Pergamon–Brassey, 1989), pp. 51–60.

29 J. Phillips, 'Blackshirts chic struts catwalks in the new Italy', *The Times*, 16 July 1994.

30 For Mussolini's ubiquitous 'presence' see, for instance, R. De Felice and L. Goglia, *Storia fotografica del Fascismo* (Bari and Rome, Laterza, 1982); *id.*, *Mussolini. Il mito* (Bari and Rome, Laterza, 1983); and G. Di Genova, *L'uomo della Provvidenza. Iconografia del Duce, 1923–45* (Bologna, Bora, 1997). See also Italo Calvino's interesting account of Mussolini's official portraits: 'The Dictator's Hats', *Stanford Italian Review*, 8:1–2 (1990), pp. 195–210.

31 His remains were publicly displayed in the Piazzale Loreto in Milan hanging upside down, and subjected to verbal and physical abuse, on 29 April 1945. During the night of 24 April 1946, on the first anniversary of the Liberation, they were snatched by a group of neo-Fascists. See M. Isnenghi, 'Il corpo del duce', in *id.*, *L'Italia del Fascio* (Florence, Giunti, 1996), pp. 405–19; and S. Luzzatto, *Il corpo del Duce. Un cadavere tra immaginazione e memoria* (Turin, Einaudi, 1998), both of which also deal with the 'symbolic body' of Giacomo Matteotti.

32 See anon., 'In the pink for Italy's election campaign', *The Times*, 29 May 1987.

33 C. Maltese, 'Il nude look della politica', *La Repubblica*, 22 November 1995.

34 Anon., 'I giovani di AN in mutande davanti Montecitorio', *La Repubblica*, 7 November 1996.

35 On the Church's use of nudity and the 'body beautiful' for doctrinal reasons see: C. Eisler, 'The Athlete of Virtue. The Iconography of Asceticism', in M. Meiss (ed.), *De Artibus Opuscola XL. Essays in Honour of Erwin Panofsky* (New York University Press, 1961), vol. I, pp. 82–97;

M. R. Miles, *Carnal Knowing. Female Nakedness and Religious Meaning in the Christian West* (Tunbridge Wells, Burns & Oates, 1989); S. Haskins, *Mary Magdalen. Myth and Metaphor* (London, HarperCollins, 1993); L. Steinberg, *The Sexuality of Christ in Renaissance Art and in Modern Oblivion* (University of Chicago Press, 1996, 2nd edn); R. Rambus, *Closet Devotions* (Durham, NC, Duke University Press, 1998); and J. Darriulat, *Sébastien le Renaissant* (Paris, Lagune, 1998).

36 Zeri, *I francobolli italiani*. See also G. Ottolenghi and G. Moscati, *Postal History of the Nazi Antisemitism* (Carnago [Varese], SugarCo, 1996), which deals with the Nazis' use of stamps and postmarks for propaganda purposes in Italy and elsewhere in Europe.

37 See L. Coen, 'Francobolli postfascisti', *La Repubblica*, 5 April 1995, who notes that on 14 December 1994 Tatarella had publicly expressed the wish that Italy might become a more united country through the new stamp issue.

38 Colour reproductions of the membership cards of the MSI have been provided to the editors of this volume by the party in question. For illustrations of the cards of other parties see: 'Anon. from Romagna', *Amarcord del PCI. Le tessere del Partito dal 1921 al 1991* (Ravenna, Il Monogramma, 1991); various authors, *Le immagini del Socialismo. Comunicazione politica e propaganda del PSI dalle origini agli anni Ottanta* (Rome, PSI, n.d. [1983]), pp. 370–7, 432–3, 478–9; G. Spadolini, *Tessere repubblicane. Un percorso in immagini* (Ravenna, Circolo Culturale C. Cattaneo, 1981); C. Dané (ed.), *Parole e immagini della Democrazia Cristiana in quarant'anni di manifesti della SPES* (Rome, Broadcasting & Background, 1985), unpaginated.

39 For the importance attached by the Socialists to the backdrops of their congresses see M. V. Carloni, 'Metti in scena Bettino!', *Panorama*, 14 May 1984, pp. 211–12. The article includes an informative interview with Panseca. On the Craxi myth see C. Mariotti, 'Il culto della Craxità', *L'Espresso*, 10 June 1984, pp. 137–43, which also refers to the wealth of publications that had appeared on the Socialist leader and Prime Minister by that time.

40 See A. Destro, 'A New Era and New Themes in Italian Politics: the Case of Padania', *Journal of Modern Italian Studies*, 2:3 (1997), pp. 358–77.

41 See the useful survey by U. Eco and P. Violi, 'La controinformazione', in V. Castronovo and N. Tranfaglia (eds), *Storia della stampa italiana*. Vol. 5, *La stampa italiana del neocapitalismo* (Bari and Rome, Laterza, 1976), pp. 97–172. On the individual forms of appropriation of public space see the bibliography, in the sections 'Myths, symbols and rituals', 'Graphics' and 'Language'.

42 See C. De Gregorio, 'La rabbia dell'Italia in un'ondata di fax', *La Repubblica*, 16 July 1994; anon., 'Ed il popolo del fax torna a protestare. "Attacco arrogante" ', *La Repubblica*, 7 October 1994; C. De Gregorio, ' "Mani ferite". Urla il popolo dei fax e l'Italia va in piazza', *La Repubblica*, 7 December 1994. For an analysis of this phenomenon see F. Erbani, 'Siamo tanti, siam faxisti', *La Repubblica*, 20 October 1994.

43 See *Strano Network, Net Strike. Pratiche antagoniste nell'era telematica* (Bertiolo [Udine], AAA Edizioni, 1996); and *Zip! Hot Web. Guida ai siti alternativi e radicali su Internet* (Rome, Castelvecchi, 1997). For more general (and scholarly) accounts of the use of the Internet for political mobilisation purposes see K. A. Hill and J. E. Hughes, *Cyberpolitics. Citizen Activism in the Age of the Internet* (Oxford, Rowman & Littlefield, 1998); S. Bentivegna, *La politica in rete* (Rome, Meltemi, 1999); L. Pucci, *La sfera telematica* (Bologna, Baskerville, 1999); and A. De Rosa, *Fare politica in Internet* (Milan, Apogeo, 2000).

44 See anon., 'www.ammazzateli.it', *L'Espresso*, 25 March 1999, p. 52.

45 See S. Gundle, 'Italy', in D. Butler and A. Ranney (eds), *Electioneering. A Comparative Study of Continuity and Change* (Oxford, Clarendon Press, 1992), p. 195.

46 On the funding of political parties from 1948 to the present see: G. P. Ciaurro, 'Public Financing of Parties in Italy', in H. E. Alexander, with J. Federman (eds), *Comparative Political Finance in the 1980s* (Cambridge University Press, 1989), pp. 153–71; M. Rhodes, 'Financing Party Politics in Italy. A Case of Systemic Corruption', *West European Politics*, 20:1 (1997), special issue *Crisis and Transition in Italian Politics*, pp. 54–80; and Teodori, *Soldi e partiti*.

47 The system established by the laws of 1993, 1996 and 1999 is supposedly based on the reimbursement of campaigning expenses to candidates, rather than on subsidies to parties (which the referendum had rejected). An analysis of 'reimbursements' from 1993 to 1996, however, has shown that they substantially exceeded the actual expenses incurred by candidates; the unspent amounts were retained by parties, functioning as old-style subventions. See Teodori, *Soldi e partiti*, pp. 180–1.

48 See anon., 'Soldi ai partiti, via libera alla legge', *La Repubblica*, 27 May 1999.

PART I

Party propaganda and political discourse

2

Italian modernisation and the propaganda of the Marshall Plan

David W. Ellwood

When the European countries signed up to the Marshall Plan (officially known as the European Recovery Program, ERP), in the spring of 1948, each of them accepted a clause which allowed for the dissemination within their borders of 'information and news' on the workings of the plan itself. From these premisses, barely noticed at the time, there sprang the greatest international propaganda operation ever seen in peacetime.[1] None of the sixteen countries[2] participating in the Marshall Plan was untouched by this campaign, but one in particular, because of the exceptional conditions prevailing there, saw the greatest effort of them all: Italy.

Now that what is left of Marshall Plan documentation can be freely consulted in the archives of Washington, we can discover what sort of image of Italy the Marshall Planners assigned to the country brought with them on their arrival, and what they conceived their task to be. We may then ask what variety of culture accompanied these new missionaries of the American way of life (their office in each of the participating countries was known in fact as a 'Mission'), and how they represented their subsequent impact on Italy to their Congressional and public sponsors, in their efforts to justify the continuing support of the American taxpayer.

The Italy which greeted them in 1948 must have seemed a land of baffling contradictions: post-Fascist and pre-democratic; ex-enemy and ex-'co-belligerent', republican in sentiment in the North, monarchical in the South; a supplicant at the Paris peace conference, but apparently without remorse for its part in the war; in desperate need of every aid dollar available, but without a reconstruction plan; bereft of the spiritual, political, economic or military resources needed for life in the atomic era, but already radically divided in two ideologically. It was in these terms that reality in Italy had usually been described to American public opinion by returning diplomats and military men, and above all by the correspondents of the prime newspapers of the era.

No one doubted that the Italians had shown a great will to carry forward their reconstruction process and that three years after the end of the war they had taken giant steps along the chosen path with their gifts of improvisation, dedication and hard work. But the political battle under way, and the precariousness of the economic situation, were such – no less than in other European countries; in some ways more so – that the Americans on the spot had gradually become aware, in this context too, of the inadequacy of the first-aid methods they had applied hitherto to help the Old World back on its feet. In this sense the plight of the Italians was one of the more prominent among the hard cases which had eventually produced the Marshall Plan.

The birth of that initiative signalled a qualitative change in the nature of West European–American relations, an intensification of the American commitment to Europe which in some ways corresponded to what European governments themselves had wanted the Americans to do, in some ways did not. The United States, enjoying one of the most pragmatically creative phases of its modern foreign policy history – in reaction to the partial failure of the great wartime visions of Roosevelt, the uncertainties of the first Cold War phases and the embarrassments of the Truman doctrine – had invented with the ERP a new method of projecting its power into Europe.

But in order to ensure the effectiveness of this new method, a quite new awareness was required of the contexts in which it would operate, of their historical and contemporary conditions, of the men likely to be available to carry it out, of the appropriate strategy they should adopt. Otherwise there was the risk that effort would be wasted, friends alienated, enemies on all sides encouraged. So how was the Italian situation seen by the agency called upon to administer the Marshall Plan on the ground, the European Co-operation Administration (ECA)?

Readings of Italian identity in 1948

The US ambassador to Italy, the influential career official James C. Dunn, had written to Washington in May 1947:

> The population in general and the most responsible part of the financial and industrial ruling class have completely lost faith in the government and are afraid of making new investments or of putting more money in existing ones. A flight from the lira is beginning; the inflationary spiral is unchecked. . . . Such is the shortage of food products in the country that the most serious observers are extremely worried over the risks of a general famine situation arising at some point in the coming months.

But in the ambassador's view the essential problem was obvious: 'there could easily arise a new confidence in the future if it were not for the political agitation of the Communists'.[3]

In the light of the very poor results secured by Prime Minister Alcide De Gasperi on his first-ever trip to Washington in January 1947, the promises of the Marshall Plan naturally justified new kinds of hope. But such was the gravity of the economic and social situation throughout the winter of 1947–48 that – as elsewhere in Europe – the Americans were forced to supply 'interim aid'. And here we see the first signs of an approach to the local context in conflict with that being applied by the government on the spot. The deflationary approach insisted on by De Gasperi's Christian

Democrats and their allies was simply ignored and there were new American programmes to relaunch agriculture, stimulate the South and help rebuild the transport sector. But at this point the attention of Washington began to concentrate much more intensely on the country, since the first national elections to be held under the new republican constitution were about to take place, and it was clear that a major Cold War clash was likely to break out, with each of the two major parties, Christian Democrats and Communists, backed by its respective superpower sponsor.

When the new National Security Council (NSC) had started its work in November 1947 its first paper concerned Italy, the 'pre-revolutionary' conditions said to exist there, the possibility that the Communists could come to power by legal or extra-legal means and the impression that Italy had first priority in Cominform strategy. The NSC was convinced that 'the majority of the Italian people . . . are ideologically inclined towards the Western democracies, friendly to the United States and conscious of the fact that US aid is vital to Italian recovery'. The Council was also clear that 'the prevailing economic distress' was what gave the Communists their mass support.[4]

But as the elections came nearer the emphasis in NSC deliberations changed. With a parliamentary victory appearing ever more probable, a vast propaganda effort was set in motion with a significant new clandestine dimension supplied by the CIA and a part of the American trade union movement. The official campaign included the promise of revision of the peace treaty, an appeal – signed also by Britain and France – for Trieste to be returned to Italy, and a host of publicity-winning minor gestures such as the return of Nazi-seized gold, a gift of merchant ships, and the redistribution of *Ninotchka,* Ernst Lubitsch's anti-Communist film parable of 1939 starring Greta Garbo. The State Department made it clear that Communist voters would be banned from emigration to the United States, and Marshall himself declared that, should the left win, Italy would be excluded from the benefits of the ERP.[5] But these were just elements in what turned out to be 'the most hectically fought political campaign that ever took place in Europe', according to the leading CBS journalist on the spot at the time, Howard K. Smith, writing a year later. And it was Smith who identified 'the frank, open entrance of America' into it as the most important and unprecedented factor in the entire battle.[6]

American experts in 'counter-insurgency' looked back ten years later on the Italian campaign of 1948 as opening a new era of 'psychological warfare'. They make it clear that no overall propaganda strategy existed: whatever it took to stop the left was allowed. A pattern of action emerged based on 'explanation, terror and reassurance'. Covert funding of the governing Christian Democrat party (DC) and the break-away right-wing Socialists (PSLI), began to the extent of $1 million, and there was a great effort (though not as great as Washington would have liked) to supply the forces of law and order with the equipment to face down an insurrection. The use of military force was 'never completely ruled out', writes James Miller in the most detailed study of the campaign based on American sources. In fact a number of situations were envisaged which 'would compel American military intervention'. While the US Air Force had already indicated its requirements for bases in southern

Italy, the US Navy proved adept at showing its presence at moments considered appropriate.[7]

The private campaign set in motion by the Italo-American community was even more remarkable, not least for its originality. Ten million letters and cables were sent from individual Italian-Americans 'to relatives and acquaintances in Italy begging them to vote against the Communists'. Famous stars such as Frank Sinatra and Gary Cooper recorded radio programmes; the Vatican and the American propaganda agencies United States Information Service (USIS) and Voice of America ran campaigns in parallel. 'Freedom flights' carrying air mail from America were organised with the co-operation of the US Post Office and TWA, and the red, white and blue 'Friendship Train' distributed piles of gifts gathered on its tour of America.[8]

When the uproar died down and the true impact of the conservative victory on 18 April could be measured, it became clear that not all the American plans had worked. The DC victory – for the only time in their history the Christian Democrats secured an absolute majority – was based on the mobilisation of the Vatican more than on outside aid, while the American money and support poured into the right-wing splinter group from the Partito Socialista disappeared almost without trace. In terms of international politics, the event demonstrated that the Soviet Union had done nothing to aid the PCI – refusing to surrender Trieste, renegotiate the peace treaty or aid Italy's admission to the United Nations – while the West Europeans, specifically the British and French, though willing to recognise that Italy was one of their weaker brethren, had proved powerless to come to the country's aid in its hour of need. The Americans for their part had demonstrated a quite new and infinitely ingenious capacity for projecting their power into such situations. The long-term implications of the effort did not, however, look encouraging to thoughtful commentators.

The influential economic counsellor in the American embassy, Henry Tasca, complained that the industrialists, large landowners and other elements of the ruling groups were concerned exclusively for their own immediate short-term interests, and that they were capable of any compromise rather than recognising the need for long-term reform and social modernisation.[9] The CBS commentator Howard Smith went further, denouncing America's alliance 'with social elements in Italy whose aims have nothing to do with democracy'. By such methods the United States had compromised its long-held faith in self-determination and plunged into an open-ended commitment to the Christian Democrats. Foretelling the future with accuracy, Smith declared that, without its own self-sustaining reform process, the country would be 'an object of our charity for many years to come'.

Like most American observers Smith was convinced that democratisation as such was not a problem:

> I know of no people in Europe who so painfully want to be democratic. They have had their dictatorship, and it is my firm impression that from right to left the whole people is deathly sick of it. . . . But the naked circumstances of earning a livelihood are against them.

In eloquent detail Smith went on to list the age-old problems of overpopulation, underdevelopment, poverty and alienation between North and South, and showed how badly the impact of world war and civil war had compromised the fragile web of improvisation which alone had conserved stability up to that time. 'The social consequences of this dire struggle of man against man for jobs and survival inside Italy are obvious,' Smith went on, echoing long-standing American official analyses of politics throughout Southern and Central Europe:

> It induces the privileged to hold on blindly to every advantage they possess in the struggle; to the point, if necessary, of supporting right-wing dictatorship to guard it for them. In desperation it drives the poor to the other extreme – towards Communism and confiscation. The slack necessary for social compromise, which is the first requisite for democracy, does not exist.[10]

In its comment on the Italian elections the *Atlantic Monthly* criticised De Gasperi for his lack of sensitivity to social problems and noted how many of Mussolini's old supporters had enthusiastically converted to Christian Democracy. The prestigious Boston journal worried about the future of the school system and about press freedom; it denounced the control held by 'a restricted group of business potentates' over the 'bizarre' price structure. All these problems spelled out danger for the future of Italian democracy 'and in view of the new awareness of our responsibilities' – according to this authoritative voice of east coast liberalism – 'we should keep them under check'.[11]

The Marshall Plan and social modernisation

But the key question in Italy, according to a *New York Times* correspondent, Michael L. Hoffmann, writing in June 1949, was not the defeat of Communism. It was instead whether the country could develop its own authentic, viable form of capitalism. A real capitalist mentality, unafraid of risks, enthusiastically in favour of individual initiative, was 'as rare in Italy as a Communist on Wall Street', according to Hoffmann's sources. The market was divided horizontally, a huge gap separating the luxury level from that of the workers and peasants:

> Italian industrialists have never shown much interest in the job of adapting their products to the mass market, with the result that the scale of their operations remains small and their costs high. The idea of persuading the low income consumer to feel the need for something he's never had, using advertising, and then to give it to him at a price he can afford, could be the Marshall Plan's biggest contribution to Italy – if it gets anywhere.

Italian conservatives were far too inclined to use force to hold Communism down, Hoffmann insisted, instead of trying the remedy of mass consumption and mass production. Italian industrialists rigged what feeble market there was and encouraged the unemployed to emigrate. If this mentality could be changed, Marshall Plan administrators expected other obstacles such as high interest rates and the obsession with frugality to disappear as a consequence, Hoffmann reported.[12]

For John Gunther, author of one of the most famous portraits of inter-war Europe's ruling classes, *Inside Europe*,[13] the principal challenge before the ERP in Italy was to find an alternative to emigration for the 400,000 people born every year. Almost all the foreign observers commented on this theme of overpopulation, which Gunther, citing anonymous 'experts', estimated at 13 million out of a total population of 45 million. De Gasperi apparently told Gunther that he would willingly give up all the Marshall Plan aid if he could 'export' those 400,000 every year. Knowing that overpopulation aggravated poverty and therefore enlarged their political market, it was logical in Gunther's view that the Communists had aligned themselves with the Catholic Church in opposing family planning. Without ERP aid the local ruling classes would never be capable of defeating Communism. In France Communism could not hope to win without violence and the threat of civil war, while in Italy it could come from one day to the next like an evil spell. Why? Because such was the suffocating weight of the old educational system that no one could ever discover what the reality of Communism was like. Politics could not be discussed in the schools, and in the absence of open debate and of a new, modern, reforming leadership which could abolish the prevailing superstition and defeatism, it was up to the United States to supply examples, ideals and inspiration along with its bread.[14]

So the Marshall Plan, when it finally began, was never just an abstract affair of economic numbers: loans, grants, investment, production, productivity, etc. – even if these were its key operating tools. Nor was it merely another weapon in America's Cold War anti-Communist crusade, though all concerned were well aware that, operating as an 'indigenous group', the Italian Communists had an immense psychological and political advantage over the transatlantic superpower.[15] Hence the effort aimed to get as close as possible to the people it was benefiting – at all levels of society, and particularly in relations between the citizen and the state – in order to channel attitudes, mentalities and expectations in the direction Americans understood, the direction of mass production for mass-consumption modernisation. 'You Too Can Be Like Us': that came to be the message of the Marshall Plan, specifically of the vast propaganda effort which accompanied the plan in Italy, the largest of its kind in any European country.[16]

'What the European worker wants first of all,' wrote Henry S. Reuss, one of the directors of the ERP field headquarters in Paris, was 'a promise of a larger stake in his country's economy – enough income to enjoy better food, a new suit, a picnic or the movies, less cramped living quarters, a chance to retire when he is old.'[17] Beyond anti-Communism, beyond the figures for production and trade, beyond even the vision of a new era of European co-operation, this was the promise of the Marshall Plan in its heyday and it was the task of the propaganda effort to bring that promise home to Europeans everywhere. The administrator Paul G. Hoffman wrote in his memoirs:

> They learned that this is the land of full shelves and bulging shops, made possible by high productivity and good wages, and that its prosperity may be emulated elsewhere by those who will work towards it.[18]

The propaganda project in Italy

From the propaganda point of view, the key ERP countries were considered to be France, the Anglo-American military bi-zone in Germany, and Italy, followed by a second band containing Greece, Turkey, Austria, Trieste (a separate entity for ERP purposes) and the French zone of Germany, a third including Britain and Sweden, and a fourth grouping the rest. But it was in Italy that the largest Marshall Plan information campaign emerged, the one considered 'tops' in the Paris headquarters of ERP.[19]

At its head was Andrew Berding, an energetic former head of the Rome bureau of the Associated Press, co-author of ex-Secretary of State Cordell Hull's memoirs and himself a future Assistant Secretary of State for Public Affairs. Berding and his small staff were extraordinarily active and inventive. Within a month of starting work in August 1948 they had established a daily survey of the Italian press, made contacts with radio, film, press and news organisations, prepared a three-room exhibition with accompanying placards and photos, set up documentary film production facilities and agreed with the Italian national radio network on an eight-language weekly short-wave broadcast and a fifteen-minute weekly programme in Italian.[20]

They came to think in terms of tens of documentary films, hundreds of radio programmes, thousands of mobile film shows, millions of copies of their pamphlets, tens of millions of spectators for their exhibitions and films. Between June 1948 and the end of 1950, to quote a typical report, 'the Mission installed and operated 45 exhibits frequented by 6,744,000 visitors. In these exhibits 16,049,555 pieces of ERP literature were distributed. Cost of the operation was . . . $537,239.30. The expenditure was in Counterpart . . .' (in other words in that part of the funds obtained from the sale of Marshall Plan goods which the administration kept for its own uses, the source of money for almost all the huge effort).[21]

There is no mystery about the operating principles which Berding and his staff applied in their campaign. They were arrived at fairly quickly in Italy, were spelled out more clearly than elsewhere and, although similar to the methods used in the other ERP countries, were probably applied more intensively after the experience of the 1948 elections. They changed little up to the outbreak of the Korean War. A January 1950 report from the Rome mission insisted: 'Carry the message of the Marshall Plan to the people. Carry it to them directly – it won't permeate down. And give it to them so that they can understand it.'[22] The basic thrust then was for a truly mass programme using 'every method possible . . . to reach Giuseppe in the factory and Giovanni in the fields' or, as the Paris office put it, 'slugging it out way down among the masses'.[23]

In his January 1950 summary, prepared for a Congressional presentation, Berding also listed the other key operating principles:

1 To convince the average Italian 'that the Plan is his as well as Mr. Marshall's', in other words to increase the sense of national identification with the plan and to encourage a personal stake in its outcome.
2 To demonstrate the depth and seriousness of Italian–American co-operation: 'Thus the signs which the Mission has induced the Italian Government to put

up by the many hundreds over the ERP Counterpart fund projects carry the color of both countries, side by side, on the same shield.'

3 To make use of local identities, particularly regional ones, by demonstrating the work done in each area.

4 To direct special attention to key 'target groups', particularly organised labour, Communist and non-Communist; agricultural workers; housewives, as runners of the 'economics of the household'; management in business and industry, 'in whose hands lie the guidelines of productivity', and finally children, following the example of the Church, which 'has always maintained that the best way to win and retain followers is to convince while they are young'.

5 To avoid direct confrontation with the massive waves of Communist propaganda directed against the plan. Thus 'when the Communists said the Marshall Plan was a plan of war, the Mission never said it was not a plan of war but over and over again, in thousands of inhabited centers, with every medium at its disposal, the Mission put across the slogan – "ERP means peace and work".' America's response – the Korean War – could not have been a more unfortunate development from this point of view.

6 To avoid accusations of interference in Italian internal affairs. Not surprisingly, this was the principle which gave the publicity men most difficulty, especially since they were under pressure in Congress to step up their labelling of goods and services originating in the United States with American flags.[24]

When applied on the ground the methods proved extremely flexible and no idea seemed too large or too daring for the Information Program in its heyday. Besides the traditional media there were ERP concerts and ERP essay contests, ERP art competitions and ERP variety shows on radio, ERP trains and ERP ceremonials. There were calendars, cartoon strips, postage stamps and atlases. There were troubadours singing the story of ERP-sponsored miracles in Sicilian villages:

> Ah poor Mariella! She loves Giovanni, who loves another. Mariella leaps into the river to end it all. She is saved and Giovanni realises at last how much he loves her. Then (the guitar goes somber) tragedy! The icy water has given Mariella double pneumonia. The doctors shake their heads: she is about to die.
>
> But wait! (the guitar goes faster). Up comes a burly hero marked 'ERP' – the European Recovery Program, the Marshall Plan. From a gigantic hypodermic needle labelled 'ERP Penicillin from the USA' he treats the dying Mariella. She recovers! She marries Giovanni!'[25]

Even mobile puppet shows were provided: 'to bring the Marshall Plan message ostensibly to children but actually through the children . . . to semi-literate or illiterate adults . . .'. This was 'Operation Bambi', run in agreement with the Ministry of Education, which according to its supporters did not 'bring the children statistics or dry commentaries on international economics. It brings them entertainment they have never seen before, and educates them with modern techniques.'[26]

Choosing its media very carefully, the Information Division of the Rome ERP Mission assigned to the cinema the principal role in putting over its message.

Before treating this experience specifically, brief mention must be made of the other significant means of communication of the ERP campaign in Italy. Radio, for example, was exploited only up to a point, since the listening audience was not high, owing to the cost of sets, and a Parliamentary Control Committee supervising the monopoly state network included Communist deputies. Nevertheless thirty-four different types of show were produced, mostly of a documentary nature, 'utilising on-the-spot recordings, original music and commentary'. The Mission thought that radio was 'ideal for wide, immediate distribution of general information and for stimulating a predisposition to acceptance of a message'. But they thought it weak for explaining the details of difficult problems.[27]

For these purposes the Information Division preferred exhibits, which were styled to cater for what the ERP staff believed was a particularly Italian love of colour, movement and humour. They did not hesitate to use a Mickey Mouse cartoon if possible, becoming expert at shifting from the amusing to the serious quickly but subtly. This was a particularly pressing necessity, since the substance of the exhibitions, as of the ERP itself, was inevitably heavily technical, economic and abstract. Concepts such as 'counterpart funds' (the sums of money in local currency, equivalent to the dollar value of exports provided by the ECA), the 'dollar gap' (the shortage of dollars in the international financial markets), 'productivity' and 'European integration' were in fact not only quite new to European ears but difficult to communicate in the best of circumstances. Now they had to be put over in a situation in which the greatest part of the population was still 'absorbed in the difficult daily problems of finding enough food, keeping warm and making ends meet under conditions of inflation and unrest', as a report to Congress explained afterwards.[28]

Berding explained the Mission's solution to this problem with an example:

> Instead of using statistics to tell about the Counterpart fund, the exhibits show a huge safe, from which on an endless belt pours a cascade of thousand-lire notes, which dissolve into models of the Counterpart projects financed with the funds.

Little wonder that the ERP information directors in Washington felt that 'we have become in surprising measure . . . the principal fount for education about the big economic problems and developments disturbing the world today'.[29]

Opening up an ERP pamphlet or visiting a Marshall Plan exhibition in the months down to June 1950, what were the themes one would always find? What was the 'message'? A booklet distributed at the Venice exhibition on ERP in summer 1949 opens with a dramatic quantification of the dimensions of American aid: three ships a day, $1,000 a minute, two weeks' salary from every worker. The goals?

> By utilising American free supplies of foodstuffs and raw materials, Italy and the other nations included in the ERP plan hope to attain by the year 1952: a higher standard of living for the entire nation; maximum employment for workers and farmers; greater production, through exploiting all their energies and by a close economic collaboration with all the other ERP countries.

The essential mechanisms of the plan are then outlined: how supplies of wheat and raw materials from the United States turn into lire deposited in a special fund at the Bank of Italy, which is then used for public works and other 'productive improvements aiming to diminish unemployment'. The details follow, underlining how work has been restored to lifeless industries, how new machinery has modernised factories and how greater output needed to be integrated Europe-wide to facilitate emigration and stabilise economic life on a continental scale. The concluding message states that:

> ERP is a unique chance offered to European nations toward reconstructing their economy, raising the standard of living among the masses, and attaining by the year 1952 an economic stability which is the foundation of political independence .... Every worker, every citizen is bound up in this rebirth. The future and the peace of Italy and of Europe, the general well-being of all, depend on the will and the work of each single one of us.[30]

The reference to the masses and to workers illustrates the crucial importance the ERP as a whole attached to changing the balance of power, the structures and the attitudes prevailing in the world of organised labour. Here information activities were only part of a vast operation directly aided by the American trade unions which actively sought to organise non-Communist trade unions where hardly any had existed before. Without entering into the merits of this long-controversial undertaking, which was largely a product of the Marshall Plan's Cold War dimension, it is worth noting that the entire thrust of the effort was to create trade unions with different ideological objectives from those dominated by the left parties which emerged after the fall of Fascism. The creation of a single non-political organisation devoted to 'the economic improvement of the job holder' was to be the aim, and a furious propaganda and political battle developed on this front from 1949 onwards.[31]

The theme of ERP information on the subject was that non-party, economically oriented trade unionism made for 'better working conditions, better wages, peaceful labor–management relations, higher productivity and a more vital democratic life', as the long 1950 report explained.[32] But if convincing the workers of this unheard-of story at a time of massive unemployment and general dislocation was hard, persuading the industrialists of their role in promoting higher living standards was barely less difficult.

The key words here were mass production, scientific management and above all productivity. A typical portable exhibition on the subject would explain what productivity was, 'how it has given the United States a high standard of living, how increased per man output can result in betterment of living conditions, social progress, strength and ability to defend democratic institutions'. There were specialist reviews of the subject, joint committees, trips to inspect American factories, conferences and eventually even 'productivity villages' where model factories and workers' communities could be seen in action.[33]

And there were constant exhortations and even reprimands for the industrialists, pushing them in the direction of modernising their attitudes and their practices.[34] In October 1950 the ERP Mission Chief in Rome, H. L. Dayton, went so far as to accuse business and industrial leaders of paying lip service only to the need for 'raising the standard of living and to the basic principles of low cost and high production'. And he asked why it was that shoes arrived in the shops with up to 500 per cent profit margins added, and why an automobile cost the equivalent of 1,000 days' work in Italy – for an industrial worker – compared with 100 days' in the United States. 'Something to justify their support of democracy,' Dayton demanded, referring to the 'little men and women who are the backbone of the country', and he recommended to his audience at the Chamber of Commerce in Genoa a new publication entitled *Productivity*.[35]

Although financed by counterpart funds, this review was published by the Italian government, and it was to the state that the ERP directed a third major effort in modernising attitudes and practices. The efficiency and credibility of the state were seen as fundamental in reconciling individuals to their democracy and to their government, as well as creating the infrastructure and environment in which business operated. 'Soundness and efficiency of government administration, improvement in fiscal systems, correction in taxation policies and administration, social security programs and administration, aids to small business, safeguards against monopoly': these were just a few of the desirable objectives the Italian Mission saw for an effective push in this area.

There was no question here of a major publicity operation, but in arranging exchanges, sending expert advisers and dedicating a good part of the elaborate 'technical assistance' programme to government reform, particularly in the fiscal sector, the ERP sought consciously to place the old relationship between the state and its citizenry on a new basis of confidence and mutual respect.[36] But, without knowing it, the Mission had stumbled at this point on what would emerge as the crucial historical problem of the first Italian Republic; little wonder then that they had to admit their substantial failure in such areas of tax reform by the end of 1950.

The choice of cinema as the key means of persuasion

As we have already seen, from the beginning of its endeavours the Information Division of the ERP Mission in Rome had been clear that the press and the radio, although not negligible, could not bear the central weight of the planned offensive: only one newspaper was sold per day for every twelve Italians and the distribution of radio sets was limited to about half the population. The national government's idea, however, was to concentrate precisely on those two media: the Foreign Minister went so far as to propose buying up half the country's dailies to make sure that the right message was put over. This suggestion was never taken seriously by the ERP men. They insisted that visual messages were the key to the situation, especially in a country where illiteracy still stood at 15 per cent. Only the cinematographic medium, they made clear, possessed the power of communication, of suggestion and of persuasion – if correctly deployed – to penetrate the 'most mentally closed' social groups, the Communist worker or the peasant farmer isolated in his remote mountain village.[37]

In the early phases the film effort relied on the existing cine library of the USIS, care being taken to select only materials free of any political content whatsoever (not always an easy task in view of the official priorities of the agency in favour of explaining US foreign policy), material which could appeal to a wide range of interests in any audience, and which possessed an obvious technical and didactic function.

Applying this method, 'a huge success' was achieved by the ERP information officers who participated in the Padua Fair of October 1948. Their programme consisted of about forty documentaries, covering subjects as diverse as tourism in New York, new methods of breeding poultry, a sample of American newsreels, the latest techniques in plastic surgery. There were a significant number of titles dedicated to showing progress in American agriculture. But in reality, no matter what the subject, an ever-growing public 'continually asked to see them again, quoting other people who had already seen them'.

For the occasion a special programme of technical films was put together for the 15,000 workers of the nearby Marzotto textile mills, the huge majority of whom were Communist by persuasion. At the same time five prizewinners in a factory competition, offered the choice of a three-month trip to America or Russia, were about to embark for the United States.[38]

On the basis of this experiment, a group of industrialists from the major steel and engineering companies in the country were invited to select a programme of forty further films from a package of seventy-two sent for the purpose from the United States. The aim was not to teach the latest techniques in aeroplane maintenance, to cite one example, or to offer an introduction to electronics, as in another case, but to find a non-propagandistic point of contact with the Communist worker. 'Even though these films do not openly praise the American way of life,' explained the embassy in Rome, 'they reflect a part of it in the way the workers dress, the shining conditions in the factories, the technical excellence of the machinery etc.'[39] In front of such a suspicious and militant audience only a tangential approach could be tried, and an MGM product of 1950, *Meet King Joe*, was rejected as too provocative because it depicted in bombastic style the American worker as the best paid and best treated in the world.[40] For this reason, too, the Mission in Italy began to think from the very beginning of its operations of constructing its own repertory of film materials, and from November 1948 onwards it set out to realise the ambition.

Unfortunately the documentation which has come down to us from this project reveals little of the strategic or operational choices which lay behind it. In general the documentation of the Marshall Plan is extremely variable in quantity and quality, and while the ERP Mission in Italy has left numerous traces of its existence, they are rarely substantial or coherent. The Rome Information Division, for example – in contrast to its peers in other countries – apparently left no autonomous archive of its own. Only partial lists of films completed have been discovered so far. In the official archives of Washington and Rome, only a few dozen of the results of the extensive production campaign can be consulted. From the records currently available it would appear that sixty-three documentaries had been produced by April 1952 (forty of them by the end of 1950), but only forty-two are visible in the National Archives in Washington, depository of the largest collection.[41] However, from the correspondence between the Rome Mission and the headquarters in Paris and Washington, and from the reports prepared for Congressional hearings, certain facts and patterns can be traced.

In the first year of activity it appears that eighteen documentaries were completed, all made so as to demonstrate the effects of the ERP at work in concrete situations:

> One film, for instance – entitled *Rails* – shows the progress achieved with ERP contributions on one stretch of the Italian railroads, and the importance the railroad occupies in the daily industrial, agricultural, commercial, tourist and domestic life of the communities along the line. Another describes pictorially the assistance given by the United States generally in the rehabilitation of the Italian railroads.[42]

The first documentaries, in 16 mm black and white film, were distributed as trailers to accompany the main feature in first-run and second-run cinemas in towns up and down the country. With the aid of two USIS vans (which quickly became six) the films were also transported into the tiniest and remotest villages, since it was calculated that only 2,000 of the 9,000 towns possessed a cinema of their own. Internal audience estimates talked of 'four, five or six million spectators' for each product (though without specifying the time span in which films were shown).[43]

Berding told a Congressional committee in January 1950:

> The Italian people like color and life, hence the Mission decided that they must be informed through color and life. . . . The Italians like entertainment, and this fact has been remembered, too. In the movie projections put on by the sound trucks of the Mission, it is not unusual – and it is very gratifying to the crowd – to see a Mickey Mouse animated cartoon. The Mission induced Italy's most noted comedian, Eduardo De Filippo, to make a documentary movie in which he dramatizes his initial inability to understand the Marshall Plan and ends up by being convinced.[44]

The use of famous personalities in this way was, however, extremely rare. The majority of documentaries confined themselves to illustrating the physical and moral impact of American aid in specific contexts.

A typical example was *Miracle of Cassino*, produced at the beginning of 1950. Showing the recovery of the famous monastery town six years after the devastating bombardment, the film dwells on building activities, on the railway, on the market. The popular will to recovery is highlighted, with shots of the efforts made by the people themselves, whilst the ERP contribution to the general welfare, especially public housing and the railway station, are presented as an integral part of the entire story. The symbolic importance of the town and its fame throughout the world made it a perfect subject for the propaganda campaign.

Still more meaningful from the viewpoint of the ERP men was the film dedicated to Sicily, *Village without Water*, also produced between the end of 1949 and the beginning of 1950. (Many of the films carry no production date.) This documentary, narrating the arrival of a mains water supply in a small town in the centre of the island, illustrated, according to a Mission telegram:

> reconversion of that island from feudal agricultural community to modern farm production. . . . Important to note that ERP appreciated probably more in Sicily than in any other part or any other country under Marshall Plan. Tie in troubadours which we use extensively on island and which typical Sicilian outgrowth.[45]

In the Senate in Washington meanwhile, in words reminiscent of Lenin and Mussolini as well as the American President Woodrow Wilson, the cinema was being lauded as 'the most powerful means we have' for communicating 'the American story' to the world. In a long presentation on the Senate floor in July 1950, Senator Wiley of Wisconsin paid tribute to the Hollywood industry, to America's film culture and to the role of the government in using cinema abroad in the Cold War struggle. The speech was accompanied by a detailed State Department report on its activities in this area, complete with reports from the field illustrating the effectiveness of the material used in various countries. The Italian example reads as follows:

> When USIS advertised a film showing in a small town near Florence, the local Communist Party immediately announced the showing of a Sovexport film at the same time. When the showings were held 250 spectators came to the USIS show while 15 attended the Communist exhibition. It was later discovered that many who attended the USIS show had contributed to the rental of the Soviet picture.[46]

In the wake of this expression of Congressional confidence Andrew Berding, having meanwhile become Deputy Director of the Information Division at the Washington headquarters, wrote to Wiley to tell him that in the whole of Western Europe fifty ERP documentaries and newsreels were circulating, which were seen every week by upwards of 40 million people, divided between 30 million for the newsreels and 10 million for the documentaries. 'Our enquiries in various countries,' Berding stated, 'have shown to us the great potential of the cinema in transmitting information in ways that spectators can understand, believe and remember.'[47]

Judgements on the first phase

Summing up the results of its efforts after two years of activity, the Information Division in Rome calculated that at least 30 million citizens could by then be counted as 'well informed' on the Marshall Plan. Of the entire population 52 per cent considered it good for the country, while 15 per cent perceived it negatively. 'It is on that 37 per cent . . . which has no specific opinion on the ERP that the Information Division will concentrate its efforts in the months to come,' promised the report, which repeated a long-standing conviction that women and young people should be considered the key target groups from a long-term perspective. At the strategic level, the objectives had evolved, now being defined as 'the mobilisation of the Italians around the idea that only on the basis of a free economy can a strong, democratic and free Italy be constructed, together with a peaceful and prosperous Europe'. In particular, 'This division, in the coming months, will put before the Italian people the example of economic integration represented by the forty-eight American states, an example which Europe might follow with profit.' In fact, the division considered the enthusiasm of the Italians for European unity (together with the growth of a non-political trade union movement where none existed before) among its greatest successes.[48]

But in private there were many doubts about the effectiveness of the message and the overall results. Just explaining what the Marshall Plan was turned out to be far harder than expected. The first head of the information effort in Europe, the well known journalist Al Friendly, commented later: 'The idea that one nation would transfer part of its current output to a group of other nations, with very few strings attached and for the benefit of all, was too paradoxical for easy acceptance.'[49] A high-level official in the Paris headquarters noted as early as February 1949: 'The European worker listens listlessly while we tell him we are saving Europe, unconvinced that it is his Europe we are saving.'[50]

An opinion poll carried out by the ECA in mid-1950 interviewed almost 2,000 people, including citizens of France, Norway, Denmark, the Netherlands, Austria, Italy and Trieste. On average, approximately 80 per cent of those selected knew of the ERP and 75 per cent approved of it. (Outside France, which stood as a special case in view of the intensity of opposition to the Marshall Plan, 55 per cent was the minimal level of approval.) Between 25 per cent and 40 per cent of those interviewed understood its functioning. But as the official sponsors of the poll commented, it was among the minorities 'not on the team' that the most important groups for the persuasion strategy were still to be found: the workers and the peasants. They it was who doubted most profoundly the motives behind American action, just as Communist propaganda prompted them to do.[51]

It would in fact be easy to portray the Marshall Plan in deep political crisis by the middle of 1950, unable to bring about the sought-for shifts in attitudes, expectations and behaviour. Even in Italy, where so much effort was spent, government, industry and labour 'persist in taking a very dim view of productivity', a Labor Division inspector from Paris reported in June. According to this observer the fundamental economic and political context of the Marshall Plan effort there had to be changed, since it was up against 'the prime flaw of Italian industry . . . , its parasitic nature, its monopolistic structure, practices and outlook' and its distribution system, 'an heirloom of the 13th century'.[52]

The crisis of the Marshall Plan

But the greatest challenge to American action in Italy from summer 1950 onwards was the battle against the effects of the war in Korea. It is impossible to overestimate the impact throughout Europe and on the Italian front in particular of this decisive moment in the Cold War escalation process. The war brought in its wake a qualitative change, an unprecedented intensification of the ideological and psychological commitment to the anti-Communist crusade, and specifically a stepping-up of the propaganda offensive. Expenditure on the persuasion effort across the participating nations passed from roughly US$1 million to almost US$6 million per annum; in Italy alone almost US$1 million was being spent at an annual rate by the end of 1950.[53] For their part the local left-wing forces seized upon the occasion with great energy to proclaim their identification with the very strong anti-war sentiment expressed by various parts of the Italian population, insisting that the entire episode confirmed their predictions that an Italy in NATO would inevitably be dragged into America's wars.

Henceforth the problems of military security would take over from economic reconstruction at the head of America's priorities in Europe: that was the consensus which quickly emerged at ERP headquarters in Paris. But the militarisation of all the effort, coming together with the prospect of general rearmament, cost the promoters of general prosperity as the solution to all ills very dearly.

Throughout ECA it was recognised that the strain of rearmament could produce 'internal security crises' in countries such as France and Italy, or at best sceptical neutralism of a kind evident in public opinion in a number of countries, and articulated most effectively by *Le Monde*.[54] But the ECA men on the ground had already decided that there was no conflict between the defence and the ERP objectives: it was just a matter of bending the existing policy goals to the new requirements. An August 1950 paper produced in Paris showed how, in order to increase European 'stability, self-confidence and, therefore, self-respect', the existing policy themes might be transposed:

> 1. Marshall aid and military assistance are good for you because they give you – as Europeans – a fighting chance to make Europe strong enough to discourage any aggression. 2. But this strength can only be achieved through unity. As separate, rival powers, the nations of Free Europe are weak, are dangerously exposed. 3. Productivity must increase because more food, more machines, more of nearly everything is needed to make Europe so strong it will be unassailable.[55]

Realising that mobilisation for rearmament was a challenge to established attitudes and expectations as much as to economic goals, the Marshall Plan men in Europe intensified their propaganda offensive in very specific ways. Henceforth they openly referred to it in terms of 'psychological warfare', not least because it also embraced a permanent, large-scale 'black' or subversive dimension with a substantial intelligence-gathering capacity.[56]

But the Americans were under no illusions as to the difficulties they faced. In a top-level analysis of two and a half years of effort carried out for the Paris headquarters, it was admitted that knowledge of the Marshall Plan and its popularity were by that time – November 1950 – stagnant. While the percentage of the population opposing the plan in countries such as France and Italy was smaller than the Communist vote, still doubts persisted in 'much too great a segment of the European population' round the question of

> whether [US] policy was aimed at progressive improvement in general living standards, or was designed more to shore up economic and social systems which are not popular and to restore to power reactionary and conservative vested interests.[57]

The top Americans in Europe considered they had been 'led down the garden path' in countries such as France, Germany and Italy, where their investments showed so few signs of paying visible social or political dividends. They believed, said a British observer, 'that really strenuous efforts . . . from the masses cannot be expected unless "social justice" figured as part and parcel' of all future schemes to raise production for defence.[58]

Adapting the propaganda project

Only in the third and fourth year, however, did the awareness take hold that the effectiveness of the messages depended in the first instance on their being adapted to local circumstances. In the early months it had been considered more important to have available press articles, formulas for radio shows, exhibitions and films which could be used in any country in Europe and even be shown on American television on occasion. Hence the importance attached to the newsreels specially commissioned from the 'March of Time' organisation and from Fox-Movietone. It was one of these in fact which opened the television series *The Marshall Plan in Action*, shown successfully by the ABC network for thirteen weeks from June 1950.[59]

From that year on, however, the organisation of the information campaign changed in response to the recognised need for more effective contact with local reality. The director of the information campaign at the European level explained later that the effort had

> tended more and more to become a working alliance with various European groups, including labor unions, groups working for European unification [*sic*] and various anti-Communist elements. More and more its propaganda technique was indirect, and more and more its objectives were to change basic political, social and economic attitudes in Europe rather than to merely advertise or explain American policy.[60]

In a country like Italy a system of subcontracts began to delegate to local script-writers and directors the fabrication of film propaganda material, using schemes furnished by the sponsor but translated into the symbolic, visual and spoken language of the Italian context. In this way the Organizzazione Epoca was born, set up not to proclaim but to conceal the American origins of its operations. Naturally no one was taken in. A *Newsweek* writer commented after a visit to Italy that 'even the most sincere friends of the United States sometimes find it hard to appreciate what they are getting'.[61]

Among the friends in difficulty were to be found on occasion even the Italian authorities. A number of conflicts took place between those responsible for state broadcasting and the Information Division over the approach employed by certain radio programmes, where the former took offence at a variety of deleterious social conditions which the programmes alleged to exist in the country they governed. Too often, protested the Minister of Posts and Telecommunications in February 1950, the scripts concentrated on the negative aspects of the prevailing situation rather on the reforming activities being undertaken by the authorities themselves, for instance in agriculture.[62] In the cinema too there was occasionally trouble. The documentary *People of Venafro*, of September 1950, describing the impact of ERP aid on a poor area of the South, was objected to by the relevant Ministry because it described the local Church and ruling classes in unflattering terms, and suggested the town was hopelessly squalid before the Americans arrived. Over Mission grumbles about 'censorship' the film was modified to avoid giving offence to anyone.[63]

In its search for impact and effectiveness the Information Division went as far, in the second half of 1950, as to produce five expensive films in Technicolor. Almost nothing is known of these films; only two are certain to have survived. But the official reasoning behind the choice of colour emerges from the documents and is significant:

> (1) Color shorts are a rarity in this country, with greater commercial distribution possible than for black and white; greater acceptability by the audience, and especially by the spectators in movieless towns reached through ECA sound and movie trucks; (2) a sample of opinion showed that the Italian spectator is much more interested in subject matter presented in color; and (3) color permitted the competent treatment of certain subjects such as the processing of silk and the making of steel which would have been rather flat in black and white.[64]

The range of subjects treated began to evolve after 1950. There was talk of film projects to stimulate tourism, making use of the well-known Hollywood stars who were by now to be found in the Rome production studios. On the broader European level there was discussion of how to translate into film language the two abstract concepts which were the most difficult to treat and yet the most important for the entire ERP project: European integration and productivity. *Productivity, Key to Plenty* was the outcome of this debate, a documentary seen in all the participating countries and including examples from a number of them. But by this time the overwhelming emphasis in the information effort had been shifted to the struggle to explain rearmament.

An October 1951 telegram from Rome to Washington illustrated the productions under way at that time aimed at reorienting the 'information' campaign. New truck convoys had been organised to carry the story of NATO up and down the country. They offered two colour documentaries and two in black and white on subjects such as the reconstruction of Italy's armed forces, including illustrations of the new motorised units, the renovated Alpine divisions and the rebuilt navy and air force. Meanwhile, on the radio, twelve weekly documentaries offered more on the same subjects, with special programmes for all branches of the armed services. For background use additional films were being prepared: 'color documentary *A Ship is Born* and *Naples's other Face* (steel); in production *Nossa* (zinc for defense); *Cornigliano* (steel for defense)'.

In the so-called 'Special media' category certain initiatives were proposed and carried out which would never have been imaginable in countries with more sophisticated mass media cultures, or whose sovereignty was treated with greater respect:

> 1952 calendars emphasise productivity, Eur unity, defense; paper doll cutouts for girls called 'friendship chain' illustrate Eur unity; postcards illustrate unity and strength, production dials compare strengths of free world, Soviet; 9000 shields posted on ERP projects and machinery carrying message 'For the Free People from USA – Prosperity, Strength and Freedom.'[65]

But no one apparently, either at the time or afterwards, ever chanced a serious analysis of the reception of all this inventiveness in the minds and hearts of the peoples to whom it was addressed with so much fervour. In private, however, scepticism was widespread.

At the highest official level, the ERP men found an unlikely adversary in the head of the principal industrialists' association (Confindustria), the formidable and influential figure of Angelo Costa. Exasperated by the ceaseless preaching and pressuring of the Marshall Planners, which increased visibly after the Korean War outbreak, Costa accused them in a series of private letters of understanding little or nothing of the context in which they were operating.

Costa explained that, to begin with, unlike those of the American constitution, the institutions of the Italian state did not rest on a firm foundation of historical legitimacy; instead the laws of Rome were regarded as a form of legalised robbery, and as such were systematically evaded. As for the economic planning demanded by the ERP, with targets for investments, GNP, imports, etc., it could only cause harm, and in fact the country had already recovered from the war without any of that.

> In a land where history has created a delicate balance between industry and agriculture, a dense network of relationships which are not only economic but also social in character, measures of innovation brought in from above can only create disorder.

Costa was implicitly opposed to the spread of large-scale industry and urbanisation, and now expressed all his scepticism concerning the culture of productivity and high wages. No matter how cheap synthetic fibres became, he insisted, Italian women would always prefer clothes made in the home with natural materials; tinned food might be sold very cheap, but Italian traditions of cooking would always be preferred. Small firms and traditional artisan skills would be central to Italy's future just as they had been in the past. As for the concept of productivity, it ignored the basic difference between Italy and America: there, capital was cheap, labour dear; at home the situation was the opposite.

But the Americans did not give up, and, much against his better judgement, Costa too was to be found among the delegates at the great conference on 'Productivity' organised by the ECA in New York in 1952.[66]

Assessing the results

At the beginning of his final year at the head of the Rome embassy, Ambassador Dunn offered his own estimate of the results obtained up to that point and of the principal problems still facing Italy. He wrote:

> Astonishing economic recovery of Italy has concealed relatively much slower progress in psychological and moral recovery. Stimulating effect of General Eisenhower's appointment in Europe [as Supreme Allied Commander in NATO] and vigorous start which was given to rearmament for common defense has virtually petered out. Support of public opinion for NATO has not waivered, but most of officialdom and leaders of democratic parties are convinced that expenditures for social purposes must have priority over additional defense expenditures.

For Dunn the dimensions of the economic problems were still such as to intensify 'the sense of discouragement', with the result that all the parties fell back ever more often on appeals of a nationalistic type to hide their difficulties. Under attack from the extremes of both right and left for its alleged 'servilism' towards the United States, the government felt the need to demonstrate on every occasion its independence at the international level, particularly *vis-à-vis* the Americans.[67]

A few months after Dunn's report, the head of the ERP Mission in Rome concluded his own term of office with another long written analysis, this time for the benefit of his successor – the head of the new 'Mutual Security' Mission. Entitled 'The Italian Problem Today', this panoramic survey presents a picture of a country with extraordinary achievements behind it in terms of reconstruction, financial stabilisation and material production, but with almost all its structural problems – even understood in strictly economic terms – still to be tackled. Whilst great progress was in evidence in terms of democratisation and the wish to be part of Europe, true political stability remained far away. Poverty and unemployment were still rife and far too many still had no choice but to emigrate. The underlying reason was evident: the refusal of the vested interests in politics, industry, agriculture and the bureaucracy to embrace the Marshall Plan vision of mass production for mass consumption based on free enterprise and constantly increasing productivity.[68]

In its discussion of these contradictions, today's Italian historiography emphasises the capacity of the centrist governments of the era to elude, neutralise or ignore the American directives, even in an emergency such as that provoked by the Korean War. No comprehensive or coherent plan was ever drawn up for the use of American aid, in spite of incessant ECA pressure in this sense. Very few of the reforming, modernising methods proposed by the Americans for the state and the economy were ever adopted.[69]

Yet it is widely recognised that, in a more diffuse, cultural sense, the Marshall Plan in all its manifestations did help put modernisation permanently on the public agenda. The static vision of the country's industrial prospects proposed by personalities such as Costa, rooted as it was in an idea of national identity where frugality was the supreme moral principle and where individual savings were the fount of all wealth, clashed in reality with the new expansionism being demonstrated by a private industrial sector which was anxious to leave behind the protectionism of the autarchy era and take advantage of the opportunities offered by rapidly expanding world markets. By 1953 Italian industrial production had doubled compared with 1938 and the annual rate of productivity increase was 6·4 per cent, twice the British equivalent. At Fiat production per employee quadrupled between 1948 and 1955, the fruit of intense application of American technology underwritten by Marshall Plan aid – but also of much more intense disciplinary control of the workplace.[70]

Today it is possible to calculate with greater accuracy the overall impact of the Marshall Plan on the participating countries, an impact understood not only in macroeconomic terms, but also as a form of cultural model or psychological lymph fluid. Above all, the limits of its innovating capacities have become clear, as has the crudeness of its insistence on the American way as the solution to every problem.

Yet no one doubts the underlying effectiveness of the energising impulse from outside. Government, industry and the public all 'bet on the future' in those years, to adopt the expression of the economic historian Vera Zamagni. The results of course only became clear with the passage of time. In northern Europe 1953 was the year when the new post-war horizons of production and consumption began to open up. In contrast, in Italy that year saw the second round of general elections of the republican era and a clear reversal of the predominant trends of 1948. The Communist vote went up 10 per cent and the extreme right also advanced. A furious Ambassador Luce (Clare Boothe Luce, the formidable wife of the founder of the *Time-Life* empire) asked what had been the use of all the millions of dollars poured into the country since the war.[71]

But when there began the years of the economic 'miracle' – called such because it was so unexpected at the time – it soon emerged that since the war the same psychological processes had been going on in Italy as in other Western countries: the transformation known as 'the revolution of rising expectations', in the phrase invented in 1950 by Harlan Cleveland, a high official of the Marshall Plan. And its origins were all American. As the English economist Michael Postan wrote in the following decade:

> Transatlantic inspiration to European policies of growth . . . came not only from what the USA gave or preached but also from what the USA was. . . . Both openly and discreetly the wish to catch up with the USA became the ambition of governments and the public. . . . American affluence and American levels of consumption – motor cars, domestic gadgets, and all – were held up as rewards to come. In short, America's very presence provided an impulse to European growth and a measure of its achievements.[72]

In spite of its outward traditionalism and dedication to Catholic ideals of austerity and humility, most of the DC was looking forward to the prospect of modernisation on the American pattern without reserve.[73]

The outcome of Italy's 'miracle' has led some historians to include that nation as among the most Americanised of all the Western European countries in those years. Its need for a strong development model became more deeply felt as expectations rose and the technological possibilities of fulfilling them became more readily available. Urbanisation (7–8 million moved to the cities in the 1950s), the expansion of welfare, the development projects and the DC system of spreading its influence by distributing public money, all pushed consumption upward. Wages grew less than productivity, but still consumption increased on average by 5–6 per cent per year. It was high social mobility which made the American model seem so appropriate and attractive, says Vera Zamagni, providing 'a common pattern which succeeded in homogenising the Italians and at the same time preserved their localistic traditions'.[74] In no country was the impact of the motor car revolution more tremendous, led by a company, Fiat, which had been a privileged beneficiary of ERP aid and made no secret of its admiration for American methods of production, distribution and selling. Yet the car which put the Italians on wheels, the Fiat 600 of

1955, was a small utility model, in no way resembling the Detroit product. As functional model, what America offered was always adopted as far as it was useful and no further.

In a long and interesting analysis of European attitudes to America supplied to the US intelligence services by an anonymous Bolognese observer just after the elections of June 1953, particular importance was attached to the role of the cinema in the functioning of this filtering and appropriation process: 'Ninety-five per cent of all Europeans – friends and enemies of America – judge American society by what they see at the cinema.' From Hollywood's products many had taken away a dreadful impression of the country, of its crime and corruption, and of the venality and brutality of its ruling groups in particular. But the medium

> was useful above all in reinforcing the European admiration for the American standard of living, for American technology. A Plymouth or a Chevrolet is considered a great luxury even in countries, such as Italy, which have important car industries of their own. The possession of a refrigerator is sufficient on its own to identify a family as belonging to the richest levels of the bourgeoisie. Undoubtedly film has given the United States a propaganda triumph, to the extent that it has reminded Europeans of their traditionally optimistic vision of the 'American paradise'.[75]

'The American myths kept their promises and won through,' proclaimed Enzo Forcella, a veteran left-wing intellectual, at a post-Cold War conference held in Bologna in 1990 to discuss the impact of American culture in all its forms in the ideologically radicalised Italy of the 1950s. Forcella was referring specifically to the images purveyed by ERP documentaries of the American way of life, particularly those showing workers arriving at factories at the wheel of their own car, an unthinkable notion in the Italy of 1949.[76]

Whatever the pattern of adoption and rejection of America's apparently limitless offerings, Forcella's opinion confirms the essential role played by the cinema in all its forms as a transmitter of the American inspiration and example. While it is clearly impossible to separate the functions of Hollywood from those of the Marshall Plan documentaries (there was apparently no operational link of any kind between the two), what we can suggest is that if the inspirational message of the ERP films embodied an invitation to follow the American example all the way, the feature films on the same programme demonstrated, for better or for worse, where the road might lead.

Alternatively, we might hypothesise that whilst the concept of productivity furnished the key modernising concept on the supply side of the transformations under way, a force like the cinema worked on the demand side of the same social and economic changes, accelerating and channelling the evolutions of mentality and behaviour. Up there on the screen, where myth and model fused, the new civilisation of opulence was on show. If there were those who did not like what they saw – and how many cultural critics founded their careers denouncing it? – then it was simply up to the Europeans to come up with something different.

NOTES

Earlier versions of this chapter appeared in N. Pronay and D. W. Spring, *The Political Re-education of Germany and her Allies after World War II* (London, 1985), and in R. Kroes et al. (eds), *Cultural Transmissions and Receptions. American Mass Culture in Europe* (Amsterdam, VU University Press, 1993). I am grateful to Ms Babbettli Azzone for providing some of the additional research included in this edition.

1 No propaganda or 'information' effort was included in the early stages of planning for the European Recovery Programme, either in the United States or among the European participants. The necessity of such a campaign – identified in phrases such as the urgency of 'a Marshall Plan of the spirit' – was foreshadowed in the first American discussions but not acted upon until the programme effectively began. Cf. Allen W. Dulles, *The Marshall Plan*, an analysis of early 1948, now reprinted and edited by M. Wala, (Providence, RI, and Oxford, Berg, 1993), in particular chapter 7, 'Man cannot live by bread alone'.

2 The participating countries were: Austria, Belgium, Britain, Denmark, France, Greece, Iceland, Ireland, Italy, Luxembourg, the Netherlands, Norway, Portugal, Sweden, Switzerland, Turkey. The Anglo-American bi-zone of Germany was also included, under Allied military supervision.

3 Report, Dunn to State Department, 3 May 1947, in *Foreign Relations of the United States* (FRUS), vol. III (Washington, DC, 1947), p. 890.

4 NSC 1/1, 1 November 1947, in *ibid.*, p. 724; NSC 1/2, February 1948, in *ibid.*, p. 766.

5 D. W. Ellwood, 'The 1948 Elections in Italy: a Cold War Propaganda Battle', *Historical Journal of Film, Radio and Television*, 13:1 (1993), pp. 19–33.

6 H. K. Smith, *The State of Europe* (New York, Knopf, 1949), pp. 205–6.

7 J. E. Miller, 'Taking off the Gloves. The United States and the Italian Elections of 1948', *Diplomatic History*, winter 1983, p. 48; R. T. Holt and R. W. Van de Welde, *Strategic Psychological Operations and American Foreign Policy* (University of Chicago Press, 1960), chapter VI.

8 Ellwood, 'The 1948 Elections', pp. 20–2.

9 J. L. Harper, *America and the Reconstruction of Italy, 1945–48* (Cambridge University Press, 1986), p. 157.

10 Smith, *The State of Europe*, pp. 207–11.

11 Anon., 'Italy', *Atlantic Monthly*, June 1948, pp. 5–7.

12 M. L. Hoffmann, 'Test of Capitalism foreseen in Italy', *New York Times*, 3 June 1949.

13 J. Gunther, *Inside Europe* (New York and London, Harper, 1936).

14 J. Gunther, 'Inside Europe Today', *New York Herald Tribune*, 10 and 11 February 1949.

15 H. B. Price, *The Marshall Plan and its Meaning* (Ithaca, NY, Cornell University Press, 1955), p. 246.

16 There is no history, official or scholarly, of this operation. I have offered an introduction in 'The Marshall Plan and the Politics of Growth', in P. M. R. Stirk and D. Willis (eds), *Shaping Postwar Europe. European Unity and Disunity, 1945–57* (London, Pinter, 1991). This treats further some of the material discussed in the following paragraphs.

17 Memo, Henry S. Reuss to A. Friendly, 25 February 1949, in National Archives (NA), Record Group (RG) 286, OSR Information Division, Office of Director, 'Publicity and Information 1949' sub-file.

18 P. G. Hoffman, *Peace Can be Won* (London, Michael Joseph, 1951), p. 53. Hoffman was head of the European Co-operation Administration (ECA), which supervised the ERP programmes.

19 'Principles on Guaranties for Information Media', 13 September 1948, in NA, RG 286, OSR Information Division, Office of Director, General Subject Files 1948–49, 'Huse (Personal File)'; letter, F. R. Shea, Chief, Field Branch, European Information Division, to Berding, 11 February 1949, in NA, RG 286, OSR Information Division, Retired Subject File (Information), 'Italy II' sub-file.

20 'Notes dictated by Berding for use in Congressional presentation', 16 January 1950, in NA, RG 286, OSR Information Division, Information Subject Files, 'Previous Testimony' sub-file; Monthly Report, Information Division, ECA Mission to Italy, 1 September

1948, in NA, RG 286, OSR Information Division, Mission Files (OSR 471), 'Italy 1948–49' sub-file.

21 Letter, Shea, Chief, Field Branch, European Information Division, to Berding, 24 February 1949, in NA, RG 286, OSR Administrative Services Division, Communication and Records Section, Country Files 1948–49, Italy, 'Publicity and Information: Radio – Film' sub-file; Report, 'A Review of the Activities and Performance of the Information Division of the Special Mission to Italy from June, 1948 to December 31, 1950, with particular emphasis on the last six months of 1950', n.d. (but 1951), in NA, RG 286, ECA Washington, Information Division, Office of Director, Informational Country File, 'Italy' sub-file. I have published this lengthy summary in E. Krippendorff (ed.), *The Role of the United States in the Reconstruction of Italy and West Germany, 1943–49* (Freie Universität Berlin, 1981), pp. 274–302.

22 As note 20.

23 Letter, F. R. Shea, cited in note 21.

24 As note 20.

25 G. Gaskill, 'Our Marshall Plan Hucksters', *American Magazine*, December 1949, p. 46.

26 'Notes dictated by Berding' (cited in note 20); 'A Review of the Activities' (cited in note 21).

27 'A Review of the Activities'.

28 Economic Co-operation Administration, *A Report on Recovery Progress and United States Aid* (Washington, DC, 1949), p. 178.

29 Comment by R. Mullen, Director, Office of Information, in 'Budget Estimate, Fiscal 1950', in NA, RG 286, ECA Washington, Information Division, Information Subject File, 'Previous Testimony' sub-file.

30 Copy of pamphlet 'ERP in Italy' in NA, RG 286, ECA Washington, Information Division, Office of Director, Informational Country File, 'Italy' sub-file.

31 Memo, 'Labor Information', 19 December 1949, in NA, RG 286, OSR Information Division, Mission Files, 'Italy: Publicity and Information' sub-file.

32 'A Review of the Activities'.

33 *Ibid.*

34 Cf. V. Zamagni, 'The American Influence on the Italian Economy, 1948–58', in C. Duggan and C. Wagstaff (eds), *Italy in the Cold War. Politics, Culture, and Society 1948–58* (Oxford, Berg, 1995), p. 84.

35 Text of Dayton's speech in NA, RG 286, OSR Central Secretariat, Permanent Country Subject File, 'Italy 1951' sub-file. The speech aroused considerable controversy in Italy and a protest from the head of Confindustria, the employers' association.

36 Memo, Stone to Zellerbach and Barrows, 19 April 1949, in NA, RG 286, OSR Central Secretariat, Country Subject File, 'Italy: Administration' sub-file; telegram, Zellerbach to OSR, Paris, 3 May 1949, in NA, RG 286, ECA Washington, European Program Division, Mediterranean Branch, Subject files pertaining to France and Italy, 'S-37 Technical Assistance' sub-file (quotation from this telegram); W. J. Hoff, Director, Technical Assistance Division, ECA Washington, to S. McRosen, Bureau of the Budget, 10 October 1950, in NA, RG 286, ECA Washington, Office of Director, Technical Assistance Division, 'Italy; General' file.

37 'A Review of the Activities'.

38 Letter, Rome embassy to State Department, 10 November 1948, in NA, RG 469, European Program Division, Mediterranean Branch, Country Subject Files, 'Italy. ERP Publicity – S 47' sub-file.

39 Telegram, Dunn to State Department, 2 February 1949, in NA, RG 469, Director of Administration, Communication and records Unit, Geographic Files 'Italy – P.R. – Motion Pictures' sub-file.

40 Letter, Berding to Evans, Chief, Information Division, G.B., 19 September 1950, in NA, RG 286, Office of Information, Office of Director, 'Chronological File 1 September 1950–28 February 1951'.

41 Figure of sixty-three cited in telegram, MSA (Mutual Security Agency) Rome, to MSA, Paris, 4 June 1952, in NA, RG 469, Mission to Italy, Office of Director, Subject Files (Central Files) 1948–57, 'P.R.: Radio and Films' sub-file; figure of forty cited in doc. cit. note 38. Only eighteen films were visible until a few years age, but twenty-four additional ones have since emerged. I am grateful to Linda Christenson of Washington, DC, for this and other relevant information.
42 Report by Berding to ECA Washington, 20 June 1949, in NA, RG 286, ECA Washington, Office of Information, Office of Director, Country Subject Files, 'Italy' sub-file.
43 'Notes dictated by Berding'.
44 *Ibid.* The film has never been located, and may not have survived.
45 Telegram, ECA Mission, Rome, to ECA Washington, 21 March 1950, in NA, RG 469, Director of Administration, Administrative Services Division, Communication and Records Unit, Geographic Files 1948–53, 'Italy – P.R. 1950' sub-file.
46 Extract from *Congressional Record* of 20 July 1950 conserved in NA, RG 469, Director of Administration, Administrative Services Division, Communication and Records Unit, Subject Files (Central Files) 1948–53 'P.R. – Motion Pictures 1950' sub-file.
47 Letter, Berding to Wiley, US Senate, 24 July 1950, in NA, RG 286, ECA Washington, Office of Information, Office of Director, Chronological File 1950.
48 Telegram, ECA Information Division, Rome, to OSR, Paris, 18 August 1950, in NA, RG 286, OSR Information Division, Office of Director, General Subject Files 1948–49, Publicity and Information 1949–50, 'Congress' sub-file.
49 Cited in Price, *The Marshall Plan*, p. 246.
50 Doc. cited in note 17.
51 Minutes, Conference of Information Officers, Paris, 28 August 1950, in NA, RG 286, OSR Information Division, Office of Director, General Subject Files 1948–49, Publicity & Information 1948–49, 'Information Officers' sub-file.
52 Report, 'Productivity trip to Italy, 11–16 June 1950, in NA, RG 286, OSR Labor Information, Office of Economic Advisors, Country Subject Files 1949–50, 'Italy Productivity (General)' sub-file.
53 *Ninth Report to Congress of the Economic Co-operation Administration*, quarter ending 30 June 1950, dated 17 November 1950 (Washington, DC, 1950), p. 39; ECA, *Overseas Information Program of the ECA*, Second Year, 1950 (Washington, DC, 1950), p. 45.
54 *Le Monde*, 5 April 1950. (Debate in France summarised in *Summary of International Affairs, 1949–50*, Oxford, 1953, pp. 145–50.)
55 Memo, F. V. Norall to R. Drummond, 1 August 1950, in NA, RG 286, OSR Information Division, Retired Subject File (Information), 'Mission Memoranda' sub-file.
56 A. Carew, *Labour under the Marshall Plan. The Politics of Productivity and the Marketing of Management Science* (Manchester University Press, 1987), pp. 126–30.
57 'Notes for Ambassador Katz regarding information', n.d. (but end 1950), in NA, RG 286, Central Secretariat, Subject Files 1948–52, 'Public Relations' sub-file.
58 M. J. Hogan, *The Marshall Plan. America, Britain and the Reconstruction of Western Europe, 1947–52* (Cambridge University Press, 1987), p. 411.
59 Press release 'The Marshall Plan in Action', April 1950, and letter, Berding to ECA Information Division, Rome, 27 July 1950, in NA, RG 286, ECA Office of Information, Office of Director, 'Chronological File 1950'.
60 Cited in Price, *The Marshall Plan*, p. 247.
61 J. B. Phillips, 'Italy. Making the ECA Visible', *Newsweek*, 11 November 1949, p. 45.
62 Correspondence in NA, RG 469, ECA Mission to Italy, Office of Director, Subject Files (Central Files) 1948–57, 'Public Relations: Radio and Film' sub-file.
63 Letter, Berding to Gervasi, Information Division, Rome, 11 September 1950, in NA, RG 286, Office of Information, Office of Director, 'Chronological File 9/1/50–2/28/51'.
64 'A Review of the Activities'. The two surviving films are *Silkmakers of Como* and *A Ship is Born*.

65 Telegram, ECA Rome to ECA Washington, 9 October 1951, in NA, RG 469, Director of Administration, Administrative Services Division, Communication and Records Unit, Geographic Files 1948–53, 'Italy – P.R. 1950' sub-file.
66 Correspondence, ECA Mission Chief to Costa, and translated text of Costa speech, Rome, 8 November 1951, in NA, RG 469, ECA Mission to Italy, Office of Director, Subject Files (Central Files) 1948–57, 'Productivity Drive' sub-file.
67 Telegram, Dunn to State Department, 22 January 1952, in NA, RG 286, OSR Central Secretariat, Permanent Country Subject File, 'Political Affairs' sub-file.
68 Report, 'The Italian Problem Today', 7 June 1952, in NA, RG 469, ECA Mission to Italy, Office of Director, Subject Files (Central Files) 1948–57, 'Italy: Economic Problems' sub-file.
69 P. P. D'Attorre, 'Il Piano Marshall: politica, economia, relazioni internazionali nella ricostruzione italiana', in E. Di Nolfo, R. H. Rainero and B. Vigezzi (eds), *L'Italia e la politica di potenza in Europa, 1945–50* (Settimo Milanese, Marzorati, 1990) pp. 520–35; B. Bottiglieri, *La politica economica dell'Italia centrista, 1948–58* (Milan, Comunità, 1984), pp. 10–12. In her latest work Vera Zamagni is more positive; see 'The American Influence', pp. 77–87.
70 V. Zamagni, *Dalla periferia al centro. La seconda rinascita economica dell'Italia, 1861–1981* (Bologna, Il Mulino, 1990), pp. 418–20.
71 V. Zamagni, 'Betting on the Future. The Reconstruction of Italian Industry, 1946–52', in J. Becker and F. Knipping (eds), *Power in Europe? Great Britain, France, Italy and Germany in a Postwar World, 1945–50* (Berlin and New York, de Gruyter, 1986); on the 1953 elections see Ellwood, 'The Politics and Economics of Limited Sovereignty', in Duggan and Wagstaff (eds), *Italy in the Cold War*, pp. 25–46.
72 M. M. Postan, *An Economic History of Europe, 1945–60* (Cambridge University Press, 1966), p. 49.
73 This is argued by P. Ginsborg, *A History of Contemporary Italy. Society and Politics, 1943–88* (Harmondsworth, Penguin, 1990), pp. 205–6, 222–3.
74 V. Zamagni, 'The Italian "Economic Miracle" Revisited. New Markets and American Technology', in E. Di Nolfo (ed.), *Power in Europe?* Vol. II, *Great Britain, France, Germany and Italy and the Origins of the EEC, 1952–57* (Berlin and New York, de Gruyter, 1992), pp. 197–226.
75 Report, 'European Attitudes toward the US', sent 10 June 1953, in NA, RG 469, ECA Mission to Italy, Office of Director, Subject Files (Central Files) 1948–57, 'Public Relations' sub-file.
76 Forcella's informal intervention is conserved on tape at the Istituto Gramsci, Bologna. For the conference papers see P. P. D'Attorre (ed.), *Nemici per la pelle. Sogno americano e mito sovietico nell'Italia contemporanea* (Milan, Franco Angeli, 1991).

3

Government propaganda: official newsreels and documentaries in the 1950s

Maria Adelaide Frabotta

The year was 1950: Italy entered the first decade of peace with the hope that post-war reconstruction would bring about a definitive support structure for the country. Alcide De Gasperi, Prime Minister for the sixth time, faced the task of governing a population which was still scarred by the moral and material devastation of the war, a population riven by opposing foreign occupations and military activity and, thus, barely conscious of its own national standing. Guido Piovene, in his celebrated *Viaggio in Italia* (Travels in Italy), published in 1957, wrote that Italy's unity was never really under threat:

> not even a war with catastrophic consequences had seriously undermined it. It was a case, however, of a form of unity which was essentially passive in nature, since Italians did not have sufficiently strong or deep-rooted reasons to force a split, such as the one which led to the separation of England and Ireland. A bit of sentiment and a lot of rhetoric also helped. However, the very same reasons which acted to safeguard the physical unity of the nation were an impediment to its moral unity, a form of unity which implies the pursuit of a common purpose.[1]

So it was necessary to re-establish the grand economic and social values as collective assets. Italy had to be reunified by bridging the gap between the advanced North and the chronically underdeveloped South with a principal objective in mind: to rebuild the state machinery as a service and as the expression of national identity. Above all, the new nation-state had to move from being a quasi-sacred entity which lorded it over individuals and society to becoming an entity which respected individuals' freedom of initiative. The constitution itself, which took effect in 1948, provided the fundamental guiding principles for the adoption and enforcement of this path.

The politics of the 1950s, however, give the impression of having lost sight of these ideals, of having opted instead for a system which upheld the principles of centralism and bureaucracy, which were merely a continuation of pre-Fascist and Fascist administration. As before, the government of the day imposed its own political agenda and passed it downwards to a passive population. The government did not communicate, rather it propagandised its own unique, absolute ideas and set in motion a system of forced persuasion which alienated civil society. The Italian people again found themselves in a situation of being governed, rather than being able to participate in government.

This lost opportunity for change is apparent in the area of official information. In 1950 De Gasperi set out his ideas on the question in the belief that he had finally distinguished between the logic of propaganda and public information in an interview given to the daily *Il Messaggero*:

> The Government has the duty to make known what it is doing and why it is doing it, and it will not be a bad thing if, through an impartial documentation, the public is kept well informed of the problems of public administration and the solutions adopted or envisaged.[2]

De Gasperi, however, took only the first step: he said nothing about the need to place citizens at the centre of institutional action through dialogue with them, which would make it possible to monitor the quality of the service provision. The organisation of the bodies of official information to which he referred are a clear case in point.

In 1952, De Gasperi presented a bill for the reorganisation of the Presidenza del Consiglio, the Prime Minister's Office, as a supreme co-ordinating organ of government policy to the first permanent commission of the Chamber of Deputies. He described the aims of that office thus:

> The information services are a most valuable and indispensable instrument for a State that is the political expression of a people, a State that seeks to participate with dignity and honour in the community of nations, to protect its interests, both national and international.[3]

He then talked about the new Centro Documentazione which he had set up and inaugurated in August 1951. Its purpose was not to provide a news service, he explained, but to look at activity which was already being carried out by the public administration, with the aim of supplying the general public with the salient points. In his view, the Centro Documentazione was meant to meet the need for a national information agency enabling the government to liaise with citizens and supply a good product through the efforts of highly professional staff.

The first head of the Centro Documentazione was Gastone Silvano Spinetti. This official began his career in Mussolini's government: he worked in the press office, and later also held important posts in the Ministero della Cultura Popolare. He was, therefore, experienced in the areas of information and propaganda. He survived four changes of government from 1951 to 1957, but his best professional efforts occurred under the De Gasperi regime, whose aims he understood well. In 1954 he wrote in *Documenti di vita italiana*, the centre's official publication, in the full knowledge that it was not distributed solely to government Ministries and public bodies but, above all, to Italian communities and the civil service abroad, that the Centro Documentazione was created 'to document and disseminate, both at home and abroad, information on activities of the public administration, with a special focus on reconstruction'.[4]

To carry out the Prime Minister's plans Spinetti used all forms of documentation, but he favoured visual media especially. Photography, posters and newsreels were the most effective ways of communicating with the people, so the photographic and film department of the Centro Documentazione flooded cinemas, post offices, railway stations and just about any public meeting place with its output. De Gasperi endorsed this frenetic activity: as in every large-scale reconstruction, it was necessary to create myths and offer projects which promised a better future, and the film medium was especially apt in this respect.

De Gasperi first set out his ideas on the subject as early as 5 October 1950, at the celebrations for the 500th issue of the *Settimana INCOM*, the most popular newsreel of the time, which was produced by INCOM, a privately owned enterprise. In the course of his address he stressed how well suited the medium was to convey educational messages quickly and across the length and breadth of the country.[5] For Sandro Pallavicini, the company's chief executive, this was the start of a collaboration with the Prime Minister which led to INCOM's newsreel being produced under the government's aegis. Domenico Paolella, who was the editor-in-chief and had himself directed some of the *Settimana INCOM* newsreels, described Pallavicini in these terms:

> Pallavicini's parents sold electrical home appliances. He was very likable and good at public relations. . . . He was convinced that it was necessary to make newsreels in a true journalistic fashion, namely with an editor, editor-in-chief and correspondents, with the freedom to film real events. The company was small but solid, financed by a Swiss-Milanese group of people with great business acumen, especially the Cedraschi family. And in those days our newsreels represented the only audio-visual medium that showed Italians what was going on, given that television only started in 1954.[6]

Pallavicini was also the first film maker to cultivate contacts overseas. After the war, with the short entitled *Thanks, America* – a testimony to Italians' indebtedness and gratitude to Americans for their financial contribution to reconstruction – he went to New York. Gian Piero Brunetta remarks in his *Storia del cinema italiano*:

> During the election period, in particular, Pallavicini made much use of materials supplied by the Americans themselves to emphasise the United States' contribution to the democratic development of Italy. Immediately after the 1948 electoral victory he presented himself to the Americans to claim the credit promised to him. The American ambassador in Rome, in a letter dated 27 April 1948 to the State Department, stressed Pallavicini's pro-American sentiment and urged his government to contribute more financially, and on a more regular basis.[7]

Pallavicini's pro-American sympathies were well known to the Italian viewing public from the *Settimana INCOM* newsreels. The first number, dated February 1946, started with Pallavicini interviewing Ellery Stone, Admiral-in-Chief of the Allied

Command, and its title was even more significant: *L'Italia muove i primi passi sulla strada per la democrazia* (Italy takes its first steps on the road to democracy). The arrival of Teresio Guglielmone as company chairman in 1947 put a decisive political stamp on INCOM's output. Guglielmone, a Turin banker elected to the Senate as a Christian Democrat, succeeded in introducing American-style newsreels into the Italian political and institutional arena, and thus provided both his party and the government with an effective tool of persuasion.

In 1952 the photographic and film department of the Centro Documentazione began to produce shorts on an intensive basis. Spinetti, however, did not rely exclusively on INCOM to make them; he also initiated contact with other studios. During his tenure, eighty-five out of 140 documentaries were made by private film companies. The preferred studio of the Prime Minister's Office was Documento Film. Other studios – Astra, Orizzonte Cinematografico, Atlante and Gamma – were used later, albeit on a more occasional basis. The Istituto Nazionale Luce, which had made the Fascist propaganda newsreels, the *Giornale Luce*, shown in all cinemas on behalf of the Ministero della Cultura Popolare, was put into liquidation in 1945, and then into receivership. It carried on working but only on small commissions, having been overtaken by the private-sector film-making companies, whilst awaiting the approval of a Bill for its reorganisation and relaunch as the sole supplier of official newsreels. Giulio Andreotti gave his personal support to the relaunch of the Istituto Luce as early as 1952, when, as an Under-Secretary to the Prime Minister's Office, he was also responsible for the performing arts.[8]

Directives were issued to guarantee maximum distribution of the newsreels throughout the national territory. Documentaries, first and foremost, had to accompany feature films with guaranteed box-office returns in the cinemas which premiered films. The production agencies had to send the lists of films to the heads of the press offices in the prefectures, specifying the dates and projection venues in the various localities of the respective provinces. The agencies then had to send the same information every week to the photographic and film department of the Centro Documentazione. They also had to ensure that the films were shown in the cinemas for at least four days. Each short was usually distributed to 1,500 cinemas.

The earliest films were aimed mainly at Italians living in Italy, in view of the ever-growing role cinema as a form of entertainment played in their lives. The number of film venues had in fact risen from 14,676 in October 1952 to 15,500 in September 1953 – a record figure, with the lion's share in the North and the Centre. Rome sold the highest number of tickets, followed by Naples. After 1954, when colour replaced the black and white of traditional documentaries, the network of distribution was enlarged to include Italian communities abroad as well as foreign audiences through 'cultural programmes' organised by the Italian Cultural Institutes.

Ieri e oggi (Yesterday and Today, 1952), directed by Giorgio Ferroni, marked the start of the long series of shorts made by the Istituto Luce. Thus a notable archive of images recording government policy on Italy's reconstruction was created. The films had ultra-positive messages and faithfully reflected the political line of the various Prime Ministers in the 1950s. It is no accident that one of the last shorts of the series was *L'Italia è in cammino* (Italy on the Move, 1958), directed by Giovanni

Paolucci: the reconstruction had been completed and Italy was on the march to economic development.

The Centro Documentazione may have believed that it had reached and persuaded Italian audiences with its messages; however, the real country bore little resemblance to the one depicted in the shorts. Only feature films managed to show Italy's true face, by revealing its geographical diversity. Unlike the newsreels of the last few years of Fascism, which presented a studio-reconstructed reality, they showed a wounded and traumatised country. Neo-realism revealed that there was no distinction between the public and the private: whether in council flats, the new neighbourhoods of the urban periphery, the streets, the squares or the places where people mingled, every element became an indicator of a more general condition. In other words, the post-war films told of the dynamics and transformations in the lives of Italians in terms of their behaviour and collective mentality, not unlike a public diary in which real events and images of possible worlds overlap and are distilled, and where different perceptions of reality are represented to form the common denominator of a nation in search of a new identity.[9]

After the years of rags, pain and hunger came the years of some hope and the first visible changes in people's lives. Italian films also told stories which looked to the future with more optimism, which encouraged consumerism and introduced new life styles. The urban landscape changed, as did dwellings, ways of speaking, travel, clothing and norms of behaviour in the workplace. Indeed, Italian cinema was always ready to represent the story of every individual on the screen.[10] The warmth of everyday life was completely absent from the government films. Their optimistic messages lacked authenticity and the reality that they represented did not match the everyday experience of the viewing public. If anything, they seemed to want to avoid any identification with the viewers.

The reactions to *Ieri e oggi* are interesting in this respect. Two newspapers, the Communist *L'Unità* and the Christian Democrat *Il Popolo Nuovo*, reported the controversial screening of the newsreel at a Turin technical college. The *L'Unità* article, which appeared on 21 February 1953, was entitled 'I fischi parlano' (Booing speaks volumes). It described the event with sarcasm:

> A few days ago the students of a technical college were invited to the Massimo cinema for a film morning organised by their college. After the film, however, a documentary was shown. It was a newsreel of blatantly obvious government propaganda called *Ieri e oggi* which, through a generous amount of effrontery and bad faith, sought to show that 'thanks to the diligent efforts of the government' Italy had completely recovered from the damage of the war; housing was now available for everyone, and the bridges, streets and abbeys destroyed during the war had been rebuilt. All this was offered up as proof of how much the Christian Democratic government had achieved. The first murmurs were heard in the audience – was this a film morning or a rally of the Christian Democrats? Then, when the film's narrator said that the government had brilliantly solved the problem of youth unemployment by setting up 'schools-cum-workshops' (in the few that existed in Piedmont, attendees are paid 500 lire for ten to twelve hours' work![11]), there was a salvo of booing to underline the colossal electoral lie.

After a few days, on 25 February 1953, *Il Popolo Nuovo* fought back with a piece called 'Fischi e fiaschi de *L'Unità*' (*L'Unità*'s booing and fiascos): 'From beginning to end, the story of booing and some students leaving the cinema in protest is pure invention. Quite the opposite, the audience was very pleased with the film and the heads of the school thanked the cinema's management.' Both articles, notwithstanding the heated political tones which were typical of those years, are a telling account of filmgoers' reactions to newsreels. Most of all, they show just how wide the distribution network established by the Prime Minister's Centro Documentazione was: there were as many screenings for entertainment purposes as special educational days on the subject of reconstruction.

The golden years of the Centro Documentazione began in 1952. Unfortunately for the government, it closed well before it had fulfilled its objectives because of De Gasperi's premature death on 19 August 1954. During this period, shorts accounted for 60 per cent of its activities in the 1950s. 'Reconstruction' was the by-word, but also the proof of the pivotal role that the state continued to play in public works. In a 1953 issue of *Documenti di vita italiana*, De Gasperi wrote:

> Seven years ago, when the rubble was still before our eyes, and we were weighed down by the worry that supplies would not be enough to provide meagre rations of food, and the anxiety that social disorder and the abuse of power would lead to the break-up of the family that is our nation, it seemed impossible to predict when reconstruction would be achieved. But now the phase of reconstruction is behind us and our country is in the process of development and rebirth. Age-old demands of forgotten people are being met; in addition to rebuilding what was destroyed, new works are being undertaken; essential public services are being brought to towns and suburbs which had none. Italy is modernising its industrial and agricultural equipment; production and national income are on the rise; and we are rebuilding our glorious armed forces to safeguard independence and peace in a climate of international solidarity between free peoples.[12]

Ieri e oggi and *Meglio di ieri* (Better than Yesterday), which was also made in 1952, brought the positive results of post-war economic and social reconstruction to the screen by celebrating the iron will demonstrated by Italians at that difficult point in time.

Meglio di ieri was produced by Documento Film and directed by Romolo Marcellini, who had made a few of the Istituto Luce newsreels. The film has an interesting script which, despite its propagandist tone, effectively blends the newsreel and fiction-film genres. The protagonist of the film is Nalin, a Piedmontese factory worker in the Dora valley who wants to change his dire economic situation and has faith in the process of reconstruction. Nalin represents the economic miracle that De Gasperi was in the process of bringing about. The key points made by the film are: economic progress can be guaranteed only if all Italians contribute to the development of industrial activity, which, in turn, belongs exclusively to the nation; and the plan for reconstruction envisages the intervention of private capital – the only possible way to inject dynamism into the country's economy. *Meglio di ieri* created a stereotype which was to last for a long time: namely, that Italy was an economically efficient industrial nation, made up of self-made men who worked hard for their own well-being and that of their motherland.

In 1952 Italy was a desolate place. Its population was 47·5 million, of whom 2 million were still unemployed, 1 million were underemployed and 1 million were hired hands or casual labourers in agriculture. However, *Braccia e lavoro* (Arms and Work, 1952), a twelve-minute black-and-white film in the traditional style of an Istituto Luce newsreel, explained how the government had succeeded in the fight against unemployment. The first few frames show the agonised, dejected faces of people looking at their idle arms. The soundtrack and commentary evoke the drama of the country's predicament. The mood becomes calm again when, much like the happy ending of a fairy tale, the state's efforts against unemployment are shown.

The film *Ricostruzione edilizia* (Housing Reconstruction, 1952), on the other hand, explains government intervention in housing provision. It recalls (with some exaggeration) that almost 50 per cent of families had lost their homes in the rubble. The old post-war hovels had been demolished and in their stead the houses of the future were being built, not just on the basis of primary need but, more important, as a symbol of growing consumer well-being. The short's director was Vittorio Sala, who had trained under Fascism at the Centro Sperimentale di Cinematografia, the national film school.

La scuola dei grandi (School for Grown-ups, 1952) addressed the subject of school education. The percentage of those who had attended school was still low. However, according to the film's narrator, 'only' 77 per cent of pupils left school after gaining their primary school certificate, whilst 13 per cent were still illiterate.

Poverty, too, continued to be a serious problem. It predominantly affected one area: the South. The 1951 parliamentary inquiry found that 5·8 per cent of poor families lived in the North and a startling 50·2 per cent lived in the South. In *La terra nuova* (The New Land, 1952), the government showed the development of southern agriculture and publicised the activities of the Cassa per il Mezzogiorno, the development fund which was set up in 1950 for the economic development of the South.[13]

The Italian economy was still predominantly agrarian but industrialisation was on the increase. It was necessary to publicise the economic transformation. In 1953 the Centro Documentazione printed more than 3,000 copies of the booklet *La rinascita dell'Italia, 1945–52* (Italy's Rebirth, 1945–52), a veritable hymn in figures to Italy's economic and social reconstruction. Results were reported by region and province. During the same year shorts were made on the various regions: Lombardy, the Veneto, Liguria, Tuscany, Umbria, the Marches, Abruzzo and Molise, Latium, Campania, Apulia, Basilicata, Sicily and Sardinia. These were all depicted as areas where agriculture would have to coexist with industry, whose development was close at hand. The protagonist of change was once again the state, which carried on as the arbiter of its own evolution and as the sole distributor of funds.

Economic development led to private consumerism whose potential the government extolled. *I nostri divertimenti* (Our Leisure Pursuits, 1953) introduced the first consumer models of everyday leisure. Moreover, Italians were getting taller (average height: 1·7 m), they were buying goods (4 per cent of families had a washing machine and 14 per cent a refrigerator) and they were going about ever more frequently in motor cars (in 1950 there were ten motor cars per 1,000 inhabitants).

L'Italia e il mondo (Italy and the World, 1953) exalted the international importance that Italy had attained, and *Made in Italy* (1953) told of the success of Italian exports.

Economic development and consumerism transformed the main cities. Urbanisation had begun, and after only a year it was possible to see how fast the phenomenon was spreading. In the countryside new towns were being built and served as the driving force of the new Italian society. The government did not initially view urbanisation favourably. An article in the December 1953 issue of *Documenti di vita italiana* noted:

> The distribution of population in the cities and the countryside is a very important factor for the economy. In almost every civilised country in recent decades there has been a strong trend of mass emigration from small localities to the cities. This phenomenon, known as urbanisation, has, however, certain negative consequences for the economy.[14]

The article maintained that there was a fall in migrational flows from 1936 to 1951. It also showed that the population was concentrated in three main cities: Milan, Rome and Naples. The statistical data provided were, however, merely indicative of a trend. Italians at the time still preferred to live in their home villages, the countryside being their main source of support. They identified with particular, narrow territorial areas having their own centuries-old municipal traditions. A local feeling of belonging was still stronger than national identity.

De Gasperi acknowledged both realities, but was also aware that urbanisation could make it possible to harness state centralism to the economic process that was under way. His government programme proceeded apace. Reconstruction did not mean getting rid of the old values, but combining them with new ones, that is to say, progress where there was respect for tradition, an industrial economy working alongside agriculture, new categories of work and retraining for artisans, adopting the newly emerging consumer goods and the continuation of popular customs.

Rome, the seat of national government, was often the chosen urban landscape for the shorts made by the Centro Documentazione. However, the future economic centres also began to be featured. Milan and Naples, for instance, were used as symbols of a North and South unified by national reconstruction. *Non siamo lontani* (We're Not Far Off, 1953) and *Comunicare a distanza* (Communicating at a Distance, 1953) dealt with the new roads being built and the modernisation of telecommunications throughout the country. *Oggi in Lombardia* (Lombardy Today, 1953) illustrated the economic change. It underlined the effects of recovery in Lombardy, where 80 per cent of industrial plant had been destroyed during the war. Milan is praised as the moral and economic capital of the nation: a city of economic and social culture. 'It is not just a case of rebuilding the old,' the narrator stresses, 'but also of building the brand new.'

The first message promoting urban expansion was launched: 'Houses, houses, everywhere' – these were the words accompanying images of the new Milanese suburbs. From 1945 to 1953 the state concentrated its funding in Lombardy on the construction of habitable rooms: 26,652 rooms in the state sector and 40,000 in private dwellings, with some pretence of more.

In Milan the motor car was no longer a luxury but the expression of better living standards. More generally, the essence of urban life was articulated by the phrase 'the well-being and tranquillity here are the signs of a solid and lasting prosperity'. The images of *Oggi in Lombardia* well illustrate the development of this northern metropolis of the future and, with that, the idea of a vast urban space. The city is described as a composite community having interests which, even though seemingly at times in conflict with one another, were providing new opportunities for growth and development.

Campania industriale (Industrial Campania, 1953), on the other hand, describes a 'Naples that was working, working hard'. An unusually snow-covered Vesuvius serves as a backdrop, but it is a view that is no longer merely picturesque – this is a city in which, as the commentator stresses, 'the overriding imperative is to rebuild, rebuild'. The film claims that Naples had resumed its rhythm as an industrial metropolis of the South; the iron foundries of Pozzuoli stood alongside the busy textile factories and power stations, all ready to serve the vast area of the Campania region. Economic development, as a result, had revolutionised the urban space, creating new types of neighbourhoods on the outskirts, far from the unhealthy slums of the city centre. 'The city of the future' would from then on be located in healthy, expansive and sunny areas such as the Vomero. The government had invested a great deal in the change. In the words of an article in the February 1953 issue of *Documenti di vita italiana*:

> The typical region of the South, which because of its specific circumstances has contributed to the Southern Question, is Campania. Its capital, Naples, is a city whose economy has greatly suffered as a result of Italy's unification and after eighty years its problems have not yet been resolved. The criteria followed for its industrialisation and urban development have always been wrong. The reconstruction may have solved its basic and immediate problems, but it has laid bare the need to radically tackle with far-reaching measures the problems that have gone unresolved in the past. A series of new construction works must be started if Naples and Campania are to be raised to a level of economic importance on a par with northern regions.[15]

De Gasperi was insisting on the observance of principles of national unity: Italy's main expanding urban areas had to be served with the same positive models of social life. Especially with reference to areas of the South, it was essential that a different speed of development did not result. The industrial development policy pursued by the state was one by which factories would be created or expanded both in the North and in the South.

The idea of space and leisure time for all the inhabitants in large urban areas underwent a radical change at the beginning of 1954. *Ai margini della città* (At the

Edge of the City, 1954) was the first government short to encapsulate this. The images of pressing urbanisation are explained in terms of an inevitable and unstoppable condition of change, in spite of the commentary, which often indulges in images of the idyllic countryside being relentlessly eaten up by concrete, with an air of nostalgia for something which unfortunately was rapidly disappearing. Colour, which was effective, although still not quite realistic, was chosen over black and white to suggest the importance of the radical change in the countryside it described. 'The metropolis is at hand,' declares the speaker, Giorgio Stegoni, the well-known voice of many a Fascist newsreel, 'and here we are still in the countryside. It is covered in dust and sand at the edge of the city.' The initial shot opens with a comparison of two kinds of dwellings and the scenery around them. A long sequence of new blocks of flats separates the old and the new, clearly distancing the peasant dwellings from the luxury urban flats. Around this two scenes dominate: one ordered ('every country lane is instantly converted into a road'), the other bucolic ('the august nostalgia for the ruins of ancient aqueducts'). The city chosen is Rome, but it is barely recognisable from the 'bustling and wholesome' life of its new housing estates, far from the charms of the old city centre. The short's message is clear: Italy must turn itself into a country of rapidly expanding cities. Reconstruction, which challenged the old models of the agricultural system, offered in their stead industrialisation, which would profoundly alter the face of cities and their hinterlands. At the edges of cities lived nomadic shepherds and itinerant people who made a living from casual artisan activities. Dignified in their poverty, they were nevertheless ready for the change, already half countrymen and half town-dwellers with a 'healthy zest for life' in the ordered web of the metropolis.

Thus the government entered into the daily lives and life styles of Italians by suggesting new and revolutionary ways of using space and time, and notions such as abundance and quality of life. The country was still essentially traditional, owing to its peasant base: frugality and moderation in consumption were the fundamental values of its culture. Typically, the peasant population carried out their activities near their homes, or at any rate in places that could be reached on foot or with traditional modes of transport, and they certainly had no vacations to while away somewhere else. On the other hand, the changes in the urban landscape revolutionised the habits of its inhabitants, who began to commute daily to their place of work. The need for city-to-city transfers, hitherto rarely experienced, became commonplace and was solved by the use of the private motor vehicle. The industrial development of this product, which was no longer a luxury but a fundamental means of transport, brought motor scooters to the Italians in the large cities, which in the ensuing decade were to be replaced by motor cars. *Ai margini della città* conveyed the idea of the two worlds – the urban and the rural – simply by the representation of faces: the inhabitant of the new periphery and the travelling artisan of many trades. The film was made by Documento Film. The number of copies made was high, in view of the conditions of distribution imposed by the Centro Documentazione, with which the film company had to comply.

In 1954 the theme of economic development began to feature in government films. The productivity of the industrial cities of the North, Milan and Turin in particular, was bombastically eulogised. Such celebratory emphasis contrasted markedly with the way these metropolises were depicted in quality feature films: they were presented in negative terms, as places both physically cold and lacking in human warmth. Turin and Milan were cities where the strong process of industrialisation brought with it a transformation wherein the human dimension had given way to anonymity and alienation. As for Rome, directors depicted it as the embodiment of all vices that had dogged Italy during the course of its history. Rome wanted to free itself from the image of a city of monuments and watercolours. It was the top-ranking mega-city with a backward service sector and a petty bourgeoisie made up of ministerial aides and bureaucrats; in government shorts, however, it took on the role of the place of all places, and was always depicted as the locus of all the positive contrasts and negative contradictions of the country. The old neighbourhoods, where the boundaries between public and private had never existed, had to survive alongside the new isolated neighbourhood conurbations where individualism and guaranteed well-being triumphed over collective solidarity, a necessary sacrifice for modern development. Towering over all this was the magnificent papal architecture which made Rome the *Urbe* – the city *par excellence*. In 1955 *La Roma del Bernini* (Bernini's Rome) was distributed: Bernini's architecture provided an opportunity for expounding on the benefits of the reconstruction of Rome and Naples.

Meanwhile, the number of immigrants in the capital grew rapidly. People driven on by the mirage of plenty and consumerism instead found themselves trapped and waiting for work in the web of the inhospitable and inhuman suburbs. The social and cultural backgrounds of the new arrivals presented significant problems; policy on infrastructure and services was unable to cope with the rapidly growing demands of both the old and the new urban population. Consumerism was steadily gaining ground, so government propaganda abandoned the theme of reconstruction in favour of that of comfortable living. From 1955 to 1959 its shorts talked principally of economic progress.

Giro in Italia (Tour of Italy, 1955) used the popular annual cycling event of the *Giro* to show a renewed and reunited country under the banner of economic and social development. Italians were said to recall the sad times of the war only as a distant memory. They had reacquired their leisure habits, from playing the lottery (*Il lotto*, The Lottery, 1955) to their great passion for football (*La partita dello scudetto*, The Match for the Championship, 1956). Television sets were no longer a luxury but had become a major part of the household; they affected everyday rhythms and created small-screen myths (*Giovedí sera*, Thursday Evening, 1956).

The country was rich: it had natural gas (*Una fiammella si è accesa*, A Small Flame has Started to Burn, 1957), the roads were by then motorways (*Strada panoramica*, Panoramic Route, 1955; *L'autostrada del sole*, The Sun Motorway, 1959) and Italians finally had the vehicles to take advantage of them (*Cicli e motori*, Bikes and Cars, 1956). In short, Italy was on the march, as the title of a significant INCOM newsreel of 1958, *L'Italia è in cammino*, proclaimed. The last newsreel of 1959 was *Il domani non fa più paura* (Tomorrow No Longer Holds Any Fear, 1959): the country was eager to leave the 1950s behind and plunge headlong into the economic boom of the 1960s.

With the end of the 1950s, however, the government's film output declined drastically. Its documentaries were so lacking in content that the press derided them as a useless activity. The left-wing daily *Paese Sera* reported on 12 December 1961: 'Our paper has published several official letters from various Italian embassies protesting at the shoddy quality of documentaries sent abroad to show how much our country has developed.'

The following decades saw no alternative forms of institutional communication. As recently as 11 October 1995 an advertisement published in the Roman daily *Il Messaggero* read: 'Dear Italian State, it seems to us that your capacity to communicate with your citizens is four times lower than in England.' Alas, one thing is clear: public information for citizens remains at the level of celebratory accounts of government activity and fails to communicate effectively.

NOTES

1 G. Piovene, *Viaggio in Italia* (Milan, Mondadori, 1957), p. 28.

2 Quoted from A. De Gasperi, 'Presentazione', *Documenti di vita italiana*, 1 (1951), p. 1. On this magazine see below.

3 Quoted from R. Lefevre, 'Origini e sviluppi del servizio governativo per le informazioni in Italia', *Saggi e studi di pubblicistica*, 2 (1961), pp. 204–5.

4 The editorial staff of *Documenti di vita italiana* was housed in the first division of the Centro Documentazione, whose responsibilities included: the gathering of data on reconstruction, the running of a cuttings and official data archive, the analysis of statistical data and the issuing to all the provinces of communiqués on reconstruction. The fourth division of the Centro Documentazione dealt with foreign administrations and translated *Documenti di vita italiana* into French, English, German and Spanish. On the tasks of the service divisions of the Centro Documentazione, see M. A. Frabotta, 'Il cinegiornalismo degli anni cinquanta', in A. Mignemi, *Propaganda politica e mezzi di comunicazione di massa tra Fascismo e democrazia* (Novara, Istituto Storico della Resistenza, and Turin, Gruppo Abele, 1995), pp. 206–28.

5 The text of his address was published in *Settimana INCOM Illustrata*, 42 (1950), p. 35. The film production company INCOM was founded in 1938 on the initiative of Luigi Freddi. The first *Settimana INCOM* newsreels were made in 1946, and in the same year *La Settimana INCOM Illustrata*, a weekly magazine, also began to appear. On the INCOM newsreels see M. A. Frabotta, 'Il cammino dei cinegiornali italiani nel paese e in Europa', in G. P. Brunetta (ed.), *Identità italiana e identità europea nel cinema italiano dal 1945 al miracolo economico* (Turin, Fondazione Agnelli, 1996), pp. 173–9; *id.*, 'Il cammino dei cinegiornali', *Cinema e Cinema*, 67 (1993), pp. 53–74. On INCOM newsreels' international reports see M. A. Frabotta, 'L'Italia e il mondo nella dimensione degli anni cinquanta: i cinegiornali INCOM', in E. Di Nolfo, R. H. Rainero and B. Vigezzi (eds), *L'Italia e la politica di potenza in Europa, 1950–60* (Settimo Milanese, Marzorati, 1992), pp. 371–89. On INCOM's general structure see G. P. Bernagozzi, 'Le "settimane" del terrore', in G. Tinazzi (ed.), *Cinema italiano degli anni cinquanta* (Padua, Marsilio, 1979), pp. 210–34. See also L. Quaglietti, 'Lo scandalo dei documentari e cinegiornali', in *Storia economico-politica del cinema italiano, 1945–80* (Rome, Editori Riuniti, 1980), pp. 122–42.

6 D. Paolella, 'Foglia di fico per il cronista', in F. Faldini and G. Fofi (eds), *L'avventurosa storia del cinema italiano* (Milan, Feltrinelli, 1979), p. 133.

7 G. P. Brunetta, *Storia del cinema italiano* (Rome, Editori Riuniti, 1993), vol. 3, p. 5.

8 The Bill, entitled 'Istituzione dell'Istituto Nazionale Luce', was introduced by De Gasperi, Guido Gonella (Minister of Education), Mario Scelba (Interior Minister), Ezio Vanoni (Finance Minister) and Giuseppe Pella (Treasury Minister); examined in the Senate on 14 July 1949 and presented by the Prime Minister in November 1950. The Istituto

Nazionale Luce came into being as a private company in 1924 with the aim of producing cultural and educational films. Later, by a decree of 1925, it was transformed into a state-controlled enterprise directly accountable to the head of the government until it became, via a royal decree of 1929, the sole photographic and film service of the state. In 1936 it was made directly answerable to the Ministero della Cultura Popolare, though it maintained the characteristics of a state-controlled enterprise. Its film activities included: the screening of newsreels (four per week, of an average length of not more than 300 metres); documentaries on every subject; and the production and distribution of educational films in association with the ministries of education and popular culture. On relations between the state and the Istituto Luce under Fascism see M. Argentieri, *L'occhio del regime. Informazione e propaganda nel cinema del Fascismo* (Florence, Vallecchi, 1979).

9 On Neo-realism see D. Overby (ed.), *Springtime in Italy. A Reader in Neorealism* (London, Talisman, 1978, 2nd edn); R. Armes, *Patterns of Realism* (New York, Garland, 1986); D. Forgacs, 'The Making and Unmaking of Neo-realism in Post-war Italy', in N. Hewitt (ed.), *The Culture of Reconstruction. European Literature, Thought and Film, 1945–50* (London, Macmillan, 1989), pp. 1–87.

10 See M. Liehm, *Passion and Defiance. Italian Films from 1942 to the Present* (Berkeley, CA, University of California Press, 1984); P. Bondanella, *Italian Cinema. From Neorealism to the Present* (New York, Continuum, 1990); and M. Landy, *Italian Film* (Cambridge University Press, 2000).

11 Casual agricultural labourers, the lowest-paid wage earners at the time, received about 120 lire per hour.

12 A. De Gasperi, 'Presentazione', *Documenti di vita italiana*, 14–15 (1953), p. 1.

13 See M. A. Frabotta, 'L'ora del Sud: informazione governativa italiana per il Mezzogiorno negli anni '50', *Sud*, 5 (1993), pp. 7–43.

14 *Documenti di vita italiana*, December 1953, p. 19.

15 *Ibid.*, February 1953, p. 22.

4

Italian propaganda abroad: the case of the surrogate 'voice of Italians' in post-war Britain

Lucio Sponza

The changes introduced in 1993 in Italy's electoral system failed to empower its over 5 million citizens living abroad to vote for the Italian Parliament in their country of residence, and left them only with the usual non-option of returning to Italy to exercise their most basic political right. In the face of the high hopes of such expatriates, and the indifference of their home-based compatriots, the proposed legislation was not passed, as it fell short of fifteen votes in the Senate in November 1993. The issue returned to the fore in 1997, against the backdrop of the discussion to revise Italy's constitution, which took place within an *ad hoc* parliamentary commission. Expectations were once again dashed in July 1998, when the renewed proposal failed to secure the approval of the Chamber of Deputies – this time by twelve votes.

Had the Bill become law, it would have been interesting to see how the political parties set about organising their electoral campaigns in places as far apart and diverse as Canada, Argentina and Australia. As for European countries with large numbers of Italians (notably France, Germany, Switzerland and Belgium), selective and spasmodic political propaganda has been hurriedly arranged on the eve of parliamentary elections since the 1950s, its intensity being in inverse proportion to the distance of the host country.

Unlike the ordinary strategy of political influence pursued within the peninsula, those erratic campaigns consisted of attempts to persuade the expatriate electorate to return to Italy to vote, as much as to vote for the 'right' party. The former Communist Party used to arrange mass transport by hiring train carriages and coaches, encouraging emigrants – as the slogan went – 'To return to vote. To vote to return.' But that was typical of the 1960s, the last decade of substantial Italian emigration.

Italy's low-key interest in the issue of the expatriate vote 'in loco' is reflected in the absence of studies of the dissemination of general information, let alone on political communication, directed at Italians abroad.[1] The case of Italians in Britain is no exception; nor is it surprising, given the relatively small number involved. Yet anyone considering the matter would discover how a community that is in continuous need of defining itself can easily fall prey to forces which then impose an identity which best suits the agent rather than the community. That is what this chapter is about, although I shall concentrate on the first post-war decade, focusing on the one newspaper which significantly began to circulate within that community in 1948 and which has remained the only major medium of information and ideology ever since: *La Voce degli Italiani*. First, however, it is necessary to outline three interconnected contexts: the idiosyncratic nature of the Italian presence in Britain; the role of the Roman Catholic Church; and the combination of prejudice against Italians and post-war Britain's manpower shortage.

The migration of Italians to Britain never reached massive proportions and their overall presence even diminished in the inter-war period. By the time Italy declared war on Britain, in June 1940, fewer than 18,000 Italians were assumed to be living in the country:[2] most of them were engaged in catering (as waiters, cooks, restaurant keepers and hotel managers) and shopkeeping (mainly small food stores and ice-cream parlours). Nearly half of them resided in London, notably in Clerkenwell, Islington and Soho, but there was also a substantial presence in Manchester, South Wales and Scotland (especially in Glasgow). The vast majority came from two mountain districts: the Apennine valleys between Parma and Lucca, and the Liri valley, between Rome and Naples. It was a century-old example of 'chain migration' based on an originally temporary and itinerant influx, and developed through kinship and village ties. This fragmented background was not remedied by the Italians' general involvement in independent and self-contained activities – which resulted in detachment from the host society – or by the scant attention the pre-Fascist Italian authorities paid them.

Fragmentation, isolation and near oblivion were not conducive to any sense of common belonging, unless within the religious tradition – and even then it was more a case of passive rituality than of genuine fervour and social commitment. A veneer of proud and common identity existed in the 1930s, a consequence of several factors: the praise lavished on the consolidation of the Fascist regime by British opinion-makers, with few exceptions (they changed their tune only after the Italian invasion of Abyssinia in 1935); the welfare policies implemented by the Fascist authorities in favour of the emigrants in the areas of health, education and leisure (though ideologically motivated); and above all, the signing of the Lateran treaties in 1929, which enabled the Duce, the King of Italy and the Pope to be seen as an interdependent and inspiring triad by Italians in general and emigrants in particular (with the exception of the few political exiles, anarchists and other revolutionaries, in Britain). Their alienated condition could thus be sublimated into a sense of belonging and an identity represented by national and spiritual symbols.

Italy's declaration of war on Britain was a terrible blow, and in many cases shattered the very unity of the family, which had been the community's backbone: thousands of men were interned in the Isle of Man, others were deported to Canada and Australia. Hundreds of families were devastated and few remained unscathed by the loss of loved ones due to the catastrophic sinking of the *Arandora Star*.[3] The shared grief was a powerful and painful agent of community awareness, and left a scar on what after the war became to be known as the 'old Italian colony' in Britain. In memory of the nearly 500 men lost, a tablet was placed at the entrance of

St Peter's (the 'Italian church') in Clerkenwell, London. One of the victims was a missionary priest, a symbol of the participatory role of the Roman Catholic Church in the vicissitudes of the emigrants' life, and death.

Furthermore, the central position of the Church in the eyes of many Italians was strengthened by the collapse of all the other institutions which had provided them with a sense of order and continuity, if not also with a sense of identity. The defeat of Fascism had brought about the disintegration of the Italian state and the destruction of the monarchy. From these massive ruins emerged the figure of Pope Pius XII and his Church, to whom, therefore, so many people now looked for a glimpse of hope and inspiration for revival. But the role of the Vatican could not be confined to spiritual matters, now that the advance of Communism in Europe was perceived as a greater threat to Christian civilisation than Fascism had been. Nor was Western liberal thought regarded with sympathy, or even understanding, by a Pope whose 'apocalyptic vision meant that he was unable to find much good in the contemporary world'.[4]

So the Church threw all its weight behind the Christian Democratic Party, which was facing the challenge of the left-wing Front in the 1948 general election. A direct consequence of the victory of the Christian Democrats and the Vatican was the intensification of deflationary monetary policies, which aimed to keep the national debt under control and the lira steady, notwithstanding that the substantial financial aid received under the Marshall Plan would have enabled the Italian government to provide job-creating investment without causing inflationary pressure. Consequently, poverty and unemployment found an outlet in emigration, which continued to be a major feature for nearly two decades.

Nor did the Christian Democrats' triumph of 1948 serve as an encouragement to restraint by the Roman Catholic Church in its efforts to influence all aspects of social life. On the contrary, now that the levers of power were firmly controlled by the new crusaders, the objective was set for the edification of a holistic Christian state, on the grounds that a state cannot 'have a different conscience from that of its citizens'.[5] In this attempt 'the network of parishes became a ramified and ubiquitous labour exchange, a parson's *raccomandazione* (testimonial) became the key to open otherwise closed doors'.[6]

This was not confined to Italian affairs, as far as Italian workers were concerned; the British government resorted to thorough vetting of would-be Italian immigrants under official schemes introduced in the early post-war years to meet labour shortages which threatened to undermine the recovery of the economy.[7] The purpose was to weed out Communists and similar troublemakers. Before they were screened by British officials in Italy, both men and women were investigated by the police, which relied on the views of the local religious authorities and organisations. Later, women were spared the examination. The discreet collusion between the British and Italian governments can be seen in the following letter addressed by W. H. Braine, the British labour attaché in Rome, to an official at the Ministry of Labour in London, suggesting that the Italian authorities should be entrusted with the whole procedure:

> On the question of screening for political sympathies, this could be undertaken by the Italians mainly through the Local Police and Carabinieri and counterchecked by the local Church representatives, e.g. the Parish Priest, *Azione Cattolica* (AC) and/or *Associazioni Cristiane Lavoratori Italiani* (ACLI). What is most important and must be emphasised throughout is that no mention of such screening should appear in any official communications to the Italians or in any records of conversations or other memoranda. Publicity on this point could be sufficient to bring the Government down. A counter-check as to the political sympathies of the men could, to some extent, be exercised by the appropriate section of the Embassy here and the various contacts of that section.[8]

The vetting of Italian immigrants had been obsessively required by the Home Office and by MI5, but Braine himself – who supervised the recruitment of Italian workers for British industry – thought that the procedure seriously delayed the operation and was actually ineffective.[9] The Rome-based labour attaché himself had on several occasions criticised the procedures, as will be shown later. Not to mention the fact that more Italians came to Britain outside such government-sponsored schemes through the mechanism of individual labour permits for which no screening was envisaged.

Yet at a time of persistent labour shortages for hard and menial occupations, Italy offered the possibility of cheap labour, after the reservoir of Poles and other Eastern Europeans (mostly recruited through the British government-sponsored scheme 'European Volunteer Workers') had been exhausted. Several private recruiting agencies, as well as government departments, were actively pursuing such a course. Some even tried to cash in on the real or imagined subversive danger. One such instance was the Benedict Bureau, based in the Republic of Ireland but mainly active in Britain, which claimed to have good credentials and contacts with 'reliable' institutions in Italy.

The Bureau was introduced to the British government by its manager as 'quite a large [agency] run on Christian principles, [which] co-operate[s] very closely with a number of official emigration organisations in other countries'. Their contact in Italy was with the Comitato Assistenza Emigranti, a government-sponsored institution based in Turin. As for the Communist-free 'merchandise' they offered, it was added that: 'We supply male and female, skilled and unskilled, labour, and in this connection we would say that all work and character references are checked and the emigrants are guaranteed to be without Communist affiliations.' The reply by the Ministry of Labour was that the government-sponsored schemes of recruitment were adequate and no external contribution was necessary.[10] In fact, officials there had become sceptical for some time as to the danger of importing Communism from Italy. Two years earlier it was pointed out that: 'There has been substantial migration of Italians to many other countries and . . . we have not yet heard of any difficulty having arisen as the result of any of these recruits having subsequently busied themselves in propagating Communist doctrines'. The point was also made, for good measure, that Italian women were even less likely to cause trouble, as they were 'not so politically minded as their menfolk'.[11]

The letter was addressed to the Ministry's Regional Officer for the East and West Ridings, where wool industrialists had enquired about the arrangements for excluding Communist agitators. Concern had arisen when two Italian women engaged in the Lancashire cotton industry were reported to be politically motivated troublemakers. The accusation came from the Italian woman official who had accompanied them in their journey to Britain. The view of W. H. Braine was solicited, and he promptly obliged, advising caution:

> It is so easy to describe as Communist or Fascist, as the case may be, anyone who has sufficient independence of character to take a stand or who is just bloody-minded. Before we start a witch-hunt we should have clear evidence that a particular individual is conducting political propaganda or is deliberately acting as the agent of a particular political party.

There was no such evidence, but one of the two women was sent back to Italy. As to the remedy for the malaise among the workers, the labour attaché expressed his surprise 'that little or nothing [had] been done to arrange for these Italian women to meet Italian-speaking people and have regular visits from an Italian-speaking priest', as the workers themselves had repeatedly expressed this desire.[12]

The Italian clergy and missionaries in Britain were taken by surprise by the new wave of immigration, notably by that of young women workers, which started in 1949. In the immediate post-war years their concern was to restore the network of contacts within the old Italian colony which had suffered so much during the war, both materially and psychologically, to the extent that it was now mute and disoriented. An important step towards that recovery and the rekindling of the immigrants' pride in being Italian *and* Roman Catholic was the launch of a newspaper: *La Voce degli Italiani* (hereafter *La Voce*).

La Voce first appeared as a small-size monthly in January 1948,[13] but its ambition was to reach Italians throughout Great Britain. Its founder and director was Padre Domenico Valente, of the Pauline Order, who was based at St Peter's, although services there were administered by the Pallottini Fathers. The early issues of the paper provided readers with useful information on consular services, legal practices and health; they also contained items of historical and entertainment value, but religious and pastoral items were prominent. St Peter's had been the main focus of the London-based Italian community for the best part of the preceding 100 years, as its opening went back to 1864. Yet never before had the Italian missionaries launched such an ambitious newspaper, possibly because the only previous attempt at addressing Italians in Britain (as opposed to those living in London, or elsewhere in the country), namely a weekly entitled *L'Italia Nostra*, upheld Roman Catholic values and comprehensively informed its readers of official religious events. The fact that this was also the mouthpiece of the Italian Fascist party in Britain and the instrument of vehement political propaganda[14] did not bother the Italian priests and missionaries.

The leading article in the first issue of *La Voce* made it clear that patriotism and traditional faith went hand in hand, and that therefore its message was addressed to wherever 'there was an Italian heart still throbbing for these two loves: God and Country'. Still, in a system of belief based on hierarchical structure, there was no doubt as to the order of that dual loyalty: 'We are above all God's children; we are both Italian and Catholic and must take pride in it; as Catholics we are more united in brotherhood because our religion provides us with a bond more everlasting [*sic*] than our nationality.' Divisive factors were also mentioned and rejected: '[This paper] will not concern itself with politics of any kind: politics come between us, whereas religion and the love of our country unite us. We seek to form a family bond.'[15] Indeed, the family, together with God and country, made up the triadic icon the emigrants were meant to worship if they wanted to preserve their Italianness.

The resolution to avoid politics was expedient, superfluous and disingenuous. It was expedient because the infatuation with Fascist propaganda had left a painful legacy among the Italians who had been in Britain a long time. In addition, conjuring up old ghosts might have caused embarrassment to some of the leading contributors and founders of the paper, since they had also written for the Fascist sheet and had not spared any eulogies to the Duce. It was superfluous because most Italians coming to work in Britain were either apolitical or, as we know, had already been screened. Even when, in the 1950s and early 1960s, Italians migrated to Britain in relatively large numbers, 'political life as such, be it local or national, [did] not concern [them] much'.[16] Finally, the resolution not to discuss politics was disingenuous because it assumed that to defend and promote values stemming from religious principles would not involve ethical and political judgements. Even when it came to party politics, *La Voce*'s editors could not refrain from clear statements on what to support and what to condemn at certain junctures.

The first test came only a few months after the paper's establishment, on the occasion of the momentous election of April 1948. Before polling day it was written that the political conflict was no mere electoral competition, but 'the dramatic contrast between two civilisations, two life philosophies, two worlds of irreconcilable enemies', and the article concluded with the invocation 'God bless Italy'. After the Christian Democrats' victory, the voters were praised in the following terms: 'despite the fact that we are poor, we know how to resist the temptations of the devil in Communist attire'.[17] While accepting that these words were written with sincerity and empathy, the rhetorical device of assuming common cause with the readers and faraway compatriots was pushed too far when this cloak of shared poverty was donned by a very rich woman.

The writer of those lines was in fact Donna Marcella Carr Salazar, a wealthy Italian who had married into the English aristocracy and lived in a mansion, Ditchingham Hall, in Norfolk. She was one of the founders of *La Voce* and an assiduous early contributor who liked to sign her articles 'Donna Nennella', and describe herself as 'a mother and grandmother'.[18] Her daughter – the Marchioness of Lothian – was also a fervent supporter of *La Voce*. Family harmony, religious fervour and a certain philosophy of life were the causes which 'Donna Nennella' felt impelled to act upon on behalf of her compatriots married to British men. At the end of December 1947 she circulated a letter to as many Italian 'war wives' as she could reach, inviting them to meet regularly at the Club of Italian-British Families, which she herself had set up. Incidentally, this was the first post-war organisation which sought to establish a network of contacts among Italians in Britain. The meeting was to take place at the Brompton Oratory in South Kensington, London. Their children and husbands were also welcome, and as a possible bait for the latter she informed them that a billiard room would be at their disposal. The newspaper was to act as the link among the various local 'Family Circles' which Donna Nennella hoped would spring up.

Meanwhile, for the women who were writing to her expressing sadness and homesickness, Donna Nennella's advice was to 'pray and remember that so much depends on us, as Roman Catholic women, if this world is ever to improve; remember, too, that it is the same the world over, that life is desperately hard everywhere'. As for correspondents who asked for help to find work, the reply was: 'We shall do all we can for those who need it, but I beg to repeat the exhortation to those of you who can afford it, to dedicate all your time to your husband and to your children.'[19]

At one point Donna Nennella was encouraged by Padre Valente to communicate to her readers the 'wise words' for married couples attributed to the famous tycoon and moralising philanthropist, Andrew Carnegie. This was in the form of a double decalogue quiz; the first set of questions were addressed to the husbands, the second to the wives. The husbands were urged to be kind and considerate; to show their love through flowers and gifts at anniversaries; to make an effort to understand their companions' 'voluble frame of mind'; to avoid any embarrassing comparison with other women (notably with their own mothers); to show gratefulness for all the little services their wives rendered, 'such as, for example, sewing on buttons to your shirt, mending your socks, washing your clothes'. The wives were advised always to be caring; to make home life pleasant for their spouses (even by making an effort to prepare varied and unexpected meals); not to interfere unduly with their husbands' work, but to be able to discuss it with them; indeed, even to keep abreast of politics and intellectual interests which their husbands might cultivate; to try to maintain good relations with their in-laws (especially with their mothers-in-law); to choose their own clothing, bearing in mind their husbands' tastes in terms of colours and fashion.[20]

It was not necessary to serve up Carnegie's wisdom. Only a year earlier the Catholic journal with the largest circulation in Italy, *Famiglia Cristiana*, had published the 'Decalogue of the Christian [i.e. Roman Catholic] bride' expounding almost verbatim the philanthropist's philosophy on matrimonial matters. This is not surprising, since one would expect conservative and reactionary thinkers, whether professing worldly or spiritual inclinations, to put forth obedience and subordination both as virtues in themselves and the foundation stones of a stable social order. Yet when it came to the 'war wives' a conflict of loyalties could have undermined such instructions. In one of the regular reports Donna Nennella received from the various and expanding Family Circles it was revealed that sometimes British husbands objected to their wives' going to Mass on Sunday morning. In her role as agony aunt she suggested a three-pronged strategy. First, the unhappy wife should pray to the Lord for a change in her husband's attitude. If that did not work, she should talk her husband out of his obstinacy by stressing that there is only one Church for Roman Catholics, wherever they happen to live. Finally, 'if you fail to persuade him with your kind ways, have the courage to make him understand that not even marital authority can force you either to renounce your Religion or to forget your Country'.[21]

Worse was the case of the correspondent whose marriage had been celebrated in an Italian Protestant church (because the couple's arrival in Britain was imminent and there was no time for the bureaucratic procedure required by the Roman Catholic ceremony). Padre Valente replied by stating categorically that: 'your marriage is only valid in terms of civil law; it is invalid before God. Consequently, you and the gentleman with whom you live are not husband and wife.' The remedy of a proper Roman Catholic marriage was suggested.[22]

With almost the same zeal shown in Italy in the fight against atheism and Communism, the Italian Roman Catholic authorities in Britain fought against secularisation and Protestantism. For this purpose to claim that Catholics had a monopoly over the Christian God was not enough; it was also argued that only *Italian* clergy and missionaries could be entrusted with the task of keeping the traditional faith alive among the emigrants. The authority of the arch-conservative Cardinal Piazza was called upon, by quoting him as saying that 'Experience teaches that when [Italian] emigrants are left without the religious services administered by [Italian] priests, all too often they lose their faith and fall victim to religious indifference or Protestantism.'[23]

Yet for all this concern, as we have already noted, the Italian Catholic authorities were criticised by W. H. Braine for neglecting the young women employed in the textile industries of the north of England. The thin distribution of new Italian immigration over wide areas, far from the mainly urban centres which had a tradition of an Italian presence, did pose logistic problems for the religious authorities. It was only just before Christmas (1949), several months after the arrival of the first workers, that an Italian missionary from St Peter's Church (Don Ermete Bonomo) ventured forth to Lancashire to visit the young Italian women there. He candidly admitted that the trip was suggested by the Italian ambassador (Tommaso Gallarati Scotti) and by the Bishop of Nottingham (Monsignor Ellis), who chaired the Catholic Committee on European Volunteer Workers. As for his impression of the Italian textile workers, Don Bonomo stated that he was very happy as far as their religious life was concerned and praised the women in Italy belonging to *Azione Cattolica* for having encouraged their emigrating fellow citizens to stay loyal to their common faith. The missionary priest was particularly touched by the workers' promise that they would take Holy Communion at Christmas. He was also confident about the positive role to be played by the new Committee for the Assistance to the Italians in Great Britain. This was set up by the ambassador and chaired by his wife; it included the wives of other diplomatic and consular officials and the wives of the most distinguished members of the Italian colony. The main purpose of these endeavours was to avoid that 'anyone of those young women should find herself in a painful condition of isolation, something which is the biggest danger for anyone forced to work and live far away from his or her family'.[24]

Yet when by the end of 1951 Italian Roman Catholic missions were established in Liverpool and Leeds to look after Italians in northern England, their reports sometimes expressed concern about the women workers. The best known of such cases was raised by Padre Tolmino Taddei, who was the missionary priest based in Leeds. First of all he criticised the fact that on their arrival in Britain Italian women were exposed to the presence of young male refugees from Eastern Europe, 'mingling not only in the industrial towns but also in the same factories, among the looms on the same floor, and I dare say even in their dwellings'. As a result,

> So many girls have lost their youth, many of whom will only return to Italy when forced to do so by the police. Others have had to settle for invalid unions, for marriages which are likely to be temporary. Only God can know how many abortions have occurred and how many are still taking place. I know of several cases in which girls have become sterile as a consequence of botched abortions. Nor should it ever be forgotten that England, especially in the industrial districts, is the land of divorced people, of bachelors, of adventure-seeking foreigners, even of negroes from the West Indies, etc.[25]

Even if the Italian authorities fully shared Padre Taddei's views, down to his openly racist remark, they were unable to control the workers' lives abroad; nor were they willing to accede to the missionary's suggestion that the emigration of women under the age of twenty-one should be prohibited. Unable to twist the arm of the Italian authorities as they were successfully doing within Italy, the Roman Catholic Church could only resort to its own channels to campaign among the emigrants and warn them against the temptations of an alien environment, in which the supposedly most cherished values of the Italian tradition (the holiness of the family and the purity of womanhood) were at risk. The defence of national identity was therefore regarded as one and the same thing as the defence of the Roman Catholic faith.

There was no mention of this disquiet in the pages of *La Voce*. On the contrary, in the articles on the women workers a light-hearted, patronising tone was adopted: women were portrayed as a childlike, cheerful and pious lot. Reporting on a Boxing Day party organised in London by the Missionary Sisters of Verona, it was pointed out that it was as if the young women were looked after by good mothers. Indeed, 'all of them shared the same naive enthusiasm for the magnificent Christmas tree allowing them the illusion of becoming children again'. The gaiety and pleasant chit-chat in various Italian dialects were only interrupted by the big cheer which arose to welcome Padre Mario Bigarella, who 'had come to honour the nice party with his presence' and who made 'their hearts resonate [with his] simple and warm words of reassurance and encouragement to continue along the path of a virtuous and laborious life'.[26]

Monsignor Bigarella had arrived in Britain only a few months earlier to co-ordinate the work of the newly established Italian Roman Catholic Missions: the response to the growing wave of Italian immigrants to Britain (notably for employment in brickworks around Bedford and Peterborough) and to the perceived grave peril which confronted them. This, in his own words, was that the Italians might be disoriented when faced with 'so many sects [*sic*], each practising different and even juxtaposed forms of Christianity'. They might come to believe that, in the end, it was only a question of personal opinion and choice, but he warned them: 'From this condition it would be only a matter of time before religious indifference, total abandonment of the faith, out-and-out paganism were reached.'[27]

The Chief Missionary knew that it was impossible for his clergy to keep in regular contact with individuals and small groups belonging to a dispersed community of immigrants. He therefore supported the religious integration of Italians with British Catholics at the local level. He explained his reasons in *La Voce*, showing particular concern for the young women workers in distant districts who married Poles, Ukrainians and Yugoslavs, and – raising the customary alarm concerning non-Catholic marriages – he pointed to the invalidity of the bond before God and the virtually inevitable slippery slope to 'the desertion of the Catholic Faith'. Yet however desirable the integration of Italians with the indigenous Catholics, he also added that his recommended course could not succeed easily because the British 'are well-mannered and polite, but keep the foreigners at a distance'.[28]

Monsignor Bigarella also pressed the Vatican authorities for a clear statement in favour of his suggestion, but his words fell on deaf ears.[29] This was hardly surprising: by criticising the segregationist course adopted by the Roman Catholic authorities, Bigarella hit at the very heart of the plan which equated the preservation of the emigrants' Italian identity with their religious allegiance to the Church of Rome.

Would Italians in Great Britain have become less isolated from the host society had the Vatican not made efforts to provide them with their own churches, parishes and opportunities for social interaction? Probably not, since other, more powerful and interlocking factors contributed to the Italians' general failure to integrate into British society. These were: their tendency to concentrate on their families and work, ignoring any larger commitment; their self-deceptive and unrealistic determination to return to Italy after few years; the nature of their idiosyncratic occupations, which kept them tightly together where the employment was in specific industrial sectors, or dispersed in a myriad of small, family-based units in food dealing and shopkeeping; the unintrusive nature of British institutions and civil society, which can be easily interpreted as indifference or even hostility; the language barrier, which made sustained interchange very difficult.

For all these reasons it was said that: 'It was the various Italian Missions which looked after the social needs of the new [immigrant] communities, and also provided recreational and sporting facilities in some cases. This help was invaluable in providing a sense of security for the immigrant.'[30]

Whether the right balance was struck between that sense of security and the need to break down the isolation is difficult to say. What is certain, in the light of the subsequent overall history of the Italians in Britain and the pervasive role of the Catholic Church and its affiliated organisations, is that the permanent condition of detachment from British society is paired with a growing alienation from Italian society as well. The profound social and economic changes which began in the mid-1950s have transformed Italy into a completely different country. Yet the mass of emigrants who arrived in Britain between the late 1940s and throughout the 1960s have remained almost as if in a time capsule. The Catholic clergy's and missionaries' singleminded pursuit of a narrowly defined course of traditional values contributed, in the end, to that double dislocation – an inevitable result, perhaps, of the emigrants' condition of physical and emotional displacement.

NOTES

1 The lack of comprehensive studies of the press and other media among emigrants is hardly redressed by the yearly surveys of the Italian press abroad published by the Federazione Unitaria della Stampa Italiana all'Estero. The best-known work on the subject, *La stampa italiana all'estero dalle origini ai nostri giorni*, by V. Briani (Rome, Istituto Poligrafico dello Stato, 1977), badly needs thorough revision. For a historical outline of Italian press in Great Britain see L. Sponza, 'La présence italienne en Grande Bretagne à travers ses journaux, 1890–1990', in A. Bechelloni, M. Dreyfus and P. Milza (eds), *L'Intégration italienne en France* (Brussels, Complexe, 1995), pp. 389–97. More generally, on the limited interest shown by Italian political institutions towards Italians abroad, see G. Tassello, 'Esiste una politica italiana verso gli italiani all'estero?' in *Studi Emigrazione*, 127 (1997), pp. 487–99.

2 The figure did not include the children of Italians, if born in Britain.

3 The *Arandora Star* was transporting Italian, German and Austrian internees to Canada when it was hit by a torpedo and sank on 2 July 1940. See P. and L. Gillman, *'Collar the Lot!' How Britain Interned and Expelled its Wartime Refugees* (London, Melbourne and New York, Quartet Books, 1980), chapter 17; A. Bernabei, *Esuli ed emigrati italiani nel Regno Unito, 1920–40* (Milan, Mursia, 1997), chapter 17; L. Sponza, *Divided Loyalties. Italians in Britain during the Second World War* (Berne, Peter Lang, 2000), chapter 4.

4 P. Hebblethwaite, *In the Vatican* (London, Sidgwick & Jackson, 1986), p. 33.

5 Quoted in a thorough reassessment of the role of the Roman Catholic Church and Pius XII in the first decade of post-war Italy: G. Miccoli, 'La Chiesa di Pio XII nella società italiana del dopoguerra', in F. Barbagallo (ed.), *Storia dell'Italia repubblicana*, vol. I (Turin, Einaudi, 1994), p. 561.

6 *Ibid.*, p. 568.

7 See T. Colpi, *The Italian Factor. The Italian Community in Great Britain* (Edinburgh and London, Mainstream, 1991), pp. 144–9.

8 Public Record Office (henceforth PRO), LAB 13/833; letter by W. H. Braine to G. D. E. Ball (Overseas Department of the Ministry of Labour), 26 August 1950. It is part of correspondence concerning the proposal to recruit Italians for coal mining.

9 Various documents on this criticism are included in the PRO files of the Ministry of Labour (LAB), namely: 8/1214, on iron-foundry workers; 8/1713 and 13/822, on women for the cotton industry; 13/833–4, on coal mines; 8/1798, on brickworkers. See also, for general considerations, 13/804, 'Italian recruitment: Home Office [HO] security check and questions arising on delay in recruitment, 1951–60'.

10 The correspondence, dating from August 1951, is in PRO, LAB 13/817, file No. 91.

11 PRO, LAB 8/1713; copy of a letter by P. Goldberg to H. Stevens, 29 July 1949.

12 PRO, LAB 13/822; letter by W. H. Braine to G. D. E. Ball, 13 October 1949. Fifty young Italian women had arrived in Lancashire in June 1949. The scheme was successful, and further recruitment followed. The Italian official was a Professor Magnino, personally chosen by the Italian Minister of Labour (Amintore Fanfani) to shepherd the cotton workers. She was described by Braine, in the same quoted letter, as 'of the studious, professional type, rather remote from everyday life and very probably out of sympathy with the working class'.

13 *La Voce degli Italiani* started to appear fortnightly in 1957, and continues to do so.

14 As far as the contents of *L'Italia Nostra* was concerned, there was little the missionaries objected to and much that met their enthusiastic approval. Unofficially and at a higher

level, however, relations between the Fascist authorities, on the one hand, and the Vatican and missionary orders of Italians abroad, on the other, were sometimes tense and marked by reciprocal suspicion. See: P. V. Cannistraro and G. Rosoli, *Emigrazione, Chiesa e fascismo* (Rome, Studium, 1979), especially chapter 4; G. Rosoli, 'Santa Sede e propaganda fascista all'estero tra i figli degli emigrati italiani', *Storia Contemporanea*, 17:2 (1986), pp. 293–315.

15 'Ho cambiato il cielo ma non il cuore', *La Voce degli Italiani*, January 1948, p. 1.

16 B. Bottignolo, *Without a Bell Tower. A Study of the Italian Immigrants in South West England* (Rome, Centro Studi Emigrazione, 1985), p. 63.

17 'Diciotto aprile' and 'Circolo della famiglia', *La Voce degli Italiani*, April 1948, p. 3, and June 1948, p. 5, respectively.

18 In other words, this lady was a typical aristocrat 'divid[ing] her time between caring for her own children [and grandchildren] and charity work on behalf of the poor' (with whom she identified so closely), as is argued, with reference to the vehicle of Roman Catholicism in Italy, by Stefano Pivato, 'Strumenti dell'egemonia cattolica', in S. Soldani and G. Turi (eds), *Fare gli italiani* (Bologna, Il Mulino, 1993), vol. II, p. 365.

19 'Circolo delle famiglie Italo-Inglesi', *La Voce degli Italiani*, January 1948, p. 5. Regular and often lengthy articles under the same title appeared for a couple of years.

20 *Ibid.*, July 1949, p. 7.

21 *Ibid.*, August 1948, p. 5.

22 *Ibid.*, March 1948, p. 2. This advice featured in the column 'Letters to the Director'. Only short extracts from the letters were reproduced, followed by lengthy answers. A section entirely devoted to the readers' views would have been out of keeping with the pontificating tone of the paper. Even when, in the mid-1970s, such a section was introduced, only a few sympathetic letters were published.

23 'Con gli italiani di Londra', *La Voce degli Italiani*, December 1950, p. 5.

24 'Come stanno le lavoratrici italiane in Gran Bretagna (intervista con Don E. Bonomo)', *La Voce degli Italiani*, February 1950, p. 5.

25 Archivio Centrale dello Stato, Ministero del Lavoro, Direzione Generale Collocamento Manodopera, Div. IX, box 20, folder 96. The report, dated 17 September 1952, was sent to the ACLI, which forwarded it to the Italian Ministry of Labour. Incidentally, by 1951 the Italian-born population in Britain had increased to 34,000; of these 21,000 (61 per cent) were women.

26 'Un'ora lieta per le lavoratrici italiane a Londra', *La Voce degli Italiani*, February 1952, p. 7.

27 'La nuova emigrazione italiana in Gran Bretagna', *La Voce degli Italiani*, February 1952, p. 7. Three missionary districts had been set up, based on London, Leeds and Liverpool. By the end of 1954 they had increased to five: Leeds, Rochdale, Birmingham, Bedford and London. Four years later there were nine, now reaching into Scotland: Glasgow, Rochdale, Bradford, Leicester, Birmingham, Bedford, Peterborough, Bristol and London.

28 'Le missioni cattoliche in Gran Bretagna', *La Voce degli Italiani*, January 1955, p. 9.

29 See P. Doyle, *Post-war Italian Immigration to Britain*, Bedford Environment and Community Research Unit, 1989, pp. 13–14. I am grateful to Dr Doyle for providing me with a copy of this cyclostyled study.

30 *Ibid.*, p. 14.

5

The Italian Communist Party in propaganda films of the early post-war period

Mino Argentieri

The Italian Communist Party (PCI) was the first political party in Italy to set up a film division, at its headquarters in the Via delle Botteghe Oscure, Rome. Between 1947 and 1948 the division was run by Marcello Bollero, later by Giuseppe Alessandri. This small division was part of the Press and Propaganda Department and had numerous responsibilities. It made documentaries and propaganda shorts, including the so-called *filmine* (short films with fixed images and captions), appointed film critics, wrote film reviews for the Communist and allied press, and dealt with economic, technical and legislative problems. In addition, it was responsible for the development of the cine-club movement, the *Amici del Cinema* (Friends of the Cinema), and ran the film production and distribution company Libertas Film[1] and the Cooperativa Spettatori Produttori Cinematografici (Film-makers and Audience Co-operative). The latter made two of Carlo Lizzani's early films: *Achtung! Banditi!* (Beware! Bandits! 1951), a fictional account of Resistance activities in Liguria, and *Cronache di poveri amanti* (Tales of Poor Lovers, 1954), which was adapted from a novel by Vasco Pratolini and dealt with life in a quiet street of Florence in the early years of Fascism.

Between 1947 and 1957 many of the PCI's film-related activities were smothered by restrictive government measures.[2] Libertas Film, for example, had to close down because most of the films on its lists were rejected by the censors.[3] The Cooperativa Spettatori Produttori Cinematografici also folded when export licences were refused for *Achtung! Banditi!* and *Cronache di poveri amanti*. Some documentaries were banned. Among them were: *La lunga lotta* (The Long Struggle, undated) produced by Federterra, the old left-wing union of rural workers, which dealt with the problems of peasant labour; Gillo Pontecorvo's *I fatti di Celano* (The Celano Incidents, 1950), an account of the May Day rally of 1950 in Celano (Abruzzo region), which led to two agricultural labourers being killed by the vigilantes of local landowners; and Sergio Grieco's *Il cammino della libertà* (The March of Freedom, 1951), a chronicle of the thirtieth anniversary of the PCI. Moreover, over half was cut from Lizzani's *I fatti di Modena* (The Modena Incidents, 1950) – the part reconstructing the massacre of six striking factory workers by the police.

The censors' offensive, which penalised Neo-realist and foreign films as much as those produced by the PCI, led to more *filmine* being produced, since the law did not affect this glorified magic-lantern type of material. It explains why the PCI's film output from 1947 to 1957 was intermittent.

None of the films made during the years immediately following Italy's liberation are extant. During that period the partisans' association, ANPI, together with the film company Titanus, produced a full-length documentary on the Resistance entitled *Giorni di gloria* (Days of Glory, 1944–45). The project was co-ordinated by Giuseppe De Santis and Mario Serandrei, together with Marcello Pagliero and Luchino Visconti. ANPI also produced two feature films: Aldo Vergano's *Il sole sorge ancora* (The Sun Still Rises, 1946), a tribute to the Resistance movement, and De Santis's *Caccia tragica* (Tragic Hunt, 1948), a political melodrama set in the immediate post-war period.

Three shorts, including one directed by Aldo Vergano entitled *Chi dorme non piglia pesci* (The Early Bird Catches the Worm), can no longer be traced. They were prepared for the 1948 election campaign and shown from mobile units in the squares.[4] Also lost are the only two reels released of the *Cinegiornale del popolo* (The People's Newsreel). Made in 1949, they were intended to be alternatives to *La Settimana INCOM* and other pro-government cinema newsreels.[5] The shorts made by amateur film makers from within the Communist ranks and trade union organisations have also vanished.

The catalogue of the Archivio Audiovisivo del Movimento Operaio e Democratico[6] contains the titles of sixteen films centrally produced by the PCI from 1948 to 1960. In chronological order they are:[7]

1 *Quattordici luglio* (The 14th of July, 1948), directed by Glauco Pellegrini. (Discussed below.)
2 *Togliatti è tornato* (Togliatti is Back, 1948), made up of clips shot by different directors and edited by Carlo Lizzani. (Discussed below.)
3 *Nel Mezzogiorno qualcosa è cambiato* (Something has Changed in the South, 1949), directed by Carlo Lizzani. (Discussed below.)
4 *Viva 'L'Unità'* (Long Live *L'Unità*, 1949), anonymous. A documentary about the distribution of the Communist daily by activists in various Italian cities.
5 *Amici dell' 'Unità'* (Friends of *L'Unità*, 1949), directed by Carlo Lizzani. This documentary deals with the distribution of *L'Unità* in the country and in the workplace.
6 *Gioventù in marcia* (Youth on the March, 1949), anonymous. A chronicle of the demonstration by the Communist youth organisation Alleanza Giovanile.
7 *Modena, città dell'Emilia rossa* (Modena, a City of 'Red' Emilia, 1950), directed by Carlo Lizzani. (Discussed below.)
8 *I fatti di Modena* (The Modena Incidents, 1950), directed by Carlo Lizzani.
9 *Il cammino della libertà* (The Road to Freedom, 1951), directed by Sergio Grieco.
10 *Omaggio a Cesare Manetti* (A Tribute to Cesare Manetti, 1953), directed by Piero Cristofani and produced by the Castelfiorentino branch of the PCI. Manetti was a local Communist leader murdered by the Fascists.

11 *Giovanna*, 1955, directed by Gillo Pontecorvo. This medium-length film about the political education of a woman during the occupation of a textile plant was later incorporated into *Die Windrose* (The Windrose, 1956), an international, multi-episodic work co-ordinated by the Dutch political film maker Joris Ivens and financed by the state-owned East German film organisation DEFA.
12 *Gli uomini vogliono la pace* (People Want Peace, 1958), anonymous. A documentary on the subject of war and peace, produced for the 1958 election campaign.
13 *Gli uomini vogliono vivere* (People Want to Live, 1958), anonymous. Another documentary on war and peace.
14 *Milano 1959* (Milan 1959, 1959), anonymous. A documentary on the city council of Milan, produced for the 1960 local election campaign.
15 *Tre anni di storia: dall'8° al 9° congresso del PCI* (Three Years of History: from the Eighth to the Ninth congress of the PCI, 1960), anonymous. An account of the two Communist congresses and of the main events of 1958–60.
16 *Carosello elettorale* (Election Roundabout, 1960), anonymous. A PCI election propaganda short parodying well-known television advertisements.

The government's control over radio and television and its stranglehold over the cinema, newsreels and documentaries, which lasted until 1960, hindered the use of cinema for propaganda purposes. This explains why the PCI preferred to rely on newspapers, posters, flyers, banners, housing-block and farmstead meetings and public rallies. However, as the above list shows, the PCI did not give in altogether – not even in the most difficult moments, such as after the electoral setback of 1948.

Looking at the early PCI films, it comes as a surprise to see how little they were influenced by Neo-realism. Neo-realism showed an Italy tormented by persistent problems of a social, economic, human and psychological nature, largely unknown to many Italians. It also provided the means of openly confronting those problems. The PCI's films, however, lay outside the fiction genre, and as examples of propaganda they were axiomatic – they did not inform, and documented little. Their discourse, like that of the speeches made at party rallies, was simple, declarative and lacking in argumentation. Whether such propaganda was effective is open to question.

Rarely did the shorts react against either the arguments of the other political camps or the stereotyped images of the PCI. They were geared to audiences already on the left and sympathetic to the PCI. The image of the party and the workers' movement which they promoted was free from radical excesses and sectarianism. What they represented was a kind of 'in' conversation, which, while failing to stamp out existing prejudices and antiquated opinions, succeeded in reinforcing new political convictions. (This, indeed, is more propaganda than consolidation.) Their ends were also pedagogic: activists and supporters were encouraged to conform to the 'model' being presented and to learn to change in the light of new circumstances; in other words, they were meant to free themselves from an anachronistic style and the romantic stereotype of the revolutionary Communist.

The early films were somewhat starchy and reminiscent of news reports. However, their objectivity was feigned, as the point of view they put across was strictly in accordance with the official party line. The first clues in this respect are found in the declamatory tone of the voice-over commentary and in the directors' assertive roles. Amazingly, ordinary people, the protagonists in these films, never speak a word, not even to endorse the party's views. First-hand accounts (e.g. interviews) and live sound recordings were never used, save in the filming of leaders' speeches or their contributions to debates. These admittedly expensive techniques were common practice in English, American and Soviet documentaries of the 1930s and 1940s and in the newsreels of the New Deal. They were employed rather less in Italian cinema, though frequent use was made of them in the *Settimana INCOM* newsreels.

The absence of sound recording of personal accounts was not due to lack of technical or financial resources. It was a case of a deliberate choice: as a disciplined organisation the PCI favoured stentorian pronouncements from above. In the depiction of events and gatherings, the directors indulged in 'choral' images, namely massive protest marches and huge crowds of people. Rarely was attention ever paid to anything which might personalise the masses by isolating any of their individual participants. At most, the crowd was compartmentalised into socially and culturally identifiable groups. This formula was eschewed only to film the party leaders, and would be accompanied by commentary on the echelons they occupied in the hierarchy, their popularity and political fortunes.

In *Togliatti è tornato*[8] the vice-secretaries Luigi Longo and Pietro Secchia are supporting actors to Palmiro Togliatti in the starring role; he truly towers over them. Velio Spano, Mauro Scoccimarro, Mario Alicata, part of the film's galaxy of leaders, were on an even lower scale of importance, which meant that less film footage and fewer minutes of attention were given over to them.

The prevalence of shots of the masses in both *Togliatti è tornato* and *I fatti di Modena* is in keeping with the content of the narration. The camera, by means of extreme long shots, makes individuals disappear into a single mass of people. These films show the vast popular participation in the celebrations for Togliatti's return to active politics after the attempt on his life in July 1948,[9] and in the funeral of the Modena factory workers who succumbed to police bullets in January 1950, respectively. The film on Togliatti sought to deliver an image of strength, but also one of jubilation and serenity, in order to mirror the PCI's roots in the lifeblood of society. Cinematic structure was treated as less important than the unfolding of a rite and a day's events overflowing with emotion and expectation.

Togliatti è tornato is a carefully choreographed, folksy spectacle aiming to portray the PCI as a varied social and geographical entity. Amidst the marchers and in the film generally there are metalworkers and intellectuals, Milan factory workers (in overalls, marching in step) and dockers from Civitavecchia, young people and women, Emilian peasants and Sicilian farm labourers, the Neapolitan *pazzariello*[10] and allegorical floats not dissimilar to parades in the Soviet Union. The high point of the afternoon's games was a medieval joust, known as the *Giostra del Saracino*. This paid homage to historical traditions and showed that the changes which the

PCI was seeking to bring about presupposed a critical reappropriation of traditional culture, including that of the earliest class struggles. The film is also a valuable source of information on Communist collective rituals in the early post-war period and on the most recurrent symbols of that time.

Togliatti è tornato, clearly, has no artistic pretensions: there is no hint of a narrative or poetic idea, nor of a style attributable to a single inspirational personality.[11] Rather, it is a chronicle filmed by several directors from different angles tied to the schedule of the day's ceremony. If there was a unifying hand, it was that of Mario Serandrei, who had political control over the editing process.[12] In reporting terms, *Togliatti è tornato* follows an event over twenty-four hours and has a joyous but combative mood. It presents the PCI as a brotherhood – united, solid, serene, settled and disciplined – a party made up of the most hard-working people in the nation, an organisation that was an integral and natural component of Italian society, history and culture. Nevertheless, the cinematic techniques used were old, if not antiquated. Typical negative features of this and other films were a 'tripod-style' camera work (the camera was rarely moved about), a dearth of detail and an almost non-stop voice-over commentary. The spoken commentary was the politico-ideological fulcrum of these films. It was polished, carefully balanced and usually written by party officials or journalists. Only in the 1970s did the style of the spoken commentary of Communist documentaries change.

The technical quality of *Togliatti è tornato* is more than adequate, but its style – impersonal, enumerative and deferential – remains that of a report or a newsreel. The film editor had the upper hand over the news reporter only when it came to shooting the sequence in which Togliatti praises the Soviet Union, its contribution to the liberation from Fascism, the conquests of Socialism, Stalin and the need to maintain peace. The building of Soviet Socialism is presented in mythical terms, as a guiding beacon. This was a recurrent and obligatory theme in post-war Communist films, part and parcel of the tributes to Stalin. It was the thread that linked Italian workers with the revolutionary movement – victorious in a large section of the world – to a feeling of supranational solidarity and with a major power which was eager to establish peaceful relations with other countries.

This acritical, far from impartial approach can also be found in Sergio Grieco's *Il cammino della libertà*. The film tells the PCI's story for the masses and is the fastest-moving of the series. Through the use of news reports, photographs, superimposition, moving texts, as well as close-ups of hands, feet, uniforms and objects, the director reconstructs the trials before the Fascist Special Tribunal and the anti-Fascist conspiracy. None the less, the general historical profile is simplistic, the references to the Soviet Union and its first five-year plan are hagiographic, and the omissions are too numerous to count. The battle fought by the PCI and the USSR against Fascism is depicted heroically and emphatically. The film provides no new insights; it is rather a mythologised account interspersed with real events, often charmingly described. Like *Togliatti è tornato*, *Il cammino della libertà* evoked an image of tenacity, strength and invincibility, enlarged by references to the Soviet Union. These two films, in their systematic praise of the USSR, were not shining examples of propagandistic cunning, as they ignored the justifiable unpopularity of Stalin's regime and the fears of millions of Italians which were fuelled by the anxieties of the Cold War on the international front, as well as by the social tensions within Italy. The persistent idealisation of the Soviet Union may have met with the approval of the left-wing electorate, but it failed to reassure the waverers and reinforced existing anti-Communist and anti-Soviet attitudes. This disjunction was due more to the PCI's politics than to its propaganda. Documentaries such as *Togliatti è tornato* and *Il cammino della libertà* did try to reassure the more open-minded and the floating voters, but they sought to do so by whitewashing what the right and the centre had painted black. Exaggeration and counter-exaggeration made up the debate on social and economic policies, as well as on the role of the Soviet Union.

Pure romantic propaganda may be the most apt description of Carlo Lizzani's *Modena, città dell'Emilia rossa*. To praise the admittedly admirable achievements of the Communist-led local government the film embarked upon grand eulogy, running the gamut from the ruins of imperial Rome, the splendour of the Italian medieval city-states, Alessandro Tassoni's *Secchia rapita*,[13] the Este dynasty, artistic treasures in the city museums, Ciro Menotti (a Modenese martyr of the Risorgimento), to the stone memorials of those killed during the Resistance. It was intended as an historical compendium, as well as a legitimation of the new local ruling class.

In this film, too, the director and the narrator seek to reassure. Was Modena really a city where the wake of civil war carried on long after Liberation? Were there really trenches filled with the bodies of collaborators, priests and landowners in Modena, Reggio Emilia and other Emilian towns? The film refutes accusations and insinuations: the Modenese are not a bloodthirsty lot, but 'good, friendly and hard-working people', and 'Modena is not the Mexico of Italy'. Lizzani's Modena is depicted as having the largest livestock market in Italy, and as a place where deals involving billions of lire are made with vigorous and righteous handshakes. The film then proceeds to catalogue municipal merits: the planning stage of the largest cattle market in Italy was complete and building work was about to begin, the peasants were battling to extend cultivation to untilled land, and factory workers were toiling to get the factories running. The viewer is shown an old gasworks where the workers are slaves to outdated technology and backbreaking tasks, but is then reassured by the voice-over that in 'Modena all this belongs to the past' because the city council has modernised its industrial plant and services.

'The factory workers,' the narrator notes, 'have emerged from the depths of Vulcan's cave as if from a prison and now, faces beaming, they gather round the mayor and *Ingegnere* Malagodi, chief executive of the factories now under the municipality's control.' The factory workers 'used to be slaves to soul-destroying machines, now they preside over perfect, easy to operate equipment'. Modernity, efficiency, industrial progress: these are seen as the means to overcome every form of ideological bias, but they were also the distinguishing features of a model which mixed rustic bonhomie with social evolution, straddling the Scandinavian model of democracy and the glorious traditions of reformist Socialism in Emilia.

The class struggle is sacrosanct, but the film's commentary tries to find allies for the working class even from the scores of entrepreneurs: 'Modenese industrialists have had no trouble in placing their trust in modern workers to achieve bold projects. From a technical viewpoint, Modenese factory workers are highly skilled, intelligent, dynamic and dignified, with a sense of real trade-union commitment'. The survey continues: a gigantic motor-racing track is being built, along with hospital wards and housing for workers. And 'where once there were stagnant water and refuse there is now a place where children can play and people can go for a stroll. The old tram tracks are being taken up and soon no one will remember the lumbering green trams; in their place there will be fast, splendidly modern trolley buses.' As for the bags of rubbish, 'They will go too, to be replaced by ultra-modern sturdy bins which will be easier on the eye, with no loss of practical utility.' And we are shown dustmen going about their business with carts, tricycles and vans. Then come the skating rinks, the *pensioni* charging reduced rates for the summer holidays at Riccione and Rimini, a mobile out-patient unit for children and holiday camps at seaside and mountain resorts. And yet more children – stretched out in the sun, eating heartily, playing, having fun and singing. Thus the first part of the film ends with a seaside sing-along, an exultant hymn to the future. 'When children sing it's like a downpour or the roar of a waterfall. It's a healthy sign when children shout with wild abandon like birds.' And the hope is that 'all the children of Emilia and Italy can sing in this way'.

Children at summer camp, having spent a month at the seaside or in the mountains, are shown hugging their parents, and the ending of the second part of the film anticipates 'a tomorrow full of song', a phrase taken from the letter of a partisan who was condemned to death, while the film homes in on a parade of motor cyclists with red banners, women in white clutching peace banners, gymnasts and young men marching in formation.

This propaganda film lays itself open to much criticism. The triumphalism is irritating, despite the good record of the Communist-led local governments in Emilia-Romagna and Tuscany. Every social problem appears to have been solved and there is not the slightest hint of self-criticism. The civic spirit and social awareness which the people of Emilia and Romagna have displayed throughout the century are missing, and the raw material of the documentary is depersonalised and largely detached from its historical context. Not one face lingers in the mind, not one story told emblematically represents the whole. Worse still, the film is an unwitting reminder of the Fascist newsreels and documentaries which dealt with 'the achievements of the regime', and echoes the stylistic excesses of Socialist-realist cinema.

What stuns the viewer is the fact that no link is ever made with the ideals of Socialism, with the heritage of the Socialist struggles, or with the identities of the Communist and Socialist Parties which had governed Modena since the end of the Second World War. A sense of shame on the part of film makers or the PCI's propagandists does not account for this, since much contemporary printed material proves otherwise. Propaganda films, however, tended to dilute red to pink and camouflage Socialist-Communist policy behind a semblance of modernity, in an attempt to make the left appealing, to calm and free public opinion from doubts, phobias and panic. In so doing, they took on an unhealthy rhetorical style.

Social conflict was acute in 1948–49, yet it is absent from *Togliatti è tornato* and *Modena, città dell'Emilia rossa*. We get an inkling of it in Lizzani's *I fatti di Modena* and in Glauco Pellegrini's *Quattordici luglio*.[14] The latter is a tame account of what happened on the day the right-wing student Antonio Pallante shot Togliatti.[15] Pellegrini and the scriptwriter, Felice Chilanti (who also wrote the commentary), imagined a situation where news of the attack arrives at the editorial offices of *L'Unità* just when a delegation of peasants from a remote part of Sicily is in Rome to talk to Togliatti. This was a narrative pretext for introducing the Sicilian peasants into the demonstrations in which Italian workers were giving vent to their anger. But let us proceed step by step.

This documentary does not fight shy of mixing theatrical fiction with real footage to create a didactic narrative. From the PCI's headquarters in Rome the scene moves to a place in Sicily. Arrogant *mazzieri* and *gabellotti* (middlemen in the semi-feudal system of the large estates), wearing dark glasses, meet to exploit the peasants' poverty with the aim of setting up a blackleg labour organisation, peddled as an 'unshackled' trade union, whose purpose is to force peasants back into the old-style agrarian slavery. Alarmed, the comrades have scraped some money together for Armando, Franca and Giovanni to go to Rome and tell Togliatti what is afoot. The scene then closes and the action returns to Rome. 'Yes, you must talk to Togliatti,' they are told by a party official who greets them. Because the Communist leader is in the Chamber of Deputies, they are advised to come back around one o'clock; in the meantime, if they wish, they can visit the editorial offices of *L'Unità*.

At this point the film does more than simply show the place where the PCI's party paper is produced. The viewer is treated to a rapid account of the workers' movement from the Fascist dictatorship to Liberation, through the device of a quick flick through copies of the paper. In the offices of *L'Unità* the telephones are ringing furiously when word spreads that Togliatti has been shot. For a few minutes we leave Armando, Franca and Giovanni, who have run into the street to distribute the special edition of *L'Unità* announcing the assault. Pellegrini did not have much footage of the real event at his disposal, so he had to resort to symbolic reconstruction.

Thousands of grieving Communists are shown marching in silence in front of the hospital where Togliatti is being treated. Whilst he is in the operating theatre the camera focuses on the party secretary's empty desk in his Botteghe Oscure office. The narrator reads the telegram in which Stalin chides the PCI's leaders for not having watched over Togliatti's safety. But Togliatti is now out of danger. In an interview with the *Settimana INCOM* he thanks the surgeon, Professor Valdoni, the other doctors, the nurses and all who have helped to save his life and who have surrounded him with affection. Then he promises to take up his post again as soon as he is well.

Armando, Franca and Giovanni return home; the popular uprising has put the wind up the *mazzieri* and *gabellotti*, who are now making more reasonable demands. The film ends with Togliatti recuperating – his return to the struggle is imminent – and with a glorifying show of red flags and peace banners.

Quattordici luglio is more than just a short documentary; on account of the ingenuous devotion that inspires it, its vibrant commentary and the dramatisation of events through the use of a careful *mise-en-scène* and a well thought out script, it has all the qualities of a short feature film. The highlight of *Quattordici luglio* is the general strike by the Communist union CGIL, the masses having already stopped work of their own accord. By eschewing an accurate rendering of events and representing them symbolically, Pellegrini's film evokes a solemn 14 July. The mood in the workers' movement is one of anger, but of quiet and disciplined anger. It is a mood of clear-headed, self-confident and law-abiding indignation. Such formidable self-control is a significant detail; it does not offer any insights into the protest that erupted during those two or three days, but helps in the evaluation of the virtuous image promoted by the party leaders. This restraint imposed from above contrasted with *L'Unità*'s reports on the trials of the culprit, which repeatedly called for solidarity with the hundreds of Communists arrested after 14 July who were condemned to long prison terms for having shouted one 'Long live . . .' or 'Down with . . .' too many times during a demonstration.

It would be unfair to blame Pellegrini for the smoothing over of the historical reality. This was a recurrent practice in Communist propaganda films, which may have been induced by the censorship rules that banned feature films or documentaries containing any real or presumed incitement of class hatred or criticism of the state and its institutions (e.g. the police and the army). It may equally have been motivated by concern that plain-speaking visual documentaries might harm the protagonists of the fiercest political battles of the time.

Nevertheless, the cinematic portrayal of the workers' and peasants' struggle varied according to the vehicles of communication employed. Party publications (*L'Unità*, *Vie Nuove*) and the pro-Communist press dealt with burning issues in an outspoken way, as did the posters announcing strikes, occupations of land or factories, or denouncing murders of workers and women. The graphic artists, however, especially at election time, frequently played down the militant image of the PCI by dressing it up with images drawn from its rhetorical repertoire: the peasant or factory worker and the typical Italian family (usually consisting of a young couple with at least one small child in its mother's arms) – all confidently looking to a bright future if the people vote Communist. The optimistic fairy tale of the electoral posters was, however, counteracted by the funereal imagery arising from the bitter social tensions and political confrontation.

As one moves from the party headquarters in Rome, the heart of the propaganda machinery, to local branch level, the discrepancy in the nature of the propaganda material becomes apparent. However minimal, it was not fortuitous; it was the result of greater autonomy at the local level of the party's organisations, notwithstanding their strong loyalty to the party's central bureaucracy. In the cyclostyled tracts and oral testimonies there is sometimes passion, anger, class resentment and determination which gradually disappear as one ascends the bureaucratic ladder. This is not to say that the propaganda produced by Central Office sought to avoid controversial issues. No attempts were made to conceal social injustices, or even internecine political and trade union quarrels. However, the emphasis was on symbolic images liable to defuse conflict. Activists were depicted as serene and strong men convinced of their own invincibility; outsiders had to be reassured that the party would never think of arbitrating social conflict except by democratic and legitimate means. The PCI's political line was not betrayed by this cinematic self-representation, though there are some political observers who accuse the early post-war Communists of double dealing. Historians attempting to investigate the climate of the period through the use the PCI's film output will need to take into account the more restrained and conciliatory tone of the propaganda discourse originating from the centre.

Quattordici luglio intrigues historians because it is a documentary which uses virtually two languages to address two different audiences. The first is the appeasing idiom mentioned earlier, aimed at the public at large; the second is more veiled and directed at militants and party officials. The film offers a political, rather than historical, reading of events. In essence, it argues that social tensions have increased because the industrial and agrarian reforms envisaged by the constitution have not been implemented, and that Italy's subordination to the United States threatens to drag the republic into a third world war.

The narrator quotes from the speech Togliatti made in Parliament on 10 July 1948, using Jacobin tones: 'Today the response to the imperialist war should be one of revolt and insurrection for the sake of peace, independence and the future of our country.' But what was this revolt, this insurrection for peace? The concept manifested itself in a then still nebulous interpretation of the events of 14 July, but one which had official blessing: the Communist leadership, in short, turned what was a spontaneous mass movement into a new and powerful political reality. This reality was unequivocally represented by the masses who protested on 14 July. However, it is only just before the film ends that the political problem is made clearer. Pellegrini included a few homely sequences shot in the gardens of the PCI's training school at Frattocchie, a few kilometres from Rome. Togliatti is still convalescing; we see him looking rested, smiling and happily enjoying the sun. With him are the party vice-secretaries, Pietro Secchia, Luigi Longo and another party chief, Edoardo D'Onofrio. The four chat intermittently whilst starting to play chess.

Unintentionally, at least on Pellegrini's part, the game of chess acquires symbolic significance. It is unintentional because, at the time the film was being made, the party leadership was aware that on 14 July thousands of Communists were showing signs of great political restlessness in the belief that the hour of revolution had arrived, and also because very few people knew the party's highest ranks were divided as to what policies and aims should be pursued after the electoral defeat of the 18 April. Only several years after the dramatic events of the summer of 1948 did the members of the PCI learn of these disagreements, which set Togliatti apart from other Communist leaders, the hard-liners who had not yet been won over to the gradualist, democratic, parliamentary approach to political struggle, to which the party secretary had committed himself in an attempt to hasten the realisation of Socialism.

These differences of opinion are echoed in the script edited by Chilanti, which must have had the approval, if not of Togliatti himself, then of the main leaders of the PCI. They are first voiced during the chess-game sequence; Secchia is shown reading aloud the following lines from a newspaper article: 'The general strike marks the beginning, not the end, of a great battle. It has demonstrated that the forces for freedom and democracy in our country are powerful.' We are then told by the voice-over that Longo, 'a dab hand on the chessboard', had declared in the Chamber of Deputies that 'Revolutionary situations are born out of the political ineptitude, brutality and violence of the ruling classes, who are unable to resolve in a responsible manner the social and political problems which have come to a head. And we as Italian Communists will not shirk from our duty of leading the struggle on new terrain.' The narrator then introduces a judicious Togliatti into the dialogue, who reassures listeners that 'It is in everyone's interest that, as soon as possible, I rejoin the comrades who are leading the party so competently.' He adds: 'For this to happen I must be allowed for a while to concentrate my energies on getting well, so I can get back to work.' This is a personal prologue, but it prepares the ground for his reply to Secchia and Longo. The commentary continues: 'In the peace and tranquillity of this gathering Togliatti's powerful words resonate: "Today the most progressive sections of society stand with us; they wanted a Republican constitution and now demand its full implementation. Tomorrow all of Italy will be with us."'

The words uttered by the three men, enigmatic and opaque to the outside world, reveal differences of opinion which the film's commentary does not try to smooth away. Secchia was in favour of a general strike, that is to say, one of the hardest forms of social and political struggle, and talked not of the end but of 'the beginning of a great battle'. Longo attributed the responsibility for 'revolutionary situations' (the crisis of 14 July was certainly not one) to the shortsightedness of the ruling classes, promising that the Communists would lead in 'the struggle on new terrain'. Togliatti responded to the ambiguity created by these propositions with an explanation which harked back to constitutional principles, and to the masses who were demanding the implementation of the Constitution and who were destined to join the PCI until it came to represent the whole of Republican Italy. This was tantamount to delivering a hammer blow to the revolutionary palingenesis, but it was also a reference to differences and antagonism at the heart of the party's secretariat and leadership. For historians this cinematic testimony is of special interest, since those disagreements were kept under wraps.

In the documentaries discussed so far, the productive effort was extraordinary and was made possible thanks principally to the voluntary work and enthusiasm of the legions of working men and women seen in the films. As a result, the reconstruction of the events almost coincided with the unfolding of actual occurrence, with the exception of the summary reporting of collective events, such as the celebrations for Togliatti's return to active politics in September 1948 or the funerals of the workers killed by the police in Modena. In the latter type of documentary, work was organised according to the tried and tested practice of the Istituto Luce, which dated back to the parade to celebrate the proclamation of the Empire (1936) and the prolix accounts of Hitler's visit to Italy (1938). But it was in Lizzani's film *Nel Mezzogiorno qualcosa è cambiato* that something well and truly changed.

Nel Mezzogiorno qualcosa è cambiato is more than the documentary work of an accomplished director; it has a formal plot and complex structure. It is the account of a political event, namely the initiatives which marked the South's rebirth at Crotone, Salerno, Bari and Matera, presented in accordance with the canons of socio-journalistic investigation. Using the event as a starting point, it examines a whole range of problems, giving a broad overview of the South. The core of the film is characterised by a spirit of enquiry, which, owing to its poignancy, recalls Neo-realist feature films and documentaries. The film makes an impact by denunciation, its persuasiveness owing more to the simple visual imagery than to the ideological and political soundtrack. The viewer is in for a disappointment when both director and narrator cast aside their impressionistic travel accounts to delve into the causes of the social inequities. The explanations they provide are sketchy and too propagandistic.

Nel Mezzogiorno is Neo-realist in so far as it informs as much as it tries to instil social values. It depicts working-class life, the desolation of Naples' slums, rural poverty, the plight of agricultural hired labour, the dwellings where human beings and animals live side by side, the soulless suburban districts crawling with refugees, the hovels in the mountain hamlets, the shanty towns on the edges of cities and the cave dwellings of Matera. Neo-realism is also evoked by the hard social facts which are provided, and by the illustration of the Southern Question by means of statistics, diagrams, super-impressions and special effects. There is linguistic variety in the various sequences, and the editing reveals the influence of British and American social documentaries of the 1930s, but mediated by Italian Neo-realism. This film freed the cinematic efforts of the PCI from an overtly propagandistic approach and replaced it with one where socio-economic data also played a part. *Nel Mezzogiorno* is a model of cinematic journalism, though it does not quite manage to be analytical, and contains features which are typical of propaganda cinema such as the frequent use of invective and a mood of optimism.

Nel Mezzogiorno is remarkable for its terse writing style and concrete images of society. Such qualities are all the more apparent when the film is compared with others on the Southern Question, with their propensity for flamboyant allusion and lyrical effusion. Lizzani's film combines sociological enquiry with the exigencies of propaganda. It is a model which the PCI hesitated to adopt as its own but was to return to in the 1970s, on the crest of the latest novelty: television reporting of unresolved social problems.

NOTES

This chapter focuses on a few shorts only, those I am directly acquainted with. The remaining films – some of which have disappeared without trace – are referred to in passing, by way of information only.

1 Libertas Film's first cycle of activity was in 1947–49. It was co-ordinated by the producer and director Alfredo Guarini, who had already represented the PCI in the film section of the Comitato di Liberazione Nazionale (CLN), the national Resistance organisation, during the German occupation and immediately after the liberation of Rome. It was replaced by another organisation, Specchio Film, which was run by Marcello Bollero and produced documentaries and newsreels. Libertas Film resumed its activities in the mid-1950s when

Specchio Film closed down, but this time without the participation of Guarini and his collaborators.

2 The censorship law, which was passed on 16 May 1947 and remained in force until 1962, had the same aims as the law approved by the Fascists in 1923, soon after they took power. Paradoxically, it was a carry-over from the Liberal era of Giolitti, and concerned all forms of 'incitement of class hatred' in Italian and foreign films. By adhering to this type of prohibition it was easy for those in power during the post-war era to reject cinematic material in which the censors saw elements capable of upsetting class relations. The law went as far as banning a Soviet documentary about a football match because the victorious team was Russian. Prime Ministerial circulars were issued by Giulio Andreotti, then Under-Secretary with special responsibility for the performing arts, to ban the screening in private cinemas and cine clubs of any Italian or foreign film deemed unacceptable by the censors. Cine clubs lost the small amount of freedom which they had enjoyed until 1948, and many were persecuted.

3 The films the company distributed included: Jean Renoir's *La Marseillaise* (1938), a film about the French Revolution commissioned by the Communist union CGT; Karel Steklý's *Siréna* (The Siren, 1947) on the factory- and mine-workers' struggles in Czechoslovakia; and various Soviet films.

4 Vergano's short is about a customer who sleeps whilst a barber gives him a shave. He dreams that the Fascists have returned, but when he wakes up he breathes a sigh of relief because the Popular Front has prevented them from coming back.

5 On these newsreels see Maria Adelaide Frabotta's chapter in this book, which includes a bibliography in note 5.

6 This library, based in Rome, houses the largest collection of material on Italian political and social struggle with a leftist orientation.

7 No films were made by the PCI in 1952, 1954, 1956 or 1957. In the period under consideration some shorts and medium-length documentaries were also produced by trade unions: Florestano Vancini's *Delta padano* (The Po Delta, 1951), whose export was banned because it examined age-old problems such as poverty, malaria and typhoid in the Polesine marshlands; Pontecorvo's *Missione Timiriazef* (The Timiriazef Mission, 1952), a chronicle of floods in the Po valley; and Massimo Mida's *Di Vittorio* (1957), a tribute to the left-wing trade unionist Giuseppe Di Vittorio.

8 This film is now readily available, being featured in the video-cassette that accompanies the volume by N. Tranfaglia (ed.), *Il 1948 in Italia. La storia e i film* (Florence, La Nuova Italia, 1991).

9 See note 15 for a bibliography of this attack.

10 The *pazzariello* character is a pedlar of wine, pasta, etc., dressed either in eighteenth-century or in multicoloured costume, followed by musicians with drums and flageolet.

11 As is also the case, for instance, with Leni Riefenstahl's *Triumph des Willens* (Triumph of the Will, 1936) and the film of the Mexico City Olympics (1972) made by Miloš Forman, Kon Ichkawa, Claude Lelouch, Yuri Ozerov, Arthur Penn, Michael Pileghar, John Schlesinger and Mai Zetterling.

12 Similarly, *L'Italia con Togliatti*, a documentary on Togliatti's funeral which the PCI produced in 1964, was co-ordinated by Glauco Pellegrini using material filmed by Gianni Amico, Libero Bizzarri, Francesco Maselli, Lino Miccichè, Elio Petri, Sergio Tau, Paolo and Vittorio Taviani Marco Zavattini and Valerio Zurlini.

13 The *Secchia rapita* (Pillage of the Wooden Bucket) is a mock-heroic poem published in 1662. It recounts the war between Guelph Bologna and Ghibelline Modena, set off by Modena's theft from Bologna of a wooden bucket.

14 This film is also included in the video-cassette issued with Tranfaglia (ed.), *Il 1948 in Italia*.

15 On this event, and the reactions of the Communist leadership and party supporters to it, see especially: M. Caprara, *L'attentato a Togliatti. 14 luglio 1948: il PCI tra insurrezione e programma democratico* (Venice, Marsilio, 1978); W. Tobagi, *La rivoluzione impossibile. L'attentato a Togliatti: violenza politica e reazione popolare* (Milan, Il Saggiatore, 1978); and G. Speroni, *L'attentato a Togliatti* (Milan, Mursia, 1998).

6

Political identity and communication

Jeff C. Pratt

At an informal level Italian political communication unfolds in a myriad of public events: the coded remark thrown at a passer-by in the street, the heated arguments in a square, the careful scrutiny of who is present at a gathering. These everyday conversations and actions are by turns witty and obsessive, passionate and cynical – they are both the substance of everyday political communication and reflections of deep-rooted political cultures. Sometimes the remarks seem arcane and elusive, sometimes banal and commonsensical, in both cases they are merely fragments of a wider discourse. For that reason any analysis of such communication needs to widen the frame of reference and explore the *context* in which the events are generated, which includes both what was not said (at the time) and a range of factors which shape the form and content of the communication. Obviously this is an open-ended task, and the analysis offered here has to be very selective. The main focus of this chapter is a discussion of the political identities which are communicated and contested in these events, and the most important context for analysing them is the party political system itself.

Two images of Italian party political life coexist rather uneasily. In the first, the various parties represent significantly opposed interests within Italian society, and they have generated systematic and rival ideologies. The parties have deep roots within society, they have permeated almost all organisations as well as the consciousness of Italian citizens, so that a person's political allegiance is a fundamental part of his/her identity, and will shape almost all that person's actions and conversations. In this sense Italy is seen as a highly 'politicised' society, where politics connotes difference and the differences are substantial. The second view is more cynical and has been greatly reinforced by the corruption trials of the early 1990s. Politics is not about the articulation of collective interests, but about the realisation of individual interests. The apparently deep-seated ideological conflicts of public debate are a façade, a verbose illusion behind which the real business of politics proceeds as usual, the struggle for power and resources. All politicians are self-serving, and the surface differences of Italian political life hide basically similar aspirations. In this perspective too Italy is seen as highly politicised, but in a different sense, namely as a very individualistic and competitive society run by politicians unusually skilled in the arts of manipulation and deception.

These contrasting images of party politics are found both among those who are part of political life and among those who comment on it. They reflect both major variations in Italy's political life and differences of interpretation. This chapter can offer only a selective and personal account of some of these themes. My own understanding of Italian politics has been shaped by immersion in the highly polarised reality of small towns in Tuscany, starting with Montepulciano, where I began anthropological research in 1970. The experience of this political culture, where major social divisions were reflected in, and shaped by, party politics, and where most people's political allegiances were stable, is not typical of all Italy in all periods, but it will provide a framework for asking questions about other situations and other interpretations.

Montepulciano is the centre of a *comune* which then had 15,000 inhabitants. It was contested by two main political forces. The first was the Communist Party (PCI), which had run local administration since the war, and whose political support came chiefly from the countryside beyond the city walls. The local party was certainly in transition and a new generation of leaders was emerging, but the party was still vigorously articulating class-based interests, talking the language of Socialism more than that of administrative efficiency: it was more closed and monolithic than open and dialogue-seeking. The opposition to the Communists consisted of local businessmen, the main land-owning families and the local clergy. It was a predominantly urban elite which controlled most of the local economy and was organised around the Christian Democrat Party (DC). Although united by anti-Communism, it contained a wide variety of interests and political positions, including a minority who showed some nostalgia for a more traditional, hierarchical society, and who viewed the occupation of the Renaissance town hall by all those peasants and Communists as little less than a barbarian invasion.

This political configuration had been consolidated a generation earlier, first in the partisan movement, and then in the protracted struggle to end the sharecropping system which dominated the countryside. The fight for land reform was shaped by the increasingly bitter national and international divides of the Cold War period. A complex and multi-layered set of ideological oppositions emerged. The left articulated a class-based ideology which stressed national and international solidarities. The centre-right developed an organic model which stressed the interdependence of different parts of society, the value of local identities, and allegiance to Catholic teaching. The centrality given to the family and to morality in the construction of the opposition between Communism and Catholicism has been analysed in detail elsewhere.[1]

In the working environment, on farms and in factories, most people found themselves alongside those who were politically like-minded, and this pattern of segregation was found in many other contexts. Regular churchgoing denoted allegiance to the DC, while both the Church and the left established a range of organisations, recreational circles and bars where their supporters gathered in the evenings. Civic associations, from sports clubs to burial societies, tended to be associated with one of the major political groupings. Even shops were often identified with the political 'colour' of their owner and drew their customers accordingly. Of course there were exceptions: some DC supporters among the labourers and sharecroppers, and some left-wing supporters amongst the urban middle class. Occasionally even families were politically divided, but that was thought to put considerable strain on the relationship between husbands and wives and was the subject of banter.

I now want to turn to the way judgements and comments which reflected a particular political and ideological position permeated everyday conversation, drawing material chiefly from those occasions which involved participants from different political parties. In central Italy in this period almost all areas of social life were potentially subject to ideological contestation, and I shall start with three short examples.

On one summer evening I was talking to a Communist activist opposite the famous Renaissance church of San Biagio, just below Montepulciano, and made a remark about the beauty of the place. To my surprise, he disagreed strongly. 'Look at the size of the doors,' he said. 'There is nothing in the whole building which is built to the scale of man. When you go inside it is all too vast, you immediately feel ill at ease. Anyway, the important thing about that place is that it was built with Medici gold, and built to the glory of the Medici. And the men who built it, the labourers, lived on grass and roots, that is the important thing to know about that building. What would I do with it? I would turn it into a grain store for all the farms in this part of the *comune*.' This is of course very different from the dominant discourse (then and now) about the town's history and the achievements of its citizens as recounted by the local elite, the official guidebooks and art histories. For a period, at least, history and aesthetics became a contested arena within which judgements based on radically different political positions were expressed.

In the mid-1970s I was living in a 'politically mixed' village when a local man married a woman from another district, not in church but in a civic ceremony in the town hall. It was the first civic marriage in the locality, and gave rise to recurrent comment in the streets and bars. 'What does he think marriage is, some kind of contract like buying a pig?' The remark is so loaded that if said to a person's face it would normally lead to violence. Left-wing ideology had long contained a component of anticlericalism, but Pius XII's pronouncement in 1949 of an anathema against supporters of Marxist parties and the selective suspension from the sacraments of Communist militants led to new tensions. Most Italian Communists were not anti-Catholic as such: they were baptised, married and buried by the Church, and subscribed to many of the same moral precepts as the rest of the population. Twenty years later a small minority began to break with the Church, but in the 1970s civic weddings in the smaller centres of Tuscany were still extremely rare. It remained a delicate issue which the left would attempt to treat as an essentially private matter and the Catholic forces treated as a fundamental demonstration of the moral error of their opponents.

A third context where political difference emerges is the relative importance attached to local identity and the social occasions which celebrate it. In central Italy there is a diffuse notion that the inhabitants of a town share common characteristics which set them apart from their neighbours, part of a complex phenomenon known as *campanilismo*, which involves the idea that the *campanile* or bell tower provides the point of reference or orientation for people's lives. It became a contested discourse in the post-war period. Although some elements of the discourse – for instance, the notion of shared local identities – were part of the 'common sense' of all sections of the population, this very easily shifted into the view that local identities were the fundamental grounds for the construction of political interests, and it was this phenomenon which the left contested. In elections the centre-right often used symbols of local identity for their campaigns, and claimed to represent the true interests of the local population. This was combined with the representation of society as an organic unity, internally differentiated, hierarchical, where harmony reigned if everybody worked together and knew their place.

Any appeal to identity constructed on the basis of a person's place of birth or residence became suspect within large parts of left-wing discourse, and the subject of critical comment. However, we are dealing not just with sensitivity to verbal formulas, but with practices which marked out alternative constructions of society. For example, the processions to celebrate the town's patron saint or the complex festivities during carnival were seen by the purists on the left as reinforcing not just the importance of territorial boundaries but the fundamentally harmonious class relations within the locality. Left-wing ways of occupying public space represented an antithesis to both these constructions. The two major forms of political action in the repertoire of those who opposed the existing social order were the strike and the demonstration. These were usually combined, and represented a moment of rupture. All economic activity in the town ceased, and the streets were occupied by a group of people who defined themselves around a class identity, for example agricultural day labourers (*braccianti*), bussed in from all over the province. Anti-Fascist demonstrations were organised on the same principles, and were experienced by some townspeople as an invasion, and palpable proof that there were alternatives to the construction of identities and interests on the basis of local harmony. The most spectacular events of this kind were the national *Feste dell'Unità* – in the mid-1970s the *corteo* (march) on the last day brought together more than a million people, a proclamation of unified political purpose with the banners of the metalworkers of Turin, the rice planters of Vercelli, the miners of Sardinia, the *braccianti* of Apulia.[2]

The aesthetics of a building, the celebration of a wedding, the value attached to local identity, all emerge as contexts where people's judgements and practice could indicate their political allegiance and become the focus for competing claims about the truth of different political ideologies. The arguments which erupted in public places became highly oppositional: they supposed a world divided into two camps, contrasted as positive and negative, with no middle ground. The most banal remark could trigger an argument whose content focused on the errors of the opposing parties: a comment on the deficit of the local administration led to a reply about the obscurity of Vatican finances. Such discussions could escalate across the whole range of the opponent's political world, and it paid sometimes to change the direction of attack: 'In Russia you are not be allowed to criticise anybody's finances,' to which the reply might be: 'If you looked at what the Church did during the Inquisition, it has no right to lecture anybody on liberty.'

In these kinds of exchanges the speaker was held responsible for all the actions of the political world with which he or she was identified. For a Christian Democrat this included the Catholic Church and the Pope, conceived of as an integral part of Italian society. Communism was represented as a unitary phenomenon, realised in the Soviet bloc, to which local Communists were loyal and obedient, so that Russia, an external power, was portrayed as revealing the true nature of Communism and was the main point of attack. Exchanges of this kind rarely followed a linear theme but had built into them a tendency to escalation, since each speaker would attempt to move to the highest possible ground in terms of values and morality, reflecting the dominant discourses of the Cold War, which portrayed these political differences as a contest between good and evil. They involved particular political skills, the ability to move sideways when boxed in on one terrain, to set traps by staying on ground where the opponent thought he was strong yet finding unexpected ripostes, and in having the last word, the exit line from the escalation. Verbal skills of this kind, *finezza*, are much valued in a variety of contexts, but needed ideally to be combined with a deep knowledge of the political history of your own party. If in the middle of a referendum campaign your opponent suddenly stated that the late secretary of the PCI, Palmiro Togliatti, had been opposed to legalising divorce, you could lose a great deal of authority by showing surprise or by not having an answer. Obviously not everybody had the same rhetorical ability or political knowledge, and we can now turn to a consideration of the ways in which they were acquired.

For Communists there were two main ways to acquire greater knowledge of their political world: reading and attending meetings. Taking out a subscription to the party newspaper, *L'Unità*, was a good indicator of commitment, and when correctly folded and placed in a jacket pocket with the title showing it functioned as a badge of membership. The ideological premise of this newspaper was an 'imagined community', but an international community of the working class rather than Benedict Anderson's community of the nation.[3] What constituted news were the struggles of the working class, with greatest coverage given obviously to Italy, but also with an explicit international scope so that an account of tin miners in Bolivia or a union agreement in Britain would take precedence over news of Italian celebrities in the Via Veneto. The simplest and constantly repeated lesson from this news was the need for solidarity, but it was combined with some notoriously esoteric analysis of the Italian political process. Attendance at party meetings also played a vital role in the dissemination of information about the political culture of the party, especially for men, who made up the vast majority of the active membership in Tuscany. Discussion meetings before elections or the PCI's national congress placed party policy in the context of a long didactic history of party strategy and the changing balance of forces and alliances within Italian society.

Members went to the party section not just for regular meetings but for information at critical junctures, such as on election days, or in the periods of tension which followed the bombing of civilian targets in the 1970s. There existed an organisational structure and communication network which was seen very explicitly as an alternative to that of the state. Dropping in at party headquarters was an act of solidarity; like many other practices, such as the display of *L'Unità*, the use of the term *compagno* (comrade) or the informal personal pronoun *tu*, it was part of a process of inclusion and exclusion, recurring markers of political identity. There was hierarchy as well as solidarity, and party headquarters were of course also a place where leaders explained the correct line on strategic issues to the rank and file. They did so using a very distinctive lexicon and syntax, a 'left-wing' register of the Italian language. It was acquired by local activists through attendance at party schools and was considered one of the attributes of a *compagno preparato*. I have analysed elsewhere some of the characteristics of this speech form and its role in decision making at meetings[4]. In these discussions local aspirations were placed in a wider perspective, and at the same time those aspirations were also redirected and often transformed according to wider strategic objectives which were established by a highly centralised party apparatus.

For the centre-right the main forum of ideological elaboration was the Catholic Church, its parish clergy, parish newspapers, its flanking organisations like the *Comitati Civici* and *Azione Cattolica*. It was here that for Catholics local experience was placed in a wider context, made relevant to a wider political struggle, and here that for Catholics that experience was also reinterpreted and transformed according to wider political objectives. When the villager's civic wedding is likened to buying a pig, there is an enormous weight of ideological elaboration behind the insult. In Catholic dogma marriage is a sacrament; parish priests in their sermons and informal conversations insisted that only sexual unions which they had sacralised were legitimate. Membership of a family based on a sacralised marriage was a precondition for a moral life, and those not in such a state were outside the moral community. Pastoral letters elaborated on the theme that the primary moral relationships are family relationships and that the primary experiences and obligations of life are family-centred. Catholic social doctrine in all its ramifications since the end of the nineteenth century had held up the family as the ideal economic unit – the independent peasant proprietor, the small artisan – and advocated organic patriarchal work relations. All these religious, political and economic strands were pulled together in the great Catholic ideological crusade of the Cold War, which was still reverberating through small-town life in the 1970s. The family was the cornerstone of a moral Christian society; Communists were opposed to it and as such were evil.

The political life I have described so far is specific to a particular period (the 1970s) and to certain regions of Italy (Tuscany, Umbria, the Marches and Emilia-Romagna, the so-called 'red belt'), and we can now summarise its characteristics. The majority of the population were identified with one of the major political groupings; it was part of their social identity and correlated closely with their social position. Political difference was not confined to a restricted domain of social life but tended to permeate a wide range of social interactions and reflected different interpretations of a very broad spectrum of relationships. A great deal of value was attached to *coerenza*: people who were *coerente* demonstrated a high level of political commitment and this was reflected in all their attitudes and in their relationships at work or at leisure. The major political groupings had themselves developed wide-ranging ideologies: this 'totalising' aspiration was most conspicuous with the PCI, the DC and to a lesser extent the neo-Fascist MSI, but less well developed among the minor parties, which did not offer a distinctive perspective on all aspects of society and tended to move in the gravitational field of one of the larger parties.

It has sometimes been said that there was a ritualistic quality to the expression of political difference in this kind of environment, but this judgement needs to be interpreted very carefully. It is true that the political views of the rank and file were often expressed in terms of the consistency of a person's political identity and the moral superiority of that commitment. It is also true that political disputes were sometimes fought out at a very high level of abstraction, that in elections there was a tendency towards global ideology rather than programmatic manifestoes on taxation and expenditure. In public speeches there was a penchant for rather abstruse formulations. For example, in the 1970s the political battle was fought between the proponents of a *compromesso storico* or 'historic compromise' (this phrase encapsulated the PCI strategy of an alliance with the Christian Democrats, but was subject to radically different interpretations within the party) and those who advocated *convergenze parallele* or 'converging parallels' (the phrase referred to the DC's relationship with the left, but its theological niceties were really understood only by Aldo Moro, their then leader).

All these characteristics of political dispute could suggest that form was more important than substance, and that much activity was symbolic gesturing which did not reflect the 'real business' of politics. I think this misrepresents a political culture in which organisations and ideologies had the totalising quality I have described, where one aspect of a person's behaviour could stand for the whole, and misinterprets also the kind of 'restricted linguistic code'[5] which most of the population used when expressing political difference. However, it does lead us to the second version of Italian political life which I set out in the introduction: the view that the apparently deep-seated ideological conflicts are a façade behind which politics proceeds as an undistinguished scramble for personal advantage.

In this view the motivation of politicians becomes the key feature of political life, the ground on which everything is judged. This view could be found in central Italy in the 1970s, and there was a vocabulary to describe it. On the left, a politician accused of being self-seeking would be described as bourgeois, lacking the qualities of sacrifice and solidarity necessary to be a true comrade; for the Church such a person was tainted by the errors of individualism and egoism. Both sides acknowledged the existence of this dimension of political activity, but neither considered it either general or natural. For some in the local community politics did connote a cynical world of personal advantage, a view found especially among those who were not permanently identified with any party. 'All politics is dirty', they would say. 'All politicians look after their business' (*affari loro*), a politician always 'carries water to his own mill' (*porta acqua al suo mulino*). Here then we find generic judgements about politics and about the self-interest of those who participate in it, but the key phenomena which provoke these judgements are patronage and clientelism.

Social science writings on Italy have documented the patronage system as a complex phenomenon which permeates many areas of social life. The aspect which concerns us here is the use of state resources, either at the centre or locally, by political parties to favour particular individuals and groups in a way which consolidates support for that party and the resources of specific politicians within it. There are two main ways in which this can happen. The first is the direct distribution of state resources, such as jobs in the public sector, pensions or health care to party supporters in return for votes, other forms of political support or financial gain.[6] The second is the use by political parties of state agencies to award permits and contracts in the public sector to companies which often have a long-standing relationship with a party, in return for substantial *tangenti* (kickbacks).

Clientelism was, and is, widespread in Italian public life, even if not uniformly distributed. Its representation in everyday discourse and practice takes a very different form from the previous examples and rests on a number of premises. First, that society is hierarchically ordered, with a chain of patrons between the client and the great national leaders or bosses. Secondly, the world is characterised by intense competition for resources such as jobs or welfare payments; these are always in short supply, and the competition is not regulated by the kind of impersonal rationality which is formally supposed to operate in a state bureaucracy. Clientelistic practices have made both these premises true. The third premise is that individuals are motivated by the desire to maximise personal gain – this applies particularly to all politicians and is seen as common sense. Fourthly, common sense also suggests that action to obtain resources takes place within the terms of the existing power structure: pragmatism militates against collective action to obtain resources in any other way.

Politicians present themselves as tireless defenders of their regions and of their constituencies, and campaign for greater state investment in industry and infrastructure. The support they receive, in the form of preference votes and party membership cards 'in their pocket', is the basis of their bargaining position inside the national party and government.[7] Their agents at the next level down are the key officials in state agencies who have control over the allocation of resources in return for political support. In these circumstances the political identity of the client is an identification with the power and career of a particular politician, not just of a party such as the DC, or even of a faction within it, but with the key local patron. Political identity is the product of a person's search for help among a group of power holders who are differentiated only by their relative resources and availability. It is the result of participation in power fields which are shaped by hierarchical integration into vertical blocs, rather than by definition around class or other collective interests.

In this context, political communication focuses on who you know, who can fix a particular problem, whether their power is waxing or waning, what their help will cost. Successful clients have to put a good deal of work into obtaining information, and into controlling the amount of information available about themselves in order to keep their options open. This is the political communication not of the demonstration and the open piazza but of the quiet conversation in a bar or a shop when the other customers have left. Of course, at some points the client may be required to be visible – at party headquarters, in church, at public meetings or for the visit of dignitaries, in order to show where they stand. Sometimes these clientelist relations build up over time; they involve the allegiance of families and extended kin, and may be consolidated by the long-term moral obligations of godparenthood. More generally it is best that those who do not need to know of a particular allegiance should not know; hence a client will attempt to conceal what is known about his movements and contacts in a local society where a person's movements are the subject of constant scrutiny and comment. Clients attempt to control information about themselves and also obtain as much information as possible about changes in the personnel of the power field that surrounds them.

Specific clientelist practices are embedded in a complex discourse about power and morality, and when we look at everyday representations of political life we find some striking ambivalences. The client may be deferential when approaching a patron, but the relationship is nevertheless also represented as between autonomous individuals: they choose to help each other. There is a request for help – the normal channels for obtaining something seem to be strangely blocked – and the debt is partly repaid by the offer of help in return: the family's vote, the membership card, perhaps more energetic support at election time or a gift. The two people may describe themselves as *amici*, trust has built up, there are mutual advantages in the favours they do each other, and if the favours are slightly irregular, the world is not perfect and only saints or fools practice altruism; it is up to everybody, and especially those with 'families on their shoulders' to try to look after themselves. So in this way relations of dependence are referred to as exchanges, and the moral judgements made on those exchanges are highly dependent on context. Clientelist practices are at odds with the official way of obtaining resources, but they are eminently sensible; they are legitimate as a personal strategy even when as a system they are considered illegitimate.

This is a highly politicised environment in the sense that a very wide range of resources are under the control of political parties, and the average citizen is forced to enter into relationships with local politicians in order to gain a livelihood. The competition for these resources means that success depends on manipulative skills. However, that does not imply that in this environment the bedrock of political action is exposed, or that we can be satisfied with a universalist model of 'economic man' which both local people and external commentators have sometimes invoked to explain political allegiance. Where clientelism flourishes it is not a natural phenomenon but the product of a variety of social forces – a fragmented class structure, the long history of particular civic and religious institutions, and alongside these the political and cultural history of the region.[8] It is also worth stressing that the shaping of personal political identities by clientelism needs to be placed in a wider cultural context. When we look at the representation of power and morality within these relationships we see how they unfold within cultural constructs of the person. These discourses of the person include those concerned with honour, *omertà* (code of silence) and cunning; the moral evaluation of hierarchical relations of kinship, patriarchy and paternalism; the moral evaluation of egalitarian relations such as comradeship and friendship (although the latter is an uncertain translation of *amicizia*). These constructs and practices, which vary even within Italian regions, are an integral part of the different traditions which make up Italian political life; they are an essential context for understanding the banal comments about self-interest which make up everyday representations of clientelism.

The confrontation brought about the political turmoil of the early and mid-1990s focused on the corruption of the body politic. Conversations revealed a demand for exorcism of the corrupted parts, but the demand for exorcism was a complex and evolving discourse. In part it was aimed at individuals; it was the desire to identify and punish those who had profited, and whose base self-interest had turned political difference into a charade. The highest in the land ceased to be untouchable and the feeling grew that a 'clean-up' was not just possible but happening. There can now be little doubt that the public language of help and favours characteristic of clientelism coexisted with what James Scott has called a 'hidden transcript' which expressed strong resentment.[9]

It is an excellent legal principle that individuals are held responsible for their actions, but there were those on the left who doubted that the prosecution of a few hundred could end a political system. The excitement that 'we' the citizens can finally nail 'them', the corrupt (either as individuals or as a generic *classe politica*), offered a limited analysis of the recent events. For a start, as Umberto Eco wrote in *L'Espresso*, you would never guess from the uproar about Giulio Andreotti, the seven-time Prime Minister charged with Mafia activity, whom all the people now shouting 'thief' had actually voted for in the last forty years.[10] However, Eco's own answer – that these practices had lasted so long because people had 'all drawn some advantages from this way of doing things', and consented to it – is also inadequate. I have suggested that the moral judgements made on clientelistic practices varied according to context, and we need to understand how the legal attacks on the existing power relations may alter those judgements. Above all the left has insisted that patronage was a power relation, and those caught up in it did not all draw advantages from it, and that the decried practices had material consequences. Between those who say there were a few thieves and they must be punished, and those who say everybody was responsible, there is space for analysis of a political system in terms of who benefits, and whose interests are served.

On this terrain it was the Lega Nord which achieved the first breakthrough. It combined popular discontent with the inefficiency and malpractice of the public sector with a strong appeal to regional identities, and as a result a new set of political differences came to dominate the political agenda in the 1990s. Italian unification, they argued, was a mistake because there existed marked differences in the political and cultural traditions of the peninsula and these differences continue to exist. In this movement's response to the corruption scandals there was a call for exorcism, but on a different plane from the other parties. The errors were the result of the imposition of a national government on northern people's legitimate aspirations, and specifically the imposition of a corrupt southern political culture on the good people of the North. There were attacks on all other political parties in so far as they attempted to maintain Italian unity in its existing form. As a political movement the Lega contained – and still contains – a variety of positions on the future of the Italian state, on the distinct characteristics of northern culture, and on racism. There are a complex mixture of ideological strands, and a rapidly evolving electoral base, so the long-term success and physiognomy of the League are hard to predict.

This chapter has sketched two forms of political communication. The first was the product of a highly oppositional Cold War ideology, within which a person's political identity correlated with other social attributes, was generally fixed and stable, and *coerenza* was valued. It was a totalising ideology, in the sense that all opinions and social action, from aesthetic judgements to participation in a *Festa*, could be interpreted in terms of political difference, and this contributed to the coded form of much communication. The second set of examples, which concentrated on clientelism, were much less totalising or stable, and influenced a narrower range of personal identity. They were also often coded, both because they rested on knowledge which should not be revealed, and because they invoked a world of self-interest which was undifferentiated and largely unspoken. I have tried to suggest that these discourses, while invoking a commonsensical universalism, in practice rested on culturally specific constructs of the person and morality. Both these forms of political communication have been presented in the past tense. The old forms of political difference crystallised in the Cold War are now much attenuated, even in Tuscany. Clientelism is not dead, but the old semi-private language in which it was semi-legitimised has been brought into full public gaze, and its more deferential modes are unlikely to survive unchanged.

NOTES

1 See J. C. Pratt, *The Walled City. A Study of Social Change and Conservative Ideologies in Tuscany* (Göttingen, Herodot, 1986), chapters 7 and 8.

2 The Communist *Feste dell'Unità* were extremely popular in the 1970s, and were organised on every level from the ward, or neighbourhood, to the *comune*, province and nation. Even when their more didactic political purpose (debates and speeches) began to decline, and the recreational side dominated, their wider political purpose in terms of creating *presenza* remained important. For this phenomenon in Bologna see D. I. Kertzer, *Comrades and Christians. Religion and Political Struggle in Communist Italy* (Prospect Heights, IL, Waveland Press, 1990, 2nd edn).

3 B. R. O'G. Anderson, *Imagined Communities. Reflections on the Origin and Spread of Nationalism* (London, Verso, 1991, 2nd edn).

4 J. C. Pratt, 'Some Italian Communists Talking', in R. D. Grillo (ed.), *Social Anthropology and the Politics of Language* (London, Routledge, 1989), pp. 176–92.

5 See B. Bernstein, *Class, Codes and Control* (London, Routledge, 1974, 2nd edn).

6 J. Davis, *Land and Family in Pisticci* (London, Athlone Press, 1973), reports the case of the priest who wanted the first month's salary of everyone for whom he had fixed a job at the Christian Democrat-controlled petrochemical plant. There is no clear dividing line between the small-scale trading of jobs for votes I have described here and the major corruption scandals reported at the national level. Accounts of clientelism at the grass-roots level can be found in a wide range of studies by anthropologists and others using a fieldwork methodology. They include the following: for the Friuli region, D. Holmes, *Cultural*

Disenchantments. Worker Peasantries in North-east Italy (Princeton University Press, 1989); for Tuscany, Pratt, *The Walled City*, and R. Wade, 'Political Behaviour and World View in a Central Italian Village', in F. G. Bailey (ed.), *Gifts and Poison. The Politics of Reputation* (Oxford, Blackwell, 1971), pp. 252–80; for Umbria, S. Silverman, *The Three Bells of Civilization. The Life of an Italian Hill Town* (New York, Columbia University Press, 1975); for the Abruzzo, C. White, *Patrons and Partisans. A Study of Politics in Two Southern Italian Comuni* (Cambridge University Press, 1980), especially chapters 5 and 11; for a village in Piedmont, F. G. Bailey, 'What are Signori?' in *id., Gifts of Poison*, pp. 231–51; for Basilicata, E. C. Banfield, *The Moral Basis of a Backward Society* (New York, Free Press, 1958), and Davis, *Land and Family in Pisticci*, especially chapter 9; for Campania, P. Allum, *Politics and Society in Post-war Naples* (Cambridge University Press, 1973); for Sicily, J. Boissevain, 'Patronage in Sicily', *Man*, 1 (1966), pp. 18–33, and P. and J. Schneider, *Culture and Political Economy in Western Sicily* (New York, Academic Press, 1976). I have extracted some general points from these ethnographies, but the various authors offer strikingly different analyses of the phenomenon.

7 See Allum, *Politics and Society*.

8 See R. D. Putnam, *Making Democracy Work. Civic Traditions in Modern Italy* (Princeton University Press, 1993).

9 J. Scott, *Domination and the Arts of Resistance* (New Haven, CT, Yale University Press, 1990).

10 U. Eco, 'Italiani, ma chi ha votato per Andreotti in tutti questi anni?', *L'Espresso*, 11 April 1993, p. 218; now reprinted with the title 'Chi votava per Andreotti?' in U. Eco, *La bustina di Minerva* (Milan, Bompiani, 2000), pp. 47–8. In October 1999 Andreotti was cleared of colluding with the Mafia. (He was also acquitted of murder in a separate, concurrent trial.)

7 Political rituals

David I. Kertzer

Political life is rooted in the manipulation of symbols, and in this symbolic process ritual plays a central role. All too often, however, political observers and analysts regard ritual lightly, typically identifying it with pre-modern societies – emperors and kings surrounded by superstition and spectacle. In this view, the ritual element in modern political life is, at best, something of a quaint survival, a bit of puffery that has little influence on the real stuff of contemporary politics.

In this chapter I would like to argue against this conventional wisdom by demonstrating the importance of ritual to political life in Italy today, and by identifying those aspects of ritual that make it so politically potent. In short, I will sketch a theory of the political importance of ritual by examining Italian politics, focusing in particular on one of the major political developments in Italy in the early 1990s, the transformation of the Italian Communist Party (PCI) into a post-Communist party, the Partito Democratico della Sinistra (PDS).[1] This is not to suggest that ritual is necessarily more important to the PCI than to other political forces in Italy – the Christian Democrats, neo-Fascists and other groups could just as easily be viewed from this perspective, and indeed before concluding I will take a brief look at the use of ritual in the transformation of the Movimento Sociale Italiano (MSI) to the Alleanza Nazionale (AN).

In examining PCI ritual, and the use of ritual in the battle over the transformation of the party, we adopt a concept of ritual that is not limited to religion. Following many other analysts of ritual, and especially work on the political uses of ritual, I take a broader view, seeing ritual as symbolic behaviour that is socially standardised and repetitive. Indeed, it is through ritual that symbols come to be defined, diffused and energised.[2] The series of events that provide our focus here began in November 1989, in the wake of the dismantling of the Berlin Wall and in the midst of the break-up of the Soviet bloc regimes. Party secretary Achille Occhetto, speaking at a ritual commemorating a battle of the Resistance in Bologna, announced what came to be known as *la svolta* (the turning point), the initiative that would transform the PCI into a post-Communist party. He called for a new political entity, which initially came to be referred to simply as *la cosa* (the thing), since a decision on the name of the new party proved to be a ticklish problem in itself. His proposal sparked a bitter struggle at all levels of the party, with the opposition staunchly opposed to giving up the party's Communist identity.

The battle over the *svolta* was waged to a great extent as a battle over symbols and fought to a considerable extent through ritual. Ritual provided the primary means through which the party leaders were able to tap the passions of the members and sympathisers. But, as we shall see, ritual does more than simply stir the emotions. Let us look first, then, at the features of ritual that make it so powerful.

The power of ritual

Previous analyses of the political role of ritual have focused primarily on its use in reinforcing the *status quo*. In this view, ritual shores up existing power holders and power systems by surrounding them with the aura of legitimacy. Yet the political importance of ritual goes well beyond this, for the successful use of ritual is equally crucial for movements of political change. Four features of ritual are of special relevance for understanding their political value: their power (1) to represent political groups, (2) to provide legitimacy, (3) to build solidarity, and (4) to shape people's perceptions of political reality. We look at each of these briefly.[3]

REPRESENTING THE PARTY

Political parties can exist only through symbolic representation. They can be conceived of, and seen, only through their associated symbols. Rites are crucial to this process of associating individuals with symbolic entities such as parties, religions or nations. Through the party-associated rites, individuals both identify themselves and become identified by others with the party. Rituals allow individuals to come in contact with the holy symbols that bond them jointly to this symbolic entity. They provide a context in which the myths that sustain the party can be validated and energised. They also perform a crucial organisational function in marking the in-group from the out-group, distinguishing those associated with the party from all others, by making public the link between member or sympathiser and party symbol.[4]

During the Fascist years, for example, people publicly affirmed their identification with Fascism through a whole series of rites. A plaintive illustration comes from the case of the destitute young Italian mother of three small children who, taking her last breath on a hospital bed, the hospital director at her side, lifted up her arm in the Fascist salute and proclaimed 'Viva il Duce! Viva l'Italia!' Presumably, it was her hope that, through performing this rite, she might attract favourable attention of the authorities for her soon-to-be-orphaned children.[5]

For the leaders of the PCI, the centrality of ritual in defining the party and in providing a means of linking large numbers of people with the party had profound implications. For the new 'thing' to be considered in fact new, it required new symbolic representation, yet at the same time the existing rites linking PCI members and sympathisers with the party were threatened by any rejection of the earlier symbolism on which the rites were based. Party rites without red flags, without the singing of various old revolutionary songs, without the old symbolic representation of the Communist heroes and the imperialist villains, would not appear to be rites of the party at all.

LEGITIMACY AND MYSTIFICATION

The value of ritual in conferring political legitimacy was well understood by kings, popes and rulers of various kinds through the millennia. The aura of sacrality that people tend to confer on the powerful is nourished and strengthened by ritual performance. By manipulating and claiming ownership of the holy symbols, power holders demonstrate their special power and legitimise their claim to authority. At the same time, ritual forms – from inaugurations to imperial processions – structure the contact between the power holders and the masses.

Ritual not only legitimises its sponsors but confers legitimacy on its participants as well. Consider the plight of the heir to the Italian kingdom in the aftermath of World War II. Badly needing to shore up the legitimacy of the monarchy in the wake of its connivance with Mussolini and, later, its cowardly behaviour in running from the Nazi threat in 1943, Prince Umberto sought appropriate ritual means of legitimation. Opportunity appeared in the form of a demobilisation parade of 'patriotic' military forces in Milan, scheduled for Sunday 6 May 1945. Umberto sought to stand in review of the troops in the parade, thus identifying himself with the anti-Fascist, anti-Nazi forces, and showing that the throne represented all Italians, both left and right. Yet leaders of the Resistance forces refused to allow the prince to ritually review their troops. Rather than bring this rejection into such clear public symbolic view, Prince Umberto retreated. A year later, of course, a national plebiscite would end the Italian monarchy.[6]

As this case shows, the struggle for legitimacy through ritual takes place in part through efforts to claim the mantle of an existing ritual. The durability of ritual amidst political change means that ritual itself becomes a political prize, a kind of holy grail. Political competitors, then, not only fight through ritual, they also fight over ritual, that is, over their right to identify with powerful rites.

SOLIDARITY AND AMBIGUITY

Participating together in ritual fosters a feeling of oneness. The heightening of emotion, the use of various aural and visual stimuli, the chemistry of the crowd, all these give ritual unusual potency in creating and renewing bonds of solidarity. These are hardly new insights, for they lie at the heart of Durkheim's classic view of ritual.[7]

Less well appreciated is the fact that ritual produces such solidarity without requiring the people thus brought together to share the same interpretation of the rite's meaning. Communist Party members and sympathisers who came together in a central piazza, waved red flags, and sang revolutionary songs had their bonds of solidarity with one another greatly strengthened, as well as their sense of identification with the party. However, while some of them viewed their participation as contributing to the demise of capitalism, others simply viewed it as a pleasant way to spend an evening.[8]

Perhaps the simplest, yet one of the most powerful ritual devices employed by the Communists for this purpose was the use of the term *compagno* (comrade). Indeed, the more threatened was the party's solidarity, it seemed, the more incessant became Occhetto's use of the term. All who addressed party members were obliged to begin their speeches with 'Care compagne e cari compagni' (Dear comrades), thus establishing the solidarity of speaker and audience. In his speeches to various gatherings during the crisis over the party's transformation, Occhetto commonly began every section of each speech with this ritual incantation. The habit reached its height at his opening speech to the 1991 party congress, where the PCI was to be dissolved: Occhetto addressed his audience as *compagni* six times in the final section of the speech alone.

At moments of transition the use of ritual to produce solidarity becomes especially pronounced. A good example of just such ritualised mechanisms for expressing solidarity comes from the reaction to Stalin's death in 1953. The party's relationship to Stalin was, indeed, publicly defined through ritual, and his death was greeted with a frenzy of ritual activity. The PCI sent its entire leadership to the funeral ceremonies in Moscow; at the insistence of the PCI, the Italian parliament adjourned for a day in deference to the death. Commemorative observances were held simultaneously throughout the country, from the Central Committee in Rome to the smallest rural party section. Hundreds of thousands of Italians signed memorial books which were then ceremonially handed over to the Soviet embassy in Rome.

RITUAL CONSTRUCTION OF POLITICAL REALITY

As the case of the ritualisation of Stalin's death shows, in addition to creating solidarity, ritual encourages certain views of political reality. It was through ritual, for example, that the view that Soviet Communists, Bulgarian Communists and Italian Communists were all part of the same movement was most powerfully expressed. Likewise, it was through ritual that the United States could be most effectively identified as the enemy. Togliatti could show the extent of the PCI's loyalty to the Soviet Communist party through the kinds of ritual described above. Three decades later, Berlinguer could show the PCI's new distance from the Moscow-directed Communist movement by choosing to spend his summer holiday in China.[9]

Rituals highlight certain events and interpretations and conceal others, leading us to focus our attention on some things and ignore others. A history of the PCI's international position can be read from a history of the public demonstrations that the party organised. It sponsored demonstrations of mourning for Stalin's death, yet none for Mao's. And, while the PCI publicly claimed to be happy about the demise of the Communist regimes of Eastern Europe, the fact that not a single public ritual was held to celebrate it spoke volumes about the party's actual position. The PCI had, in fact, sponsored thousands of demonstrations against the presence of US troops in Vietnam, yet not a single demonstration against Soviet troops in Afghanistan. The party had spoken out against the Soviet invasion of Czechoslovakia, yet initiated not one public demonstration against it. The word lacks the force of the rite.

The power of symbolism and ritual to define political reality was evident in 1990 in a revealing *contretemps* over the commemorations in Bologna of the tenth anniversary of the railway station bomb that killed scores of people there. In the immediate aftermath of the explosion, with emotions running high, the Communist officials of Bologna branded the act as the work of the 'Fascists', although no credible claim of responsibility for the bombing had been made and there was no immediate evidence as to the identity of the authors. Huge demonstrations were organised in Bologna, channelling popular rage over the massacre into an expression of solidarity around the PCI and city officials, who were given powerful ritual occasions on which to speak out on behalf of the population against the evil in their midst.

The ritual commemorations of the tenth anniversary of the explosion were challenged, however, by leaders of the MSI. A Communist deputy in Parliament called for a moment of silence to commemorate the anniversary. In response, an MSI deputy called for a parliamentary order to alter the commemorative plaque marking the shrine that had been erected in Bologna's main piazza in response to the bombing. The MSI demanded the removal of reference to Fascist responsibility for the bombing. To the anger of the Communists, the Christian Democrat Prime Minister, Giulio Andreotti, agreed and a heated debate about the proper ritualisation of the bombing ensued.

In reaction, thousands of people gathered before the shrine in the main piazza of Bologna. Their response to the proposal to remove the term *fascista* from the plaque, according to the *L'Unità* account, was 'Rage, astonishment, and rage again'. 'It is a shameful method,' the head of Bologna PCI Federation proclaimed. At the same time, the head of the organisation of relatives of the bombing victims announced: 'We will defend that plaque and keep it the way it is. And we will view all those who have gone along with Rauti's [leader of the extreme right of the MSI] request as friends of the Fascists.'[10] In battling over symbols, ritual is a potent weapon. The aim is to fix the symbols, and thereby establish the symbolic definition of reality, and in so doing equate one's own political group with good and the other with evil.

Central to this symbolic battle is the ability to define history. A good example of just such ritual combat over history arose in September 1990. Newspapers were filled with new charges (actually, a rehash of old charges) directed at long-dead PCI leader Palmiro Togliatti. Togliatti, who had served as Minister of Justice in the first post-war government, was accused of complicity in protecting the Communist killers of large numbers of political enemies following Liberation in 1945. The area that experienced the largest concentration of such killings, in the heart of Emilia-Romagna, became known as the Triangle of Death.

While the PCI could and did deal with these charges through a raft of denunciatory press releases and interviews, ritual offered the most effective vehicle for responding. Only through ritual could the party demonstrate its claim to speak for a greater mass of people. Moreover, such public ritual could whip up the emotions of the members and sympathisers in a way other forms of communication could not. Party leaders announced that a national demonstration would be held in Reggio Emilia, at the heart of the triangle of death, where all party forces – regardless of their division over the *svolta* – would come together 'in defence of the Liberation struggle'.[11]

For its part, the MSI could hardly pass up the symbolic possibilities offered by the occasion, and promptly announced that it would hold its own national 'conference' and procession in Reggio Emilia on the same day. The ritual battle was joined. Scores of ageing *partigiani*, their medals dangling from their chests, marched through the streets, along with large numbers of supporters. Their procession ended at the central piazza, with its shrine on which are engraved the names of the 600 local people martyred in the Resistance. Shortly after the official procession had passed, demonstrators from the extreme-left Democrazia Proletaria party marched by, ritually exhibiting their militancy by chanting such old favourites as 'Camerata basco nero, il tuo posto è il cimitero' (Comrade with a black beret, your place is in the cemetery).[12]

Meanwhile the MSI held its 'conference' on the triangle of death in a hotel near by in the centre of the city. Large numbers of anti-Fascist demonstrators gathered outside, with police lines set up to keep the two groups apart. When the MSI members made their way out of the hotel and entered the piazza they were immediately greeted with whistles, shouts and slogans from the crowd. The *Fascisti* reacted in proper ritual role by giving Roman salutes, arms outstretched, and launching into songs from the Fascist years. In the anti-Fascist crowd, youths exhibited their militancy by wrapping red bandannas around their faces, while others did ritual battle by countering the Fascist songs with louder renditions of songs identified with the Resistance. As some of the bandanna-clad youths gathered stones, the police moved in to disperse them. Just a few metres away, at the central piazza, the partisans' association ANPI continued its vigil.[13]

That all this had some instructional utility to the PCI was clear from the comments of the head of the party's provincial leader for Reggio Emilia. The day after the party had assembled thousands of demonstrators in the city's central piazza, he explained that the events had had a positive effect. A new generation had 'learned to love the Resistance in a new way'.[14]

Party congresses

With the exception of the years of Fascism, when they were suppressed, national party congresses represented the holiest of the rites of the PCI. They defined the party organisation through a series of symbolic presentations of the structure of leadership and by linking members with the party through a capillary procedure of preparatory local-level meetings electing delegates to higher levels. They legitimised the party leadership and its line by providing a mechanism to demonstrate the support of the membership, and by allowing the leaders to identify themselves with the holy symbols of the party. They increased the solidarity of the members, whose bonds were renewed through the panoply of rites surrounding the congresses. And the whole structure of symbols bound up in the ritual defined friends and enemies, the nature of world and national events, leading members to certain constructions of political reality.

It is not surprising, then, that party congresses were at the centre of the efforts to transform the PCI into the PDS. It was through the congresses that the new party could be legitimised as the heir of the old, while defined in a new way. At the same time, in the heightened emotional context of such powerful rites, the opposition was given an important opportunity to assert its own claims to legitimacy and its own construction of political reality.

In the wake of Occhetto's November 1989 announcement of the *svolta,* the wave of opposition forced him into the immediate scheduling of an 'extraordinary' national party congress. For the opposition the congress seemed to offer the only hope of defeating Occhetto and his allies, since supporters of the *svolta* had a clear majority on the party's Central Committee. But the holding of a congress had value for the majority as well, allowing them to use the party's principal ritual to legitimise the *svolta*, retain party solidarity, and define a new political reality for member and non-member alike.

The process began, as in previous congresses, with the holding of local party section meetings throughout the country. There members debated the major proposals before the congress, voted on them, and elected representatives to the next higher body, the Federation (or provincial-level) gatherings, where the procedure was repeated. The ultimate result was the election of 1,100 delegates to the national congress.

All told, 400,000 of the 1,422,000 party members cast their votes in local section meetings, with 66 per cent voting in favour of Occhetto's proposal (motion one), and the bulk of the rest (31 per cent) for the main opposition motion (motion two). The third motion, identified with the hard-line Communist Armando Cossutta, received only 3 per cent of the vote. Occhetto had a large majority, but never before had there been a PCI congress with such a large and organised faction publicly dedicated to opposing the party head's programme.[15]

Occhetto and his allies sought to use the congress, held in Bologna, to transform the symbolism of the party, but in doing so they faced an opposition intent on using the power of that symbolism against them. As the congress got under way, many of the old symbols were gone. Among other discarded symbols were the previously obligatory representatives of 'fraternal' Communist parties. They had now become an embarrassment, their solidarity no longer ritually desirable.

As it turned out, Occhetto and allies were not fully up to the challenge of competing with the minority on the rich symbolic terrain of a national party congress. While attempting to abandon many of the symbols and rites which had given past PCI congresses their identity, and which had bound the members to the congressional activities, the leaders of the majority lacked any powerful new symbolism to replace the old. They proposed no new party name, no new symbol, no new song, nor any new rites for expressing party identity or membership solidarity with the party. All the rites and symbols of solidarity, legitimacy and identity were the old rites, rites which had now become identified with the opposition.

The basic structure of the congress itself did not change. It opened and closed with long speeches by the party head, with scores of short speeches by party delegates in between. Occhetto's problems were clear from his three-hour opening speech, which engendered little more than respectful applause. The potent symbols were largely lacking and, indeed, the first interruption for applause came only twenty minutes into the speech, when Occhetto invoked the sacred names of Nelson Mandela and Daniel Ortega. The next applause came when he praised the heroic struggle of the Palestinian people. In short, that part of his speech which invoked the standard party icons, which remained within the hallowed ritual frame, allowed the delegates to transport themselves into special, ritual time. By contrast, his oratory regarding the dropping of traditional party symbols and identity and his criticism of the parties of Eastern Europe produced only discomfort in his audience.[16]

By contrast with Occhetto's plight, leaders of the opposition were well positioned to take advantage of the symbolic forum offered by the congress. In the session following the secretary's uninspiring speech, Pietro Ingrao, leader of the 'no' forces, denounced the *svolta*. As he concluded his remarks, his supporters leapt to their feet to sing 'Bandiera rossa' (the Red Flag) and the Internationale, creating an emotional sea into which many members of the majority were swept. The prolonged display proved a bitter trial for Occhetto, who, after polite applause, remained disconsolately perched over a crowd which had exploded in joyful celebration. Other party leaders went up to shake Ingrao's hand, but Occhetto remained in his seat, wincing as the crowd bellowed 'Pie-tro! Pie-tro!' By the time Occhetto returned to the podium for the concluding speech on the last day of the congress he was clearly on the defensive. He could say nothing critical about the history of the PCI, nothing to mar the holy symbolism of the party. When he mentioned the Soviet Union, it was only in a positive vein, to congratulate Gorbachev. He never mentioned the United States except to express criticism. In short, in warding off the attacks of the opposition he sought to position himself on the familiar symbolic terrain of the party.

Rather than having a single congress which would sanction the proposed *svolta* and give birth to the new party, Occhetto had been compelled by the opposition to devote two special congresses to the task. Following the nineteenth congress, which voted in his favour but at which there was as yet no concrete plan for the new party in place, a frenetic period of symbolic battle occurred. Occhetto and allies developed and announced the new name (Partito Democratico della Sinistra, PDS) and new party emblem (a leafy oak tree with the old PCI symbol at its base). Meanwhile the opposition argued that only now was the party in a position to make a final decision on the change. In short, in the view of the minority, the *svolta* had not been fully legitimised by the nineteenth party congress; that decision awaited the twentieth, held ten months later in the Adriatic coastal town of Rimini.

The twentieth congress took place in a period not only of great internal party tension but of unusual international tension as well. The US-led allied assault on Iraqi forces in Kuwait and Iraq had begun only days earlier. Revealingly, the reformist forces within the party, which might have used the repulsion of the Iraqi conquest of Kuwait as a means of showing the new international collocation they sought through the creation of the PDS, instead fell back on old rhetoric and old symbols. It was apparently judged more important to deal with the threatened schism of the anti-reformists within the party than to send any message outside.

Accordingly, when Occhetto took the podium for the opening speech to the gathering that was to give birth to the new party and, presumably (though he could not admit it), mark the death of the old, he devoted the first half-hour to a denunciation of American military intervention. In short, opposition to the US military became the symbolic means of constructing solidarity in the fractious party while burnishing Occhetto's leftist credentials in the face of attacks from his enemies that he was no better than a Social Democrat.

The symbolic structure of the twentieth congress combined an attempt to reinforce the sagging solidarity of the old party with an effort to demonstrate what was supposed to be the novelty of the new party: the bringing in of new groups of pacifists, environmentalists, Catholic leftists and assorted others. The mixture of symbols, though, was not entirely successful.

In deference to the old, the congress began with the playing of the Internationale, followed by the showing of a series of videos on a huge electronic screen hanging over the convention hall. First came the scene of recently deceased party hero Giancarlo Pajetta at the previous autumn's party *Festa* (a major political ritual I unfortunately cannot go into here), with 'Thank you, comrade Pajetta' super-imposed in huge letters. A video history of the PCI followed, leading into the pacifistic picture of youths singing 'All we are saying is give peace a chance' (in English!). At the last 'All we are saying . . .' the lights over the platform gradually went on and the formal programme began.

The congress's liminality was evident in the hall's decorations. The stage was draped in red, but the podium and the tables for all the delegates were covered with green, recalling the reaching out to the environmentalists. Use of the green also had the effect of providing an alternative (to the Communist) interpretation to the red, for green and red (and white) are the colours of the Italian flag. A symbol of the PCI was affixed to one side of the stage, but it was balanced by the symbol of the PDS on the other side. No party name nor slogan hung above, but rather a single word, in a kind of stylised script: 'Twentieth'.

Occhetto's opening speech similarly wove together symbolic claims of continuity with the past and references to the new. The former prompted enthusiasm in the audience, the latter did not. Calling for an end to the military nature of NATO drew applause, as did his mention of the recent celebration of Gramsci's hundredth birthday. Indeed, he repeatedly invoked Gramsci to legitimise his proposal and express continuity: 'We will bring Gramsci with us into the new party.' By contrast, his repeated allusions to the Pope (in connection with the pontiff's presumed opposition to the invasion of Iraq), and to the need for an environmental movement, were greeted with considerably less enthusiasm.

The death of a Communist

In the liminal period between the nineteenth and twentieth party congresses, with symbols in flux and party members' identity threatened, the need for emotional release and reassurance through rituals of solidarity was great. The party congress, which had previously served to bring party members together under the old symbols, renew their bonds of solidarity, reinvigorate their construction of history and legitimise the party leadership, had become an arena of factional struggle. What remained was death, as ever before a creator of a sacred time which ties past to present. It was the death of a Communist that would, for a fleeting but exalting time, allow party members to enter into a kind of communion that would soon be lost to them.

In September 1990 Giancarlo Pajetta, the seventy-nine-year-old legendary Communist Party leader, died. Pajetta embodied in his person much of the mythic structure of the PCI itself and, as more than one observer noted, his death seemed symbolically appropriate, coming at the time the PCI itself was about to expire. As one of the last surviving leaders of the Resistance, and one of the last survivors of the PCI leadership from the Fascist period, Pajetta had become the symbolic point man in the party's continued identification with the anti-Fascist struggle and the Resistance. Occhetto, for example, told the press in response to the news of Pajetta's death: 'We pay tribute to him not only as the fighter for the PCI, but the man of the Resistance and the anti-Fascist struggle as well.' In this symbolic fusion the military struggle against Mussolini and Hitler continued uninterrupted via the PCI over the past half-century.[17]

On the morning of 14 September Pajetta's coffin was placed on view in the rotunda of the PCI headquarters in Rome. It was covered with the red flag of his local party section. Thousands of party members filed by, some of the older ones with their fists raised, tears streaming down their faces. In the afternoon the funeral procession began, taking the coffin from the national PCI headquarters in the Via delle Botteghe Oscure to the piazza in front of the Parliament building where Pajetta had served for decades as Communist deputy. As the Internationale was played to a slow funereal beat the banners of the cities of the Resistance led the procession, followed by delegations of *partigiani*. Banners proclaiming 'Goodbye *partigiano* Nullo [Pajetta's *nom de guerre* in the Resistance]' and 'Long live the glorious Resistance' dotted the march.

Occhetto, meanwhile, had to make the most of this ritual opportunity, though he had to take care that nothing in his remarks to the throngs assembled in the piazza could be seen as divisive or self-serving. His central task was to identify himself with Pajetta and the symbolism attached to him, and to take advantage of the power of the emotions generated by the rite. Tapping into the emotional power of the death, he turned to Pajetta's family and spoke, in a voice cracking with emotion, of their importance to the nation's history. Here he recalled Pajetta's mother, who, in addition to suffering through Giancarlo's long years of imprisonment during Fascism, saw another son killed by the Fascists and a third deported and tortured by the Nazis.

It was, proclaimed Occhetto, a moment for party unity. Sadly noting Pajetta's own anguish at the crisis that had overtaken the party – though not mentioning that

Pajetta objected to the *svolta* and regretted having backed Occhetto for party head – Occhetto concluded: 'I think that even if our vision today of the party differs from that which men like Pajetta, formed in trying times, had . . . , we cannot fail to interpret, in the light of our own experience, that value of unity that he strenuously championed.' The ceremony – beamed to the nation live on television – concluded with the playing once again of the Internationale. The red flag-draped coffin, with red roses atop, made its way out of the piazza as thousands raised their fists and sang 'Bella Ciao!' and 'Bandiera rossa'.[18]

From Movimento Sociale to Alleanza Nazionale

The PCI was not the only Italian party eager to change its identity in the period of rapid political flux following the fall of the Berlin Wall. The changed international political climate, the transformation of the Italian Communist Party and the implosion of the Christian Democratic and Socialist parties – linked with the corruption scandals of *Tangentopoli* – all contributed to a new situation, and new opportunities, for the Movimento Sociale Italiano as well.

Founded in 1946 by veterans of Mussolini's Social Republic (1943–45), the MSI regularly drew about 5 per cent of the vote nationally. Stigmatised as neo-Fascist by the other parties, it had long been isolated from the Italian political mainstream.[19] However, the demise of the DC and the end of the Cold War presented leaders of the MSI with new opportunities for growth and influence. MSI candidates came close to winning the mayoral elections in Rome and Naples in 1993. At the beginning of 1994 Gianfranco Fini, the able party secretary, saw that by altering the party's image he could enter into a coalition with Silvio Berlusconi's Forza Italia and thereby not only take a huge leap in respectability for his party but also take the MSI out of its ghetto and, for the first time in its history, aspire to become part of a national government.

In order to take this leap, however, Fini had to remake the identity of his party, jettisoning its uncomfortable Fascist legacy. This, too, could be done only through ritual. Issuing proclamations was not enough. Public rites had to be performed, new symbols invented and displayed.[20] Aware of this, Fini first arranged, as part of the move to ally with Forza Italia, to change the name of the political label under which the party would run in early 1994, coining the new name of Alleanza Nazionale in the place of the heavily freighted label of Movimento Sociale. To sanction the demise of the old symbolism and the birth of the new, Fini called for a national convention, to be held in the spa town of Fiuggi, in January 1995.

The parallels between the PCI's Rimini convention of 1990 and the MSI's Fiuggi convention five years later are striking. Both were organised by a party leader eager to remake his party's identity. Both were rites of transition, burying the old and inaugurating the new; both faced the thorny problem of dealing with the appeal of the old symbols and rites to the party membership; and both faced a minority of the leadership keen on keeping that old symbolism alive.

As in the case of the PCI convention in Rimini, there were two groups of delegates to the Fiuggi conference. A large majority represented the MSI membership, but a second group was added to symbolise the new forces that were joining with the old to create the Alleanza Nazionale. The first half of the meeting, billed as the seventeenth national convention of the MSI, had the task of burying the old party, while the second half was billed as the first national convention of AN. Each of the two was opened and closed by the same person, party head Gianfranco Fini. Here the analogy with the PCI experience was again a close one, for while the unchanged national leadership meant that there was less problem with continuity, it made it more difficult to make the case that anything really new was actually being established. Fini had to do all he could to manipulate the rites of the convention to demonstrate the validity of his claim that AN was not simply old wine in a new bottle.

To accomplish this, a number of the best known of the old rites of the party had to be eliminated. One could not have a non-Fascist party while retaining the rites identified with Fascism. Speakers at the convention should no longer address the delegates as *camerati*, as they always had done. And the Roman salutes of old, long part of the neo-Fascist nostalgia, could no longer be tolerated, nor could the use of the colour black. The old MSI anthem, 'Sole che sorgi' (O Rising Sun) had to be ditched, and a new one introduced. The French extreme right-wing leader, Jean-Marie Le Pen, formerly the darling of the MSI, and a fixture as a guest at recent MSI conventions, was conspicuously absent. The party's own history also had to be redefined while the continuity of old and new was demonstrated. A video of long-time MSI leader Giorgio Almirante, veteran of the Italian Social Republic and Fini's mentor, was played on a huge screen and brought tears to the eyes of the delegates. Alessandra Mussolini blessed the change by saying that her grandfather was a man of innovation and change who always looked to the future. And, as in the PDS, the new AN symbol would conserve, at its base, the old tricoloured flame of the MSI.

Yet for many of the old MSI faithful, giving up the cherished old rites and symbols was emotionally painful, a fact that opponents of the change seized upon at the convention. Here, too, the parallels with the forces opposing the PCI *svolta* are clear. Opposition leaders, by addressing the delegates as 'camerati' and pronouncing that they were proud to be called 'Missini' (members of the MSI), triggered the strongest emotional response in the crowd. And when the final vote for the change was taken, and the opposition lost, they sang the old MSI anthem, exerting a strong emotional pull on those present. And, like Cossutta and the others who broke with the PCI over its new course, Pino Rauti and his colleagues of the MSI opposition threatened legal action against the old party leadership so that they could retain the use of the old party name and emblem.

Conclusion

In Italy, as elsewhere, ritual provides people with powerful means to influence the political process. Yet we often overlook the political power of ritual, especially its importance in periods of political change. In the liberal tradition, political ritual has been viewed with suspicion, identified with irrationality and the dangers of the crowd, a relic from a benighted past that is best overcome as soon as possible. In the Marxist intellectual tradition, political ritual is likewise treated condescendingly, associated with the apparatus involved in the creation of false consciousness.[21] Yet as the Italian case shows, there can be no politics without symbolism, and in the construction of symbols, and in the battle over symbolic construction ritual plays a central role. It provides a means of making palpable that which cannot otherwise be seen, it affords a potent mechanism for producing legitimacy and solidarity, and it helps us construct political reality out of what must otherwise appear as chaos.

NOTES

1 A fuller examination of the role of symbolism in the birth of the PCI can be found in D. I. Kertzer, *Politics and Symbols. The Italian Communist Party and the Fall of Communism* (New Haven, CT, Yale University Press, 1996).

2 For a fuller discussion of the definition of ritual use here see D. I. Kertzer, *Ritual, Politics and Power* (New Haven, CT, Yale University Press, 1988). For a review of concepts of ritual see C. Bell, *Ritual Theory, Ritual Practice* (Oxford University Press, 1992). For an analysis of local-level Communist rites in Italy in the early 1970s see D. I. Kertzer, *Comrades and Christians. Religion and Political Struggle in Communist Italy* (Prospect Heights, IL, Waveland Press, 1990, 2nd edn).

3 For other recent works on political ritual see the bibliography under 'Myths, symbols and rituals' at the end of this volume.

4 R. A. Rapaport, 'Liturgies and Lies', *International Yearbook for Sociology of Knowledge and Religion*, 10 (1975), p. 88, puts the matter this way: 'participation in ritual demarcates a boundary . . . between private and public processes. . . . Participation is the outcome of a dichotomous choice.'

5 D. Biondi, *La fabbrica del Duce* (Florence, Vallecchi, 1967), p. 257.

6 On Prince Umberto's abortive visit to Milan see C. F. Delzell, *Mussolini's Enemies. The Italian Anti-Fascist Resistance* (Princeton University Press, 1961), p. 547.

7 E. Durkheim, *The Elementary Forms of Religious Life* (Glencoe IL, Free Press, 1974 [1915]). See also the discussion of Durkheim's ritual theory and the role of solidarity in Kertzer, *Ritual*, pp. 61–7.

8 For a classic statement on the use of rites in producing solidarity without consensus see J. Fernandez, 'Symbolic Consensus in a Fang Reformative Cult', *American Anthropologist*, 67 (1965), pp. 902–29.

9 On Berlinguer's China holiday see J. B. Urban, *Moscow and the Italian Communist Party* (Ithaca, NY, Cornell University Press, 1986), p. 338.

10 A. Guermandi, '"Non spetta al governo decidere su queste cose"', *L'Unità*, 3 August 1990.

11 M. Smagiassi, 'Il PCI adesso dice basta: "Non si può screditare la Resistenza"', *La Repubblica*, 6 September 1990.

12 J. Meletti, 'Il giorno più amaro di Reggio Emilia. La rabbia dei partigiani: "Giù le mani dalla Resistenza"', *L'Unità*, 9 September 1990.

13 D. Mastrogiacomo, '"Finiamola col mito della Resistenza"', *La Repubblica*, 9–10 September 1990, p. 9.

14 J. Meletti, 'Migliaia in piazza a Reggio', *L'Unità*, 9 September 1990, Bologna section.

15 R. Armeni, 'PCI: prossimo venturo', *Rinascita*, 11 March 1990, p. 5.

16 I attended both the nineteenth PCI congress in Bologna in 1990 and the twentieth in Rimini in 1991. Descriptions of these congresses in this chapter are based in large part on this direct observation. For a more detailed examination of the symbolism employed in the nineteenth PCI congress see D. I. Kertzer, 'The Nineteenth Congress of the Italian Communist Party. The Role of Symbolism in the Communist Crisis', in F. Anderlini and R. Leonardi (eds), *Italian Politics. A Review*, vol. 5 (London, Pinter, 1992), pp. 69–82.

17 B. Miserendino, 'Pajetta, il grande ribelle', *L'Unità*, 14 September 1990.

18 This description of the Pajetta funeral rites is based on S. Marroni, 'Il funerale di un comunista vero', *La Repubblica*, 15 September 1990, and B. Miseredino, ' "Ciao, Gian Carlo, non ti scorderemo." Il lungo corteo, l'emozione e gli applausi per l'ultimo saluto', *L'Unità*, 15 September 1990.

19 For more background on the MSI see P. Ignazi, *Il polo escluso* (Bologna, Il Mulino, 1998, 2nd edn).

20 An analysis of some of the symbols of the MSI can be found in L. Cheles, ' "Nostalgia dell' Avvenire". The Propaganda of the Italian Far Right between Tradition and Innovation', in L. Cheles, R. Ferguson and M. Vaughan (eds), *The Far Right in Western and Eastern Europe* (London, Longman, 1995), pp. 41–90.

21 In Antonio Gramsci's writings, however, there is recognition, at least implicitly, of the political importance of ritual. For a discussion of some of these issues see D. I. Kertzer, 'Gramsci's Concept of Hegemony. The Italian Church–Communist struggle', *Dialectical Anthropology*, 4 (1979), pp. 321–8.

8
The political press

Mario Isnenghi

All the press is political, not just that section of it which proclaims itself to be so by a party reference in its name. This political link, whether or not consciously sought, has been part and parcel of the history of journalism in Italy since the country's unification. Rarely has there been an editor, leader writer or opinion maker who has kept himself at one remove as might a reporter or a mere witness who has not entered the arena of dispute himself as a protagonist.[1] One could say, for example, that Luigi Albertini, co-owner and editor of the leading bourgeois daily *Corriere della Sera* from 1900 to 1925 – its most authoritative phase – was himself, along with his influential paper, an unofficial voice of the Liberal Party in Italy.[2]

Editors of *Avanti!*, the official newspaper of the Socialist Party (PSI), such as Benito Mussolini (1912–14), Giacinto Menotti Serrati (1914–23) and Pietro Nenni (1923–26), eventually became party leaders, and even, in Mussolini's case, head of the government. Antonio Gramsci, one of the founders of the Communist Party (PCI) in 1921, who worked on the *Grido del Popolo, Avanti!* and *L'Ordine Nuovo*, also proved to be a journalist of originality and a keen theorist. He saw newspapers as a driving and direction-giving instrument for a political group intent on gaining self-awareness and extending its influence in society.

If we scan the history of the Italian press briefly from the early decades to the present day it is obvious that, while party newspapers have often struggled to survive, newspapers supporting a particular party have prospered and are the norm. Newspaper editors such as Indro Montanelli, who was first at *Il Giornale* and then at the short-lived *La Voce*,[3] Eugenio Scalfari at *La Repubblica*, Luigi Pintor, Valentino Parlato and Rossana Rossanda at *Il Manifesto* and more recently Vittorio Feltri, a quarrelsome bully who moved from *L'Indipendente* to *Il Giornale* and then to *Libero*, have behaved like fully-fledged politicians; they would not tolerate their dailies being treated merely as information broadsheets.

It is true that the hypothetical distinction between 'facts' and 'comment' is vaunted as a motto each time a newspaper is born, or reborn with a new editor. (Typically, in such cases, reference is made to the supposed splendour of English-language journalism.) However, it does not take long to realise that the formula cuts no ice and does not last. The most recent case, that of *L'Indipendente*, is typical. When it came into the world in 1991 it made great show of its highly virtuous, sober, London-inspired aplomb. Within a few short months of its launch, however, it was on the verge of bankruptcy. A new owner and editor attempted to relaunch it as a militant vehicle of the Lega Nord. However, the paper finally collapsed in 1996.

At this point it is necessary to set out the fundamentals of the press system in Italy within the temporal and political cycle which began with the fall of Fascism and the monarchy, and the birth of the Republic.

The journalistic landscape to emerge from the Second World War and the bloody clash between Fascists and anti-Fascists of 1943–45 was more than ever before one of *la politique d'abord*. On the extreme right, those nostalgic for the Fascist regime and the Italian Social Republic, RSI (the state founded by Mussolini in northern Italy shortly after he was deposed by the king in 1943), entrusted their raging recollections and inalienable rancour to a form of political journalism which at the outset was semi-clandestine, its aim being to keep alive, for decades, the recriminatory bitterness arising from their refusal to accept what had taken place. Thus a kind of half-voluntary, half-constrained ghetto was formed, consisting of a separate and parallel Italy which, for a long time, appeared lost in a tortuous historical past, but which (as the results of recent elections have shown) does not live solely in the past.

Within the confines of this isolated world, however, one could find various right-wing weeklies commanding considerable circulation figures and influence, such as *Il Borghese* and *Candido*, or the less radical and politicised *Oggi* and *Gente*, favoured by the petty bourgeoisie for their entertainment value. These publications were written and read by conservatives and downright reactionaries, resentful of, and impervious to, party democracy – in other words, by people for whom anti-Fascism would never become an acceptable substitute for Fascism, the latter being perceived as guilty of having lost the war.

There were dailies which specialised in providing a haven for the least reputable veterans of the Fascist press: for example, the *Roma*, published in Naples and owned by the monarchist shipping magnate and populist mayor Achille Lauro, and in the capital, *Il Giornale d'Italia* and *Il Tempo*. The latter, founded in 1944, may be said to have been already 'old' then; its venomous anti-Communism was unmatched by anything else on the right.

So far, I have limited the discussion to the world of right-wing politics and the press. However, a good many journalists from the Fascist era managed to ply their trade, more or less openly, in centre and centre-right journalism which addressed itself to its middle-class peers (the professions and employees, namely those who harboured, with greater or lesser propriety and conviction, the same illusions and generational failures), as well to the vast 'grey area' of those who, in 1943–45, when choices had to be made, preferred to be passive observers and wait to be 'liberated' by the Anglo-American forces.[4]

In Rome moderate opinion was represented by the old and well-established daily *Il Messaggero*, also read in other regions of central Italy, which included local pages.

In the post-war period the paper relied on an illustrious *revenant*, Mario Missiroli, a theorist and practitioner of every possible kind of transformism. Under Fascism he spared no bowing, scraping or appeasing gestures in an effort to get those in power to restore him to the editorial position of which he had been deprived at the beginning of the regime. He did not succeed in this, but after the collapse of Fascism that failure became his alibi as well as his good fortune. After the Second World War those in power (both the new guard and the old) who practised the liberal maxim of *heri dicebamus* – in other words, a 'let's carry on as if nothing happened' approach – recycled him at the top as a doyen of the bloc of the pro-government press (i.e. almost the whole of the press). From 1946 to 1952 he was at *Il Messaggero*, and then, for the next ten years, he held the most coveted and authoritative journalistic post, that of general editor of the *Corriere della Sera* in Milan. This is an early indication of the professional and communication strategies set in motion by the Christian Democrats and their government allies. Former Fascist editors were also made editors of large regional dailies, a typical example being Giovanni Ansaldo, appointed to the Naples paper *Il Mattino*, which served as a ministerial mouthpiece for the whole of the Campania region. Even former chief reporters of the Italian Social Republic were recycled: Attilio Tommasini, for instance, was made editor of *Il Gazzettino* of Venice, which, on a semi-monopoly basis, controlled the staunchly Catholic and politically moderate Veneto region.

It was, however, not simply a case of skilful chameleon-like behaviour on the part of individuals. The crisis of the Fascist regime and the military defeat had the effect of displacing the internal components of the power bloc, and changed party references. Nevertheless, the most popular and influential papers were more or less the same ones as before.

Founded at the end of the nineteenth century and locally based, the press passed without too much ado from Liberal Italy to Fascist Italy, and then to post-Fascist Italy, remaining all the while the voice of the economic and political masters. In the 1950s newspapers continued to refer to themselves as 'independent', but it was purely a nominal description, since 'politicking' was perceived as being more akin to an opposition movement, i.e. as something vaguely dirty and disquieting (the influence of a Fascist upbringing). Honest folk, on the other hand, were supposed to put themselves forth as apolitical and pro-government: in other words, they were Christian Democrats *faute de mieux*, given that the Liberal Party (PLI), in principle ideologically closer to several of these newspapers and journalists, was too small and elitist, and did not have behind it the large rank and file which only the Catholic Church, source of moderate power and true antagonist of the leftist bloc, could deliver. The advice which Montanelli, the most influential and best loved of the bourgeois opinion makers and veterans of the Fascist press, gave on the eve of the 1976 elections when the Communists seemed likely to win – 'Hold your nose and vote Christian Democrat!' – accurately expresses such an attitude, one of nausea and cynicism.

The forces of the left, for their part, quickly lost the supporting papers which arose from the 1945 upswing – a time when radical renewal seemed to be just round the corner. Assorted small dailies, youthful in approach and cash-starved, sprang up in various Italian cities. Armed with enterprising spirit and zest, they set out to fight the noble battle for progressive democracy against the older newspapers and the old foxes of the profession who were hardened to all experience. It was an electrifying period, albeit brief and unrepeatable. The historian Carlo Zaghi, who lived through it personally in Milan, the capital of the Resistance and of the so-called *Vento del Nord* (the sweeping wind of change brought about by Partisans fighting in the North) wistfully compared these years to the Jacobin period:

> It seemed as though we were back to the three-year reign of the Jacobins when the Revolution had swept away the tyrants, and newspapers became an expression of freedom, dignity, and human, civil and political progress. They emerged from the ghetto that absolutist sovereigns and the Church had locked them in for centuries, becoming a forum of free and open discussion. Milan became again the capital of the free, patriotic and democratic press. In the space of a few days, dozens of newspapers of all types, tendencies, colours, dimensions and descriptions – up-front, radical and violent – had sprung up in the Lombard capital; they were a sign of maturity, verve and awareness. They were sought after and read avidly at the newsstands by an impatient population. They made a laughing-stock of the grey, flat and monotonous uniformity of the Fascist press.[5]

The clearest, relatively successful example of a journalism born of an active involvement in the transition from Fascist to post-Liberation Italy was *Il Nuovo Corriere*. This was set up after the war in Florence by the Tuscan writer Romano Bilenchi, one of a considerable number of former 'left Fascists' (dissident intellectuals of the 1930s supporting the radical Fascism of the early 1920s) who joined the political class in opposition, via the palingenesis of the Resistance.

With the electoral defeat of 18 April 1948, the dashed hopes of 1945 and the entry into the long and difficult tunnel of the Cold War, the financial resources of the PCI and PSI, and their trade union, the CGIL, had to be deployed on other, more pressing fronts. Left to their destiny, very few newspapers of the left succeeded in making a name for themselves or even surviving in the market place. One of the few which did was the Rome-based *Il Paese*, later *Paese Sera*. Despite its ups and downs and numerous editorial mishaps, it succeeded in securing an appreciative popular readership, particularly in the capital, with a reportage style of journalism that mixed social commentary, ideology and human-interest stories. Though it was owned by the PCI, it made itself accessible to a wider and more heterogeneous readership than the party's 'hard core' militants.[6]

The opposition press was not the only one to be outside the market system. It is worth remembering that the market for daily newspapers in Italy has traditionally been narrow and static: overall figures for printing and distribution fluctuated for decades at around 5 million copies until television came on the scene, draining away capital, advertising and readers. A few new titles, such as the aforementioned *La Repubblica* and *Il Giornale*, were created in the 1970s to good effect. They pushed the circulation figures up a little, but without substantially changing the situation: the three or four most widely read titles sell around 400,000–700,000 copies a day, with a maximum of 750,000 copies. These figures are a far cry from the very high figures attained in other countries.

To return for a moment to the situation in the 1950s, the older, immutable papers continued to dominate. In the main they were not commercially viable: they were run for political rather than financial gain, and thus tended to be highly specialised, 'ideology-led' enterprises. Their respective owners, who were never 'merely publishers', kept them going in order to support the general political choices in which they felt they had a stake, and their specific sectoral interests. Large-scale industry owned the leading newspapers, with the motor industry in first place (notably Fiat, owner of *La Stampa*), followed by the textile, cement and petroleum sectors. As for the scores of regional dailies, they tended to be owned by industrial and banking concerns, and wealthy families. These newspapers were more likely to be profitable, since, as in the case of *L'Arena* in Verona, or *La Prealpina* in Varese, they could rake in all the local advertising.

Provincial newspapers made up the largest proportion of papers sold on newsstands. To their readers they were generally 'the' paper. As they had no competition, this situation remained virtually unchanged in the first fifteen to twenty years of the post-war period. These papers abhorred 'politics' and would have been horrified by the idea of being seen as 'party papers' linked with any kind of 'propaganda'. Yet many of them received pre-prepared material for their domestic and foreign economic coverage from outside bodies and agencies connected with Confindustria (the Confederation of Italian Industry) or the DC. Thus, in addition to being a 'spontaneous' force biased in favour of the government of the day, their choice of camp also had solid structural foundations.[7]

It may be difficult for a British reader, whatever his or her political background – be it Conservative, Liberal Democrat or Labour – to appreciate the anomalous case which Italy represented. The country had the largest Communist Party in the West, a Socialist Party which for a long time was unwilling to see itself as social democrat, the strongest left-wing trade union confederation (the CGIL), three 'red' regions (Emilia-Romagna, Tuscany and Umbria) and many small cities run by the left. The world of culture, art and publishing was dominated by the recognisable and prestigious presence of left-wing ideas and personalities, as a consequence of which the very expression 'right-wing intellectual' – let alone 'intellectual of the centre' – sounded, until quite recently, like a contradiction in terms. Yet the press was dourly presided over by an anti-Communist, pro-American, Atlanticist and clerical mix.

To exemplify this paradox, it is sufficient to mention that, though the regions just named consistently enjoyed stable left-wing regional government, they were 'ruled', journalistically speaking, by an occupying force of old traditionalist and fiercely reactionary newspapers: *La Nazione* in Tuscany, *Il Resto del Carlino* in Emilia-Romagna, and, in Umbria, the bourgeois papers published in Rome, Florence and Bologna. This situation persisted to the extent that in the long run the antagonistic stance of these right-wing papers did not succeed in affecting local power relations, nor did the forces of the left manage to prevent their electorate from reading a local press so strongly biased against them. In these regions, more than elsewhere in the country, people grew accustomed to reading the party dailies – especially *L'Unità* (PCI) and *Avanti!* (PSI) – in addition to, or instead of, their local paper. The differing strength of these two parties was reflected in their respective papers. In terms of number of pages, standard of information, printing quality and distribution strength, the long-standing Socialist daily did not match up to its younger sister paper.

Mention must also be made at this point of a daily which, though not tied to a specific party, played an important political role: *Il Giorno*. Founded in 1956 in Milan as the mouthpiece of public capital (one of its co-founders was Enrico Mattei, head of the chemical giant ENI), the paper championed the cause of a shift to the left of the government axis, and called for a centre-left reformist alliance between the Christian Democrats and the Socialists.[8] *Il Giorno* was modern, agile and attractive: it won over readers from the camps of friends and foes alike. It lived up to expectations and eroded part of *Avanti!*'s natural readership. However, in the 1950s and up to the early 1970s, people continued to look forward to reading the Socialist daily, especially its Sunday edition, when the italicised letters of its time-honoured masthead appeared in red for the leading articles signed by some of its best-loved popular tribunes, such as Pietro Nenni, and the future President of the Republic Sandro Pertini. During its happier days *Avanti!* also succeeded in animating discussion, and printed the views of maverick left-wing intellectuals such as Raniero Panzieri, Gianni Bosio and Franco Fortini, who were unlikely to appear in the more orthodox and regimented pages of the Communist paper. The 'felicitous' openness of the PSI, which catered for everything and everyone, had clearly had an impact on *Avanti!*

The PSI's entry into the government majority in 1963 put an end to this. The nonconformist intellectuals abandoned the party, and, especially during the leadership of Bettino Craxi, *Avanti!* became little more than an order paper which no one read unless out of political professionalism or for party representation. Despite a dramatic drop in its circulation, the old flagship newspaper of the left continued to appear, riding on the wake of memory and habit.[9] It became what the Christian Democrat daily *Il Popolo* had always been: a bureaucratic voice which no one, save party stalwarts, wanted to read, because nearly all the television news programmes and daily papers were sympathetic to the political views of *Il Popolo*'s readership, and because their reporting was better.[10] People considering themselves to be Catholic first and supporters of the Catholic party second, who wanted to consolidate their identity and cultural interests, would have done better to turn directly to the source of ethico-religious legitimation: the Vatican's *L'Osservatore Romano*.

The real make-up of political power in the Catholic party came to be something other than its original founding ideal. It should not be imagined that the average Christian Democrat, during the eras of Alcide De Gasperi and Amintore Fanfani or, less remotely, of Ciriaco De Mita and Mino Martinazzoli, was an avid reader of the pompous and austere Vatican paper. Those who did not see themselves simply as party stalwarts, and whose staple diet did not consist solely of stock exchange lists and gossip from the corridors of power and the party factions, would read *L'Avvenire*, an anomalous daily linked with CEI, the Standing Conference of Italian Bishops. Its coverage enabled readers to keep abreast of what was happening both at Church hierarchy level and within the overall context of *Azione Cattolica*, the widespread social organisation of laity and clergy.

In terms of dailies, the journalistic landscape in Italy which can properly be described as Catholic has been in a habitual state of suspended animation. This is partly due to the strategic decision, made at the turn of the nineteenth and twentieth centuries, to reach the 'non-reader' through popular periodicals. These are of three main types: weekly diocesan magazines, which until fairly recently totalled 1 million copies; publications from the shrines, such as *Il Messaggero di Sant'Antonio*, which appears in several languages and has the highest circulation in Italy; and national periodicals, the most important of which, *Famiglia Cristiana*, sells more than better known 'secular' weeklies such as *L'Espresso* or *Panorama*.

The 'cross' borne by the Catholics for being in government had no small impact on the Catholic press. It made the pragmatism of the clerical/industrial/pro-NATO mix more expedient than a journalism of ideas.

Before turning to more widely read party newspapers, it is worth focusing on *La Voce Repubblicana*, the slim and elegant daily of the Republican Party (PRI), which was developed by Ugo La Malfa and later, in turn, by his son Giorgio and Giovanni Spadolini. The paper did not attempt to be available on newsstands, which are largely geared to the neutral reader. Using greater flair than its Christian Democrat counterpart, it chose to provide a sophisticated platform for the pronouncements and political and parliamentary initiatives of the party's top-ranking politicians. The latter, though few in number, were long-lived, and super-committed to the many roles ascribed to them by the disproportionate space and political power enjoyed by their small party – a party which dated back to the Risorgimento and was called upon to represent large-scale industry and 'secular' finance in government coalitions.

Another party paper, the *Secolo d'Italia*, has been more successful than *La Voce Repubblicana* in building a distinct readership of its own. Since 1952 it has been a companion to, and an outlet for, the troubled existence of Mussolini's 'orphans' who, depending upon the individual and the generation of monarchic or republican Fascism, look back nostalgically either to the anti-Communist 'cudgel' or to the ideals of the Italian Social Republic, and are further divided between anti-American nationalists and extremist supporters of the Western alliance.

The 'opening to the left' which reflected the gradual parting of Communists and Socialists in the 1960s was a turning point in the political history of the second half of the twentieth century. The Socialists went over to the side of the Christian Democrats, Social Democrats and Republicans, and were later joined by the Liberals. The PCI remained in opposition, but at trade union, local and regional administration levels the Socialist-Communist front was not affected.

Despite the crisis of 1956, which reduced the PCI's hold over intellectuals, and the end of the political alliance between the PCI and PSI, which had led them in 1948 to dream of winning a majority and government power, the situation remained constant in the post-war period until the mid-1990s. The distinctive factor was undoubtedly the relative inertness of voting behaviour: over one-third of the electorate consistently confirmed its political preferences, which were feared by the right, and hoped for by the left, as liable to lead to a radical transformation of the system. It is not possible here to examine the many nuances, internal variants and transitional phases of a political situation in which the parties of the left were, for a time, the founders of the anti-Fascist Republic, and co-authors and principal guarantors of the constitution and democracy, and yet also marked by the utopian aspirations of that 'otherness' which bore the name, history and strength of the Soviet Union. The victorious revolution was a myth which Bologna and the other 'red' cities articulated in the parochial and homespun terms of 'good government'. It was a myth which was no less active among, and influential over, the progressive component of the working classes than the concurrent 'American myth' of freedom and consumerism was among the supporters of the centre parties. Even the least sympathetic historians of tomorrow will have to pay tribute to the Communists, as the nationalist-Fascist historian Gioacchino Volpe did between the wars with regard to the historic role played by the Socialists. The Socialists talked of revolution, but in practice contributed to the political education of the masses by teaching them a civic 'alphabet' and bringing them into the fold of the state.

After the Second World War the PCI did not talk of revolution, not even at its party conferences or in its manifestoes. What it did do was to channel class-based demands into forms of mass democracy and a robust guarantee to counter, at first, the authoritarian aspirations of Pope Pius XII and a notable part of the Catholic world (already strongly clerico-Fascist) and, later, the right-wing subversive tendencies of that section of the ruling class which was vulnerable to pressure from outside forces. This task of educating the workers, peasants and petty-bourgeois masses through successive variants of something which, in the academic and positive sense used by scholars of language and communication, could be defined as a 'rhetoric' of democracy and anti-Fascist unity, was carried out in considerable measure in the party paper; it was recognisable in expressions such as 'new party', 'dialogue with the Catholics', 'historic compromise', 'national solidarity' and 'constitutional spectrum'.

No other political force in Italy throughout the post-war period had a militant newspaper of the type envisaged by Gramsci comparable to *L'Unità*.[11] The paper's pervasive presence within society fuelled its staying power and capacity for involvement to such an extent that, far from being reduced to a bulletin for a restricted few, its overall print run and circulation figures put it not far behind the stronger pro-government papers. Indeed, on key anniversaries and special occasions – 1 May, Liberation Day (25 April), the days immediately following an election, etc. – it broke all records in reaching and going beyond the 1 million mark. But these respectable circulation figures do not reveal the central role played by this paper, with its unique way of encouraging mass participation and self-representation.

One of the reasons why people were so loyal to *L'Unità* was the way in which the paper made itself a vital tool of awareness, bridging the gap between the grass roots and the centre via a constant two-way flow. There was a movement from the centre to the grass roots. ('Democratic centralism' and the strong leadership typified by Palmiro Togliatti and his successors made this inevitable almost right up to the 1990s.) There was, however, also a movement from the grass roots towards less peripheral spheres of awareness, solidarity and action, because, unlike in the other parties, branch life in the PCI long remained a reality. From the provincial federations, local branches and factory sections flowed a considerable volume of news, suggestions and requests. The task of the political press management (the running of *L'Unità* was one of the chief roles which high-ranking party members were expected to take in turn) was one of co-ordinating and marshalling people's extraordinary desire to contribute, to be known and to count. In the past, therefore, *L'Unità* appeared in different editions in Rome, Milan, Turin, the North East, etc. in an attempt to keep pace as far as possible with the multiplicity of circumstances. Later this was no longer seen to be a priority owing to production costs, but also because the PCI's isolation came to be a minor issue: the party was no longer 'in the trenches' and Communists' views could be aired via other channels (e.g. private radio and television channels/networks).[12]

For at least as long as the PCI lasted (its embarrassed heir, the Partito Democratico della Sinistra, PDS – later Democratici di Sinistra, DS – is more 'secular' in its approach) the relationship between *L'Unità* and its readers, in terms of the paper's relevance to everyday life and the level of people's identification with it, was unparalleled. *L'Unità* had a certain militant mystique: it was a symbol, a declaration of identity, a kind of life assurance, rather than simply an official party paper extolling the party line. For this reason, for many years, much like the piously zealous women of the 'wholesome' diocesan press, only more so, or the Jehovah's Witnesses nowadays, a good number of activists were recruited for *L'Unità*'s Sunday door-to-door distribution – an activity that served as an accurate gauge of the individual members' commitment at branch meeting level. This was especially true in the distant past when public acceptance of 'Communists' was low and there was a risk in being seen with the paper of 'class struggle' in factories, schools or even offices. From the 1970s onwards this individual form of proselytism declined, not solely on account of a relaxation in ideological tensions but also because the generation of 1968 invested greater hope and passion in the then emerging dailies of the New Left, especially *Lotta Continua* and *Il Manifesto*.[13] The latter, incidentally, continues to enjoy a good following after three decades.

In the context of the general political evolution and changed times, in which it was striving to be a 'party of government' rather than a protest party, the PCI sought new ways of communicating with, and involving, the public. Thus the frequent and very well attended *Feste dell'Unità* came to have an important place in the party's activities.

The *Feste* have been held all over Italy; they range from the small-town or neighbourhood type to the crowded provincial ones, and the massive national event, which is held in a different city each year, as proof of the party's organisational strength. People going along to the *Feste* include not just paid-up party members and supporters but whole families whose sympathies may be described as vaguely democratic and anti-Fascist. They can choose to pay to get in, and so voluntarily contribute to the party press. Once inside they can eat sausages or fried fish, drink, dance, go for rides on the roundabout, enjoy painting exhibitions, drink *Cuba libre*, play the tombola, have a go at archery, peruse the 'sacred texts' on the bookstalls or listen to, or take an active part in, political and cultural debates. Marx, Engels, Gramsci, Berlinguer and, depending upon the period, Fidel Castro, Ho Chi Minh, Mao Tse-tung and other important personages of the family gallery have benignly presided over these rites, which are intended to strengthen the sympathisers' political identity and sense of solidarity.

The irreducible Communist 'difference' has faded into the past; indeed, it has become commonplace at the *Feste* to have round-table discussions with priests, industrialists and parliamentarians from within the so-called 'constitutional spectrum' (which from 1994 also included the 'post-Fascists' of Alleanza Nazionale, AN).[14] These events provide an opportunity for people to sit under the trees with the sound of skewered meat sizzling in the background, just as one might on a pleasant day out – in short, a Sunday for politics.

Now, as regards *L'Unità*, the days of the fire and sword of yesteryear seem far away, and many 'comrades' are more likely to be seen with a copy of *La Repubblica*, the wealthy and progressive daily newspaper of 'advanced capitalism' which pushed for the PCI's entry into government, envisaging a PCI free from foolish radical ambitions well before it became the PDS.[15] We will stop here. At present the political situation in Italy appears to be dominated by the fickle and frivolous imaginary worlds created by television rather than by the traditional written word – to the extent that newspapers and periodicals vie with one another to imitate the delights of these 'ephemeral' and virtual worlds.

NOTES

1 *Editors' note.* The masculine form is used here because there have been no major female leader writers/opinion makers in Italy. On the role of Italian women journalists in the male-dominated world of the press see M. Buonanno, L. Grifo, M. Mafai and F. Nirenstein, 'Le giornaliste in Italia: molta visibilità, poco potere', *Problemi dell'informazione*, 18:3 (1993), pp. 271–95.

2 See L. Albertini, *I giorni di un liberale. Diari, 1907–23*, ed. L. Monzali (Bologna, Il Mulino, 2000).

3 *La Voce* was set up in March 1994 and ceased publication in April 1995.

4 C. Pavone, *Una guerra civile. Saggio storico sulla moralità nella Resistenza* (Turin, Bollati Boringhieri, 1991).

5 C. Zaghi, *Terrore a Ferrara durante i 18 mesi della Repubblica di Salò* (Bologna, Istituto Regionale 'Ferruccio Parri' per la Storia del Movimento di Liberazione e dell'Età Contemporanea in Emilia-Romagna, 1992), p. 435.

6 For a historical account of this daily, which folded in 1994, see E. Parpaglioni, *C'era una volta 'Paese Sera'* (Rome, Editori Riuniti, 1998).

7 M. Isnenghi-Belfagor, *Giornali e giornalisti. Esame critico della stampa quotidiana in Italia* (Rome, Savelli, 1975).

8 On *Il Giorno* see V. Emiliani, *Gli anni del 'Giorno'. Il quotidiano del Signor Mattei* (Milan, Baldini & Castoldi, 1998), and G. Melega, *L'anima m'hai venduto* (Milan, Feltrinelli, 1998), which deals with the paper's early years.

9 *Avanti!* ceased publication in 1992 in the wake of the collapse of the PSI, and was re-established in the spring of 1997; however, it appears somewhat irregularly. For a concise survey of this daily from its beginnings to 1992 see M. Ridolfi, 'L'*Avanti!*', in M. Isnenghi (ed.), *I luoghi della memoria. Simboli e miti dell'Italia unita* (Bari and Rome, Laterza, 1996), pp. 317–28.

10 After the break-up of the DC in 1994 *Il Popolo* appeared as the organ of the Partito Popolare Italiano (PPI), which was borne out of the old party's left-wing faction. It ceased publication in 1998.

11 On *L'Unità* see L. Paolozzi and A. Leiss, *Voci dal quotidiano. 'L'Unità' da Ingrao a Veltroni* (Milan, Baldini & Castoldi, 1996).

12 In an attempt to boost sales the newspaper reintroduced local pages in Tuscany and Emilia-Romagna in September 1998, shortly after it was acquired by a private consortium.

13 On the press of the New Left see U. Eco and P. Violi, 'La controinformazione', in V. Castronovo and N. Tranfaglia (eds), *Storia della stampa italiana*, Vol. 5 *La stampa italiana del capitalismo* (Bari and Rome, Laterza, 1976), pp. 97–143.

14 At the 1995 national *Festa dell'Unità*, held in Reggio Emilia, for the first time the leader of Alleanza Nazionale, Gianfranco Fini, was also invited. See M. Smargiassi, 'Che festa rossa! C'è anche Fini . . .', *La Repubblica*, 26 August 1995.

15 For the early story of *La Repubblica* see E. Scalfari, *La sera andavamo in via Veneto. Storia di un gruppo, dal 'Mondo' alla 'Repubblica'* (Milan, Mondadori, 1986).

9

Picture battles in the piazza: the political poster

Luciano Cheles

Though political campaigns, in Italy as elsewhere, today tend to be dominated by television, the poster continues to play a role in them (Figure 1). Various reasons account for its survival. The poster is a low-tech, inexpensive medium, yet its potential impact and effectiveness are considerable, because of the dominance of the visual over the verbal (images are notably more memorable than words), its accessibility and inescapability (being on public display, it is seen even by the most politically recalcitrant passer-by), and its relative permanence (it is displayed for a certain length of time during which it enjoys legal protection against destroyers).

1] Florence, Piazza Santa Maria Novella: propaganda for the 1996 elections

The poster is, arguably, a quintessentially Italian medium. Its widespread use as a means of mobilisation may in fact be explained in the light of the Catholic Church's centuries-old tradition of using artistic forms for persuasive ends (both religious and political).[1] It should, moreover, be related to the outdoor nature of much of recreational life in Italy: the ritual of the *passeggiata* alone justifies the parties' investment in this form of communication.[2]

Political posters, notably, attract graffiti, which, though illegal, are a form of feedback.[3] They unwittingly fulfil a function not unlike that of the Pompeian city walls, on which the citizens aired their political views. One is also reminded of the Pasquinade tradition – the practice, especially current in Renaissance Rome, of writing comments and gossip on placards hanging from a statue located in a city-centre piazza.[4]

The presence of a multitude of parties no doubt fostered the use of the poster in Italy: before the advent of television, this medium provided political movements with strong visual characterisations, especially through the depiction of party emblems, thus rendering them more easily recognisable by the electorate.

It should also be noted that, until the mid-1970s, posters were for the opposition parties the principal means of making their views known to the general public, since a large proportion of the so-called independent press, and the state-owned broadcasting service in its entirety, were biased in favour of the ruling coalition (the Democrazia Cristiana, DC, and its allies).

2] Milan: propaganda for the 1948 elections. The building covered with posters functioned as a polling station

In the early post-war period the relatively high level of illiteracy (about 15 per cent; and a substantial portion of the rest were only semi-literate) made the poster with its simple, striking imagery the obvious 'universal' vehicle of political communication.

Finally, the parties' extensive use of the poster may be explained in terms of continuity with wartime propaganda practices, those of the Fascists in particular.[5]

Posters are not produced by parties exclusively during election and referendum campaigns; they are also issued to announce meetings, rallies and congresses, to voice reactions to topical events (a political scandal, an international crisis, etc.), and to commemorate special occasions (e.g. 8 March, Women's Day; 25 April, the Liberation from Fascism; 1 May). This survey, however, will deal largely with election and referendum posters, focusing especially on those produced nationally, since the greater effort that usually goes into their design makes them potentially more revealing of the aspirations and official attitudes of a given party, and of the image it wishes to project of itself.

1946–48

In the early post-war years the use of posters (and indeed of other forms of propaganda) in referendum and election campaigns was almost completely unregulated. There were no laws ensuring that parties had equal opportunities to promote their political views, no rules with regard to the format of the posters and the locations where they could be displayed. The results was a free-for-all: party activists of all political tendencies went round armed with ladders, brushes and glue pasting posters on the most eye-catching surfaces – the buildings in the city centre were an obvious target (Figure 2). The only regulation was intended to safeguard freedom of expression: a decree law passed on 10 March 1946 (No. 74, art. 72) stipulated that preventing the diffusion of propaganda by removing or destroying posters was punishable by imprisonment for a period of one to five years and a fine of 3,000–15,000 lire.[6]

The earliest political contests of the post-war period – the local elections of March and April 1946, and the elections to the Constituent Assembly and referendum on the monarchy which took place concurrently on 2 June the same year – saw a limited use of the poster. Mass rallies, meetings, leafleting, newspapers and *altoparlanti mobili* (cars equipped with loudspeakers sending out slogans, news and songs) were the principal instruments of mobilisation. The DC also benefited from a more informal, but highly effective, propaganda vehicle: the Church's vast, all-encompassing parish network.[7]

The poster campaign of the Communist Party (PCI) for the June elections and referendum was especially low-key. Pietro Secchia, who was in charge of the party organisation at the time, argued in a report on the campaign of the administrative elections that it was 'more useful to spend money to assist the needy than on posters', and warned that the showy, American-style political advertising used by some parties had evoked the propaganda practices of Fascism.[8] The PCI leader, Palmiro Togliatti, for his part expressed the fear that an excessive display of propaganda material might lead to accusations that the party received funding from Moscow.[9]

Though the DC also made modest use of posters in 1946, it did not fail to recognise the potential of the medium. Amintore Fanfani, then head of the party's propaganda department, the Ufficio SPES, stressed in a circular that the poster was 'extremely valuable'.[10]

The 1946 election posters give a distorted view of the intensity of the political battle that was being fought between the two main opposing forces: the DC and the left (PCI and the Socialist Party, PSI). They suggest an absence of acrimonious antagonism. By their tame and, at times, even conciliatory approach the posters, in contrast with other forms of propaganda, seem to reflect the tacit agreement among the parties that made up the outgoing coalition (DC, PCI and PSI) that they should form another government together.[11]

The DC propaganda dealt with such uncontroversial themes as freedom, reconstruction, the future, justice and peace, while the Communist propaganda urged voters to oppose Fascism, though the neo-Fascists did not actually field any candidates in the elections. The far-right vote found refuge in Guglielmo Giannini's L'Uomo Qualunque (Man in the Street) party, whose political philistinism and strong law-and-order stance appealed to the middle and lower middle classes.[12]

An interesting feature of the propaganda of 1946 is the widespread use of Christian-inspired iconography. Clearly, the pivotal role religion played in Italian society made this sort of imagery a potential vote catalyst. The hieratic peasant woman wearing a headscarf and holding one of her two children on one arm before the logo of the DC – the crossed shield – recalls the image of the Virgin and Child (Figure 3). The aim was to identify the party with womanhood and with Christianity.[13] The PSI went much further: it presented class struggle as one of the tenets of Christian doctrine. A poster featuring Christ in a setting that included smoking factories in the background reminded voters that 'a rich man shall hardly enter into the Kingdom of Heaven' (Matthew, 19:23), and exhorted them to vote for Socialism so that the poor might be freed from the exploitation of the rich (Figure 4).[14] The PCI did not actually use Christian imagery in its propaganda, but was keen to stress, in order not to antagonise the Catholics, who seemed to be increasingly identifying with the DC, that the majority of its members were Catholic, and that the party condemned religious intolerance and anticlericalism.[15]

One Communist poster, issued by the party's Parma branch, did feature an image blatantly inspired by Christian iconography. However, it was not connected, at least not directly, with the 1946 elections or referendum: it was issued to advertise the local *Settimana della compagna* (Communist Women's Week) (Figure 5). The picture is worth dwelling upon in view of its complexity; it is in fact revealing of the diverse range of visual traditions from which 'militant' graphic artists drew their imagery.

The image of the audacious young woman transfixing an octopus symbolising war, injustice, oppression, ignorance and poverty (*miseria*) – as the inscriptions on the tentacles make clear – with the pole of her red flag is modelled on the popular genre of St Michael/St George slaying the snake/dragon. The celebration of the *compagna*'s heroic fight against the evils of society has been reinforced by reference to the story of David and Goliath: the position of her left arm echoes, in fact, the gesture of defiance featuring in Donatello's and Verrocchio's famous bronze statues of the biblical hero (both in the Bargello Museum, Florence).[16] The arm (or arms) akimbo, suggesting boldness and self-assurance, was also Mussolini's most characteristic posture. The artist, who designed the poster only a year or so after the collapse of Fascism, is unlikely to have been unaware of this ambiguity. The gender inversion and the Christian/Renaissance allusions must have been deemed sufficiently strong to discourage any possible Fascist reading of the detail.

It is partly to offset the references to male warriors that the woman has been depicted in an anabashedly sensuous manner. The *compagna*'s erotic allure, as well as her free-flowing hair, serve to portray her as the allegory of liberty, and sexual and social emancipation. (The word *oppressione* featuring on one of the octopus's tentacles was no doubt intended in terms of gender relations as well as in a more generically political way.)[17] The woman's blossoming figure, moreover, probably symbolises youthful vitality (an essential quality for an activist) and, possibly, even prosperity (as the tentacle bearing the word *miseria* that writhes round her left leg seems to suggest).

While fulfilling allegorical functions, the image of the attractive woman also belongs to the realm of private sexual fantasies. (The graphic artist, a certain 'Musolino', was most probably a man; female artists were then rare.) It in fact derives from

3] 'For the future of your children, vote for the Christian Democrat Party.' Poster, 1946

4] 'Vote for Socialism, which frees the poor from the exploitation of the rich.' Socialist Party poster, 1946

the genre of erotic illustrations: the figure's features – the close-fitting top, thin waist, wind-blown skirt and shapely legs – echo, in a slightly more restrained form, those of the hugely popular pin-ups drawn in the 1930s by Gino Boccasile (Figure 6).[18]

Through the thoughtful use of colour the image also seeks to refute the traditional accusation that patriotism and internationalism are mutually exclusive: the woman's green dress and the flowing red banner she is holding 'naturally' complement each other to form, together with the white background, the tricolour.

This Communist adaptation of traditional religious themes (St Michael, St George, David), also involving a reversal of the heroes' gender, was probably meant as tongue-in-cheek. It is worth recalling that the poster addressed itself to the Communist women of a city – Parma – with long-established secular and left-wing credentials. The image in question would have been deemed unsuitable for electoral propaganda aimed at the general public nationwide.

To return to the political contests of 1946, mention should be made of one of the referendum posters that were produced by the pro-monarchy camp. It portrayed King Umberto II (Vittorio Emanuele III had abdicated on 9 May) together with his wife, Maria José, and four children, and aimed to present the monarchy as a symbol of traditional values and national unity (Figure 7). The homely and slightly sentimental nature of the family portrait attempted to counter the dramatic

5] Poster advertising a 'Communist Women's Week.' Parma, 1946

6] Gino Boccasile, cover of the magazine *Le grandi firme*, 22 April 1937

7] Pro-monarchy poster, 1946 referendum

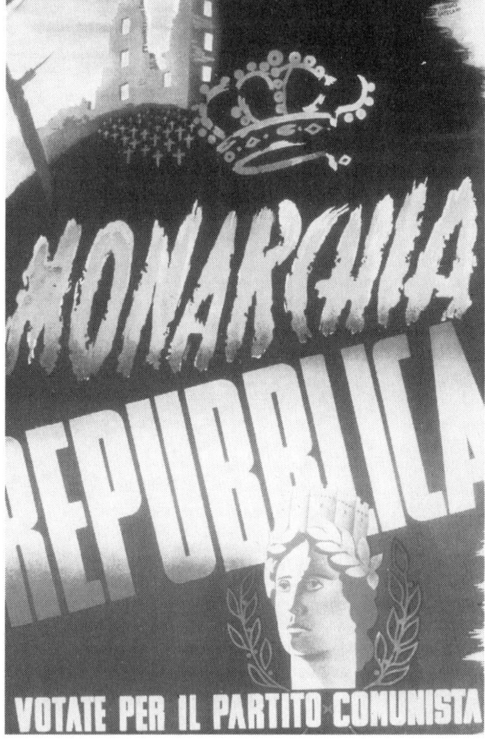

8] Communist poster, referendum and elections, 1946

propaganda of the left which drew attention to the monarchy's close association with Fascism and the tragedy that ensued (Figure 8).[19]

The elections of 1948, by contrast, were bitterly fought. Following the left's expulsion from government in 1947, politics became rigidly polarised into two blocs: the Christian Democrats on one side, and the Socialist and Communist alliance or Fronte Democratico Popolare on the other. The DC, supported by the *Comitati Civici*, sought to present the electoral contest as a choice between civilisation and barbarism, between good and evil, between Christianity and atheism, between patriotic feeling and an 'alien' ideology intent on destroying Italian civilisation. Their propaganda visualised this through powerful apocalyptic imagery, some of which was inspired by religious iconography (Figures 9, 10, 12, 13).[20]

The poster output of the Fronte, which adopted Garibaldi's effigy as its logo,[21] was minimal and quite tame: peace, freedom and work were the main themes featured in it (Figure 14).[22] As in 1946, the PCI's principal means of mobilisation were pamphlets, newspapers, magazines and political rallies – a word-dominated propaganda that was no match to the visual onslaught of the opposition.[23]

Stylistically and thematically, many of the posters produced by the DC and the Civic Committees were dependent on the propaganda of Fascism (Figures 10, 11). This was hardly surprising, given that, as Umberto Eco has pointed out, not only had many of the artists who designed the posters worked for the Fascist regime, but the public De Gasperi was addressing was the same anonymous masses who, only a few years earlier, had responded favourably to the demographic policies of the regime, and passively endorsed the campaign for the purity of the race.[24] A DC poster featuring Garibaldi and his army chasing an 'alien'-looking Togliatti (Figure 15) – one of several that were produced in 1948 by the centre and right-wing parties to delegitimise the left's use of the hero's effigy (Figure 16) – provides a particularly striking endorsement of Eco's remarks. The spectral image of the Communist leader holding his briefcase under his left arm is almost identical to that of the Jew caricatured in an illustration that appears in a 1939 issue of the antisemitic magazine *La difesa della razza* (The Defence of the Race) (Figure 18).[25] Togliatti was represented in much the same way in a DC poster of 1950 attacking the Communists for voting against agrarian reform (Figure 17): the pointing gesture of the Gargantuan peasant echoes the huge accusing hand depicted in the Fascist illustration, thus providing incontrovertible evidence that the latter acted as a model. The three images may have been devised by the same artist.

1950s and 1960s

The campaign for the elections of 1953 was as virulent as the previous one, but was approached quite differently.[26] The catastrophism that had characterised the earlier poster output of the DC and the Civic Committees disappeared, as did much of the Christian imagery. Even the Christian Democrat woman shed her Madonna-like appearance to be depicted in a poster as an elegant, tall and slender figure that seemed to have come out of a fashion magazine, and juxtaposed, in a glaringly 'classist' way,

9] 'The Christian worker.' Civic Committees poster, 1948

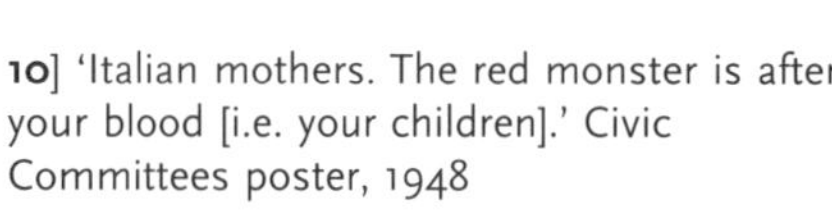

10] 'Italian mothers. The red monster is after your blood [i.e. your children].' Civic Committees poster, 1948

11] 'Bolshevism against the family. "The family is the greatest abomination to have been created in civilised countries" – Lenin.' Italian Social Republic poster, *c.* 1943

12] '[The Italian Republic, presented as the embodiment of the Fatherland, the Family and Freedom]: "Defend me!".' Christian Democrat poster, 1948

13] The Soviet bear tramples on Rome's *Altare della Patria* (Italy's cenotaph). Civic Committees poster, 1948. A giant bill-board featuring the same image was erected in Piazza Venezia, Rome, opposite the monument itself, to give greater immediacy and emotional intensity to the threat.

14] 'For peace in Italy.' Communist/Fronte Democratico Popolare poster, 1948

15] 'The tombs open, the dead arise' (words from the national anthem). 'Get out of Italy, get out you foreigner!' The illustration depicts Palmiro Togliatti being chased by Garibaldi and his army. Civic Committees poster, 1948

to a short and corpulent Communist woman, of obvious peasant or working-class stock. The text warned women that their femininity was at risk if they voted Communist (Figure 19).[27]

The PCI, abandoning its earlier reticence, made full use of the poster as a means of attack and counter-attack.[28] Propaganda became a game of visual-verbal repartee, of witty tit-for-tats, in which slogans and satirical images (cartoons supplanted the descriptive realism that dominated the poster campaigns of 1946 and 1948) were boomeranged back to their senders suitably modified. The DC launched the convenient formula of its equidistance from the neo-Fascist Movimento Sociale Italiano (MSI)[29] and PCI, thus positioning itself at the heart of democracy (Figure 20). The Communists replied to this attack by associating Christian Democrats, Neo-Fascists

facing **16]** '[Garibaldi]: "Voters, beware! That guy is nothing to do with me!" Give your votes to the Blocco Nazionale so that they may not be wasted.' Poster produced by the Blocco Nazionale, an alliance of the Uomo Qualunque Party and the Liberals, 1948

17] 'You [Togliatti] have voted against agrarian reform.' Christian Democrat poster, 1950

18] The Jew. Illustration from *La difesa della razza*, 20 September 1939

ELETTORI!
BADATE, IO NON HO
NIENTE A CHE FARE
CON QUELLO LÌ!
DATE PURE I VOSTRI VOTI AL BLOCCO NAZIONALE
PERCHE' NON VANNO DISPERSI
Votate
BLOCCO NAZIONALE

tu
hai votato
contro la
RIFORMA
AGRARIA
DEMOCRAZIA
CRISTIANA

and monarchists, and depicting them as obedient servants of the same capitalist master: a poster featured the cartoon drawing of a grinning American in a top hat, manipulating the parties puppet fashion (Figure 21). The MSI counter-attacked with a cartoon of De Gasperi as a puppeteer pulling the strings to which the leaders of his outgoing coalition parties (PLI, PSDI and PRI) are attached (Figure 22).

A major theme of the 1953 elections was that of corruption. A series of Communist posters caricatured DC officials as fat, clawed figures handling bags of money (Figure 23), or else represented them armed with giant forks, spoons and knives, symbols of their greed (Figure 24). The Christian Democrats answered back with similar images: a poster depicted the PCI as a huge red pig feeding on the votes of the PSI (Figure 25), while another caricatured the obese Georgi Malenkov, Stalin's successor, at his dining table about to tackle Italy, having gobbled up China and the countries of Eastern Europe; the *forchetta* became in yet another poster a weapon with which to run through the 'Reds' (Figure 26). The neo-Fascists jumped on the bandwagon and lampooned De Gasperi as carving up a chicken representing Italy (Figure 27).

None of the election posters of the PCI drew from the rich figurative traditions of the left (e.g. Constructivism, Expressionism and Socialist Realism). In order to reach the widest public, the party preferred to rely on the same conventional figurative idioms used by its opponents. A booklet distributed to the organisers of evening courses for election campaigners set out the PCI's policy clearly: the propaganda was to be 'simple and concrete', 'made by party members and all other citizens too'; the aim was 'to campaign with all voters'.[30]

19] 'Italian women . . . even your femininity depends on your vote.' Christian Democrat poster, 1953

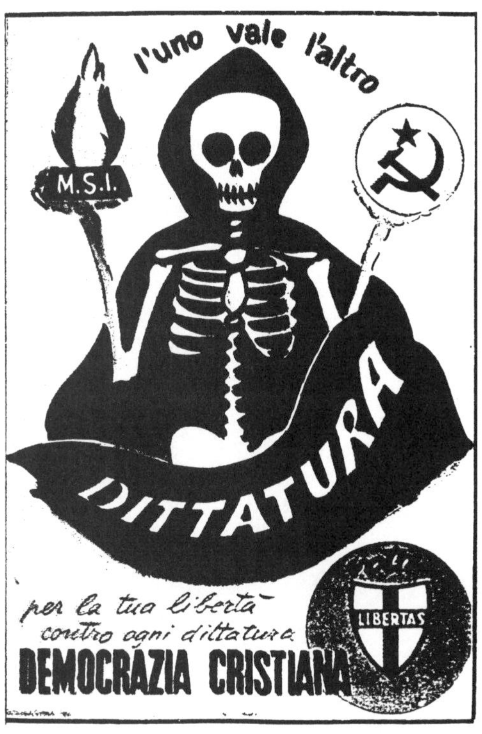

20] 'Dictatorship: "They [Neo-Fascism and Communism] amount to the same thing." For your freedom, against all dictatorships, vote for the Christian Democrat Party.' Poster, 1953

21] 'The capitalist: "This one or that one . . . all the same to me!"' (a modified quotation from Verdi's *Rigoletto*). The three puppets represent Neo-Fascism, Christian-Democracy and the monarchy. Communist poster, 1953

22] 'You must vote MSI.' 'The Christian Democrat puppeteer [De Gasperi].' Poster, 1953

23] 'Let's keep the Christian Democrat profiteers and Fascist bosses out of the feeding trough.' Communist poster, 1953

24] 'For honesty, against corruption, vote Communist.' Poster, 1953

25] '[The Communists] feed on the votes of the Socialists.' Christian Democrat poster, 1953

26] 'Communist gallows' and 'Italian fork.' Christian Democrat poster, 1953

27] 'Against Christian Democrat greed, vote MSI.' Poster depicting De Gasperi, 1953

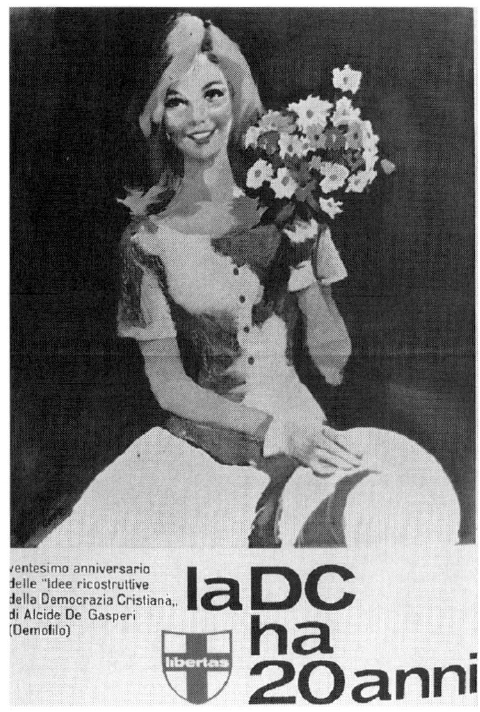

28] 'To remove the stains of clerical corruption, use your Communist vote.' Poster, 1958

29] 'The DC is twenty years old.' Christian Democrat poster, 1963

30] 'The PRI: showing our country the way.' Republican Party poster, 1970

Such was the quantity of posters that had been produced for the 1953 campaign, and the unruly scramble to paste them on to the most prominent public surfaces, that a law was passed in 1956 regulating the nature and use of election propaganda. The posters were to have the same format (70 cm × 100 cm) and be posted exclusively on boards erected for the occasion in the most frequented areas. The number of boards was to be proportionate to the size of the population, and each party was to be allocated the same amount of display space.[31] The aims were to reduce the wastage of propaganda material, ensure equal opportunities all round, and enable the public to view the posters arranged side by side, like pictures in a gallery.

Perusal of the poster output of the main parties in the late 1950s and early 1960s – there were parliamentary elections in 1958 and 1963, and local ones in 1960 – shows a consolidation of the earlier practice of addressing voters using popular and universal figurative modes and of avoiding styles and iconographies associated with specific ideological traditions. An interesting innovation was the adoption of idioms, both verbal and visual, inspired by commercial television advertising. The playfully alliterative slogan 'Io dico, tu dici, DC' (I say, you say, DC) used by the Christian Democrats in their 1960 poster campaign is a case in point.[32] At times the borrowing was explicit and tongue-in-cheek: a Communist poster of 1958 parodies an Omo washing powder advert to urge the public to use their votes to remove the stains of the DC's corruption (Figure 28).

Despite the growing interest in the verbal and visual codes of commercial advertising, none of the parties entrusted its campaign to an external agency.[33] The posters were produced within the propaganda departments or designed by anonymous artists politically close to the commissioning parties. No conscious efforts were made to devise uniform styles that might give individual parties an immediately recognisable identity. Nevertheless, the 1963 elections saw the first attempt to use marketing techniques in a political campaign.

In order to revitalise its image, the DC turned for professional advice to Ernst Dichter, founder of the celebrated Institute for Motivational Research in New York, which applied psychological experiments to advertising. Dichter's research suggested that the DC was perceived by the public as old and staid, and therefore needed 'rejuvenation'. To launch its new image, a poster was produced featuring a young woman with a bouquet of flowers, and the slogan 'La DC ha vent'anni' (The DC is twenty years old) (Figure 29). Its consequences were disastrous: all over Italy the posters invited graffiti, the most recurrent of which were 'Allora bisogna farle la festa', translatable as 'Then we must throw a party for her' but also as 'Let's give her one, then', and 'È ora che vada a farsi fottere', which has in Italian the same ambiguous meaning, 'It's time she got screwed'.[34]

This incident aborted what might have become a new trend in the way of approaching propaganda. In 1968, interviewed by the magazine *Budget*, Michele Pellicani, co-director of the Press and Propaganda Department of the PSI, expressed his scepticism at the idea that politicians should call on the services of professional admen. Though conceding that the parties could learn from advertising campaigns, he remarked:

> While to force a bar of soap or a stock cube on to customers the persuader need not be convinced of the quality of the product, to 'sell' an ideology, a political programme or a party he must himself be persuaded. Of course, the question of communication is one that must be confronted by parties too; however, advertising technique does not solve the question of propaganda, since parties are driven by ideals.[35]

It was a view that would also have been endorsed by the other parties until the beginning of the following decade. However, from the mid-1960s two parties came to realise that their graphic propaganda could be approached more professionally, while being dealt with by artists who endorsed their political views. They turned to graphic designers who were making a name for themselves outside the world of politics, choosing them first and foremost on the basis of the quality of their work.

The first of these parties was the PRI. In 1965 its National Secretary, Ugo La Malfa, an economist and former research officer at the Banca Commerciale Italiana, called on Michele Spera, a graphic artist with a training in architecture, to translate his vision of the PRI as a party of managers, industrialists and technocrats in figurative terms. Throughout a period of over thirty years (the collaboration with the party ceased when Giorgio La Malfa – Ugo's son – took over the party leadership in 1994) Spera designed colourful rationalist and Op Art-inspired images which recalled the industrial design and advertising of a progressive high-tech firm such as Olivetti (Figure 30). Spera adapted the same graphic style not only to the posters, which dealt with a wide range of events, but to the whole visual output of the PRI: brochures, the party daily *La Voce Repubblicana*, the stage settings of the party congresses, etc. This integrated approach was to give the PRI a striking image, or 'corporate identity' – a concept borrowed from the advertising world.[36]

The PSI was the second party to enlist the assistance of professional graphic designers to give itself a clearly identifiable image. From 1969 to 1973 Sergio Ruffolo produced a series of Bauhaus-inspired posters which owed much of their impact to the carefully planned layout, the simplicity of the images and the logical interaction between image and text.[37] He was succeeded by Ettore Vitale, who strengthened the visual identity of the PSI through the creation of innovative imagery and the adoption of a consciously co-ordinated approach of the type pioneered by Spera.

While mostly drawing from the traditional Socialist visual repertoire, Vitale interpreted the images modernistically so as to stress both the party's glorious history and its contemporary relevance.[38] His idiom is symbolic, yet never over-cerebral and obscure. Thus a poster of 1974 commemorating the fiftieth anniversary of the murder of the outspoken Socialist deputy Giacomo Matteotti by the Fascists featured in dramatic close-up a well-known portrait of the martyr, cut across by a broken red line (Figure 31). An early 1980s poster celebrating Women's Day reproduced a detail from one of the icons of Italian Socialism, Pellizza da Volpedo's painting *Il Quarto Stato* (The Fourth Estate, 1898–1901), in reiterated and suitably updated form: the 'token woman' marching along with her male comrades was polemically shown without the child she holds in the original painting (Figure 32).

In the wake of the PRI and PSI, the DC and PCI also strove to update their graphic propaganda in the 1960s and early 1970s. The results of their efforts, however, were on the whole unremarkable, rarely going beyond the routinely modernistic. The posters were characterised by a sober, rationalist style. In terms of colour, those of the PCI tended to rely on a combination of red and black (the agitational colours *par excellence*), and those of the DC on blue (the colour of the mantle of the Virgin, the Queen of Heaven, and of the Savoy household).[39]

The MSI, too, modernised its propaganda, in order to widen its appeal. Under the leadership of Giorgio Almirante[40] it relinquished its overtly Fascist images (a poster produced for the local elections of 1970, depicting a heroic male figure waving the tricolour and rescuing a man (Figure 33) is among the last examples of a genre that derives directly from the propaganda of Fascism) to replace them with others inspired by a range of reputable visual sources (film posters, Renaissance art, etc.). These 'new' images were not always 'innocent', as will be shown later.[41]

It is worth pointing out that the visual propaganda of the late 1960s and early 1970s, a period heavily marked by the growth of new political and counter-cultural movements, was virtually unaffected by the innovative images which many of these engendered. The graphics of the Cuban revolution, of the French May '68, of the American underground and of the anti-Vietnam protest movement had become cult images among the young, in Italy as elsewhere,[42] yet one would be hard put to find

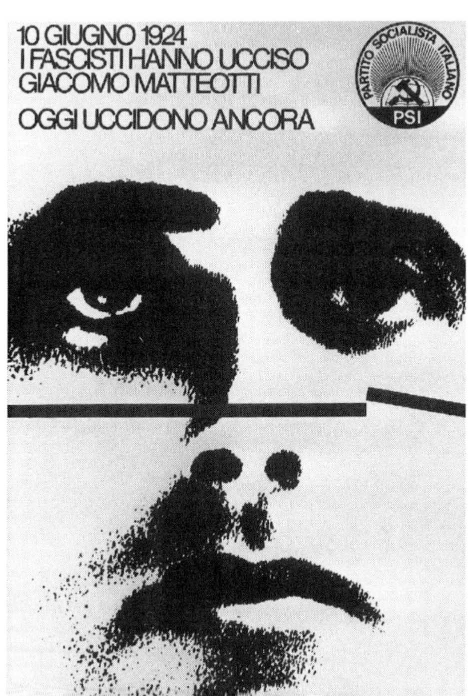

31] '10 June 1924: the Fascists killed Giacomo Matteotti. Today they still kill.' Socialist Party poster, 1974

32] 'From the women's movement to women on the move.' Socialist Party poster, 1982

any trace of them in the posters of the parliamentary left. This is revealing both of the PCI's and PSI's uneasiness with regard to radical political and counter-cultural groups, and of their inability to comprehend and acknowledge youth culture. It is equally true that the parties made little effort to address the youth audience specifically at the time – the fact that the voting age was not lowered to eighteen until 1975 provides a partial explanation. Revolutionary graphics did, however, have an impact on the printed literature of the extraparliamentary left, the civil rights groups (feminist, gay, pacifist, ecological, etc.) and the more militant trade union organisations.[43] In the late 1970s and in the 1980s they were also to be appropriated by the MSI, in particular its youth wing, the Fronte della Gioventù, and its trade union organisation, CISNAL, to project an up-to-date militant image, since the culture of the left had achieved a hegemonic position (Figures 34, 35).[44]

Though the posters produced in the 1960s and early 1970s were, in the main, more professionally and attractively produced, they tended to be less informative and persuasive than those of earlier periods. Their role had changed: no longer were they devised on an *ad hoc* basis and used as means of dialectical exchange, to counter attacks from the opposition and engage in quick repartee with it, and, ultimately, to proselytise. The posters now fulfilled a more generic and allusive function: they merely acted as reminders of what a given party stood for, often using a subtle and even playful idiom that addressed itself to a select audience – one made up largely of sympathisers.[45] The bulk of political argumentation and persuasion was now taking place

33] 'Join us before it's too late.' MSI poster, 1970

facing

34] 'May Day 1985: Work for everyone, so that it may become everyone's celebration.' CISNAL poster, 1985

35] 'May '68. The start of a long struggle.' Atelier Populaire poster, Paris, 1968 on television (a law passed in 1960 gave equal airwave access to all the parties, including those in opposition which had hitherto been excluded from the broadcasting media)[46] and in the press.

The mid-1970s

The poster resumed its original role as an instrument of political mobilisation during the referendum campaign for or against the repeal of the divorce law, in spring 1974.[47] Various reasons account for this revival. It should be noted first of all that, on account of the crucial importance of the issue, *all* vehicles of communication were deployed and used to their fullest potential. Two of the poster's traditional practical virtues – cheapness and permanence – made this medium particularly appealing to a range of organisations, such as the Coltivatori Diretti (Small Independent Farmers' Association), the Lega delle Cooperative (Co-operatives' League) and the partisans' association ANPI, which were eager to be actively involved in the campaign, and would probably not have been able to make their (pro-divorce) voices heard otherwise.

The poster medium was also well suited to an issue which, by its nature (it affected the social, religious and emotional spheres), seemed to invite visualisation. The referendum campaign was undoubtedly the most 'graphic' since those of 1948 and 1953. Finally, thanks to the mnemonic potential of visually presented information,

the poster was apt to explain to the public the referendum question's equivocal formulation: a 'yes' vote was a vote against divorce (i.e. in favour of its abolition), and a 'no' vote one calling for the law to be retained.

Most parties, including the PSI, employed advertising agencies on this occasion – an indication of their awareness that the attractive posters which their propaganda departments and professional graphic artists had been churning out in recent years were, in persuasive terms, a blunt weapon and, as such, unsuitable for the fierce battle that lay ahead. The spin doctors called upon by the pro-divorce parties faced the arduous task of having to devise campaigns based on the instinctively unappealing term 'no', and having to compete with the cunning slogan of the Civic Committees, who fought alongside the DC and the MSI for the abolition of divorce: 'Sì, come nel giorno di nozze' (Say 'yes', as on your wedding day).

The campaign of the *anti-divorzisti* was, predictably, dominated by images of suffering children, dejected wives (Figure 36) and sentimental wedding scenes (Figure 38). These images were in part astutely deflated by the pro-divorce parties. A PSI poster reproduced the photo of a child with the pre-emptive comment: 'Tireranno fuori la foto di tuo figlio per farti votare come vuole Almirante' (They'll get out a picture of your child to make you vote as Almirante wants you to) (Figure 37).[48] Another PSI poster featured the photo of smiling bride and groom with the accompanying text: 'Chi crede nel matrimonio non ha paura del divorzio' (Those who believe in marriage are not afraid of divorce) (Figure 39).

As well as using emotional imagery, the *anti-divorzisti* resorted to blatant deceit. One poster depicting the Communist flag appealed to 'comrades' to vote against the 'bourgeois' divorce law (Figure 40). Another featured a photo of the late PCI leader Togliatti together with an anti-divorce quotation of his taken out of context (Figure 41).[49] The purpose was to mislead naive left-wing sympathisers into believing that the PCI disapproved of divorce.[50] Yet another poster invited the public to vote in favour of the repeal of the divorce law by using the bureaucratic register and visual layout of official civic announcements (Figure 42). The three posters, whose true origin was indicated only by the letters 'CNRD' in minuscule print, the little known acronym of the anti-divorce umbrella organisation Comitato Nazionale Referendum Divorzio, was withdrawn following legal action by the PCI.[51]

The anti-divorce lobby, aware that Italy had become a secular society, avoided giving their campaign overtly religious connotations and turning it into a 1948-type crusade against the Infidel. They opposed divorce on the grounds that it was 'bad for the family'. However, religious images, albeit veiled, were not entirely absent from their visual propaganda. A DC poster depicting a seated woman with a baby on her lap and an older child leaning on her knees as if to seek protection and comfort (Figure 43) is based (in reverse) on Leonardo's celebrated National Gallery cartoon for the *Virgin and Child, with St Anne and St John* (Figure 44). Similar images were to be used in 1981 by the Movimento per la Vita (Pro-life Movement) during the campaign for the referendum on abortion. These allusions to Christian iconography, which, one presumes, were meant to be perceived subliminally, suggested that the institution of the family and pregnancy were sacred. They also implicitly proclaimed the need to protect traditional values because, like the art of the Renaissance, they were an essential feature of Italian civilisation.[52]

The MSI, which campaigned vigorously for the abolition of divorce in the hope that a victory of the *sì* front would confer on the party political legitimation after three decades of marginalisation, also used allusive and symbolic imagery, though of a different nature. The designs of some of its posters, though apparently unimpeachable, 'secretly' harked back to Fascism. One poster produced by the youth wing of the party sported the reiterated phrase 'Alt al Comunismo' (Stop Communism) with a superimposed large black 'SI' in the middle (Figure 45). This layout recalled that of a giant billboard which the Fascists erected in 1934 on the façade of the Palazzo Braschi in Rome, the party's national headquarters, to call for a 'yes' vote in a plebiscite for or against the list of new deputies proposed by the Great Council for the following parliamentary term (Figure 46).[53] Here it is the 'SI' that is reproduced in repeated form, while pride of place is given to a stylised portrait of Mussolini. Another poster issued for the same occasion indicates that the similarity is not coincidental. It featured a large 'SI' with the superimposed slogan: 'I Comunisti vogliono fare del referendum un'arma per imporre il loro ingresso al governo, gli italiani debbono fare del referendum un plebiscito contro il Comunismo' (The Communists want to use the referendum as a weapon to impose their entry into the government. The Italians must use the referendum as a plebiscite against Communism) (Figure 47). The word *plebiscito*, which in contemporary Italian has only the meaning of 'landslide victory', has here been used ambiguously to mean also 'referendum'. The likely aim was to establish a parallel with the *plebiscito* of 1934, when the *sì* amounted to 96·25 per cent of the total vote (a result achieved partly through intimidation and vote-rigging). The very fact that the referendum on divorce was taking place exactly forty years after the plebiscite must have been interpreted by the MSI, out of some kind of number mysticism, as a good omen. A final confirmation that the MSI poster just described alludes to Fascism is provided by the unusual three-dimensional letters 'SI': they have been copied from the poster produced by the Fascists to announce triumphantly the results of the plebiscite, and featuring a photomontage of Mussolini (Figure 48).[54]

The MSI was henceforth to resort frequently to the practice of alluding to Fascism – and even Nazism – in coded form. The creation of visual propaganda incorporating two levels of meaning served to project a modern and 'respectable' image for the benefit of the public at large while reassuring the *cognoscenti* that the old ideals had not been repudiated.[55]

The mid-1970s were a turning point for the two main parties, as far as the nature of their propaganda imagery was concerned. A year after its divorce referendum defeat, the DC, keen to project an unstuffy, progressive image, and appeal to the younger generation in particular, produced for the local elections (15–16 June 1975) a series of posters, each carrying a different slogan, which featured the party's crossed shield logo as if it had been improvised with a spray can (Figure 49).[56] The change of approach was confirmed in the parliamentary elections of 1976:[57] the DC posters were characterised by the dominant use of red and black colours and a rational layout

36] '"He cheated on me, he forced me to get a divorce, he's left me with two children, and all I get is a pittance of alimony." Vote Yes against divorce, to save the family.' Poster produced by the National Committee for the Referendum on Divorce, 1974

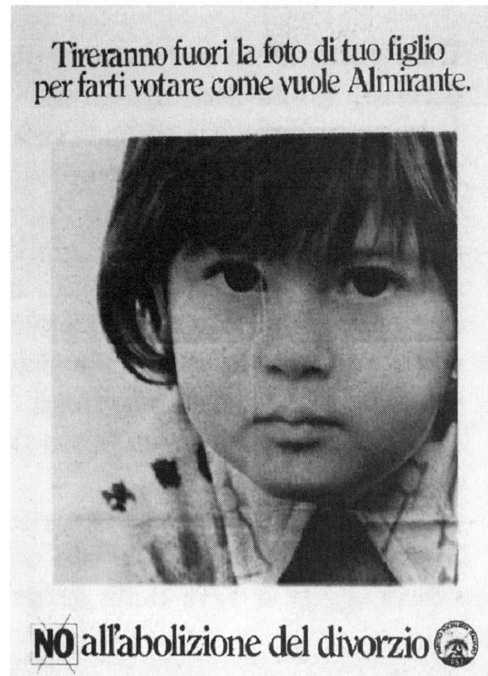

37] 'They'll get out a picture of your child to make you vote like Almirante wants you to do. Say No to the abolition of divorce.' Socialist Party poster, 1974

that gave them a left-wing appearance. The purpose seems to have been mainly to lend the DC campaign dialectical and modernly aggressive overtones.

Paradoxically, whilst the DC chose to adopt a visual approach normally associated with the left, the PCI, whose victory seemed close at hand after its successes in the regional elections of 1975,[58] sought to reassure the moderate electorate by opting for soft-focus, pastel-coloured images of smiling youths, reminiscent of shampoo and condom adverts (Figure 50).

A feature of the 1976 campaign was the multitude of posters aimed specifically at women. The growth of the feminist movement, the divorce referendum, the ongoing heated debate on abortion, the designation of 1975 as International Women's Year had all contributed to placing women's issues firmly on the political agenda. Parties keenly competed for the votes of a more politicised electorate whose choices were likely to be less influenced by tradition and/or by the voting behaviour of the male members of their families. Unlike earlier posters aimed at a female public, which tended to depict women as mothers and nurturers,[59] the new ones featured them as active participants in social, political and economic life: women were shown demonstrating, debating and engaging in professional activities. The most interesting of such posters was issued by the DC: it depicted a young and attractive candidate – Silvia Costa, who was to be in charge of the Ufficio SPES in the 1980s

38] 'Say yes, like you did on your wedding day!' Anti-divorce poster, National Committee for the Referendum on Divorce, 1974

39] 'Those who believe in marriage are not afraid of divorce.' Socialist Party poster, 1974

40] 'Comrades! Politics have nothing to do with it. It's the family that's at stake. Vote yes, against the bourgeois and the unpopular divorce law.' Anti-divorce poster produced by the National Committee for the Referendum on Divorce, 1974

41] '"Divorce is unnatural and harmful" (Palmiro Togliatti). Against the bourgeois and unpopular divorce law, vote yes.' Anti-divorce poster poster produced by the National Committee for the Referendum on Divorce, 1974

Vista la Legge n. 898 del 1 - 12 - 1970 "Disciplina dei casi di scioglimento del matrimonio„ il C. N. R. D.

RENDE NOTO

che tale legge consente

1) - IL DIVORZIO AUTOMATICO:
perchè un coniuge può chiedere e ottenere il divorzio per il solo fatto che sono trascorsi 5 anni di separazione;

2) - IL RIPUDIO:
perchè può chiedere il divorzio anche il coniuge colpevole.

DICHIARA

che la Legge Fortuna - Baslini è la peggiore legge divorzista del mondo

INVITA

gli elettori e le elettrici in occasione del Referendum del 12 Maggio a VOTARE

SI

all'abrogazione della Legge FORTUNA-BASLINI

42] Anti-divorce poster in the guise of an official notice. National Committee for the Referendum on Divorce, 1974

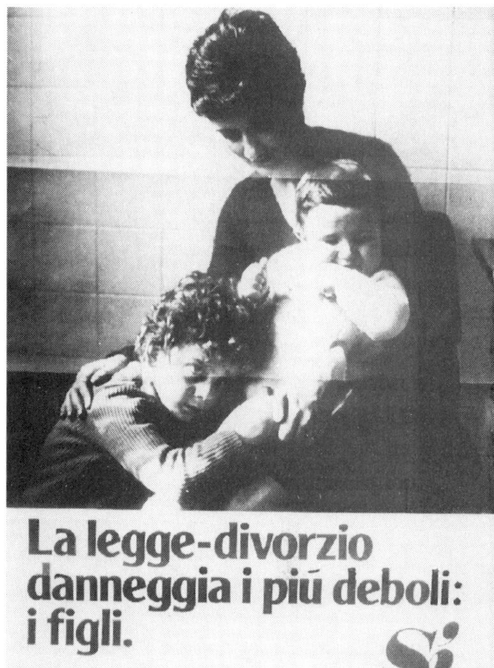

43] 'The divorce law hurts the weakest: the children.' Christian Democrat poster, 1974

44] Leonardo, cartoon for the *Virgin and Child, with St Anne and St John* (National Gallery, London)

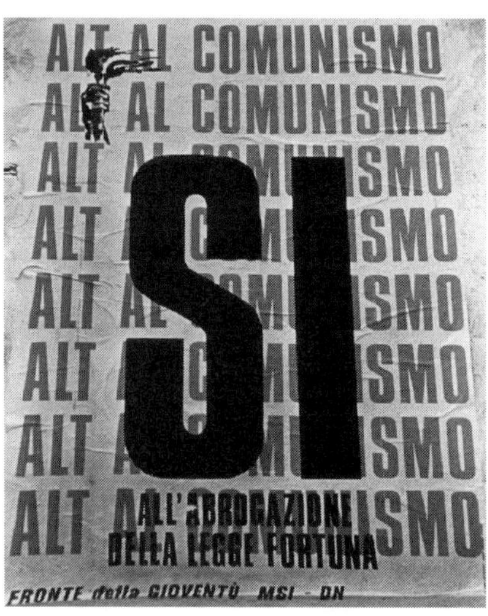

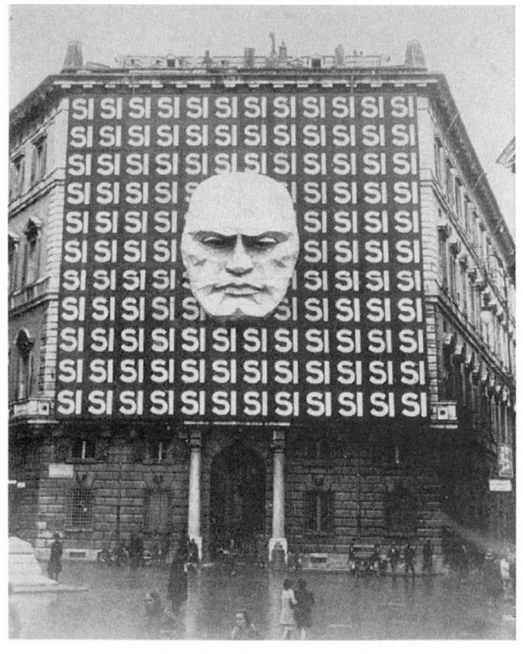

45] Anti-divorce poster, Youth league of the MSI, 1974

46] Fascist billboard on the Palazzo Braschi, Rome, during the plebiscite of 1934

47] Anti-divorce poster, MSI, 1974

48] Fascist poster announcing the result of the plebiscite of 1934

49] 'When the DC is strong, violence is weak.' Christian Democrat poster, 1975

50] 'Build your present and your future with the PCI.' Communist Party poster, 1976

51] 'Come with us. True revolution builds, it does not destroy. The new DC has already started. We women will carry it forward.' Christian Democrat poster, 1964

– talking to a small group of women in an urban setting (Figure 51). This unlikely scene was probably intended to evoke a well-known advertisement genre: that of the housewife praising the virtues of a commercial product (e.g. a washing powder) to others. The fact that the poster was the only one in the whole election campaign to be in full colour would confirm this interpretation; it suggests that it was aimed at the vast lower middle and middle-class readership of the numerous women's glossies which feature the type of advertisement in question.

The 1980s

Political campaigning underwent radical changes in the 1980s. Most parties – the PCI was the main exception – relied heavily on advertising and marketing professionals,[60] following the trend successfully established by Margaret Thatcher and François Mitterrand. They also placed greater emphasis on the leaders' and the candidates' personal profiles. This was a major departure from a party-centred system where parties represented specific ideologies and the subcultures in which they were rooted. Private television networks also contributed to the change of approach. While RAI, the state-run television, did not carry political advertising and strictly regulated its coverage of election campaigning, commercial stations enjoyed considerable freedom: they introduced paid political advertisements (*spot elettorali*) and produced programmes to which politicians were invited to contribute to discuss concrete issues in plain language. This led to the 'spectacularisation' of politics, since many relied on gimmicks to attract attention.[61] The emergence of a candidate- and leader-oriented approach to campaigning was to affect the nature of the posters being produced.

The first poster campaign to focus extensively on political leaders[62] was that of the parliamentary elections of 1983. The Socialists were the most aggressive pursuers of this approach. Colour portraits of Bettino Craxi, the youthful, plain-speaking leader who had set himself the task of relaunching the party as a modern left-wing alternative to the PCI, featured unabashedly in the party's visual propaganda.[63] His style of presentation was new: the broad smile and open shirt suggested self-assurance (the main slogan of the campaign was 'PSI. L'ottimismo della volontà', 'PSI. Optimism of the will'[64]), informality and down-to-earthness, while the close-up spelt approachability (some of the posters also depicted him leaning forward towards the viewer, Figure 52).[65] This extrovert and dynamic style of campaigning was inspired by American propaganda.[66]

The PRI also placed its leader, Giovanni Spadolini, at the core of its campaign: like his predecessor Ugo La Malfa, he was no ordinary politician, having been a university professor and an editor of the prestigious daily *Corriere della Sera*; the fact that from June 1981 to November 1982 he had been the first non-Christian Democrat Prime Minister for thirty-six years added lustre to his personality. Curiously, the leaflets and newspaper advertisements emphasised Spadolini's political stature by reproducing two photographs showing him in the company of Margaret Thatcher (Figure 53) and Helmut Schmidt. The photographs did not, however, feature on the posters.

The PRI campaign was mostly dealt with by the advertising agency Pirella-Göttsche, which had earlier (1976) worked for the PSI, and was later to be approached by the Partito Radicale.[67] This was a far cry from the long-held, universally accepted view that the promotion of a particular party could be done effectively only by an organisation ideologically aligned with it.

The European elections of 1984 marked a turning point in Communist campaigning: the party propaganda was entrusted to an advertising agency, Filmedia,

52] 'PSI. Optimism of the will.' Socialist Party poster featuring the portrait of the leader, Bettino Craxi, 1983

53] 'Giovanni Spadolini. An Italian politician unlike other Italian politicians.' Republican Party advertisement, 1983

which devised a series of brightly coloured posters dealing with issues such as unemployment, nuclear disarmament and the environment in an fresh and unconventional way. The party logo remained unchanged, but was reproduced in diminutive form (Figure 54).[68] The PCI, however, with its belief in 'the masses', continued to reject personalisation. The charismatic leader Enrico Berlinguer did not feature on the party's publicity material until after his sudden death on 11 June 1984, on the eve of the Euro-elections.

The propaganda of the 1987 parliamentary elections[69] will be remembered especially for the DC's campaign based on the slogan 'Forza Italia! Fai vincere le cose che contano' (Come on, Italy! Put what counts on the winning side), from which Silvio Berlusconi was later to derive the name of the party he founded in order to fill the political vacuum left by the collapse of the centre parties in the wake of the *Tangentopoli* trials. The DC campaign was entrusted to Marco Mignani of RSCG Italia, affiliate of the French multinational agency led by Jacques Séguéla which had helped Mitterrand make it to the Elysée Palace in 1981.[70]

In contrast with the triumphant and self-congratulatory campaign of the PSI, which stressed the political stability, economic progress and low inflation achieved by Italy during the previous parliamentary term under the government led by Bettino Craxi (the slogan devised by the Armando Testa agency was 'Cresce l'Italia', 'Italy is growing'),[71] Mignani created one which relied on images evoking a wholesome life style and traditional family values: a wedding, a pregnant woman with her child, a group of nursery school children with their teacher (Figure 56), etc. As well as on posters, these themes featured on party election broadcasts – signed by Gianni Quaranta, production designer of James Ivory's highly successful *A Room with a View* – for mutual reinforcement. A surprising feature of the DC campaign was the blatant patriotism, as expressed especially by the football-derived slogan 'Forza Italia!' The overt celebration of Italianness, which had been avoided in the past because it was associated with the MSI's ultra-nationalism,[72] was now legitimised by the self-confident and optimistic mood generated by economic prosperity.

The graphic output of the other parties was unremarkable; but then the 1987 campaign was dominated by television advertising, and this is where most creative energies appear to have been channelled.[73]

As pointed out, the PCI had been wary of cultivating the image of its leaders. The Rubicon was however crossed in September 1988: a close-up colour portrait of Achille Occhetto, who had succeeded Alessandro Natta as Party Secretary in June, featured in a poster advertising his rally at the conclusion of the national *Festa dell'Unità*, held in Florence.[74] A booklet including the text of his speech and an interview, entitled *Achille Occhetto. Per il nuovo PCI*, even took the unprecedented step of showing on its spread-out front and back covers the leader addressing a huge and attentive crowd. The following year, the portraits of some of the PCI candidates who stood for the European Parliament featured on the election hoardings.

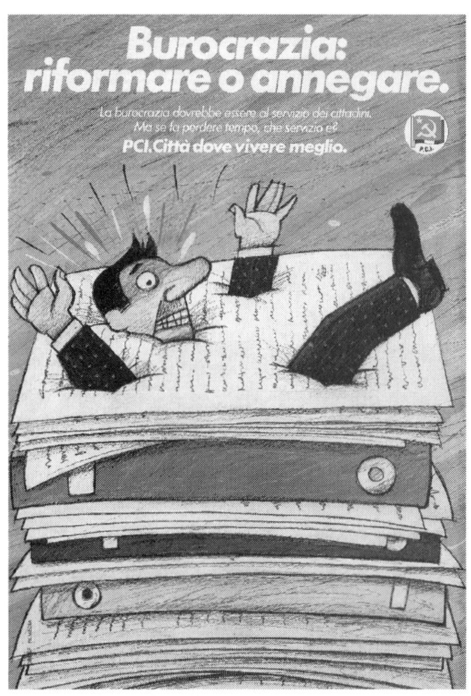

54] '*Homo demens*? Vote PCI. It's a sign that you want peace.' Communist Party poster, 1984

55] 'Bureaucracy: reform it or sink.' Communist Party poster, 1985

56] 'Come on, Italy! Put what counts on the winning side.' Christian Democrat poster, 1987

The 1990s

The campaign for the 1992 elections was almost entirely candidate-centred. This gave the poster a new lease of life, for no medium was better suited to provide aspiring parliamentarians with the visibility they needed. Almost invariably, in fact, the posters featured their portraits.

The strong emphasis on the candidate was partly the result of a change in the electoral system, which accelerated the trend towards personalisation and spectacularisation. The referendum of 9 June 1991 had abolished multi-preference voting, which had lent itself to corrupt practices, to replace it with a system by which the voter picked only one name from a ballot slip.[75] This brought about fierce competition among candidates,[76] and led them to outdo one another with gimmicks in an attempt to attract the attention of the public and secure their preferences.[77] Hence the elaborate ways in which many chose to have themselves represented in posters and other literature.

Italian politicians had tended to be portrayed half length, set against a neutral background. During the 1992 campaign, however, the need to distinguish themselves from their rivals led to the proliferation of different poses, gestures and props (which made it necessary to depict the figure in fuller form), as well as of significant backgrounds.[78] These features alluded to the status and supposed qualities, achievements and aspirations of the sitter. Usually the more important the candidate the more visually complex, or even 'spectacular', the portrait.[79] Thus Giorgio La Malfa had

57] '"I want to unite honest Italians and make them win through" – Giorgio La Malfa.' Republican Party poster, 1992

58] 'The quiet force. Mitterand for President.' French Socialist Party poster, 1981

59] 'A police superintendent in the Senate: Ennio di Francesco.' Socialist Party poster, 1992

60] 'Let's vote Cristofori to get things done together. A turning point for Ferrara's future.' Christian Democrat poster, 1992

himself represented before an idyllic landscape complete with country church, to evoke a simple and genuine life style, this being implicitly contrasted with hectic and corrupt urban civilisation (Figure 57). The picture was blatantly derived from the celebrated 'Force tranquille' poster and election broadcast of Mitterrand's 1981 presidential campaign (Figure 58).[80] The Socialist candidate Ennio Di Francesco, a former police superintendent who had been involved in the fight against drug barons, terrorism and the Mafia, was depicted in a poster in a three-quarter view emphasising his right elbow, forearm and clenched fist (Figure 59). The posture, which was meant to denote strength, determination, assertiveness and defiance, was inspired by a well-established Renaissance portrait type;[81] the allusion to such an illustrious visual tradition probably served to temper the aggressiveness of the message. Finally, a poster promoting the DC candidate Nino Cristofori depicted him three-quarter length, his raised right arm pointing towards the onlooker (Figure 60) – an oratorical gesture traditionally connoting authoritativeness and a sense of leadership.[82]

Not all parties, however, followed the trend of depicting their candidates on the posters. The Partito Democratico della Sinistra (PDS) by and large resisted it,

61] 'The North pays for everyone. Enough of taxes paid to Rome. We want fair taxes, we want them paid to Lombardy.' Lega poster, *c.* 1992

62] 'Shut up and pay, you Lombard ass-head, or you'll be accused of racism. The Lombard hen is laying golden eggs for Rome and further down! They'll all get fried in a pan, and we'll never see them again!' Lega poster, local elections, 1988. The poster was also produced with a text in Lombard dialect, and in versions that suited other Northern regions (e.g. Romagna). The cartoon of the 'Roman' peasant in her traditional costume collecting the golden eggs has since featured in countless other Lega literature (posters, brochures, etc.).

preferring to use solely their names. The few portraits that were shown were of the old, no-frills, half-bust type. Two politicians did get the fuller-length portrait treatment, but they were not members of the PDS: a poster reproduced photos of the DC chiefs Arnaldo Forlani and Giulio Andreotti in their youth smiling smugly, in order to remind the electorate that they had been in power for a long time. None of the candidates of Rifondazione Comunista, the hard-line Communist splinter group, featured on their printed propaganda. Interestingly, though, the party chose to illustrate the issues it focused upon – women's exploitation, unemployment, the health service, etc. – through anonymous portraits emblematically representing different categories of people.

The Lega Nord polled 8·7 per cent of the national vote in 1992 – its first major breakthrough in a parliamentary election – making little use of posters (or of election broadcasts, for that matter) and preferring to rely, as it had in the previous two years, on the free publicity provided by the media's reporting of Umberto Bossi's outrageous style of campaigning.[83]

The poster had been one of the Lega's main vehicles of political mobilisation, especially in its early years (the 1980s). This was partly due to necessity (until the party became a force to be reckoned with, press and television tended to ignore it), but above all it reflected the Lega's desire to distance itself from other political groupings which were increasingly relying on election broadcasts and television chat shows. The posters were quite unlike those of other parties. At a time when printed and other types of propaganda were almost universally entrusted to professional agencies, the Lega chose to devise its own internally, making few aesthetic concessions. The posters had (and continue to have) a consciously amateurish feel. Most consisted solely of the logo (the armoured portrait of the twelveth-century knight Alberto da Giussano, who, having stood up against Emperor Frederick Barbarossa, was an apt symbol of local rebellion against central power), and of texts crudely laid out, printed in one or two colours only, and with lettering in a nondescript, no-nonsense typographical style. The language was pedestrian, being characterised by simple syntax and everyday vocabulary (a conscious reaction against *politichese*, the obscure jargon of many Italian politicians), a charged emotional style and a Manichaean structure (e.g. productivity/parasitism, equated with North/South) (Figure 61). A few of the posters featured simply drawn cartoons illustrating the party's *leitmotif* of the 'idle South' exploiting the industrious North through the central fiscal system (Figure 62).[84] These crudely produced posters are part and parcel of the Lega's self-representation as a protest movement. They are the printed equivalent of graffiti, a vehicle of communication the party has also used on a systematic basis to make its views known.[85]

The campaign for the 1994 elections has attracted much attention, both scholarly and journalistic, though it has focused almost exclusively on the role of television, the victory of Berlusconi's centre-right coalition having been attributed by many, in varying degrees, to the tycoon's unscrupulous use of the networks he controlled.[86] Yet the campaign's graphic output was not without interest, and deserves to be commented upon.

Before dealing with the posters, some general remarks should be made about the logos of the new political groupings that took part in the contest. Most of them – including the logo of the Progressisti, the left-wing alliance – featured the tricolour in some form or other.[87] The full rehabilitation of this symbol of patriotic fervour is largely a reaction against the Lega's secessionist threats.[88] Blue is another colour that was revived in 1994 for patriotic purposes (it is worth recalling that Catholicism was, until recently, the state's official religion). It featured prominently in the logo of the Partito Popolare Italiano (PPI), and in that of Alleanza Nazionale (AN). Berlusconi referred to Forza Italia's aspiring parliamentarians as *Azzurri* (the Blues), one of several sports terms he adopted to give his party a patriotic, supra-ideological appeal.[89]

The trend towards personalisation was strengthened in 1994. Two main factors account for this: in the first place, the demise of some of the old parties and the general disenchantment with political ideologies, which led to even greater emphasis being placed on the alleged qualities of the candidates; secondly, the new electoral system, based predominantly on the British-inspired 'first past the post' principle,[90] which placed the candidates supported by the various alliances in strong competition with one another. As in 1992, it was mostly the posters of the parties on the centre and right of the political spectrum that reproduced the effigy of the candidates. The PDS eschewed the practice, despite acknowledging the importance of personalisation in a manual produced for distribution to its campaigners.[91]

Forza Italia's poster campaign was as slick and professional as its television one. The design of the posters was co-ordinated. The candidates were presented in a similar way, to heighten the party's 'corporate identity'.[92] They all wore formal, well-cut clothing, looked well groomed and smiled gently. They were also all depicted half length, standing in a three-quarter-view posture – the female ones placed on the right-hand side of the poster, turned to the left, and the male ones on the left-hand side, in a symmetrical arrangement (Figure 63). This gender-led spatial organisation of the candidates was repeated a few weeks later in the posters for the Euro-election campaign. It is of interest because it happens to correspond to the position that a woman and a man conventionally occupy in relation to each other (notably that of the bride and groom when they come before the altar), an arrangement which assigns to the man the traditionally superior right-hand side.[93] The poster featuring Berlusconi mostly followed the same typology: he distinguished himself from the other candidates only by his broad smile – the attribute of the self-satisfied, successful entrepreneur, as well as of the star of the entertainment world, exuding optimism and *joie de vivre*, and promising the dream of a fulfilled life (Figure 64).[94]

The posters devised by Forza Italia for the Euro-elections are also worth discussing briefly. They differed from those produced for the Italian elections mainly in so far as the candidates were represented behind a blue sky, whose realistic rendering (it featured a few clouds) only thinly disguised the colour's political symbolism. The sky also fulfilled a generic celebratory function, since it traditionally evokes positive values.[95] The poster featuring Berlusconi sought to distinguish

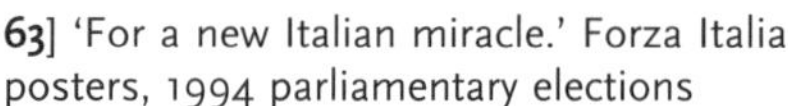
63] 'For a new Italian miracle.' Forza Italia posters, 1994 parliamentary elections

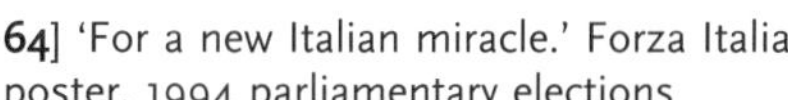
64] 'For a new Italian miracle.' Forza Italia poster, 1994 parliamentary elections

65] 'For more clout in Europe.' Forza Italia poster, 1994 European elections

66] 'Ignazio La Russa. [The] right [choice to] beat the left-wing coalition.' Alleanza Nazionale poster defaced by the Lega sticker, 1994 parliamentary elections

67] 'A right fit to govern. At last. To rebuild Italy: Alleanza Nazionale.' Poster, 1994 parliamentary elections

him as much as possible from the other candidates. Not only did he beam broadly, but he filled a larger proportion of the pictorial space, confronted the viewer (a typically hieratic mode) instead of being shown sideways, and, in a reversal of the convention, was allocated the right-hand side of the poster. Finally, and obviously enough, Berlusconi alone was depicted before a forest of microphones, to stress the international attention which his meteoric rise to political stardom had attracted (Figure 65).

The graphic propaganda of AN was also carefully thought out. The party was keen to project an image of respectability in order to profit from the opportunity to enter the government after half a century of political exile. Thus the poster advertising Marco Cellai's candidature in Florence depicted him before one of the city's highlights, the Church of Santa Maria Novella. The poster promoting the Milan candidate, Ignazio La Russa, featured him in shirtsleeves, his jacket nonchalantly thrown over his shoulder in an attitude of informality, and thus 'modernity',[96] that was intended to dispel the stuffy and pompous image the right used to evoke (Figure 66). The visual emphasis thus given to the white of his shirt was probably meant as a sign that his party had relinquished Fascism (white being the chromatic opposite of black) – a point picked up by local Lega activists, who covered part of La Russa's posters with a red strip of paper declaring: 'Alleanza Nazionale = MSI =

Museo sepolcri imbiancati' (AN = MSI = [stuffy old] Museum [of] whited sepulchres).[97] The defacing of AN propaganda by the Lega was particularly outrageous given that the two parties were part of the Berlusconi camp. (In view of their antagonism the leader of Forza Italia had actually formed two separate alliances – a Forza Italia–Lega in the North, and a Forza Italia–Alleanza Nazionale in central and southern Italy, where the MSI's strength was concentrated.)

Interestingly, the 1994 elections also saw a return of the practice of secretly alluding to Fascism for the benefit of those who needed reassurance that the party had not betrayed its past. This practice had been interrupted in the late 1980s, probably because the increasingly relaxed and 'tolerant' political climate allowed the MSI to come out into the open.[98] The most outrageous example is provided by the poster featuring Fini, which was produced for nation-wide distribution (Figure 67). The picture incorporating the leader's portrait is divided diagonally in two. The upper 'triangle' is filled by a portion of the European flag (an element included to give the party a fashionable international dimension). In the background of the lower half is an arm that incongruously extends from Fini's left shoulder, and which should be interpreted as a disguised Fascist salute. The detail is not readily perceivable because it is blurred, and because the elbow and that part between the inner curve of the arm and the left-hand side of Fini's face have been filled in with amorphous elements whose purpose was probably to distract the viewers' attention from the detail. That the arm should not be viewed as an accidental and innocent element of the background is indicated by the fact that the full picture is not a single photograph but a photomontage.[99]

One of the most striking posters of the 1994 elections was produced by a party at the other extreme of the political spectrum, which took part in the campaign merely to advise the electorate to abstain: the Maoist Partito Marxista-Leninista Italiano. The poster depicted a hand clutching a red flag, whose pole functioned as a spear piercing a dragon (the 'Second neo-Fascist Republic') (Figure 68); this is a humorous conflation of the St George/St Michael-slaying-the-dragon/snake theme with Chinese iconography, both traditional (the dragon, actually a symbol of auspiciousness) and revolutionary (the muscular arm and red flag), and seems to argue that Maoist doctrine is applicable to the Italian context.[100]

The most distinctive and significant posters of the elections of 1996[101] were those featuring the leaders of the parties/party alliances. Berlusconi had himself represented sitting at his desk, his right hand holding a pen and resting on a set of sheets (the text of a speech he has been fine-tuning, as some crossed-out words indicate); a document bearing the logo of Forza Italia lies near by (Figure 69). He smiles, but only moderately: the beam that characterised his 1994 campaign would have been ill-suited on this occasion, not only because his portrait as statesman required a certain *gravitas*[102] but because his short-lived experience as head of government and the pending investigations for corruption would have given his pronounced optimism a hollow ring.

Another politician who had himself portrayed in a 'presidential' style was Lamberto Dini, the outgoing head of the caretaker government formed after the collapse of Berlusconi's coalition (of which he was Treasury Minister) in December 1994, and leader of Rinnovamento Italiano, one of the parties in Romano Prodi's centre-left Ulivo (Olive Tree) alliance. The setting is the Prime Minister's office, as the presence of the flag seems to indicate (Figure 70). This is no formal portrait, though. Unlike Berlusconi, who makes full use of the desk as a symbol of his position and as a distancing device, Dini stands, somewhat casually, *before* his desk, so as to be perceived as accessible. Hands in portraiture tend to connote status and power.[103] Dini's however, do not fulfil their symbolic potential to the full: they occupy a marginal position within the pictorial space and are cut off by the lower edge of the picture.

Prodi might have been represented in his professorial study, surrounded by books, so as to draw attention to his distinguished academic career. Instead the poster featured a close-up of his podgy face[104] which emphasised the squint beneath the thick old-fashioned glasses, the greying hair and the five o'clock shadow (Figure 71). Prodi's campaign organisers and the graphic artist who designed all printed publicity, Andrea Rauch, had clearly taken note of the advice he was given when he agreed to stand as leader of the centre-left coalition in February 1995: he was not to emulate Berlusconi, who had been groomed and 'rejuvenated' by his spin doctors to be marketed like a star, perfect and inaccessible; Prodi was to turn his physical imperfections to advantage by stressing his ordinariness, transparency and authenticity.[105]

Pier Ferdinando Casini, the most prominent figure of the Centro Cristiano Democratico (CCD), was also represented in close-up (Figure 72). The purpose here was diametrically opposed to Prodi's, namely to show off his good looks.[106]

Fini was depicted standing relaxed, leaning against a wall, arms folded (Figure 73). The attitude is so unusual – no post-war leader in Italy has ever been represented in such a manner in formal or semi-formal portraits – that it should be treated as significant. The folded arms are said to evoke 'defensiveness, unwillingness to be open or change one's mind'.[107] It is an interpretation that fits in admirably with Fini's intransigent stance on constitutional reform (his advocacy of a political system giving the President of the Republic considerable executive powers), a stance that had led to the resignation of Prime Minister designate Antonio Maccanico in February 1996, and the consequent calling of new elections. But one may go further, and see in Fini's folded arms also an allusion to Mussolini. Though not as frequent as the arm(s) akimbo, this was in fact one of the canonical attitudes of the Duce, and was intended to connote a resolute, no-nonsense character. It featured in a number of official portraits, was imitated by blackshirts and lampooned by caricaturists (Figures 74, 75).[108] The relaxed manner in which Fini stands (when Mussolini's crossed his arms the torso always stayed rigid) only serves to camouflage the allusion and give the portrait the necessary respectability.

No such ambiguities were to be found in the visual propaganda of the Movimento Sociale Fiamma Tricolore (Social Movement Tricolour Flame), the hard-right splinter group of the MSI, led by the vociferous and charismatic Pino Rauti. The posters featured images and slogans of overtly Fascist inspiration, i.e. of the type used by the MSI before Almirante's modernisation (Figure 76).

68] 'Choose Socialism. Abstain. Reject the Second neo-Fascist Republic.' Poster produced by the Italian Marxist-Leninist Party, parliamentary elections, 1994

69] 'My pledge: to work for five years to transform Italy in everyone's interests.' Forza Italia poster, 1996

70] 'We do as we say.' Lista Dini, Rinnovamento Italiano poster, 1996

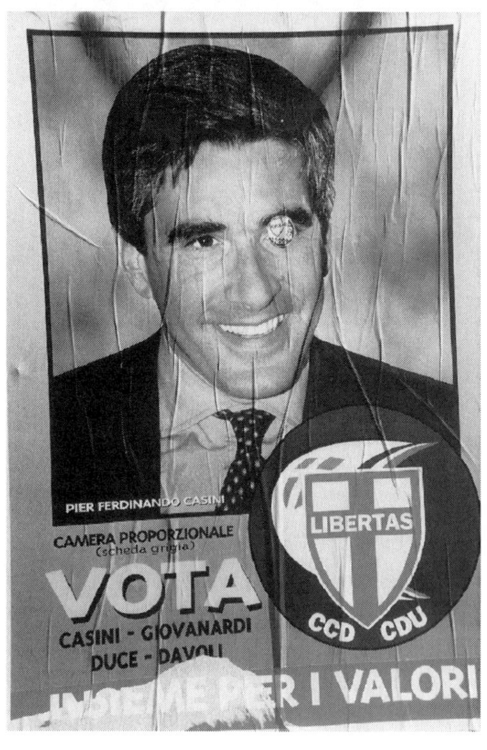

71] 'Romano Prodi.' Olive Tree alliance poster, 1996

72] 'Together to defend our values.' Poster issued jointly by the Centro Cristiano Democratico and the Cristiano-Democratici Uniti, 1996

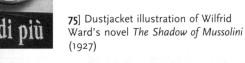

73] 'We are clear and true to ourselves, in favour of a presidential system. For an Italy that deserves better.' Alleanza Nazionale poster, 1996

74] Mussolini in his study, *c.* 1924

75] Dustjacket illustration of Wilfrid Ward's novel *The Shadow of Mussolini* (1927)

76] 'Italy is getting old and dying! Zero birth-rate, abortion, homosexuality: because of all these, in fifty years' time we won't be here any more. The State should support families with policies protecting traditional values. Proletarian Italy, on your feet!' Movimento Sociale Fiamma Tricolore poster, 1996

Conclusion

While remaining a constant feature of Italian political campaigning, the poster has served different functions in the past half-century. In the early post-war period it was a vehicle of attack and counter-attack, as well as information. These roles were largely taken over, in the 1960s, by televised political debates. The growing practice of entrusting printed publicity to professional graphic artists, rather than to party activists with some artistic skill, led to its aestheticisation. As a result, political posters, like their commercial counterparts, sought to attract attention through the use of inventive images and texts. Ultimately, they aimed to create or consolidate a 'corporate image'. More often than not, they addressed themselves largely to the party faithful.

The rise of the party election broadcast in the early 1980s has not brought about a decline of the political poster. The personalisation of political campaigning, accelerated in the 1990s by changes in the electoral system, has on the contrary revived its fortunes, since the medium is well-suited to promote party leaders and other candidates through their portraits – as the campaign for the election of 31 May 2001 confirmed. In any case, in political propaganda, as in commercial advertising, new means of communication do not supplant 'old' ones: the same messages may be expressed concomitantly, through the different media, in a variety of forms (some more articulate than others), thus reinforcing one another and ensuring that they reach the widest public.[109]

There is, therefore, little reason to believe that the newest means of communication, the World Wide Web, which all Italian parties now employ to disseminate information about their activities and programmes, will erode the poster's role. Given its practical advantages and the importance of street life in Italy, the political poster is as unlikely to die out in the near future as its commercial counterpart.

NOTES

I should like to thank the Scouloudi Foundation for a Historical Award which enabled me to undertake research for this chapter in Italy.

1 It is worth recalling that the term 'propaganda' originates from the Catholic Church. It was first used in 1622 by Pope Gregory XV when he established the Sacra Congregatio de Propaganda Fide with the aim of countering the Protestant Reformation in Europe and disseminating the Christian doctrine in the recently discovered lands. See E. Leso, 'Alle origini della parola "propaganda"', *Quaderni Costituzionali*, 16:3 (1996), p. 337.

2 The piazza is, notably, a focus of political activism as well as the social heart of an Italian city. See M. Isnenghi, *L'Italia in piazza. I luoghi della vita pubblica dal 1848 ai giorni nostri* (Milan, Mondadori, 1994). The political poster is not, of course, the only type of poster to thrive in such an outdoor-oriented culture: commercial and 'public interest' posters (*manifesti di pubblica utilità*) also feature strongly in the urban landscape. Mention must also be made of the death notices (*annunci mortuari*) tradition, about which see M. Lange, 'Italian Death Notices', *Design Issues*, 5:1 (1988), pp. 30–3.

3 No other form of political communication provides opportunities for totally free and spontaneous reactions – not even party rallies, since, being usually heavily policed, they tend to discourage uninhibited manifestations of disapproval.

4 For the suggestion that posters may be treated as a modern adaptation of the Pompeian custom and the Pasquinade tradition see H. Risatti, 'The Contemporary Political Poster in Italy', *Art Journal*, 44:1 (1984), special issue on 'The Poster', p. 11.

5 See M. Isnenghi *et al.*, *L'Italia in guerra, 1940–43. Immagini e temi della propaganda fascista* (Brescia, Fondazione Luigi Micheletti, 1989); *id.*, *1943–45. L'immagine della RSI nella propaganda* (Milan, Mazzotta, 1985).
6 *Lex. Legislazione italiana* (Turin, Utet), 34 (January–June 1948), p. 234.
7 On the propaganda for the 1946 elections and referendum see: E. Di Nolfo, *La repubblica delle speranze e degli inganni. L'Italia dalla caduta del Fascismo al crollo della Democrazia Cristiana* (Florence, Ponte alle Grazie, 1996), pp. 199–204; A. Ventrone, 'La liturgia politica comunista dal '44 al '46', *Storia contemporanea*, 2:5 (1992), pp. 779–836; and P. L. Ballini (ed.), *1946–1948. Repubblica, Costituente, Costituzione* (Florence, Polistampa, 1998), pp. 178–205.
8 Quoted in Ventrone, 'La liturgia', p. 810.
9 *Ibid.*, p. 811.
10 The text of the document is reproduced in C. Dané (ed.), *Parole e immagini della Democrazia Cristiana in quarant'anni di manifesti della SPES* (Rome, Broadcasting & Background, 1985), pp. 15–17. The Ufficio SPES was founded in 1945 by the then deputy Secretary of the DC, Giuseppe Dossetti. 'SPES', as well as being the acronym for Studi di Propaganda e Stampa (Propaganda and Press Studies), is the Latin word for 'hope'. The choice of an acronym with punning possibilities is likely to have been inspired by the name of another propaganda organisation: the Istituto Luce, which produced the newsreels of the Fascist regime. 'Luce' stood for 'L'Unione Cinematografica Educativa' but also translates 'light' in Italian.
11 The printed and 'permanent' nature of the poster medium appears to have given it an 'official' status that discouraged its use as negative propaganda. The fact that the illustrated posters were produced centrally probably also explains their moderate tone. On this question, see Mino Argentieri's chapter in this volume, pp. 82–3.
12 On this party see S. Setta, *L'Uomo Qualunque* (Bari and Rome, Laterza, 1995, 2nd edn).
13 Women were enfranchised in 1946. The DC, realising that they were a potentially rich pool of votes to draw from, produced then and in subsequent elections a number of posters that were specifically addressed to them.
14 The theme of Christ as a Socialist *avant la lettre* was not new: it had featured in Socialist literature at the turn of the century. See S. Pivato, *Clericalismo e laicismo nella cultura popolare italiana* (Milan, Franco Angeli, 1990).
15 A copy of a poster featuring such reassurances is in the archives of the party's Press and Propaganda Department.
16 For illustrations of these statues in an accessible publication see C. Avery, *Florentine Renaissance Sculpture* (London, John Murray, 1970), pp. 83 and 133, respectively. Notably, in Renaissance Florence David symbolised the city's vigilance against tyranny.
17 On the alliance between the erotic and the political in visual representations of women there is a substantial literature, much of it focused on Eugène Delacroix's 'Liberty Guiding the People'. With reference to this painting, see, for instance, M. Warner, 'The Slipped Chiton', in *Monuments and Maidens. The Allegory of the Female Form* (London, Weidenfeld & Nicolson, 1985), pp. 263–93, and M. Pointon, 'Liberty on the Barricades: Woman, Politics and Sexuality in Delacroix', in *Naked Authority. The Body in Western Painting, 1830–1908* (Cambridge University Press, 1990, pp. 59–82).
18 See A. Faeti, 'L'inventore delle gambe', in *Gino Boccasile. La Signorina Grandi Firme* (Milan, Longanesi, 1981), pp. vii–xvii.
19 The DC produced no posters for the referendum campaign, having opted for a free vote on the question of monarchy *v.* republic.
20 On the campaign of the DC and the Comitati Civici see especially: L. Romano and P. Scabello (eds), *C'era una volta la DC. Breve storia del periodo degasperiano attraverso i manifesti elettorali della Democrazia Cristiana* (Rome, Savelli, 1975); J. C. Pratt, *The Walled City. A Study of Social Change and Conservative Ideologies in Tuscany* (Göttingen, Herodot, 1986), chapter VIII; D. W. Ellwood, 'The 1948 Elections in Italy: a Cold War Propaganda Battle', *Historical Journal of Film, Radio and Television*, 13:1 (1993), pp. 19–33; *Trenta Giorni*, 16:3 (1998), special issue on the 1948 election campaign.

21 The reasons for such a choice are explained in the Introduction to this volume (p. 2).
22 On the genesis of the poster illustrated here, the main one of the Communist campaign, see C. Lizzani, 'Raf, Edith e Luisa. Così nacque il manifesto-simbolo del 1948', *L'Unità*, 16 April 1998. On the campaign of the PCI see A. Ventrone, 'Il PCI e la mobilitazione delle masse, 1947–48', *Storia contemporanea*, 24:2 (1993), pp. 243–300. For a first-hand account of Communist preparations for the campaign see *Quaderno dell'attivista*, February 1948, special issue *La campagna elettorale*, pp. 2–31.
23 Carlo Felice Casula has argued that the propaganda of the PCI was over-intellectual: see 'I Comunisti e la comunicazione', in N. Tranfaglia (ed.), *Il 1948 in Italia. La storia e i film* (Florence, La Nuova Italia, 1991), pp. 135–6.
24 U. Eco, 'La diga', *L'Espresso*, 20 April 1975, pp. 80–3.
25 *La difesa della razza*, 20 September 1939, p. 11. On this magazine see D. Bidussa *et al.*, *La menzogna della razza. Documenti e immagini del razzismo e dell'antisemitismo fascista* (Bologna, Grafis, 1994).
26 On the 1953 election campaign in general see P. Facchi (ed.), *La propaganda politica in Italia, 1953–58* (Bologna, Il Mulino, 1960).
27 That Communism, being a 'perverse' and 'unnatural' ideology, 'masculinised' women was a recurrent theme of the propaganda of the time. Shortly before the 1948 elections, on 4 April, the right-wing weekly *Oggi* featured an illustrated article entitled 'Le reginette del Cominform' (The Cominform's Beauty Queens) lampooning the physical appearance of some high-profile Communist women, such as Rita Togliatti, wife of the Communist leader, and 'La Pasionaria' (Dolores Ibarruri).
28 See especially D. G. Audino and G. Vittori, *Via il regime della forchetta. Autobiografia del PCI nei primi anni '50 attraverso i manifesti elettorali* (Rome, Savelli, 1976), and E. Novelli, *C'era una volta il PCI. Autobiografic di un partito attra verso le immagini della sua propaganda* (Rome, Editori Riuniti, 2000), pp. 84–95.
29 The MSI, which had been founded in December 1946 by Mussolini's closest collaborators, had six deputies in the outgoing Parliament, having polled 2 per cent of the national vote in 1948 elections.
30 See *Come si fa propaganda elettorale. Tre conversazioni per i propagandisti delle sezioni e delle cellule* (Rome, Sezione stampa e propaganda, PCI, 1953), p. 8. The PCI did not, however, reject the pictorial traditions of the left entirely. Graphically the election posters may have been somewhat unadventurous, but the material produced by the party and its sister organisations – e.g. the trade union CGIL (Confederazione Generale Italiana del Lavoro) and the women's association UDI (Unione Donne Italiane) – for an audience made up largely of sympathisers, was more modernistic in inspiration. The use of photomontage, of lettering treated pictorially, of broken lines, of foreshortened figures and of words superimposed on images reveal the debt to Constructivism. The posters' modernism was, however, merely a watered-down version of their radical models. Togliatti was, notably, strongly hostile to artistic experimentation, as he believed it to be inaccessible to the masses. Albe Steiner, the left-wing graphic artist whose innovative work was inspired by photomontage artists such as John Heartfield and Alexander Rodchenko, was not invited by the Central Office of the PCI to design posters until the early 1960s. On the PCI's attitude to the arts in the early post-war period see: N. Misler, *La via italiana al realismo. La politica culturale artistica del PCI dal 1944 al 1956* (Milan, Mazzotta, 1973); N. Ajello, *Intellettuali e PCI, 1944–58* (Bari and Rome, Laterza, 1979), chapter VIII, and S. Gundle, *Between Hollywood and Moscow. The Italian Communists and the Challenge of Mass Culture, 1943–1991* (Durham, NC, Duke University Press, 2000). On Albe Steiner see: M. Accolti Gil, 'La grafica di Steiner', *Mondoperaio* (November 1976), pp. 43–57; M. Huber and L. Steiner (eds), *Albe Steiner. Comunicazione visiva* (Florence, Alinari, 1977).
31 For full details of this law (No. 148), passed on 31 March, see *Lex. Legislazione Italiana* (Turin, UTET), 42, 1956 (I), pp. 525–8. An attempt to regulate the poster propaganda had been made in March 1952. See P. Calamandrei, 'Disciplina della propaganda elettorale per mezzo dei manifesti murali', in *Scritti e discorsi politici*, vol. I, *Storia di dodici anni*, book I, ed. N. Bobbio (Florence, La Nuova Italia, 1966), pp. 508–13. The-free-for-all

which the Bill was meant to put an end to was vividly described by Calamandrei, 'Un caso di follia collettiva', in *Scritti e discorsi*, vol. I, book 2, pp. 316–19.

32 The slogan may also have been influenced by that of Eisenhower's 1952 presidential campaign – 'I like Ike' (which in turn was inspired by the culture of advertising). The DC poster is reproduced in C. Dané (ed.), *Parole e immagini della Democrazia Cristiana* (unpaginated).

33 The question as to whether parties should seek the advice of advertising consultants was, however, debated as early as 1948. See R. Pomé, 'Tecnica pubblicitaria e propaganda politica', *L'ufficio moderno*, No. 7 (1948), pp. 251–5.

34 For an account of the gaffe, told by Adolfo Sarti, the official then in charge of the Propaganda Department of the DC, see 'Quando la DC aveva vent'anni', in Dané (ed.), *Parole e immagini della Democrazia Cristiana*, pp. 38–41.

35 Cited from L. Sollazzo, 'Pubblicità elettorale', *Sipradue*, November–December 1968, pp. 27–8.

36 On Spera's work see: G. Picciotti (ed.), *Una politica, un'immagine. Materiali grafici di Michele Spera per il Partito Repubblicano Italiano* (Rome, La Ragione, 1987), and *Michele Spera. 194 storie di un segno* (Rome, Socrates, 1996).

37 On Ruffolo's work for the PSI see Various authors, *Le immagini del Socialismo. Comunicazione politica e propaganda del PSI dalle origini agli anni Ottanta* (Rome, PSI, n.d. [but 1983]), pp. 432–49. Ruffolo was also a talented newspaper layout artist. His theoretical grasp and aesthetic sensitivity come across in his volume *Vestire i giornali* (Turin, Gutenberg 2000, 1986).

38 For a survey of Vitale's work for the PSI till 1983 see Various authors, *Le immagini del Socialismo*, pp. 450–7, 472–546, and A.C. Quintavalle, *Ettore Vitale* (Milan, Electa, 2000).

39 For the visual propaganda of the DC see Dané (ed.), *Parole e immagini della Democrazia Cristiana*. For the output of the PCI see *PCI '81. Almanacco del 60°* (Rome, PCI, 1980), pp. 49–80, and Various authors, *Vedere a sinistra. Bruno Magno. Dal PCI al PDS. I manifesti e altre immagini, 1971–91* (Rome, Salemi & Editori Riuniti, 1991).

40 Almirante was re-elected leader in 1969 (he had first led the party in 1948–50) and remained in office without a break till 1987. He was quite experienced in the field of 'political persuasion', having been in 1944–45 Ministerial Private Secretary in the Ministero della Cultura Popolare of the Italian Social Republic, whose activities consisted largely of orchestrating the propaganda machinery.

41 For a general account of the visual propaganda of the MSI see L. Cheles, '"Nostalgia dell'avvenire". The Propaganda of the Italian far Right between Tradition and Innovation', in L. Cheles, R. G. Ferguson and M. Vaughan (eds), *The Far Right in Western and Eastern Europe* (London, Longman, 1995), pp. 41–90.

42 On these graphics, see for instance: D. Sterner, *The Art of Revolution* (London, Pall Mall, 1970); R. Cirio and P. Favari (eds), *L'altra grafica* (Milan, Bompiani, 1973); and L. Gervereau *et al.*, *Les Sixties. Britain and France, 1962 to 1973* (London, Philip Wilson, 1997).

43 *L'immagine della politica. Il manifesto della nuova sinistra, 1968–77* (Florence, Centro Studi e Archivio Storico 'Il Sessantotto', 1988); L. Canapini and G. Ginex, *Cipputi communication. Immagini, forme, voci per i lavoratori* (Milan, Mazzotta, 1997).

44 This point was explicitly acknowledged by Almirante in a speech at a party conference in April 1970, reproduced in the party's daily, *Il Secolo d'Italia*, 7 April 1970. The question of the MSI's plundering from the culture of the left is discussed at length in Cheles, '"Nostalgia dell'avvenire"'; see also *id.*, 'Le geste commémoratif dans l'extrême droite italienne', in J. Davallon, P. Dujardin and G. Sabatier (eds), *Le Geste commémoratif* (Lyon, Centre d'étude et de recherche de l'Institut d'études politiques, 1994), pp. 149–79.

45 A. C. Quintavalle, 'Le guerre dei manifesti e delle loro marche', in Various authors, *Le immagini del Socialismo*, pp. 348, 362.

46 D. Novelli, *Dalla TV di partito al partito della TV, 1960–95* (Florence, La Nuova Italia, 1995), pp. 1–35.

47 On this campaign see: M. Clark, D. Hine and R. E. M. Irving, 'Divorce – Italian Style', *Parliamentary Affairs*, 27 (1973–74), pp. 333–58; P. Mancini, *Il manifesto politico. Per una semiologia del consenso* (Rome, ERI, 1980).

48 On the use of children in this campaign see: G. Borgese and G. P. Meucci, 'Bambini "sì", bambini "no". La strumentalizzazione dell'infanzia nella campagna per il divorzio', *Corriere della Sera*, 29 April 1974.

49 Togliatti expressed his opposition to divorce on 7 November 1946 at a meeting of the sub-committee of the *Costituente* (the assembly in charge of preparing the new constitution). His accommodating stance on the thorny issue of divorce reflected his desire not to antagonise the DC, with which he wished to continue to govern.

50 The pro-divorce lobby, too, attempted to woo the voters of the opposite camp by arguing on their own ground – though without resorting to trickery. The PCI issued a brochure entitled *Cattolici e divorzio* which illustrated the open debate that was taking place worldwide among Catholics on this issue. A number of Italian Catholic intellectuals publicly declared their pro-divorce stance.

51 See: m.a. [*sic*], 'Il cavallo di Troia', *Corriere della Sera*, 18 April 1974; anon., 'Un decreto del pretore di Roma accerta il falso contro il PCI', *L'Unità*, 9 May 1974.

52 These allusions to Renaissance art are likely to have been noticed by a tiny proportion of the public; as far as I am aware, they have escaped the attention of scholars and journalists who have written on the referendums in question. Unlike British visual propaganda, which strives for clarity and tries to address the widest audience, Italian political (and commercial) posters, not unlike works of art, at times delight in hidden meanings accessible only to the initiated. On Italian propaganda's not infrequent reliance on Renaissance iconography see L. Cheles, 'L'uso delle immagini rinascimentali nell'iconografia del manifesto politico', in R. Varese (ed.), *Letture di storia dell'arte* (Bologna and Ancona, Il Lavoro Editoriale, 1988), pp. 39–58; see pp. 49–50, Figures 35–7, for the anti-abortion posters referred to above.

53 On this plebiscite see R. De Felice, *Mussolini il Duce. Gli anni del consenso, 1929–36* (Turin, Einaudi, 1974), pp. 311–13.

54 For a fuller account of the referendum campaign of the MSI see Cheles, '"Nostalgia dell'avvenire"', pp. 59–62.

55 For a detailed discussion of this practice, see *ibid.*

56 Umberto Eco wryly remarked: 'Since every technique connotes an ideology, if you draw the fasces with a spray-can they will inevitably acquire a vaguely underground air and a whiff of marijuana'. See 'La diga', *L'Espresso*, 20 April 1975, p. 80. The slogan 'Quando la DC è forte, la violenza è debole' (When the DC is strong, violence is weak) used in one of the posters in the spray-can series has a law-and-order message that conflicts curiously with the rebellious attitude evoked by the 'graffiti'.

57 On these elections in general see H. R. Penniman (ed.), *Italy at the Polls. The Parliamentary Elections of 1976* (Washington, DC, American Enterprise Institute for Public Policy Research, 1977).

58 The PCI obtained a relative majority in seven regions, and gained control of major cities, including Rome, Venice and Naples, which had been run by DC-led coalitions for decades.

59 On the representation of women in posters see A. Sartogo, *Le donne al muro. L'immagine femminile nel manifesto politico italiano, 1945–77* (Rome, Savelli, 1978), and E. Baeri and A. Buttafuoco, *Riguardarsi. Manifesti del movimento politico delle donne in Italia* (Siena, Protagon Editori Toscani, 1997).

60 For the main parties' views on the question of whether political campaigns should be entrusted to admen see anon., 'Onorevoli opinioni', *Stato e comunicazione*, 2:2 (1983), pp. 16–21.

61 G. Statera, *La politica spettacolo. Politici e mass media nell'era dell'immagine* (Milan, Mondadori, 1986); G. Mazzoleni, 'Emergence of the candidate and political marketing.

Television and election campaigns in Italy in the 1980s', *Political Communication and Persuasion*, 8:4 (1991), pp. 201–12.

62 Leaders had hitherto rarely been represented on posters. The fear of evoking the ghost of Mussolini largely accounts for the parties' reluctance to celebrate them as charismatic figures. Another reason is that the presence on the political scene of so many parties (and, within some parties – especially the DC – of factions), and the ensuing need to mediate and compromise in order to form electoral pacts, discouraged the promotion of individual personalities, since imbalances in their exposure would have put the alliances at risk. See T. De Mauro's preface to R-G. Schwartzenberg, *Lo stato spettacolo. Carter, Breznev, Giscard d'Estaing: attori e pubblico nel gran teatro della politica mondiale* (Rome, Editori Riuniti, 1980), pp. vii–xvii, and G. Pasquino, 'Alto sgradimento: la comunicazione politica dei partiti', *Problemi dell'informazione*, 13:4 (1988), pp. 487–9. A party which had no qualms about exalting its leader was the MSI. Traditionally a believer in the cult of charismatic leadership, since the 1970s it had featured Almirante on its printed publicity, at times depicting him addressing a huge audience from a raised platform to evoke one of the canonical images of Fascism: that of the Duce haranguing a *folla oceanica* (sea of faces). Another party was the PRI: Ugo La Malfa was frequently represented in posters in the 1970s. The fact that he had been a 'technocrat' seems to have rendered his 'cult of personality' more acceptable.

63 On the PSI campaign of 1983 see Various authors, *Le immagini del Socialismo*, pp. 540–4.

64 This was based on Antonio Gramsci's aphorism 'Optimism of the will and pessimism of the reason'.

65 On the significance the close-up portrait in propaganda see P. Fresnault-Deruelle, 'Têtes d'affiche', in *id.*, *Les Images prises au mot. Rhétoriques de l'image fixe* (Paris, Médiathèque-Edilig, 1989), pp. 181–95.

66 See K. Melder, *Hail to the Candidate. Presidential Campaigns from Banners to Broadcasts* (Washington, DC, and New York, Smithsonian Institution Press, 1992), and G. Yanker, *Prop Art. Over 1000 Contemporary Political Posters* (London, Studio Vista, 1972), which affords a useful comparison between the American way of representing candidates and the approaches followed elsewhere.

67 M. Chierici, 'Li trucco e li vendo', *Panorama*, 9 November 1986, pp. 222–8.

68 See anon., 'Hanno vinto le sottilette Kraft', *Stato e Comunicazione*, June 1984, pp. 28–30. The propaganda of the local elections of 1985 was also entrusted to Filmedia, and similarly approached (Figure 55). See M. Mucillo, 'Il nuovo look comunista. C'era una volta la falce e martello', *La Repubblica*, 1 March 1985.

69 For an analysis of this election see P. Corbetta and R. Leonardi (eds), *Italian Politics. A Review*, vol. II (London, Pinter, 1987), chapters 4–6.

70 On this and later campaigns devised by Séguéla for Mitterrand see J. Séguéla, *La Parole de Dieu. Quatorze ans de communication mitterrandienne* (Paris, Albin Michel, 1995). Like Séguéla's agency, RSCG had made a name for itself with a number of striking commercial advertising campaigns, such as those for Slip Eminence and Amaro Ramazzotti. On Mignani and his DC campaign see R. A. Prevost, *I creativi italiani* (Milan, Lupetti, 1987), pp. 86–92, and D. M. Masi and F. Maffioli, *Come 'vendere' un partito* (Milan, Lupetti, 1989), pp. 73–92.

71 On Craxi's image during his period as Prime Minister (1983–87) see G. Statera, *Il caso Craxi. Immagine di un Presidente* (Milan, Mondadori, 1987).

72 See L. Cheles, 'The Italian Far Right. Nationalist Attitudes and Views on Ethnicity and Immigration', in A. G. Hargreaves and J. Leaman, *Racism, Ethnicity and Politics in Contemporary Europe* (Aldershot, Edward Elgar, 1995), pp. 159–75.

73 On the 1987 campaign in general see: C. Incerti, 'Video, dunque voto', *Panorama*, 17 May 1987, pp. 218–23; N. Prevost, 'Vincitori e vinti', *Comunicare*, July–August 1987, pp. 15–21.

74 This turning point was noticed by the left-wing press. See, for instance, G. Moltedo, 'Occhetto a Firenze', *Il Manifesto*, 17 September 1988.

75 On this referendum and its implications see P. McCarthy, 'The Referendum of 9 June', in S. Hellman and G. Pasquino (eds), *Italian Politics. A Review*, vol. 7 (London, Pinter, 1992), pp. 11–28.

76 Previously, prospective deputies standing for the same party in a given constituency also seemed to vie with one another for preferences. In actual fact they formed pacts among themselves: the area each person had to cover during campaigning was agreed in advance, and the resources available were pooled. See S. Brusa Delli, 'E se vince Paperone?' *Panorama*, 22 March 1992, pp. 54–8.

77 G. Pansa, 'Ma lo daresti il voto a un profilattico?', *L'Espresso*, 5 April 1997, pp. 21–3.

78 The comments that follow concerning the elections of 1992, 1994 and 1996 are based on the posters I saw mainly in Emilia-Romagna and Tuscany.

79 Such developments interestingly echo in part the evolution of the Renaissance portrait. Peter Burke has convincingly argued that the democratisation of this pictorial genre (by the early sixteenth century even tailors and craftsmen were commissioning portraits of themselves) led to the members of the upper classes having themselves depicted in the grand manner in order to stand out from the hoi polloi. Theatrical postures, eloquent gestures and such prestige items as books, clocks and statues became standard features of their portraits. See P. Burke, 'The Presentation of Self in the Renaissance Portrait', in *The Historical Anthropology of Early Modern Italy* (Cambridge University Press, 1987), pp. 150–67.

80 On the political-figure-before-a-landscape genre see: F. Cachin, 'Le paysage du peintre', in P. Nora (ed.), *Les Lieux de mémoire*, vol. I, *La Nation* (Paris, Gallimard, 1997), pp. 957–96; P. Fresnault-Deruelle, 'Le visage et le paysage. Quelques réflexions sur l'image de François Mitterrand en 1981', in *Les Images prises au mot*, pp. 159–70.

81 See J. Spicer, 'The Renaissance Elbow', in J. Bremmer and H. Roodenburg (eds), *A Cultural History of Gesture* (Cambridge, Polity Press, 1991), pp. 84–128.

82 Roman emperors were at times represented with an index finger pointing. A well-known example is the so-called 'Prima Porta Augustus' (Vatican Museums), which Cristofori's portrait may well have wanted to evoke. On the pointing gesture see L. Cheles, 'Tipologia dei ritratti nella fascia inferiore del Ciclo dei Mesi di Palazzo Schifanoia', in A. Gentili, P. Morel and C. Cieri Via (eds), *Il ritratto e la memoria, 2* (Rome, Bulzoni, 1992), p. 82.

83 G. Mazzoleni, 'Quando la pubblicità elettorale non serve', *Polis*, 6:2 (1992), pp. 291–304.

84 On the Lega posters see S. Piazzo and C. Malaguti, *La Lega Nord attraverso i manifesti* (Milan, Editoriale Nord, 1996). The cartoons recall those of the Uomo Qualunque party, with which the Lega has some affinities: a distrust of traditional parties and of politicians, an anti-fiscal stance, and a 'commonsensical', populist attitude. On the language of the Lega see especially P. Desideri, 'L'italiano della Lega', *Italiano e oltre*, 8 (1993), pp. 281–5; 9 (1994), pp. 22–8.

85 Piazzo and Malaguti, *La Lega Nord*, pp. 94–5.

86 See, for instance: A. Lyttelton, 'Italy. The Triumph of TV', *New York Review of Books*, 11 August 1994, pp. 25–9; M. Morcellini (ed.), *Elezioni di TV. Televisione e pubblico nella campagna elettorale '94* (Genoa, Costa & Nolan, 1995); M. Livolsi and U. Volli (eds), *La comunicazione politica tra la Prima e Seconda Repubblica* (Milan, Franco Angeli, 1995).

87 For a full survey of the party and coalition logos see C. Branzaglia and G. Sinni (eds), *Partiti. Guida alla grafica politica della Seconda Repubblica* (Florence, Tosca, 1994). The symbol of the Progressisti combined nationalism with internationalism: it consisted of two brushstrokes, one red and one green – the red one thicker and above the other – against a white background so as to evoke the tricolour.

88 A law passed in January 1998 making it compulsory for public buildings (town halls, schools, etc.) to display the Italian flag was also a response to the Lega's attempts to undermine national unity, and provides further evidence that patriotism is no longer exclusively associated with the far right. To pre-empt any possible ultra-nationalist sentiment, this law requires that the flag of the European Union be displayed alongside the tricolour.

89 See P. McCarthy, 'The Languages of Politics', chapter 11 in this volume, p. 200.

90 See L. Lo Verso and I. McLean, 'The Italian General Election of 1994', *Electoral Studies*, 14:1 (1995), pp. 81–6.

91 See C. Chiappelli, M. Rodriguez and L. Paganelli, *Il libro delle elezioni* (Rome, PDS, 1994), section 4.1.

92 It should be noted that a number of posters from the same party would be displayed on the same hoarding: those of the various candidates contesting the seats allocated on a proportional basis in the Chamber of Deputies; that of the candidate seeking to win the Chamber of Deputies seat attributed on the basis of the first-past-the-post system; finally, that of the candidate standing for election to the Senate following a part-majoritarian and part-proportionate system. Even when candidates were supported by a party alliance rather than a single party (as was the case with all those who contested the single seats in the lower Chamber, and some of those who sought election to the Senate), their specific party affiliation was usually made clear.

93 On the symbolism of right and left in Western culture see *Sfera*, 12 (1990), special issue entitled *Destra e Sinistra*.

94 S. Gundle, 'Il sorriso di Berlusconi', *Altrochemestre*, 3 (1995), pp. 14–17. That Berlusconi should have been represented in the posters as *primus inter pares* is surprising, given that throughout the campaign he assumed a 'presidential' stance. See C. Freccero, 'Il presidente virtuale', *Micromega*, March–April 1994, pp. 134–7.

95 F. Rigotti, *Metafore della politica* (Bologna, Il Mulino, 1989), chapter III, 'Metafore spaziali di alto e basso'. Great leaders, e.g. Mao and Mitterrand, were often depicted against a vast expanse of sky.

96 On the theme of the politician in shirtsleeves see P. Fresnault-Deruelle, 'Des hommes politiques en bras de chemise', in *Les Images prises au mot*, pp. 171–80.

97 During the 1995 local election campaign the young stewards who ensured the smooth running of Fini's rallies wore white T-shirts with the words 'Servizio d'ordine' printed in small black letters as a uniform.

98 The triumphal launch of Alessandra Mussolini, the Duce's granddaughter, in 1992 was tantamount to a proclamation of the party's allegiance to Fascism.

99 The Fascist salute featured in disguised form in other AN posters. See Cheles, '"Nostalgia dell'avvenire"', pp. 80, 82, figs 43, 44.

100 The PMLI has issued a number of such 'syncretistic' posters in past years. On the propaganda of revolutionary China see S. L. Landesberger, *Chinese Propaganda Posters. From Revolution to Modernization* (Armonk, NY, Sharpe, 1995).

101 For useful concise accounts of these elections see A. Stille, 'Italy. The Convulsions of Normalcy', *New York Review of Books*, 6 June 1996, pp. 42–6, and S. Warner and F. Varese, 'The Italian General Election of 1996', *Electoral Studies*, 15:4 (1996), pp. 562–9.

102 There is no study of official representations of Italian statesmen. For some useful insights into the iconography of the genre with reference to France see P. Fresnault-Deruelle, 'Les portraits officiels des Présidents de la République', in *Les Images prises au mot*, pp. 143–57.

103 See N. M. Henley, *Body Politics. Power, Sex and Non-verbal Communication* (New York, Simon & Schuster, 1986), p. 127.

104 During the campaign Prodi's chubby face was much lampooned by AN. The Bologna candidate Filippo Berselli printed 30,000 leaflets on thick *delicatessen* shop wrapping paper featuring a slice of *mortadella* with a portrait of the Ulivo leader on it. Slices of *mortadella* were also to be distributed in Bologna town centre as a stunt; the idea was resisted at the last moment. It should be noted that a decree law passed shortly before the election campaign forbade all negative propaganda.

105 Prodi was advised by a group of semiologists and sociologists from the Department of Communication at Bologna University, who also monitored every stage of his campaign. See: R. Di Rienzo, 'Vado in diretta, faccio una cassetta . . .', *L'Espresso*, 17 February 1995, pp. 49–50; m.s. [*sic*], 'Caro Prodi, non imitare Occhetto', *La Repubblica*, 12 February 1995, p. 7. For first-hand information on the 'philosophy' behind Prodi's campaign see the manual produced by the Ulivo for distribution to its campaigners: O. Calabrese, M. Rafaiani and L. Sacchetti (eds), *Orientamenti di comunicazione politica* (Bologna, Grafiche Damiani, 1996). For an insider's account of the campaign see R. Grandi, *Prodi. Una campagna lunga un anno* (Milan, Lupetti, 1996). Andrea Rauch was eminently suited to design the printed publicity of Prodi's glamour-free, 'honest' campaign, having throughout his

career worked exclusively for humanitarian and cultural organisations. On his work see: F. Taborda, 'Studio Graphiti', *Novum Gebrauchsgraphik*, 61:11 (1990), pp. 10–17; various authors, *Quattro stelle. Graphic Design in Europa* (Milan, Electa, 1993), pp. 34–49.

106 The poster here reproduced was photographed in the Piazza Trento e Trieste in Ferrara. Of the many posters displayed on the boards, it was virtually the only one to have been substantially defaced. The 'horns' daubed on Casini's head with the spray can, and the sticker of the Partito Popolare Italiano (the left wing of the old Christian Democrat party) glued on his left eye, monocle-fashion, vilify and ridicule him, implicitly warning passers-by not to be taken in by the candidate's handsome features.

107 Henley, *Body Politics*, p. 127. That the folded arms evoke an uncompromising attitude is confirmed by the Italian phrase 'incrociare le braccia', meaning metaphorically 'to go on strike'.

108 As well as the illustrations referred to, see GEC (Enrico Gianeri), *Il Cesare di cartapesta. Mussolini nella caricatura* (Turin, Edizioni Veca, 1945, 2nd edn), pp. 135, 150, 242, 271, 285, 288, and U. Silva, *Ideologia e arte del Fascismo* (Milan Mazzotta, 1973), figs 115–16.

109 On the use of posters and billboards during the election campaign of 2001 see Anon., 'That's Italian poster politics, signori', *The Economist*, 3 February 2001, p. 38. It is worth remarking that even in a country like Britain where propaganda, especially since Margaret Thatcher's 1979 campaign, is approached in a sophisticated high-tech fashion, the printed image for public display plays no small part in political campaigning. Small posters showing the likeness of election candidates (or simply their names) are sellotaped by supporters on window panes so as to be seen by passers-by, while billboards featuring striking images and/or slogans usually attacking political opponents are strategically placed in public sites. These hoardings, large enough to be seen from a passing car, actually enjoy a 'double life': they are usually unveiled officially by party leaders or other prominent politicians in the presence of journalists, so as to benefit from media exposure as well. It should be noted that the Conservative and Labour Parties' expenditure on poster advertising increased dramatically in the 1990s – a sign of their strong belief in the power of this medium. See anon., 'Tories' Writing is on the Wall', *The Independent*, Media supplement, 3 March 1997.

10

Advertising politics on television: the party election broadcast

Isabella Pezzini

Politics and television broadcasts: an odd couple?

If television commercials have now established themselves as a sparkling genre, the same cannot be said of party election broadcasts (*spot elettorali*), which aspire to be treated very seriously. Propaganda, traditionally associated with suspect insincerity, arouses caution and distrust. The opacity of a politician's discourse is regarded as potentially more dangerous than that of a salesman: an inducement to buy something and inducements to vote in a particular way are not perceived to be manipulations of the same order, despite the fact that, as will be shown later, the use of marketing techniques is now commonplace in politics, and has affected the form and content of the political message.

While in other countries election broadcasts have been a feature of campaigning for some time (in the United States they have been used since 1941), in Italy they are a relatively recent phenomenon, having first appeared in 1983. Indeed, it can be argued that political communication in Italy generally lags behind, despite the 1994 election victory of the media mogul Silvio Berlusconi, which forced practically all the parties to speed up the pace of change and think more about questions of communication and image.

The party election broadcast is an especially interesting form of communication, on account of its textual characteristics (its conciseness and linguistic syncretism foster creative expression, thus making the message highly memorable), and the mode of its output (repetition leads to recognition, familiarity and appreciation). Despite the poor quality of some election broadcasts, particularly those produced at local level, they are a significant record of the climate, events and protagonists of past electoral contests, and of political imagery intended for popular consumption. The broadcasts have been much debated in Italy of late: the focus of the concern has been the conditions of equal access to the media by the various parties. Though research into the impact of the media on voting behaviour has been careful not to rush to any conclusions, some would argue that a good communication and image strategy alone can deliver election victories. Paul Virilio, for instance, has interpreted

Berlusconi's 1994 election victory as a prime example of a '*coup d'état* by the media'.[1]

This chapter will analyse some election broadcasts in chronological order, and consider the main studies that have appeared on the subject. These *spot elettorali* will be examined as texts, with a focus on their internal make-up as communicative artefacts – an approach based on a semiotic 'archaeology of meaning'.

Italian politics on television

The use of party election broadcasts must be considered in the light of the new role played by the media in political communication. The earliest television programmes devoted to politics were the *Tribune politiche*. These were sessions where leading politicians were interviewed by journalists from a range of newspapers, and first took place during the four weeks preceding the local elections of 6–7 November 1960. The *Tribune* were jargon-ridden, but disciplined by a fairly strict system of turn taking and air time.[2] These rules, the outcome of an agreement between the political parties that had become increasingly aware of the propaganda potential of television (then still a state monopoly), had been codified by the parliamentary broadcasting watchdog, the Commissione parlamentare di vigilanza delle Radiodiffusioni.[3]

By the 1970s the format of the *Tribune* had come to be perceived as too rigid. It could not withstand such political upheavals as the students' and workers' unrest, the civil rights protest movement, terrorism and the economic recession. The programmes' run ended symbolically in 1979 with the sight of a gagged Marco Pannella, leader of the Partito Radicale, in front of the television cameras – an act of protest against the unequal treatment doled out to the smaller political groupings by the public information services. This was a turning point in political communication: it marked the beginning in Italy of the spectacularisation of politics.[4]

A significant event of the 1970s was the campaign for the referendum on divorce (1974). Though fought mostly in the press rather than on television, it demonstrated that it was possible to move political debate to the media arena – a phenomenon that was summed up by Carlo Marletti as the 'transformation of the media into a political party'.[5] Persistent criticism of the state's television monopoly led to the reform of the RAI, the national broadcasting corporation, in 1975.[6]

The period 1979–81 was characterised politically by three main events: the first European elections (1979), local elections (1980–81) and the referendum on abortion (1981). Commercial television stations, though still organised on a small-scale and semi-professional basis, had started to spring up and would later contribute to the far-reaching changes in the use of television for election purposes – an impetus to change which would force even the RAI to introduce new formulas for political coverage, within a poorly organised regulatory framework. Gradually personalisation, secularisation, spectacularisation and the use of marketing techniques took over political communication, in the wake of the American and European experience.[7]

Turning a political leader into a Hollywood-style star is no easy matter; yet the task of the new spin doctors, the political communication consultants who were called to identify and play up the 'saleable qualities' of the individual candidates, was precisely to transform politicians into celebrities. In 1980 a mere 1·5 billion lire (£750,000 at the exchange rate of the day) were spent on campaign publicity. The time was ripe for the use of advertisement-like political broadcasts. These *spot elettorali* made their début in the 1983 general election campaign.

The 1983 parliamentary elections saw the development of new trends in political communication. The image of the leader became more important than that of the party. The pool of the so-called 'opinion vote' increased, and aspects of political communication which had earlier been perceived as of lesser importance were given more weight and subjected to 'adjustment' by the needs of television.

The communication strategy of the parties was gradually forced to shift its focus from general political issues to the so-called 'policy issues', which had a more direct impact on the daily lives of the voters. The very methods of communication also changed dramatically. In the words of Gianpietro Mazzoleni:

> Speeches at public rallies were supplanted by interviews in the television studios (where non-politicians called the shots); posters were replaced by billboards; and leafleting by party activists gave way to mail-shots of newsletters and brochures sent to a public targeted by computer-aided marketing consultants. The result was not a simple updating of methods but a radical alteration of political communication itself, which relinquished its informative and persuasive character to become a form of entertainment and fiction, where the things that mattered most were gimmicks and image-making.[8]

The content also changed: politics ceased to be an 'abstract good' and became a 'material good', whereas advertising had always sought to endow consumer goods with 'mythical' qualities. This paradox merely emphasised the similarity between the two camps.

Party election broadcasts are, in advertising terms, features of the marketing campaign rather than of the creation of a brand image. They constitute an advertising investment which is almost entirely pinned to a desired election outcome; their purpose is to 'sell' the product (win votes). Yet they could also be used as an effective instrument of communication with the electorate during non-election periods. This would make it possible to maintain an ongoing relationship with the voters and to plan a longer-term strategy – one not exclusively dictated by electoral necessities.[9] It is likely that what may appear to be a lack of awareness concerning the need to inform the public may in actual fact be a deeply held belief on the part of some politicians that they can rely on other, more effective, vehicles of communication: namely the 'real' centres of power and their personal contact networks, through which they can exert influence and control. In the case of the parties of the left, ideological reasons lie behind their reluctance to use the media.[10]

Party election broadcasts make their debut, 1983

The 1983 elections, called early because of a crisis provoked by the Socialist Party (PSI), were important for political communication, for a variety of reasons. To start with, the mix of a partly public and partly private broadcasting system was by then well established, and made it seem possible that the traditional political discourse would be juxtaposed with a new media discourse. Private-sector television companies were still not permitted to make live broadcasts, so information in the narrow sense remained largely a monopoly of the RAI and monitored by the parliamentary watchdog. The commercial television companies did, however, contribute to the campaign with programmes featuring discussions, speeches, interviews, etc. They also sold advertising time to political parties.[11]

In their programmes the private-sector networks encouraged debate on concrete issues, and thus increased contact between politicians and the viewing public, and began to undermine the abstract and woolly political jargon which was incomprehensible to most people.

The data gathered by Mazzoleni on this two-month electoral campaign are as follows: the RAI provided 1,645 minutes of air time at no cost to the parties. In addition to that figure 1,860 minutes were provided by the private-sector operators. In terms of the traditional advertising media, there were 1,023 *spot elettorali* on national RAI channels, as well as 6,149 advertisements in daily newspapers and 157 in magazines. The overall costs allegedly amounted to 10 billion lire (£4,760,000); the actual figure is likely to have been much greater.[12] The sum of 2·5 billion lire (£1,200,000) was spent on election broadcasts alone, the principal novelty of the campaign.

Altogether, thirty-nine *spot elettorali* were shown nation-wide. The breakdown was as follows: Christian Democrats (DC), seven; Communists (PCI), six; Socialists (PSI), twelve; Republicans (PRI), seven; Social Democrats (PSDI), six; and Liberals (PLI), one. There was none at national level on behalf of the Partito Radicale, the far-left Democrazia Proletaria (DP), the Partito Nazionale dei Pensionati (National Pensioners' Party), or the Movimento Sociale Italiano (MSI). The *spot elettorali* of 1983 used different and clearly identifiable approaches. Those of the three major parties are worth examining here.

The DC opted for short broadcasts in the suspense-film mould. They depicted scenes of imminent small catastrophes, averted at the last minute, and had a voice-over to interpret the action: 'Fortunately Italy has a party that safeguards your security.' They closed with an incisive slogan uttered first by a male voice and then repeated by a female voice: 'Decidi DC!' (Decide DC!). The PCI, too, went for dramatic fiction. A series of disturbing scenes sought to exemplify the DC's misdeeds. They were accompanied by a voice-over of facts and figures on the issues raised: 'The DC has failed. There is an alternative. Vote Communist.' The PSI, in its series of election broadcasts entitled *L'ottimismo della volontà* (Optimism of the Will), featured Bettino Craxi, other leading party figures, as well as endorsements by celebrities from the worlds of entertainment, sport and business.

Paolo Mancini in 1984 examined the *spot elettorali* shown at national level on the basis of three content or structural variables: the themes dealt with, the presence or absence of film-clips, and the presence or absence of references to political opponents.[13] With regard to the themes dealt with, Mancini did not find significant differences between the parties (though only the PCI broached the subject of the Mafia). He noted a widespread disinclination to discuss programmes and concrete issues. There were two exceptions: the PSI (which did deal with them to some degree) and the PCI (which supplied factual information capable of swinging voting behaviour). The DC, on the other hand, exploiting its traditional image as a party transcending specific political issues, concentrated on emotive themes, such as security, continuity and clarity.[14] As for the visual structure of the *spot elettorali*, namely their exclusive or concomitant use of film clips and images of people, the parties showed clear-cut preferences: the DC and the PCI made extensive use of film clips, while the PSI favoured images of individuals.

The narrative structures of the various election broadcasts were, on the whole, quite elementary, and exploited conflict. The PCI had a sole 'enemy' – the DC, which had 'reneged' on its election promises. The DC, on the other hand, relied on an element of suspense to cast itself as a rescuer who would save Italy from the dangers to which she could fall prey – an approach often used in the propaganda of the Cold War years.[15] Political communication should concentrate on outlining future perspectives; Mancini found, however, that in these broadcasts the focus was on the need to overcome the then current situation, which was depicted as dire.[16]

Certain traditional motifs, such as the Communist menace, the 'bosses' and the working class, did not figure in the campaign (although they reappeared in 1994). In 1983 the political contest concentrated on ways of communicating the message rather than on specific themes or programmes. In other words, from the beginning, the party election broadcasts were approached as a form of glamorous entertainment. This went hand in hand with the process of 'personalisation', that is to say, with the promotion of individual candidates or leaders to whom were attributed the 'celebrity qualities' required for media attention, to the detriment of purely ideological and political considerations, which had hitherto been at the core of campaigns.

The 1987 election campaign

Early elections were also called in 1987, brusquely ending the second government led by Craxi. Overall, this was a television campaign,[17] even though the media were still a long way from being a voice independent of government. In this campaign individual personalities played a dominant role, as seen in the clashes between Craxi and the DC leader, Ciriaco De Mita. This polarisation of personalities was not entirely reflected in the parties' propaganda output. The PSI exploited the image of its leader, but the DC made the tactical decision not to be drawn into the fray and devised the non-issue-specific slogan 'Forza Italia! Fai vincere le cose che contano' (Come on Italy! Put what counts on the winning side).

As far as television was concerned, 1987 signalled the high point of an explicit carving up of the broadcasting 'cake' between the parties: the DC was given virtual control of the RAI 1 channel, the PSI of RAI 2 and the PCI of RAI 3. This was also the year that *Samarcanda*, a RAI 3 chat show presented by Michele Santoro, was broadcast, quickly becoming one of the most popular current affairs programmes.

Above all, however, 1987 is noteworthy because it was the first year of real participation by private-sector television in the election campaign. The RAI's involvement was strictly regulated in terms of what could be shown (debates, press conferences, programmes made by parties themselves, final appeals, etc.) and the format of programmes (for political debates the ritualistic formula of question–answer–rebuttal between journalists and politicians was observed; speaking time was closely monitored; there were no direct confrontations between political opponents; and there was no direct intervention by the public). The entire programme schedule was reviewed for the campaign and purged of anything that could have been perceived as implicit propaganda. Political programmes were shown during prime-time hours, and paid political advertising was prohibited.

The private-sector networks showed programmes created specifically for the campaign, such as *Elettorando* (About the Election), *Voti e volti* (Votes and Faces) and *Faccia a faccia* (Face to Face), as well as their usual current affairs programmes, such as *Dovere di cronaca* (Duty to Report), *Parlamento in* (In Parliament) and *TV tv*, with contributions from some of Italy's best-known journalists (e.g. Giorgio Bocca, Mino Damato, Gianni Letta, Arrigo Levi and Vittorio Zucconi).

Though the dominant model remained that established by the RAI's *Tribune politiche*, commercial television, not boxed in by official regulation, had a freer hand: the candidates were presented as individuals rather than as party representatives, and reference was often made to their private lives. Moreover the questions were more direct, sometimes provocative and teasing, and debates were open to the general public as well as to the usual 'delegates' (journalists, moderators and experts).[18] The private-sector networks made full use of their prerogative of broadcasting paid political advertising. They invested considerable effort in election broadcasts and experimented with new communicative styles and strategies.[19]

The duel between the DC and the PSI, fought out in a campaign which was obviously very expensive for both, is best illustrated by the different approaches of their *spot elettorali*. The DC entrusted its propaganda to Marco Mignani, one of Italy's top admen, who came up with a very polished and emotive campaign modelled on commercial advertising. Its key slogan was 'Forza Italia!' (Come on, Italy!), which Berlusconi adopted six years later as the name of his own political party. The campaign essentially consisted of one *spot elettorale* produced in half a dozen slightly different versions, following a 'mythologising' micro-narrative model. A peasant opens the door of an outbuilding, and instantly transforms the darkness into a bright rural landscape. From this point a series of micro-stories begins. Their segments were spliced in a variety of ways, and depicted life punctuated by heart-stirring images (a marriage, a child's birthday, grandparents). At the core of the stories was identification between personal and collective values, a synthesis that can be expressed by the equation of DC = Italy = You. These 'back to basics' images, overflowing with mawkish sentiment, were highlighted by the music of Ennio Morricone and a choral song: 'For a smile, for freedom, for love and a great future, for an untroubled life . . . homes, jobs and the future of your children! Come on, Italy! Come on, Italy! Come on, Italy!' At the end of the choral outpouring a mellow voice familiar from films dubbed into Italian declaimed: 'Put what counts on the winning side. Vote DC!'

The PSI's strategy was just the opposite. It favoured a structured argument centred on the gains (progress, modernity, stability) achieved by the outgoing PSI-led government and the danger of losing them if the PSI was not re-elected to power. The main series of *spot elettorali* was dominated by the image of the party leader. With all the prestige associated with being the incumbent Prime Minister, Craxi was repeatedly interviewed by Gianni Minoli, a well-known RAI journalist. (The RAI, as noted earlier, did not transmit paid political advertising and was at pains to avoid any obvious association between its own journalists and politicians, at least during election time.) No expense was spared in making these interviews. The venue varied according to the topic under discussion, and ranged from a factory (for employment and economic development) to a supermarket (for consumer prices and inflation). The interviews were structured in two parts: first a few questions (or, more accurately, opportunities for soundbites) and answers, followed by a few, sometimes amusing, comments on the carnation, the PSI's new symbol. This was an openly 'seductive' conclusion chosen to offset the core political argument.

The PCI's main slogan was: 'C'è un'altra possibilità . . .' (There is an alternative . . .). One election broadcast depicted, in succession and with a suitable sound track, a flower-filled meadow, work going on in a factory and, finally, the serene, slightly enigmatic face of a graceful and ordinary young woman, suddenly shown to be surrounded by other women. The voice-over then affirmed: '. . . let's eliminate pollution, not the environment. There is an alternative: let's create more jobs, not just profits. The PCI: a party removed from intrigue and in close touch with the voters.' The script avoided a narrative style and personalisation, and criticised the *status quo* only in very general terms, without identifying specific political opponents.

The 1992 election campaign[20]

During the campaign of 1992 there was an increase in the use of *spot elettorali* by comparison with the 1987 campaign. This was also the result of the so-called 'Mammì law' of 1990 (put forward by the then Minister of Posts and Telecommunications, the Republican Oscar Mammì), which had fully legitimised private-sector television companies, authorising them to broadcast live programmes and provide comprehensive information.

Well-known journalists, such as Maurizio Costanzo, who presented *Elettorando* on Canale 5, revolutionised the way politics were discussed. Their programmes were centred entirely on individual candidates, who were now treated with greater familiarity, while being forced to respect the time allotted and to accept interruptions for commercial breaks. This was in part the outcome of the new electoral rules, especially the introduction of the single-preference vote for seats in the Chamber of Deputies,[21] which also had the effect of reducing the number of party election broadcasts shown at national level and of increasing the number at local level. The data available mostly concern nation-wide broadcasts: DC, two; PSI, three; Partito

Democratico della Sinistra (PDS), seven; Partito Social-Democratico, three; Partito Liberale, one; Lega Lombarda, two; Rifondazione Comunista, two; Federalismo Pensionati Uomini Vivi (Live Pensioners for Federalism – one of several, ephemeral local parties), seven; Lista Sì Referendum (another short-lived party), one; MSI, two.[22]

With unintentional foresight of the storm that the *Mani Pulite* (Clean Hands) or *Tangentopoli* (Bribesville) investigations would unleash on politics and the business world, all the *spot elettorali* except those of the DC praised the virtues of change. The basic themes remained those which represented the differences between the parties, but little attention was paid to proposals and programmes. The process of personalisation carried on apace. This strategy was pursued by the PSI (Craxi was a central figure in almost half the party's electoral broadcasts), the Partito Social-Democratico, the Partito Repubblicano, the Lista Sí Referendum, the Federalismo Pensionati and by the Lega Lombarda, whose leader, Umberto Bossi, vaunted the image of an 'unpolished' man of the people. The Lega Lombarda and the PDS were the only parties which dealt with specific issues. In general, parties went for the conative, aesthetic or emotive approach. The propaganda of the DC especially, with its strongly anti-Lega Lombarda and family-centred discourse, epitomised this approach. Compared with previous elections, less use was made of techniques which equated parties with consumer goods (for example, through the association between party symbols and attractive imagery), and greater emphasis was placed on argumentation; the latter was, however, of a somewhat Manichaean nature. Overall, the communicative approaches were more concrete: the language of advertising gave way to the language used for televised information. Many of the images featured in election broadcasts were recycled in posters and press advertising, and segments from their sound tracks were used on the radio. This multimedia approach was another sign of the parties' increased professionalism and media awareness.

The 1994 elections and Silvio Berlusconi

The 1994 elections were a turning point: they marked the transition from the First to the Second Republic. The country had been set ablaze by the *Tangentopoli* scandals, and a radical redrawing of the Italian political map ensued, which affected even the parties that survived. The following political alliances were formed:

1. The Progressisti, made up of the PDS, Rifondazione Comunista, La Rete (The Network: an anti-Mafia party of the South), Alleanza Democratica (AD, formed by left-wing intellectuals), the Cristiano-Sociali (ex-DC left-wingers), the Verdi (Greens) and the PSI.
2. The centre, consisting of the Partito Popolare Italiano (PPI: born from the centrist faction of the old DC) and the Patto Segni (a grouping built around the maverick Mario Segni).
3. The centre-right, whose electoral cartel was represented by two sub-alliances; the Polo delle Libertà (Pole for Freedoms) in the North, made up of Forza Italia, Lega Nord, Centro Cristiano Democratico (CCD, formed from the right wing

of the old DC), Unione di Centro (ex-Liberals); and the Polo del Buongoverno (Pole of Good Government) in the South, represented by Forza Italia, Alleanza Nazionale (AN), Centro Cristiano Democratico and Unione di Centro.

These were also the first parliamentary elections to be conducted on the new, mainly majoritarian system, which had partly been put to the test in the mayoral elections of 1993.[23] This system accelerated the processes of polarisation, personalisation and spectacularisation of politics.

The electoral campaign was dominated by television: never before had public and private-sector television played so major a part in the political contest.[24] This brought with it the serious problem of unequal access to the airwaves for all the political contenders, despite the newly approved legislation intended to guarantee a level playing field.[25] No network or television programme escaped the accusation of bias. In this unprecedented situation, politicians (many of whom were newcomers) and television presenters found themselves having to use professional techniques of communication, and to invent new forms of debate and public participation.

Berlusconi made much use of the expertise of communication and marketing professionals well before the campaign started. He relied heavily on market surveys to mould his new political movement.[26] Opinion polls also played a central role in his strategy. This tool, which had never before been used to such an extent, produced its own celebrities, but, more importantly, it enabled Berlusconi to fine-tune his campaign while it was in progress.

With regard to the *spot elettorali*, those of Forza Italia in particular followed the dictates of electoral marketing and figured within a coherent strategy. In an Italian context, characterised by dilettantism and distrust or – at the other extreme – by unrealistic expectations of the impact of political advertising on voting behaviour, Berlusconi's party election broadcasts seemed the height of perfection. One might even say that the credibility he was seeking through the imagery he used was not grounded in reality but was more akin to that of the fiction serials, soap operas and game shows that had been the daily fare of his television channels for years.

The breakdown of the number of *spot elettorali* shown during the campaign is as follows: Progressisti, one; Rifondazione Comunista, one (produced in four variants); La Rete, one; Centro Cristiano Democratico, one; Lega Nord, two (one of these, entitled 'What the Lega has Achieved', had several variants); Lista Pannella/Riformatori (a small, independent grouping built around the charismatic Marco Pannella), two (one, solely on behalf of the Lista Pannella, was produced in several versions); Forza Italia, seven in the 'Club Forza Italia' series (these clubs were local associations patterned on the football fan clubs of AC Milan, the team owned by Berlusconi) and ten featuring Berlusconi himself (one of which was made in four different versions).[27] These figures show the great disparity between the different camps: the campaign was dominated by Forza Italia virtually without competition.[28]

The new political map meant that all groupings had to make a major choice between identification and recognition. Whether new parties, older parties or alliances struck for the election under the new voting system, they all saw the need to offer voters someone or something that they could identify with. This did not necessarily mean identification with a leader. Moreover, although Forza Italia was in a position to adopt a range of approaches, the older parties had to content themselves either with a statement made by their party leaders (as did the Lista Pannella, Lega Nord and Rifondazione Comunista, for instance) or with a film clip of a more or less 'realistic' nature (Centro Cristiano Democratico, La Rete, Progressisti). When comparing the scripts of the various *spot elettorali*, it becomes clear that these constraints led the parties to avoid concrete issues and to concentrate on the past (surprisingly described in positive terms) rather than the future – the theme so wilfully pursued by Forza Italia.

A comparative analysis of the texts of the different *spot elettorali* may start from the consideration that they can be viewed as variations on a basic narrative scheme, whose core is represented by the trial. By means of this particular act, the subject acquires, conquers or loses something which he/she considers of value. Before and after the act of gaining or losing, there is room for manipulation: someone or something activates the subject's desires or sense of duty, inducing him/her to acquire a specific competence, represented in terms of modality, that is to say, of wanting to, having to, or being able to, with a view to the impending test. An opportunity for sanction is also provided: this is the space in which the subject is judged, appreciated and rewarded, or otherwise. The text of each *spot elettorale* focuses the attention on a particular aspect of the basic scheme: the acquisition, the conquest or the loss.[29]

Let us now examine the texts of some of the election broadcasts.

PROGRESSISTI

> [Sung] We're the ones, we're the fathers and sons . . . We're the ones doing the talking, 'Bella Ciao!' . . . history . . . [Spoken] Working together for Italy's rebirth. It's a tremendous challenge. Let's rise to it and win with the Progressisti.

This *spot elettorale* begins with the words of a popular song – 'La storia', sung by Francesco De Gregori – which fades into the background to make way for the brief, slogan-like spoken text. Here a collective subject is present at all levels: in the song lyric, with the use of the pronoun 'we' and references to history and the Resistance ('Bella Ciao!' is a well-known partisans' song), and in the scene of children colouring the coalition's logo (three brush strokes in red, white and green) on a piece of glass. There is no dialectical exchange between speaker and public. The text fulfils two main functions: that of inviting identification as well as exhorting people to resist when put to the test; the latter is represented as conflict that needs to be overcome, but without any indication of an enemy. The word 'challenge' (*sfida*) is an interesting choice: the challenge consists of putting a value to the test, a value that presupposes the existence of a sense of pride, an awareness of self-worth and the courage to expose these to the risk inherent in the challenge. Thus the value, attributed or presupposed, is a moral one. The scenario is that of the impending trial, and the communicative model is one of general encouragement.

LEGA NORD

> [With a picture of the Chamber of Deputies in the background, Umberto Bossi is standing with his arms held slightly behind his back.] There's an enormous amount of confusion. The old parties, the swindlers, are changing their names and passing themselves off as new, as liberals, as supporters of federalism, but it's all lies. [He points to the viewer.] Don't be taken in: vote Lega!

The style here faithfully follows the approach adopted by the party in previous election campaigns: it seeks to make an impact through its coarseness.[30] The brief spoken text tries to unmask the old parties, implying that the Lega has the authority and ability to do so. This is reinforced by Bossi's pointing finger, betokening communication on the direct and personal level of I–you. The scenario invoked in this election broadcast is the present rather than the future, thanks to the photograph of the Chamber of Deputies.

FORZA ITALIA

The two series of *spot elettorali* made by Forza Italia were similar in style and included some of the most striking features of the electoral publicity used by the DC in the 1987 campaign – especially the impassioned language.

The first series aimed to promote the formation and membership of the Club Italia, and shows the precision with which consensus on the leader was sought. The electorate was provided with an opportunity to participate and, most of all, win – as if the event in question were a competition for prizes. Three very short *spot elettorali* relied principally on graphic illustrations (apart from the closing footage of a fluttering flag and Forza Italia's signature tune in the background, which was used in all the Forza Italia election broadcasts, including those in the Berlusconi series) and the slogan: 'Per dare forza all'Italia, scendi in campo; anche nella tua città dài vita a un club Forza Italia' (To give Italy the heart to win, take part; start a Club Forza Italia in your city too!).

Three others in the same series relied mainly on film clips, recalling those used by the DC in 1987: a montage of Italian cities (Venice, Florence, etc.) alternated with images of happy people (couples, young families, members of the affluent society) and moving crowds, as well as with glimpses of glamorous, high-tech working environments (computers, factories, etc., set against dramatic sunsets). The sound tracks consisted of the party song, different segments of which were played. Its basic lyrics were as follows:

> Come on, let's get moving! The future stands before us; let's enter it! Come on, my Italy, my hand in yours. We have what it takes to be bigger, bigger! Come on, my Italy; there are so many of us who believe in it! In your history lies a new history: we'll write it together! Come on, my Italy; it's time to believe. Come on, Forza Italia! There are so many of us! And we all have fire in our hearts. Our hearts are sincere and free and beat for you. Come on, Italy: be free! Come on, Italy: you can grow! Come on, Italy: find your dream in us! Belong to your people who are reborn in you. Come on, Italy: stand with us!

The spoken commentary at the end then seeks to rouse viewers with 'Forza Italia, risveglia il tuo orgoglio' (Come on, Italy: awaken your pride).

The ten election broadcasts in the Berlusconi series, on the other hand, had a uniform and carefully worked-out make-up, particularly in their presentation of the leader. In keeping with television-style language based on serialisation and repetition, the format was varied slightly to include different themes. These were very specific and pitched at particular cross-sections of the population: small entrepreneurs, shopkeepers, the elderly, young people, women and the undecided. They employed a structure which enabled each *spot elettorale* to function as a jigsaw piece within a wider narrative. The scripts were read with great attention to elocution: their rhythm was well paced and matched to the background music. The intent was clearly aesthetic as well as communicative.

Let us consider one of these broadcasts to illustrate the kind of topic chosen to rally support. The issues of employment and taxation were dealt with by proposing 'simple' solutions, dictated by common sense and an optimistic approach.

> [The *spot elettorale* opens and closes with FI's symbol on a blue background and a catchy tune with a sing-along refrain. Berlusconi appears, his right side turned slightly to the left. He is standing in his study, and behind him, just above shoulder height, is a photograph of him with his children at the seaside, along with other knick-knacks. We later see him seated at his desk, with his hands on a bundle of papers to symbolise the 'knowledge' he acquired prior to his entry into politics. He is elegantly dressed in a dark double-breasted suit, a light-coloured shirt and a dark tie, in other words, in what is to become the Berlusconi uniform. He speaks:]
>
> To get our economy really going again we have to encourage and support the activities of small business, shopkeepers, professional people, artisans and the self-employed.
>
> [The camera moves backwards as he straightens up slightly and puts down a sheet of paper on to a pile of papers, hitherto out of view, to the right of his desk.]
>
> We have to stop penalising them by taking their incomes away, because they are the driving forces of our economy. They are the ones who create jobs for our young people. So [vote] Forza Italia for this reason, too! To get the economy going again and defeat unemployment!

It is worth remembering that when Berlusconi announced his entry into politics he recorded the speech on video, which he distributed widely.[31] His election broadcasts referred back to that speech, to create the impression that they were an integral part of it. This technique also served to strengthen his image as an authoritative figure – an image underscored by the visual element, as well as by what Berlusconi said and how he said it. Even an unsophisticated viewer could see that these *spot elettorali* were concocted as if the man, then merely a candidate, were already Prime Minister. Indeed, the inter-textual references evoked the traditional New Year's Eve address of the President of the Republic.

Berlusconi entered the fray using the strategy of 'seduction', that is to say, subtle manipulation based on the ability to persuade someone to do something without resorting to coercive methods.

The Ulivo wins without party election broadcasts, 1996

The progress of party election broadcasts in Italy came to a halt with the elections of 21 April 1996, which were won by the Ulivo (centre-left alliance) comprising Partito Popolare Italiano, Rinnovamento Italiano (Italian Renewal: a grouping founded by the outgoing caretaker Prime Minister, Lamberto Dini), Verdi and Sinistra Europea (a party consisting of some former Socialists). The Ulivo, led by Romano Prodi, defeated the Polo della Libertà headed by Berlusconi, consisting of Forza Italia, Alleanza Nazionale, Centro Cristiano Democratico and Cristiano-Democratici Uniti (CDU).

Law 515 of 10 December 1993 on electoral campaigning introduced a distinction between *pubblicità* (advertising, which was forbidden), *propaganda* (which was disciplined) and *informazione elettorale* (electoral information, which was required to be thorough and impartial). The parliamentary commissioner charged with overseeing the law's implementation (*Garante*) justified the prohibition on 'advertising' in these terms:

> The media should be prevented from being used to degrade an election, that is to say, from turning a debate on ideology or political programmes, for which moral and intellectual consensus is sought, into a battle fought with spectacular elements and captivating, often misleading, slogans in the mould of commercial advertising, whereby the voting public are treated as mere 'electoral consumers'. Far from encouraging or increasing democratic participation, such a situation demeans the intended recipients of the message.[32]

The distinction between 'advertising' and 'propaganda' was bad news for party election broadcasts, and it was difficult to apply in practice.[33] On 26 February 1996, before the start of the electoral campaign, the *Garante* announced the new rules of the *par condicio* (regulations on equal access to the media) for the period leading up to 18 March, the deadline for the submission of the lists of candidates, and for the period thereafter. Opinion polls were prohibited during the last fifteen days of the campaign, but party election broadcasts were permitted on commercial television channels, both national and local, until 21 March. Each broadcasting station was permitted to show up to two such broadcasts for any single political party. The party alliances fighting for seats under the first-past-the-post system (mainly the Ulivo and the Polo) were allowed three broadcasts; individual parties contesting under the system of proportional representation were permitted an additional one, from 18 to 21 March. The broadcasts were not to last more than forty-five seconds, and they could be shown only between 1.00–2.00 p.m. and 6.00–11.00 p.m.

In the meantime, the Ulivo announced that it would not be making any *spot elettorali*, to underline its desire to establish new forms of contact with the electorate and to avoid 'telepolitics'. The Ulivo's big electioneering idea was its campaign bus, in which Prodi travelled to 100 cities to talk to the voters.[34] In addition to the difficulties of applying the new rules on television access, the Ulivo's decision not to use *spot elettorali* was the reason why other parties did not invest in that form of communication, which Berlusconi had perfected only two years earlier.

In terms of television, the 1996 campaign will be remembered especially for the reappearance on the state-run channels of *Tribune politiche*-type programmes, as well as for the political chat shows chaired by well-known presenters during peak viewing hours.[35] Some of these chat shows invented entertaining gimmicks. *Porta a porta*, for example, introduced the candidates who were guests on the programme with suitable accompanying music (approved by the candidates themselves). Thus, for the PDS leader Massimo D'Alema, there was a piece with a catchy beat by the French band Tambours du Bronx; for Lamberto Dini, a Louis Armstrong number; for Umberto Bossi, an extract from the Carl Orff's *Carmina Burana*; for Silvio Berlusconi, pieces sung by Tina Turner and the Neapolitan singer-songwriter Pino Daniele; and for the leader of Alleanza Nazionale, Gianfranco Fini, a tune from Hugh Hudson's film *Chariots of Fire*.[36] The Ulivo, though discouraging its candidates from appearing on television, invested in other forms of communication, too: it adopted as its 'anthem' Ivano Fossati's song 'La canzone popolare', set up links on the Internet, and continued to use its campaign bus. Shortly after the election a documentary was made of the bus campaign, entitled *Viaggio in Italia* (Travels in Italy). It was sold as a video-cassette with *L'Unità*, the PDS daily.

To conclude, it may be said that the gradual 'mass-mediatisation' of Italian politics has not come to a complete stop; rather, it has created a new awareness of the importance of communication on the part of all political players. The Media situation in Italy is currently troubled by the fact that one of the two major television companies, Mediaset, is directly controlled by Silvio Berlusconi, leader of the centre-right alliance and Prime Minister-to-be at the time of writing. This conflict of interest has negatively affected the creative use of political advertising on television. The latest law on *par condicio* (February 2000), approved after laborious negotiations, has attempted to regulate political communication more effectively. It has drastically limited the opportunity to make use of *spot elettorali* and introduced a new, strictly regulated type of advertisement known as *messaggio autogestito* (self-managed message). Owing to limited visibility (off-peak viewing slots and limited broadcasts) it is proving unattractive to politicians.

NOTES

I wish to thank all those who helped me in the gathering of information and audio-visual material: Valentina Agostinis, Lucia Corrain, Romano Frassa, Marco Mignani, Maurizio Sala (Directors' Club), Michele Sorice and, especially, Paolo Mancini, the Director of the Archivio per la Comunicazione Politica of the University of Perugia. I should also like to thank the editors, Luciano Cheles and Lucio Sponza, for their helpful comments on a draft of this chapter and for their assistance.

1 P. Virilio, *Lo schermo e l'oblio* (Milan, Anabasi, 1994), p. 168.

2 In the first ten minutes the party secretary would set out his party's platform; a twenty-minute debate would then follow with journalists in the studio. See A. Grasso, *Storia della televisione italiana* (Milan, Garzanti, 2000), p. 127.

3 For a detailed description of the situation which led to access for all parties, including the opposition, to television and radio, the procedures for access and how the *Tribune politiche* were conducted, see Various authors, *Dieci anni di Tribuna Politica, 1960–70* (Rome, RAI – Radiotelevisione Italiana, 1971); E. Novelli, *Dalla television di partito al partito della televisione. Televisione e politica in Italia, 1960–95* (Florence, La Nuova Italia, 1995), pp. 1–35.

4 G. Statera, *La politica spettacolo. Politici e mass media nell'era dell'immagine* (Milan, Mondadori, 1986).

5 C. Marletti, *Media e politica* (Milan, Franco Angeli, 1984). Also worthy of note in this context is the approval on 2 May 1974 of law 195 on the public funding of political parties, which substantially increased the parties' resources.

6 Law 103, passed on 14 April 1975, had three main strands: it stated that only the RAI had the right to broadcast programmes at national level; it recognised local needs (hence the eventual launch of the regional channel of RAI 3, and the granting of permission to set up cable television networks where the number of potential subscribers was at least 150,000); and it authorised the relaying of foreign television programmes. These revolutionary provisions were intended to meet the demands of political parties and viewers alike. See: F. Monteleone, *Storia della radio e della televisione in Italia* (Venice, Marsilio, 1999), 2nd edn, p. 389.

7 In France the symbolic culmination of this new mode of campaigning occurred during François Mitterrand's successful presidential campaign (1981) with the felicitous oxymoron of *La force tranquille* (the quiet force), created by Jacques Séguéla, one of the gurus of contemporary advertising philosophy. See J. Séguéla, *Hollywood lave plus blanc* (Paris, Flammarion, 1983); *id., Demain il sera trop star* (Paris, Flammarion, 1989).

8 G. Mazzoleni, *Comunicazione e potere. Mass media e politica in Italia* (Naples, Liguori, 1992) p. 166.

9 There are exceptions to this tendency. A few weeks after the 1994 elections Berlusconi, the first Italian Prime Minister to have an advertising expert on his staff (Bob Lasagna, formerly at the Saatchi & Saatchi agency), tried to use short televised slots to 'inform' the citizenry of his government's achievements. They were discontinued because the broadcasts were seen as propagandist rather than informative. Berlusconi also made available to the press a series of videos which showed highlights of his time in government. In his last few weeks as Prime Minister he frequently explained his position through the use of video-tapes, which were conceptually very similar to his electoral broadcasts, and which were repeatedly shown on his own channels as well as on those of the RAI.

10 One of the outcomes of the 'mass-mediatisation' of politics is the phenomenon of personalisation (see below). The left, in favouring 'the masses', has traditionally been wary of this. The focus on the party leader reawakens the old hostility to the 'cult of personality'.

11 At that time Canale 5 was owned by Berlusconi, but Rete 4 and Italia 1 were controlled by the publishers Mondadori and Rusconi respectively.

12 Mazzoleni, *Comunicazione e potere*, p. 152.

13 P. Mancini, 'La "prima volta" degli spot politici', *Problemi dell'informazione*, 9:1 (1984), pp. 7–31.

14 *Ibid.*, pp. 20–1.

15 See L. Romano and P. Scabello (eds), *C'era una volta la DC. Breve storia del periodo degasperiano attraverso i manifesti elettorali della Democrazia Cristiana* (Rome, Savelli, 1975).

16 Mancini, 'La "prima volta" ', p. 25.

17 See E. Cheli, P. Mancini, G. Mazzoleni and G. Tinacci Mannelli, *Elezioni in televisione: dalle tribune alla pubblicità. La campagna elettorale televisiva 1987* (Milan, Franco Angeli, 1989).

18 See *ibid.*; S. Bartezzaghi and L. Corrain, *Per un'analisi semiotica della campagna elettorale 1987* (unpublished paper, University of Bologna, 1987).

19 For an analysis of this campaign compared with that of 1992 see: A. Notarnicola, 'La contesa delle immagini. Gli spot televisivi dei partiti per le elezioni politiche del 1987 e del 1992', *Quaderni di scienza politica*, 1:3 (1994), pp. 395–488.

20 For reasons of space this chapter deals only with party election broadcasts in general elections. Political advertisements were also shown on television during the 1989, 1994 and 1999 European elections, and in the local elections of 1990, 1993, 1995, 1997, 1999 and 2000. See *Comunicazione politica*, 1:1 (1991); 3:1 (1994); 4:1 (1995); 6:1 (1997); 7:2 (1998); and P. Guarino, 'Gli spot politici: 1999–2000', in I. Pezzini, *Lo spot elettorale. La vicenda italiana di una forma di comunicazione politica* (Rome, Meltemi, 2001), pp. 75–125.

21 The old multi-preference system was repealed by the referendum result of 9 June 1991.

22 These figures and accompanying information are from G. Tinacci Mannelli, 'Di che cosa parlano gli spot televisivi?', *Comunicazione politica*, 2:2 (1992), p. 17.

23 Laws 276 and 277 of March 1993 introduced the system of majority voting with a proportional element. In June, November and December that year there were local elections and direct elections of mayors and provincial presidents, with the possibility of a run-off ballot in the absence of an absolute majority, and a bonus of additional seats for the winner.

24 There is a substantial literature on the 1994 election campaign. See especially: A. Abruzzese, *Elogio del tempo nuovo. Perché Berlusconi ha vinto* (Genoa, Costa & Nolan, 1994); G. Statera, *Il volto seduttivo del potere* (Rome, SEAM, 1994); J. Farrell, 'Berlusconi and Forza Italia: a New Force for Old?', *Modern Italy*, 1:1 (1995), pp. 40–51; M. Livolsi and U. Volli (eds), *La comunicazione politica tra la prima e la seconda Repubblica* (Milan, Franco Angeli, 1995); M. Morcellini (ed.), *Elezioni di TV. Televisione e pubblico nella campagna elettorale '94* (Genoa, Costa & Nolan, 1995).

25 Law 515 of December 1993 (especially articles 1, 2, 8 and 15) restricted access to, and publicity in, the mass media during election campaigns with the object of 'guaranteeing conditions of parity within the limits of what is practicable' for the various political contenders. The RAI, the publishers of dailies and periodicals and local/national television/radio licence holders were all made subject to specific regulations. The RAI was to abide by the rules stipulated by the parliamentary watchdog, and the private-sector television stations were to be answerable to the parliamentary commissioner for publishing and broadcasting.

26 This provoked criticism even from experts in this field. Some researchers employed by Berlusconi were accused of having contributed to his success by using techniques traditionally deployed to expose communication strategies, rather than construct them. See, for example, M. Farina, 'Forza Italia è nata in Francia?', *Sette*, 15, supplement to *Corriere della Sera*, 14 April 1994, pp. 38–43.

27 The Polo's output was produced by the same source, which was under the control of Fininvest, Berlusconi's holding company.

28 In the absence of official figures, my analysis is based on the *spot elettorali* recorded on video-cassette and on those made available to me by FI.

29 The narrative theory in question is that of Algirdas Julien Greimas, set out in *Du sens: 02. Essais sémiotiques* (Paris, Seuil, 1983).

30 Bossi's 'rough' image was in marked contrast to the smooth, serene and distant image cultivated by Berlusconi.

31 On this speech see M. Deni and F. Marsciani, 'Analisi del primo discorso di Berlusconi', in Livolsi and Volli (eds), *La comunicazione politica*, pp. 227–41.

32 Chapter 2 of 'Relazione annuale al Parlamento per la radiodiffusione', in *Vita italiana – istituzioni e comunicazioni*, 1 (1994), pp. 86–92.

33 To quote Carlo Fusaro, the law's distinction between 'advertising' and 'propaganda' is a 'commendable effort to define the indefinable', made all the more complex by the provision for exceptions which 'make getting round the prohibition child's play, since debates, round-table discussions and conferences are all excluded from the ban, as are the illustration of manifestoes and the presentation of candidates'; see 'Media e spese elettorali', *Rivista italiana di scienza politica*, 23:3 (1994), p. 439.

34 For an inside view of Prodi's campaign see R. Grandi, *Prodi. Una campagna lunga un anno* (Milan, Lupetti, 1996).

35 See M. Livolsi and U. Volli (eds), *Il televoto. La campagna elettorale in televisione* (Milan, Franco Angeli, 1997).

36 G. Battistini, 'Rock o tamburi per far colpo sui teleschermi', *La Repubblica*, 13 April 1996.

11

The languages of politics: from *politichese* to the 'discourse of serenity'

Patrick McCarthy

The 1996 election campaign was a struggle between two different kinds of language as well as between centre-right and centre-left. To oversimplify, the campaign pitted an aggressive Silvio Berlusconi against a reassuring Romano Prodi and an ostentatiously rational Massimo D'Alema, while Umberto Bossi jeered from his mythical Padania, the free and pure kingdom of northern Italy, purged of immigrants, idle southerners and meddlesome Rome bureaucrats. Anger and calm were strategies that conveyed contrasting ways of looking at the world. Behind arguments about taxes and magistrates the languages of the coalitions contained their view of the totality of policy, of the movement of change that began in 1992 and of the Italian state itself.

Political discourse is an invention, ceaseless although not free. There are certain things that it hides – the *non-detto*. The things it does say – the *detto* – it is trying to call into existence.[1] They may be said to exist if listeners are convinced.

In the April 1996 elections the languages of centre-right and centre-left had the same starting point. This was the rejection of the 'old' political language, which was used in Italy until the crisis of the state – a crisis that was also linguistic: it is orthodoxy in Italy to view the old language as empty, wordy and obscure, and to refer to it disparagingly as *politichese* (politics-speak). By contrast the new political protagonists – Berlusconi, Prodi and Bossi – are united in using a language that is supposedly simple, concrete and direct.[2]

The reality is more complex. The old language was often rich in meaning, while the new language – or more correctly languages – is/are often empty. Moreover, their simplicity is the result of hard and sophisticated work. We shall begin with a glance at the language of pre-1992 Italian politics, then we briefly trace the evolution of political discourse before examining in that context the various kinds of discourse used in the 1996 elections.

The obscurity of the post-war regime

Aldo Moro, the Christian Democrat leader and Prime Minister kidnapped and murdered by the Red Brigades in 1978, is considered the incarnation of obscurity.

Explaining why he failed to interrogate him, Mario Moretti, his chief jailer, stated: 'Moro speaks in code, concrete things are swallowed up in a sea of vagueness.'[3] At the outset of the post-war regime the speeches of Alcide De Gasperi had been erudite but clear. As the decades wore on, the Christian Democrat Party's sense of its mission to rebuild Italy after military defeat and economic chaos faded, and its language became obscure. Of course it used many languages, and Giulio Andreotti, who was less concerned with mission than with power, was terse and ironic.

Moro, who understood his party's degeneration, used obscurity as one weapon among several. His last speech, delivered to the DC parliamentary group on 28 February 1978, mingles emotional intensity – a prophetic 'io temo' (I fear) repeated three times in one paragraph – with a deliberate vagueness. The agreement with the Communists is described as 'un qualche accordo parziale su cose da fare, per un certo tempo' (just a partial agreement to do certain things in a limited time). The verbs are a maze of subjunctives and conditionals, and the prepositions do not define the precise relationship between the nouns.[4]

The speech acts on various levels. To DC voters the jumble of words is reassuring, for it seems unlikely to provoke change. To DC parliamentarians there is a precise message: they must support the new agreement with the Communists, the *compromesso storico* (historic compromise). For the Communist leadership there is a trap: the agreement is indicated only as 'un'area di concordia, un'area di intesa' (an area of agreement, an area without conflict). By not spelling out what this area is Moro strands the Communists in a wasteland between government and opposition.

So Moro's language was far from empty and its obscurity served precise goals. One may, however, argue that, since those goals could not be acknowledged, the DC was tempted by solipsism. The same fate befell the Communist Party (PCI), whose Gramscian vocabulary left it increasingly unable to analyse an Italy that was changing in ways Gramsci had not anticipated. Phrases like 'rinnovamento civile e intellettuale' (civic and intellectual renewal), 'blocco storico' (historic bloc), 'classe dirigente' (ruling class) and the abused 'egemonia' (hegemony) became frozen. They were strung together in rhetorical sentences full of ritual allusions to 'tutte le forze antifasciste e democratiche' (all democratic and anti-Fascist forces), or 'tutte le masse popolari' (all the popular masses) or 'tutte le energie patriottiche' (all patriotic energy) – terms that were used in the Resistance and lost meaning as the decades passed.[5]

During the period of the historic compromise (1976–79), the PCI leader Enrico Berlinguer succeeded in injecting into the ossified Gramscianism an urgent moral discourse. Around the key word 'austerità' (austerity) he marshalled a struggle between 'individualismo sfrenato' (unbridled individualism), 'lo sperpero e gli sprechi' (waste and squandering) and 'la follia del consumo' (the folly of consumerism), which were the marks of bourgeois capitalism, and 'lavoro' (work), 'solidarietà' (solidarity) and 'rigore' (rigour), which indicated the values of the working class.[6]

This language breathed life into a new historical protagonist: the Communist militant who had more duties than rights was to serve as an example to the wasteful Italy of the post-1973 oil crisis. However, Berlinguer was unable to transform his ethical appeals into a political programme or to build a bridge between his language and Moro's.

The language of the post-war order was richer than contemporary politicians have been willing to admit. Yet the DC's obscurity and the PCI's Gramscianism marked, by their solipsism, the end of a regime. They invited a populist reaction: the new language had a limited vocabulary, shorter periods and an aggressive tone. Speeches in the piazza became less important than television talk shows (which is why the quotations in this chapter are short). Still, just as the emptiness of the old language had been exaggerated, so the new simplicity could not in itself offer a valid substitute. It soon ran into difficulty, as Berlusconi would discover. Moreover, simplicity, which in fact entailed much craft, was merely a common starting point after which the various languages diverged.

The barbarian hordes march on Rome

The old words had already been attacked. The Movimento del '77, a second New Left upsurge, particularly strong in Rome and Bologna, satirised the PCI's Marxist heritage in graffiti like 'Groucho Marx vive' (Groucho Marx lives) and 'Dopo Marx, aprile' (After Marx, April). Berlinguer's discourse of rigour was debunked in slogans like 'Autoriduzione' (self-reduction) where customers themselves were supposed to set prices in cinemas and restaurants, or like 'Espropriazione proletaria' (proletarian expropriation) where Movimento militants helped themselves to consumer goods in the name of the working class.[7]

But this was a self-conscious irony, too fragile to survive. It was left to the Lega Lombarda, later Lega Nord, to launch a sustained onslaught on the old political discourse. When he began organising in the early and mid-1980s, Bossi followed the example of the traditional regionalist movements, like the Partito Sardo d'Azione, and he cultivated his local dialect. But the Lombardy dialect was not strong enough to provide the cultural focus of a movement which was in any case less a matter of a region than of protest. So Bossi's language must challenge the regime discourse. It must be violent.

Bossi's early experience instilled into him the view of language as transgression. Scribbling graffiti on walls and battling with opposing militants in order to stick posters on billboards taught him that he must write quickly and crudely. The Lega's language would be popular, but it would also contain what Herbert Marcuse had called magical elements.[8] As such it would be doubly subversive: less intellectual than the old discourse but more emotional and more mythological. It would bind together the new community and cut it off from the 'Italian' nation.

Bossi began using the language of the bars in the Milan hinterland and he blended with it the myth of the northern cities uniting against the emperor Frederick Barbarossa in the twelfth century. He added a note of menace: when the magistrates investigated the Lega's finances, Bossi began holding up a bullet before applauding crowds and explaining that a magistrate's life was worth no more than the price of the bullet. Following the principle of magic that if one controls an opponent's name one controls her or him, Bossi distorted the names of rival politicians: Berlusconi was shortened to 'Berlusca' or ridiculed as 'Berluscosa' (Berluscwhat) or else his vanity was mocked by the title 'Berluskaiser'.[9]

Since the Lega had no money for the cool medium of television, it used transgression in order to gain publicity. Bossi littered his statements with 'cazzo' (prick) and 'stronzo' (shit). When a law restricting the rights of immigrants was passed, it was too soft for Bossi, who called it 'una presa per il culo del paese' (a phrase literally translatable as 'the country is being buggered', meaning that Italians were being conned).[10] Lega spokesmen were aggressively masculine, casting doubt on their opponents' virility and excoriating gay men. This did not prevent the Lega from depicting itself in feminine terms. One militant explained this: 'Umberto is like a mother. He only punishes you because he thinks you've done something wrong.'[11]

Faith found an outlet in the periodic gatherings at Pontida, a small town in the Bergamo province. Whereas Italian children are taught that the most important and most unfortunate event of the Middle Ages was their country's failure to form a nation-state,[12] Bossi and his followers celebrated the alliance of the northern cities, the pact they sealed at Pontida and their victory over the Holy Roman Emperor at Legnano, near Milan.

The Lega's myth contained an element of protest. Myths of various kinds are an integral part of political discourse: De Gasperi created the myth of Catholic Italy where, so he claimed, Italians would be unable to read Dante if the Communists came to power.[13] However, Bossi's myth had two special traits: firstly, as we shall see later, he added to it new pieces drawn from ordinary life and, secondly, it was slightly ridiculous, which allowed people to cultivate it while one part of them mocked it. This mental reservation allows voters to support the Lega while not believing in an independent Padania.

Berlusconi: from a populism of government to a new solipsism

Bossi's was the language of protest and not of government. When he entered politics in 1993 Berlusconi wanted to build a new order on the ruins to which the Lega and the magistrates had reduced the old regime. He wished to preserve Bossi's direct language but to eliminate the insults and obscenities, and to change the myths. He achieved the second goal by adopting a tone of exaggerated courtesy, prefacing his every remark with 'mi consenta' (if I may be permitted). He spoke of 'misura' (measure) and 'equilibrio' (equilibrium).[14]

Berlusconi dismissed Moro's language as incomprehensible and condemned the old political class for indulging in chatter. His own language was a discourse of action: key words were *organizzare* (to organise) and *realtà* (reality). Forza Italia is described as a 'movimento di gente certamente concreta, certamente pratica, certamente di grande esperienza, con un'esperienza forgiata nella trincea dei mestieri, delle professioni, del lavoro' (a movement of people, certainly concrete, certainly practical, certainly with lots of experience, their experience forged in the trenches of the trades, the professions or work).[15] Berlusconi's language talked about action, but it did not move quickly from point A to point B. It did not resemble popular spoken Italian, and the simplicity, evident in the restricted vocabulary and the repetitions, did not prevent Berlusconi from making allusions to war ('la trincea'), to management ('organizzare') and especially to soccer ('Forza Italia', Come on, Italy; 'squadra', team; and 'gli Azzurri', the Blues, from the colour of the national sports team).[16] This was a language about, rather than of, action. One model for Berlusconi's simplicity may have been the AC Milan supporters' clubs, whose language was '*L'italian basic*, quattrocento parole che anche gli incolti capiscono' (basic Italian, four hundred words that even the uneducated understand).[17]

Supposedly rational and modern, Berlusconi created a myth in which the principal character was Silvio Berlusconi, the great entrepreneur who had created the Fininvest holding company out of nothing and who would now save Italy from corrupt politicians and the economic crisis. An analysis of the speeches Berlusconi made on behalf of his advertising agency Publitalia[18] reveals that they are less a description of what Publitalia could do for its clients than the depiction of a charismatic leader in whom the clients could place their trust. Similarly Berlusconi's speech at the Rome convention that launched Forza Italia[19] was less an outline of policy than the creation, via language, of the leader who would conjure up a million jobs.

Much space has been given in interpretations of Berlusconi's success in the 1994 elections to the theme of spectacle: as the owner of three television networks and of AC Milan he was already a master of spectacles. The analysis of his language, however, stresses other reasons for his victory. The cultivated simplicity of his speeches fitted the moment of reaction against the language of the old regime. With the political class discredited, it was natural for Italians to turn to an entrepreneur, a member of a much-admired social group. Berlusconi played on this theme both by reminding his audiences of the economic miracle and by offering to use managerial methods to reform the state. He understood that the post-1992 turmoil was in part a crisis of modernisation, and he offered himself as the person best equipped to lead Italy into the age of twenty-four-hour capital markets and of the international assembly line.

Until his election victory in March 1994 Berlusconi's language was controlled. The transition from Bossi's populism of protest to a populism of government was successful. Meanwhile the Partito Democratico della Sinistra (PDS) had failed to find a substitute for the Gramscian jargon it had given up.[20] By contrast Forza Italia's allies were faring better. Bossi captured the mood of protest, and the solemn statements of the 'post-Fascist' Gianfranco Fini were gaining legitimacy for an Alleanza Nazionale (AN) that also deployed the rabble-rousing oratory of the hard-liner Teodoro Buontempo or of Alessandra Mussolini.

Meanwhile populist simplicity was invading many kinds of Italian discourse after 1992, which proves that there are links between political language and other kinds of language, and also that in a time of confusion a country often turns back to its cultural traditions. Two cases deserve mention.

The Clean Hands investigation could be symbolised only by a man of the people. Of the leading magistrates, Francesco Saverio Borrelli came from an established bourgeois family and Gherardo Colombo was an intellectual. But Antonio Di Pietro had to be a southern peasant who, like millions of other poor southerners, had come to the North. 'He had the nice chubby face of a Molisan peasant, almost a face from a bygone age, the face of a country boy,' writes a well-known journalist.[21] Di Pietro lived up to his reputation: his oratory was less polished but more forceful than was usual in his profession. He also sprinkled his conversation with country sayings such as 'Quando l'acqua non arriva più al mulino, il mulino non macina più' (When the water no longer reaches the mill, the mill cannot grind any more).[22]

Of ironic interest is the language used in 1995 by Eugenio Scalfari, then editor of *La Repubblica* and one of Berlusconi's great enemies, to describe the changes he was about to make in his paper. He was introducing colour because it was 'a more modern and immediate way to communicate with the public'. But communication, which must be 'fast', was not in itself enough. The paper would also offer 'positive, concrete solutions'.[23] Berlusconi could hardly have said it better! However, not all kinds of Italian discourse changed in that way. For example, doctors and academics held firm to their traditional language.

During his period as Prime Minister Berlusconi's language altered greatly, and the origins of the linguistic clash in the 1996 elections are to be sought in the autumn of 1994. One example of change lies in Berlusconi's body language, in particular in his smile. Berlusconi's clothes do not change: from 1993 to 1996 he wore suits, frequently blue, with buttoned shirt collars and vaguely regimental ties, or else he wore expensive track suits and running shoes. In 1993 his smile was dazzling, his permanent sun tan indicated not merely health but wealth, and he radiated self-confidence.[24]

In 1996 the smile was featured on countless Forza Italia posters, and other politicians, such as the handsome Pier Ferdinando Casini, a leader of the Centro Cristiano Democratico (CCD), imitated it. But by now the real smile was a grimace that Berlusconi was flashing on and off. It was too mechanical to be convincing, and during the 'off' periods he looked haggard. The decline had begun when he discovered that being Prime Minister did not protect him against the magistrates and that his government offered hostile journalists an easy target.

The change in body language dented the myth of the entrepreneur-saviour of Italy. Berlusconi responded with ever more attempts to revitalise it. He appealed over the heads of his political rivals to 'la gente' (the people). Who were/was 'la gente'? They were neither individuals nor clearly defined groups or classes. Classes had been dissolved, so Berlusconi maintained, by the general prosperity which Fininvest helped shape by its advertising. 'La gente' were the adolescent girls who watched Ambra, the teenage pop star, on Berlusconi's television and wrote the 600 letters she received each week, or the AC Milan supporters who worshipped the footballers Franco Baresi and Paolo Maldini. In short, 'la gente' needs a leader. Unlike a body of citizens who seek dialogue with the government, it endorses the leader's monologue. It is an obedient version of Jean Baudrillard's silent majority.

Thus Berlusconi, who had none of Baudrillard's irony, could claim that state television 'doesn't appeal to the people, it is against the government for whom the people have voted'.[25] This means that those elected by 'la gente', even if I have argued that 'la gente' cannot confer legitimacy, are in Berlusconi's eyes 'unti dal Signore' (anointed by the Lord).[26] The leader–people relationship is exalted and intermediaries like magistrates or opposition parties are merely harmful. Berlusconi's language grew ever more religious. He compared himself to Christ, who drank the bitter chalice, carried the cross and was betrayed by Judas-Bossi.

Alternatively Berlusconi's sense of himself began to falter. In 1995 he compared himself to Snow White and Mother Teresa, denied that he was a new Don Quixote and was compared by Walter Veltroni, the deputy leader of the centre-left coalition, to Forrest Gump. Berlusconi's narcissism remained, but he saw himself as a victim, not a saviour: the magistrates, the press, state television, left-wing intellectuals and Juventus supporters were all his enemies.

Even before March 1994 violence lurked in the background of his speeches. Populism is Manichaean: if the people are to be good, there must be an incarnation of evil. Berlusconi located it in Massimo D'Alema, whose physical being he excoriated in his weekly magazine *Panorama*. He spoke of D'Alema's 'ghigno vendicativo' (vindictive sneer) and his 'baffi sottili che tremano' (thin moustache that quivers).[27] When he was forced out of power in December 1994 Berlusconi saw Communists under every stone.

Whereas his 1994 campaign was marked by a calm self-confidence that reassured voters, in 1996 he embraced and strengthened the mood of protest. Initially this appeared a legitimate gamble. Polls showed that the number of voters who considered themselves adequately represented by Parliament and government had gone down from 17 per cent and 14 per cent respectively in 1992 to 7 per cent and 4·5 per cent in 1995.[28] In March 1996 the campaign began with the tax revolt of the self-employed, who put Romano Prodi to flight in Turin. Berlusconi called for 'una ventata liberatrice' (a liberating gust of wind) to sweep away the government regulation that damaged small business.[29] However, in Italy, where distrust of the state is equalled only by reliance on the state, such a stance loses some supporters.

The next issue in the campaign did not work for Forza Italia. A Rome magistrate, Renato Squillante, was arrested on charges of taking bribes to fix trials; among those accused of offering bribes was Fininvest. To Berlusconi the magistrates were simply trying to sabotage his campaign, and he compared some of them to the policemen-turned-criminals of the 'white Fiat Uno' murders, much talked about in the early and mid-1990s.[30] This remark was thrown back at him throughout the campaign.

Even so, Berlusconi's statements on particular issues were less damaging than his general tone of aggression and paranoia, which was taken up by some of his supporters. In October 1995 he had declared Italy a police state and D'Alema a product of the Soviet Union.[31] A few days before the elections he warned that 'if the left wins, there is a risk there will be no more elections'.[32] Meanwhile the 'wets' of Forza Italia, like Vittorio Dotti, had lost out to the hawks, such as Cesare Previti. They emulated Berlusconi's new language: Previti declared that, if the centre-right won, it would take no prisoners, while Filippo Mancuso compared the men who had driven him from office to mass murderers.[33]

The surprising thing is that in-house documents of Fininvest and Forza Italia reveal that Berlusconi's experts knew he was on the wrong track. Memos warned him to set himself above polemics and to win trust in the country. The electorate wanted reasons for hope, but all Berlusconi offered them was wars. His advisers told him to stay off television but he appeared more and more often and looked more and more bitter. Raffaele Della Valle, Forza Italia leader of the House and a 'wet', blamed the election defeat on Berlusconi's choice of language: 'Do you want to know what our first mistake was? Our language. [It was] often truculent, arrogant.'[34] An isolated Berlusconi was talking to himself. His was not the solipsism of the old DC, but it was still solipsism.

The language of Alleanza Nazionale was significantly different and yet it was tainted with rage. When Berlusconi denounced the magistrates, Fini was careful to keep his distance. He tried to maintain the solemn, statesmanlike pose that had been successful in legitimising his party in 1994. When he speculated on what would happen if the centre-left won, Fini limited himself to suggesting, 'I do not believe there would be the renewal that the country needs.'[35] Fini wore dark suits with a collar and tie, his wife was elegant, and to humanise his image he was photographed attending Lazio soccer matches. Such photographs, however, contained a message to the initiated. The Lazio supporters come from the outskirts of Rome where the MSI had been strong, and the fans behind the southern goal have often given mass Fascist salutes.

Alleanza Nazionale started the campaign burdened with blame for having refused the constitutional compromise worked out by Berlusconi and D'Alema. To intransigence Fini added protest when he endorsed the Turin tax revolt. When he was accused of exploiting any and every grievance, he found excuses, although, in its post-election autopsy, Alleanza Nazionale admitted that its leader had been over-zealous.[36] Fini found a safer target when he denounced 'the state-aided capitalism of the great families'.[37] But a suggestion that income tax should not be deducted at source[38] cast doubt on his competence and revived the view that his party was nothing but a vehicle for protest.

A further problem for the right was that a different and even more authentic version of the discourse of rage was offered by the Lega. Bossi deployed all his weapons: vulgarity ('Il Nord si è rotto le palle,' literally 'the North has had its balls broken', meaning that the North had had enough); a simple target ('I want to massacre, to decapitate Rome'); a Manichaean structure (Rome versus 'Padania [which] has recognised itself as a nation'[39]), as well as religious allusions to the God of Padania who makes Himself manifest at Pontida.

As well as sprinkling his speeches with time bombs and Winchester rifles trained on Rome, Bossi introduced into his Pontida myth, itself expanded to include the fantasised 'Mantua parliament', the myth of the Scottish – initially Bossi seemed to think he was Irish – rebel William Wallace. Bossi took the film *Braveheart* and wove it into Italian politics, of which it became, in the Lega's eyes, the dominant metaphor. The part of Wallace was taken away from Mel Gibson and awarded to Bossi, who announced, however, that he had no intention of being hanged, drawn and quartered. Scotland became Padania, London was Rome and the centre-right and centre-left leaders were a collective version of the English king.[40]

Once again only the diehard supporters of the Lega would take the fictional personage of Wallace-Bossi literally, but many more might maintain a minimal disbelief while suspending the rest. Bossi's clothing had changed. Since he was now the leader of the Padanian nation, he wore a tie more frequently. But his rumpled suits and his old pullovers were an explicit subversion of the norms of elegance.[41]

The centre-left: God's cyclist, two Americans and an ex-Communist in search of reason

Berlusconi laid down a language for the election, and the centre-left responded. In this sense Berlusconi was still the key figure in Italian politics. The centre-left's strategy was sketched out the previous spring when Romano Prodi declared himself a candidate to lead the opposition. Prodi depicted himself as an anti-Berlusconi: whereas the head of Forza Italia was closed in his resentment, Prodi would be open. He would present himself as an ordinary person, not as a charismatic leader. He too favoured track suits and running shoes, but his were not expensive. His wife's clothes were less stylish than Daniela Fini's and she rode around Bologna on a bicycle.

The carefully constructed contrasts extended into the field of sport. Prodi, too, used words like *squadra* (team) and *allenatore* (coach), but to soccer he opposed cycling, which was less glamorous. Against AC Milan's victories in the European Champions' Cup Prodi pitted his Sunday rambles over the mountains near Bologna, surrounded by friends. He flaunted his knowledge of the great cyclists. He talked of Rik van Steenbergen, whose speciality was the Paris-Roubaix race. He declared that Gino Bartali was his special favourite but, remembering his PDS allies, he had a kind word for Fausto Coppi, who in the ideological 1940s was widely, albeit incorrectly, considered to be a Communist merely because he was the rival of the arch-Catholic Gino Bartali.[42] Mostly Prodi described cycling as escape and fun, a brand of sport very different from the extreme professionalism of AC Milan, which left ordinary people with no role but to watch and cheer.

Against Berlusconi's narcissism, Prodi presented himself as the man of dialogue. He did not promise to create a million jobs but rather warned that sacrifices would be needed. Where Berlusconi had united Italy with his television networks, Prodi hired a bus and drove around the 'hundred cities'. Implicit was the promise of a different kind of leadership. Because the decisions at Finivest were handed down from the top, Prodi talked not about IRI (the state-controlled holding conglomerate he had headed) or his consulting firm, Nomisma, but about the university, where there is (supposedly!) collegiality. Similarly Prodi's Catholicism was post-Vatican II and stressed the importance of community.[43]

Sometimes Prodi's blend of ecological cycling and parish-hall togetherness was too Franciscan to be true. However, as well as offering a serenity that contrasted with Berlusconi's growing bitterness, Prodi suggested that Italy should be governed not by a leader who demanded that his followers must trust and obey him but by a team captain who could bring together southerners and northerners, Catholics and Communists. It was a choice that emerged from Italian history: two Prime Ministers of the late nineteenth and early twentieth centuries come to mind: the authoritarian Francesco Crispi and the liberal-minded Giovanni Giolitti.

Prodi's election campaign continued his initial challenge, although he widened his range. He claimed credit for his years as president of IRI and he reiterated the Catholic view of the interventionist state.[44] He used strong language to suggest that Berlusconi's private life and his television networks were morally offensive.[45] But neither Prodi nor any other centre-left leader abandoned the strategy of meeting aggression with calm reason: 'We shall defeat hatred with ideas'.[46]

The strategy consisted first of linking the centre-right's aggression with ideology, and then with a lack of policies and of competence. By contrast the centre-left associated calm with programmes and practical ability. The 1996 campaign reversed the 1994 campaign: now the centre-left captured common sense. The PDS's slogan 'Un'Italia forte e serena' (A strong and serene Italy) was a conscious borrowing from Mitterrand's 'La force tranquille' (Figure 58).[47]

Veltroni introduced one of the two main American variants. The week before the elections *L'Unità*, of which he was the editor, distributed a book about Woody Allen.[48] One of Bobby Kennedy's daughters came to Italy and appeared at the centre-left's rallies. Veltroni declared that his ideal was the Democratic Party. He did not hide his liking for popular American culture and commented that 'the day will come . . . when, as in a Western film, the good will win and the bad will lose'.[49] Veltroni was following a PCI tradition that went back at least to the 1940s. This was 'the other America', or 'democratic America', that the writer Elio Vittorini had celebrated in his magazine *Il Politecnico*; it was the America of Roosevelt and Hemingway.[50] The difference was that there was no Togliatti to rein Veltroni in.

Veltroni's America was different from that of the outgoing Prime Minister Lamberto Dini. Dini flaunted the years he had spent in Washington at the IMF to demonstrate his competence in economic issues. Since his role in the centre-left coalition was to win over centrist voters and to inspire confidence in international capital markets, he had to appear learned and authoritative. So he buried Berlusconi's spendthrift policies under English phrases like 'supply-side economics'. Yet since he was no longer a technocrat but a politician, Dini had also to appear human. He achieved this by the American tactic of introducing his wife and family into the campaign. Donatella, whose Valentino clothes caused ironic murmurs on the left, fell into the Hillary Clinton category. But Dini used sentimental language to talk about their marriage.[51]

The most interesting brand of language came from Massimo D'Alema. Ecumenical to the point of meeting with a group of managers of Berlusconi's Mediaset,[52] D'Alema presented tolerance as an essential trait of any party that, like the PDS, claimed to be a party of government. Other traits were efficiency and the ability to inspire trust. The stress laid by D'Alema on the PDS's governmental vocation revealed that the PCI's haunting fear of illegitimacy was still alive. To legitimise the PDS, D'Alema shunned Marxist and even Gramscian vocabulary. Although he invoked 'the great world of work'[53] he avoided the term 'class' and abandoned to Rifondazione Comunista the traditional language of the Italian left. Thus Rifondazione spoke of constructing 'a class-based alternative to the market economy' and of replacing capitalism with 'a planned economy run democratically by the producers'.[54]

The discourse of class was pushed to the fringe of politics, while D'Alema used a seemingly neutral vocabulary. He talked of *regole* (rules) and his favourite word was *quadro* (framework): social conflicts were to be placed in 'a frame of reference, a system of agreed rules'.[55] He was not alone in using this vocabulary, but no other centre-left leader used it as much. It depicted society as a coherent whole organised around fixed but flexible principles. Clearly D'Alema wanted to win over voters who were troubled by Berlusconi's rampant individualism or by an anarchical market.

Like the PCI leaders, D'Alema presented an ordered society, but the forces creating order were no longer derived from Gramsci. They were to be an integral part of the new Italian state, which is a proof that the PDS takes seriously its task of reforming that state. Conflicts of interest and domination of the media would be banished. Yet D'Alema did not spell out what the economic and social structures of the new Italy would be. D'Alema's rationalism masked a *non-detto*: the PDS lacked a vision of how society worked. In this it was no different from most European left-wing parties. But the PDS's uncertainty hung over the Prodi government.

The centre-left was not afraid to be serious. In 1994 it had been too serious and had been outmanoeuvred by an opponent who used the media better. This time the centre-right appeared gimmicky. Prodi performed badly on television, but Berlusconi was little better. The contrast between the two manifestoes, studied as visual objects, worked to the centre-left's advantage. The centre-right's manifesto cover, as in 1994, depicted a blue sky with white cumulus clouds. In place of the sun there was a circle containing part of the Italian flag and a blue inscription: 'Polo per la Libertà'. It contained 100 proposals: a magical, round number. The booklet had 216 pages compared with the seventy-eight pages and forty-six propositions of 1994. The 1996 centre-right manifesto was still easier than the centre-left's, but it was more daunting than that of 1994.

Once more the centre-left turned seriousness into a virtue. It offered eighty-eight propositions which were 'theses for the delineation of the platform and programme of the Olive Tree, presented by Romano Prodi'. The language was bureaucratic, while the manifesto looked like a school exercise book: part of each page was lined and left blank so that the reader could take notes; at the end there were six lined, blank pages. The didactic dreariness was banished, however, by the splendid dark green colour of the covers. On the front was a white circle with a green olive plant and the word *L'Ulivo* in blue. The only touch of red was the apostrophe. As a visual object the centre-left's manifesto was more original and it said more: it told voters that politics were difficult and they must make an effort.

Conclusion

So simplicity was not, after all, the leitmotif of the campaign language. Green is considered by psychologists to be restful, and another key word in D'Alema's vocabulary was 'serene'.[56] Whereas the centre-right tried to launch a crusade, the centre-left offered dialogue. By stressing ideas it set political discourse apart from the conversations in the AC Milan supporters' clubs. This was unlikely to last, because, as Italy began to change, so did the language of its politics. The immediate problem the centre-left faced was to find a discourse which could give meaning to economic austerity.

Finally, the elections offered theatre. As is traditional in Italy, they enriched the round of daily life and mingled the real and the imaginary. This was symbolised by the way D'Alema's gesture of blowing on his hands was widely taken up. First *Striscia la notizia* (Sneeky News), a satirical programme on one of Berlusconi's television networks, used it as a motif between sketches, and then people used it as a greeting. It soon lost all connection with D'Alema, and its original significance, whatever it may have been, was forgotten.[57] As a greeting it signified that the person who made the gesture was following and enjoying the elections and wanted to talk about them. It was body language that had changed bodies and become the sign of political theatre.

NOTES

I wish to thank Cynthia Lazo, who worked as my research assistant on this chapter. Also Roberto Paganini for studying the two programmes. Finally Emanuela Poli, who read the draft and suggested improvements.

1 The many methodological problems, the various sub-categories of political discourse, its links with other kinds of language as well as with accent, clothing, gestures and body language cannot be treated in this short chapter. For the *detto* and the *non-detto* see my 'Il linguaggio di Margaret Thatcher', *Europa Europe*, 2:2 (1993), pp. 151–70.

2 On the vacuity and opacity of the old language see U. Eco, 'Political Language: the Use and Abuse of Rhetoric', in *Apocalypse Postponed*, ed. R. Lumley (London, British Film Institute, 1994), pp. 103–18 (essay first published in Italian in 1973); M. Baldini, *Parlar chiaro, parlare oscuro* (Bari and Rome, Laterza, 1989), chapter 2.

3 Mario Moretti, interviewed by C. Mosca and R. Rossanda, *Brigate rosse. Una storia italiana* (Milan, Anabasi, 1994), p. 159. Exercising their writers' prerogative to use the literary language in order to pass judgement on political language, Pier Paolo Pasolini and Leonardo Sciascia both denounced the language of the DC as a form of non-communication. See P. P. Pasolini, *Empirismo eretico* (Milan, Garzanti, 2000 [1972]), *passim*; L. Sciascia, *L'affaire Moro* (Palermo, Sellerio, 1978), pp. 11–22.

4 A. Moro, 'Ultimo discorso', in *L'intelligenza e gli avvenimenti*, introduction by G. L. Mosse (Milan, Garzanti, 1979), pp. 374–91. On Moro's language see P. Desideri, 'Il discorso politico. Profilo linguistico di Moro, Craxi, Pannella', *Italia contemporanea*, 174 (1989), pp. 7–11.

5 Both kinds of vocabulary were used by the Communist leader Palmiro Togliatti, who added to them a crude, polemical note derived from the Third International. For instance, he invited Gide to limit himself to the theme of pederasty and he dismissed dissidents as lice. For his language see P. Togliatti, *Da Salerno a Yalta* (Rome, Editori Riuniti, 1984).

6 E. Berlinguer, *Austerità, occasione per trasformare l'Italia* (Rome, Editori Riuniti, 1977), *passim*.

7 There was much parody in the language of the Movimento del '77, which renewed the protest but not the utopianism of 1968. If 1968 was 'l'imagination au pouvoir', 1977 was

irony in power. For a longer discussion see R. Lumley, *States of Emergency. Cultures of Revolt in Italy from 1968 to 1978* (London, Verso, 1990), pp. 295–312. Here again Nanni Moretti used the medium of the cinema – see *Ecce Bombo* (1978) – to pass sarcastic judgement on the various brands of the New Left language.

8 H. Marcuse, *One-dimensional Man* (London, Routledge, 1991), p. 85.

9 See R. Iacopino and S. Bianchi, *La Lega ce l'ha crudo!* (Milan, Mursia 1994), which is indeed better on the crude than on the magical ingredients in Bossi's discourse. On the language of the Lega see also S. Allievi, *Le parole della Lega* (Milan, Garzanti, 1992).

10 C. Brambilla, 'E Bossi ordinò ai suoi', *L'Unità*, 18 November 1995.

11 U. Bertone, '"Umberto non sbaglia mai"', *La Stampa*, 27 November 1995.

12 See a textbook used by twelve-year-old children: G. Ferrari, A. Marinelli and G. Monti, *Pagine del tempo* (Novara, De Agostini, 1985), p. 95.

13 A. De Gasperi, 'La Linea del Partito' (speech at the 1946 DC congress), *Discorsi Politici* (Rome, Cinque Lune, 1956), vol. I, p. 97. Dante is actually more frequently seen as a founder of the secular view of the world.

14 For an analysis of Berlusconi's language in 1993–94 see my 'Il Linguaggio di Berlusconi', *Il Regno*, 15 May 1994, pp. 276–8, and 'Silvio Berlusconi: la parola crea l'uomo politico', *Europa Europe*, 3:3 (1994), pp. 241–56.

15 Speech by Silvio Berlusconi to Forza Italia local government representatives, 26 October 1994. Text provided by the Forza Italia press office.

16 On Berlusconi's use of the language of football see E. Semino and M. Masci, 'Politics is Football. Metaphor in the Discourse of Silvio Berlusconi in Italy', *Discourse and Society*, 7:2 (1996), pp. 243–69, and N. Pozzo and P. Russo, 'Berlusconi and Other Matters: the Era of Football Politics', *Journal of Modern Italian Studies*, 5:3 (2000), pp. 348–70.

17 G. Fiori, *Il Venditore* (Milan, Garzanti, 1995), p. 134.

18 See S. E. D'Anna and G. Moncalvo, *Berlusconi in Concert* (London, Otzium, 1994).

19 'Discorso del 6 febbraio 1994'. Text supplied by the Forza Italia press office.

20 To my knowledge there is no serious study of the language of the so-called *svolta* (the turning point, i.e. the change from PCI to PDS). A close reading of the speech of the party leader Achille Occhetto at the 1990 Bologna congress would reveal a linguistic confusion from which the PDS had not emerged in 1994. On the *svolta* see D. Kertzer, 'The Nineteenth Congress of the Italian Communist Party. The Role of Symbolism in the Communist Crisis', in F. Anderlini and R. Leonardi (eds), *Italian Politics. A Review*, vol. 5 (London, Pinter, 1992), pp. 69–82, and the same author's chapter in this book.

21 G. Pansa, *I bugiardi* (Rome, *L'Unità*–Sperling & Kupfer, 1993), p. 189.

22 F. Manzitti, 'Di Pietro farà politica', *La Repubblica*, 21 September 1995.

23 E. Scalfari, 'Comincia una nuova stagione', *La Repubblica*, 26 September 1995.

24 S. Gundle, 'Il sorriso di Berlusconi', *Altrochemestre*, 3 (1995), pp. 14–17.

25 C. de Gregorio, '"Faziosi e indebitati". Berlusconi annuncia l'attacco finale alla RAI', *La Repubblica*, 8 June 1994.

26 V. Testa, 'Berlusconi-Scalfaro: la tregua', *La Repubblica*, 26 November 1994.

27 'Intervista', *Panorama*, 4 February 1994, pp. 9–14.

28 Censis, *Rapporto sulla situazione sociale del paese, 1995* (Rome, Censis Foundation, 1995), p. 12.

29 S. Tropea, 'Berlusconi plaude: "È un segnale chiaro e forte"', *La Repubblica*, 5 March 1996.

30 F. Verderami, 'Berlusconi attacca Dotti e il pool', *Corriere della Sera*, 15 March 1996.

31 A. Longo, 'Ormai è una persecuzione', *La Repubblica*, 7 October 1995; V. Testa, 'Il pool vuole distruggermi', *La Repubblica*, 1 October 1995.

32 S. Marroni, 'L'Italia al voto in mezzo al veleno', *La Repubblica*, 26 March 1994.

33 b.pal. [*sic*], 'Ma davvero chi vince non farà prigionieri?', *La Repubblica*, 16 April 1996; S. Marroni, 'Bufera su Scalfaro. E Mancuso attacca Dini: "Sono in pericolo"', *La Repubblica*, 1 April 1996.

34 C. Brambilla, '"Traditi dalla protervia"', *La Repubblica*, 27 April 1996.

35 R. Capitani, 'Match sul lavoro tra D'Alema e Fini', *L'Unità*, 27 March 1996.

36 A. Longo, 'Ma dov'è finita la Destra sociale?', *La Repubblica,* 24 April 1996.
37 M. Fucillo, 'Con Dini la nomenclatura della vecchia Italia', *La Repubblica,* 3 March 1996.
38 M. Caprara, 'Fisco e stipendi, bufera nel Polo per Fini', *Corriere della Sera,* 7 April 1996.
39 G. Passalacqua, 'Bossi dorme e annuncia la cravatta padana', *La Repubblica,* 21 April 1996; U. Bossi, 'A Pontida c'era il dio della Padania', *Corriere della Sera,* 26 March 1996.
40 'Il Senatur fa un errore', *La Repubblica,* 5 December 1995; U. Bossi, 'La canaglia romana', *La Repubblica,* 29 February 1996; C. Brambilla, 'Bossi: "Torno in pista, la secessione è legittima"', *L'Unità,* 12 January 1996; 'Sellano i cavalli i guerrieri di Braveheart', *La Repubblica,* 17 April 1996.
41 For a fuller political analysis of Bossi's sartorial style (and that of other politicians) see Maria Pia Pozzato's chapter in this book.
42 See S. Pivato, *Sia lodato Bartali. Ideologia, cultura e miti dello sport cattolico, 1936–48* (Rome, Edizioni del Lavoro, 1985), and D. Marchesini, *Bartali e Coppi* (Bologna, Il Mulino, 1998).
43 See my 'Il professore e il Cavaliere: la guerra filologica', *Il Regno,* 15 June 1995, pp. 338–40.
44 See 'Uno stato leggero ma attento alle regole', in R. Prodi, *Governare l'Italia* (Rome, Donzelli, 1995), p. 24.
45 M. Smargiassi, 'Berlusconi ha fatto i soldi con sesso e violenza in TV', *La Repubblica,* 16 April 1996. Private lives were dragged into the campaign more than is usual in Italy.
46 'Vinceremo l'odio con le idee. Dalla Convention dell'Ulivo le proposte per l'Italia', *L'Unità,* 24 March 1996.
47 D'Alema offered this as proof that the PDS was now a part of the European left. See A. Longo, 'Fini e D'Alema: niente patti con Bossi', *La Repubblica,* 18 April 1996.
48 Woody Allen, *Elementi di paesaggio,* 12 April 1996.
49 S. Di Michele, 'La piazza nelle mani dei giovani', *L'Unità,* 19 April 1996.
50 See my 'America: l'altro mito della cultura comunista', in P. P. D'Attorre (ed.), *Nemici per la pelle. Sogno americano e mito sovietico nell'Italia contemporanea* (Milan, Franco Angeli, 1991), pp. 217–34; and S. Gundle, *Between Hollywood and Moscow. The Italian Communists and the Challenge of Mass Culture, 1943–1991* (Durham, NC, Duke University Press, 2000).
51 Dini claimed that he had wooed his wife with the music of the singer Ornella Vanoni, thus blending American frankness and Italian popular culture. See r.r. [*sic*], 'E Lamberto duetta con Ornella', *La Stampa,* 11 March 1996.
52 The company was set up by the magnate to run his television empire (the advertising agency Publitalia and his three television networks), while offering blocs of its shares on the market (July 1996). Fininvest, Berlusconi's family holding company, retains control of Mediaset.
53 Television debate, 9 April. Author's notes.
54 *Falce Martello,* 25 April 1996.
55 'Intervista a Massimo D'Alema' *L'Unità,* 23 March 1996.
56 It recurred in his 17 April speech at Bologna. Author's notes.
57 Conversely, the expression *porto delle nebbie* (port of mists) was a metaphor waiting to be used. Literally a translation of the title of a 1930s film by Marcel Carné, *Le Quai des brumes,* which depicted a real port, 'porto delle nebbie' was used to describe the knavery of the Rome magistrates' office. When this became a campaign motif the metaphor began a new life.

PART II

Persuasion through symbolism and spectacle

12

Meetings of desire

Umberto Eco

Of late the weekly magazine *L'Espresso* has received a good many requests for help from readers whose activities require them to take part in meetings. It is an experience common to many. Whereas in 1968 the only meetings held were those in universities and factories, nowadays one can find oneself attending a neighbourhood meeting, a residents' association meeting, a parents of pupils meeting (the so-called *decreti delegati*), a pupils and teachers meeting, a hospital meeting or even a prison meeting. There are also women's meetings (feminist or otherwise), meetings of those charged with the enforcement of public order, meetings of homosexuals, theatre-company actors, co-op members, editorial meetings, etc. Even to write this article, friends and collaborators were contacted and a meeting was called of people experienced in attending meetings. The contents are the result of a collective vote, its authors having been delegated by the meeting to write it. In the end, one author delegated the other to do the writing.[1]

Thus described, this trend may seem ridiculous, and some people already talk of a 'meeting mania' and view the meetings which are taking place up and down the country as innocuous, albeit boring, parodies of the soviet, whilst those in power carry on as if nothing has happened, and terrorist groups use direct individual action (or oligarchic action) in preference to the spuriously democratic meeting.

Yet, though we live in an age when the Marxists of 1968 are ashamed of having been Marxists, the former masters of Stalinist demonstrations maintain that they do not care about the working class any more, and the terms 'class' and 'mass' are becoming inappropriate for polite conversation, it should be said that the proliferation of meetings has been a positive development.

Although a slogan such as 'presa della parola' (taking the floor to have your say), loaded with all the naivety of someone who may have said it once upon a time, is now open to witty transformations such as 'presa per il sedere' (to be the focus of a 'piss-take'), the great meeting mania has made for greater public participation. It has challenged the principle of authority, at least on a psychological level. It has taught many, who never had the courage before, to express their opinions and make their voices heard. It has led many to feel that they are making political statements, even when they are talking about their own personal problems. In a word, we the authors prefer a country where there are too many meetings to one where there are none.

Having said that, the proliferation of meetings produces its own neuroses, and it is vital to be aware of this.

A meeting is a political act which aims to involve also those who are not career politicians. Inevitably, however, political professionals seek to exploit meetings by using all the tricks (legitimate or otherwise) at their disposal.

In principle, at least, no one can say that they are wrong in so doing. The problem for the others, i.e. the non-experts, is, if anything, that of knowing the same rules in order to be able to participate in the game. But what is the game?

Is there a standard type of meeting which exemplifies 'correct' procedural rules? The answer is no. There is a difference between meetings held at a university and at a flat in the Via Roma. Some meetings are called to criticise a structure perceived to be outdated. Others aim to make a particular body about whose worthiness everyone agrees (a neighbourhood committee, a co-operative, the editorial panel of a radical left-wing newspaper) function democratically. There may be meetings made up of groups which are united by a common revolutionary cause, and meetings of groups belonging to different political tendencies, whose purpose is to 'compare notes'. There are 'polar' meetings (students *v.* lecturers, tenants *v.* management), meetings characterised by their homogeneity (members of a theatrical co-operative), as well as Leninist and Liberal Party meetings.

In terms of models, there are meetings of the 1968 type and the 1977 type. The 1977 type, prevalent in the universities, will not necessarily be the most suitable type for a local school, where, for the first time, parents sit down with the headmistress to discuss the purchase of textbooks. Nor should it be assumed that in 1977 all the meetings held in Italian universities excluded those of the 1968 type.

So the first question to be clarified is: in what kind of meeting am I participating? We can identify three abstract types of procedure, bearing in mind that real meetings will often be a blend of two or three such categories. It is up to the participants to identify the trends of their own meetings and work out what they are trying to achieve. In the profiles at the end of this chapter we have set out for each type the normal operative rules and tactics which the 'professionals' generally use to control meetings. This is not to say that 'tricks' are necessarily bad, since the very format of a meeting lays itself open to manipulation.

The first type is the Judicial Meeting. This is listed first because the first meetings of 1968 were of this type. The judicial meeting is polar in nature, with accusers pitted against the accused. This may mean students pitted against lecturers, tenants of a building against the management, hospital patients against the doctors, and so forth. The grammatical tense of the judicial meeting is the past: 'What did you do in years gone by?' The judicial meeting seeks to modify power relations, to put new relations in their stead and to break the entrenched relations of authority. Its most frequently used technique is the trial: force predominates and the vehemence of the accusations forms the basis of its procedure. Yet the judicial meeting is not tantamount to a people's tribunal. The latter arises when one side gets the upper hand and destroys the opposing side, as, for example, in the French Revolution. The judicial meeting, on the other hand, usually does not seek to deny the existing relations of power: the management is still the management; the lecturers are still the lecturers. It is, rather, a case of formulating these relations along different lines, by showing that the behaviour of those in power is criticisable and correctable.

The second type is the Deliberative Meeting. It is not usually polar (i.e. white *v.* black, white representing absolute authority). It does put diverse forces into play, but the confrontation is with equal weaponry. It has been designated as the second type because historically it comes after the judicial-style meeting. For example, school pupils may initiate a judicial meeting to pass judgement on their teachers. This will lead to two different possibilities: they can either meet and deliberate their problems autonomously, or they can meet with their teachers in a sole meeting with equal voting power. The deliberative meeting then becomes homogeneous (equal forces), without removing its conflictual nature. Its grammatical tense is the future: the focus of the deliberation is what needs to be done tomorrow.

In 1977, however, a different type, the Impulsive Meeting, came to prevail, although some examples of the type had been in existence earlier. The impulsive meeting is concerned not with the past or the future, but with the present. Neither the trial process nor deliberation is attempted; instead the participants confront each other at the level of personal confessions. In the impulsive meeting each person puts his/her own ego on display; the personal dimension is more important than the political; the confession dominates over the purpose. Deliberative and judicial-style meetings both use so-called *sinistrese*, left-speak, typical phrases of which are: 'nella misura in cui' (to the extent that), 'argomentazioni serrate' (coherent arguments), 'ricorsi a principi di autorità' (recourse to principles of authority), 'il pensiero di Lenin' (Lenin's doctrine), and 'lotta di classe' (class struggle). The impulsive meeting, on the other hand, uses what may be termed *libidinese*, libido-speak, through which all the flows of desire, human need, untrammelled impulses and liberatory crises are vented.

In meetings where left-speak is used, the impersonal third person singular or the first person plural prevails: 'si deve ritenere che' (one must presume that), 'noi vogliamo che' (we demand that), 'è certo che la situazione attuale è la seguente' (without question the present situation is as follows), etc. Whereas in the impulsive meeting the first person singular is the most frequently used form: 'io penso che' (I think that), 'voglio dire che' (what I'm trying to say is), 'permettetemi di dire che' (let me say that), etc.

Left-speak is dialectical and syllogistic, whilst libido-speak is narrative. Left-speak explains what needs to be done and sets out the reasons why; libido-speak explains what an individual is feeling and why he/she is talking about it.

Left-speak speaks (or pretends to speak) after having spoken a lot. The speaker puts himself forward as a guarantor of the truth he/she is saying (bolstered by references to philosophical or political authorities – remember Godard? 'Lénine a dit . . .'). Libido-speak, on the other hand, purports to speak or speaks as if it were the speaker's very first attempt at speaking out: 'Comrades, I'm sorry if I can't put into words what I want to say, my ideas are a bit mixed up, it's the first time I've stood up and spoken in public, I'm a bit paranoid, but I want to tell you what my feelings are at this moment . . .' Left-speak structures itself on a series of interventions and answers, libido-speak on a series of narrations and counter-narrations (my experience against yours). An address in left-speak tends to establish a leadership, but one in libido-speak avoids doing so (the impulsive meeting reacts forcefully against the possibility of any leadership being established). Obviously, the rhythm also varies: in left-speak it is fast, as in the chanting of slogans during a demonstration; the rhythm is one of ideas linked together syllogistically. The syntactic model is that of Cicero. In libido-speak the rhythm is slower, even broken. The syntactic model varies from Proust to Beckett.

The interjections, though, do not vary between the two linguistic styles: 'cazzo' ('fuck', literally 'prick'), 'cioè . . . perché, dico compagni . . .' (I mean . . . because, as I say, comrades . . .). Through these linguistic constants, left-speak and libido-speak meet and recognise each other. In technical terms, one could say that the two styles differ in vocabulary and syntax, but their punctuation marks and 'contact' signals remain unchanged (so, ultimately, all types, impulsive or deliberative, are united as part of the same 'movement').

Another difference is that in meetings conducted in left-speak there are pre-defined 'groups' (Lotta Continua, Il Manifesto, Movimento Lavoratori per il Socialismo), whereas in meetings held in libido-speak groups tend to form and disperse on fortuitous impulse. The impulsive meeting is dominated by flows of desire; it is a machine which cuts and expels without recourse to any set agenda; it does not judge, but latches on to things according to its inclination.

There are, of course, numerous possible combinations of the two; there can be brusque changes of regime between left-speak and libido-speak and reversals of roles. When, during a meeting predominantly in libido-speak, interventions are made in left-speak, the offending contributions are derided and labelled – cries of 'Scemo, scemo!' (Moron, moron!), are an illustration of this. A meeting in libido-speak can take a deliberative turn, but it is usually for deliberation of a march and the calls of 'Corteo, corteo!' (March, march!) signal the end of the meeting, but it leads to a new occasion of impulsive aggregation (whereas in left-speak a march is decided beforehand, it is never improvised). For the specialists: the deliberative and judicial meetings held in left-speak have a tree-like structure, whilst impulsive meetings in libido-speak have a structure which is rhizome-shaped.

What happens to the leader in impulsive meetings? A leader does not appear to exist. Nevertheless, there are historic leaders who have an ability to influence even impulsive meetings. But whilst in deliberative meetings the leader sets the agenda ('This or that needs to be done'), in the impulsive type of meeting the potential leader, at best, manoeuvres the passage between the two meeting types: 'Comrades, we have to come to a conclusion' (transformation from impulsive to deliberative) or 'Comrades, we don't have to reach a conclusion' (passage from deliberative to impulsive).

At this juncture it is clear that it is pointless to say whether one type of meeting is preferable to another. A meeting is a response to the needs of a situation. Some situations require free expression of all the feelings pertinent to them, with the meeting taking on a therapeutic function ('Together at last!'). Other situations require concrete decisions to be taken to avoid group frustration. The art of participation in a meeting consists in knowing what is at stake.

Concluding remarks? There are at least two. The first is political in nature. In recent years there has been an upsurge in impulsive-type meetings. Though lost to mass meetings, the functions of deliberation and judgement have been taken up by oligarchic groups: terrorist groups with their people's tribunals seem to be doing, at leadership level, what many meetings no longer do at mass level, namely judging and deliberating punishments and interventions. It is a problem which needs pondering on.

The second observation is biological in nature. There is no need to search for ideological reasons for the transformation of many meetings from the deliberative to the impulsive type, since there are material explanations. In the university context, where gatherings are disproportionate to the confined spaces in which they are held, the meeting inevitably becomes impulsive: people casually move in and out of small groups (those here today may not be the ones who are here tomorrow, and there is not the space to have the whole lot together). In meetings of other types (neighbourhood, factory, secondary school), the rules may differ precisely because of a different space-to-participant ratio.

So, since a meeting is determined also by the material conditions of where it is held, it is necessary to evaluate how the relationship between social circumstances, physical space and psychological reactions determines the type of meeting one can expect to find. Even the space in which a meeting is held (whether freely chosen or imposed) constitutes a political and psychological problem.

The judicial meeting

Object: the past; model: a court of law; ideal: Plutonic.[2]

OPERATIVE RULES

1 Ask the speakers to clarify the terms they use and to give concrete examples, so that the accusations are not generic (risk of transformation into an impulsive meeting).
2 Ensure that the accusations are turned into a *cahier de doléances* (list of demands, those responsible, injustices, etc.) and that solutions are proposed.
3 If the accused accepts the challenge of confrontation, he/she must either criticise himself/herself or criticise the *cahier de doléances.*
4 The accuser must allow the accused to put forth his/her own critique, or else the accused will harden his/her stance of resistance and dialogue will become impossible. N.B. the preceding rules do not apply if the judicial meeting is in essence a people's tribunal, in which the accuser is in a position of strength and aims to destroy the opponent – in this situation a supplementary rule applies.
5 Do not set up a would-be people's tribunal if you are not starting from a real position of strength, otherwise the accused will play along, but later re-establish their power, and the judicial meeting, rather than a people's tribunal, becomes an impulsive meeting steered by the opposition.

TRICKS AND STRONG-ARM TACTICS

1 Strong interventions which put the accused on the psychological defensive. For example, if those accused excel in the art of irony, the accusers must put their case with severity and without smiling, branding every attempt at irony as bourgeois perversion. If, however, the accused have no sense of humour, the accusers must overwhelm the accused with teasing irony. When this trick works, the meeting becomes a people's tribunal.
2 Submit evidence of a highly emotive nature to put the accused in psychological difficulty, even if the accused are not directly responsible for the proven deed. Examples: the unexpected arrival of a wounded comrade; first-hand testimony by sufferers of grave injustices; letters from comrades in gaol.

INTERRUPTIVE PLOYS

The ploys used in the deliberative type of meeting (see below) also apply here. Inevitably they transform the judicial meeting into one in the impulsive mould.

The deliberative meeting

Object: the future; model: mock parliament; ideal: Apollonian.

OPERATIVE RULES

1 Fix rules for speeches: the duration of each speech, the number of speeches per motion, their overall duration.
2 Set an agenda, leaving ample time for 'any other business' to be discussed after the other items on the agenda.
3 Elect a chairperson capable of observing rules 1 and 2.
4 Do not begin unless there is a quorum (otherwise anyone could invalidate the decisions taken).
5 Distinguish between routine motions and those of substance.
6 Vote on each point of the agenda separately, but only after having read through all the proposals so that deciding on one point does not make it impossible to decide on the others.
7 For each item, if possible, put forward conflicting motions so that those who vote are aware of what they are accepting and rejecting.
8 When the debate becomes confused, call a halt to enable the formation of groupings of opinion (or of elected committees) able to draft motions that already have some chance of being supported.

TRICKS AND STRONG-ARM TACTICS

1 Time and a rock-hard bum. Those who are able to resist right up to the end, wearing the others out, will be able to present their own motions at a moment when most of the opposition will have already left.
2 Confound your opponents with a storm of motions one after the other so that, when the time comes for the decisive motion, they will be tired and confused.

3 Put to the vote ambiguous, seemingly harmless motions which, however, invalidate subsequent motions.
4 Encourage the meeting to divide into groups for the purpose of drawing up motions, but make sure that you have representatives in every group, so as to influence the motions as required.
5 Make sure that two fictitious groups propose opposing motions which will essentially lead to the same result. The opposition will believe that it has made a choice.

INTERRUPTIVE PLOYS

1 To transform a deliberative meeting into an impulsive one:
   (a) Organise unexpected happenings.
   (b) Yell 'Scemo, scemo!' at every intervention.
   (c) Yell 'Corteo, corteo!'
   (d) Laugh; mew like cats; turn on transistor radios; bring animals into the meeting hall; at the same time, feign epileptic attacks in different parts of the meeting hall.
2 To change a deliberative assembly into a judicial one:
   (a) Strongly criticise the chairperson's methods.
   (b) Complain about the short time allowed for interventions, saying that it favours articulate elites and puts marginalised individuals, who have difficulty in expressing themselves, at a disadvantage.
   (c) Ask for the quorum to be verified (point out, for instance, that students who live some distance away are absent).
   (d) Ensure the impromptu arrival *en masse* of a group of people having the right to attend (their absence is justified by serious reasons, e.g. clashes with the police below), who will proclaim their opposition to the decisions taken. (This works if the chairperson failed to verify the quorum earlier.)
3 To regain moral unity during the meeting:
   (a) Yell 'There are Fascists down there!'
   (b) Sing the Internationale (other songs are permissible at meetings of Catholic organisations such as the ACLI, Comunione e Liberazione, etc.).

The impulsive meeting

Object: the present; model: a festive get-together; ideal: Dionysian.

OPERATIVE RULES

Generally there are none, but when they do arise, they are on a par with tricks and strong-arm tactics. Every rule is seen as a trick. At best, there are criteria for survival or psychological balance.

1 Do not become a victim of your traditional rules.
2 Do not saddle others with your rules.

3 Do not be led to believe that the impulsive meeting is a deliberative one. Decision-making kills it off.
4 Do not confuse the impulsive meeting with a judicial one, since there is no clear distinction between the participating parties (your accuser may also be your ally).

The impulsive meeting does, however, have a series of distinctive criteria, namely an implicit decalogue of its own, or rule of irregularity.

1 The primary aim of the meeting is that meeting.
2 It is not necessary for the meeting to end with a decision being taken, nor is it necessary for any decision which is taken to be implemented.
3 The secondary aim of the meeting is to call the next meeting. Meetings do not, of course, follow on: the new one simply discusses the same problems all over again.
4 The meeting defines the groups which constitute that meeting. (Groups or tendencies pre-existing the meeting do not define the nature of the meeting. In other words, a meeting is not called because groups want to air their views, rather it is a case of groups wanting to air their views precisely because there is a meeting.)
5 The right to be at the meeting belongs to all those people who are actually in it.
6 To take part in the meeting, one must physically enter the space in which it is taking place. To enter does not mean that one has to stand there. Simply walking through it is enough.
7 The right to vote at the meeting applies to anyone who happens to be walking through it at that moment.
8 It is not possible to have a decentralised meeting linked by closed-circuit television; impulsive meetings do not permit bicameralism. Every other space marks a separate meeting, which is opposed to the first.
9 Two categories of individuals are excluded from the impulsive meeting:
(a) Anyone who is not there.
(b) Anyone who tries to give it rules or impose a leadership upon it. (Latent and apolitical leadership can arise which imposes limits on the uninhibited, impulsive expression of individuals. For this reason, pushers or rapists reported by feminist groups are, as a rule, expelled.)
10 Public pronouncement of the nine points set out hereinabove is prohibited, the penalty being the death of the meeting.

INTERRUPTIVE PLOYS

There are none, that is to say, every possible type of interruption is a correct one.

NOTES

This essay originally appeared in *l'Espresso*, 25 December 1977. It is reprinted here for the first time in English by kind permission of Umberto Eco.

1 This study was born of shared experience while at university and was conceived and discussed with Paolo Fabbri, who, to all intents and purposes, is its co-author.

2 *Editors' note.* 'Plutonic' is here used to refer to an ideal of harsh judgement. In classical mythology Pluto was the ruler of the underworld.

13

Persuasion by violence: terror and its texts

David Moss

Between 1969 and 1988 Italy witnessed some 16,000 acts of broadly defined political violence, at a cost of nearly 400 deaths, 5,000 injuries, and damage to property and individual victims estimated at $600 million.[1] Other types of post-war violence (separatism in the Tyrol, Mafia in the South) had had political consequences, but the violence of the period 1969–88 reached more people and represented a more sustained attempt to infiltrate the country's social and political conflicts. Its forms, authors, targets and objectives of terrorism, spread out over two decades, were very diverse. The overwhelming majority of attacks were directed against the property of individuals and organisations by their antagonists on the extreme left and extreme right. In the early years of violence, between 1969 and 1975, these assaults were largely the work of the extreme right, accompanied by indiscriminate bombings which left 45 dead and 349 injured. In contrast, the years between 1976 and 1982 were dominated by the extreme left and its increasingly lethal attacks on a widening array of human targets (though this period also saw the worst of all massacres perpetrated by the far right: the Bologna Station bomb of 2 August 1980, which killed eighty-five people). Thereafter, undermined by the mass defections and confessions of its protagonists, violence declined rapidly, vanishing altogether after a final clandestine murder in 1988.[2]

Some two-thirds of the deliberate attacks on people and property were designed as acts of 'armed propaganda'.[3] They were attempts simultaneously to persuade a wide spectrum of victims and potential victims to act and reflect in new ways, and to convince particular audiences that the assailants' diagnoses of the problems of Italian politics and society were accurate and required resolution through violence. The attacks were carried out clandestinely, accompanied by the diffusion of documents bearing the name of the group responsible and explaining its reasons for the choice and timing of the action. For this type of clandestine political violence, which will be the focus of this chapter, the production of texts – or in some cases the deliberate refusal to produce texts – was an essential element in the strategy of persuasion by violence.

The documentary dimension of communication by clandestine violence deserves more analytical attention than it has generally received. First, because acts of violence need accompanying texts in order to be identified as political, each successful communication by violence depends on combining roles that can be played by different people and need to be co-ordinated. Two-thirds of convicted left-wing activists in Italy played no part in attacks on individuals and two-fifths had no direct role at all in any violent attack.[4] They did, however, often play an essential role in researching, composing and disseminating the texts that provided violence with its meanings. Second, the demand for texts to supply contexts for the interpretation of violence varies, allowing us to track communicative constraints and the changing importance of specific categories of authors. Third, treating texts as strategic productions makes relations between flesh-and-blood authors, signatures on texts and acts of violence much less straightforward than they are sometimes made to appear. In violence there need not be a direct correspondence between writer and author: in one sample of left-wing violence, for instance, 23 groups used 125 different signatures for their actions.[5] Such discrepancies emphasise the need to treat the documentary dimension as an independently important feature of any violent communicative act. Acts of violence prepare an individual to serve as a bearer of meaning, but the meaning itself is achieved only, if at all, with the help of the accompanying text. This feature does not convert acts of violence into (harmless) texts, as is sometimes suggested, but should lead us to examine the various ways in which texts make or fail to make those acts persuasive.

To take this approach is to examine in more detail the symbolisation process, regarded as the key distinctive characteristic of clandestine political violence. The very familiarity of the definition seems to have distracted attention from investigating the actual practices of symbolisation, the range of meanings that symbols are supposed to carry and the distribution of the understanding of symbols among the people who witness their creation. This shortcoming reflects the generally rather undeveloped analysis of symbolisation.[6] Moreover, accounts of Italian violence which do pay attention to its semiotic dimensions do not go beyond the study of a single episode.[7] My aim is to extend this line of analysis to cover more violence and a longer period.

Violence as ritual: frame and interaction

In liberal democracies the deliberate use of violence against people for political aims represents a dramatic rupture of routine political conflict. This rupture has both macro and micro dimensions. On one hand, it opens up the possibility of a new communicative field, unstructured by obvious conventions or constraints. At the micro level, acts of violence separate victims sharply from their social assumptions and relationships, sometimes in ways which may be extremely hard to reverse,[8] producing a lasting sense of insecurity and isolation. Both levels of uncertainty are heightened when the attack is delivered clandestinely. The elements of separation, marginalisation and symbolisation strongly suggest that clandestine political violence may be analysed as an instance of ritual action, organised according to the tripartite sequence of separation–marginalisation–incorporation identified by Arnold Van Gennep.[9]

Rituals are created to stand apart from ordinary social activity to provide a context for reflection on, and transformation of, matters of identity, time and authority. First, they are characteristically designed to organise, confuse and reorganise the relationship of the protagonists with (other members of) their own community. They accomplish the transformation of individual or collective identities by shifting their bearers back and forth across boundaries of various kinds before reintegrating them in a new social status.[10] Participants and spectators are also likely to encounter beings whose only direct intervention in social life comes in the ritual context. Second, a characteristic element of ritual is the disruption of time, frequently shifting the actions within the ritual into a different time frame. And, third, rituals are a standard context for delivering and eliciting authoritative, usually uncontestable affirmations of basic values. Can the communicative dimensions of Italian political violence be illuminated as a limiting case of ritual action?

Prima facie evidence certainly points to the characteristic features of ritual structure and content. The bomb massacre of Milan's Piazza Fontana in 1969 was widely regarded as the opening move in a new phase of Italian politics, marked by tension and disorder. Political identities among those who used violence (were the Brigate Rosse – BR, or Red Brigades – really red? were they and Autonomia allies in a single 'partito della lotta armata' – party of armed struggle?) and their opponents (how revolutionary was the Communist Party; how sympathetic to Fascism was the Christian Democratic party?) became problematic.[11] The political boundary between actors and spectators was often queried: could Italians remain neutral observers of the confrontation between users of violence and the state? The flow of time, too, appeared to have been upset. Diego Novelli, mayor of Turin in the most violent period, met the representatives of every organised group in the city to ask that their activities should continue in a normal way, 'to give the feeling of life continuing to flow, that it had not stopped'.[12] Social scientists, too, displayed similar perception by making the 'blockage' of normal political development a cause and consequence of violence.[13] Finally, the authors of clandestine violence routinely delivered apodictic statements about Italian politics, protected from direct contradiction because of the reluctance of opponents to appear to be coerced into direct dialogue. The attacks themselves provided the context for the opponents of violence to state their own fundamental social and political values. Those features suggest that the prolonged use of violence as a technique of political persuasion after 1969 can be plausibly described as an extended ritual, partly insulated from, and partly intertwined with, non-violent politics.

To develop this description requires some analytic terms. I shall track the evolution of communication through clandestine violence in terms of an initial contrast between macro-violence and micro-violence, distinguished by function rather than scale of damage. Acts of macro-violence play the role of shifters,[14] delocalising devices which create new frames for communicative action. Each frame is inhabited by actants – semiotic jargon for the group signatures and individual battle names which flesh-and-blood authors use to sign their actions. Interaction within each frame is carried by acts of micro-violence, building up the actants' identities, clarifying membership boundaries, and trying to coerce the social categories represented by the victims into acknowledging some kind of direct relationship. Shifts of frame move the communicative context progressively further from its initial point of departure in non-violent politics. They are marked by the appearance of new actants, the re-organisation of relations within and between frames, and new communicative centres. Successive shifts of frame – I shall identify three – increase confusion over identities and thus lead to greater difficulties in authoring persuasive messages. Ritual closure is achieved by the shifting in, and dismantling of, actants, returning their authors to the society from which their use of violence had wholly or partly separated them.

Shift 1: Piazza Fontana, 1969

The bomb set off in a Milan bank in December 1969, killing sixteen and wounding eighty-eight, transformed the practice and understanding of political violence. Hitherto it had been mainly a fringe component of public mobilisation, serving to express ideological hostility as directly as possible in the course of political and industrial conflict or direct confrontations between extreme right and extreme left. After Piazza Fontana, general mobilisation declined, and violence on occasions of mass demonstrations gave way increasingly to violence by small groups. As Donatella Della Porta and Sydney Tarrow conclude: 'The more dramatic forms of violence arise when the mass phase of the protest cycle declines. . . . As mass mobilisation winds down, political violence rises in magnitude and intensity.'[15]

The features of the Piazza Fontana bomb opened up the possibility of a new field of political communication. The deliberately indiscriminate use of violence, breaching all conventional limits of political conflict, also upset the routine distinction between protagonist and spectator: anyone might be a victim, regardless of political opinions and responsibilities. Confusion was aggravated, first, by uncertainty over the responsibility for planting the bomb, first attributed to the left, then to the right, and, second, by the investigative failure (some argued, the active obstruction of investigations) by police, judiciary and security services. That placed under suspicion the values and commitment of all major parties, casting doubt on their proclaimed political identities. Furthermore, since the bombing was not connected with any particular local conflict, and since the scale of damage created an immediate national audience, the use of violence was wrenched out of a purely local frame of reference. Piazza Fontana converted its instances from random supplements to local confrontations into common refractions of a co-ordinated national strategy.

To the activists of the extreme right the Milan bomb, followed by the death of the anarchist Giuseppe Pinelli in police custody, conveyed a hitherto unsuspected degree of support in key institutional positions for their confrontation with the left. The impression of powerful protection at all levels, including the external support of authoritarian regimes in Greece, Spain and Portugal, was strengthened at regular intervals by the further four neo-Fascist massacres between 1970 and 1974, by the revelations of *coups d'état* (planned, aborted, serious, comic), and by the apparent judicial immunity of their authors. The response to these messages of support was clear: rising levels of neighbourhood assaults on left-wing activists by neo-Fascist militants – ten times more frequent than left-wing attacks on the right between 1969 and 1974; and the appearance of the first clandestine signature for right-wing attacks, the Squadre d'Azione Mussolini (SAM).

The distinction between clandestine and legal politics on the right was very weak. The new secretary of the Movimento Sociale Italiano (MSI), Giorgio Almirante, encouraged his extremist organisations (Avanguardia Nazionale, Ordine Nuovo), and the users of the SAM signature were themselves mainly activists in legal extreme-right groups.[16] All this violence, signed and unsigned, was designed to persuade observers of the collapse of the post-war conventions of Italian politics. The use of bombs, coupled with the historical evocation of the SAM signature, signalled a return to wartime conditions, erasing the distinction between combatant and civilian, politics and war. The derangement of political categories and identities marked the liminal phase preparing Italians for a rite of reaggregation – the return of the extreme right to the political arena from which it had been largely excluded since the establishment of democracy in 1945.

For the militants of the extreme left Piazza Fontana signalled three communicative tasks: to unmask the local, national and international connections on which the extreme right traded; to disseminate a proper understanding of the co-ordinated class war already unleashed against the working class; and to display determination to resist the attack. Some militants, e.g. the anonymous authors of the volume *La strage di Stato* (State Massacre), devoted themselves to patient investigation;[17] others (the members of the 'defence squads' of such extraparliamentary groups as Lotta Continua, Potere Operaio, Avanguardia Operaia and Movimento Studentesco) showed readiness to resist,[18] and a very few, taking the name of Red Brigades, combined these tasks with active counter-violence. Like the SAM on the right, the BR dominated clandestine violence on the left, claiming responsibility for four-fifths of all left-wing clandestine attacks between 1970 and 1974. Again like the SAM, their primary time reference was the past: Renato Curcio, the BR leader, took his first battle-name ('Armando') from his partisan uncle murdered by the Germans in 1945, and the early Red Brigades weaponry was handed over directly by former members of the Resistance who designated Curcio and Alberto Franceschini their political heirs.[19] Those historical references made the new actant more substantial.

In deliberate contrast to the right-wing terrorists, who used violence to communicate disorder, the BR paid great attention to making their own violence orderly. Targets were chosen according to known shop-floor hostilities to accredit their claims to be the delegates of the working class; levels of violence were carefully restrained. The message that violence could be creative of order was most widely communicated in the four kidnappings between 1972 and 1974. Each instance was a miniaturised exemplification of successful persuasion by violence. The victims were separated from society by violence, persuaded to reflect on their political role, shown publicly (via a widely circulated 'confession') to endorse the kidnappers' claim that a co-ordinated class war against the working class was in progress, and released unharmed to live out their new awareness. The kidnappings, which relied on the absolute separation of audience and protagonists to disseminate their messages, also countered the extreme right's attempt to demolish this distinction.

Despite the availability of a new, unexplored frame for political action, few Italians were persuaded of its necessity. Its use and consequences remained highly circumscribed. Almost all clandestine violence took place in Milan or Turin; predictability was established by repeated use of the bomb/kidnapping contrast; and the extreme right and extreme left were each represented by a single actant, whose authors carried out the acts and composed the minimal texts required to explain them. In this first phase the authors and actants were directly linked, and the frame for clandestine action was firmly anchored to legal politics. The SAM responded to the strategies of the parliamentary and extraparliamentary right; the inventors of the BR preserved alternating identities between violent and non-violent politics, participating in grass-roots activism and using their individual battle-names and collective signature for the shift into clandestine mode. No doubt this alternation was especially accessible and appealing to militants who had migrated to Milan from other parts of Italy and had no clear local political identity in the city itself (Curcio, Mara Cagol, Franceschini, Mario Moretti, Antonio Paroli, Prospero Gallinari, Fabrizio Pelli, Alfredo Bonavita). The coherence of their communications, addressed to specific factory audiences, could be sustained precisely because they failed to attract recruits or support from the local, more deeply rooted segments of the extraparliamentary left.

Shift 2: Pedenovi and Coco, 1976

The murders of the MSI provincial councillor Enrico Pedenovi and the magistrate Francesco Coco in 1976 signalled a shift of frame for the use of violence. The new frame was populated by new actants (Prima Linea was responsible for the murder of Pedenovi) and new levels of attack (Coco was the first deliberate murder by the BR). Competition among left-wing signatures and widening repertoires of violence were a response to pressures on the earlier frame of violence; they also prompted some increasingly complex communicative demands.

In the mid-1970s the frame of the relatively limited violence of the earlier years was undermined at many points. Its primary axis – the projection of the right–left antagonism from ordinary politics – collapsed in the wake of the withdrawal of support for extremist violence by the MSI and the end of tolerance of right-wing organisations by local police and judiciaries. The protagonists of the radical right, the symbols of determination to restore Fascism, were killed, arrested or forced into exile, depriving followers of their direct relationship with the bearers of the historical meanings for their violence.[20] Neo-Fascist assaults diminished sharply; the SAM signature vanished; clandestine attacks were restricted to the single city of Rome. Repudiating any intention to influence national politics, and devoting their violence either to gestures of hostility to the newly unsympathetic state or to pure self-affirmation, the extreme right abandoned any more general communicative ambitions for violence.[21] Whatever political messages were contained in the final bomb massacres in 1980 (Bologna station) and 1984 (the Naples–Milan train) remained entirely obscure.

The disappearance of the extreme right removed the initial rationale for clandestine violence on the left. More or less simultaneously the temporal reference for armed struggle had to be erased: the communicatively far more powerful PCI reappropriated the rites and symbols of the Resistance to legitimise its return to collaboration with Catholics and Socialists and sponsored committees in all major cities to mobilise opposition to violence in the name of Resistance values. Furthermore, the political arena to which the early Red Brigades had anchored their use of violence changed rapidly. The extraparliamentary left turned parliamentary or disintegrated; mass political and industrial conflict diminished; and grass-roots politics fell increasingly under the control of the political parties in the wake of administrative decentralisation and the victory of the left in major city elections in 1975. The ability to sustain an alternating identity between legal and illegal politics was thus undermined on both sides of the divide.

The collapse of the extraparliamentary left did, however, make available for clandestine violence members whose active roles in its quasi-military 'defence squads' had made familiar to them the idea of violence as a dimension of political activity. The new activists, mostly employed and intent on trying to combine participation in violence with work and with legal politics, could be found in most of the cities of central and northern Italy which had not hitherto been the scene of clandestine attacks. Armed struggle was therefore offered an unexpected source of support; but its members also posed problems for the alignment of authors and actants required to produce intelligible and persuasive messages.

As far as the BR were concerned, this co-ordination was already experiencing difficulty. By 1976 most of their original members had been arrested; others had been identified by the police and disappeared into full clandestinity.[22] Recruitment from the extraparliamentary left (Lotta Continua, Potere Operaio, Autonomia) distributed authors still more widely, adding factories, public bureaucracies and universities to the contexts to which violence had to be made responsive. Coco's murder, planned as commemorative revenge for the death of Cagol and coinciding with the court appearance in Turin of the BR members whose demands he had thwarted during the kidnapping of the magistrate Mario Sossi in 1974, showed the first use of violence as a means of internal communication among users of the signature.[23] Raising violence to the level of murder reflected the disconnection between the attack and any attempt to seek approval from factory or political audiences. It also presaged the increasingly serious violence to come as users of the BR signature tried to find targets which would appeal to all their now very differently located affiliates: those targets would have to be independent of the idiosyncrasies of local conflicts and would have to be attacked with sufficient violence for the message of solidarity to carry widely. The redirection of attack towards 'state' representatives (politicians, magistrates, police) was thus designed to persuade an increasingly fragmented set of local users that they shared a common set of antagonists.

Accompanying the violence came ever lengthier documents, spelling out the relationships and responsibilities of different groups of users ('columns', 'fronts') and different kinds of activists ('regulars', 'irregulars'). The political analyses became longer and denser, supplying an interpretive context for violence which had not previously been necessary. In the first phase, communications had been shaped with only narrow factory audiences in mind, whose sentiments and reactions could be directly gauged. By the mid-1970s, however, fellow users of the signature were required to identify both the justification and consequences of violence: pitching them at an increasingly general level served to protect them from direct confutation by local experience.

The murder of Pedenovi, attributed later to the nascent signature Prima Linea, revealed the existence of left-wing activists who accepted the use of clandestine violence but rejected any supra-local frame of reference. The affiliates of the groups associated with Autonomia preferred purely local audiences for their attacks, tying them directly to factory and neighbourhood conflicts. The consequence was a dramatic increase in the number of (mostly short-lived) actants: between 1976 and 1979 the number of signatures each year climbed from 24 to 217, authoring 1,647 increasingly serious attacks.[24] This attempt to preserve the contiguity between the legal and illegal politics of earlier years encountered the increasing hostility of political parties and trade unions, which began to scrutinise their members more carefully for signs of sympathy with violence, especially once the first cases of deliberate murder and serious injury appeared. Efforts to provide potential recruits with decisive experience of 'state repression' by deliberately turning demonstrations into violent confrontations with the police ensured that fewer demonstrations were organised. Efforts to persuade by violence tended therefore to hamper the forms of non-violent political protest, further increasing the opposition to violence in the residual extreme left.

The multiplication of signatures was nonetheless only achieved at the price of a loss of focus for the use of violence. BR texts did not reveal clearly whether violence was still in the phase of 'armed propaganda' or had progressed to the stage of 'prolonged civil war'. The primary target of attack wavered between the state, the DC and the PCI. Disagreements surfaced over whether the primary audience for violence should still be the traditional working class or a new category of *operai sociali* (young recruits, often from the South, who were less attached to the old-style working-class unionism and politics). The multiple clarifications which had to be carried by any given act of violence to internal and external audiences interfered with each other and confused its communicative impact, already weakened by the growing distance between legal and illegal politics. The action which was intended to mark the shift to a new reorganised frame where the conditions for effective persuasion would be established was the kidnapping of the DC president Aldo Moro.

Shift 3: Moro, 1978

By taking Moro as a 'political prisoner' the Red Brigades returned to a tactic familiar from earlier years. Their immediate objectives, too, remained similar: the demonstration of their 'military' capacity to defy the state, the willing transformation of the victim, the endorsement of their analyses of political reality, and the demonstration of the power to influence ordinary politics. In fact, although intended to resolve some of the difficulties besetting persuasion by violence, the kidnapping only revealed them more clearly. Far from clarifying the aims and capacity of communication by violence, the details of the kidnapping and its conclusion gave rise, then and later, to intractable conflicts over the identity and intentions of its authors, sabotaging the attempt to establish a clear communicative authority for acts of violence.

Within the Red Brigades themselves the kidnapping enabled the original members, on trial in Turin, to identify themselves in a new role and assume overall authority for the BR signature. As Franceschini put it, 'We decided to become, once and for all, the "historic leaders" of the BR [and] recite the part that "history had assigned us".'[25] But the kidnapping immediately revealed the fragility of the consensus among their likely followers, despite the attempts by the 'historic leaders' to produce ever more abstract contexts for violence from their prison cells. Disagreements over the conduct and conclusion of the action provoked the first public defections from the Red Brigades. They were soon translated into attacks to publicise internal contrasts: the murders of Renato Briano and Manfredo Mazzanti in 1980 and the five kidnappings of 1981 represented the primary use of violence to resolve factional conflicts. This strategy reached its terminus with a double murder in Turin in 1982, carried out simply to diffuse a charge of treachery against a recently arrested BR activist. Targets who had once been carefully selected to persuade local audiences were now randomly chosen instruments of internal communication among the declining residual supporters of armed struggle. The consequence was the disappearance of the single BR signature: the warring factions divided, while the 'historic leaders' refused to supply further meanings for the signature they had created.[26] The final attacks signed by the rival groups, concluding in 1988, were directed at targets with solely national or international connections, without reference to any specific audience.

The kidnapping was no more successful in persuading the users of other signatures to accept BR direction for their violence, either spontaneously or in self-defence against more effective state repression. Indeed, the desire to convey dissent from Red Brigades objectives led to a further increase in violence and in new signatures. The new actants were, however, created by disillusioned users of previous signatures rather than by new recruits to the armed struggle. Heightened competition among signatures for the dwindling number of potential users generated yet more serious violence.[27] The range of political and institutional targets widened to include members of the left, while state repression provoked frequent revenge attacks on magistrates, police and prison guards. Almost no social category escaped inclusion in the category of potential victims, bringing left-wing users of violence by a different route to the same undifferentiated communicative strategy that their extreme right opponents had employed a decade earlier.

Ironically, too, just as Piazza Fontana had impelled the BR to seek the co-ordinated strategy behind right-wing violence, so the Moro affair persuaded others to do the same for left-wing violence. In an interview shortly after Moro's murder the magistrate Pietro Calogero suggested that the apparent disorder among users of violence was in fact serving as a deliberate disguise for a single group of BR and Autonomia activists to direct the variously dubbed *partito della lotta armata, partito della guerra civile* (party of civil war) or simply *l'organizzazione*.[28] That interpretation, applied retrospectively to all types of violence from the early 1970s, bound together – more effectively than any left-wing signature appears to have achieved – the frames of local activism, clandestine militancy, the jailed intelligentsia and the alleged super-directorate. The theory of a perfectly co-ordinated set of frames, which was taken seriously enough to lead to the incrimination and five-year preventive detention of some of Autonomia's leaders, remained publicly controversial, however – as did the wilder analogous speculations, also provoked by the choice of Moro as a target and the failure to protect or rescue him, that the real occupant of this frame was the CIA or KGB.

Shifting in: Peci, 1981

Defections from the armed struggle, and appeals to fellow participants to defect, had begun some time before the first formal measure to encourage exit became law and the first significant *pentito* (supergrass), Patrizio Peci, had availed himself of its benefits. The eventual three laws (1980, 1982, 1987) offered reduced penalties to an increasing range of former activists in return for the unequivocal repudiation of violence and the confession at least of individual responsibilities. Since confessions had to be verified in open court, these measures provided both the incentive and procedures for rituals of individual re-incorporation. The mass trials, filling courtrooms across Italy throughout the 1980s, thus became the scene of public reconstruction of identities. Abandoning the argot of armed struggle and accepting re-description of their pasts in legal terms, the repentant activists announced the beginning of their social reintegration. Because left-wing activists had paid more attention than right-wing militants to establishing details of their signatures, confessions and repudiation of the past came much more commonly from the left.[29]

In the course of divesting individuals of their clandestine identities the trials also dismantled the frames themselves. They reduced the independent reality of the actants to the joint agency of particular individuals, bearing varying levels of responsibility. As defendants took advantages of judges' latitude to tell their individual stories, orderly meanings were recovered and fixed for even the apparently least explicable attacks. Indeed, the presentation of the past as an intelligibly organised reality reflected not only the precision of legal language but also the pressure on defendants to convey with the greatest clarity the nature of the past that they were now rejecting. Moreover, since by judicial agreement each trial dealt only with local violence, any disputes about the meaning of specific attacks tended to be resolved in terms of local determinants. The explanations for some attacks (for example, the murder of the journalist Walter Tobagi) nonetheless remained bitterly controversial.

Restoration of local meanings to violence was reinforced by the failure of the two attempts to establish the achievement of national-level frames of violence. Calogero's hypothesis of a single 'armed party' was rejected in court in 1984; later, a parallel charge against all 426 users of the BR signature that they shared the single national project of an armed insurrection against the state was also dismissed. No doubt these failures provided one reason for the reluctance to support proposals for a general ritual of reconciliation between the political class and its armed antagonists. Court proceedings had been highly individualist in their outcomes, indeed leaving serious discrepancies in the treatment of apparently similarly responsible activists. Equally individual had been the well-publicised private reconciliations between assailants and their victims or victims' kin; in any case, these *rapprochements* were prevented from assuming a general public significance by the open criticism that victims had come to level at the political elite for its reluctance to compensate the people whom they had once used to symbolise the state itself. Thus the initiative of the then President, Francesco Cossiga, in 1991 to manufacture a form of ritual closure by granting an unsolicited politically motivated pardon to Curcio encountered little support and considerable opposition. Since 1987, when the last law in favour of *pentiti* was passed, measures to reduce penalties further for the dwindling number of former activists in prison have been regularly proposed to Parliament but have found little support. In sweeping away the political class which had directed the responses to violence in the 1970s and 1980s, the elections of 1994 and 1996 helped to mute the residual communicative power of more recent violence. The allocation of individual responsibilities for the entire string of still unpunished neo-Fascist massacres, and the solution of the alleged outstanding puzzles of the Moro kidnapping, remain to be achieved. But the extended ritual sequence inaugurated by Piazza Fontana has effectively found its closure in those other rituals of the courtroom and ballot box.

NOTES

1 C. Hewitt, 'The Costs of Terrorism. A Cross-national Study of Six Countries', *Terrorism*, 11 (1988), pp. 169–80.
2 In May 1999 a government adviser on labour law reform, Massimo D'Antona, was killed in Rome; the self-styled 'Red Brigades for the Construction of the Fighting Communist Party' claimed responsibility for the murder.
3 D. Della Porta and M. Rossi, 'I terrorismi in Italia tra il 1969 e il 1982', *Cattaneo*, 3:1 (1983), p. 28.
4 D. Della Porta, *Il terrorismo di sinistra* (Bologna, Il Mulino, 1990), pp. 167–8.
5 *Ibid.*, pp. 91–2.
6 See J. Davis, *Exchange* (Buckingham, Open University Press, 1992).
7 See D. Moss, 'The Kidnapping and Murder of Aldo Moro', *Archives européennes de sociologie*, 22:2 (1981), pp. 265–95; and R. E. Wagner-Pacifici, *The Moro Morality Play. Terrorism as Social Drama* (University of Chicago Press, 1987).
8 See S. Lenci, *Colpo alla nuca* (Rome, Editori Riuniti, 1988).
9 E. Leach, 'Time and False Noses', in *Rethinking Anthropology* (London, Athlone Press, 1961), pp. 132–6.
10 B. Kapferer, 'Ritual Process and the Transformation of Context', *Social Analysis*, 1 (1979), pp. 3–19.
11 The strategies of the BR and Autonomia were conventionally regarded as contrasting projects for the left-wing use of violence. The BR favoured a rigid organisational structure, avant-garde status and political targets. Autonomia, a loosely linked array of short-lived local groups originating in the mid-1970s and reaching its widest appeal in

1977–78, encouraged 'spontaneous' violence in the course of neighbourhood and factory conflicts. In practice, distinctions in the use and motivations of violence were far less sharp than the ideologues of either side claimed. For documents produced in the name of Autonomia see G. Martignoni and S. Morandini, *Il diritto all'odio* (Verona, Bertani, 1977). R. Lumley, *States of Emergency. Cultures of Revolt in Italy from 1968 to 1978* (London, Verso, 1990) describes the political-theoretical setting.

12 D. Novelli, *Vivere a Torino* (Rome, Editori Riuniti, 1980), p. 29.

13 L. Bonaparte, 'Some Unanticipated Consequences of Terrorism', *Journal of Peace Research*, 16:3 (1979), pp. 197–211.

14 See B. Latour, 'A Relativistic Account of Einstein's Relativity', *Social Studies of Science*, 18 (1988), pp. 3–44.

15 D. Della Porta and S. Tarrow, 'Unwanted Children. Political Violence and the Cycle of Protest in Italy, 1966–73', *European Journal of Political Research*, 14:5–6 (1986), p. 620.

16 See E. Pisetta, 'Militanza partitica e scelte eversive nei terroristi neofascisti', in R. Catanzaro (ed.), *Ideologie, movimenti, terrorismi* (Bologna, Il Mulino, 1990), pp. 191–215; and F. Ferraresi, *Threats to Democracy. The Radical Right in Italy after the War* (Princeton University Press, 1996).

17 *Strage di Stato* (Rome, Samonà e Savelli, 1970) was a very influential 'counter-investigation' of the links between the extreme right, sections of the state apparatus and neighbouring right-wing regimes in Italy's political violence between 1969 and 1972. It was compiled by a group of left-wing activists who wanted to demonstrate the falsity of the charges against the extreme left, reveal the contradictions in the testimony of key witnesses and publicise evidence of right-wing responsibilities. The book went through five editions in one year and provoked many legal actions for libel.

18 On the main extraparliamentary left groups, including details of antecedents, origins and differences, see: W. Tobagi, *Storia del Movimento Studentesco e dei Marxisti-Leninisti in Italia* (Milan, Sugar, 1970); G. Vettori, *La sinistra extraparlamentare in Italia* (Rome, Newton Compton, 1973); and M. Monicelli, *L'ultrasinistra in Italia, 1968–78* (Bari and Rome, Laterza, 1978).

19 See A. Franceschini, *Mara, Renato e io. Storia dei fondatori delle BR* (Milan, Mondadori, 1988), pp. 3–11; R. Curcio, *A viso aperto* (Milan, Mondadori, 1993), pp. 18, 71.

20 In 1974 and 1975 Ordine Nuovo and Avanguardia Nazionale – founded in 1956 and 1960, respectively, by rebel members of the MSI – were dissolved by court order. For a description of their relations with Fascist practice and ideology, and the fate of their leaders, see Ferraresi, *Threats to Democracy*.

21 See Pisetta, 'Militanza partitica', and Ferraresi, *Threats to Democracy*.

22 Among the early Red Brigades members, Curcio, Franceschini, Maurizio Ferrari, Giorgio Semeria, Pelli, Roberto Ognibene and Bonavita had been arrested by 1976; Gallinari was arrested in 1974 but escaped in 1977 and was rearrested in 1979; Franco Bonisoli and Lauro Azzolini were captured in 1978; Moretti was apprehended in 1981.

23 Mara Cagol, who married Curcio in 1969, had been a founder member of the BR. In 1975 she was killed in a police raid on the house where the BR were holding a kidnap victim, Vittorio Vallarino Gancia. Sossi was released unharmed by the BR over a month after his kidnapping. The public prosecutor, Francesco Coco, had opposed the decision of the Appeal Court in Genoa to grant provisional release from jail to the left-wing activists named by the BR in exchange for freeing Sossi.

24 M. Galleni, *Rapporto sul terrorismo* (Milan, Rizzoli, 1981), pp. 176, 277.

25 Franceschini, *Mara, Renato e io*, p. 153.

26 *Ibid.*, p. 203; Curcio, *A viso aperto*, p. 192.

27 D. Moss, *The Politics of Left-wing Violence in Italy, 1969–85* (London, Macmillan, 1989), pp. 72–3.

28 G. Palombarini, *Sette Aprile. Il processo e la storia* (Venice, Arsenale Cooperativa Editrice, 1982), pp. 169–78.

29 Pisetta, 'Militanza partitica', p. 213.

14

The last laugh: *Cuore* and the vicissitudes of satire

Robert Lumley

Ed egli avea del cul fatto trombetta (Dante, *Inferno*, 21.139)

Political satire has a short life. It belongs to a particular moment and when that moment passes, deprived of its context, it loses meaning. The politician whom we would have instantly recognised at the time from his hunchback or way of speaking becomes a stranger. The allusions to an event or incident have now to be reconstructed. Only exceptionally will a caricature in words and pictures capture the imagination years later because it has successfully combined 'the topical and the permanent, the passing allusion and the lasting characterisation'.[1] However, satire can provide a rich and fascinating object of study. Because of its ephemeral nature, a cartoon often proves to be a sensitive barometer of the humours and discontents of a particular moment.[2] The use of visual images as well as the printed word also offers that special quality of embodying the figure of speech in front of our eyes.

The satirical magazine that I want to analyse and discuss, *Cuore*, makes no claim to immortality. It has been in existence since January 1989 as an insert in what was then the Communist daily, *L'Unità*, and since January 1991 as an independent weekly. It occupies a minor place within the Italian press and its fortunes have been closely bound up with daily political events. Yet *Cuore*, I would argue, is a very interesting example of a magazine of satire because of the constituency it represents, its language, and the particular historical moment in which it flourished. While the circulation of *Cuore* is comparatively small at around 150,000, reaching a peak of 180,000, its actual readership is much larger. If it is also borne in mind that the readers are mainly young people and are characterised by a high level of identification, as shown by polls and letters, *Cuore* can be said to have a significant influence within a determinant area – the young who associate themselves with the left or with oppositional values more generally.

It is, however, the historical events in Italy in the period 1989 to 1994 that gave *Cuore* its special role. These years saw the dissolution of the Communist Party (PCI) and the formation of the Democratic Party of the Left (PDS) followed by the crisis of the Republic under the impact of the *Tangentopoli* corruption scandals and rise of the Lega Nord. In rapid time a political class was wiped out, with three out of every four politicians of the governing parties charged with criminal activities.[3] In these unprecedented circumstances *Cuore* became a point of reference for a left searching for a new identity and a sharp-tongued critic of the old regime. For a while it even seemed to be riding the crest of a wave, feeling a strong sense of direction in the midst of the chaos.

The aim here is to explore *Cuore* as an example of political satire. The first section will deal with political crisis before and in the early stages of the *Tangentopoli* scandal, although reference to subsequent developments will be included. The second section will examine the language of *Cuore*, notably the use of recurrent metaphors based on the lower half of the body. In the third section the readership's relationship with the magazine will be considered by analysing the letters page and the annual readers' poll. Each section will provide a particular vantage point from which to analyse *Cuore*, but all will be shown as closely interrelated: the use of the body metaphor for talking about politics and politicians; the establishment of a special relationship between *Cuore* and its readers through a certain type of language and through open-ended politics. In the fourth section some general observations will be made on the problems and difficulties besetting not only *Cuore* but any satirical venture of its kind.

Collapse of 'Il Palazzo'

Although in the 1980s political corruption took on a systematic character, few outside government at the time seem to have suspected what later came to light after the launch of the *Mani Pulite* operation in 1992.[4] If there were suspicions there was no hard evidence of its scale or judges were thwarted in their efforts by the political class. It was therefore the satirist with a nose for what was going on rather than the journalist or opposition politician who drew a picture of corruption at work. For *Cuore* there was little doubt that political corruption was rife. In its issue of February 1989, dedicated to the Christian Democrat national congress, this party of government was depicted as a shark swallowing the magazine's masthead (Figure 77). Under a headline 'School for thieves' there are data on corruption: 'sixty per cent of the cases from 1945 to 1978 involve Christian Democrats. They amassed 926 billion lire worth of rake-offs in the magic 1970s. . . . But the Socialists are fast catching up and are now implicated in fifty per cent of corruption cases.' The space traditionally occupied by editorials in the daily press is given over to an extract from Pier Paolo Pasolini's prophetic denunciation calling for leading Christian Democrat politicians to be put on trial. Giulio Andreotti, founder member of the party and seven times Prime Minister, was a favourite target (Figure 78).

But not all the attacks were directed at the Christian Democrats, the historic enemy of the left. By the time *Cuore* was founded, the relationship between the Socialist Party (PSI) and the Communists had become embittered. Bettino Craxi, head of the PSI, led vituperative campaigns against the PCI in the 1980s. Not surprisingly, *Cuore* took pleasure in people getting their comeuppance for the *Tangentopoli* scandals in which the Socialists, as the leading party of government in Milan, were heavily implicated. A Vincino cartoon prior to these events (Figure 79) had already shown a map of the city in the hands of the Socialist 'mafia' families: an underground station has been named 'Boboburg', after Craxi's son Bobo, who was Secretary of the Socialist Party in Milan, while the Via Fatebenefratelli ('Be charitable to your brothers'), the party's nerve centre in the city, has been renamed 'Fatebenecognati' ('Be charitable to your brothers-in-law') – an allusion to Paolo Pillitteri, Craxi's brother-in-law and then Socialist mayor of Milan. With the arrest in February 1992 of Mario Chiesa, an administrator caught red-handed receiving a *tangente* (rake-off) in return for a local government contract, the satirists went to town. Bobo Craxi's comment on Chiesa's arrest (quoted in *Cuore*), 'It's just a caricature and the PSI still remains the most modern party, the party of the modern person,' was too good to be true. Michele Serra, the editor of *Cuore*, reported on the crisis of overabundance hitting satire as revealed by an official industry communiqué, which concluded with the following proposal:

> That the PSI undertakes to abide by a moratorium for the period of a year covering thefts and other crimes relating to public property. This brief interval of abstinence would, apart from allowing our Socialist comrades a well-earned holiday, enable satirists to restock their warehouses with products worthy of a modern nation.[5]

Jokes at the expense of the PSI reach a high point with the inclusion of a free poster, a photograph of their leaders behind bars and the slogan 'HELP THE COMRADES IN PRISON: VOTE PSI'. The allusion is to the historic campaigns of the left in favour of the victims of repression and injustice as well as to the contemporary protestations of Craxi that the Socialists were being framed. The irony has a sharp edge.

The satire, however, is directed at the whole governing political class and its methods, and not just at particular personalities or parties. This world was lampooned regularly in Vincino's weekly map entitled 'Palazzo'. The architecture of power (topped by the clock of Montecitorio, the Chamber of Deputies' building) is depicted as crumbling if not falling while desperate figures cling to balustrades. The apparent solidity is shown to be a sham. The structures are nothing more than theatre scenery or cinema backdrops. A cartoon of a television studio at the time of the Gulf War exposes the reality effect for what it is – a trick (Figure 80). It is not even that there is something to be shown, for there is really nothing there. Emptiness, void, hollowness, containers without contents – these are the metaphors for the last years of the 'First Republic'. The acronyms referring to the various parties of the *Pentapartito*, the five parties that governed Italy for most of the 1980s, have become comic, as in the possible coalitions prognosticated by *Cuore*:

> Dc, Psi, Pli, Pri, Psdi
> Oppure [Or]: Dsi, Plsdi, Pro, Plis, Paf
> Oppure: Pres, Trin, Plif, Pnsl
> Oppure: Dsdi, Psfi, Pi, Pa, Pu, Pif, Pam, Pum[6]

Acronyms metamorphose into comic-strip captions; the words no longer have referents in the real world but refer only to one another.

77] *'Bon appétit.' Cuore*, 13 February 1989

78] Giulio Andreotti. Cartoon by Perini, *Cuore*, pre-1992

This semantic void is figured in Vincino's 'Il grande inciucio'. *(Inciucio* is a Neapolitan word now used to refer to the wheeling and dealing of political opponents in cahoots with one another.) The cartoon shows the politicians of Montecitorio all saying to one another, 'Ciu, ciu,' (Figure 81). The bird's-eye view creates a revision of scale whereby the (self-) important politicians are reduced to being 'elementary forms of life'.[7]

This picture of the Italian parliament evokes the images of late nineteenth-century polemics.[8] However, there is no equivalent moral discourse based on a vision of the world divided into good and evil. The satire has the light touch of irony and there is a recognition that Parliament is representative. An accompanying article by the editor of *Cuore* criticises the term 'Palazzo' as a convenience that lets everyone else off the hook: 'The crime of corruption provides for corrupt power and a

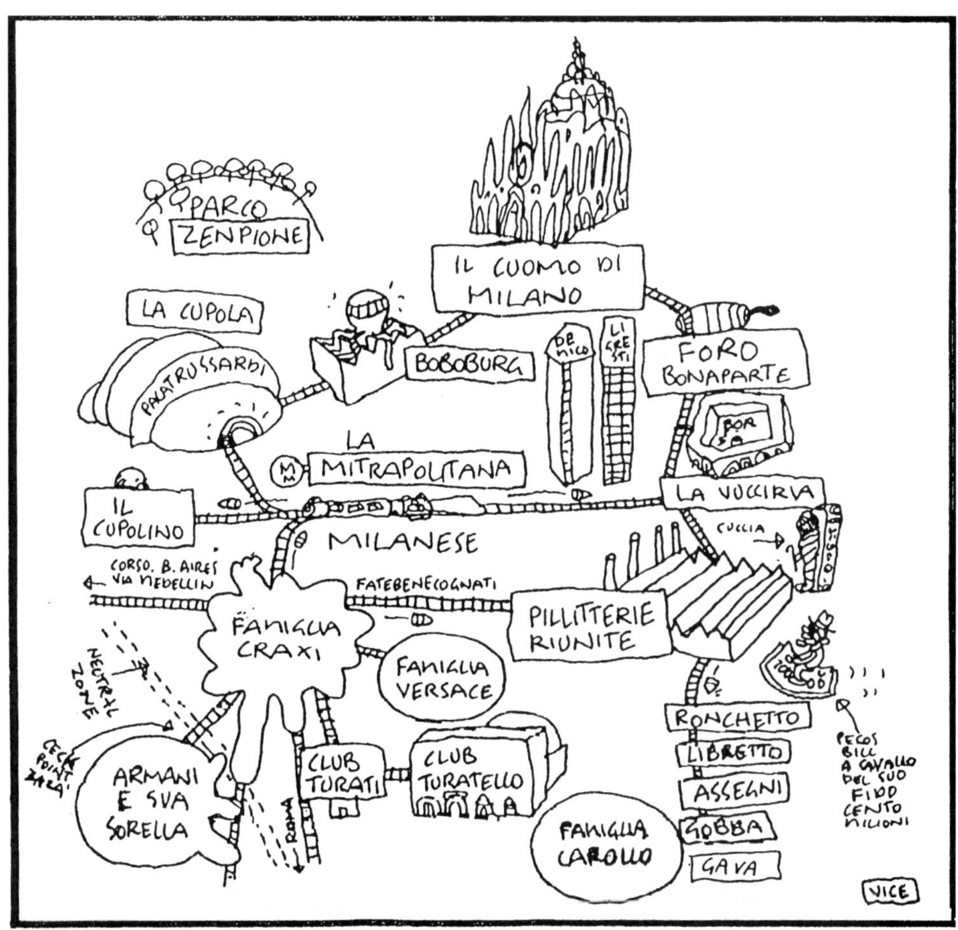

79] Map of Milan. Cartoon by Vincino, *Cuore*, 1992

corrupting society; so long as the corrupting society regards itself as led astray by the Palazzo rather than as a willing accomplice, nothing will change.' It concludes: '"You are all involved." Open the windows: if you're aware of a nasty smell, it comes from you.'[9]

The spread of disillusionment and the confirmation of 'cynical reason'[10] was perhaps an inevitable accompaniment to the assault on the Palazzo in which *Cuore* played its part. The nihilistic and anarchist streak was there. *Cuore* too could be said to sometimes use (albeit unconsciously) those weapons of caricature that induce

80] 'Applaude.' Cartoon by Vincino, *Cuore*, 4 March 1991

81] 'All in it together.' Cartoon by Vincino, *Cuore*, 27 April 1992

82] 'What a man!' 'Berlusconi: "Soon the *carabinieri* will be on my side."' Cartoon by Vauro, *Cuore*, 18 December 1993

83] '[Berlusconi]: "Forza Italia is undoubtedly, indisputably, by far the largest party in Italy."' Cartoon by Vincino, *Cuore*, 5 February 1994

'physiognomic reactions' equating 'sensuous and moral quality or feelings' to the point where we are 'hardly aware of their metaphorical or symbolic character'.[11] Yet the growth and legitimation of a cynical view of politicians and politics was not a development which was always welcomed by satirists. Michele Serra lamented (forgetting for a moment the political poverty of the left) that it was not just money but ideals that had been stolen: 'The biggest robbery of the century is the one that took away the hope of belief in politics as something positive.'[12] Unfortunately very few on the left realised the dangers, and wishful thinking blunted political sensibilities. The collapse of the 'First Republic' did not, as events unfolded, automatically favour its enemies, those outside the Palazzo. In the run-up to the decisive election of 27–8 March 1994 the weakness of a certain form of satire showed itself. The caricatures of Berlusconi, for instance, are remarkable for their crudeness. The blade of wit is exchanged for the blunderbuss. Berlusconi is depicted as a man in chains and as a hot-air balloon ready to be deflated (Figures 82 and 83). As the threat of a right-wing victory grew into reality the tone got quite desperate. Then in defeat *Cuore* offered the worst consolation of all, namely that the majority had been duped.

Bodily language

Cuore, the heart, alludes to a bodily organ that is associated, together with the head, with the more elevated or noble aspects of human behaviour. Yet both word and image have acquired kitsch associations. For Italians it is indissolubly linked with Edmondo De Amicis's tear-jerker for children, *Cuore*. The choice of this title for a satirical magazine was not, therefore, entirely fortuitous. Michele Serra recalls:

> We were thinking of De Amicis because he's the most satirical thing imaginable, he makes you want to die laughing, all pathos, unspeakable. So *Cuore* is a quotation, but I also liked the word because it means strong feelings, having a heart.[13]

The higher register is not entirely absent from *Cuore*. Contributors have included Natalia Ginzburg and Franco Fortini, writing respectively about death and Communism. Apart from anything else there is a delight in words that is intolerant of a restricted vocabulary. However, the literary tends to appear as pastiche or in conjunction with other registers that bring fine-sounding expressions down to earth.[14] Unlike the cultural pages of the national press, *Cuore* started life as a publication designed not for and by intellectuals (the left-wing literary critic Alberto Asor Rosa is a favourite *Cuore* target) but for a wider readership and with intellectuals participating on the magazine's terms. On the same page or within the same sentence there often coexist a range of registers. Of these, elements of 'popular' or 'vulgar' speech (*brutte parole*) and the images of what Mikhail Bakhtin called 'the material bodily lower stratum'[15] – play a crucial role.

The fact that certain words and their image equivalents crop up in *Cuore* would not be significant but for their frequency and prominence; they positively exhibit themselves before the reader. They are given, as we shall see, the phatic function of prompting *cuoristi* to identify themselves with the publication by mimicking elements of their way of talking.[16] Even seemingly gratuitous usages of *brutte parole* are useful in this role. On the other hand, the choice of such words for communicative purposes is their explicit *raison d'être* for *Cuore* writers and cartoonists. They are seen as indispensable for the expressive charge they can give to a headline or caption.

Bakhtin provides invaluable insights in helping us to think about the deeper reservoirs of bodily imagery in European cultures. He writes:

> Wherever men laugh and curse, particularly in a familiar environment, their speech is filled with bodily images. The body copulates, defecates, overeats, and men's speech is flooded with genitals, bellies, defecation, urine, disease, noses, mouths and dismembered parts. . . . The common human fund of familiar and abusive gesticulations is also based on sharply defined images.[17]

This generalisation is applicable to contemporary societies as well as to the early modern period of Rabelais that is Bakhtin's object of study. The area of language subject to interdict has increased, with euphemism becoming more complex and widespread in relation to the sexual and the scatological – concepts of bodily decency, for instance, are much stronger in modern urban societies. Meanwhile the magico-religious taboo has declined in importance. There is, though, remarkable continuity in how and why people laugh and curse.[18] The continuity is also evident in the vocabulary and the patterns of association:

> Generally there are recurrent identifications in this use of forbidden vocabulary: the sexual organs, whether male or female, are synonymous with stupidity (*coglione, testa di cazzo* – pillock or dickhead), with anger and ill-humour (*incazzarsi*).[19]

This recurrence is, it seems, a feature not only of Italian but of all European languages. However, use of this bodily language has differed according to variables such as context, gender, generation and, crucially, social class. For Bakhtin it was rooted in the popular and folk culture of the Middle Ages and continued to be used by the 'people' while another more cerebral and 'classical' idea of the body prevailed in the dominant or official culture.[20] For Nora Galli de' Paratesi, writing of the early 1960s, the popular matrix of the use of direct language remains strong. It is not that members of the upper class do not use direct expressions, especially among close friends, but the plain talking of the market place and everyday life is that of the popular classes.

The point of this detour is not to suggest that *Cuore* is somehow seeking to embody or revive an older popular culture. Rather it is to suggest a link which is metaphorical and which has its origins not in a mythical popular culture but in the youth culture of the late 1960s and 1970s. The world to which Bakhtin referred was a distant memory in a modern Italy whose peasantry had largely disappeared. On the other hand, the kernel of Bakhtin's thesis according to which the bodily language of the popular classes represented something alive (in a state of 'becoming') and fundamentally antagonistic to official culture and its values of individualism was widely shared. Bakhtin's work might not have been known,[21] but one need only look at Dario Fo's theatre – *Mistero Buffo* (Comic Mysteries), for instance – to see affinities.

The 'working class' or 'popular masses' stand for a subversive materialism of which bodily language is an authentic expression.[22] The conflation of political and sexual freedom, a hallmark of radical movements in the wake of the 1960s, found a basis in a wholesale challenge to all forms of authority, whether parental, institutional or economic; in the words of Peppino Ortoleva:

> The rupture of linguistic taboos . . . involved subverting order and hierarchy, dramatically marking the explosion onto the public stage of the 'lower regions', of even the most despised forms of bodiliness.[23]

A representative voice of this new politics in Italy was a magazine called *Re Nudo* whose politics of transgression can be illustrated with two images: a poster available to readers in which Disney characters indulge in every kind of sexual activity (Figure 84), and a front cover showing a woman holding a giant penis (Figure 85). The first clearly expresses the sacrilegious urge behind ideas of sexual liberation, with Disney representing puritan and repressive values; the second is more ambiguous but it is probably another example of the 'phallocracy' against which the incipient women's movement of the time was to react.

Cuore can be traced back to this earlier moment when American counterculture and the new politics of women's and gay liberation were introduced to Italy. A goodly percentage of contributors, including the former editor of *Re Nudo*, were young participants in the 1968 rebellion, and the broad parameters of that anti-authoritarianism and libertarianism live on, not least in the bodily themes of *Cuore*. However, it would be a gross simplification to leap from *Re Nudo* to *Cuore* without mentioning the experience of *Il Male*, the satirical magazine born of the youth protest Movimento del '77 whose brief existence subsequently became legendary. Much of the style of *Cuore* – the savage irony, the use of fakes and photomontage, the wilder flights of fantasy – come from this forerunner.

The representation of the 'lower bodily stratum' firmly anchors the satire of *Cuore* to everyday life. Perhaps no part does this more effectively than 'il culo' (translatable as bum or arse), which is the main protagonist of this section. And by 'culo' I mean not just the anatomical part itself but its functions and products. I will start by analysing the use of the word and then look at how some cartoons have developed the associated imagery.

Cuore came out on 8 April 1991, in response to the fortieth government crisis, with the headline 'HANNO LA FACCIA COME IL CULO' (literally, 'They've got a face like an arse') and the subheading 'And, as if that's not enough, it's an ugly arse.' Very soon afterwards a new government was constituted, made up of the same faces, and *Cuore* responded with 'HANNO LA FACCIA COME IL CULO/2' and the subheading 'They're re-running the same government, so we're re-running the same headline'. When I asked why *Cuore* made so much use of sexual and bodily metaphors, the editor replied with reference to this particular episode:

> *La parolaccia*, the swear word, is indispensable. It often has a linguistic power that other words lack. That particular example was an amazing semantic success: 'avere la faccia come un culo' means saying someone has no shame, is totally shameless.

84] Cartoon from *Re Nudo*, March 1971

RE NUDO

giugno 1971 - n. 6 (n. 1 nuova serie) - Lire 200

COLPO DI MANO!

(diventa ogni giorno più difficile resistere con le parole)

GIU' LE MANI DAL «MOVEMENT»! / TESI SULLA COMUNE / SERVIZIO SPECIALE: PRINCIPI DI CANNABISMO / LA COMUNE DI OVADA / FRONTIERE-REPRESSIONE / S. VITTORE: NUOVA PROVOCAZIONE / IL NOSTRO SOUND LA LORO MUSIKA / e ancora: notizie, documenti, lodi e delazioni.

85] Front cover of *Re Nudo*, June 1971

> But running the headline 'Shame' wouldn't have worked. Using a swear word in order to shock is idiotic, but if it serves a purpose then it should be put in.[24]

The face is, of course, the privileged, higher part of the body historically associated with a person's soul or character as celebrated in the art of portraiture.[25] But it has also long been regarded as an instrument of deceit. The expression 'faccia come un culo', as in this example, acts to deface and debase the authority figure concerned.

The cartoonists' play on the word 'il culo' shows their dependence on verbal expressions. Altan, a regular contributor to *Cuore*, is a good example of someone who makes a virtue of this subordination of the image to spoken language. This can be seen in a cartoon for *Cuore* centred on the notion of 'inculare' (buggery) in which an umbrella is aimed like a lance by one character at another's 'culo', carrying the caption 'Don't move, I've just got to revive the centre' (Figure 86). The action works both on the literal level (the act of 'inculamento') and that of the figure of speech meaning 'to take advantage of' and/or 'deceive'. An active ('inculare') and passive ('inculato') are both depicted, exemplifying Galli de' Paratesi's observation: 'Impotence or the passive sexual condition . . . are synonymous with misfortune, lack of ability or anyway with the situation of someone who is tricked or wronged; active sexuality is synonymous with cunning and prowess'.[26]

The expression itself and its associations have a history going back centuries – operating at what Gombrich would call a mythic level[27] – while being in common use. Altan's skill consists in linking this level of meaning with the topical: 'the centre' incorporates both the image of the 'centre of the culo' (the 'arsehole') that is targeted and the idea of the 'political centre' which was then a fashionable term among commentators. One could deduce, in conclusion, that the notion of a political centre is not worthy of much respect, and that, as the dress codes tell us, the 'common man' is vulnerable to the ruses of the powerful.

Other parts of the 'lower bodily stratum' feature in *Cuore* and there is no shortage of 'cazzi', 'palle' and 'coglioni' (pricks, bollocks and balls). In fact, it is worth noting that the male rather than the female body is predominant. 'Il culo', for instance, is hairy and male. It is rare to find images of the female body or female parts. While the word 'figa' (cunt) and associated words ('sfiga', 'sfigato') are found quite a lot, what is notable is the relative absence of direct expressions and representations featuring women, suggesting editorial policy or agreed practice. Moreover, the male body is unflatteringly presented (Figure 87). As often as not, the individual members have acquired a life of their own and fly off in all directions. The body is disembodied, dismembered, especially in the work of Perini (as will be seen in the illustrations of the readers' poll in the following section). Far from having the male body in its Renaissance glory, an object of admiration, we have a Bakhtinian body – a body that is grotesque, excessive, comic or, simply, banal. The phallus, in particular, is 'uncrowned'; in the words of Syusy Blady, regular *Cuore* contributor: 'The prick is declared stupid, aggressive, inept, a mere nothing in fact'; yet: 'Him, the prick as prick, has a life of his own, feelings of his own, and is much less of an idiot than his proprietor.'[28]

86] 'Don't move, I've just got to revive the centre.' Cartoon by Altan, *Cuore*, 27 November 1993

'Cuore' identity

Every publication is produced with readers in mind and employs certain devices and forms of address as appropriate.[29] In the case of *Cuore* this relationship is marked by its explicitness. The very language of *Cuore* is meant to be the language of its readers. The individual 'I' becomes the collective 'we *cuoristi*'. However, there are two *Cuore* spaces for reader participation that encapsulate that process of identification and identity creation – the letters page and the annual readers' poll. Analysis of these two genres will, moreover, enable us to review the earlier discussion of the political crisis and the use of bodily language in a new perspective.

Although the questions raised in the letters page are too numerous to summarise, it is possible to examine a good many of them under the heading of 'identity'. A preoccupation with political identity, sexual identity, personal identity, the identity of *Cuore* or simply with lack of identity is recurrent. Put plainly, readers ask, 'Who am I?' 'Who are we?' 'Where (if anywhere) are we going?'

The preoccupation with identity is not new. Think of the heart and mind searching over political identity following the revelations about Stalin. However, it could be argued that the years we are concerned with represent a special moment of crisis taking place in a context in which notions of identity had become problematic. The conditions of postmodernity spell a society in flux in which stable and fixed identities have given way to fragmented and multiple ones.[30] By the end of the 1980s this conception had migrated from the books of philosophers into the everyday lives of people like the readers of *Cuore*. Such views had therefore become widespread before the collapse of the Berlin Wall and the crisis of the political system in Italy. The hiatus of 1989–94 was political in that suddenly first Communists and then Catholics found themselves without their traditional parties, or, rather, with parties changing their names, symbols, structures and identities. Yet to read the ensuing debate around the problem of identity in exclusively political terms, even if the language was that of politics, would be to miss the novelty of the situation. It was not, as it was for the majority of Communists after 1956, a matter of reconstituting the existing forms of identity, but a matter of reconceptualising the notion of identity. Furthermore, many felt that collective identities had become inconceivable.

87] 'Sale time.' Cartoon by Mannelli, *Cuore*, 13 January 1992

It was in this context that *Cuore* played an important role as a point of reference for a young readership that felt itself to be 'on the left' when no one knew any more what exactly 'the left' meant[31]. For Michele Serra this role too was not entirely new: 'I think that the whole history of Italian satire in the last twenty years or so – *Male, Tango, Cuore* – is the history of the ideological crisis of the left; . . . we have attempted to turn the tears into laughter'.[32] But while *Cuore* aimed to make readers laugh (whether hysterically, angrily or happily), the letters page is the place where the 'tears are used to water something that's alive'. It is the 'cuore' of *Cuore*. It is also where, in the guise of 'agony uncle', advice, consolation and wisdom are imparted.

Some examples can illustrate this pedagogic function. Patrizio Roversi, the letters editor, replies to a call for the paper to stop publishing pro-Lega Nord letters by saying that the Lega is heterogeneous and that ambiguity is interesting; in short, '*Cuore* è una rivista poliformoperversa, cioè piena di contraddizioni' (*Cuore* is a polymorphous perverse publication, full of contradictions).[33] And here he is replying to another political purist:

> *Cuore* is a free-trade area, just as satire is. That doesn't mean no ideological tariffs at all, but it does mean no duties of a narrow political stamp. At a time of great confusion and mix-up nobody has yet explored the frontiers inhabited by people of good faith who are totally pissed off with what's happening.[34]

When *Cuore* was an insert of *L'Unità* its political position was circumscribed; readers who bought the PCI daily paper were usually expressing a political preference. When, however, it became an independent publication (albeit with *L'Unità* as a major shareholder) *Cuore* doubled its circulation and acquired a new and politically variegated following. Roversi's replies can be interpreted as part of this opening up of frontiers.

If in the early days of the independent *Cuore* the identity issue was dominated by the dissolution of the PCI, the formation of the PDS and the creation of an 'area' on the left in the place of an old-style party, its very success posed new problems. Many readers were sick of politics as such. Here is a letter from Giuseppe ('call me Josh') from Buttrio, province of Udine, which is worth quoting at length as Roversi evidently regarded it as symptomatic:

> Dear good people, a big thanks from the heart to the young and not so young who let rip in this paper that gives us the chance to shout in silence. Thank you all for stopping me feeling alone and abandoned in this vale of shits where the heaviest like me can't keep afloat and sink to the bottom. Twenty-seven Christmases and no commitment, not to the Left nor to the Right, Centre, North or East, nor even emotional/romantic. World events and those here pass me by and I hold my nose so as not to see or hear them. Perhaps I'm part of one of those vegetable zombies created by computer that wander through space in search of who knows what or maybe of just tits, arse, cunt, love, the end of Andreotti, money and freedom, peace, eating, shitting, sleeping. When it comes down to it, everything goes but everything's already lined up and programmed. . . . If someone has an itchy bum, let them borrow the crown of thorns from Christ and sit on it, but please turn off the TV first. Best wishes to everyone. Love and kisses.[35]

Roversi comments on the acidity of tone and the vein of disillusioned cynicism running through the letter:

> All in all, it is laced by a sense of guilt and contains hints of aggression towards the self and others (see the metaphor of the vale of heavy shits). There's a rejection of politics, ideology and the philosophy of commitment. There's an allusion to cyberpunk. A proud laying of claim to the minimalist centrality of the private/experiential. There's an odour of Italian-style resignation (see the 'everything's already lined up'). There's even an explicit rejection of anyone who risks moral or paternalistic judgements. . . . I'm just like Giuseppe in many ways, but I'm ten years older and I've got a job. Perhaps the only real difference is that he is a heavy piece of shit and I'm a light one that manages to stay afloat.

Roversi concludes by suggesting, 'without much conviction but with sincere goodwill', that Giuseppe would do well to go to a *Festa dell'Unità*, where he might discover people active in politics without being full of pretensions.

This letter and Roversi's response is interesting on a number of counts: it exemplifies the phatic use of bodily language to establish a commonality of speech between *Cuore* and *cuoristi*, and between generations (an average ten to twenty years separate most readers from the majority of writers and cartoonists); it also shows how *Cuore* could win consensus for its attacks on politicians and the political system but not for its promotion of an alternative vision of society. Above all, it highlights the tricky tightrope that *Cuore* has had to walk. On the one hand, there are the readers who feel that right is on their side and want to construct an imaginary wall that excludes those who do not belong (i.e. those seeking an exclusive political identity); on the other, there are the readers like Giuseppe for whom the distinctions 'left' and 'right' have little meaning and for whom the world is stupid, ridiculous and therefore to be laughed at. Roversi's 'solution' is to invite participation in a social gathering in which the political aspect is secondary.

How a publication is meant to be read and how it actually is read are, of course, very different things. This is especially the case with satire, which, as Roversi writes, 'is simply a piece of aggressive witticism, a blow that can land anywhere'.[36] In fact *Cuore* has been at its best (and worst) when it has refused to set itself up as an arbiter of political correctness and has allowed contradictions and collisions of opinion free rein. Such an approach implies acceptance of cultural complexity together with the risks of genuine pluralism.

Cuore's 'Giudizio universale' or Last Judgement is a case in point. This was the annual free-for-all when the magazine opened up its pages in an unusual experiment in readers' democracy. Readers were asked to send in their own list of 'five reasons for living'. In 1991 it resulted in some 110,000 replies, and 300,000 in the following couple of years. In the 1991 issue the league table of the top twenty reasons was published on the front page and other replies filled several inside pages.[37] Here is the table with the number of readers giving the reason in brackets:

1 Love (15,792)
2 Friends (10,024)
3 Sex (8,810)
4 Cunt (*figa*) (8,591)
5 The end of Andreotti (5,661)
6 Music (5,293)
7 Money (4,530)
8 Travel (4,468)
9 Freedom (3,473)
10 Fucking (3,360)
11 Health (3,025)
12 Juventus (2,788)
13 Family (2,475)
14 Women (2,417)
15 Cunt-licking (2,396)
16 *Cuore* (2,376)
17 Tit-touching (2,374)
18 Dope (2,287)
19 Laughing (2,246)
20 Peace (2,187)

In addition here are some of the replies taken at random from the inside pages. The following were among reasons that received six votes: 'Beatification of [the Venetian philosopher and politician] Massimo Cacciari – Beautiful weather – Bonus petrol – Ingmar Bergman – Blondes – Beer – BMW 850 – Umberto Bossi sodomised by a gorilla.' Politicians crop up regularly, as in the following: 'Picking up Andreotti dressed as a prostitute in the Piazza di Spagna – Bettino Craxi – Begging – Shitting on [President] Cossiga – Hanging up [the Socialist economist] Giorgio Ruffolo by his balls . . .' But there is also 'Hanging my husband up by his balls.' Hardly an obscenity is missing and transgressive sexual imagery is heavily represented (as in Perini's illustrations (Figures 88, 89 and 90)). It is an explosion of bodily language in which the world is turned upside down and inside out. Almost everything is reduced to the level of the 'material bodily stratum' and, at the same time, all that is base and vulgar is elevated.

The *raison d'être* of this experiment is explained by the editor:

> As for 'political' control, it's just absurd and moralistic even to suggest it. When the microphones are turned on, they're on, and that's it. You've got to be ready for everything, even for the worst – and the worst is there all right. As a result the 'Giudizio Universale' (Last Judgement) has become a cultural *monstrum* that reflects in rather an exhaustive manner the social and intellectual bedlam of this end-of-century moment. [Appropriately, a cartoon shows God having a break and a drink at the bar – Figure 91].

On the negative side, Serra points to the prevalence of violence:

> Metaphorical violence (often witty, sometimes sublime, sometimes terrifyingly gratuitous) but always violence, testifying to the fact that the 'bad teachers' are an invention of bigots and that the real problem are the 'bad pupils' – all of us, in other words.[38]

The ultimate justification of the 'Giudizio Universale' is, therefore, that readers are brought face to face with themselves.

Impossible normality

On the walls of the *Cuore* office in Bologna there is an Altan cartoon in which a character looks at himself in the mirror and reflects: 'The Italians are an extraordinary

88] Cartoon by Perini, *Cuore*, 30 December 1991

89] Cartoon by Perini, *Cuore*, 30 December 1991

90] Cartoon by Perini, *Cuore*, 30 December 1991

Una rara immagine di Dio durante la pausa mensa.
(foto Ansa-Perini)

91] 'A rare picture of God having a break at the canteen. Photo by Press Agency Ansa-Perini.' Cartoon by Perini, *Cuore*, 30 December 1991

people. I only wish they were a people like all the others.' These are precisely the sentiments of Michele Serra, editor of *Cuore* until July 1994. Italians are maddening because they oscillate between *moralismo* and *immoralità*, between dogmatic application of bureaucratic rules and an absolute disregard for the law and the common good; the ruling class is weak, selfish and incapable of a wider vision of society. Italians, unlike the citizens of the 'mature democracies', have yet to come to an agreement about how to live together.[39]

Whatever the merits of this catalogue of ills, it gives some idea of the broad agenda of *Cuore*. What is at stake is not minor disfunctions or grievances; conflicts quickly touch fundamentals so that satire naturally deals with bigger issues rather than with the foibles that feed *umorismo*. As those of *Cuore* argue, it is impossible to produce satire that is not political. Everything from the language of officialdom to issues of sexual identity is potentially political.

This raises two orders of difficuly. Firstly, there is the problem of promoting political positions, especially when that means supporting a political party or campaigning *for* rather than *against* someone or something. *Resistenza umana* is ultimately the *raison d'être* of the producers and core readers of *Cuore*, who would also subscribe to the values associated with the historic Resistance. Yet a significant swathe of readers (the Giuseppes) do not want to be told how to behave, either politically or in any other way. At the same time, *Cuore* would cease to be *Cuore* were it perceived as party-political and therefore as propaganda. Its nature as satire depends on it being an 'open' and not a 'closed' text.

Secondly, and more fundamentally, it is politics with a capital P that looms large in Italian satire, with the abuses and failures of the political elite providing the regular targets. And if this is inevitable and welcome when in the midst of the events of *Tangentopoli*, the obsession with this Politics has its cost. As Serra commented in his introduction to the *Cuore* compact edition of May–July 1991:

> Only someone who produces satire can understand the real (unresolved) dilemma: the talking endlessly about the same old ugly sewer called Power. Eccentric, on the margins, but looking towards the centre. Outside the mainstream media, but up to the neck in the media, just like the character who in order to appreciate how bad the shit is tastes a spoonful every day.[40]

Another dilemma facing *Cuore* has been how to produce political satire that does not speak a predominantly male language. There are women cartoonists, such as Elle Kappa, and writers such as Syusy Blady (though the clear majority are men). There is also an awareness of gender issues: firstly, *Cuore* does not exploit women's bodies, either in the form of advertising (there is none) or in that of erotic imagery; secondly, the male body is used as a source of comic representations in which the Italian tradition of associating political power with virility (Craxi and Bossi exemplifying this in recent times) is mercilessly pilloried. None the less, *Cuore* is read mainly by young men. It is their fantasies that fill the 'Giudizio Universale' we looked at earlier. In fact, the bodily language of the publication relates closely to male forms of speech, especially the use of direct expressions and euphemism[41].

This dilemma presents particular difficulties because not only *Cuore* but the satirical tradition in Italy (as in most countries) is predominantly male. Nor is it just a matter of attitudes. The language itself is shaped by centuries of use and is slow to change. One answer could be to pursue an editorial policy of 'political correctness'. Certain words and expressions could be banned and others promoted in the interests of women readers. However, such an approach would fail to take account of the very nature of words (and images), namely their polysemy or capacity to acquire new meanings[42]. The much harder but more intelligent strategy would involve trying to subvert existing usage in order to take more account of women's speech. Far from excluding certain words and images from the publication, this might entail including a wider range of representations.

It may be the case, on the other hand, that *Cuore* is due to end its days. Satirical publications, like *Charlie Hébdo* or *Le Canard enchaîné*, that have survived over decades are extremely rare. The pattern, certainly in Italy, is short but intense bursts of activity followed by a rapid demise. Usually the publication's life is closely bound up with a moment of acute crisis or conflict. When the moment passes, the sense of purpose is lost and disbandment ensues, often amid much acrimony. Hopefully *Cuore* will be an exception to the rule. Whatever transpires, however, the *raison d'être* of satire remains so long as there is inequality and abuse of power: in the words of the founding editor of *Cuore*: 'The good old rule of satire is that the poor man who trips up isn't funny, but when the rich man trips it makes you laugh.'

Postscript

Since this chapter was finished *Cuore* has folded. The demise was sad but seemingly inevitable – falling sales, loss of direction, decline of quality, exhaustion of the patience of the owner. In an interview with *La Repubblica* on the same day Michele Serra noted that sales had already been falling when Berlusconi was Prime Minister, and that the attempt by the then editor, Claudio Sabelli Fioretti, to turn the weekly into an Italian version of *Le Canard enchaîné* had been fundamentally misconceived. The writing had been on the wall for some time.

Of course, *Cuore*'s end retrospectively puts everything written here into the past tense. Yet it seemed best to leave the account in the present, to leave questions open rather than close the lid on the final speculative remarks. What's more, the chapter is about *Cuore*'s defining moment (the years 1989 to April 1994). In so far as *Cuore* will be remembered, it will be for issues like the one that, exploiting the ambiguity of the term *legale* in the phrase 'ora legale' (summer time), announced when the clocks changed: 'Scocca l'ora legale, panico tra i Socialisti'.

NOTES

I am very grateful to the following for their comments on a draft of this chapter: Luciano Cheles, Clare Coope, Paul Ginsborg, Laura Lepschy, Claudia Nocentini and Enrico Palandri.

1 E. H. Gombrich, 'The Cartoonist's Armoury', in *Meditations on a Hobby Horse* (London, Phaidon, 1971), pp. 137–8.
2 See A. Brilli, *Dalla satira alla caricatura* (Bari, Dedalo, 1985).
3 L. Ricolfi, *L'ultimo Parlamento. Sulla fine della Prima Repubblica* (Rome, La Nuova Italia Scientifica, 1993).
4 M. Eve, 'Comparing Italy. The Case of Corruption', in D. Forgacs and R. Lumley (eds), *Italian Cultural Studies. An Introduction* (Oxford University Press, 1995), pp. 34–51.
5 M. Serra, 'Verso un accordo tra satira e PSI', *Cuore*, 24 February 1992.
6 *Cuore*, 10 July 1989.
7 *Ibid.*, 27 April 1992.
8 See J. Dickie, *Darkest Italy. The Nation and Stereotypes of the Mezzogiorno, 1860–1900* (Basingstoke, Macmillan, 1999).
9 M. Serra, 'Siamo tutti coinvolti', *Cuore*, 27 April 1992; the term 'Palazzo', which refers to the political establishment, was coined by Pasolini and entered common currency.
10 For a discussion of cynicism as a cultural and political phenomenon see P. Sloterdijk, *Critique of Cynical Reason* (London, Verso, 1988).
11 Gombrich, 'The Cartoonist's Armoury', pp. 138–9.
12 *Cuore*, 11 May 1992.
13 Author's interview with Michele Serra, 6 July 1994.
14 Apart from his great ability as an editor, Michele Serra himself was a brilliant contributor; see, for example, the collection of his pastiches, *44 Falsi* (Milan, Feltrinelli, 1991), also his short stories, *Il nuovo che avanza* (Milan, Feltrinelli, 1989).

15 M. Bakhtin, *Rabelais and his World* (Bloomington, IN, Indiana University Press, 1984), p. 368.
16 In the words of Stuart Hall: 'Just as our sense of the identity of a person depends to a great extent on his appearance, style of being-in-the-world, how he presents himself, in the same way the collective identity of a newspaper rests not simply on *what* is said . . . but on *how* what is said is presented, coded, shaped within a set of signifying meaning-structure'; in A. C. H. Smith, *Paper Voices. The Popular Press and Social Change* (London, Chatto & Windus, 1975), p. 21.
17 Bakhtin, *Rabelais and his World*, p. 319.
18 N. Galli de' Paratesi, *Semantica dell'eufemismo* (Turin, Giappichelli, 1964), p. 66.
19 *Ibid.*, p. 48. I owe to Claudia Nocentini the following comment: 'In Italian there is no equality in this respect: only male parts denote stupidity, whereas the female ones, by contrast, denote *astuzia* (shrewdness) and enviable qualities; if, for instance, *figo* is used of a man, it signifies handsome or cunning.'
20 Bakhtin, *Rabelais and his World*, p. 321.
21 *Rabelais and his World* was first published in Italian by Einaudi in 1979; for the influence of Rabelais on comic writing in Italy in the 1970s see the work of Gianni Celati, notably *La banda dei sospiri* (Turin, Einaudi, 1976).
22 See the interview with Dario Fo, 'Dario Fo à Vincennes', *Cahiers du Cinema*, No. 250 (1974), pp. 16–25.
23 P. Ortoleva, *Saggio sui movimenti del 1968 in Europa e in America* (Rome, Editori Riuniti, 1988), p. 140; see also, R. Lumley, *States of Emergency. Cultures of Revolt in Italy, 1968–78* (London, Verso, 1990), pp. 70–100.
24 Author's interview with Michele Serra, 6 July 1994.
25 See J-J. Courtine and C. Haroche, *Histoire du visage* (Paris, Rivages, 1988).
26 Galli de' Paratesi, *Semantica dell'eufemismo*, p. 48.
27 Gombrich, 'The Cartoonist's Armoury', p. 129.
28 S. Blady and S. Toni, *Vocabolario sessuato. 99 sguardi sul mondo della femminista e del misogino* (Milan, Feltrinelli, 1993), p. 45.
29 See U. Eco, *The Role of the Reader. Explorations in the Semiotics of Texts* (London, Hutchinson, 1981).
30 See M. Perniola, *Enigmas. The Egyptian Moment in Society* (London, Verso, 1995); also A. Giddens, *Modernity and Self-identity* (Cambridge, Polity Press, 1991).
31 See N. Bobbio, *Left and Right. The Significance of a Political Distinction* (Cambridge, Polity Press, 1996).
32 Author's interview with Michele Serra, 6 July 1994.
33 *Cuore*, 9 November 1991.
34 *Ibid.*, 11 February 1991.
35 *Ibid.*, 20 September 1991.
36 *Ibid.*, 12 August 1991.
37 *Ibid.*, 30 December 1991.
38 M. Serra, 'Cosa succede in città', *ibid.*, 30 December 1991.
39 Author's interview with Michele Serra, 6 July 1994. The list of maladies is not new, of course; see G. Bollati, *L'italiano. Il carattere nazionale come storia e come invenzione* (Turin, Einaudi, 1996, 2nd edn).
40 M. Serra, *Cuore compact* (Milan, Cuore Corporation, 1991), p. 5.
41 Galli de' Paratesi, *Semantica dell'eufemismo*.
42 'Each living ideological sign has two faces, like Janus. Any current curse can become a word of praise, any current truth must sound to many people as the greatest of lies': V. N. Voloshinov, *Marxism and the Philosophy of Language*, quoted in C. Woolfson, 'The Semiotics of Working-class Speech', *Working Papers in Cultural Studies*, 9 (1976), p. 170.

15

The centre cannot hold: music as political communication in post-war Italy

Alessandro Portelli

On screen and behind glass

In Gianni Amelio's film *Lamerica* (1994) a truckload of men round a bend on a mountain road. They are singing a song by Toto Cotugno, runner-up in a San Remo Italian Song Festival: 'Lasciatemi cantare/con la chitarra in mano./Lasciatemi cantare/sono un italiano' (Let me sing/With my guitar in my hand./Let me sing/I'm an Italian). Ironically, they are not Italians, but Albanians on their way to emigrate and become Italians. You can tell, because most Italians, nowadays, would not be caught dead singing in public, with or without a guitar.

Nobody sings any more in Italy. Sometimes you see us, behind the car windscreen, moving our mouths like fish only to shut up abruptly at the red light.[1] Once, they say, you could supposedly hear *stornelli* (an old form of popular singing) in the air of plebeian cities like Rome; singing was an act of expression, an extension of speech. Music was mostly self- and hand-made; washerwomen singing at the stream or amateur pianists in parlours competed only with their neighbours or peers.

When sound reproduction became possible, however, the world's best music became available in our homes, and we no longer needed to provide our own. This 'ready-made' music makes home-made sounds seem rough and incompetent: to sing in public today is to invite comparison with professionals – literally, to make a spectacle of oneself. Music becomes increasingly harder to perform without adequate equipment; songs are composed for specialists. Singing is less an extension of speech than a performance and a business.

On the other hand, everyone loves singing on television. In 1994 a programme entitled 'Karaoke', broadcast on one of Silvio Berlusconi's networks, was Italy's most popular television show.[2]

Karaoke consists of singing to a pre-recorded accompaniment: a tame relative of other ways of entering into the record, such as scratching or dubbing, a distant cousin of rap and a descendant of the old 'sing-along' albums of the 1950s. In its Japanese beginnings karaoke retained a home-made atmosphere: small groups, indoors, took turns at the mike. As Umberto Eco has pointed out, 'it was an excellent socialising tool' and allowed all 'to practise the noble art of singing'.[3] This secured karaoke a place in popular festivals run by the Church or by political parties, from ex-Communists to (ex?) Fascists.

Television karaoke, however, is a huge spectacle, staged for thousands of enthusiastic young people in large city squares and for millions of viewers at home. Rather than the pleasure of singing and entering into the recording, it entails the pleasure of entering the screen and *being seen*. It replaces a dialogic short-range exchange with the unilinear flow of mass communication. While dubbing or rap imply creative improvisation and change, karaoke creates a pre-established space, an authoritative model, well-defined boundaries. No wonder that, at the peak of this genre's popularity, network owner Silvio Berlusconi was also Italy's Prime Minister.

Now, a small dose of passivity can do no harm; it can even be rather fun. Hegemony, however, succeeds not by forcing unpleasant things down our throats, but by offering pleasant, desirable things. Because karaoke is a nice and harmless toy, it has been allowed to expand and crowd all other forms out of social and semantic musical space, and become virtually the only social space of expression for masses of young people. While young people are increasingly marginalised, television karaoke provides them with an illusion of centrality. No wonder that, while the left has been divided between criticism and defence of karaoke, the right has unanimously come out for it: filling the Piazza San Giovanni in Rome with singing teenagers rather than angry workers is a perfect metaphor for the politics of populist consensus of the new and the old Italian right.[4]

Karaoke has also erased all other musical discourse from the sphere of language: any act of public singing automatically becomes karaoke. When, in 1994, Pope John Paul II joined the singing throngs at a mass gathering, an approving front-page headline in *L'Unità*, the newspaper of the Partito Democratico della Sinistra (PDS), announced that 'The Pope joins karaoke in the stadium' – homage less to God than to karaoke master of ceremonies Fiorello.[5] John Paul II did not mind: like all great communicators, he knows the power of stardom, and latched on to the idea. Two weeks later, huge screens in St Peter's square helped the faithful sing along with the Pope. Applauding this 'karaoke of the spirit', *La Repubblica* called it 'The Pope's great show'.[6]

Singing, then, is authorised only when on screen and under guidance. Singing in any space other than the privacy of the automobile or the publicity of television – such as the social space of the streets – is tantamount to breaking through the screen and invading the public sphere. For instance, a journalist from *La Repubblica* reported on 25 April 1994 that

> singing [the partisan song] 'Bella Ciao!', in driving rain, 300,000 Italians walked the streets of Milan to Piazza Duomo. . . . The band came forward, in wavering, broken lines; instruments and musicians were soaking wet, the notes were ancient – old, rather. But at 3.30 p.m., in a broad Milan boulevard, 'Bella Ciao!' no longer sounded like a plain old marching tune, but a song for youth.[7]

The 25th of April 1994 was no ordinary anniversary of Italy's liberation from Fascism. For the first time since World War II, the government included members of the neo-Fascist party. Mass demonstrations reaffirmed the value of anti-Fascism, and music was a crucial form of expression. In Milan, partisan and working-class anthems mixed with 1960s protest songs, topical parodies of pop tunes, and songs by left-wing *cantautori* (singer-songwriters). Young people danced to 'Bella Ciao!' reinforced by a salsa rhythm section. In Rome, partisan songs were joined by Afro-Cuban drums brought by African and Latin American immigrants. Meanwhile, back in Milan, an alternative parade staged by the *centri sociali* (youth centres) crossed the city to the sound of rap music.[8]

The political music of the middle ground

Mario Pirani wrote in *La Repubblica* in January 1995:

> When I was a child, the echo had not yet vanished of an ugly song of the 1920s: 'Fascisti e Comunisti giocavano a scopone./Vinsero i Fascisti con l'asso di bastoni'. (Fascists and Communists were playing cards./The Fascists won with the ace of clubs.) Years went by, and the game between Fascists and Communists was regulated by the machine-gun instead of the truncheon. The Communists won, and sang: 'O partigiano/portami via/Bella ciao, bella ciao . . .' (Partisan, take me with you, bella ciao, bella ciao . . .) The defeated black brigades raged desperately: 'Le donne non ci vogliono più bene/perché portiamo la camicia nera./Dicono che siamo da catene./Dicono che siamo da galera' (Women do not love us any more/because we wear black shirts./They say we ought to be in chains./They say we ought to be in jail.) Then, fortunately, came the San Remo song festival, rock and roll, and karaoke.[9]

This leading article in a respected liberal newspaper places the partisan eulogy 'Bella Ciao!' and the Fascist hymns to knives and grenades in the same category: it views them as the 'singing prehistory, bloodshot, womanish and peasant', of a 'feud' between extremists which did not concern right-thinking, respectable liberals. It is a late manifestation of what the historian Stefano Della Torre has described as a 'grey area' – the non-political, uncommitted middle group that stayed out of the Resistance, waiting to see who would win.[10] Pirani couches this attitude in a musical metaphor: 'political' songs on the fringe, pop music in the middle ground. He has a point: the San Remo song festival and karaoke were indeed the sounds of the grey area, the political music of the extreme middle.

Discussing karaoke's appeal, Umberto Eco noted: 'It is as though, instead of playing ball, the audience went out to watch others play.' However, whereas football spectators 'give up playing in order to admire others who play extraordinarily well', in karaoke 'one gives up singing (not too well, perhaps) in order to admire others who sing worse'.[11] Eco does not attempt to explain why anyone should do such a thing. But he had already done so in a celebrated 1961 essay on the quiz-show star Mike Bongiorno:

> Worshipped by millions, this man owes his success to the fact that from each and every action and word of his television persona there transpires such absolute mediocrity . . . that no viewer, no matter how backward, is ever made to feel inferior.

We may easily apply Eco's conclusions about Mike Bongiorno to karaoke star Fiorello: both offer the viewer 'a portrait of his own glorified and officially sanctioned limitations'.[12] Mediocrity becomes a virtue, averageness a coveted goal.

Just before Bongiorno's heyday, the grey-area politics of mediocrity and non-involvement were embodied by the San Remo song festival – truly a musical institution. Inaugurated in 1951, the festival promoted 'traditional' Italian popular music, half-way between degraded *bel canto* and diluted folklore (both represented by its most celebrated star, Claudio Villa),[13] with an occasional tinge of American swing and crooning.[14] San Remo helped create a unified national mass culture based on shared sounds, feelings and attitudes. The music was easy and singable, the lyrics sentimental, the tone mostly melancholy, with a hegemony of the heart and a (diminishing) sprinkling of generic God, Country and Mother. Its implicit rural nostalgia is not unlike Nashville country music, without its occasional irreverence and lower-class energy, and further removed from folk roots.

This kind of music was the only one allowed on the radio. Though disseminated via a modern vehicle, music conveyed a sentimental resistance to modernity; it would have been hard to imagine that Italy was going through a dramatic period of industrialisation and urbanisation, fraught with conflict and dislocation. The politics of popular music consisted in the avoidance of anything controversial, over-intellectual or potentially divisive, in favour of 'universal' feelings, to which even Communist workers could, and indeed often did, subscribe. Anything outside this provincial melodic lower middle-class consensus was a deviation from 'common' sense, and denied mass cultural citizenship.[15] Thus, to classify San Remo and karaoke as right-wing would be to attribute to them an ideology and a political stance which they sternly resist. They are, rather, organic to that broad and formless area of opinion that treasures the belief that its ideas are not 'political' but commonsense, and shares its votes between the conservative centre and the backward-looking right – between the Christian Democrats and the bourgeois neo-Fascism of the Movimento Sociale Italiano, and later between Forza Italia and Alleanza Nazionale. The fact that the audience of San Remo and karaoke includes social and generational strata otherwise ideologically oriented only increases their hegemonic potential.

Times, however, were a-changing even around San Remo. In 1958 Domenico Modugno took the festival by storm with the surreal and erotic 'Nel blu dipinto di blu' (Into the Blue [Sky] Painted Blue), universally known as 'Volare' (Flying), and Italian music was changed for ever.[16] According to the Communist official and popular music historian Gianni Borgna, the conflict between tradition and modernisation (embodied by Claudio Villa and Domenico Modugno) turned the San Remo festival from a 'pillar of Christian Democrat hegemony' into the ground of 'a real struggle for hegemony between the old and the new, the backward and the progressive'.[17]

Actually, in San Remo as well as in society, the struggle was less between 'the old' and 'the new' than between different combinations of both, in which the incorporation of new language preserved the essence of the old power. Modernisation took place under the aegis of traditional and conservative socio-political forces; likewise, the apparent conflict between old crooners of the Claudio Villa school and new *urlatori* (shouters) or mavericks like Domenico Modugno resolved itself in a historic compromise: by 1962 Modugno and Villa were singing the same song and winning the festival together.[18] Whatever could not be assimilated into the 'new' was pitilessly thrown out: in 1967 Luigi Tenco, a progressive and intelligent singer-songwriter, committed suicide when his song was excluded from San Remo's final run. The winner that year was Claudio Villa; the presenter – as almost every other year between 1963 and 1979 (and again in 1997!) – was Mike Bongiorno.

By then, however, San Remo was losing relevance: rather than generating the 'new', it was vainly endeavouring to incorporate changes originating elsewhere. International stars, the courting of young audiences and a phoney social commitment did not succeed in revitalising it. In 1965, while San Remo crowned Elvis look-alike Bobby Solo, everybody else was listening to the Beatles. In 1970, at the height of the students' and workers' unrest, Adriano Celentano won by singing 'Chi non lavora non fa l'amore' (If you go on strike, you won't make love). Although San Remo remains a huge television event – 'a sheer, sharply virtual TV reality, a parallel world' that has little to do with music[19] – it has ceased to be the sound of the times.[20]

And yet, in at least one area San Remo music has prevailed: in the streets. In the turbulent year of 1977 steelworkers marched in Rome singing protest verses to the tune of 'Papaveri e papere' (Poppies and Ducks, runner-up in San Remo, 1952) or 'La donna riccia' (The Woman with Curly Hair), an early 1950s Modugno piece. In Bologna rebelling students parodied popular songs that were old before they were born.[21]

The tradition of political parody is well-rooted in radical culture, at least since the 1920s, mainly through the work of the Communist song-maker Raffaele Offidani, alias Spartacus Picenus.[22] Parody, allowing rapid circulation and instant singability, was the dominant form of the 'golden age' of Communist singing (1946–53):[23] the 1952 San Remo winner 'Vola, colomba bianca, vola' (Fly, White Dove, Fly) became 'Vola, bandiera rossa, vola' (Fly, Red Flag, Fly).[24] The price paid by opposition culture was implicit homage to commodified culture.

It was a surprise, however, to hear the revolutionary generation of the Movimento del '77 singing to the very tunes which they would not be caught dead listening to. The secret of the staying power of this music is melody, anathema in the days of rap, rhythm and dance music. Because they were banal they were singable; because they were not memorable they were easily, almost unconsciously, remembered. They had never really been 'new'; what made them ironically functional in the midst of struggle for social change and justice was their uncanny ability to grow old.

Alternatives from above

In 1964, while 'the new' was asserting itself in San Remo through Gigliola Cinquetti singing 'Non ho l'età' (I am Too Young [to Love You]), the real scandal was created at another, highbrow festival, the Spoleto Festival of the Two Worlds, by a ballad half a century old entitled 'O Gorizia, tu sei maledetta!' (O Gorizia, You're Cursed!). This sorrowful song protesting against the war and the army featured in Bella Ciao, a folk song concert presented by the Nuovo Canzoniere Italiano, a Milan-based group which specialised in the research and presentation of folk music. As Michele Luciano Straniero sang, the elegant audience began to shout and protest and the police climbed on to the stage threatening to arrest the performers.[25] Apparently, what was truly unbearable was not 'the new' in popular culture but the unshakable resistance of the old in the culture of opposition.

If San Remo was the sound of the average and the middle, the alternatives could come only from above, from below and from without: the creation of more intelligent songs, the rediscovery of the culture and music of the non-hegemonic classes, and the advent of strange foreign sounds. Let us begin with the alternatives from above.

In 1957 a group of musicians and intellectuals based mostly in Turin – including the musicians Fausto Amodei and Sergio Liberovici and the writers Emilio Jona, Italo Calvino and Franco Fortini – created the 'Cantacronache' collective in order 'to infuse the unreadable, cliché-ridden lyrics of Italian-style songs with the hard experience of the news, and everyday events in ordinary people's lives'.[26] It was the first attempt to restore intellectual and moral dignity to a debased yet popular and therefore important form, and to find a popular outlet for poetry.

Most of the performers and authors were politically committed, but the material was not openly so. The infusion of sophistication, realism and humour in the unreal world of popular song was, however, an implicitly anti-hegemonic act. Other more overtly political experiments involved 'serious' music (Luciano Berio, Luigi Nono), jazz (Giorgio Gaslini) and theatre (Laura Betti, Ornella Vanoni, Milva).[27] These experiments were unable to reach a mass audience, partly because of a media boycott and partly because of their own elitism; rather than influencing the tastes of the masses, often the innovators were only marking their distance from them.

The music business itself, however, was becoming aware that old-style popular music was becoming irrelevant, young people no longer bought it, and new forms of dissemination were breaking the monopoly of the state radio. The 45 rpm record and the jukebox became an alternative form of musical consumption, and paved the way for American rock and roll and popular music;[28] television made music a more visual experience, favouring a generational shift among performers; advanced recording technology created new spaces for intensely personal artists or small alternative bands; clubs, discos and arenas linked music with new forms of socialisation.

Unconventional voices such as Gino Paoli, Luigi Tenco, Fabrizio De André, Enzo Jannacci, Giorgio Gaber and Lucio Dalla were thus able to achieve a degree of success. Supported by companies seeking new markets, *cantautori* managed to break into radio, where even their tamest material sounded like a breath of fresh air. Their influences included French *chansonniers*, swing, soft rock, jazz and folk songs. They sang about suburbia and marginalisation, shattering the pop illusion of average and timeless common sense. A later generation of *cantautori* influenced by the student and workers' movements – Francesco Guccini and Francesco De Gregori were the most prominent among them – broke the taboo of politics. But even before them a commercial pop star like Gianni Morandi had been able to sing about Vietnam: his 'C'era un ragazzo che come me amava i Beatles e i Rolling Stones' (There was a Boy like Me who Liked the Beatles and the Rolling Stones) was both a celebration of the new British sounds and an anti-war protest. It was censored on television, and turned into a world hit by Joan Baez.

The music was too easily romantic, the lyrics oscillated between everyday speech and the clichés of school poetry,[29] the politics were shaky or vague, the temptations of commercialism hard to reject. Yet it seemed at times as if the project of Cantacronache had been achieved in reverse: rather than bringing poetry to song, song was being raised, if not to the level of poetry, at least to that of social relevance and verbal articulation, catering for the younger generation's yearning for a synthesis between ordinary feelings, music and politics.[30] The *cantautori* refused to be cast as spokesmen for a generation or an idea; but songs like De Gregori's 'Pablo' (a eulogy for a young dead comrade) or Guccini's 'La locomotiva' (the story of an anarchist railroad engineer who drives his locomotive into a luxury train) became radical anthems for one or two generations.

Alternatives from below

In its search for alternative expression the Cantacronache group had also tapped a rich vein of protest material that existed in oral tradition. Owing to the mass appeal and class roots of anarchism, Socialism and Communism, Italian folk music was distinguished by a wide repertoire of explicitly political songs that were also genuine folk songs, such as the working-class anthem 'Bandiera rossa' (The Red Flag) or the revolutionary 'eight-hour' song 'Le otto ore'. This tradition of *canto sociale* (social singing) also incorporated hymns and parodies composed by revolutionary musicians and poets, such as the aforementioned Spartacus Picenus or the anarchist Pietro Gori.[31]

The partisan repertoire of 1943–45 included reworked folk ballads ('Bella Ciao!'), hymns from the songbook of the international left ('Fischia il vento', The Wind Blows) and parodies of popular and even Fascist songs ('La Brigata Garibaldi', The Garibaldi Brigade). As the ethno-musicologist Diego Carpitella has noted, the song repertoire of the Resistance was a ragbag of rural and urban genres and styles – folklore, peasant and artisan traditions, popular music – unified by a shared ideology.[32] Together with the pop song parodies and the radical repertoire of occupational groups such as the *mondine* (seasonal ricefield workers), the songs of the Resistance defined *canto sociale* as 'a frontier between official cultures (both dominant and oppositional) on one hand, and people's cultures on the other'.[33]

By the late 1950s, just when this tradition was showing signs of becoming exhausted, it was rediscovered (and recorded) by Cantacronache and by radical intellectuals such as the historian Gianni Bosio, the ethno-musicologist Roberto Leydi and the anthropologist Alberto Cirese. Bosio advocated an interdisciplinary and radical approach to the history of the non-hegemonic classes, based less on the role of leadership and organisations than on the experience and culture of the rank and file;[34] Leydi and Cirese sought to revive the fieldwork started by Alan Lomax, Diego Carpitella and Ernesto De Martino.

While adopting the more explicit political material for immediate intervention, Bosio and Leydi identified folk music as a whole as an expression of class culture, and therefore as politically relevant. They created a magazine (*Il Nuovo Canzoniere Italiano*), a record label (Dischi del Sole) and a number of musical and cultural events. The Nuovo Canzoniere Italiano was also the name they gave to an organisation for the collection and promotion of folk and political music through fieldwork and performances, which made its debut with the already mentioned controversial performance at the 1964 Spoleto Festival. In 1966 Bosio also founded the Istituto Ernesto De Martino with the aim of promoting the critical study and the alternative presence of popular and working-class culture.[35] Throughout the 1960s and 1970s the collective produced records and books, organised concerts and other cultural events, and created what was to become Italy's largest archive of oral, folk and working-class culture. Despite myriads of financial, organisational and political difficulties, the Istituto De Martino remains active today.

Bosio's and Leydi's project has remained viable because it was rooted in mass movements rather than in parties and other political organisations. The Nuovo Canzoniere Italiano and the Istituto De Martino have managed to be a meeting ground for the old and the new left (unlike political song collectives arising from the 1960s movements, a good example being the Canzoniere del Proletariato, with its ties to the far left group Lotta Continua). People's history and experience were more important than the songs' political line: Ivan Della Mea's 'O cara moglie' (Dear Wife), Gualtiero Bertelli's 'Nina', and Paolo Pietrangeli's 'Valle Giulia' (a location in Rome where violent clashes between students and the police occurred in 1968), 'Uguaglianza' (Equality) and 'Contessa' (Countess) combined political passion with an articulate individual point of view. At their best, these songs shared with working-class folklore the sense of personal involvement in the experience of history, in which not only was the personal political but the political was intensely personal too.[36]

A major controversy raged over the question of whether performers should seek personal expression or endeavour to document and reproduce faithfully the sound of folk informants. Were new songs supposed to adopt a 'folk' style of simple chords, basic instrumentation, singable tunes, or were they to allow space for the influence of contemporary sounds? How important was musical quality, aside from its political message?

The artist who best combined musical creativity with radical politics was Giovanna Marini, a great performer of folk songs and the author of complex and visionary long 'ballads' and folk operas. Marini believed that in order to politically energise folk music it was necessary to highlight its cultural and stylistic otherness, and contaminate it with classical as well as contemporary music (both 'serious' and 'popular'). She has created some of the most innovative Italian political music and poetry of recent years. In the mid-1970 her search for urban folk styles led her to invent a form of rap. Unfortunately, she was too independent for the Italian music business and political bureaucracies. She has built a very successful career largely abroad, and is seldom called upon to perform in Italy.

The demise of the Nuovo Canzoniere Italiano was mainly a consequence of the fragmentation of the movements on which it had staked its existence. After the mid-1970s, the audience for protest and folk music shrank dramatically. The fashion for the Andean music of the Inti Illimani group and for Irish music, in solidarity with struggles in Chile and Ireland, for a while seemed to fill the gap. Some of the popular *cantautori* were also influenced by the protest songs of the 1960s and continued that tradition in different ways. What remained of the folk revival was less interested in political activism than in musical research *per se*, as was the case with the Naples-based Nuova Compagnia di Canto Popolare. Conservative groups, such as the fundamentalist Catholics of Comunione e Liberazione and later the Lega Nord, promoted a localistic, traditionalist presentation of folk music. Meanwhile the discourse of social and generational protest was being pre-empted by rock. By the end of the 1970s, protest songs and the traditional political music could hardly be said to exist any more.

Alternatives: news from elsewhere

In the late 1940s the radio band leader Luigi Granozio had a hit with a song – 'Roma forestiera' (Rome the Foreigner) – about a girl named Nannarella, who is 'innamorata de 'sta musica americana' (in love with this American music) and no longer sings *stornelli* at the public fountain. It is a telling document of how, through 'this American music', Italian popular culture lost a voice and found a body.[37] Nannarella no longer washed her laundry at the fountain: she did not yet own a washing machine, but she certainly had running water – and a radio. Rather than singing in public, she listened in private to the new sounds – but probably danced to them in public.[38] The music was whatever was available, but it included the American sounds of swing and big bands. Censored by Fascism, jazz was one of the sounds of liberated Italy.[39] However, it attracted only a limited audience (Mussolini's son Romano, incidentally, emerged as a brilliant jazz pianist). With rock and roll it was a different matter.

At first, the little world of Italian popular music thought it could deal with rock and roll as it had done with other musical fashions: tame it and incorporate it as a passing novelty. The results were ludicrous: Claudio Villa's ' "Zi" Gennaro rock and roll' (Uncle Gennaro [a typical Neapolitan name] Rock and Roll) was a pathetic attempt to cast rock and roll in a familiar vernacular vein. Later, a Neapolitan musician, Renato Carosone, wrote the definitive song on the subject: 'Tu vuo' fa' l'americano' (You're

Playing at Being American) was a declaration of surrender. Its music was no longer a case of nostalgic *stornelli* like 'Roma forestiera' but a moderate soft rock idiom, parody and homage; its language was the irony of a modernised and contaminated dialect listing rock and roll as one of a number of cultural imports, from dress codes and Camel cigarettes to the English language. Americanisation was becoming a synonym for youth culture, and rock and roll carried with it a life style that accompanied Italy's transition from a rural, tradition-led society to an other-directed mass culture.[40]

'The Beatles, long hair, dance parties, nonconformist dress,' recalls a young man from a village in southern Lazio, 'these things broke the mould, and created a generation of young people who were more active, open and politically aware.' A Rome university student explains: 'I was in love with the Beatles! I had a passion for the English language as a synthesis of everything I was not, everything Italy was not, everything my adolescence was not, and as the vehicle of certain musical myths, the realm of imagination.'[41]

If what counted in the folk revival was the message, in rock and roll it was the medium: not what the music said, but what you did with it. Youth movements claimed music as a basic right: from Led Zeppelin's 1971 concert in Milan to Lou Reed's 1975 concert in Rome, mass break-ins and clashes with the police generated some of the tensest moments of social conflict. The refusal to pay the high price of concert tickets paved the way to the refusal of the concert as 'concentration camp':[42] music belonged to young people (and especially to the *proletariato giovanile,* marginalised working-class youth) who refused to just sit and listen.

The participatory aspects of the folk revival and the singer-songwriters (the beach and camp-fire guitars of the 1960s and early 1970s) grew into the ideology of *stare insieme* – being together and sharing the music – which culminated in Woodstock-style gatherings. At Licola, near Naples, in 1976, 'a huge line of people dancing to the rhythm of empty tin cans and other makeshift percussions' seemed 'the political affirmation of the basic right to mass creativity'; later, at Parco Lambro, near Milan, 'the young proletariat tried in every way to make its own music (or non-music) by itself'.[43] The punk revolution against the commercialisation and professionalisation of music reinforced this participatory dimension.

As the radical movements began to wane, music also provided an alternative form of organisation: 'people's music schools' replaced political collectives as sites of cultural freedom or resistance. Beginning with the people's music school of Testaccio (a working-class district in Rome), founded by radical jazz and folk musicians, these institutions perpetuated a democratic, participatory tradition and filled a cultural gap in a country sadly lacking in musical education.

The return of political music coincided, in the late 1980s and 1990s, with the encounter between a new form of alternative social organisation, and a new musical language: the 'social centres' and rap. *Centri sociali* are abandoned buildings occupied by collectives of young people and open to the urban context. Since the creation of the Leoncavallo centre in Milan, in 1975, these 'liberated spaces' of youth opposition have spread all over the country as 'a strange mixture of utopia, planning, political experiment, metropolitan languages, very diverse experiences and backgrounds, and a mobile world of imagination in constant metamorphosis'.[44] Punk music, and then rap, have been the musical languages associated with the 'tribal' ideology and cultural style of these alternative communities.[45]

Italian rap is aggressive, timely, often oversimplified and sloganeering (though always close to the feelings of its audiences). The Neapolitan group '99 Posse sing: 'Ho un rigurgito anti-fascista./Se vedo un punto nero ci sparo a vista' (I sense an anti-fascist regurgitation./If I see a black spot, I shoot on sight).[46] Music is again a socially shared extension of speech, expression before entertainment, 'the triumph of solidarity, of a sort of early Communism, where . . . the era of the star is over and that of the movement is back'. The 'rotating microphone' and punk-inherited 'you can do it too' approach create a situation where 'the power of the word . . . meets the dance floor'.[47] On a night like any other, in Naples's 'Officina 99' centre, the critic Goffredo Fofi noted,

> groups come and go, gather and scatter, with gentle dogs milling amongst them. We gather by the stage, between the pillars of the old factory shed, to hear two plain but earnest girls sing, or scream, their poor version of rap, introduced by a master of ceremonies who has nothing in common with his TV counterparts, and does his best to prevent the poverty of the music from becoming an excuse for sexist discrimination. Then, the event many of us have been waiting for: Almamegretta, a new group, which is getting ready for its first record but already has a steady following in town. . . . Almamegretta play a strange and original mixture of many influences: Neapolitan, Arab, with some old-time rock and a bit of Latin America and more than a sprinkling of reggae. One of their songs, 'Figli di Annibale' (Hannibal's Children), makes a strong claim for the 'African' side of Italian and southern culture.[48]

A strange short-circuit connects these postmodern youth expressions with the folk tradition: the power of the word, the role of improvisation, the formulaic use of music and language, the circular shape of the performance, the breakdown of barriers between speaking, singing and dancing, the communal ethos and environment. Many rappers are aware of the history of political and protest music in Italy; a joint concert by young rappers and Nuovo Canzoniere veterans seemed 'an incongruity' to Giovanna Marini, but her colleague Ivan Della Mea saw it as 'a spontaneous stitching together of today's new music and the tradition of *canto sociale*', where 'we tied the red knot between traditional and contemporary culture'. Later experiments were better planned and more successful: after performing together with the folk musician Ambrogio Sparagna, rapper Frankie Hi NRG recognised that 'Hip-hop is open, modular music, born of contaminations,' and can only gain by contact with folk music.[49]

Italian rock music was long unable to shake off the stigma of a cultural import (most groups chose to sing in what passed for English). Rap and its adjacent styles, however, have immediately found their roots. Almamegretta in Naples, Pitura Freska in Venice, Sud Sound System in Lecce, and many others discovered the rhythmic possibilities of dialects, and realised that, just as the power of rap or the blues stems from the history of their makers, so the alternative sound of contemporary Italy must connect with our own cultural history. These syncretistic forms, both vernacular and international (Sud Sound System, for instance, synthesises rap, reggae and *pizzicata tarantata*), are the cutting edge of musical and linguistic invention and political communication in Italy today.

From the right: anthems, jingles and punk

At the 1994 *Festa del Tricolore* (the fete of the Movimento Sociale Italiano, modelled on the Communist *Festa dell'Unità*) 'the sign of modernity was a compact disc called *Techno-Balilla* ("Balilla" was a Fascist youth organisation), in which the rhythm of disco music is adapted to songs of the Fascist era such as the colonialist "Faccetta nera" (Pretty Black Face) and "Adua", and "Lili Marlene" '. The record was advertised on local television stations with marching soldiers, Fascist symbols, portraits of Mussolini and the slogan 'Un grande impero vissuto e cantato' (Living and singing a great empire).[50]

It is no accident that alternatives to San Remo and karaoke have come mainly from the left. Fascism had an ambiguous relationship with music: it generated its own hymns and fighting songs, and promoted a nationalistic version of folklore; however, increasingly suspicious of popular expression, it censored music heavily.[51] As Michele Straniero has pointed out, 'after seizing power, Fascism had no use for the naughty, militant songs of its "romantic" and "popular" period'. It preferred to use the media, especially the radio, to drive people away from independent political activities and concerns: 'The dramatic history and news of the Fascist era are paralleled by escapist, sugary music.'[52] The omnipresent motto of the Fascist era – 'No politics allowed' – also applied to popular music.

This approach was continued after the war and the fall of Fascism: the apolitical entertainment and music that served the purposes of the Christian Democrat power system also spoke to a 'respectable' bourgeois right. The old Fascist songs were used to cultivate political nostalgia, but there seemed to be no place for new right-wing militant protest music.

Things began to change in the late 1970s and 1980s, with the growth of the new, young radical right. Like their left counterparts, some of these groups stressed social and generational marginality, alternative life styles and dress codes, and outspoken criticism of 'the system'. They appropriated texts from the counter-culture, from Jack Kerouac's *On the Road* to J. R. R. Tolkien's *The Lord of the Rings*. The most popular group which played at youth gatherings bearing the name of Campo Hobbit was called Compagnia dell'Anello (Fellowship of the Ring) – half-way between the folk revival and the *cantautori*.[53] As the right increasingly addressed the anger and alienation of marginalised city youth the very sounds that spoke to the radical left often acquired a meaning for young people on the right, who could identify with them both generationally and socially. This was facilitated by the fact that protest in contemporary music, especially of the punk or heavy metal varieties, is often generic and vague enough to serve all purposes.

One sector of youth culture into which the radical right made inroads was football supporters. In the 1970s some groups of fans so identified with the left as to carry portraits of Che Guevara; they also sang parodies of left songs. By the end of the 1980s, however, most organised football supporters were hegemonised by the right, and 'right' and 'left' signs, symbols and slogans lost their political distinctiveness to mingle in 'broad, huge, warlike excess'.[54]

This mixture is reflected in football singing: the tunes are drawn from diverse sources, based on the main requisite of singability (the Cuban revolutionary song 'Guantanamera', the Beatles' 'Yellow Submarine', Frank Sinatra's 'My Way'), but the words are dominated by the 'warlike excess' of organised random. Occasionally the most ideological fringes break into outright Fascist songs like 'Faccetta nera'. Whatever the sources, there is a direct continuity between the bloodthirsty songs of the early Fascist movement and football songs that, for instance, rhyme 'libri di scuola' (school books) with 'pistola' (gun). On the other hand, the violence of these songs also resonates with the anger and aggression that underlie most marginalised and antagonistic youth culture today.

Sometimes it takes a very shrewd listener to distinguish Fascist protest songs from radical rap. The 'Naziskin' (Skinheads) band SPQR, for instance, sings:

> Anni di torpore, anni di appiattimento,
> una generazione senza sentimento.
> Non ci sono fasci, non c'è più tensione,
> per il combattimento non c'è più la ragione.
> La rivoluzione è come il vento.
> Signori del sistema non ci avete piegati.
> La rivoluzione è come il vento.
> Riaffiorano i ricordi degli anni di passione,
> di quanto è vecchio il sogno di rivoluzione.
> Ricordi senza fine di gente che ha pagato.
> Non mollare adesso la lotta a questo Stato.
>
> (Years of slumber, years of flatness,
> a generation without feeling.
> No more fasces, no more tension,
> no more reason to fight.
> Revolution is like the wind.
> Masters of the system, you haven't defeated us.
> Revolution is like the wind.
> Memories of the passionate years return,
> of the old dream of revolution.
> Endless memories of people who paid the price.
> Don't give up now the struggle against this State.)[55]

The very title of this song, 'Come il vento', is ambiguous: it is reminiscent both of Bob Dylan's 'Blowin' in the Wind' and of the partisan anthem 'Fischia il vento'; so is the phrase 'Masters of the system', which reminds one of 'masters of war'. The reference to fasces is the sole identifying trait. Otherwise, only a listener attuned to rhetorical nuances may recognise that the complaint about the lack of 'feeling' or the cult of the dead 'who paid the price' are more in keeping with the imagery of the right, though they have a place in the rhetoric of the left as well. On the other hand, the slogans about struggle, the state, 'revolution' are vague enough to please everyone, in keeping with the new right's strategy of imitating and appropriating the language, symbols and demands of youth movements regardless of their origin.

Strange encounters, then, take place on the contested and shared ground of cultural consumption and life styles. A group of 'Communists and anti-Fascists' in the Friuli region went to a concert by English punk bands and found themselves 'in the midst of a gathering of Naziskins', where five young punks were beaten up amid Fascist slogans and salutes. They blamed the promoters for presenting 'extreme-right bands as if they were representatives of the old, historical punk music'.[56] They probably were, since Nazi and Fascist youth also claim that punk music speaks for them.

Guido Caldiron explains that 'Nazi rock flourished in the late 1980s all over Europe', including northern Italy and especially Veneto: 'Many bands come from this area, such as Peggior Amico (Worst Friend), who recorded some of the genre's greatest hits in Italy.' Italian Nazi music has its own labels and distribution; it is promoted by British magazines such as *Blood and Honour*, 'a sort of billboard of racist music', and is linked with musical networks in France and Germany.[57]

The difference between Nazi rock and left-wing political music, however, is that the former has no audience beyond its immediate constituency, while even the most extreme left rap groups reach a (relatively) broader audience. The respectable right-wingers who dance to *Techno-Balilla* and who claim to have left Mussolini behind in Gianfranco Fini's Alleanza Nazionale reject any association with the radical right's punk scene, and 'distance themselves from the Naziskin anthems of the German heavy metal bands, whose texts extol antisemitism and violence against the Other'.[58] It is not that they do not ultimately share that punk scene's ideology, but that they reject its very claim to be an ideology, preferring to see it simply as common sense.

The new and respectable Italian right was also inventing its own forms of political music. In 1992, as one of the persons involved told me, a group of studio musicians were hired to record what they thought was an advertising jingle. More than a year went by before the song appeared on television as the soundtrack to a commercial – promoting, however, not a new brand of soap but a new political organisation: Silvio Berlusconi's Forza Italia.

Like most urban legends, the story of Forza Italia's anthem has a symbolic rather than literal truth. On the one hand, it represents Berlusconi as a devious character and his party as concocted by marketing and advertising wizards; on the other, it identifies the source of his power in the most pervasive and persuasive of contemporary musical genres: advertising jingles. 'Forza Italia' is 'the first jingle that effectively replaces a slogan, a symbol, perhaps even a platform'.[59] Obsessively broadcast on television, blared out at mass meetings, the song became a 'musical icon' of Italy's 'Second Republic', along with the megascreen image of ex-crooner Berlusconi pacing the stage, microphone in hand.

'Forza Italia' is as easy to sing and to remember as the most powerful and lasting of the San Remo hits, fulfilling the need for reassurance that motivates Berlusconi's voters. The arrangement is slightly modernised, enough to support the party's claim to represent 'the new' while restating its deep underlying conservatism. Some of the words – 'siamo in tanti' (there are so many of us), 'desiderio di vittoria' (yearning for victory) – bear echoes of right-wing rhetoric, as do the patriotic images that accompany them. The title, of course, is lifted from football: 'Come on, Italy!' Unlike most political and protest songs, it does not call upon its listeners to 'arise' and 'awaken', or to do anything. Rather, in the time-honoured Mike Bongiorno and Fiorello style, it tells them they are already perfect: there are many of us and we are beautiful (or we will be if we buy this product).

A recent recording by a leftist punk rock folk band called Ustmamò includes a tongue-in-cheek, very straight rendition of the theme song of *Heidi*, a Japanese cartoon popular in the 1970s and 1980s. Beyond the irony on the silliness of its music and theme, the group is making a generational statement: this is the music we grew up on, the music of our memories. 'Forza Italia' taps into the association between music, memory and television, which are extremely powerful in the culture of the younger generation. According to Theodor Adorno, advertising and popular music are both 'conceived for forgetters' and therefore easily remembered:[60] advertising jingles combine the memory power of slogans (political and commercial) and of popular music. Like old-time radio music, today's television music is also ostensibly apolitical: it is the contemporary sound of the grey area, of the uncommitted middle. With the advantage that, while few listen to the old melodies, children absorb it as they drink their milk. And, of course, most of it is carried by the Berlusconi networks.

'Forza Italia', then, is the crowning of the history of the non-politics of conservative popular music. Formally, it is the synthesis of the most effective commercial genres: San Remo, karaoke, football songs and advertising jingles. Ideologically, it takes the rhetoric of anti-politics one step further, by rallying the passive political middle and involving the uncommitted. It is a non-political song to end all politics.

Which side are you on?

Professor Domenico Fisichella, a member of Alleanza Nazionale, laid down the law only a few weeks into his tenure as Ministry of Culture in Berlusconi's 1994 government. He refused to allow a rock concert in Verona's Roman amphitheatre, the Arena. The monument, he explained, was reserved for *cultural* events; rock did not qualify because it was 'a contemporary art form which [had] not been sanctioned by the passing of time'. He conceded that contemporary expression might have 'a fashion value', but argued that it would take at least half a century to 'consecrate' a work of art. Such aesthetic criteria would rule out Almamegretta – as well as Italo Calvino and Federico Fellini.[61]

Fisichella was merely reaffirming the traditional conservative view (though young Naziskins might disagree) that culture is something that has already been made, a canon of finished artefacts, texts and monuments. Rock is not culture because it is process and performance, creativity in action, always new and yet endowed with its own history and memory. Rock and roll teaches that we create culture now, rather than receiving it from dead people and from the past, and therefore culture belongs to all. While denying that rock was culture, the right was praising karaoke as entertainment: let young people enjoy themselves, but leave Culture to us.

But there is a deeper message in Fisichella's ban.[62] Conservative spokespersons resented the contamination of a monument like Verona's Arena by the 'ill-mannered hordes with no sense of cultural value' who are attracted to rock.[63] Contamination, indeed, is what rock is about: a synthesis of histories, races, genres and languages. At a time when the conservative platform features the promise to keep the 'hordes' of Third World immigrants out of Italy and cultivates a 'differentialist' racism based on keeping cultures separate, rock stands for the migrations and mixtures that created the modern world. The black elements in rock – American blues, Caribbean reggae, African sounds or Malcolm X's and Almamegretta's claim that Italians are all 'Hannibal's children' – are a threat to cultural and racial 'purity'.

Today's Italian music is learning to mix national and international ingredients, *tarantella* and the blues, dialects and English, oral tradition and electronics, mass culture and avant-garde experimentation. There is more Italian identity, as it actually exists today, in the ragamuffin Sud Sound System, the folk operas of Ambrogio Sparagna, the visionary voices of Giovanna Marini, than in all the history of San Remo and karaoke put together.

The critic Gino Castaldo wrote at the beginning of 1995:

> Italian music has changed. On the one hand, there is a wave of new bands, rich in colours and idioms expressing radical and deeply rooted messages, that fully participate in the liveliest sections of a youth universe. On the other hand, there is the explosion of a phoney, falsely innocuous and absolutely commercial music, closely related to television's invasion of our daily lives.[64]

Of course, many young people consume, in varying doses, both the radical and the 'phoney' types of music: young radicals want to be entertained, and may enjoy an occasional bout of the mindless music of 883 or Robbie Williams; on the other hand, even the most political rap has an entertainment value and can be danced to. This is, however, why the struggle between the two musical discourses is irreconcilable: they represent not the conflict between entertainment and political involvement, but that between two radically different ideas and different combinations of both. Not the middle versus the extremes, but the militant defence of *status quo* against the militant struggle for change. Between these options the centre cannot hold, because it does not exist. To conclude, quoting Castaldo again:

> You don't need a crystal ball or visionary dreams to realise that a significant part of Italian music has found a new oppositional identity, political or broadly cultural. . . . We are nearing a new eruption of protest, a new, libertarian course in youth culture, one in which music will once again play an important role.

He is probably wrong. But he may be right.[65]

NOTES

1 Young people sing, not very well, on bus trips – but behind glass, and in the suspended time of travel. There is little singing in church, and it is lamentably bad.

2 Ratings dropped when overconfidence led the channel to replace the show's star, Fiorello, with his brother ('Fiorellino'), who was a failure.

3 U. Eco, 'Quasi quasi mi compro un karaoke e realizzo il sogno della mia vita', *L'Espresso*, 16 September 1994, p. 182. For a more critical view see M. Caramella, 'L'Italia di Fiorello, l'Italia di Berlusconi', *Linea d'ombra*, 96 (1994), p. 66.

4 F. Gennaccari, 'Povera sinistra che ha paura del karaoke', *Il Secolo d'Italia*, 4 September 1994.

5 A. Santini, 'Il Papa s'unisce al karaoke nello stadio', *L'Unità*, 20 September 1994; for a critical comment see M. Serra, 'Karaoke?', *L'Unità*, 21 September 1994. The front-page headline of *La Repubblica*, reporting the Pope's performance in Lecce, was '"Evviva Wojtila" a tempo di rap', 21 September 1994.

6 B. Boccacci and O. La Rocca, 'Il grande show del Papa. Centomila con lui', *La Repubblica*, 9 October 1994.

7 M. Fuccillo, 'Non ci provate . . .', *La Repubblica*, 26 April 1994.

8 L. Quagliata, 'Scenografia a tempo di rap', *Il Manifesto*, 26 April 1994.

9 M. Pirani, 'Linea di confine', column in *La Repubblica*, 2 January 1995.

10 Stefano Della Torre made this point in the talk show 'Milano, Italia' a week after Berlusconi and his (ex?) Fascist allies won the 1994 elections.

11 Eco, 'Quasi quasi mi compro un karaoke', p. 182.

12 U. Eco, 'The Phenomenology of Mike Bongiorno', in *Misreadings* (London, Cape, 1993), pp. 156–64. The essay first appeared in an Italian magazine in 1961.

13 C. Villa, *Una vita stupenda* (Milan, Mondadori, 1987).

14 According to Gianni Borgna, the song 'Grazie dei fior' (Thank you for the Flowers), the first San Remo winner (1951), 'echoes – distantly, of course – the white jazz swing of the 1930s'. See *La grande evasione. Storia del Festival di Sanremo* (Rome, Savelli, 1980), p. 37. The echoes are very faint, and it is hard to interpret as a sign of modernity the fact that this song of the 1950s echoes American music of the 1930s.

15 There is implicit continuity here with the use of the radio and the ban on politics that prevailed under Fascism. See especially: C. Monteleone, *La radio italiana nel periodo fascista* (Venice, Marsilio, 1976); A. Monticone, *Il Fascismo al microfono* (Rome, Studium, 1978).

16 There is an inextricable link between the advent of television and two images of modernity, youth and change in 1958: Domenico Modugno at San Remo, Edson Arantes do Nascimiento (Pelé) in the Rimet Cup in Sweden. Italian television, with its two main attractions, music and football, was really born then.

17 Borgna, *La grande evasione*, p. 28. When he wrote his book Gianni Borgna was head of the Communist Party deputies on the Lazio Regional Council. At the time of writing he is Assessore alla Cultura (Chair of the Culture Committee) on Rome's centre-left city council.

18 In the original format each song was performed by two different artists. The competition, officially, was between songs, not singers. Giovanna Marini, a concert-trained classical musician and a radical folk singer, points out that a compromise also took place at the musical level. Domenico Modugno 'evolved' Italian popular music, but in order to do so he had to moderate the experimentalism of his earlier pieces. See 'Due, tre, molti pubblici . . . : ovvero, come e perché Sanremo è morto', appendix to Borgna, *La grande evasione*, p. 194.

19 G. Castaldo, 'Il trucco è svelato: si fa solo tivvù', *La Repubblica*, 2 January 1995, p. 23.

20 In 1994 the festival was the non-football event with the largest television audience. In February 1997 an estimated audience of 15.6 million watched the festival's final night. The quality of the music and the irrelevance of the winners were no more remarkable than in the previous years.

21 The most popular verse satirised the Communist Party's decision in 1976 not to vote against Giulio Andreotti's Christian Democrat-led government; it was based on the

1920s hit 'La Spagnola' (The Spanish Woman). Similar parodies were still heard in later mass demonstrations, including the general strike against Berlusconi's policies in November 1994.

22 Anon. (Raffaele Offidani), 'Autobiografia di Spartacus Picenus', *Il Nuovo Canzoniere Italiano*, 3 (September 1963), pp. 39–45.

23 C. Bermani, 'Due secoli di canto sociale in Italia', *Volontà*, 47:1–2 (1993), pp. 9–33 (special issue on protest music, entitled *Note di rivolta*).

24 I recorded 'Vola, bandiera rossa, vola' from Adolfo Capitani, a steelworker, in Piombino (Tuscany) in 1972. I have discussed parody in 'Typology of Industrial Folk Song', in *The Death of Luigi Trastulli. Form and Meaning in Oral History* (Albany, NY, State University of New York Press, 1991), pp. 107–73, and in 'Osservazioni sul canto politico nell'area laziale', in Circolo Gianni Bosio, *I Giorni Cantati* (Milan, Mazzotta, 1978), pp. 131–3.

25 G. Morandi, 'Spoleto '64: "Bella Ciao"', *Quaderni della biblioteca popolare di Piadena*, January 1965, pp. 14–38; also in *Il Nuovo Canzoniere Italiano*, third series, No. 3 (1976), pp. 30–4.

26 M. L. Straniero, 'La canzone di protesta in Italia', appendix to R-U. Kaiser, *Guida alla musica* (Milan, Mondadori, 1971), p. 276; M. L. Straniero *et al.*, *Le canzoni della cattiva coscienza* (Milan, Bompiani, 1964). See also I. Della Mea, M. L. Straniero and C. Bermani, with song texts by F. Fortini, *La meta che non so: Franco Fortini*, special issue of *Il De Martino* (Bulletin of the Istituto Ernesto De Martino), 4 (1995).

27 See L. Nono (co-ordinator), 'Uso del suono nella lotta proletaria. Conversazione tra Luigi Nono, Giovanni Pirelli e due operai torinesi', in *Il Nuovo Canzoniere Italiano*, third series, No. 2 (1975), pp. 47–58.

28 Until the early 1960s contemporary musical sounds – rock and roll, American music in general – were heard on the radio not on the regular programmes but on air time bought directly by the record companies.

29 S. Dessì noted that 'Guccini's texts are those of a highly educated, widely read *liceo* student'. See 'La chitarra, il potere e altre cose', in G. Castaldo *et al.*, *Muzak. I cantautori, il pop, il jazz e il rock. Gli anni '70 nell'antologia di una rivista di musicaccia* (Rome, Savelli, 1978), p. 59. On the language of *cantautori* see T. De Mauro, 'Nota linguistica aggiuntiva', in G. Borgna and S. Dessì, *C'era una volta una gatta. I cantautori degli anni '60* (Rome, Savelli, 1977), pp. 133–9.

30 *Ibid.*, p. 58.

31 G. Bosio, 'Alcune osservazioni sul canto sociale', *Il Nuovo Canzoniere Italiano*, third series, No. 4 (1964), pp. 3–10; C. Bermani, 'Due secoli di canto sociale' and 'Bibliodiscografia del canto sociale italiano', both in *Il De Martino*, 1 (1992), pp. 44–65; R. Leydi, *Canti sociali italiani* (Milan, Edizioni Avanti!, 1963).

32 D. Carpitella, 'I canti della Resistenza e la musica popolare', *La musica popolare*, 1 (1977). This short-lived journal, published by Edizioni di Cultura Popolare (Milan), was affiliated to the radical left Movimento Studentesco organisation in Milan.

33 Bermani, 'Due secoli di canto sociale', p. 9. See also L. Pestalozza, 'Musica e Resistenza', *Il presente e la storia*, journal of the Istituto Storico della Resistenza in Cuneo e Provincia, 41 (1992), pp. 14–36.

34 G. Bosio, *L'intellettuale rovesciato* (Milan, Edizioni Bella Ciao, 1975).

35 *Per una storia de Il Nuovo Canzoniere Italiano*, special issue of *Il Nuovo Canzoniere Italiano*, third series, No. 3 (1976). Originally established in Milan, the institute moved to Sesto Fiorentino, near Florence, in 1995.

36 See A. Portelli, 'È la canzone politica la vera poesia civile di quegli anni', in S. Dessì and G. Pintor (eds), *La chitarra e il potere. Gli autori della canzone politica contemporanea* (Rome, Savelli, 1976), pp. 155–60; *id.*, 'Il "metodo" di fare cultura. Lettera al Collettivo delle Edizioni del Gallo', in *Per una storia de Il Nuovo Canzoniere Italiano*, pp. 82–4.

37 This song was honoured with a number of folk parodies. One version, which I recorded in 1969 in Genzano, near Rome, was composed by Silvano Spinetti, a Communist farm worker, and drew a connection between women's make-up, Americanisation and imperialism.

38 Ambrogio Filipponi, a factory worker from Terni, Umbria, remarked in an interview: 'Among the rubble and the ruins of the war, where you could still find dead bodies, there was a boom in music and dancing.' See A. Portelli, *Biografia di una città. Storia e racconto. Terni 1830–1985* (Turin, Einaudi, 1985), p. 296.

39 G. Castaldo, 'Motivi e ragioni per un jazz italiano', in D. Carpitella *et al.*, *La musica in Italia. L'ideologia, la cultura, le vicende del jazz, del rock, del pop, della canzonetta* (Rome, Savelli, 1978), pp. 112–58.

40 See A. Portelli, 'The Paper Tiger and the Teddy Bear', in M. Gonnaud *et al.* (eds), *Cultural Change in the United States since World War II* (Amsterdam, Free University Press, 1986), pp. 82–9.

41 Raffaele Marchetti, interview in A. Portelli, 'Cultura operaia, condizione giovanile, politicità del privato: ipotesi per una verifica sul campo', *Rivista di storia contemporanea*, 1 (1979), pp. 56–83; Chiara Midolo, interview in M. Arcidiacono *et al.* (eds), *L'aeroplano e le stelle. Storia orale di una realtà studentesca* (Rome, Manifestolibri, 1995), p. 73.

42 G. Pintor, 'Sulla musica pop', in Castaldo *et al.*, *Muzak*, pp. 69–70.

43 The first quotation is drawn from G. Pintor, 'Il pop: i tempi e i luoghi di una moda', in Carpitella *et al.*, *La musica in Italia*, p. 91; the second, originating from *La Repubblica*, 29 June 1979, is here cited from M. Grispigni, 'Combattenti di strada. La nascita delle culture giovanili in Italia', in M. Canevacci *et al.*, *Ragazzi senza tempo. Immagini, musica, conflitti delle culture giovanili* (Genoa, Costa & Nolan, 1993), p. 63.

44 A. Solaro, 'Il cerchio e la saetta. Centri sociali occupati in Italia', in C. Branzaglia *et al.*, *Posse italiane. Centri sociali, underground musicale e cultura giovanile degli anni '90 in Italia* (Florence, Tosca, 1992), p. 11. On youth centres see also S. Dazieri (ed.), *Italia overground. Mappe e reti della cultura alternativa* (Rome, Castelvecchi, 1996), pp. 126–74. Specifically on Leoncavallo see A. Ibba, *Leoncavallo, 1975–95. Venti anni di storia autogestita* (Genoa, Costa & Nolan, 1995).

45 F. Liperi, 'L'Italia s'è desta. Tecno-splatter e posse in rivolta', in Canevacci *et al.*, *Ragazzi senza tempo*, pp. 107–22.

46 For a right-wing response see F. Gennaccari, 'Odio a tempo di rap. Ma la sinistra da che parte sta?', *Il Secolo d'Italia*, 4 August 1994.

47 P. Pacoda, 'L'antagonismo in musica. Posse in azione', in Branzaglia *et al.*, *Posse italiane*, p. 72.

48 G. Fofi, preface to Branzaglia *et al.*, *Posse italiane*, p. 8. Almamegretta's 'Figli di Annibale' is based on a speech by Malcolm X in which he spoke of the invasion of the Italian peninsula by Hannibal's African soldiers.

49 G. Marini, 'Storia di una cantata-equivoco', *I giorni cantati*, 25 (1993), pp. 29–30; I. Della Mea, 'Il *Nuovo Canzoniere Italiano* e le Posse', and P. Ferrari, 'Radici con le ali, Della Mea, e le Posse a Torino', both in *Il De Martino*, 1 (1992), pp. 37–8 and 66–7 respectively; interview with rapper Frankie Hi NRG, in *I giorni cantati*, new series, 2 (1994), pp. 30–1.

50 m.m. [*sic*], 'Un po' di nero, salsiccia e tanto Tricolore', *La Repubblica*, 30 August 1994, and A. Dipollina, 'In TV lo spot destinato al "camerata"', *La Repubblica*, 27 November 1992.

51 A. Gravelli, *I canti della Rivoluzione* (Rome, Istituto Editoriale Giovanile, 1928); M. L. Straniero, 'Antistoria d'Italia in canzonetta', in *Le canzoni della cattiva coscienza*, p. 106; V. Savona and M. L. Straniero, *Canti dell'Italia fascista, 1919–45* (Milan, Garzanti, 1978); R. Leydi, 'Il fascismo contro le canzoni', *Il Nuovo Canzoniere Italiano*, January 1963, p. 35; E. Jona and S. Liberovici, 'Canzone contadina, canzone operaia, canzone d'autore a fronte dei fascismi', *Il presente e la storia*, 41 (1992), pp. 37–65.

52 Straniero, 'Antistoria d'Italia in canzonetta', pp. 53, 45.

53 For the right's appropriation of the counter-culture see especially the first-hand accounts of the activities of two of the 'Hobbit' gatherings and the 'philosophy' that inspired them: G. Bessarione, *Lambro/Hobbit. La cultura giovanile di destra in Italia e in Europa* (Rome, Arcana, 1979), and Various authors, *Hobbit, Hobbit* (Rome, Lede, 1987). For a critical investigation of such appropriation see R. Griffin, 'Revolts against the Modern World', *Literature and History*, 11 (spring 1985), pp. 101–23 (especially pp. 103–6, 112–17).

54 M. Canevacci, 'La "Nona" in Curva Sud. Egemonia ed entropia delle subculture', in Canevacci *et al., Ragazzi senza tempo*, p. 137.

55 A. Castellani, 'Ritratto di giovane inquieto. Immagini e stereotipi della condizione giovanile in Italia', in *Ragazzi senza tempo*, p. 239. For the right's use of music see also A. Castellani, *Senza chioma né legge. Skins italiani* (Rome, Manifestolibri, 1994).

56 'Fascisti in discoteca', letter to *Il Manifesto*, 5 January 1995.

57 G. Caldiron, 'Veneto, crocevia nero', *Il Manifesto*, 17 May 1994; A. Longo, 'E la sera cantavamo boia chi molla . . .', *La Repubblica*, 25 August 1995.

58 Dipollina, 'In TV lo spot destinato al "camerata"'.

59 L. Luperini, 'Niente programma, basta un inno', *La Repubblica*, 18 December 1993.

60 T. W. Adorno, *Wagner*, quoted in F. Moretti, *Opere-mondo. Saggio sulla forma epica dal 'Faust' a 'Cent'anni di solitudine'* (Turin, Einaudi, 1994), p. 148.

61 Domenico Fisichella made this statement in an interview to the *Corriere della Sera*; I quote from the Verona daily *L'Arena*, 22 June 1994.

62 Part of the controversy concerned the possibility of harm to the building. This is a serious problem, but it has nothing to do with the cultural value of the event being staged. A high-culture event such as opera caused so much damage to the Baths of Caracalla in Rome that performances had to be cancelled.

63 This definition of rock fans was given by the well-known theatre, cinema and opera director Franco Zeffirelli, a Forza Italia MP. See E. De Angelis, 'La cultura sotto chiave', *L'Arena*, 22 June 1994. According to De Angelis, Fisichella was, however, criticised by an Alleanza Nazionale MP from Verona, Nicola Pasetto.

64 G. Castaldo, 'Cambia la musica italiana. Il testimone torna ai giovani', *La Repubblica*, 30 December 1994, special supplement on the San Remo festival.

65 Not all signs are encouraging, though. In February 1997, as the congress of the PDS was taking place at the same time as the San Remo song festival, an apt postscript to this chapter may be to note that the treatment of the two events by the press and television was markedly similar. The PDS went a step further in the erasure of its working-class past by replacing its old anthems with a new song, entitled 'Un canto' (A Song). It was commissioned from Ennio Morricone (a composer well known for his film scores, who professes no political affiliation) and lyric writer Sergio Bardotti. Bardotti was also the manager of the group that won the San Remo festival that year. A certain osmosis between the two genres was noticeable. One of the speaking characters in the winning song tells another about the house they built together in spite of the errors of the past; the political allusions are not hard to perceive. The score and words of the PDS anthem, on the other hand, sounded just like those of a pop song. However, the congress, which had began with Morricone's and Bardotti's piece, closed – somewhat out of keeping with its political resolutions – with the singing of the Internationale. Old habits die hard.

16

Dress, politics and fashion, 1960–80

Cristina Giorgetti

The relationship between politics and clothes has a long and fascinating history. Clothing has always been a vehicle of political communication in societies where conflicting ideologies exist. Having to live with, and be compared with, political opponents generates the need to diversify one's language and proclaim – through posture, gesture, rhetorical style and clothing – the validity of one's own proposals. This can lead to emulation on the part of followers. Politicians' dress has also served other functions: it has helped them to control instinct and feelings, and enabled them to exploit the symbolic potential of colour, form and ornamentation to bolster their intended message and image. So nothing about the way politicians dress is a matter of chance, be it on a conscious or unconscious level.

Differences are accentuated and the message is made explicit when rival factions are pitted against each other.[1] The style of dress adopted by a political leader or a sympathiser then becomes a manifesto, a banner and the platform of the faction to which the politician belongs. Indeed, the uniform type of clothing is a feature of one-party regimes, where there is an intention to make the masses conform.[2]

Political dress today falls into two broad categories: the uniform type reflecting party ideology[3] and garments chosen independently to emphasise politicians' individuality over the credo to which they adhere. However, the heightened factionalism of post-1968 Italy shows that not even a tripartite division between right, left and centre is sufficient basis for a typology of political dress. The post-1968 right was in part associated with the upper middle classes. The fashion coverage of the international magazines during this period was strictly high fashion, so for the right-wing sympathisers it meant designer-label clothes for both men and women. Young neo-Fascist activists, however, preferred (and continue to prefer) an aggressive, bellicose look: black leather bomber jackets sometimes worn with jeans (Figure 92). The fact that jeans were also worn by left-wing supporters might lead one to conclude that this garment transcended class divisions, but jeans, which were available in a wide range, had their own political and social typology. Right-wingers wore American brands, in particular Levi's (advertised as 'America's finest jeans since 1850') and Wrangler's, both of which, in commercial terms, were at the higher end of the market.[4] In reality these 'American' jeans were manufactured in Italy under licence and distributed and sold in shops alongside other high-quality garments, such as the classic Burberry's mackintosh and Harris tweed jackets. Because of the earlier demand for jeans as an item of workwear and their new-found popularity among young people of all classes, the same Italian companies had for some time also been producing their own brands. Super Rifle jeans, made in the Tuscan town of Barberino, were typical in this respect.[5] Italian jeans resembled American ones in terms of cut and stitching but cost only half the price and represented the lower end of the market.[6]

The sympathisers of the centre parties, largely made up of the middle class and the petty bourgeoisie, still clung to the moral values of nineteenth-century Catholicism. They wore smart clothing that was not designer-label but classic in style and made of good-quality material. For young women this meant skirts longer than was strictly fashionable and reluctance to wear trousers, which, incidentally, were prohibited in state-run middle and higher secondary schools until the early 1970s. Male dress, on the other hand, was still based on the classic styles of the late 1950s,[7] and was thus devoid of innovative features. It consisted of the trio of jacket, shirt and trousers.

As mentioned earlier, colour, too, has political connotations. The right varied the combinations in accordance with the colours that were in fashion, whereas the centre stuck with the classic unchanging shades of blue, white, black and beige for women, and grey, blue and dark brown for men.

92] Far-right activists at a demonstration, mid-1980s

The styles worn in public by politicians of the right and centre tended to be similar to those worn by their supporters. It was not so on the left. The Communist leaders Enrico Berlinguer, Giancarlo Pajetta, Luciano Lama and Giorgio Napolitano adopted the combination of jacket, shirt, tie and trousers of traditional cut, in dark colours such as grey and brown. Their followers never wore clothes of this kind on protest marches. Even the future leader of the PCI, Achille Occhetto, who from 1963–66 was the President of the FGCI, the Young Communists movement, wore a white shirt, albeit minus tie, and a loose-fitting jacket, while Lucio Magri, who was to become General Secretary of the left-wing Partito di Unità Proletaria (PdUP), preferred shirts with high collars and English-style suits.

In the photographs of rallies and marches during the period 1967–69, what catches the eye are the work clothes worn by the various categories of the labouring class, especially the engineering and steelworkers. The dress style of the students in the *licei* (elite upper secondary schools) and universities, where a variety of political views could be found, was wide-ranging. Students on the right mainly wore English-style suits, which were slightly fitted. Those of the centre wore unco-ordinated jackets and trousers with woollen waistcoats. Left-wing students wore shirts, jumpers and trousers of straight cut.

The social turbulence of the late 1960s led to a new era. Left-wing ideology regarded the system behind the fashion industry as class-based and discriminatory: class-based because fashionable garments, the privilege of the better-off, immediately singled out the 'haves' from the 'have nots', and discriminatory because, as a result, fashion was contributing to the deepening of class divisions and the creation of an elite. The elegance imparted by expensive and discriminatory goods was now viewed as a fallacious aesthetic criterion, since the pursuit of that ideal diminished the importance and value of everyday reality. The new frontier of sartorial aesthetics was based on two main principles: the necessity to wear what the vast majority of people were wearing, and to express, through clothing as much as anything else, solidarity with faraway peoples who found themselves in analogous circumstances of oppression and struggle, in an effort to move away from the consumerism associated with clothing until then. Everyday reality was contrasted with the dream-like visions promoted by the fashion industry. Protesters in richer countries, such as France, Great Britain and the United States, also argued that factory workers could not afford to buy designer-label clothing, since the cost of an *haute-couture* garment was greater than a worker's monthly wage.

Other arguments also served to support young people's critical attitude towards fashion. The most important of these pointed to a 'dictatorial' mechanism which sought to impose clothing styles which 'depersonalised' individuals. The majority of politically committed twenty-year-olds of the period embarked upon various kinds of experience in order to 'find themselves' and discover new life styles. The uniformity of the clothing worn by the young protesters paradoxically underlined their individuality: it expressed their refusal to succumb to the saturation advertising of the new seasons' styles of the 'capitalist' fashion houses. The young protesters sought inspiration in what the workers were wearing, this being in stark contrast

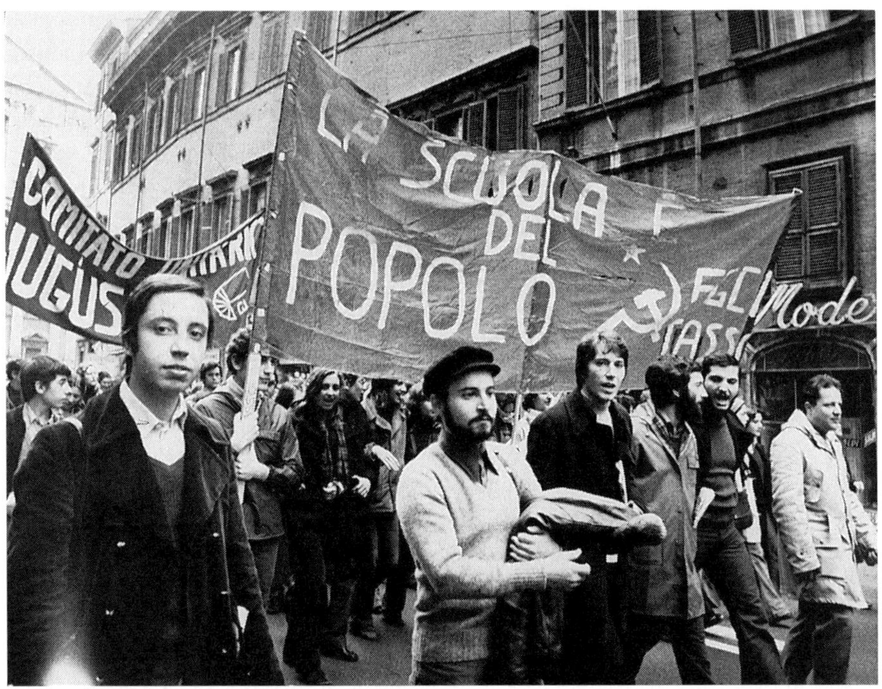

93] Communist students at a demonstration, early 1970s

to bourgeois style. Workwear came to replace the more formal and elegant garments that had been the norm until then.[8] Even the clothes worn by young people on special occasions, such as parties, ceremonies or gala openings at the theatre, echoed the styles worn by the protesters.

A favourite garment of the left's supporters from the late 1960s to the early 1970s was the anorak, the most common type of which was the so-called *eskimo* (Figure 93).[9] The origins of this rain and windproof coat lay in the traditional whale-gut coat worn by Arctic inhabitants, subsequently adopted, on account of its light weight, in a green version by the Allied troops in Northern European seas during the Second World War. Since then the Eskimo-style anorak, with its artificial fur lining or cotton nap, has been valued for its usefulness in emergencies. It became a typical workers' garment because it was cheap and practical: owing to its loose fit, men could wear it over heavy work shirts and jumpers, its detachable hood making it even more versatile.

Another typical working-class garment adopted by the left was the jumper. Heavy, hand-knitted jumpers were traditionally associated with people who toiled at the most gruelling occupations, from lumbering to Nordic fishing. Its lowly origins explain why it was not readily accepted as a sophisticated fashion item. It was successfully introduced to a wider public only through sporting activities. In the 1950s and 1960s luxury jumpers were machine-knitted and regarded as leisurewear. The protest movement not only refused this distinction, but chose as its ensign the most humble type of jumper – that worn by fishermen, which could be worn without a shirt because it had a high, round neck. Soon afterwards, the fashion industry came up with its own machine-knitted version using more expensive yarns, but the protest article continued to be a hand-knitted, cable or ribbed jumper of coarse yarn, right up to the latter half of the 1970s, when the dishevelled look became popular.

The boiler suit is also worthy of mention. It was the warm-weather version of workmen's overalls, and was made of blue or green fabric, the blue originating from the workmen's garment and the green from battledress, especially Cuban guerrilla uniforms.[10] Boiler suits were available from market stalls and shops which, as well as work clothing, sold plastic fishing boots (worn in the winter in a shorter version as rainwear), plastic raincoats, bedroom slippers and Eskimo-style anoraks.

These garments, save the jumpers knitted at home by women's deft hands, were simple on the outside and primitive on the inside (no hem or lining), but because they were double-stitched on the outside they were robust and suitable for occupations where they would incur heavy wear. These features were imitated in the garments made by the fashion industry: stitching with heavy thread and obvious quilting were to be found even in *haute-couture* articles, and the abandonment of linings meant that ready-to-wear items became even faster and cheaper to make.

To complete the revolutionary style, black berets with a star and mid-calf army boots were worn to express solidarity with such figures as Fidel Castro and Che Guevara, who were engaged in the struggle against capitalist regimes.

Accessories were also caught up in this politicising wave of change. The most popular spectacles in the early 1970s were simple, small, round and metal-rimmed, like those worn by Antonio Gramsci, the late Communist leader Palmiro Togliatti and Ghandhi, and conferred an intellectual look.[11] This typology differed from what the fashion industry was offering: commercial fashion sought inspiration from more freakish forms seen in pop art and launched showy lines of clothing.

Something quite new also arose out of the protest movement: unisex dressing. After the false liberation heralded by the mini-skirt, women began to reject a provocative look, and in the early 1970s adopted a more masculine image by wearing jeans. This was the beginning of the left-wing female reaction against the 'comrade masters', but those very same comrades were the inspiration for the women's new style of dress and mannerisms. Not until the mid-1970s – as photographs in the Italian press show – did women begin to reappraise the 'feminine' ideal. This found expression especially in the ample 'earth mother' skirt,[12] accompanied by a rediscovery of natural remedies, the rejection of make-up and a concentration on the exploration and understanding of the potential of women's own bodies. Women of the feminist era became their own 'shamans' and reclaimed all those forms of domestic crafts, from knitting to cooking, which had ghettoised them for centuries.[13] These women spearheaded the return to natural foods and principles that were forerunners of those nowadays referred to as 'ecological', and abandoned chemical hair dyes[14] for the more traditional henna. They also chose physical exercise over dieting, the craze of the previous decade.

94] Feminist march commemorating Women's Day, 1977

Women who were active in left-wing politics during this period, especially those campaigning for abortion on demand and equal rights in the workplace and within the family, looked unkempt. In actual fact, these slogan-shouting harridans had their own style of seduction: they wore traditional nightgowns as dresses and other loose-fitting clothes (Figure 94), and eschewed any kind of underwear except for skimpy pants (lingerie was seen as attire for male sexual gratification); they did not wear coloured lipstick or, at most, used lip gloss; their eyes were given a deep look by the use of kohl pencil, to show solidarity with harem 'slaves' in the East.

There is one final aspect of the first half of the 1970s still to be considered here: the mocking use by left-wing youth of military paraphernalia. Uniforms were sold cheap on the market stalls offering second-hand merchandise and altered to suit the taste of the young people buying them. Ironically, even the chevrons, symbol of hierarchy and military power, were recycled: they were often turned upside down to decorate coats and other garments.

Camouflage trousers and jackets were also popular. Their use resulted from the protests against the Vietnam War and other forms of organised and legalised violence.[15] These outfits were worn until the late 1970s, when tension due to numerous left- and right-wing terrorist attacks was at its highest. The climate of political violence in Italy brought about a rejection of clothing associated with the more aggressive military corps (e.g. the camouflage uniforms of the paratroops and infantry), along with the rejection of a philosophy which saw life as a political battle.

In 1973 styles were also largely influenced by the wave of solidarity with the people of Chile, which had fallen victim to General Pinochet's military *coup*. The demonstrations and strikes which followed the tragic *coup* contributed to the spread of typical South American garments, such as Andean hand-knitted jumpers of coarse alpaca wool, wooden clogs and the unisex poncho worn by the members of the musical ensemble Inti Illimani, whose songs helped to spread Chile's culture and plight throughout the whole world and focus attention on other Latin American countries as well.

In the closing years of the 1970s politicised dress did not disappear. The styles worn by the various opposing factions were merely reversed: members of the Red Brigades started to dress like the petty bourgeoisie so as to be able to pass unnoticed; neo-Fascists wore jumpers and jeans as camouflage; in the streets people continued to wear eskimo-style anoraks, Andean jumpers, long hand-made scarves and Palestinian keffiyehs around their necks. Men were still wearing their hair long and loose, much as they had done since the early 1970s, but the hippie-style *capelloni* (long-hairs) had disappeared.[16] In general the look was scruffy, but this was essentially limited to what was to be seen in the streets. In Parliament and on television the left had not changed its style. Luigi Longo wore dark jackets like Berlinguer; Pajetta wore tweed jackets and woollen waistcoats; Napolitano often donned a formal dark double-breasted suit. During this time the loden overcoat,[17] worn by the Communist trade unionist Luciano Lama, became common among the young of the moderate left and the centre. Factory workers attended funerals for their workmates in their work clothes, but the days when students wore boiler suits were gone.

The left, in its disenchantment, progressively abandoned a style of attire that evoked combative activism. In Rome, in December 1977, the engineering and steelworkers marched not in their overalls but in leather or cloth bomber jackets and classic-styled three-quarter-length heavy jackets; only a few wore eskimo-style anoraks. High-necked jumpers gave way to shirts, which became part and parcel of the proletarian style. The protest mode of dress was in its epilogue. The fashion industry, dominated by new designers such as Gianni Versace and Giorgio Armani, went back to churning out classic styles, which were now more affordable.[18] The craving for normality was experienced at all levels of society – these were the years of the *riflusso*, the backlash against political activism, and of hedonism.[19] In the wake of prevailing conformism, taste in matters of clothing became increasingly homogeneous. Italy became a major fashion trend-setter and exporter. For politicians and the people alike, the impelling preoccupation came to be the projection, through the medium of clothing, of a particular image, namely *il look*.

NOTES

1 For instance, the feuding alliances of families in medieval Florence, the *Neri* (Blacks, the Donati alliance) and the *Bianchi* (Whites, the Cerchi alliance), used the non-colours at the extremes of the spectrum to distinguish themselves from one another. On the symbolic use of colour see M. Brusatin, *Storia dei colori* (Turin, Einaudi, 1983), pp. 102–5; M. Pastoreau, *Dictionnaire des couleurs de notre temps. Symbolique et société* (Paris, Bonneton, 1999).

2 See, with regard to the Russian Revolution, B. du Roselle, *La Mode* (Paris, Imprimerie Nationale, 1980), pp. 151–4.
3 Examples of ideological uniforms are the red shirts worn by followers of Garibaldi, the black shirts worn by Fascists and the flowered shirts worn by hippies to proclaim their apolitical, anti-conformist and hedonistic philosophy of life. More recently the Lega Nord has adopted green shirts.
4 American jeans had for some time been regarded in Italy as leisurewear for the affluent. In the 1930s the heir to the throne, Prince Umberto, was photographed in jeans while walking with his wife in the woods.
5 This company started to produce jeans during the 1950s as workwear.
6 See Various authors, *Blu blue jeans* (Milan, Electa, 1989).
7 See C. Giorgetti, *Cinquant'anni di eleganza. Brioni* (Florence, Octavo, 1995).
8 See G. Paolini and W. Vitali, *PCI, classe operaia e movimento studentesco* (Florence, Guaraldi, 1977), p. 210.
9 See the entry *eskimo* in C. Giorgetti, 'Modavocabolario', *Mondo uomo*, September–October 1992 (unpaginated), and A. Longo and G. Monti (eds), *Dizionario del '68* (Rome, Editori Riuniti, 1998), pp. 203–4.
10 Overalls came into being in 1918 as an item of clothing for the elite. They were conceived by Ernesto Michaelles, a Futurist, who described them as 'comfortable, simple and aesthetically pleasing'. Soon afterwards, however, as well as being used for sport in the first motor races, they were declared the ideal garment for the masses by various Soviet designers. See C. Giorgetti and E. Colarullo, *La moda maschile dal 1600 al 1990* (Florence, Octavo, 1994), p. 105; J. E. Bowlt, 'Sogni industriali', in Various authors, *L'abito della rivoluzione* (Venice, Marsilio, 1987), pp. 17–35.
11 See C. Giorgetti, 'Occhio agli occhiali', in *Vision*, 2 (1993–94), unpaginated.
12 The wearing of 'shapeless' garments, such as voluminous peasant-style skirts, suited the feminists' desire to conceal their bodies so as not to be treated as sexual objects. See G. Parca, *L'avventurosa storia del femminismo* (Milan, Mondadori, 1976), pp. 131–40.
13 A. Schwarzer, *La piccola differenza* (Milan, Moizzi, 1977).
14 See S. Mambri, *Cosmesi* (Florence, Loggia de' Lanzi, 1995).
15 On the ritual of wearing military clothing for demythologising and derisive purposes, which was also an outgrowth of the hippy movement and its idealised pacifism, see F. Bonani, M.L. Frisa and S. Tonchi (eds), *Uniforme. Ordine e disordine, 1930–2000* (Milan, Charta, 2001).
16 See E. Bevilacqua, *Guida alla Beat generation* (Rome and Naples, Theoria, 1994), pp. 46–7.
17 Loden is a woollen fabric of Austrian origin.
18 See Various authors, *Histoire du jeans* (Paris, Palais Galliera, 1995). The book shows how some labels became household names; see especially pp. 69–75.
19 Various authors, *Il trionfo del privato* (Bari and Rome, Laterza, 1980).

17

Fashion and political communication in the 1980s and 1990s

Maria Pia Pozzato

From uniforms to *il look*

Whether political communication is understood as social information or as a way of seeking consensus. Since the 1980s it has been conveyed mainly via the channels of mass communication and, in particular, via television. Up to the end of the 1970s, the political television specials apart, parties cultivated their relationship with the electorate through election rallies, posters and the daily press. In the early 1980s the television-centred nature of electoral campaigning and political communication in general gave rise to concern with the physical appearance of politicians, their manner and pose, and especially their taste in clothing.

In earlier days, fashion intended as a code, i.e. a form of communication, might not have been worth a second thought. Politicians wore dark anonymous suits, the sort one associates with party officials in totalitarian regimes. There was nothing to distinguish the jacket worn by a Christian Democrat from that of a Socialist or a Communist. Only now and then would distinct traits be associated with prominent figures: for instance, Pietro Nenni, the old Socialist leader, wore a beret as a token of his exile in France during the Fascist period, while Giorgio Almirante, leader of the neo-Fascist Movimento Sociale Italiano (MSI), sported striped shirts reminiscent of the leisurewear of the pre-war bourgeoisie, suggesting a moderately hedonistic and elegant life style. But these were symbols of individuality rather than of a specific party or ideology – they were different from, for example, the red carnation worn in the buttonhole by members of the Socialist Party (PSI) in the 1980s, and from the red spectacle frames which the Socialist leader, Bettino Craxi, started to wear in those years because their colour and individualising character made them a good accompaniment to the carnation. For the first time in Italy physical appearance and the political message were closely linked. It was not by chance that the PSI's slogan for the 1987 elections was 'Forse un garofano starebbe bene anche a voi' (Maybe a carnation would suit you too).

My account here of political dress since the 1980s concerns only career politicians, for the simple reason that for two decades ordinary people have not been wearing 'ideological uniforms'. Even among the young the choice of dress today shows adherence to a 'style tribe' (i.e. to a specific group of people who express their cultural identity through clothing)[1] rather than to a political party or movement.

If we take politicians in the narrow sense, the essential difference between the present day and the pre-media age is that today dress is chosen, worn and used consciously to build a model of what a good politician should be. In other words, political actors no longer wear a particular kind of clothing because it is the uniform of a social or ideological grouping, but because their choice of a given style serves to communicate a political identity, or indeed sometimes to redefine it. The concept of dress as an image-creating device, which Italians refer to as *il look*, first emerged in a general context in the 1980s. It then asserted itself in the political sphere as well, albeit not without strenuous resistance, particularly from the left.[2]

As mentioned earlier, image-consciousness has been the result of the transformation of political communication by the mass media. However, the 1994 elections and the introduction of the first-past-the-post system have also contributed to this phenomenon.[3] The change in the electoral system has markedly shifted attention on to individual candidates and away from the parties.[4] As a consequence, aspiring politicians are now launched as commercial brands:[5] they are constantly 'improved' and adjusted to suit the requirements of the target audience, and to take into account the competing 'products'.

The politician as a product

With all this in mind, let us look at how the political spin doctors operate. In France Jacques Séguéla 'launched' François Mitterrand in 1981. His prime concern was to 'humanise the Mitterrand name' and create a 'branded product'. Mitterrand's main opponent, Jacques Chirac, was marketed as someone who would be 'useful' to France at that moment in time, and, therefore, as a 'brand object'. Séguéla tried to present Mitterrand as 'the strong-willed man', in contrast to Giscard d'Estaing, who packaged himself as 'the man everybody likes'. Séguéla analyses a candidate on the basis of three criteria: the *physical* (his objective characteristics), his *character* (the deeper side of his personality) and his *style* (especially communication style). He then divides the campaign into a corresponding number of phases: the representation of the politician's private life, his relation with the members of his own work team, and his political and emotive position *vis-à-vis* the electorate. It is interesting to note that, at the time, Séguéla saw clothing only in relation to the presentation of the private person. In the initial phase of the Mitterrand campaign he explained: 'I suggested to the future president that he change his style from one of image dressing to essence dressing. He made an appointment with Marcel Lassance, the creator of a soft, comfortable style of clothing – whose studio, to further the complicity, was located on the Left Bank.'[6]

Today, on the other hand, as we shall see, dress style pervades all three representational phases of politicians and sometimes decisively contributes to stressing, through its variations, the separation between the public and private spheres. At the beginning of the 1980s, however, Séguéla had clearly already understood the crucial importance of physical appearance and, by implication, dress style. For entertainers he recommended a style which was 'sumptuous, sensational, harmonious and over-the-top'; for politicians he recommended a more subdued approach to suit specific circumstances, without ever forgetting that 'people don't vote for ideas any more, but for personalities. However brilliant a candidate, he cannot allow himself to neglect his image.'[7]

It has been argued that the emergence of the leader as the figurehead of his party occurred in Italy during the 1983 elections, when politicians made use of paid television advertising for the first time.[8] At that time, the Pirella & Göttsche agency set a trend by focusing on Giovanni Spadolini, leader of the Partito Repubblicano (PRI), whilst the BBDO agency devised a campaign for the PSI that was loosely centred on the slogan 'Ottimismo della volontà' (Optimism of the Will) and only partly based on the personality of the party secretary.[9] It was only in 1987, when the PSI chose the Milan-based Armando Testa agency, that its electoral campaign was focused on the image of Bettino Craxi. It was also then that the decision was taken to make use of television, targeted on peak viewing times. Marco Mignani, who was in charge of communications for the Christian Democrat party (DC), made the opposite choice and eschewed a focus on specific party figures.

Until the late 1980s Italian publicists did not fully realise the importance of party leaders' physical appearance and were mostly concerned with the content of speeches. Significantly, a collection of essays which appeared in 1976 and dealt with women's political struggle in 1960–70 does not contain a single word on the matter of dress. Only the issues discussed (abortion, male–female differences, etc.) and the social categories included (housewives, female factory operatives, etc.) account for the differences between the twelve women politicians whose personal stories are recounted therein.[10] However, in the 1980s interesting studies began to appear on non-linguistic aspects of political communication, such as posture, gaze, gesture, dress, facial expression and the use of space. Looked at from this perspective, dress was merely an element within a 'system', but it sometimes assumed a primary role. For example, Gilberto Tinacci Mannelli and Enrico Cheli remarked in 1986:

> Outward appearance, especially hairstyle and dress, are very relevant in the formation of opinions about people, because these aspects are veritable signals of someone's age, social class, occupation and, above all, attitudes and beliefs, often even of his/her ideological and political stance. An excellent example is that of Bettino Craxi, who was known until June 1983 for his casual (albeit designer-label) style of dress. He often wore jeans to emphasise his dynamism and managerial style, but most of all, his break with traditional politics. When he became Prime Minister he totally changed tack and dressed in dark, formal, traditional suits, to reinforce the (deliberate) impression of *super partes*, the role he then filled.[11]

These authors went on to note, this time with reference to the DC leader, Ciriaco De Mita:

> [His] style of dress was usually sober and of rather ordinary taste, without any apparent affectation. On the whole, it was in keeping with a fairly standard model which underlined the intention to maintain an average appearance.[12]

So here was the beginning of a new awareness which brought with it the birth of a new kind of professional, the image-maker, whose full-time task was the promotion of the outward appearance of political personalities. The following passage, from a handbook compiled by Maria Bruna Pustetto which appeared in 1991, gives a good indication of the sort of advice that was being offered to politicians:

> The candidate should bring to the studio, or the place where he has decided to stage the photo session, at least two or three shirts, one of which must be white. Blue is always advisable, but it is always important to be cautious about the use of fabrics with a striped design which could emphasise corpulence. In addition to the shirts, he will need a few jackets, one of which should be in a solid colour. The number of ties depends solely on the resources and imagination of the candidate. However, the more of them a candidate has, the easier it will be to choose one suitable for the required impression. Floral patterns are a non-starter, but regimental ties are recommended. Small designs can bestow refinement when paired with very regular facial features, but can be disastrous under the chin of someone with strong features. A solid colour is always the surest bet and is indispensable where the jacket is in Prince of Wales check or of a more adventurous pattern.[13]

Clearly, the style 'gurus' were drawing up rules on the choice of certain types of garments over others. These rules could be absolute or dependent on the nature of the garments in combination, and on the relationship between the garments and the physical characteristics of the candidate. This 'sartorial grammar', which, at an academic level, had found its highest expression in the 1960s in some of Roland Barthes's most celebrated books (e.g. *Elements of Semiology* and *The Fashion System*), had filtered down to the more pragmatic level of Italian political *savoir-faire.*

The new wisdom was not to exaggerate contrasts between clothing, physical posture and setting, and to wear informal clothing only if one already had the necessary charisma and credibility. The advice was to appear in clothes which were consistent with those worn on other occasions, since 'inconsistency in what one is and the clothing one wears, inconsistency in what one is seeking to be and what one is trying to communicate, sends out an immediate message of unease, which can have negative repercussions on the voters'.[14] Nor was there any shortage of advice for women candidates, whose numbers had begun to rise in the 1960s, if slowly:

> Extravagance, eccentricity, flirty outfits or clothing which communicates veiled sexual availability must be excluded from the wardrobe of the woman who wants to make a career in politics, bearing in mind that male prejudice against women politicians is strong, and that other women are more or less openly hostile. . . . Go for the classic subdued styles, with the emphasis on quiet elegance. This does not mean that you have to sacrifice your femininity or your own need to please others or yourself, but you have to make a strategic choice so as to fit in more easily with the expectations of your party colleagues and the electorate. . . . Your hair should be tidy,

your hands manicured, facial make-up should be applied with discretion; alternatively, wear no make-up at all. The use of jewellery should be restrained; hosiery should always be perfect; shoes should betoken care and cleanliness; accessories should match and not be garish. These are but a few of the rules which a woman candidate must abide by if she wants to live up to, and so be, what voters expect of her.[15]

Much could be said about this feminine model, which seems to have been drawn from the columns of an agony aunt of bygone days (Donna Letizia or Irene Brin, for instance) or, worse still, from the romantic novels of Liala, a prolific writer in the Mills & Boon mould.[16] Female politicians in Italy have not conformed to this model very much in recent years. In fact they cover a rather broad spectrum: from the maverick deputy of Alleanza Nazionale (AN), Alessandra Mussolini (Figure 95), to decidedly less glamorous examples such as the ultra-serious Rosy Bindi (Figure 96) of the Partito Popolare Italiano (PPI). Another striking case was that of Cicciolina (Ilona Staller), the porn star who was elected in 1987 on the list of the Partito Radicale. With a little coronet of flowers on her head, her bosom exposed by pre-Raphaelite veils and generous make-up, it did seem as though she wanted to follow all the canons set out in Pustetto's manual, but in reverse.

95] Alessandra Mussolini, 1996

96] Rosy Bindi, 1997

Dress as the basis of a political model

As we have seen, in the 1980s, dress became part and parcel of the image-making process for male and female politicians. But the prescriptive approach of the publicists and image makers in general does not explain the actual use made of this secondary (yet interesting and important) tool of political communication. Above all, it must be said that analysing dress style as a form of communication is far from easy. Within a given culture it is possible to learn a good deal from the way people dress because they always try to communicate something via their style, be it a wish to please, to make a good impression or indeed to deceive. Nevertheless, it is not a rigid system of signs with a static code, but rather a flimsy, ambiguous area of communication, where meanings may seem banal if not tautological. So it is preferable to think of dress as an area of individual and collective negotiation where various strategies do not obey a code, but rather constantly challenge it – an area in which contrasts are continually created over time.[17]

Although in recent years politicians have been following the advice of image experts much more, it is likely that no rigid rule will ever define a 'correct' style of dress for the communication of specific messages. If anything, the efficacy of any particular choice is determined by contrasting considerations: for example, what message would Craxi's red spectacle frames have carried if at the time they were being worn by everybody? Or would there have been any transgressive impact in the crew-neck jumpers worn by the explosively rebellious Marco Pannella in the 1970s, when the Partito Radicale was fighting for the legalisation of divorce and abortion if this informal mode of dress had not stood out in a crowd wearing jackets and ties? And then there are also the cross-contrasts between people who usually belong to opposing camps. By way of illustration, consider the glaring contrast between the designer-label scarves, gaudy earrings and 'solid hairspray' styles of ladies such as Ombretta Fumagalli Carulli (a now nearly forgotten ex-Forza Italia deputy who was in 1994 Under-Secretary to the Prime Minister's Office in Silvio Berlusconi's government) and the no-frills style of the veteran Catholic feminist Tina Anselmi (a Partito Popolare deputy). Sometimes even a rigidly conformist way of dressing, as in the case of the double-breasted dark grey suits always worn by Silvio Berlusconi in the mid-1990s, can be used as a device of communication. But this confirms, rather than disproves, the rule that clothes communicate by departing from the norm: at a time when people dress far more informally than in the past, disciplined dressing represents a rejection of convention. In Berlusconi's case the anomaly extends even further in that he embraces a monotonous style – despite his wealth, which would permit him the widest possible choice of wardrobe. Finally, there are contrasts which are explicable in the light of the particular historical contexts in which they occur: the general increase in the use of blue in flags, banners, badges and shirts is a result of the decline in the use of Communist red.

It should also be borne in mind that dress is part of a wider image strategy. Sometimes a politician's appearance can serve to identify his or her entire personality in the public's mind. For example, it is likely that in 1994 the young Lega Nord deputy Irene Pivetti, virtually unknown prior to her election to the post of Speaker of the Chamber of Deputies in 1994, was initially identified principally by her curly hair, pastel-colour tailored suits and the Vendée cross[18] she wore round her neck – all signs of a femininity full of determination and constraint at the same time.

More generally, though, dress signs find their value within a broader context which includes character, ideology, contingent political choices, personal life style, age, sex, familiarity with the political establishment (or lack of it), level of popularity, and so forth. With some of these variables in mind, the French semiologist Eric Landowski has proposed a subdivision of contemporary political communication in four styles or 'types of popularity'.[19] Above all, he draws a parallel between politicians and actors. The problem of popularity for both is twofold: on the one hand there is the need to make one's name known, on the other the need to be loved. Thus there are two possible uses for dress style: one which depends on individualisation and distinctiveness in order to attract attention; the other which is dictated by the logic of seduction, persuasion and adaptation to the expectations of the electorate, and thus by the need to conquer and 'evangelise'. In both cases, politician and actor find themselves in a situation of needing to play a role and choose, one might say, a costume for the role. Now let us look at the four different basic 'types' of politicians.

The first is the so-called 'man of action', the doer. His visibility is due more to what he does than to what he is. He is reluctant to show his personal and private side. Contemporary media culture, which is characterised by indiscretion, obliges this type of politician to run the risk of seeming unappealing to the public or, worse still, of being perceived as not at ease with himself, or as having something to hide. If we graft on to this our considerations on dress, we see how the choice of clothing can support or weaken these impressions. To cite an example, Lamberto Dini, who arrived on the political scene as an anonymous economics expert in 1994 (when Berlusconi appointed him Treasury Minister) gradually moved away from this and was increasingly seen at social events in smart evening dress – or, at the opposite extreme, in shorts, a fishing hat and gumboots while pottering about the olive trees at his country home.[20]

Similarly, the former leader of the Partito Democratico della Sinistra (PDS) and former Prime Minister, Massimo D'Alema, who tries to promote the image of a pragmatic problem solver, is often seen in sailing gear on his own sailing boat (Figure 97). This triggers a complex series of associations: a rich man's sport pursued by a leader of the workers' party (an idea reinforced by the fact that D'Alema often wears designer-label sportswear); leisure instead of work; fitness as opposed to bureaucratic immobilism; a wealthy man from the South, a region stereotypically viewed as poverty-stricken; etc.

The second type identified by Landowski is the 'hero mediator'. This is a different kind of politician, one who pays more attention to how he/she is rated by the public, because he/she identifies with that public. So the hero mediator tries to establish some kind of organic unity with the public. He/she feels and wants to have behind him/her a community of interests and values founded on common emotive experience. This verges on the religious; the leader becomes a cult object; the people

97] Massimo D'Alema at Gallipoli, 1997

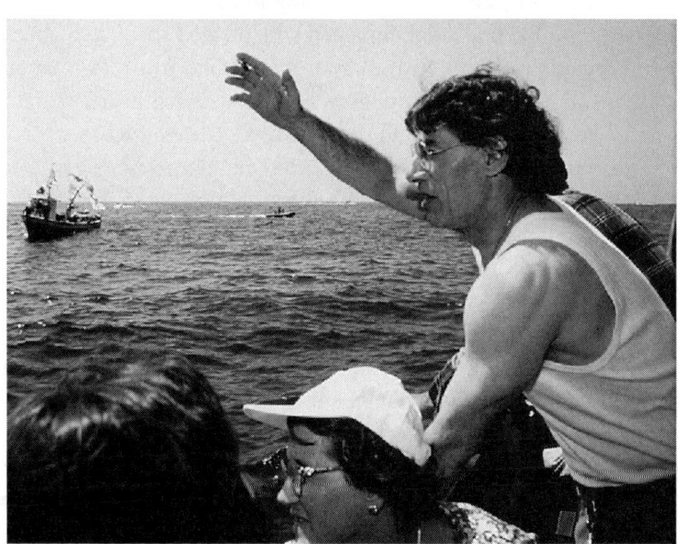

98] Umberto Bossi at Camogli, 1996

believe in him/her. Clearly, we are a long way from the pragmatic efficiency of the first political 'type'. From this second type of leader the public does not expect practical solutions so much as a role which crystallises the very existence of the group. Berlusconi is a typical example. He is a boss twice over: he is the managing director of the enterprise he created, and the leader of Forza Italia. The strong identity of both these collective realities resides solely in the leader, who personifies their ideology and faith. It is a fairly common tendency for communities to revere the public personality who most embodies and inspires – through his/her speeches, bearing, physical appearance and style – a certain togetherness, an *esprit de corps*.[21] Landowski uses as a typical illustration the British Queen, whose semi-divine status is supported by her income, palaces, genealogy and so on, but whose dress style, not by chance, is that of a British housewife in her Sunday best.

Returning to Berlusconi, he does indeed have two 'uniforms': the aforementioned grey double-breasted suit for public occasions, and the dark-coloured jumper worn without a jacket for communiqués from his villa at Arcore, near Milan. The two uniforms are a good display of the dual role (heroic and identificatory) that he fulfils as a hero mediator. But real people never exhibit such a pure typology – they tend instead to straddle two or more types. Thus, as we shall see, Berlusconi is undoubtedly, to some extent, also the third type of leader – the so-called 'political star', while the leader of the Lega Nord, Umberto Bossi, is partly a hero mediator and partly of the fourth type, the 'political clown' – but let us not anticipate too much here.

As a hero mediator Bossi is the leader of an electorate whose ethical and aesthetic values are unquestionably more popular than those expressed by Berlusconi. The life style of the *Senatùr*[22] is reflected in his modest house, outmoded hairstyle and dishevelled mode of dress whose high point is his vest (Figure 98). Bossi proudly displayed this most proletarian of garments, with its Neo-realist film associations, for the first time during the summer of 1994 when he needed to differentiate himself politically from his ally and alter-ego, Berlusconi. So one could say that Bossi, with his polka-dot ties worn with striped shirts and check jackets, is one of the politicians with the greatest awareness when it comes to appreciating the communicative value of physical appearance.[23] It is much easier to rely on a good tailor or a good fashion designer, as did nearly all the political leaders in the 1996 electoral campaign,[24] than to independently and vigorously pursue such wardrobe deregulation. While even Gianfranco Funari, who worked for a gambling den before becoming a popular political talk-show host, stopped wearing dated Ray-Bans long ago, Bossi persists in sporting his Ray-Bans unrepentently, as well as in parting his greying, not always shampoo-fresh, hair in the middle and in having kitsch posters of Alpine woods on the walls of his house.

Bossi's chosen role is that of the most genuine popular hero, someone who has not changed his tastes, not grown rich, not refined his manners after making it to the capital and who has kept his regional accent. In short, he is still a part of the social context to which his supporters belong. So in his outdated hairstyle, unfastened shirt collars and ever loose tie there lie complex political values. To mention a few: the Lega Nord's claims to being a spirited movement rather than an organised party (it is the only political grouping in Italy so far to have used catch-words such as 'insubordination', 'secession' and 'popular mandate'); its attempt to set itself up in opposition to a bourgeois and party-centred socio-political reality; its view of politics as a form of action rather than a strategic minuet; and Bossi's wish to be a leader *inter partes* instead of *super partes*.

But the purest hero mediator of all is undoubtedly Antonio Di Pietro, who, as the initiator of the *Mani Pulite* investigations, has had a fundamental political role in 1990s Italy. The dress style of the man who demolished the First Republic plays on the tension between the serious but well-groomed (indeed, solemn when he wore his court robe) magistrate and the podgy face and coarse eloquence of a peasant from the Molise region. In a sense, this was the southern version of Bossi's northern populism, but intended to promote the widest possible identification with a collective ideal that Italy has witnessed since the Second World War.

Landowksi's third type is, as already mentioned, the 'political star' – a product created by image makers when a figure is not rooted in a specific ideological tradition. This type of politician proposes himself/herself, rather than a series of values. The political star is liked, much in the way that singers or actors are liked, wears an eternal smile and has a trustworthy air. The political star openly proclaims the radical authenticity of his/her words, to the extent that his/her public and private lives coincide.

From an aesthetic point of view, this third type of politician conforms, for the most part, to the established canons on dress and good bearing. In other words, he/she tries to be in fashion or, as the magazines would say, to keep up with 'what's in'. In Italy's recent political history this type has become fairly commonplace. Its incarnation is not to be found in any specific individual, but rather is disseminated in a kind of 'mass-media cosmetic', for which gradually almost the whole of the country's political class has opted. Berlusconi's phoney good humour and the diffusion filter that he places in front of the lens of the television camera to look younger and flawless are typical manifestations of the phenomenon, as are the neatly coiffed heads and silk scarves of the female members of the Chamber of Deputies and the Senate, and the journalistic accounts of televised interviews and debates where the focus is on which politician was the most sparkling, witty and elegant, rather than on who was the most convincing.

The spectacularisation of politics is a well-known phenomenon, so we need not dwell upon it here. In Italy, since the 1994 general election, this trend has been greatly accentuated by the welding of the worlds of television and politics. Not only did the owner of three major private television networks become Prime Minister, but some television presenters became political personalities. Vittorio Sgarbi, for example, started out as an art critic and polemicist of the small screen; today he is perhaps the purest type of 'political star'. His image thrives on contrasts: dandyism and moralising invective; a good, but crumpled, suit; a hanging wisp of hair Brian Ferry-style with thick intellectual-looking spectacles; a reputation for being a *bon viveur* and a strong (but vague) anti-everything attitude. Even after having been elected a deputy Sgarbi continued to have his own daily television slot, so he has never ceased to be both a politician and a television celebrity.

The fourth and final type is the 'political clown', who resorts to bad puns, unseemly dress, crude gestures and foul language, to rebel against tradition, and discredit institutions and the political world as a whole. It is here that we find Bossi's second soul – one which bears a resemblance to a *commedia dell'arte* character because, although Bossi purports to be a new champion of the people, he is also an irreverent jester, a licensed Harlequin who uses suggestive and obscene gestures, a comic character with cascading saliva and a drawling, raucous voice like that of a 'regular' at a local *osteria*. From this perspective, even his clothing acquires further meaning: he may wear common jackets and shirts, but inside them moves a body which loves to shock and which brings to mind the mimicry of Dario Fo, rather than the restrained gestures of people from the Po valley. By this transgressive use of the body, Bossi and a few of his fellow party members are in some ways comparable to exponents of the extreme right who are often photographed pulling faces or gesturing, dressed in camouflage gear or studded leather jackets – sometimes decorated with symbolic nicknames.[25]

Moreover, even the ex-television presenter Giuliano Ferrara, a Forza Italia deputy in 1994–96, seems to fit the political clown type, on account of his verbal aggression, large cigar, long hair (until 1995) and obesity (emphasised by his penchant for red braces, often worn over a shabby shirt), which turn him into a kind of fable archetype: half Bluebeard, half Clever-clogs.

The classic anti-clowns are probably Walter Veltroni (Deputy Prime Minister in the Prodi government and then leader of Democratici di Sinistra – formerly PDS), and the leader of AN, Gianfranco Fini. Veltroni, having made it to the top, decided to go on a diet and lost about 15 kg to acquire a more serious and Kennedy-like air. Fini's clothes are generally better ironed than those of his centre-left counterparts, and Prodi, in particular, wore the grey suits of a Christian Democrat,[26] albeit with creases to suggest a dynamic personality, when he was Prime Minister (1996–98). Fini, on the other hand, wears impeccable blue shirts, suede jackets and polished brown shoes.[27] This kind of perfectionist but standard mode of dressing is in keeping with a lengthy tradition of vestimentary respectability which nowadays is not pitted against anything, but in the 1960s and 1970s was the style adopted by right-wing youth, the so-called *Fascetti*, in opposition to the scruffy, ethno-proletarian style of left-wing youth.

Conclusions

It is worth reiterating that the same sartorial signs which formerly distinguished a right-wing political stance nowadays, at most, communicate the idea of a well-groomed man. But since in the present context of Italian politics more or less everyone seems to be moving towards better grooming, it is safe to predict for the immediate future a general weakening of dress signs in political communication. To the joy of the authors of style handbooks, the choice of cut, accessories or colour combination seems to be increasingly dictated by the wish to promote a candidate from an aesthetic point of view, namely to improve his/her 'televisuality', regardless of the candidate's actual qualities and personality. In short, after the 'political star', we can expect to see the 'political supermodel' – probably the least exportable of any Italian fashion product.

NOTES

1 For the concept of the 'style tribe' and a description of the new phenomenon of youth congregating together see T. Polhemus, 'Il vestito postmoderno', in M. P. Pozzato (ed.), *Estetica e vita quotidiana* (Milan, Lupetti, 1995), pp. 123–9; *id.*, 'Sampling and Mixing', in R. Grandi and G. Ceriani (eds), *Moda. Regole e rappresentazioni* (Milan, Franco Angeli, 1995), pp. 109–42.

2 On the anti-individualist tradition of the Italian left see G. Statera, *La politica spettacolo. Politici e mass media nell'era dell'immagine* (Milan, Mondadori, 1986), who notes (p. 21): 'The 1968 movement is for the masses and their spontaneity – not for the individual, except in so far as an individual is a part of the masses. Above all, the movement is against the penetration of what is political/public by what is private/spectacular, and against personal symbols of power.' In the 1970s the popular Communist leader Enrico Berlinguer was accused of encouraging an 'impersonality cult'.

3 See G. Statera, 'Vecchi e nuovi modelli di comunicazione politica. Dalla politica degli apparati alla politica-spettacolo', in G. Pasquino (ed.), *Mass media e sistema politico* (Milan, Franco Angeli, 1986), pp. 47–73.

4 It seems to me significant that, in the course of this study, I had difficulty in finding pre-1993 photographs of politicians which were at all informative on the question of dress. For the most part, only faces appeared in the photographs. Newspapers and magazines did not deal with the physical appearance of politicians. Articles on the topic now abound. See, for instance, in the mid-1990s: G. Pansa, 'Il disperato della cannottiera', *L'Espresso*, 9 September 1994, pp. 42–4; D. Pardo, 'Lei non sa che posa ho io', *L'Espresso*, 7 October 1994, pp. 68–70; M. L. Rodotà, 'Blu, blu, i mille blazer blu', *L'Espresso*, 15 April 1994, pp. 50–1; A. M. D'Urso, 'Guarda che look', *Anna*, 28 March 1996, pp. 43–50.

5 This trend, brought about by television, had, however, been in evidence for a few years before the reform of the voting system. See D. M. Masi, *Come 'vendere' un partito. Ovvero, la teoria della comunicazione politica* (Milan, Lupetti, 1989), p. 73: 'The 1987 electoral campaign can be considered a Copernican revolution for its mode of political communication – . . . a noisy triumph of advertising with a political slant on information itself.'

6 J. Séguéla, *Hollywood lave plus blanc* (Paris, Flammarion, 1982), p. 26.

7 *Ibid.*, p. 100.

8 See, for example, Statera, *La politica spettacolo*, who also refers to the programme *Italia Parla* (Italy Speaks) on the Rete 4 channel, where the guest politicians sat in gilded armchairs.

9 For the various stages of this electoral campaign see L. Bogagni and C. Maffei, *Comunicare un partito politico* (Milan, IPSOA, 1990).

10 Various authors, *La parola elettorale. Viaggio nell'universo politico maschile* (Rome, Edizioni delle Donne, 1976). The very title of the book gives an indication of its word-centred conception of politics.

11 G. Tinacci Mannelli and E. Cheli, *L'immagine del potere. Comportamenti, atteggiamenti e strategie d'immagine dei leader politici italiani* (Milan, Franco Angeli, 1986), p. 124.

12 *Ibid.*, p. 148.

13 M. B. Pustetto, *Il manuale del candidato politico* (Milan, Bridge, 1991), pp. 95–6.

14 *Ibid.*, p. 99.

15 *Ibid.*, p. 240.

16 Liala's heroines, like Pustetto's female politicians, are obsessed with hygiene and tidiness, and opportunistically dissimulate their sensuality. The object, in their case, is marriage, and political expediency in the case of Pustetto's aspiring politicians.

17 See Ugo Volli's introduction to F. Davis (ed.), *Moda, cultura, identità, linguaggio* (Bologna, Baskerville, 1993), pp. iii–iv.

18 The Vendée cross (a cross over a heart) is the controversial symbol of reactionary Catholicism, namely of its negative attitude to the enlightened values of the French Revolution and the reformist ideas of the Second Vatican Council. After the 1996 elections Irene Pivetti, having lost her institutional role, at first re-embraced an aggressive image and role in the Lega Nord, which was more than ever determined to divide Italy into two separate republics. Thus, instead of pastel-coloured tailored suits – symbolic of institutional loyalty – she wore baggy trousers and green shirts, ecological and Po Valley symbols of the separatist movement in the north of Italy. Pivetti rejected the openly separatist stance taken by the Lega Nord in summer 1996 and was expelled from the party. In spring 1997 she founded her own party, Italia Federale, whose logo was an aggressive-looking bear. But the party did not get very far, and Pivetti's next move was to join a small Catholic party of the centre.

19 E. Landowski, 'De la représentation politique: régimes de présence et formes de popularité', in J. L. Parodi, *Présence de l'autre* (Paris, Presses Universitaires de France, 1997), pp. 219–44. The categories of politician which Landowski outlines essentially reflect the French experience and do not always closely match the situation in Italy. Nevertheless I believe they can provide an interesting starting point for discussion.

20 Since 1979 Dini had been Director General of the Bank of Italy, a post which, despite its importance, attracts little public attention. Incidentally, Dini was appointed Prime Minister after Berlusconi's fall in 1994 and later served as Foreign Secretary in centre-left governments.

21 According to Landowski, the people whose vocation it is to become 'popular' are those who know how to cultivate their image in accordance with certain widespread aesthetic and ethical values. Such individuals are more suited than others to incarnate the vision a community has of itself; cf. 'De la représentation'.

22 Lombard dialect for 'senator'. The title has stuck to Bossi even though he was a member of the Senate only in the first term of his parliamentary career (1987–92), having subsequently opted for the Chamber of Deputies.

23 On Bossi's deliberately down-at-heel look see R. Barraclough, 'Umberto Bossi. Charisma, Personality and Leadership', *Modern Italy*, 3:2 (1998), special issue *Charisma and the Cult of Personality in Modern Italy*, (eds) S. Gundle and L. Riall, pp. 264–5.

24 Thanks to the newspapers, we now know everything there is to know about the brands of shoes, shirts and ties worn by the various leaders. It is no secret who their tailors are, either. For example, D'Alema's is known to be Cenci, Berlusconi's is Caraceni, etc. In the mid-1990s the Sunday television programme *Telecamere*, on the RAI 2 channel, had a regular slot in which the stylist Michel (alias Michele Sterlicchio) manipulated the image of male and female politicians with computer graphics to recommend a particular hairstyle or style of clothing.

25 A good example of such a type is 'Er pecora' (the sheep), nickname of the AN hard-liner, Teodoro Buontempo.

26 Prodi played an influential role during the reign of the Christian Democrats. The leadership turned to him, for example, when the party had been in government forty years, for the arduous task of rationalising IRI, the state-controlled holding company. During the 1996 electoral campaign, as leader of the Ulivo coalition, Prodi made great efforts to distance himself from a past which, according to his political opponents, linked him with the old regime.

27 Fini's wife cultivates a totally different image: she wears short skirts and plunging necklines, and sports tattoos. She is often photographed dancing wildly in discotheques, or in a stadium avidly watching a football match. This up-front, aggressive style is designed to moderate her husband's formal style. The whole question of the wardrobe of politicians' wives – or husbands – is of interest and deserves separate investigation. On the political significance of high-profile wives of public men, with reference to the United States, see J. B. Gillespie, 'The Phenomenon of the Public Wife. An Exercise in Goffman's Impression Management', in D. Brissett and C. Edgley (eds), *Life as Theater. A Dramaturgical Sourcebook* (New York, de Gruyter, 1990), pp. 379–97.

18

Ritual degradation as a public display: a televised corruption trial

Pier Paolo Giglioli

Between the end of 1993 and the beginning of 1994 several million Italian television viewers were witnesses to an unusual spectacle. For almost three months the trial of Sergio Cusani, a Milan-based businessman who acted as middleman for Enimont (a large industrial group) and many political leaders was broadcast in a prime-time evening slot by the publicly owned television channel RAI 3.[1] The trial was the first and biggest to grow out of the detailed investigation of political corruption begun in Milan in February 1992, dubbed *Mani Pulite* (clean hands).[2] Viewers saw some of their most important political leaders – former Prime Ministers, former Ministers and all the leaders of the parties in the previous government coalition – confess to having illicitly accepted massive sums of money from large publicly and privately owned companies to fund their parties and, in a few cases, their own electoral campaigns.[3] Many viewers also suspected, as was subsequently borne out by the evidence, that some politicians had pocketed some of the money for their own private use.

The broadcasts of the trial were avidly followed by the public. Despite competition from prime-time evening light entertainment on other channels, the viewing figures on some evenings topped 4 million, with as much as a 16 per cent audience share. Such figures are usually the preserve of big sporting events or popular entertainment. The public prosecutor, Antonio Di Pietro, the best known of the group of Milan magistrates investigating political corruption, became a national hero, and almost all the politicians summoned before the court had their careers torn to shreds in the public glare. In short, the Cusani case represented the climax of a deep-rooted process of delegitimation (set off two years earlier by the arrest of a local government manager in Milan, Mario Chiesa, who was caught *in flagrante* pocketing a bribe), a process which, in a very short time, toppled the political regime which had ruled Italy for over forty years.

In this chapter the Cusani trial will be examined from a sociological, rather than a legal, viewpoint. I will first try to show that, for television viewers and the protagonists themselves, the trial became a degradation ritual wherein moral, rather than legal, problems were at issue. Yet contrary to what happens in traditional rituals, the outcome was in no way rigidly predetermined.[4] Certainly, bearing in mind the general disrepute in which politicians involved in the scandals were held by public opinion, the likelihood that they would escape with their honour intact was decidedly remote. Nevertheless, the trial did not inexorably produce the moral destruction of the political leaders hauled up before the court. Indeed, they sought to resist degradation and, at the end of the trial, some wound up with their reputation less damaged than others. The Cusani trial, then, must be examined both as a ritual and as a symbolic arena in which politicians fought to defend their identities and their 'face'.[5]

Degradation rituals

Degradation as a phenomenon traces its roots to the military, but even though degradation rituals rarely match the elaborate ceremony found within the army, they can occur in every sphere of social life. As Harold Garfinkel pointed out in a seminal paper,[6] they are the result of moral indignation, and all societies, unless they are totally anomic and demoralised, provide, in their routine features, the structural conditions for identity degradation.

A degradation ceremony consists of 'communicative work directed to transforming an individual's total identity into an identity lower in the group's scheme of social types'.[7] At the individual level, then, its consequence is the ritual destruction of the person degraded. At the social level, it has a dual function. On the one hand, as suggested by Durkheim,[8] the feelings of moral indignation expressed in public denunciation have the effect of reinforcing social solidarity. On the other hand, degradation ceremonies have a cognitive function, in that they confirm (or redefine) the symbolic boundaries between morality and immorality. For example, one of the most important effects of the Cusani trial (and, more generally, of the whole *Mani Pulite* affair) has been the redrawing of the boundaries of what constitutes proper and acceptable behaviour for a politician.

Structurally, a degradation ceremony comprises three main parties: the denouncer, the person denounced and the public. Their main characteristics are the following. First, since every public denunciation implies a claim to universality, the denouncer must be seen to act not as a private individual, but rather in the name of public morality, otherwise he/she may be perceived as the representative of partisan interests. Thus a recurring issue in degradation rituals concerns the resources available to the denouncer to transform him/herself from a private individual into a representative of a collective body.[9] Conversely, the impact of public denunciation can be reduced by showing the hidden links between a denouncer and vested interests which could benefit from the denunciation.

Second, for a degradation ceremony to be successful, the accused individual and his/her alleged misdeed must be removed from the ordinary realm of everyday life and made into an instance of a general category, which then is made clearer and more tangible by contrasting it with its opposite (e.g. good/evil, honesty/corruption, the public good/private interest, respect for the rule of law/unlawfulness).

Finally, the presence of the public is a necessary feature of degradation ceremonies. Usually there is a close relationship between the size of the public and the nature of the offence. For instance, if an offence occurs within a family, it is sufficient for the denunciation and degradation of the culprit to take place in front of a few close relatives. But when the offence concerns a much larger body, for instance the national collectivity, the denunciation and the degradation need to be in front of as wide an audience as possible, preferably in front of the whole nation.

The success of a degradation ritual depends on the extent to which these three conditions are satisfied. The more the accused and the event can be labelled in an exemplary way, the greater the denouncer's success in presenting him/herself as a representative of collective values, and the more the public is of the right proportions, the greater the likelihood that degradation will be achieved. Let us now see how these conditions were satisfied in the Cusani case.

The Cusani trial as a degradation ceremony

Criminal trials have a distinct ritual dimension. Consider the courtroom setting, the raised platform where the judges sit, the lawyers' and magistrates' robes, the rigid allocation of turns to speak, and so forth. The symbolic purpose of these features is to celebrate the solemnity of the law and to remind participants and the public of the clear separation that exists between everyday life and court proceedings. The frame of the trial sets it off as a world apart, a specific life form, a 'liminal' universe[10] to which external events and structures have no access, or have only limited access, which must conform to legal procedure.

The general governing principle in this world is that all citizens are equal before the law. In court, therefore, politicians are formally treated like ordinary citizens. Control of the trial's progress does not lie in their hands but in those of the judges. The politicians come into court when called, not before or after. They sit where anyone coming to court as a defendant or a witness sits, i.e. lower than the judges. Although they are well known, they must enunciate their name and their date and place of birth at the beginning of their testimony – a rite of passage which displays their transformation from wielders of power to ordinary citizens. As with other defendants, they are questioned; they cannot consult collaborators before answering; they are the focus of the audience's attention. Their words and bearing are scrutinised by the public, especially the lay public, not just for the apparent content of their answers but also for the information they inadvertently reveal.[11]

All this is in stark contrast to the public image of Italian politicians shaped by the media, especially television. When politicians are interviewed on television programmes it is usually done deferentially, or at best in a neutral tone. It is true that in the 1990s the Italian media's respect for politicians seems to have waned; some television interviewers have eschewed traditional deference and tried to put them on the spot. But, even in such cases, they are still given the chance to explain their position, to rebut accusations and to turn on their accusers. None of this is possible in a legal trial. It is, therefore, understandable that in the Cusani trial the politicians found themselves in a difficult and embarrassing position. Since degradation consists in a redefinition of the social identity of an individual as one of a lower rank, the mere fact of having to appear in court as a defendant is degrading for a politician. He no longer has a privileged status but, like every other citizen, is subject to the rule of law. Whereas the prosecutor represents the general interest, the politician represents his own particular interest: accuser and defendant have different statuses.

In the Cusani trial this asymmetrical relationship between prosecutor and defendant, which is a characteristic of criminal trials generally (surely not only of Italian ones), was further accentuated by the strong identification of public opinion with the prosecutor. This arose from various factors: in the first place, from the speed and efficiency of the Milan investigating magistrates. After only a few months from the start of their investigation they had reached the highest echelons of the political world. Between the end of 1992 and the first half of 1993 a sizeable proportion of the political ruling class – members of the Houses of Parliament, Ministers and leaders of many parties – were accused of a series of various offences: corruption, extortion, criminal association and violation of the law on the funding of political parties.[12] In a country in which public administration, including that of justice, has always been thought of as slow and inefficient this show of energy and determination on the part of the investigating magistracy inevitably had a favourable influence on public opinion.

Secondly, the *Mani Pulite* investigation took place in a climate marked by great dissatisfaction on the part of the citizenry with the traditional political order. This discontent was caused, in the main, by an increase in taxation, by ever greater realisation of the extent of the public deficit and by the state's repeated failure to deal with organised crime and the Mafia.[13] Against this backdrop, the investigation of the Milan magistrates soon turned into a moral crusade. A large section of the population, cutting across political loyalties, saw the magistrates as its avengers fighting against a corrupt and inefficient political ruling class.

Finally, this identification with the magistracy was strengthened further by the sacrificial role of a few magistrates in the battle against the Mafia. The assassination in Sicily in May and July 1992, that is, during the first few months of the Mani Pulite investigation, of two very popular magistrates, Giovanni Falcone and Paolo Borsellino, evoked powerful emotions which were dramatically vented during the funeral of Borsellino and his police escort. At the end of the ceremony, which took place in Palermo and was broadcast live on television, the politicians present were rescued with difficulty from the anger of the crowd, whereas the magistrates who were present, some of whom were of the Milan team investigating political corruption, were applauded at length. This event, which repeatedly appeared on television screens for days afterwards, was emblematic of how far the process of delegitimation of the political ruling class had gone, and how far the citizenry identified with the magistrates as a symbolic centre of the nation in opposition to the politicians.

Public support for the *Mani Pulite* investigation was vigorously expressed throughout the period preceding the trial. When the members of the investigating team were recognised in the streets of Milan, people applauded them.[14] In the daytime, groups gathered in front of the court building in Milan with placards supportive of the magistrates' efforts and attacking the politicians. When the magistrates were criticised by the Socialist Party, thousands gathered in the public squares in Milan in protest. Even the press came out on the magistrates' side. Di Pietro, the most popular of the team, was frequently featured on front pages. Further, the magistrates had the support of opposition politicians, on both the left (the Partito Democratico della Sinistra, PDS, Rifondazione Comunista and the Greens) and the right (the Lega Nord and the Movimento Sociale Italiano, MSI). This broad support meant that criticism from the few politicians who accused the magistrates of being an instrument of the PDS carried little weight.

In this way, the first prerequisite of degradation ceremonies, that the accuser should be seen as a moral representative of the collectivity, was amply fulfilled in the Cusani trial. The second prerequisite, concerning the size of the public, was met by the television coverage of the case.

The television broadcasting of the trial had several consequences. To start with, it altered not only the number of spectators – the television-viewing public was vastly greater than the number of people who could be squeezed into the courtroom – but also their status, for, although television viewers were not really 'in attendance', they could observe the event better than anyone in the area of the courtroom reserved for the public.[15] The close-ups and the attention paid by the camera to detail enabled viewers to see things about the defendants and the witnesses that otherwise would not have been visible. For instance, signs of distress, anger or anxiety such as a nervous movement of the hands, perspiration on the forehead, an eyebrow tick or the formation of saliva at the corners of someone's mouth could be detected by the television audience much better than by anyone sitting in the courtroom.

The broadcasting of the proceedings also influenced the behaviour of those in court. If a court hearing can be defined as 'talk for an overhearing audience',[16] in the Cusani trial the audience included all the people watching television. The prosecutors, defence counsel, defendants and witnesses were aware of this much wider and less technically versed audience; it sometimes led them to introduce facts and present arguments which, although irrelevant from a legal viewpoint, were essential to a public unschooled in the ways of court hearings.[17] More generally, the presence of a nation-wide audience had the effect of converting the language of the trial from one of strict legal usage to one largely anchored in morality.

This shift of register was reinforced by the fact that, as Daniel Dayan and Elihu Katz have shown, the semantics of media events are intrinsically embedded in the rhetoric of consensus.[18] Even if what is shown consists of a conflict, it is framed with reference to accepted and shared rules. In the Cusani trial such rules were not legal ones (these would have been very difficult for the lay public to comprehend) but moral ones. They had to do with the public good and with the honour, reputation and dignity of the politicians involved, not with their strictly legal responsibilities. At the same time, however, the Cusani trial was still taking place within the framework of court proceedings. So during the course of the trial there was a continual interplay of two planes of reality. On the one hand, at the level of legal proceedings, facts had to be introduced and the evidence in their support evaluated, whereas on the moral level the focus was on the character and the 'face' of the politicians.

Analytically, the moral and legal considerations were different sets of criteria; legal technicality had little importance for moral questions, while, in principle, moral questions were not to be confused with an application of the law to the facts. However, the two did, in fact, influence one another and, indeed, were often in conflict. For example, those politicians who chose strategies aimed at minimising the legal consequences of their deeds frequently lost face on a moral level, whilst those who preferred to defend their moral identity and political honour were often forced to acknowledge that they had broken the law. This point is worth exploring in greater detail.

The trial as a symbolic arena

As I suggested earlier, modern secular rituals are open-ended, their outcome is not predetermined as in traditional rituals. In the Cusani trial the politicians were not passive subjects who submitted themselves to humiliation and degradation, but individual actors determined to defend themselves. For this reason, the trial must be examined not just as a ritual, but also as a symbolic arena in which the public prosecutor and the politicians met in sharp opposition.

An accused person has at his disposal three basic strategies to minimise the effects of public denunciation. The first, which may be described as a 'sociological' strategy, consists in showing that behind the claimed universality of the accusation lie partisan interests. We have already seen, however, how the vast public support for the team of Milan magistrates made this strategy impossible. The second may be termed 'psychiatric' and consists in putting the mental health of the accuser in question. As Luc Boltanski has shown,[19] this strategy is often used in the early stages of a public denunciation which can easily lose credibility if it appears to be the product of a disturbed mind. Obviously, this too was not a strategy that could have been used in the Cusani case.

The third strategy is a semantic one. Unlike the other two, which seek to challenge the legitimacy of the accuser, this one challenges the content of the accusation and redefines the events differently from the way they are described by the denouncer. In our case, this was the only possibility the politicians had to neutralise the moral and legal charges brought against them. For, as with all 'facts', those in the Cusani trial did not speak for themselves. They became meaningful only when they were interpreted through the frames which, at the time, organised public discourse on political corruption.[20]

The basic interpretive frames used in the Cusani trial were two. They can be termed respectively 'Clean hands' and 'The costs of democracy'. Each of them typified and organised the facts in a distinct way and attributed to the protagonists in the case different legal responsibilities and moral identities. Let us briefly review them.

> *Clean hands*
>
> The law on party funding is a law of the state. Whoever violates such a law commits an offence, and the moral gravity of the offence is that much greater when perpetrated by our representatives in Parliament, the very individuals who were responsible for passing the law. The Cusani case is a symptom of the high level of corruption which lies at the heart of public life and which is posing a threat to the democratic order and the moral foundations of our country. The guilty politicians must be exemplarily punished.

This, of course, was the prosecution's frame. Note that it gave the prosecutor not only a legal role as a representative of the law, but also a moral one. In unmasking the guilty and redefining his social identity he was performing a ritual purification of public life, contrasting fundamental values and principles (moral integrity, honesty, respect for the law) with routine political practices which are often dubious and sometimes outright unlawful and illegitimate.

As we have seen, the 'Clean hands' frame was widely supported by the media and had such a cultural resonance in public opinion that only with difficulty could it be challenged by any other definition of the situation. This explains why it was accepted by many of the politicians who appeared in court. Sometimes the acceptance was explicit: political leaders such as Giorgio La Malfa, Carlo Vizzini, Renato Altissimo, Paolo Cirino Pomicino, Gianni De Michelis, Claudio Martelli[21] and others acknowledged having received illegal funds for their parties and their personal electoral campaigns. Although the admission was articulated in different ways by the various politicians, and although in the eyes of the viewing public some appeared by their demeanour to be more sincerely repentant than others, for all these men the acknowledgement of guilt implied acceptance of public degradation and the likely end of their political career.

In other cases, the agreement with the prosecutor's definition of the situation was implicit, in the sense that the politicians did not challenge his view of the legal and moral consequences of violating the law on party funding, but confined themselves to asserting their non-involvement in the charges brought against them. This was the defence line adopted by Arnaldo Forlani, the former leader of the Christian Democrats (DC), which can be summarised as follows.

> *I didn't know anything about it*
>
> I don't know that there was any illegal funding of my party during the period of my leadership. In any case, if there was any (but I don't think there was), I knew nothing whatever about it. Party funding was the business of the party treasurer, not the party leader. If the party treasurer claims that he told me about illegal funding, then he's mistaken. I didn't even know that illegal contributions were being made to other parties.

Clearly, the purpose of Forlani's position was to minimise his own legal responsibilities, but it had disastrous consequences for his moral and political image because it made him face an insoluble dilemma.

On the one hand, during his examination as a witness Forlani always ran the risk of being seen as a liar, because other witnesses and defendants, and even the treasurer of his own party, repeatedly stated in court not just that Forlani knew about the illegal funds, but that he had actively sought them. The prosecution greatly insisted on this point and in so doing seriously undermined Forlani's credibility.

On the other hand, if Forlani, who had been head of his party, a Minister, deputy Prime Minister and head of the government, was not telling lies, then his assertion that he knew nothing about a matter which was common knowledge and which had come up again and again in court left him wide open to being seen as politically naive. How was it possible to spend an entire life in politics and know nothing about the illegal funding of political parties?

Finally, Forlani's attempt to dump responsibility on the DC's treasurer served to portray him in the public eye as someone prepared to betray a friend to save his own skin, a politician too cowardly to shoulder responsibility for his own actions. In sum, this approach of 'I didn't know anything about it', quite apart from its effect on the legal plane, proved a disaster for Forlani's face both as a man and as a politician.

The other major frame used in the trial, 'The costs of democracy', provided an interpretation of the facts opposite to that of 'Clean hands'. It emphasised a realistic and pragmatic conception of politics, suggesting that the violation of the law on party funding was a minor offence, an unavoidable feature of the functioning of party machines. This frame was articulated mainly by Bettino Craxi, the former leader of the Socialist Party (PSI) and former head of government.

The costs of democracy

> A democratic political system rests upon organisations – political parties – which have become increasingly complex and costly, but which need to be maintained. Everyone in the political sphere knew that official party budgets were false. Every major party received additional funds through illegal contributions. But those funds were earmarked for political, social and cultural activities. Democracy costs money. If political parties die, we'll either turn into a society dominated by organisations which are not very democratic or into a videocracy.
>
> It's possible that there were also instances of real corruption. But one shouldn't generalise; one shouldn't put a criminal label on all political activity, not even on what from time to time occurred in violation of a hypocritical law such as that on party financing – a law which everyone broke. There are also people who have devoted their lives to politics for disinterested motives, and who have had to deal with the problem of running an organisation in the face of ever rising costs.

This frame contains three main themes which can also be found in the 'Clean hands' frames but here they are organised somewhat differently.

The first concerns the contrast between a high concept of politics as the disinterested pursuit of general goals (the politics of principles and values) and everyday politics (the politics of routine and compromise). This contrast was stressed in the 'Clean hands' frame as well, but here it means something else. In the 'Clean hands' version the opposition between these two aspects of politics was absolute and irreconcilable; in the 'Costs of democracy' version, routine politics are not perceived as the radical antithesis of principled politics, but as the condition which makes such politics possible. This frame seeks to present a vision of politics based on responsibility and technical rationality, a vision according to which the leader who lives *for* politics needs those who live *off* politics (the party machines and the money necessary to maintain them).

The second theme regards the knowledge of the illegal contributions. Unlike the 'I didn't know anything about it' position, the 'Costs of democracy' frame enabled Craxi to present himself as an expert and knowledgeable leader. This frame takes it for granted that illegal party financing was widespread, and that all politicians were aware of it from the very start of their political careers or, as Craxi put it, from the time when they were 'still in short trousers'.

The third theme deals with the shouldering of responsibility. The 'Costs of democracy' incorporates an acknowledgement that the law of the land has been breached, but it places it in an entirely different semantic context from that of 'Clean hands': instead of being repentant, the criminal proclaims his crime with pride in the name of a higher form of political morality. The conflict reappears between trying to save one's own moral face and trying to limit the legal damage of the charges, a constant theme in the Cusani trial. Craxi chose the first option, which enabled him successfully to defend his own public image; as the newspapers stated the following day, he did not come away from the courtroom humiliated, despite having been the politician most reviled by public opinion in the months preceding the trial.[22]

The same contrast between law and politics appeared in the testimony of the leader of the Lega Nord.[23] Umberto Bossi's interpretation of the facts is a subframe of the 'Costs of democracy' and can be summarised thus:

> *We're a new force*
>
> We're a new political force untainted by the corruption of the First Republic. Everybody was against us and we had a real need of funding. We sought to obtain funds in the most proper way possible. A few weeks before the 1992 election a large company made a small illegal donation to our party which, unknown to me, the party treasurer accepted. Although I was unaware of it at the time, in his shoes I'd have done exactly the same thing, because that donation meant life or death for our movement.

In some respects, there is an evident dissimilarity between Craxi's and Bossi's positions. Craxi appeared as an impassioned defender of the old political system, while Bossi was heavily in favour of political change and depicted the old regime, its practices and its political personnel as negatively as the prosecution did. But, despite this difference, Bossi, like Craxi, although stating that he was not personally involved, praised the 'political' correctness of accepting funds in violation of the party finance law. In other words, he preferred to be legally convicted rather than abdicate his political leadership.[24] And, like Craxi, at least to judge from the media's account, he came out of the trial relatively unscathed from a political point of view.

To be sure, the interpretative frames that Craxi and Bossi projected on the facts of the case were not the sole reason which explained why they were able to resist the degradation which the prosecution tried to inflict upon them. Their bearing in court was also very important. Moral judgement of the accused, especially by a lay audience, is inevitably based on how the defendants present themselves in the face-to-face encounters with judges and lawyers. Poise, *sang froid*, control of body movement and especially the ability to control the mechanisms of talk were, therefore, crucial.

In these respects, Bossi and especially Craxi performed far better than the other politicians who were summoned to court. For example, despite the fact that in criminal trials conversational rights are asymmetrically allocated in favour of the judge and counsel,[25] Craxi was able to retain control over the substance and length of his turns of talk and, to a large extent, over their thematic organisation. The result was a transformation of his testimony, via the reflexivity of talk, into a lecture on the Italian political system.

It would, however, be a mistake to separate completely the politicians' presentation of self and skill at 'impression management' from the content of their performance, since in fact they influenced each other. An example of this was Forlani's unconvincing testimony.[26] Doubtless it was due in part to his ineptitude in the witness box, but it was due even more to the implausible line he took in his defence. The tension and awkwardness which characterised his testimony arose, to a large extent, from the difficulty he had, in front of millions of viewers, in asserting not simply that he was innocent of the charges, but that he was totally unaware of the infringements of the law on party finance, something which even the man in the street was well aware of.

Similarly, Craxi's self-confidence, sometimes bordering on arrogance, and Bossi's ability to hold his own with Di Pietro were closely linked with the content of their testimonies. In particular, by redefining the object of the case as a conflict between the formal requirements of a 'hypocritical' law and the higher imperatives of politics, they succeeded in presenting themselves not just as individuals whose sole intent was to defend themselves, but also as political leaders, i.e. as representatives of collective bodies. This lessened the asymmetry in status between them and the public prosecutor and, as we have seen, it is precisely on this asymmetry that degradation ceremonies are based. The denouncer will succeed only when he incarnates public morality in the face of someone who has breached it. If the accused succeeds in presenting his action not as having been in violation of a rule but as in accordance with another system of rules shared by others, he transforms degradation into a conflict of values. This is precisely what Bossi and Craxi tried to do. They only partly succeeded, because the cultural resonance of their chosen frames was not as great as that of 'Clean hands'. But in choosing this strategy they were able to defend their political and moral identity far better than they would have done had they tried, as Forlani did, to limit themselves to asserting their innocence before the law.

Conclusion

In contrast to a narrow concept of politics as simply a conflict between social groups competing for control over scarce material resources, in recent years many scholars have highlighted the crucial role that culture plays in political life.[27] Feelings of integration into the political order and identification with political leaders can be created only by symbolic means; similarly, the collapse of political regimes and of those in power is usually accompanied by rituals which culturally codify the process of delegitimation.

In this chapter I have maintained that the Cusani trial can be interpreted as a degradation ceremony through which a whole political governing elite was removed from power. The trial forcibly expressed the principle that even the most powerful of politicians are subject to the rule of law, just like any other citizen. But the problems aired during the trial were not of a purely legal nature. The substance of the case, technically a charge of corruption, became emblematic of a whole political order. For the vast television audience watching the trial, at issue was the morality of a political regime and its leaders. The politicians summoned before the court were discredited morally and, on that basis, disqualified from participating further in political activity. In this way the Cusani trial ritually summarised and sealed a long process of delegitimation. The importance of this ritual conclusion is that it imposed a frame on the events and froze their meaning, so that after the trial any attempt to redefine the affair differently from how it was set out by the prosecution would prove extremely difficult.

Nevertheless, the outcome of the trial was not at all preordained: it depended on effective symbolic work in court. I have endeavoured to show that, of the strategies adopted by the politicians, those of Craxi and Bossi were the more effective: in challenging the prosecution's definition of the situation they transformed degradation into a contest of values. As a result, they were the two politicians who emerged from the trial the least disgraced morally and politically. Craxi was later subject to other criminal investigations and fled to Tunisia, where he died – unrepentant and resentful – in January 2000; Bossi still plays a considerable role in Italian politics.

NOTES

This chapter (written in 1996) is a much shortened version of 'Processi di delegittimazione e cerimonie di degradazione', in P. P. Giglioli, S. Cavicchioli and G. Fele, *Rituali di degradazione. Anatomia del processo Cusani* (Bologna, Il Mulino, 1997), pp. 15–73. This research was supported by a Jean Monnet fellowship at the European University Institute (Florence) in the academic year 1994–95. I also wish to thank Indaco, the Institute of Mass Communication Research of the Province of Trento, whose financial support made possible the collection and transcription of the audio-visual data of the Cusani trial.

1 There was twice-weekly coverage of the trial, in slightly edited form. A few of the more important court sessions were broadcast live, e.g. Bettino Craxi's testimony.

2 On political corruption and the *Mani Pulite* investigations, see: G. M. Bellu and S. Bonsanti, *Il crollo. Andreotti, Craxi e il loro regime* (Bari and Rome, Laterza, 1993); D. Della Porta, 'Milan: Immoral Capital', in S. Hellman and G. Pasquino (eds), *Italian Politics. A Review*, vol. 8 (London, Pinter, 1993), pp. 98–115; *id.*, 'The Vicious Circles of Corruption in Italy', in D. Della Porta and Y. Mény (eds), *Political Corruption and Democracy* (London,

Pinter, 1997), pp. 35–49; D. Nelken, 'A Legal Revolution? The Judges and Tangentopoli', and D. Della Porta, 'The System of Corrupt Exchange in Local Government', both in S. Gundle and S. Parker (eds), *The New Italian Republic. From the Fall of the Berlin Wall to Berlusconi* (London, Routledge, 1996), pp. 191–205 and 221–33; V. Onida, 'Mani pulite, Year III', in R. S. Katz and P. Ignazi (eds), *Italian Politics. The Year of the Tycoon* (Oxford, Westview Press, 1996), pp. 149–57. See also the controversial volume by S. H. Burnett and L. Mantovani, *The Italian Guillotine. Operation Clean Hands and the Overthrow of Italy's First Republic* (Oxford, Rowman & Littlefield, 1998), which argues that the actions of the Milan magistrates amounted to a *coup d'état* for explicit political ends. (Luca Mantovani is parliamentary press officer of Berlusconi's party.)

3 Technically the politicians summoned before the court were not defendants or witnesses in this trial. In Italian legal terms they were 'accused of related crimes', i.e. they would be defendants in later trials, but the evidence adduced in the Cusani trial could be used against them then.

4 On the incompleteness and open-endedness of modern rituals see J. C. Alexander, 'Culture and Political Crisis. "Watergate" and Durkheimian Sociology', in J. C. Alexander (ed.), *Durkheimian Sociology. Cultural Studies Today* (Cambridge University Press, 1988), pp. 1–21.

5 On the concept of 'face' see E. Goffman, 'On Face Work', in *Interaction Ritual. Essays in Face-to-face Behavior* (New York, Doubleday Anchor, 1967), pp. 5–45.

6 H. Garfinkel, 'Conditions of Successful Degradation Ceremonies', *American Journal of Sociology*, 61 (1955), pp. 420–4. This section summarises the main features of degradation ceremonies analysed by Garfinkel. On the same topic see also B. Gronbeck, 'The Rhetoric of Political Corruption. Sociolinguistic, Dialectical, and Ceremonial Processes', *Quarterly Journal of Speech*, 64 (1978), pp. 155–72. An important contribution to the sociological study of public denunciation is that of L. Boltanski, *L'Amour et la justice comme compétences* (Paris, Métailié, 1990).

7 Garfinkel, 'Conditions of Successful Degradation', p. 420.

8 E. Durkheim, *The Division of Labor in Society* (New York, Free Press of Glencoe, 1964 [1904]), pp. 105–10.

9 This problem is well illustrated by Boltanski, *L'Amour et la justice*, pp. 289–356.

10 On the concept of liminality see V. W. Turner, *The Ritual Process. Structure and Anti-structure* (London, Routledge, 1969).

11 On the difference between explicit communication and information given away through involuntary means see E. Goffman, *The Presentation of Self in Everyday Life* (New York, Doubleday Anchor, 1959), pp. 1–16. On a subject closely related to the one treated in this chapter see Umberto Eco's analysis of Richard Nixon's televised speech of 30 April 1973: 'Strategies of Lying', in M. Blonsky (ed.), *On Signs* (Baltimore, MD, Johns Hopkins University Press, 1985), pp. 3–11. Eco contrasts the convincing and well structured text of the speech to the embarrassment, fear and tension betrayed by Nixon's face.

12 The 1974 law on the finances of political parties provided for public funding of the parties represented in Parliament in proportion to their electoral strength. It also required political parties to make an annual declaration of all the sources and the amount of their income, a provision which was often violated.

13 Such discontent found expression in the large gains of the Lega Nord in the election of 5 April 1992, which also signalled the defeat of the traditional political forces: the DC, PSI and the PDS. Opinion polls in 1992–93 showed a marked increase in the electorate's lack of confidence in the political parties and greater support for the magistrates' initiatives.

14 The symbolic identification of ordinary people with the Milan magistrates was acknowledged and overtly accepted by the magistrates themselves. For instance, the Chief Prosecutor of Milan, Fransesco Saverio Borrelli, replied to a television journalist who had asked him how it felt to be applauded in the street: 'When people applaud us, they applaud themselves.' Borrelli also stated that the success of the Lega Nord and the partial defeat

of the government coalition parties in the 1992 elections were crucial to the success of the investigation.

15 On the ways in which television affects the conditions of spectatorship see J. Meyrowitz, *No Sense of Place. The Impact of Electronic Media on Social Behaviour* (Oxford University Press, 1985).

16 J. Heritage, 'Analysing News Interviews. Aspects of Production of Talk for an "Overhearing" Audience', in T. van Dijk (ed.), *Handbook of Discourse Analysis*, vol. 3, *Discourse and Dialogue* (London, Academic Press, 1985), pp. 95–119.

17 For example, as journalists and the presiding judge himself noted, the whole structure and many of the details of Di Pietro's closing speech seemed directed more to television viewers, who needed extra information in order to understand the legal technicalities, than to the three judges on the bench and the defence counsel.

18 D. Dayan and E. Katz, *Media Events. The Live Broadcasting of History* (Cambridge, MA, Harvard University Press, 1992).

19 Boltanski, *L'Amour et la justice*, pp. 255–65.

20 On the concept of frame (or 'interpretative package') applied to public discourse see W. Gamson and A. Modigliani, 'Media Discourse and Public Opinion on Nuclear Power. A Constructionist Approach', *American Journal of Sociology*, 95 (1989), pp. 1–37. My reconstruction of the two major frames used during the trial, which is based on a close analysis of the trial video-tapes and transcripts, is ideal-typical and thus the frames appear more internally consistent than they actually were.

21 At the time of the events examined in the trial the first three were the leaders respectively of the Republican Party, the Socialist Party and the Liberal Party; the other three were the Budget, Foreign Affairs and Justice Ministers.

22 A few of the headlines were: 'Bettino, head held high', 'A long roar', 'Roaring years' decision-maker roars again for the judges'.

23 Bossi was one of the staunchest supporters of the Milan investigating magistrates until a few days before the start of the trial, when he himself was accused, together with his party treasurer, of having received an illegal contribution of 200 million lire from the management of the Montedison Company.

24 As a matter of fact, both Craxi and Bossi, as well as Forlani, were convicted in a later trial, where they appeared as defendants, partly on the basis of the evidence collected in the Cusani trial.

25 On this point see G. Fele, 'Strategie discorsive e forme della degradazione pubblica in tribunale', in Giglioli *et al.*, *Rituali di degradazione*, pp. 135–208. On the control of conversation mechanisms in legal proceedings see also H. Molotch and D. Boden, 'Talking Social Structure. Discourse, Domination and the Watergate Hearings', *American Sociological Review*, 50 (1985), pp. 273–88.

26 According to anyone observing the trial, Forlani appeared uncertain, evasive and clearly in difficulty when asked factual questions. His physical demeanour, the subject of merciless close-ups by the television cameras, revealed a nervous and anxious man. The newspaper accounts underlined these aspects, with headlines such as 'Forlani petrified', 'Arnaldo knocked down', 'Forlani gets a grilling', 'Arnaldo: pale and scared stiff', 'Arnaldo, DC trashed and defeated'. In the *Corriere della Sera*, 18 December 1993, he was described as follows: 'His face pale, gobs of saliva at the corners of his mouth, his long sentences containing nothing at all and getting tangled up in Di Pietro's questions, he aroused the public's ire, moving some to whistle, protest, grumble.'

27 See M. Edelman, *The Symbolic Uses of Politics* (Chicago, IL, Markham, 1971); J. Gusfield, *The Culture of Public Problems* (University of Chicago Press, 1981); D. I. Kertzer, *Ritual, Politics and Power* (New Haven, CT, Yale University Press, 1988); S. Lukes, 'Political Ritual and Social Integration', *Sociology*, 9:2 (1975), pp. 289–308.

Chronology, 1945–98

	Politics and institutions	Economics and labour movement
1945	Collapse of German armies in Italy. Culmination of anti-Fascist Resistance (with strong Communist component) and execution of Mussolini (Apr.). Progressive forces (dominant in northern Italy) sapped by conservative obstruction (strong in Rome and South). Alcide De Gasperi, the leader of the Christian Democratic Party (DC) becomes Prime Minister (Dec.): his will be the longest continuous premiership in post-war Italy (nearly eight years).	Over 2 million unemployed. Industrial production at 26 per cent of pre-war level. Peasant agitations in Apulia and Sicily (July). Communist Party (PCI) adopts a moderate line and dismisses economic planning (Aug.). *Scala mobile* (wage indexation) introduced (Dec.).
1946	King Vittorio Emanuele III abdicates in favour of his son Umberto (May) but fails to save the monarchy in referendum (2–3 June): Italy becomes a republic. Pope Pius XII appeals to the electorate not to vote for 'atheistic materialism' at concurrent election of Constituent Assembly. Women vote for the first time. Election results: DC 35 per cent; Socialist Party (PSI) 21 per cent; PCI 19 per cent. A three-party government coalition (DC, PSI, PCI) is formed. General amnesty for political crimes (June). Neo-Fascist party, Movimento Sociale Italiano (MSI), is founded (Dec.).	Reconstruction of the economy begins with UN funding: northern industries benefit most. The unitary workers' union (CGIL) accepts the legitimacy of redundancies (Jan.). Plans to introduce the 'new lira' combined with tax on wealth are shelved. Foreign exchange controls are relaxed. Growing inflation. Frequent and extensive demonstrations by the unemployed and southern peasants.
1947	Formal US support for DC secured by De Gasperi while in Washington (Jan.). Socialists split (Jan.): Social Democrat faction sets up its own party (later PSDI); the main section (PSI) remains close to the Communists. The Lateran Pacts (1929 Church–state agreement) are included in the new constitution (March). PCI and PSI expelled from government: three-party coalition replaced by another led by DC, including the Social Democrats, the Republican Party (PRI) and the Liberal Party (PLI) (May). Police forces organised for tough 'law and order' action. PCI joins Cominform (Oct.). Last Allied troops leave Italy (Dec.).	High inflation in the first half of the year. Italy joins Bretton Woods agreement and enters International Monetary Fund (IMF) and World Bank (March). Harsh deflationary policies bring inflation rate down but result in further unemployment, social malaise and protests throughout the country.

Social life and civic society	Cultural life and media	
Spillover of politically motivated violence after the end of the war. PCI's first *Festa dell'Unità* is organised in September (with machine-guns hidden). In Naples Lydia Cirillo kills her British lover, Captain Sidney Lush, who intended to leave her (Oct.); at the trial the woman is applauded by the public. The Vatican newspaper, *L'Osservatore Romano*, condemns the staging of Machiavelli's *La Mandragola* (The Mandrake) (Dec.).	National Associated Press Agency (ANSA) established in Rome (Jan.). A number of new publications are launched: the popular weeklies *L'Europeo* and *Oggi*, the sport papers *Tuttosport* and *Stadio*, and the left-wing journals *Il Politecnico*, *Il Ponte* and *Società*. Carlo Levi's *Cristo si è fermato a Eboli* (Christ Stopped at Eboli) is published. Roberto Rossellini's Neo-realist film *Roma, città aperta* (Rome, Open City) is released. American feature (and propaganda) films are screened to vast audiences.	**1945**
Mussolini's remains snatched from the grave by neo-Fascists (Apr.). *Totocalcio* (football pools) introduced (May). Silvana Pampanini wins the first Miss Italy beauty contest (Sept.). Morbid general interest in the case of Rina Fort, who kills her lover's wife and three children (Nov.). Great success of Vespa motor-scooter.	First *fotoromanzi* (photo-pulp magazines) appear: *Grand Hôtel*, *Sogno* and *Bolero Film* (March). Preventive censorship of the press abolished (May). The moderate daily *Corriere della Sera* of Milan has the largest circulation (half a million copies). Many new dailies and weeklies appear, including neo-Fascist sheets (*La Rivolta Ideale*; *Il Meridiano d'Italia*). The second station of state radio starts broadcasting. Giovanni Guareschi publishes his first *Don Camillo* story: the ideological confrontation 'Church *v.* Communism' is reduced to provincial, good-natured bickering. Neo-realist cinema: Rossellini's *Paisà* and Vittorio De Sica's *Sciuscià* (Shoeshine); the latter will be the first non-American film to be awarded an Oscar. Cinema is described as 'the light that kills' in a Catholic magazine. Huge popularity of variety shows with mildly provocative soubrettes.	**1946**
Thugs hired by Mafia (led by Salvatore Giuliano, the bandit) kill several peasants who had gathered to celebrate 1 May near Palermo (May). An article in the Jesuit magazine *Civiltà Cattolica* calls for general mobilisation against Communism (June). Thousands of *Azione Cattolica* militants meet in Rome to see the Pope (Sept.). Lambretta motor-scooter launched.	Films are to be subject to preventive censorship (May). As Under-Secretary to the Prime Minister, Giulio Andreotti heads the newly established Central Office of Cinematography (June). Publication of Antonio Gramsci's *Lettere del carcere* (Prison Letters) and Primo Levi's *Se questo è un uomo* (If this is a Man). Paolo Grassi and Giorgio Strehler establish the Piccolo Teatro in Milan.	**1947**

	Politics and institutions	Economics and labour movement
1948	Republican constitution comes into effect (Jan.). Long, bitter political confrontation in view of first parliamentary election (18 April): DC and minor allies *v.* 'Popular Front' (PCI and PSI). Strong pressure from the Vatican and the United States through ideological and economic means, respectively. DC wins by a landslide (48 per cent against 31 per cent for the Front). DC-led coalition government confirmed. PCI leader Palmiro Togliatti is shot and seriously wounded (July): general strike and widespread agitation follow.	Italy joins Marshall Plan (June) and benefits from large grants and loans, but tight monetary policies are pursued. As a consequence of pro-Togliatti general strike, Catholics and moderates abandon unitary workers' union; they will eventually set up two separate confederations: CISL and UIL respectively; CGIL will then become a left-wing union, with strong Communist presence. Emigration is encouraged by the government as 'solution' to unemployment.
1949	Heated parliamentary debate on Italy's membership of NATO; protests are harshly repressed (March). PSI expelled from the International Socialist Conference for its ties with PCI (May). Communists and their allies are excommunicated by Vatican's Holy Office (July). Military Intelligence Service (SIFAR) set up; it will become an instrument of surveillance of political opponents of government parties.	State-funded 'Housing Plan' launched (Feb.). Natural gas reserves discovered near Piacenza (March). Agricultural labourers strike in the North: several are killed by the police (May–June). CGIL proposes 'Employment Plan' (Oct.). Occupation of uncultivated land in southern regions: police intervention results in several peasants killed (Oct.–Nov.). Concern for social tensions in southern Italy expressed by US Secretary of State Dean Acheson (Dec.). National strike of civil servants (Dec.).
1950	The conservative PLI, opposed to the agrarian reform that was to split large southern estates, withdraws from government. Mussolini's leading general Rodolfo Graziani is condemned to nineteen years' imprisonment as 'war criminal' (May), but is soon released because of amnesty and years already spent in captivity: he becomes honorary president of the neo-Fascist party, MSI. De Gasperi accuses the PCI of 'fifth columnism'. Defence spending boosted.	Workers demonstrating against lock-out in Modena are met with police bullets: six die, many are wounded (Jan.). Peasant agitation in southern Italy continues. Cassa per il Mezzogiorno for the South (Development Fund) launched: it will become a powerful mechanism of patronage (Aug.). Emigration encouraged by law. Industrial production reaches highest pre-war level, signalling the end of 'economic reconstruction'.
1951	Strikes and demonstrations against the visit to Italy of General Eisenhower, NATO Supreme Commander: four demonstrators are killed by the police (Jan.). Law on Italian rearmament passed (May). Growing influence over policies by conflicting factions within DC.	Large-scale internal migration from South to North and rapid urbanisation begin. Italy joins the European Coal and Steel Community (ECSC) (Apr.). Parliamentary inquiry into poverty is set up (Oct.): it will reveal a great disparity between North and South. Ten per cent reduction in import duties (Nov.). Flooding of Po delta leaves 100 dead; massive exodus from that area feeds into internal migration.

1948

Vatican-inspired *Comitati Civici* are prominent in pro-DC propaganda during electoral campaign. International sport successes deflect attention from political tensions and social disquiet: Gino Bartali's victories in *Tour de France* (July). Dancing crazes: rumba, conga, samba, tango.

Mobilisation of all media for electoral campaign: crude forms prevail (March–April). Venice Biennale re-opens. Soviet and East European films virtually banned. First neo-Fascist dailies appear (*Ora d'Italia*; *Ordine Sociale*). Major Neo-realist films: Luchino Visconti's *La terra trema* (The Earth is Shaking), De Sica's *Ladri di biciclette* (Bicycle Thieves), Rossellini's *Germania, anno zero* (Germany, Year Zero) and Giuseppe De Santis's *Riso amaro* (Bitter Rice).

1949

The activity of the *Comitati Civici* is strengthened (Jan.). The famous football team Torino perish in air crash (May). Excitement over Fausto Coppi's victories at the Milan–San Remo cycle race, Giro d'Italia and Tour de France. Lifting of bread and pasta rationing (Aug.). A DC leader, Paolo Bonomi, takes control of Federconsorzi (the Federation of Agrarian Consortia), a powerful mechanism for distributing patronage in the countryside (Dec.).

Laws to regulate and support film making (July and Dec.). Radical-liberal weekly *Il Mondo* founded. Return of commercial advertisements in newspapers. National Associated Press Agency (ANSA) is heavily subsidised – and controlled – by the government, through Under-Secretary Andreotti. Experimental television broadcast in Turin. Government circular prohibits the use of scanty bathing suits. Financial aid granted to the newly formed Association of Catholic Cinema Owners (Aug.). Trend for tear-jerker films begins.

1950

Holy Year, dominated by Catholic propaganda initiatives. *Azione Cattolica* organises congresses, exhibitions and religious tours on the theme of 'The Great Return of Christ'. Rome consecrated to 'The Heart of Mary' (May). Pius XII's encyclical *Humani generis* (On the Human Race) (Aug.) condemns modern philosophical thought. Civic Committees organise a pilgrimage to Rome of 20,000 local government officials (Oct.). The Pope proclaims a new religious dogma: Mary's corporeal assumption to heaven (Nov.).

The official version of the killing of Salvatore Giuliano, 'the bandit', is disputed by the magazine *L'Europeo*: allegations are made of collusion between police, Mafia and government. Former Fascist journalists nominated directors of important local papers (Venice and Naples). Radio entertainment intensified. First Italian film in colour is a popular light comedy: *Totò a colori*, by Steno (pseudonym of Stefano Vanzina). First illustrated weekly, *Epoca*, appears.

1951

Laura Diaz, a Communist MP, is denounced for 'offending' the Pope at a political gathering: she is tried and condemned, but pardoned (March). First post-war census of the population: 47·5 million; 42 per cent of labour force engaged in agriculture, 32 per cent in industry, 26 per cent in services; 13 per cent of total population are illiterate.

First national pop music festival – San Remo – promoted by Italian Radio (RAI): it soon becomes a glamorous media event. De Sica's *Miracolo a Milano* (Palme d'Or at Cannes Festival) and Visconti's *Bellissima* depart from Neo-realist cinema but maintain the focus on the relationship between traditional human values and changing society.

	Politics and institutions	Economics and labour movement
1952	Unsuccessful attempt by the Vatican and right-wing Christian Democrats to set up an alliance between DC, Monarchists and neo-Fascists at local election in Rome (Apr.). Law prohibiting the reconstitution of a 'Fascist Party' is passed (June). Government approves the project of replacing proportional representation with a premium-based electoral system (Oct.): the opposition prepares for all-out confrontation (and calls the Bill 'swindle law').	Industrial strikes against reduction in working hours are followed by reprisal redundancies at Fiat (March). Credit facilities are granted to small entrepreneurs and artisans (July). A network of small and medium-size industries begins to develop in the Veneto, Emilia-Romagna and Tuscany. Official unemployment around 10 per cent.
1953	The 'swindle law' passed after acrimonious parliamentary scenes, but is not implemented because DC and its allies just fail to obtain overall majority at election (7 June): DC 40 per cent, PCI 23 per cent, PSI 13 per cent. The last, short-lived Cabinet led by De Gasperi is followed by caretaker government headed by Giuseppe Pella (Aug.). Tension between Italy and Yugoslavia on the issue of Trieste: in November a protest there is repressed by British troops (six demonstrators are killed, many wounded).	National Hydrocarbons Agency (ENI) founded and led by a dynamic but unscrupulous entrepreneur, Enrico Mattei (Feb.); ENI will soon become the second most powerful state holding company (after IRI). Plant bargaining is adopted by CISL (Feb.). Special credit agencies are established to stimulate southern industrialisation (Apr.). Fiat takes steps against the members of elected workers' committees (July–Aug.). General strikes of industrial workers for wage increases (Sept. and Dec.). Industrial production increases by 8·4 per cent, incomes by 4·6 per cent.
1954	New government led by Mario Scelba, affected by anti-Communist paranoia (Jan., until July 1955). Following the pressure by US ambassador in Rome, Clare Boothe Luce, Italian companies where CGIL has strong presence are refused US contracts for the production of military equipment (Jan.). The new Secretary General of the DC, Amintore Fanfani, sets about revitalising the party (July). De Gasperi dies (Aug.). General agreement with Yugoslavia: Trieste returns to Italy, Istria stays with Yugoslavia (Oct.).	Token general strike over the killing of four people in Sicily during a demonstration (Feb.). Confindustria signs agreement on wages with moderate unions only; CGIL is excluded and isolated (June). 'Vanoni Plan' to reduce unemployment and North–South divide (Dec.), but the ten-year project will not be implemented.
1955	Pietro Secchia, PCI's vice-secretary with Stalinist leanings, is demoted (Jan.): Togliatti's rule over the party is now unchallenged. PSI's leader, Pietro Nenni, talks of 'a dialogue with the Catholics' (Apr.): PCI–PSI relationship is strained. Giovanni Gronchi (DC) elected President of the Republic with the support of the left (Apr.). Italy admitted to the United Nations (Dec.).	Launch of parliamentary inquiry into condition of factory workers (Jan.). Production of Fiat 600 car begins (March). CGIL debacle at Fiat's election to workers' committees (March). Conference of ECSC members at Messina lays down the foundation of the EEC (June).

Social life and civic society	Cultural life and media	
Civiltà Cattolica argues that the concept of equality cannot apply to religious creed (Feb.). More than 3 million radio sets are located in the North, less than 1 million in the South.	Neo-Fascist daily *Il Secolo d'Italia* established. Andreotti snipes at De Sica's film *Umberto D* for its pessimistic message (Feb.). Advertising in newspapers which criticise industrialists is discouraged at an employers' congress (June). In a newspaper interview De Gasperi suggests that to strengthen democracy special legislation aimed at curbing the press and trade unions may be necessary (July). DC-controlled press agencies mushroom. Philosopher Benedetto Croce dies.	**1952**
Sustained urban migration results in shanty towns and building speculation. A plastic statuette of the Madonna 'cries' in Syracuse and draws thousands of pilgrims (Aug.). On average 58 per cent of income is spent on food; 70 per cent of houses have no bathroom; only 10 per cent of homes have a telephone. Pius XII invites Italians to devote 1954 to the Virgin (Dec.).	Confindustria (the Confederation of Italian Industry) sets up a press agency to feed the newspapers industrialists control. Luigi Comencini's film *Pane, amore e fantasia* (Bread, Love and Imagination), starring Gina Lollobrigida and De Sica, is a box-office hit and initiates a successful series of 'rose tinted' Neo-realist films. A writer (Renzo Renzi) and the director of the journal *Cinema Nuovo* (Guido Aristarco) are condemned to several months' imprisonment by a military court for contempt of the armed forces: they had written and published, respectively, the script of a film on the Italian occupation of Greece during the Second World War (Oct.).	**1953**
The 'Montesi affair' hits the headlines throughout the year, with revelations of corruption and drug use in high places; in Sept. the foreign secretary, Attilio Piccioni, resigns because of his son's involvement in the scandal. Forty-six miners die after a gas explosion in a Tuscan mine (May). Poor performance of national football team at World Championship in Switzerland (June), partly offset by the conquest of K2, the second highest mountain in the world, by Italian climbers (July). Salerno province hit by flood: 300 dead (Oct.). The Italian Bishops' Conference (CEI) is formed: it will often pass judgement on political issues.	Television broadcasting starts: RAI-TV is a one-channel state monopoly under DC control. The Vatican condemns a show with female dancers (Jan.). Religion and sport (mainly football) are given prominence on Sundays. Guareschi, author of *Don Camillo* stories and editor of satirical magazine *Candido*, is imprisoned for libelling De Gasperi (Apr.). Giulia Occhini, the mistress of Fausto Coppi, is arrested for adultery (Sept.): the media and the public show great interest in the story. Feltrinelli publishing company is established. Two major films: Visconti's *Senso* and Federico Fellini's *La strada*.	**1954**
Rome's underground railway opened (Feb.). Socialist trade unionist Salvatore Carnevale killed by the Mafia near Palermo (May). Plan for motorway construction launched (May). Italia Nostra association founded to protect cultural heritage. The National Consumers' Union is set up.	The radical-liberal weekly *L'Espresso* appears (Oct.). *Lascia o raddoppia* (Double your Money), a television quiz show with money prize (first on air in Nov.) becomes enormously popular and newspapers begin to devote much attention to television. Luciano Berio and Bruno Maderna establish a centre for the study of electronic music at RAI studios in Milan.	**1955**

	Politics and institutions	Economics and labour movement
1956	The Constitutional Court begins to operate (Jan.). Radical Party founded, from the seceding left of the PLI: Eugenio Scalfari among founding members (Feb.). In the wake of Khrushchev's denunciation of Stalin's crimes Togliatti propels the idea of 'polycentric' international Communism (June). Discontent among Italian Communist intellectuals because of PCI's backing of the Soviet repression in Hungary (Nov.). US and Italian secret services agree to set up a clandestine anti-Communist paramilitary organisation (Gladio) (Nov.).	Confindustria and other main employers' confederations agree to sponsor their own candidates in DC and PLI's lists at elections (Feb.). A hundred and thirty-nine Italians die in a Belgian colliery (Aug.). Government intervention in economic affairs encouraged at DC congress (Oct.). Ministry of State Holdings created (Dec.): it will become a powerful instrument of political patronage.
1957	Several intellectuals quit the PCI over the Hungarian crisis (Jan.). The treaties establishing EEC and Euratom are signed in Rome (March). *L'Osservatore Romano* opposes any *rapprochement* between DC and PSI (March) and condemns the proposed separation of politics and Church teaching (Aug.).	Olivetti company reduces working week to forty-five hours, with Saturdays off and no change in wages (Apr.). Fiat 500 car is launched (July). New law provides incentives for southern development (July). National telephone system under state control through IRI (Dec.). Unemployment still at 2 million (10 per cent).
1958	EEC and Euratom come into force (Jan.). The High Council of the Judiciary is set up (March). National election without much change: DC 42 per cent, PCI 23 per cent, PSI 14 per cent (25–6 May). Pius XII dies; Patriarch Angelo Roncalli elected Pope as John XXIII (Oct.). Feuding within DC results in unorthodox regional government in Sicily, with the support of both far right and far left (Oct.).	'Independent' union established at Fiat with the support of the car company management (Sept.). Public companies set up their own agency to represent their interests and abandon Confindustria (Dec.). Oil reserves discovered in Sicily by ENI. For the first time there are more industrial employees than agricultural workers.

1956

Danilo Dolci, a sociologist and social reformer from Trieste, is arrested in Sicily, with several other people, for participating in the mass occupation of untilled land (Feb.). Liner *Andrea Doria* sinks with heavy loss of life (July). Southern immigrants are refused accommodation in lodging houses in Turin.

Law regulates the nature and use of election propaganda (March). *Il Giorno* appears in Milan (Apr.): it is the first daily owned by a public company (Mattei's ENI); it supports centre-left policies. *Il Verri* and *Il Veltro* (literary criticism journals) are founded. Cinemas meet television competition by installing television sets and showing *Lascia o raddoppia* on Thursdays.

1957

Women admitted to juries (Feb.). Eleven people are killed by a car during the Millemiglia car race (May). *L'Osservatore Romano* castigates women wearing shorts in Rome and the police authorities act (Aug.). 'Asian' flu epidemic claims several victims and delays start of school year in many provinces (Sept.).

Television advertisements in the form of a ten-minute programme (*Carosello*) are introduced. They are shown after the main evening news, and greatly appeal to children with their use of comedy, cartoons and songs. The director of the South Tyrolean paper *Dolomiten* is arrested and accused of involvement in violent separatist activities (Feb.). Pius XII fulminates against the local and central authorities for laxity of moral standards in cinema and television (March); censorship is strengthened to meet the Pope's requests. Dario Fo and Franca Rame theatre company established.

1958

The Bishop of Prato is cleared of the accusation of defamation (Apr.): he had publicly denounced as sinners a couple married in a civil ceremony. Fifteen thousand people are disappointed by the non-appearance of the Virgin at Terni (July). Many more follow the 'Giuffrè scandal' of illegal financial dealings involving the Church and leading politicians (Aug.). Legal prostitution is abolished and brothels are closed (Sept.). A Roman restaurant is also closed down after a Turkish dancer performed a near striptease at the birthday party of a Roman countess (Nov.). Opening of the first stretch of the Autostrada del Sole, linking Milan and Parma (Dec.).

Catholic dissent finds expression in two new journals: *Questitalia* and *Testimonianze*. The Holy Office prohibits the publication of Don Lorenzo Milani's *Esperienze pastorali*, which contains criticism of the use of religion for political ends. *Festival dei due mondi* (annual musical event) established at Spoleto by Giancarlo Menotti (June). A small private television station has its equipment impounded: RAI state monopoly cannot be broken (Oct.). Launching of television song competition *Canzonissima*, linked with the prizes in New Year Lottery (Oct.). Television primary education programme is also started (*Telescuola*). Boom in the sale of records of traditional pop music, but rock and roll is also popular with youngsters. Domenico Modugno wins the San Remo song festival with *Nel blu dipinto di blu* (a.k.a. *Volare*).

	Politics and institutions	Economics and labour movement
1959	The excommunication of Communists and their allies is renewed by the Holy Office (Apr.). The proposal to refuse the installation of US missiles is defeated in the Senate (Apr.). DC congress: the party is divided between those in favour of the 'opening to the left' (i.e. to the PSI) and those against (Oct.).	The Committee of Ministers for the South is established (March). First united action among the three metalworkers' federations (Apr.–May). The expression 'economic miracle' is used for the first time, by the London *Daily Mail*, in connection with Italy (May). The Ministry of Tourism and Entertainment is created (July). Financial incentives granted to small and medium-size companies (July). Car production has doubled since 1955. Unemployment is reduced to 7 per cent. Frequent metal and engineering workers' strikes.
1960	*L'Osservatore Romano* condemns the 'dialogue' between Catholics and Socialists (Jan. and May). Violent and widespread anti-Fascist demonstrations against Fernando Tambroni's government, which has sought the support of the MSI: several people are killed by the police in Reggio Emilia, Palermo and Catania; Tambroni resigns (July).	Financial Oscar given to the lira for its stability and strength (Jan.). Five-year Plan for the Development of Agriculture introduced (Jan.). Agitation and strikes in Sicily due to economic malaise and unemployment (June–July). Agreement on equal pay for equal work between men and women, signed by workers' and employers' unions (July).

Social life and civic society	Cultural life and media	
First women enter the police force. A statue of the Madonna is carried throughout Italy by helicopter, starting from Naples (April). Rowdy youngsters ('Teddy boys') infest holiday resorts; near Rome a peasant woman kills a teenager who tried to rape her (Aug.).	Two important books on the South are published by Feltrinelli: Giuseppe Tomasi Di Lampedusa's novel *Il Gattopardo* (The Leopard) and Ernesto De Martino's anthropological study *Sud e magia* (The South and Magic). The DC calls for the withdrawal of public financial support for the Crotone literary prize because the award has been conferred on Pier Paolo Pasolini for his *Una vita violenta* (A Violent Life) (Nov.). The television show *Lascia o raddoppia* is replaced by another hugely successful show, *Campanile sera*, focused on local pride and rivalry (Nov.). Nobel Prizes awarded to Salvatore Quasimodo (literature) and Emilio Segre (physics). The Ministry of Tourism and Entertainment established.	**1959**
The exclusion of women from public offices (by a 1917 Act) is declared unconstitutional (May). Olympic Games in Rome: enthusiasm for the numerous successes by Italian athletes (Aug.–Sept.).	Fellini's *La dolce vita* is released (the name of one of its characters, the intrusive photo-reporter Paparazzo, soon becomes the international word for that profession). Some MPs and the Vatican request censorial action against Fellini's film. Michelangelo Antonioni's *L'avventura* and Mauro Bolognini's *Una giornata balorda* (A Crazy Day) are impounded. Obstacles to the production of Visconti's *Rocco e i suoi fratelli* (Rocco and his Brothers) are raised in Milan. In Naples, Debussy's *The Martyrdom of St Sebastian* is banned, at the request of the local bishop, because the role of the saint is to be performed by a Soviet woman dancer. Censorship also hits Giovanni Testori's play *Ariadna* because it refers to prostitution and homosexuality. The state monopoly of television broadcasting is judged legitimate by the Constitutional Court (July). Launch of political debates (*Tribuna politica*) on television, which give opposition parties access to airwaves for the first time (Oct.).	**1960**

	Politics and institutions	Economics and labour movement
1961	First centre-left local governments, with DC–PSI alliance, in Milan (Jan.), Genoa (Feb.) and Florence (March). Electrical installations in South Tyrol hit by explosions as part of the campaign for the autonomy of that mainly German-speaking district (June); the Secretary General of the Südtiroler Volkspartei is arrested (July).	A '*Financial Times* Survey' is devoted to the 'Italian economic miracle' (Jan.). Meeting of DC leaders and economists at San Pellegrino (Bergamo) to consolidate the ideological shift to the left and to discuss economic planning (Sept.); a Committee on Economic Planning chaired by Giuseppe Ugo Papi is set up.
1962	Successful marathon speech by Aldo Moro at the DC congress to persuade the party to accept the 'opening to the left' and the alliance with PSI (Jan.). Reformist zeal of new Fanfani government (Feb.), but proposals to curb land speculation and urban sprawl will be defeated; centre-left coalition includes DC, PSDI and PRI, and is supported by PSI. As a balancing act, a conservative DC, Antonio Segni, is elected President of the Republic (May). Opening of Vatican Council II (Oct.).	PCI conference on the 'Directions of Italian capitalism' becomes a debate on the pros and cons of the DC–PSI alliance (Feb.). An Additional Note by the Minister of the Budget (Ugo La Malfa) to the general economic report advocates economic planning (May). Thirty per cent increase in pensions (Oct.). More effective taxation of shareholding introduced (Dec.). Demand for labour in the North outstrips supply for the first time ever.
1963	The economist Manlio Rossi Doria denounces the malpractices and patronage of the DC-controlled Federconsorzi (Jan.). The installation in Italy of US/NATO Polaris missiles is announced (Jan.). Parliamentary elections (28 Apr.) with strong performances by PCI and PLI, both opponents of centre-left government, from opposite positions: DC 38 per cent, PCI 25 per cent, PSI 14 per cent, PLI 7 per cent. Left-wing Socialists oppose PSI alliance with DC (June) and postpone the setting up of the first centre-left coalition with Socialist Ministers until December.	A new, hard-fought national contract for metal and engineering workers is signed: substantial wage increases are granted (Feb.). Credit squeeze to contrast inflationary tendency and balance of payments deficit (Sept.). Clashes in Rome between building workers and the police after employers' lock-out (Oct.). Capital flight abroad for fear of radical political changes under centre-left government.

Social life and civic society	Cultural life and media	
Celebrations throughout the year for the centenary of the unification of the country. The (ineffective) Fascist law restricting internal migration is abolished (Feb.). Pope John XXIII's encyclical *Mater et Magistra* (Mother and Teacher) includes expressions of solidarity with workers' rights (July). First March for Peace from Perugia to Assisi organised (Sept.). The legitimacy of the rule in the penal code which condemns only women for adultery is confirmed by the Constitutional Court (Nov.). Census reveals that 41 per cent of the labour force is engaged in industry, 30 per cent in services, 29 per cent in agriculture; total resident population: 50 million.	The deputy director of the DC daily *Il Popolo*, Ettore Bernabei, is nominated Director General of RAI: he will hold office until 1975 (Jan.). Conference organised by leading magazines and journals (including *L'Espresso*, *Il Mondo* and *Il Ponte*) to work out a cultural programme of centre-left orientation (Oct.). Second television channel launched (Nov.). The DC Minister of Justice criticises *Tribuna politica* and television variety shows 'for planting Togliatti and dancing girls in the hearts of Italian families' (Nov.). The new journal *Quaderni Rossi* marks the revival of theoretical Marxism. Successful films: Antonioni's *La notte*; Vittorio De Seta's *Banditi a Orgosolo*; Pietro Germi's *Divorzio all'italiana* (Divorce Italian Style); Ermanno Olmi's *Il posto* (The Job); Pasolini's *Accattone* (Beggar). Leonardo Sciascia's anti-Mafia novel *Il giorno della civetta* (The Day of the Owl) appears.	**1961**
Fierce trade union struggles in Turin with the massive participation of Fiat workers (many young and from the South) culminate in riots: 'siege of the Piazza Statuto' (July). Enrico Mattei dies in air crash: rumours of an international Mafia 'job' (Oct.). Law on the nationalisation of the electricity industry passed (Nov.). School reform: compulsory education extended to eight years (age six to fourteen) and single system for lower secondary schools established (Dec.).	Bolognini's film *Senilità* (As a Man Grows Older) – based on Italo Svevo's novel – is held up by the parliamentary committee on censorship but released by the Ministry of Tourism and Entertainment (March). Censorship is abolished for theatre and opera, but maintained for cinema and variety shows (Apr.). *Panorama*, a new current affairs monthly (weekly from 1967) is published by Mondadori and Time-Life (Oct.). Persistent censorship forces Dario Fo and Franca Rame to abandon their running of *Canzonissima* (Nov.). Notable films: Francesco Rosi's *Salvatore Giuliano* and Pasolini's *Mamma Roma*. Violent comic strip *Diabolik* appears.	**1962**
World-wide acclaim of John XXIII's encyclical *Pacem in Terris* (Peace on Earth) (Apr.); Pope John dies in June: Giovanni Battista Montini elected Pope as Paul VI. A car bomb explodes in Palermo, with several dead among police and bystanders: a Mafia warning (June). Two thousand people die when a mountain valley in Veneto is flooded as a result of a landslide falling into a reservoir (Oct.); subsequent inquiry will reveal responsibility on the part of the old private electricity companies. A Scolopian friar, Ernesto Balducci, is condemned to seven months' imprisonment (suspended) for writing in support of conscientious objection (Oct.). In a 'Message to the Italian people' the Church renews its condemnation of 'atheistic Communism' (Oct.).	For an episode in his film *La ricotta* Pasolini is charged with blasphemy against the Catholic religion and condemned to four months' imprisonment (suspended, and later quashed on appeal) (March). The neo-avant-garde literary Gruppo '63 is established. Successful television social inquiry: *Viaggio nell'Italia che cambia* (A Journey through Changing Italy). Three remarkable films: Rosi's *Mani sulla città* (Hands over the City), denouncing building speculation; Visconti's *Il Gattopardo* (The Leopard); Fellini's *8½*.	**1963**

	Politics and institutions	Economics and labour movement
1964	Left-wing Socialists abandon PSI and set up PSIUP (Partito Socialista di Unità Proletaria) (Jan.). Disagreement between DC and PSI over a Bill on financing private education brings the government down (July). Aborted *coup* devised by the General Commandant of the *Carabinieri* and the secret services, SIFAR (July): the plan will be uncovered only a few years later. Death of Togliatti and publication of his 'Yalta Memorandum' containing criticism of Soviet Communism (Aug.). DC splits over election of President of the Republic, prompted by Segni's illness: Giuseppe Saragat (PSDI) is elected after lengthy voting sessions (Dec.).	Strong deflationary measures are introduced, but also a mitigation of shareholding taxation (Feb.). Loans from the United States and the IMF are obtained (Feb.). First five-year plan presented (June). Balance of payments restored to sound position. Building boom, but industrial restructuring results in unemployment. 'Incomes policy' becomes a fashionable term.
1965	By nine votes to eight a special parliamentary committee rejects the request to pursue the case of ex-Minister Roberto Tremelloni (PSDI) for alleged malpractice while in office (July). The National Association of Judges is split along ideological lines (Sept.). Vatican Council II is solemnly closed (Dec.).	Financial Oscar again given to the lira for its quick recovery and stability (Feb.). 'Super-decree' to revive the economy with reflationary measures (March). Taranto steelworks opened (March). New provision for the industrialisation of the South (June). A revised first five-year plan is presented (June).
1966	DC MPs sabotage the passing of legislation to establish state nursery schools, and cause the government to fall (Jan.). PCI congress reveals split between Giorgio Amendola's 'right' and Pietro Ingrao's 'left' (Jan.). PSI and PSDI unite and form the short-lived Partito Socialista Unificato, PSU (Oct.).	Fiat signs agreement with Soviet Union to build a car plant at Togliattigrad (May). Montedison conglomerate created by the combination of Montecatini (chemicals) and Edison (ex-electrical company): it controls 80 per cent of national chemical production (July). Second plan for modernising agriculture passed by Parliament (Oct.).

Anti-military song at Spoleto Festival provokes protests by the public and a denunciation for contempt of the armed forces (June). More than a million people attend Togliatti's funeral (Aug.). First line of Milan's underground railway opened (Nov.).	Summer song festival 'Il disco per l'estate' (A Record for the Summer) is successfully launched. A new Marxist journal, *Classe Operaia*, appears. Togliatti's funeral is immortalised in a painting by Renato Guttuso. Three notable films: Antonioni's *Deserto rosso* (Red Desert); Sergio Leone's *Per un pugno di dollari* (A Fistful of Dollars), first spaghetti western film; and Pasolini's *Il Vangelo secondo Matteo* (The Gospel According to St Matthew).	**1964**
The performance in Rome of Rolf Hochhuth's play *Il Vicario* (The Representative) is prohibited for its criticism of Pius XII's silence on the Holocaust (Jan.). Tunnel through Mont Blanc opened for road traffic (July). A young Sicilian woman, Franca Viola, refuses to marry the man who had abducted her for the customary shotgun wedding. Inauguration of the first nuclear plant for the production of electricity, at Trino Vercellese (near Turin).	Literary classics in paperback appear in newspaper kiosks (Apr.). A new law on cinema makes government grants subject to 'ethico-social' principles (June). *Il Sole–24 Ore* is established as the main financial daily and mouthpiece of the Confindustria (Nov.). Marco Bellocchio's film *I pugni in tasca* (Fists in the Pocket) challenges the myth of the family. Nanni Loy's television series *Specchio segreto* (Secret Mirror) reveals hidden idiosyncrasies of Italians' private lives. A song entitled *Dio è morto* (God is Dead) is banned from radio and television. The first volume of Renzo De Felice's monumental biography of Mussolini (*Mussolini: il rivoluzionario*) appears.	**1965**
Fiery public debate when *liceo* pupils in Milan are accused of indecency for writing in their school magazine, *La zanzara* (The Mosquito), about the sexual habits of Italians (March) – they are later acquitted. One student dies after clashes between left-wing and neo-Fascist students at Rome University; the police storm the buildings occupied by students; the events arouse heated debates in Parliament, forcing the rector of the university to resign (Apr.–May). Shoddily built blocks of flats collapse in Agrigento, Sicily, and reveal extensive building speculation and corruption (July). Venice and Florence are flooded and suffer serious damage (Nov.). An entire family is murdered by bandits in Sardinia to silence a witness (Dec.).	Weekly magazine *Il Mondo* folds (March). The novelist Milena Milani and her publisher are condemned to six months' imprisonment for the publication of the 'obscene' novel *La ragazza di nome Giulio* (The Girl whose Name is Giulio) (March). Actress Gina Lollobrigida, director Mauro Bolognini and others are sentenced to imprisonment (suspended) for 'obscenity and indecency' in the film *Le bambole* (The Dolls) (Oct.). Gillo Pontecorvo's *La battaglia di Algeri* (The Battle of Algiers) is released. Mario Tronti publishes his essay *Lavoratori e capitale* (Workers and Capital). First erotic comics appear.	**1966**

1967 Pope Paul VI speaks against the introduction of divorce, an issue debated in Parliament (Jan.). The disquieting role of SIFAR in the 1964 near-coup is revealed, but the PCI's request for a parliamentary inquiry into the secret services is rejected (May).

Inter-ministerial Committee on Economic Planning set up (Feb.); one of its first decisions is to build the Alfasud car plant near Naples (despite Fiat's opposition). The Catholic Workers' Association (ACLI) declares its opposition to neo-capitalism (Aug.).

1968 Student agitations influence politics throughout the year, but the pattern of voting remains largely unchanged at national election (19–20 May): DC 39 per cent, PCI 27 per cent, PSU 15 per cent; it is a disappointing result for the PSU, which will only survive as such for another year. PCI condemns Soviet-led intervention in Czechoslovakia (Aug.).

The year is punctuated by strikes in all industrial sectors; in one case (at Porto Marghera, Venice) the aim of equal pay for all is set. At Pirelli radical and independent workers' committees are established (March). Lifting of residual tariff duties among EEC members (July). First general strike called by the three trade union confederations since 1948, on the issue of pensions (Nov.).

1967

Luigi Tenco, a singer-songwriter, commits suicide after his failure at San Remo Festival: many young people empathise with his melancholy existentialism (Jan.). Agitations, sit-ins and occupations in various universities (first at Pisa) by students protesting against a proposed reform of higher education (Feb., May). Anti-US and pro-Vietnam demonstrations become frequent (March–May). The Vatican prohibits the translation into Italian and other languages of the catechism approved by Dutch bishops (Aug.) A *liceo* teacher of philosophy, Aldo Braibanti, is accused of psychological domination of two (male) pupils who elected to go and live with him (Dec.): he will be condemned to four years' imprisonment; many intellectuals (including Alberto Moravia and Umberto Eco) will protest.

The *coup manqué* of 1964 and the role of the secret services are revealed by *L'Espresso* (May). *Lettera a una professoressa* (Letter to a Teacher), appears edited by Don Lorenzo Milani (May): a manifesto for protesting students. Allen Ginsberg is arrested for reading 'obscene' poetry at Spoleto Festival (July). Antonioni's *Blow-up*, the Palme d'Or winner of Cannes Festival, is impounded on grounds of obscenity (Oct.). The first bare-breasted women appear in a soft-porn magazine (Oct.): these publications suddenly mushroom, notwithstanding opposition from various quarters.

1968

Earthquake in western Sicily: 300 dead (Jan.). A prolonged social earthquake is caused by the 'student movement' throughout Italy. The original malaise about education develops into a political and ideological protest, combining creativity, violence and internationalism. Dissenting Catholics and feminists join in the libertarian protest. Many small revolutionary groups are established. In a controversial poem Pasolini sides with the policemen, as the children of proletarians, and against the students, as the offspring of the bourgeoisie (June). Paul VI's encyclical *Humanae Vitae* (On Human Life) reiterates the Church's condemnation of the use of contraceptives (July). Death of Padre Pio, the Capuchin monk with alleged miraculous healing powers (Sept.). Adultery is no longer a crime for women – it never was for men (Dec.).

The media are slow to appreciate the importance of the social protest of students, dissenting Catholics and women. When they do, some newpaper editors are replaced with more perceptive journalists, while a more inquisitive and critical style of reporting is adopted: Giovanni Spadolini becomes the editor of the *Corriere della Sera*, Alberto Ronchey of *La Stampa*. *L'Avvenire*, a new Catholic daily owned by CEI, appears. Nobel peace prize awarded to Danilo Dolci, well known for community work in Sicily. Pasolini's film *Teorema* is impounded for obscenity.

	Politics and institutions	Economics and labour movement
1969	PSU splits: PSI and PSDI are resurrected as separate parties (July). Aldo Moro expresses 'interest' in PCI developments (Feb.). US President Richard Nixon's visit to Italy provokes demonstrations and clashes between opposing political extremists (Feb.). Five are wounded by an explosive device at Milan Fair (Apr.). Enrico Berlinguer, the PCI deputy Secretary General, openly criticises Soviet Communism at international conference in Moscow (June). Various explosive devices are left on trains: several people are wounded (Aug.). Dissident Manifesto group is expelled from PCI (Nov.). Bomb explosion at a Milan bank in Piazza Fontana: sixteen dead, many wounded (Dec.); an arrested anarchist, Giuseppe Pinelli, 'mysteriously' falls to his death from top floor of police headquarters. The Piazza Fontana outrage is attributed by informed opinion to reactionary agents within the state and carried out by neo-Fascists ('strategy of tension'); but after prolonged investigations and trials, nobody is held responsible.	General strike over pensions (Feb.). Agreement between unions and Confindustria on abolition of regional wage differentials (March). Local general strike at Battipaglia (near Naples) escalates in violent clashes with the police: two demonstrators are killed (Apr.). ACLI sever their connection with DC (June). Fierce scuffles in Turin between the police and workers, with the participation of revolutionary groups (July). Fiat takes over Lancia (Oct.). 'Hot autumn', with extensive workers' strikes and demonstrations, results in wage increases and general improvements in working conditions (Sept.–Dec.).
1970	First local elections to provide all regions with semi-autonomous government (June). Revolt of Reggio Calabria, sparked by choice of Catanzaro as regional capital, fomented by neo-Fascists (starts in July and lasts into 1971). Numerous arrests follow mass protest on President Nixon's visit to Rome (Sept.). Farcical aborted coup led by Junio Valerio Borghese, a former commander of Mussolini's marine corps (Dec.).	Trade union confederations send a telegram to the President of the Republic to protest at the frequent harassment and arrest of workers and trade unionists as a reaction to the successful industrial negotiations of 1969 (Jan.). The president of ACLI is summoned before the CEI and criticised for his association's left-wing leanings (March). Workers' Charter becomes law (May). Taxes and tariffs increased to meet higher public expenditure (Aug.). Industrial subcontracting to medium and small-size companies, in which unions are weaker.
1971	Clashes with police at L'Aquila following the decision to make another town, Pescara, the regional capital of Abruzzo (Feb.). Law on housing reform: enhanced power of compulsory purchase to local authorities for public construction (Oct.). PCI conference on 'Communists and Europe' marks the abandonment of the party's anti-EEC position (Nov.). Former president of Montedison Giorgio Valerio accused of illegally funding political parties (Nov.). The official DC candidate for the Presidency of the Republic, Amintore Fanfani, is not supported by the whole party; in the end Giovanni Leone is elected (Dec.).	Workers' confederations introduce radical changes in their representative organisation at plant level (March). Brief general strike in support of housing reform (Apr.). New law requires industrial public companies to invest more in the South (Oct.). Tax reform approved, with the introduction of VAT and a simpler income tax (Oct.), but implementation has to wait until 1974.

Italian gradually replaces Latin at Catholic Mass. In secondary education students are given the right to hold general meetings (Jan.); the format of their final examinations is simplified (Feb.). State nursery schools established (Mar.). Public opinion outraged by cruelty to handicapped children at an institution near Rome (June). General strike called for better and cheaper housing (Nov.). Unlimited access to university granted (Dec.). Popular slogan at workers' and students' gatherings: 'What do we want? Everything!'

Je t'aime, moi non plus, sung by Jane Birkin, is **1969**
banned from radio programme and censured by *L'Osservatore Romano* for obscenity (Aug.). Julian Beck's Living Theatre expelled on grounds of obscenity (Dec.). New extreme-left journals associated with a variety of political movements appear: *Lotta Continua; Potere Operaio; Servire il Popolo; Il Manifesto*. Dario Fo and Franca Rame organise an alternative San Remo Festival; great success of Fo's satirical play *Mistero buffo* (Comic Mysteries), lampooning the Catholic Church's dogmas. Two important films: Fellini's *Satyricon*; Bernardo Bertolucci's *Il conformista*.

Mauro De Mauro, a journalist for the Sicilian daily *L'Ora*, disappears: he was investigating alleged Mafia involvement in Enrico Mattei's death in 1962 (Sept.). Divorce law passed (Dec.). Use of drugs among youngsters spreads. Almost half a million people in Rome live in unauthorised housing built by speculators with the authorities' collusion.

Journalists at RAI strike against their vice- **1970**
president, Italo De Feo, who had censured a programme (Feb.). Feminist Carla Lonzi publishes the essay *Sputiamo su Hegel* (Let's Spit on Hegel). Dario Fo's first performance of his satirical play *Morte accidentale di un anarchico* (Accidental Death of an Anarchist), inspired by the death of Giuseppe Pinelli. Italian edition of *Cosmopolitan* overtly addresses sexual issues.

Publicising and distributing contraceptives are declared lawful by Constitutional Court (March). Palermo Chief Prosecutor Pietro Scaglione and his chauffeur are murdered by the Mafia (May). The Vatican condemns ACLI for its leaning to the left (May). Census shows that, out of nearly 54 million resident population, 44 per cent are engaged in industry, 38 per cent in services and only 17 per cent in agriculture.

Il Manifesto becomes a daily (Apr.): unlike **1971**
other far-left papers it will outlive the 'revolutionary' 1970s and become a major voice in Italian political journalism. Visconti's *Morte a Venezia* (Death in Venice). Elio Petri's *La classe operaia va in paradiso* (The Working Class Goes to Heaven). *Versus*, semiotics journal edited by Umberto Eco, appears. The most popular television programme is *Canzonissima*.

	Politics and institutions	Economics and labour movement
1972	First post-war election before parliamentary mandate expires is set for 7–8 May; during election campaign left-wing publisher Giangiacomo Feltrinelli is killed by the premature explosion of a bomb he was attaching to an electricity pylon near Milan (March). Election results are marked by the rise of the far right: DC 39 per cent, PCI 37 per cent, PSI 10 per cent, MSI 9 per cent. PSI quits the government coalition led by Andreotti and the conservative PLI enters it (June). Residual Monarchists join MSI, which aims to establish a 'greater national right' (July).	EEC agreement to maintain stable exchange rates (monetary 'snake') (March–Apr.). Unitary trade union federation CGIL–CISL–UIL (July), as a step towards unification – which will not materialise. Balance of payments difficulties. Fiat installs first robots.
1973	Telephone bugging of political leaders by state officials at Ministry of Interior revealed (Feb.). Centre-left government coalition restored (July). PCI Secretary General Enrico Berlinguer launches the proposal for an alliance with DC, soon to be called 'historic compromise' (Sept.).	Lira exits from monetary 'snake' and depreciates (March). Price freeze in an attempt to check inflation (July). Further austerity measures adopted, mainly by restricting petrol consumption (Nov.).
1974	Public funding of political parties approved by Parliament (Apr.), to put an end to political bribes and pay-offs by public and private companies. (A big 'oil scandal' was the most recent case.) First high-profile action of the Red Brigades: the kidnapping of judge M. Sossi in Genoa (Apr.). Referendum on divorce (12–13 May): 59 per cent in favour of keeping divorce law; it is a serious setback for DC and the Vatican. Eight people participating in a trade union demonstration are killed by a bomb in Brescia; over 100 are wounded. A neo-Fascist group claims responsibility (May). A special anti-terrorist unit of *carabinieri* is set up, under General Carlo Alberto Dalla Chiesa (May). Two MSI supporters are killed in Padua (June). Twelve passengers are killed and many wounded when a bomb explodes in a train; extreme right group claims responsibility (Aug.).	Gianni Agnelli is elected president of Confindustria (May). Inflation at 19 per cent; deflationary measures are introduced (July). Short working week at Fiat (Oct.). The banker and Vatican financial adviser Michele Sindona flees to the United States when his financial malpractices are exposed (Oct.). Political strikes are declared constitutionally legitimate (Nov.). General strike over grievances about wages, pensions and prices (Dec.). The Constitutional Court rules that 'political' strikes are legitimate (Dec.). Informal ('black') economy develops.

1972

Police superintendent Luigi Calabresi is killed in Milan (May), extreme left groups held him responsible for G. Pinelli's 'suicide' after the Piazza Fontana massacre. Five *carabinieri* killed in an ambush near Rovigo (May). Malicious explosions in trains taking workers to trade union conference in Calabria: several wounded (Oct.). Conscientious objection declared lawful (Dec.). First gay and lesbian group, Fuori!, is formed.

Italo Calvino's *Le città invisibili* (Invisible Cities) appears. Rosi's *Il caso Mattei* (The Mattei Affair) is released. Bertolucci's *Ultimo tango a Parigi* (Last Tango in Paris) is impounded for indecency. The introduction of colour television is resisted: the government regards it as an unnecessary luxury.

1973

Violent demonstrations in Rome and Naples against the government's intention to strengthen police powers of arrest (Feb.). Clashes between neo-Fascists and anti-Fascists in Milan, a policeman is killed (Apr.). Two sons of an MSI local leader are killed by arson in Rome (Apr.). Four people are killed in Milan by a bomb thrown by an 'anarchist' with right-wing connections (May). An Alfa-Romeo official is kidnapped by the Red Brigades (June). Cholera epidemics in Naples (Aug.). The plans of the subversive right-wing network Rosa dei Venti (The Wind Rose) are exposed; high army officers are involved (Nov.). A Fiat director is kidnapped for a week by the Red Brigades (Dec.).

Gianni Agnelli, Fiat president and owner of Turin's daily *La Stampa*, acquires substantial shares in Milan's *Corriere della Sera* (May). Following Piero Ottone's appointment as editor of *Corriere* (in March 1972), the paper abandons its traditional conservative orientation; the well-known moderate journalist Indro Montanelli quits the *Corriere* (Oct.). Fellini's *Amarcord* is released. RAI broadcasts for the first time programmes on Protestantism and Judaism. Actress Anna Magnani dies.

1974

Decrees introduce elected bodies in schools giving representation to teachers, parents and pupils (May). Civil disobedience spreads during the summer and autumn, with organised 'self-reduction' of rents and prices by tenants and consumers. Feminist demonstration in Rome to press for a reform of family law (Nov.). A poster advertisement for 'Jesus Jeans' featuring the behind of a young woman causes controversy.

Montanelli launches a new daily, *Il Giornale Nuovo* (June). The Constitutional Court declares that state monopoly of radio and television is legitimate only as long as pluralism is ensured and nation-wide broadcasting is involved (July). The publisher Rizzoli becomes the sole owner of the *Corriere della Sera*. (July). Silvio Berlusconi sets up Telemilano, a local cable channel – his first foray into television. Elsa Morante's historical novel *La storia* (History) is published. Vittorio De Sica dies.

	Politics and institutions	Economics and labour movement
1975	Voting age lowered from twenty-one to eighteen (March). A young neo-Fascist savagely beaten in Milan (March) – he will die a month later. DC local leader kneecapped in Milan by Red Brigade militants (May). 'Reale law' on law and order gives more power to the police to arrest people and use weapons (May). Shift to the left at local election: in most main cities the PCI is the first party (15–16 June). Berlinguer agrees with Communist leaders of Spain and France on Eurocommunism (July). Benigno Zaccagnini replaces Fanfani as DC Secretary General and attempts to reform the party (July). Osimo Treaty between Italy and Yugoslavia to settle the old controversy over their border (Oct.).	Inflation at 17 per cent. For the first time since the war GNP decreases (by 3·5 per cent). Strengthening of *scala mobile* to favour low-paid workers (Jan.). President Leone invites Parliament to regulate the right to strike (Oct.). An Energy Plan is launched involving the construction of nuclear plants (Dec.).
1976	'Lockheed scandal': government Ministers had placed orders with the American company in a deal which involved kickbacks (Feb.); the affair eventually forces President Leone to resign. During the election campaign a young Communist is murdered near Rome by a group of neo-Fascists led by an MP of the MSI (May). Genoa's public prosecutor Francesco Coco is the first person to be killed by the Red Brigades (June). Berlinguer acknowledges the usefulness of NATO (June). At the general election (20–1 June) gap between DC and PCI narrows: DC 39 per cent, PCI 34 per cent, PSI 10 per cent. The Communist Pietro Ingrao is elected chair of the lower Chamber (July). Bettino Craxi is the new Secretary General of PSI (July). Andreotti forms a minority government with the abstention of PCI (Aug.). Split in the MSI: the moderate faction forms the short-lived party Democrazia Nazionale (Dec.).	Depreciation of the lira against the dollar. General strike of industrial workers to press for more public investment (Feb.). A former governor of the Bank of Italy, Guido Carli, becomes the new president of Confindustria (July). Austerity package introduced by the government, with the support of PCI (Oct.). The Libyan Foreign Bank acquires 10 per cent of Fiat shares (Dec.). Benetton clothing company makes major inroads into foreign markets.

1975

Heads of abortion clinic in Florence arrested (Jan.). Constitutional Court admits the legitimacy of 'therapeutic abortion' (Feb.). Twenty thousand young Catholics belonging to fundamentalist movement Comunione e Liberazione visit the Pope (March). Reform of family law establishing parity between spouses in marriage (Apr.). Horror at violence against two young women (one is killed) by three young neo-Fascists hailing from Rome's bourgeoisie (Sept.). First major demonstration of women's movement in Rome (Dec.). Law legalises possession of a small amount of soft drugs for personal use (Dec.).

Reform of RAI: control moves from government to parliamentary commission and the principle of competition among channels is adopted, culminating in the allocation of their control to political parties (mainly DC and PSI, but later also PCI) (Apr.). Pasolini murdered near Rome (Nov.); earlier in the year he had published *Scritti corsari* (Pirate writings), a collection of his articles. His *Salò* is screened posthumously – and impounded for obscenity. Nobel prize for literature to the poet Eugenio Montale. Rosi's *Cadaveri eccellenti* (Illustrious Corpses) is released. New independent local radio stations with strong ideological commitment mushroom.

1976

Feminist demonstration in Rome for the legalisation of abortion (Apr.). Earthquake in Friuli: 1,000 victims and much devastation (May). Environmental disaster when dioxin gas escapes after the explosion at a chemical plant at Seveso, near Milan (July). At an open-air music festival at Parco Lambro, also near Milan, 60,000 youngsters convene (Aug.). The extreme left group Lotta Continua holds its second congress but divisions bring about its demise (Oct.).

The new daily *La Repubblica*, directed by Eugenio Scalfari, soon competes with *Corriere della Sera* for the largest circulation (Jan.). The Constitutional Court asserts the legitimacy of local television broadcasting (June), but Telemontecarlo is widely received through relays. The Sunday variety-cum-football show (2.30–7.30 p.m.) *Domenica in* is launched by RAI 1 television channel (Oct.). Fellini's *Casanova*. Bertolucci's *Novecento* (1900). Radio Radicale starts broadcasting in Rome.

	Politics and institutions	Economics and labour movement
1977	Wave of terrorism: over 2,000 acts of politically motivated violence; eleven killed, thirty-two kneecapped. Among the victims is a leading lawyer, Fulvio Croce, originating from Turin, where the first trial against the Red Brigades is due to start in May (but will be postponed to March 1978). The Constitutional Court rules that national security cannot be used to justify covert anti-constitutional activities (May). Reform of secret services to be tightly controlled by parliamentary committee (Oct.). Berlinguer speaks in Moscow on socialism and democracy, with emphasis on pluralism and individual freedoms (Nov.).	Inflation: 18 per cent. CGIL–CISL–UIL agree to trade off diminished wage indexation for the maintenance of plant bargaining (March). IMF loan subjected to the introduction of deflationary policies (Apr.). Measures to reduce youth unemployment (June). Financial support for private industry subject to control over investment policies (July). Law is passed on equal treatment in employment between men and women (Dec.). Over 200,000 industrial workers gather in Rome to demonstrate against unemployment (Dec.).
1978	Terrorist attacks throughout the year. Reform of secret services: SISMI (military intelligence) and SISDE (internal security) replace SIFAR (Jan.). The United States says that its attitude towards Communist parties, 'including the PCI', has not changed (Jan.). DC president Aldo Moro is kidnapped by the Red Brigades; his escort is massacred (March); Moro is murdered in May, ending any prospect of an 'historic compromise', as he was the only possible linchpin between DC and PCI. Craxi strengthens his grip on the PSI (March) and soon intensifies his anti-PCI campaign. Sandro Pertini (PSI) is elected President of the Republic (July). Pope Paul VI dies (Aug.); so does his successor, John Paul I (Sept.), making way in October for the Polish Pope John Paul II (Cardinal Karol Wojtyla).	CGIL–CISL–UIL embrace a policy of wage moderation and call for investment to boost employment (Feb.). Three-year 'Pandolfi plan' aiming at curbing wages and public expenditure is launched (Aug.). The government manifests the intention to join the European Monetary System, EMS (Dec.).
1979	'Armed struggle' continues with many casualties, including a Communist worker, Guido Rossa, killed by the Red Brigades. Andreotti government's of 'national solidarity' collapses when PCI withdraws its support (Jan.). General election (3–4 June), with heavy losses by PCI: DC 38 per cent, PCI 30 per cent, PSI 10 per cent; similar results at the first European election (10 June). The Communist Nilde Jotti is the first woman Speaker in Italian Parliament (June). Craxi launches the idea of a 'great constitutional reform' (Sept.). The installation of US Pershing missiles is approved by Parliament (Dec.).	The governor and an officer of the Bank of Italy, Paolo Baffi and Mario Sarcinelli, are speciously indicted (March): they were investigating irregular political links of some credit institutions. Carlo Azeglio Ciampi is the new governor (Sept.). Sixty-one Fiat workers are sacked: they are accused of abetting political violence; the subsequent strike is unsuccessful (Oct.).

1977

Youth disaffected from traditional politics become the Movement of 1977, with an irreverent strand and a militarist wing. These are united in shouting down CGIL secretary Luciano Lama, who intended to address the students occupying Rome University: violent clashes with the police ensue (Feb.). Feminist demonstration in Rome to protest against the Senate's failure to reform the law on abortion (June). Anti-nuclear demonstration at large nuclear station near Rome (Aug.), but Parliament approves plan for the building of four new stations (Oct.). Left-wing groups organise a convention in Bologna 'against repression' (Sept.).

Colour television starts (Feb.) and local private television companies proliferate. Ninety-seven per cent of households own a television set. Dario Fo's *Mistero buffo* is shown on television and arouses vehement but sterile protests by the Vatican and the DC (Apr.). Piero Ottone is replaced by a moderate director at the *Corriere della Sera* (Oct.). The deputy director of *La Stampa*, Carlo Casalegno, is mortally wounded by the Red Brigades (Nov.). The literary critic Alberto Asor Rosa coins the expression 'two societies', to indicate the division between Italians with a secure occupation and those who are alienated from society, in particular the many young unemployed and southerners. Soft porn films begin to be widely shown in 'red light' cinemas. *Padre Padrone* by Paolo and Vittorio Taviani wins the Palme d'Or at the Cannes Film Festival. Film director Roberto Rossellini dies.

1978

Mental hospitals are to be replaced by community mental health provision, following the pioneering work of psychiatrist Franco Basaglia (May). A major feminist victory: abortion is decriminalised (May). Fair Rent Act (July). The National Health Service is instituted, based on local medical units (Dec.).

During Moro's captivity the role of the press as the main medium for the kidnappers' messages is debated. Berlusconi's Telemilano starts to broadcast on air. New magazines: *Alfabeta* (literary criticism); *Il Male* (political satire); *Il Sabato* (Catholic fundamentalism). An acclaimed film: Nanni Moretti's nonsensically entitled *Ecce Bombo*.

1979

Discontent at the arrest of Toni Negri and other Padua academics, accused of political terrorism (Apr.). A Somalian immigrant is burnt to death in Rome (May). A police chief and a judge are killed by the Mafia in Palermo within a month of each other (July–Aug.).

Rome's independent Radio Città Futura is raided by neo-Fascists and destroyed; the women who run it are wounded (Jan.). Mino Pecorelli, the editor of a sordid political magazine (*OP*), and an alleged blackmailer, is murdered (March). Television's third state channel, RAI 3, starts broadcasting (Dec.). A notable film: Ermanno Olmi's *L'albero degli zoccoli* (The Tree of the Wooden Clogs).

	Politics and institutions	Economics and labour movement
1980	Politically motivated violence continues. A decree law giving terrorists who collaborate with justice reduced sentences is approved (Feb.). National Health Service established to replace occupational health schemes (May). Eighty-five people die when a bomb devastates Bologna railway station (Aug.): extreme-right terrorists are held responsible. The left-wing terrorist son of DC leader Carlo Donat-Cattin is arrested in Paris (Oct.). PCI abandons the 'historic compromise' strategy (Nov.).	Inflation at 22 per cent. The proposal for a 'solidarity fund' to be financed by a levy on pay, supported by most trade unions, is sunk by PCI (July). The oil crisis hits Fiat, which announces substantial redundancies (Sept.): a general strike is called by the unions, but in the end workers' solidarity is sapped by foremen and white-collar employees (Oct.).
1981	Craxi's authority is reinforced at the PSI congress in Palermo: the assembly re-elects him leader with 72 per cent of the vote. Spectacular stage design and American-style side-shows characterise the congress (Apr.). Anti-abortion campaign is defeated by referendum (17–18 May). The right-wing subversive activities of the Masonic lodge P2 are exposed (May): politicians, judges, journalists, army officers, civil servants and businessmen (among them the banker Roberto Calvi and Silvio Berlusconi) are included in the 'brothers'' list. The Republican Giovanni Spadolini is the first non-DC Prime Minister: he heads a five-party coalition which includes DC, PSI, PRI, PSDI and PLI (June). Commenting on the Polish crisis, Berlinguer declares that the 1917 revolution has outlived its validity for Western socialism (Dec.).	The lira is devalued by 6 per cent within the EMS (March). A tax evaders' list featuring 20,000 names is published (Apr.). The privatisation of Montedison is announced (May). Severe losses on Milan stock market (July). Roberto Calvi is condemned to four years' imprisonment for illegal transfer of capital abroad; he is released on bail (July).
1982	A task force frees the American NATO General James Lee Dozier, kidnapped by the Red Brigades (Jan.). Ciriaco De Mita is the new Secretary General of DC: he will unsuccessfully try to reform the party and put an end to its factions. Roberto Calvi is found hanged under London's Blackfriars bridge (June). Bitter internal dissent brings down the Spadolini government (Nov.).	Vast demonstration of metal-engineering workers in Rome to defend wages and employment (March). Stern warning of the Governor of the Bank of Italy on the need to curb wage increases and public spending (May). Confindustria rescinds the 1975 agreement on the *scala mobile*: strikes and demonstrations follow (June).

1980

The Mafia kills the DC president of Sicilian region, Piersanti Mattarella (Jan.), and the chief public prosecutor, Gaetano Costa (Aug.). The world of football is shaken by revelations of extensive corruption (March). Eighty-one people die when a plane crashes in the sea near the island of Ustica (June): the cause is a mystery. New oil scandal of corruption involves high-ranking officers of the fiscal police (Oct.). Earthquake in Campania and Basilicata: 6,000 die (Nov.): reconstruction money will be largely controlled by the Camorra (Neapolitan Mafia).

A *Corriere della Sera* journalist, Walter Tobagi, is killed by an extreme-left commando (May). Berlusconi's television network grows stronger with the launch of Canale 5 (Sept.) Umberto Eco publishes his mystery novel set in monastic Middle Ages, *Il nome della rosa* (The Name of the Rose). RAI 1 variety show *Fantastico* is the most popular programme; like *Canzonissima* (which ended in 1975), it is linked with a lottery.

1981

Pope John Paul II is shot at by a Turkish terrorist (May): various conspiracy theories are put forward. A local DC leader, Ciro Cirillo, is kidnapped in Naples by the Red Brigades (Apr.): he will be released in July following the Camorra's secret intercession. The Pope's encyclical *Laborem Exercens* (The Dignity of Work) condemns both capitalism and Socialism (Sept.). The census reveals a marked increase in the number of people employed in services (51 per cent) and reductions in industry (36 per cent) and agriculture (13 per cent); resident population: 56 million. Farm holidays are increasingly popular.

The Red Brigades release a kidnapped judge, Giovanni D'Urso, when their request for documents to be published in newspapers is met; two journalists are arrested for this (Jan.). A television programme on prostitution is suspended (March). The owner and some journalists of the *Corriere della Sera* are involved in the P2 scandal: Alberto Cavallari becomes the new director (June). The Constitutional Court rules that private television can only broadcast locally (July). The American series *Dallas* boosts viewing of Berlusconi's Canale 5. Poet Eugenio Montale dies.

1982

A Sicilian Communist MP, Pio La Torre, is killed by the Mafia (Apr.). The Communist women's association (UDI) is disbanded (July). Popular enthusiasm for the Italian victory in the football World Cup (July). General Carlo Alberto Dalla Chiesa, his wife and escorting agent are killed by the Mafia (Sept.); he had been sent to Sicily as Prefect of Palermo only a few months earlier. A law introducing stricter measures to combat the Mafia is passed (Sept.). First two official victims of AIDS die (Oct.).

A journalist of the PCI daily, *L'Unità*, is arrested for publishing a forged document 'proving' that a Minister had dealt with the Camorra to secure the liberation of Cirillo. The editor of the paper is forced to resign (March). Later, it emerged that the forged document had been produced by a collaborator of the state secret service. The publisher Mondadori enters the world of commercial television with Rete 4 and screens the American series *Dynasty*. Another publisher, Edilio Rusconi, launches the commercial channel Italia 1, which is soon acquired by Berlusconi.

	Politics and institutions	Economics and labour movement
1983	General election (26–7 June), with weakening of DC: DC 33 per cent, PCI 30 per cent, PSI 11 per cent. Toni Negri is a successful candidate for the Partito Radicale and is released from jail; he will soon flee to France. Five-party government led by Craxi (Aug.).	Growing public-sector deficit has become a chronic feature of the economy. Trade unions and Confindustria accept a government package including a 15 per cent reduction in the *scala mobile* (Jan.). Heavy losses on Milan stock market follow the election results (June).
1984	Final report by the inquiry committee on P2: the subversive organisation had links with the secret services and was involved in many criminal activities to destabilise institutions (May). Enrico Berlinguer dies while campaigning for the European election of 17 June: 2 million people attend his funeral. The emotional impact helps the PCI to overtake the DC at the election for the first (and last) time. Fifteen passengers are killed and 130 wounded when a bomb explodes in a railway carriage; 'organised crime' is held responsible (Dec.).	Further reduction in the *scala mobile* divides the trade unions and causes tension in Parliament (Feb.): opposition to the measures will be defeated at a referendum in 1985. Shops are closed to protest against the government's proposal for fiscal reform, aimed at speedier tax collection (Oct.). Although economic conditions improve, unemployment increases to 10 per cent of the labour force.
1985	An economist and CISL adviser, Ezio Tarantelli, is killed by the Red Brigades at Rome University (March). Constrasting response to the Pope's peroration in favour of the 'political unity of Catholics' (i.e. solid vote for DC) (Apr.). Double defeat of PCI: at local election (12–13 May) and at the referendum promoted by them to restore the efficacy of the *scala mobile* (10 June). Francesco Cossiga (DC) elected President of the Republic at first ballot (June). Friction between Italy and the United States over the Palestinian terrorists involved in the hi-jacking of the liner *Achille Lauro*, who are not handed over to the American authorities (Oct.). Clash between Craxi and members of the Superior Council of the Judiciary (Dec.).	Inflation is below 10 per cent for the first time since 1973, but the lira weakens and is devalued by 8 per cent (July). At 15 per cent the official bank rate is the lowest since 1979. Italians increasingly invest in shares, but a report reveals that 11 per cent of the population live in poverty.

1983

Cases of corruption among local government officials emerge in Turin and Genoa (March and June, respectively): the main culprits are PSI members. Curiosity, rather than sadness, is shown when Umberto di Savoia, the exiled last king of Italy, dies in Switzerland (Mar.). The list of Mafia victims lengthens: two *carabinieri* are killed in June, a judge and his escort in July. A demonstration in Sicily against the installation of NATO missiles is harshly quelled by the police (Sept.).

Twenty-four million Italians watch *Gone with the Wind* on television, shown by RAI 2 in two instalments (Apr.). Enzo Tortora, a popular television presenter, is arrested in front of television cameras and accused of drug dealing (June): his will become a controversial legal case, eventually proved groundless. The ordeal will contribute to Tortora's death in 1988. Commercial television channels are used for the first time for party propaganda during the election campaign. Montanelli's *Il Giornale Nuovo* becomes *Il Giornale*. Mural painting on shop shutters appear in Rome to glamorise their wares and services.

1984

New State–Church Concordat is signed, revising the 1929 Lateran Pacts (Jan.): Catholicism is no longer the 'state religion'; prolonged controversy follows over religious (i.e. Catholic) teaching in schools. After the former Mafia boss Tommaso Buscetta turns state's evidence, many *mafiosi* are arrested (Sept.). Chinese restaurants open up in main cities and will quickly spread throughout Italy.

Giuseppe Fava, editor of the Sicilian monthly *I Siciliani* and outspoken critic of the Mafia, is killed in Catania (Jan.). Books on the subject of the P2 are temporarily impounded at the request of fugitive P2 member Umberto Ortolani (Apr.). Craxi introduces a decree to enable Berlusconi's commercial television (now including also Rete 4, acquired from Mondadori) to challenge the RAI at national level (Oct.); the proposal first meets Parliament's opposition, but is eventually passed. Teletext services introduced. Carlo Rubbia shares the Nobel prize for physics. RAI 1's drama series *La piovra. Il potere della Mafia* (Octopus. The Power of the Mafia) attracts large audiences.

1985

Two Sicilian businessmen who refused to pay protection money are killed by the Mafia (Feb.). 2,600 Catholics (including bishops) convene at Loreto to discuss 'Christian reconciliation and society' (Apr.). Thirty-two Juventus football supporters are crushed to death when Liverpool fans stampede just before the start of the European Cup final at the Heysel stadium, Brussels (May). Two high-ranking police officers in Palermo are murdered by the Mafia (July and August). Widespread agitation by secondary school pupils ('Movement of '85') against poor facilities at school (Nov.). At the 'maxi-trial' of the Mafia due to start in Palermo early in 1986, forty-six out of fifty designated jurors decline to sit (Dec.). Sixteen people die and seventy-seven are wounded when Palestinian terrorists shoot at passengers at Rome airport (Dec.).

The Pope deplores the showing in Rome of Godard's 'blasphemous' *Je vous salue Marie* (Apr.); later in the year apparitions of the Virgin occur in various parts of Italy. Great success of the satirical television show *Quelli della notte* (Night Folk) conducted by Renzo Arbore on RAI 2 (Apr.–June). The compact disc enters the Italian music market. Up to 16 per cent of television time is used for commercial advertising in major channels. Writer Italo Calvino dies.

	Politics and institutions	Economics and labour movement
1986	Heated debate in Parliament on the teaching of Catholicism at school: the agreement reached with the Vatican is approved only through a vote of confidence (Jan.). The Radical Party leader Marco Pannella suggests the adoption of the British first-past-the-post electoral system (Jan.). The Red Brigades kill former mayor of Florence Lando Conti (Feb.). The government resigns after being outvoted by the opposition with the support of 'snipers', but a new government, also led by Craxi, is soon in place (Aug.). 'Gozzini law' extends cases in which freedom is granted to prisoners (Oct.) Craxi's brother-in-law, Paolo Pillitteri, becomes mayor of Milan (Dec.).	'Tax on health' is introduced (Feb.). Trade unions and Confindustria sign an agreement on the *scala mobile* and on short-term contracts of employment with the purpose of training workers (May). Fiat buys back Libyan stake in the company's shares (Sept.). Raul Gardini acquires a foothold in Montedison and begins his manoeuvres to gain control of the chemical giant (Oct.). Fiat purchases Alfa-Romeo from IRI, securing a virtual monopoly of Italian car-making (Nov.).
1987	The Court of Cassation confirms that insufficient evidence exists to incriminate anybody for the Piazza Fontana massacre of December 1969 (Jan.). Clash between DC and PSI forces Craxi to resign as Prime Minister (March); a caretaker government is installed until new election. Stefano Delle Chiaie, a notorious right-wing terrorist, is extradited to Italy after his arrest in Venezuela (March): he had been in hiding for seventeen years. Inconclusive general election (14–15 June): DC 34 per cent, PCI 27 per cent, PSI 14 per cent, followed by a new five-party coalition led by lacklustre Giovanni Goria (DC). Disaffection towards institutions is shown by the election of porn star Ilona Staller (a.k.a. 'Cicciolina') on the Radical list, and by the success of two candidates of the Lega Lombarda (Umberto Bossi is elected to the Senate).	Inflation is down to 4·2 per cent, but unemployment is at 12 per cent. Five-day strike by lorry drivers paralyses the country (Feb.). Heavy stock-market losses following the Wall Street crisis (Oct.). Independent militant unions, COBAS, are set up among teachers and train drivers; they agitate throughout the year.
1988	New government led by Ciriaco De Mita (DC) but based on the same coalition around the conflicting DC–PSI alliance (Apr.). An academic adviser of De Mita, Roberto Ruffilli, is killed by the fading Red Brigades (Apr.). Two corruption cases arise: they involve former ministers, leading politicians and high state officials; kickbacks were paid by companies to secure subcontracts in prison building and railway supplies (Feb./Nov.). The recourse to secret ballots in the Chamber of Deputies is restricted to reduce the cases of 'snipers' voting against their own parties' directives (Oct.).	Chemical giants ENI and Montedison merge into Enimont (May). Berlusconi's Fininvest acquires the department store chain Standa (July). The main trade unions organise a massive demonstration in Rome to demand fiscal justice (Nov.). 'Amato law' to encourage mergers in the banking sector.

1986

Widespread demonstrations in the South against the proposed condoning of illegal house building in exchange for the prompt payment of fines: better terms will thus be introduced (March). Michele Sindona dies in jail after drinking a poisoned espresso coffee (March). The Pope and the Chief Rabbi pray together in Rome's main synagogue (Apr.). Numerous suicides among conscripted soldiers, induced by bullying, prompt the setting up of a parliamentary commission of inquiry (June). Adulterated wine causes numerous deaths.

First exhibition held at Fiat-owned Palazzo Grassi in Venice: the subject is Futurism (May–Oct.). The head of Craxi's press office, Antonio Ghirelli, becomes director of the news programmes at Rai 2 (June). *L'Unità* includes a weekly satirical supplement (*Tango*). Radio Radicale is closed down: its 'say what you like' phone-in experiment results in a shower of insults and threats. The magazine *Classe* ('Class', subtitled 'the monthly of the ruling class') appears. Bertolucci's *Ultimo tango a Parigi* is screened after a fourteen-year ban. Nobel prize for biology awarded to Rita Levi Montalcini.

1987

The dispute over religious teaching in schools reopens (July). Several referendums are held on 8–9 November: one deprives judges of their immunity from civil liability; another prevents any development of nuclear power. The 'maxi-trial' of Mafia ends with heavy sentences for 340 defendants (Dec.). Italians resort more and more frequently to alternative medicine. An increasing number of young people die of drug abuse (440 against 262 in 1986).

The monitoring of television audiences is introduced (through Auditel). First television sex show, *Colpo grosso* (Jackpot), is broadcast on a commercial channel, mixing stripping and money prizes. Successful programme of political and social debate *Samarcanda* starts on RAI 3. *Corriere della Sera* and *La Repubblica* appear with glossy weekly supplements. Writer Primo Levi commits suicide.

1988

Teachers continue their action for contract renewal; new independent unions among schoolteachers are formed. The Mafia kills judge Antonio Saetta and former leader of the 'movement of 1968' Mauro Rostagno, who had used a local Sicilian television station to denounce drug trafficking by the Mafia (Sept.). Ecological awareness spreads, with initiatives to monitor pollution.

A phone-in RAI 3 programme on social and political issues (*Telefono giallo*) resurrects the mystery of the plane which crashed in June 1980 near Ustica: public opinion suspects a cover-up (May). Bertolucci's *L'ultimo imperatore* (The Last Emperor) receives nine Oscars. A new counter-information weekly, *Avvenimenti*, appears.

1989 The Craxi–De Mita duel brings the government down (May), while a power-sharing alliance is struck by Craxi, Andreotti and Arnaldo Forlani (DC Secretary General) – hence: CAF. The prominent anti-Mafia judge Giovanni Falcone is the target of a failed assassination attempt (June); then a series of anonymous letters try to discredit him (July). Andreotti leads a new five-party coalition (July). New Code of Criminal Procedure replaces the old inquisitorial system with an adversarial approach (Oct.). In the wake of the fall of Berlin Wall the PCI leader, Achille Occhetto, proposes to accelerate the reassessment of the party's basic philosophy; the desirability of a new name is also put forward (Nov.). Various regional parties combine to form the Lega Nord under Umberto Bossi's leadership (Dec.).

Iron and steel workers protest against the planned closure of the steelworks at Bagnoli, near Naples (Jan.). Widespread general strike against prescription charges imposed by the government (May). New agreement between the trade unions and Confindustria on the *scala mobile* (July). The branch of the Banca Nazionale del Lavoro based in Atlanta (Georgia) is involved in irregular operations with Iraq (Sept.).

1990 Continual friction between the President of the Republic and the Superior Council of the Judiciary. Lega Nord's first mass gathering at Pontida, near Bergamo (March); its declared aim is a federalist Italy; six months later the stated objective is the division of the country into three republics (Sept.). A new law gives greater administrative power to local authorities (June). Perplexing casual discovery in Milan of documents pertaining to Aldo Moro's captivity in the hands of the Red Brigades (Oct.). Andreotti discloses the existence in the past of the clandestine paramilitary organisation Gladio (Oct.). Longstanding tension within the DC in Palermo induces Leoluca Orlando to leave the party and establish the movement La Rete (The Network) (Nov.).

The lira joins the narrow band of EMS (Jan.). The liberalisation of capital movements within the EC enables Italians to open current accounts abroad and invest there without restrictions (May). Lega Nord sets up its own workers' union, later known as Sin.Pa. (May). Law regulating strikes in essential public services is passed (June). Redundancies at Fiat from September. Strikes and demonstrations by metal-engineering workers (Dec.). Public debt overtakes GDP.

1989

African immigrant workers are attacked at night near Naples, one is killed (Aug.): episodes of intolerance and violence against 'non-EEC' immigrants become increasingly frequent. In December a decree (later 'Martelli law') is issued to regulate immigration and encourage illegal immigrants to legalise their status. The estimated number of non-EEC foreigners in Italy is 1 million.

Mondadori publishing group acquires the weekly *L'Espresso* and the daily *La Repubblica* (Apr.). The Olivetti head, Carlo De Benedetti, and Berlusconi begin their battle to take over Mondadori. The PCI campaigns to prevent commercial breaks in films screened on television. A young Sicilian writer, Lara Cardella, attracts much media interest with her autobiographical novel *Volevo i pantaloni* (Good Girls Don't Wear Trousers). *Cuore* appears as a satirical supplement of *L'Unità*.

1990

To protest against the government proposals to reform higher education (through greater autonomy for the institutions and stronger links with private companies) students occupy universities (Jan.). Anti-racism demonstration in Rome (Jan.). Reform of primary education: traditional single-teacher classes to be replaced by multi-teacher classes (May). For the first time referendums are made invalid by the inadequate number of voters: the proponents wanted to restrict hunting and the use of pesticides in agriculture (June). New stricter drug law (June). Young judge Rosario Livatino is killed by the Mafia near Agrigento (Sept.): suggestions that he should be canonised will be made in 1995. Growing concern about Saturday-night disco revellers' car crashes.

A controversial law crystallises Italian television as a situation of a virtual duopoly: three state channels *v.* three Fininvest (i.e. Berlusconi)-controlled channels (Aug.). The Rizzoli–*Corriere della Sera* concern takes over three major publishing companies (ETAS, Bompiani, Sonzogno). Writer Alberto Moravia dies. *Cinema Paradiso* by young director Giuseppe Tornatore is awarded the Oscar for best foreign film.

	Politics and institutions	Economics and labour movement
1991	The last Congress of PCI gives way to the Democratic Party of the Left, PDS (Feb.). Discontent as the Court of Cassation acquits the Camorra defendants accused of planting the bomb in a train in December 1984 (March), and also exculpates the neo-Fascists who had been indicted for a similar offence in August 1974 (Apr.). The Republican Party leaves the government coalition (Apr.). Multi-preference voting is curtailed through a referendum, for the purpose of weakening the patronage system (June). First symbolic step by the Lega Nord to set up a 'Republic of the North' (June). In the second half of the year a restless President Cossiga contributes to undermine the institutions by his continual criticism and hints at radical changes. The hard left of the ex-PCI sets up a new party: Rifondazione Comunista (Dec.). Gianni Agnelli and Giulio Andreotti are nominated life senators. Eight new provinces are created.	Inflationary pressure forces an increase of the official bank rate (to 12 per cent) by the end of the year. Redundancies at Olivetti and Fiat (Jan.). New workers' representative bodies at plant level: Rappresentanze Sindacali Unitarie, RSU, are set up (March). Confidustria calls for the abolition of the *scala mobile*, but Parliament refuses to lend its support (May). New issues of state bonds throughout the year are oversubscribed. Large deficit in the balance of payments. Industrial production decreases by 2·1 per cent. 'Minimum tax' is introduced on the presumed income of the self-employed.
1992	Cossiga carries on haranguing judges and his own party until his slightly early and bitter retirement in April. A local Socialist administrator, Mario Chiesa, is arrested in Milan for corruption (Feb.): this will trigger the 'Tangentopoli' (Bribesville) scandal. Salvo Lima, Sicilian DC leader, Euro MP and close friend of Andreotti, is killed by the Mafia, to which it is rumoured he was close (March). General election (5–6 April): DC 30 per cent, PDS 16 per cent, PSI 14 per cent, Lega Nord 9 per cent. An increasing number of politicians and entrepreneurs are indicted for extortion and corruption by the Milan team of judges whose most prominent figure is the public prosecutor Antonio Di Pietro emerges. Two leading anti-Mafia judges, Giovanni Falcone and Paolo Borsellino, are killed by the Mafia in separate car-bomb explosions (May and July). Oscar Luigi Scalfaro (DC) is elected President of the Republic. The Socialist Giuliano Amato is the new Prime Minister in a four-party coalition: DC, PSI, PSDI, PLI (June). Craxi receives his first warrant from Milan's chief prosecutor but reacts defiantly (Dec.).	New Fiat 500 car launched (Jan.). Redundant workers at Olivetti are to be employed by public administration (Feb.). Deflationary package to reduce state budget deficit, which is weakening the lira (July). First step towards the abolition of the *scala mobile* by agreement between government, employers and workers' unions (July). The depreciation of the lira forces it to be devalued and to leave EMS (Sept.). Severe cuts in public spending follow (especially in health care and pensions). Steep increase in discount rate (to 15 per cent). Privatisation of public companies proceeds slowly, while the Ministry of State Holdings is abolished.

1991

Two hundred thousand pacifists demonstrate in Rome against the imminent Gulf War, in which Italy participates as NATO member (Jan.). Law on equal opportunities between sexes (March). Waves of Albanian immigrants reach the Apulian shores, some are forced back, others return voluntarily (March, June and Aug.). The Anti-Mafia Commission states that the Mafia is also strong around Milan (Apr.). Three immigrant workers die in a fire at a disused factory in Modena which also functions as a dormitory (July). A Sicilian entrepreneur, Libero Grassi, is killed by the Mafia because he refuses to pay protection money (Aug.). The Anti-Mafia Investigative Directorate (DIA) is set up (Dec.). Growing popularity of mobile telephones. Census: population over 57 million; the labour force is divided thus: 59 per cent services; 32 per cent industry; 9 per cent agriculture.

At the end of a long-drawn-out battle over the Mondadori group, De Benedetti acquires *L'Espresso* and *La Repubblica*; Berlusconi gets the book-publishing component and Fininvest thus becomes Europe's second biggest media conglomerate (Apr.). A thirteen-year-old singer-dancer-presenter, Ambra Angiolini, becomes a new icon for adolescents on an early afternoon Italia 1 programme. Italia 1 also starts to broadcast regular news. A new Milan-based daily, *L'Indipendente*, appears; it will soon reflect the views of the Lega Nord. The Communist weekly *Rinascita*, established in 1944 by Togliatti, closes down. In Claudio Pavone's book *Una guerra civile* (A Civil War) the conflict between Fascists and anti-Fascists in 1943–45 is soberly analysed: the book initiates a thoughtful debate on those tragic years.

1992

The number of woodland fires almost doubles to 22,000 cases, many caused wilfully by building speculators. Over 100 cases of xenophobic acts of violence against immigrants are recorded. Nazi skinheads appear in Rome (Nov.). Anti-racism demonstration in Rome (Nov.). New Highway Code introduced (Dec.). Highest ever number of conscientious objectors (23,000).

Regular news services start on Canale 5 (Jan.) and Rete 4 (June). The authorities ask Fininvest not to expand its advertising revenues (May). Popularity of political satire programme *Avanzi* (Leftovers) on RAI 3. The most widely read weekly is *Sorrisi e Canzoni* (Smiles and Songs), with over 2 million copies (owner: Berlusconi); second is *Famiglia Cristiana* (1 million). A new weekly gives voice to the right: *L'Italia settimanale*. Lowest ever cinema attendance.

	Politics and institutions	Economics and labour movement
1993	Craxi resigns as PSI Secretary General (Feb.), but the party is sinking as corruption charges pile up. Other parties (notably the DC) are also hit; several Ministers and party leaders have to resign. Naples is revealed as another centre of systematic political corruption (March). Andreotti is investigated for alleged links with the Mafia (March). New law on local elections, enabling mayors to be elected directly by voters, is passed (March). Referendum supports electoral reform to replace proportional representation, and under a new government (led by Carlo Azeglio Ciampi, ex-governor of the Bank of Italy) a law is passed to elect MPs on a mixed system (Aug.). Massive corruption in the health service is revealed (June–July). Local elections in spring and autumn show collapse of DC, PSI and their allies with strong performance of PDS while the right is split between MSI and Lega Nord. Shock and fear in conservative circles prompt Berlusconi to declare his readiness to enter politics (Nov.).	Permanent committee on privatisations is set up, to advise the government on the implementation of the privatisation plan (June). Many industrialists and business people involved in corruption cases are arrested; ENI's former president, Gabriele Cagliari, and the head of the Ferruzzi group, Raul Gardini, commit suicide, the former while in gaol (July). Fiat takes over Maserati (May). The *scala mobile* is abolished (July). The announcement of redundancies at ENI plant in Calabria provokes workers' rebellion (Sept.). Inflation down to 4 per cent: the lowest percentage since 1968; negative national saving for the first time since 1971, but the devaluation of the lira prompts export-led revival.
1994	DC is renamed Partito Popolare Italiano (PPI), but right-wing faction forces a split and sets up the Centro Cristiano Democratico (CCD). Berlusconi's party, Forza Italia, is formed out of Fininvest staff and co-opted professionals with moderate views; its social base is the network of football clubs throughout Italy supporting AC Milan. (The team is owned by Berlusconi.) General election (27–8 March) won by Berlusconi's Polo della Libertà (mainly consisting of Forza Italia, Lega Nord and MSI; the latter is renamed Alleanza Nazionale, AN). Berlusconi becomes Prime Minister in the first post-war government to include neo-Fascists (May). Despite an even better performance by the Polo in the European elections (12 June), Berlusconi's blunders and the growing tension between Forza Italia and Lega Nord weaken the government, leading to its fall (Dec.). Public prosecutor Di Pietro resigns from the judiciary (Dec.).	Privatisation decree (Jan.). The Bank of Italy discloses that 35 per cent of small companies are part of a bigger group (March). Cross-shareholdings result in 'privatised' leading banks (Credito Italiano and Banca Commerciale Italiana) being dependent upon the secretive Milanese merchant bank Mediobanca. Thirteen million Italians go on strike to protest against the government proposal for a deficit-cutting budget (Oct.); this is followed by a mass gathering and demonstration in Rome (Nov.).

1993

The most wanted Mafia boss, Salvatore Riina, is captured (Jan.). Bombs explode in Florence, Rome and Milan with numerous casualties: they are attributed to the Mafia (May, July). A parish priest, Giuseppe Puglisi, is killed by the Mafia in Palermo (Sept.). At the start of the school year many classes are closed down because of falling student numbers; students' demonstrations throughout the autumn. The Pope's encyclical *Veritatis Splendor* (The Glory of the Truth) reiterates the Catholic Church's opposition to promiscuity, homosexuality, premarital sex and abortion. The CEI expresses alarm at the increasing number of people who are attracted by religious sects and movements and drift away from Catholicism (Nov.). Teenagers (and older people) are immersed in karaoke music, cleverly exploited by the private television network.

Reform of RAI: the rules for the nomination of the executive board are changed, in an attempt to avoid direct political influence (June). Fininvest channels are catching up with RAI's audience. RAI cameras assiduously follow the trial on collusion and corruption centred around the financier Sergio Cusani (close to PSI) and the ENI Montedison affair (from Oct.). The Catholic weekly *Il Sabato* closes down. Law to enable museums to raise private funding. Federico Fellini dies.

1994

Law sets up the National Agency for the Protection of the Environment, ANPA (Jan.). Giuseppe Diana, a parish priest, is murdered near Naples by Camorra killers (March). Students and teachers demonstrate in Rome to defend state education (May). Karaoke 'happening' in a large Roman square, with exclusive broadcasting rights for Fininvest (Sept.). Clashes in Milan between the police and young people demonstrating against their eviction from the Leoncavallo Social Centre (Sept.). Widespread university student protests against increased tuition fees (Oct.). Huge gathering convened in Rome by the trade unions to protest against the proposed budget cuts. (Nov.).

Montanelli leaves *Il Giornale* over disagreement with Berlusconi (whose family owns the paper) and establishes the technically innovative *La Voce* (March). RAI's management board is replaced with officials more subservient to the new government (July). *Liberazione* is the new daily of Rifondazione Comunista. *Caffé* is a new multicultural quarterly. The rigid duopoly in television broadcasting (RAI/Fininvest) keeps Italy at the bottom of the technological league in this field, with only 1 per cent of viewers receiving satellite television, while no cable television is yet available (against 20 per cent and 10 per cent in the United Kingdom, respectively).

	Politics and institutions	Economics and labour movement
1995	Apolitical government of technocrats headed by Lamberto Dini is supported by the centre-left parties (Jan.). Alleanza Nazionale formally replaces MSI and distances itself from neo-Fascism – only a minority led by Pino Rauti disagrees and secedes (Jan.). A Catholic economist and ex-president of IRI, Romano Prodi, is groomed to lead a broad centre-left coalition under the symbol of an olive tree (Feb.). A split in the PPI follows: its ex-secretary, Rocco Buttiglione, creates a new party, Cristiani Democratici Uniti (CDU), formally established in July; CDU moves close to CCD and Freedom Alliance. At local election (23 April–7 May) the heterogeneous centre-left formations win over Berlusconi's Freedom Alliance: with 25 per cent of the vote the PDS is the largest party. First meeting of Lega Nord's self-styled 'Parliament of the North' in Mantua (June). AN leader Gianfranco Fini is invited to the PDS's national *Festa dell'Unità* held in Reggio Emilia. In Palermo the trial of Giulio Andreotti begins: he is accused of association with the Mafia (Sept.). The Senate cast a no-confidence vote in the Justice Minister, Filippo Mancuso, who is removed from the post after acrimonious exchanges (Oct.).	Government 'employment package' to extend and regulate part-time work and short-term contracts (Apr.). Olivetti plans to enter the mobile phone market (May). A minority share in Fininvest is sold to various buyers (July). Sweeping reforms of the pension system are approved by Parliament: pensions to be based on contributions paid rather than level of salary; sixty-five will gradually become the age of retirement (Aug.). Sharp fall of the lira when the German Finance Minister suggests that Italy will not make it to the European Monetary Union, EMU (Sept.). First public offering of ENI equities fails to attract investors (Nov.). Mini-boom in production: GDP increased by 3 per cent in the year, but public debt reaches 2,000 trillion and inflation leaps to 6 per cent. Unemployment in Naples nearly reaches 50 per cent of the work force.
1996	Prime Minister Dini resigns (Jan.). Law redefines sexual violence: it is a crime against the person, no longer against morality (Feb.). Failed attempts to instal a new government prompt the President to call for new elections. The Catholic Church expresses its neutrality in the forthcoming political confrontation (March). The 'Olive Tree' coalition, supported by Rifondazione Comunista, wins the election (21 Apr.). Romano Prodi becomes Prime Minister in the first left-of-centre government for fifty years (May). The PDS is the main partner and the first national party (21 per cent of the votes). The Lega Nord remains the leading party in Lombardy and the Veneto. In Sicily's local elections the centre-right Polo della Libertà wins (June). The Lega Nord organises a spectacular three-day rally across the Po valley, culminating in Venice with a declaration of Padania's independence (Sept.). Huge anti-government demonstration in Rome, organised by the Polo and kindled by anti-tax protest (Nov.). Antonio Di Pietro resigns from his post as Minister of Public Works as he is under investigation, again, for corruption (Nov.). New law on public funding of political parties on a voluntary basis is passed (Dec.).	Gianni Agnelli steps down from Fiat chairmanship; he is succeeded by Cesare Romiti (Feb.). 'Tax Day' protest by shopkeepers (March). The newly elected government pledges to take Italy into the EMU in January 1999: sacrifices will be necessary (May). Olivetti's financial crisis leads to collapse of its share price. Carlo De Benedetti steps down as head (Sept.). Agreement among government, workers' unions and employers' unions to introduce more 'flexibility' in contracts (Sept.). A second tranche of shares in ENI is successfully sold to private investors – 24 per cent of total value (Oct.). The lira re-enters the EMS (Nov.). Unione Generale del Lavoro, a new trade union confederation incorporating all right-wing unions, is set up (Nov.). Austerity budget to satisfy Maastricht criteria for the EMU, with tightening for over 60 trillion lire; it includes a 'tax for Europe', supposed to be eventually refunded to taxpayers (Dec.). Inflation down to 2·5 per cent, the lowest level since the 1960s, but growth slows down and unemployment stays above 12 per cent.

1995

Several statuettes of the Virgin are said to be 'crying'; in the most dramatic case a plaster model near Rome is said to have wept tears of blood (Feb.): a church is quickly renovated to host the sacred image. The Court of Cassation denies single people the right to adopt children (July). The maverick Marco Pannella is arrested while openly distributing hashish to the public to attract attention and generate debate on the liberalisation of soft drugs (Aug.). The Church elevates to official dogma the barring of women from the priesthood (Nov.). A Catholic organisation reveals that over 50 per cent of Italians think that the Church has too much power (Nov.).

Bill on the equitable distribution of media time for party propaganda (*par condicio*) is passed (Feb.). The weekly *L'Europeo* closes down (Feb.); so does Montanelli's *La Voce* (Apr.). Television advertising accounts for 54 per cent of all display advertising: the Fininvest network has the lion's share. The majority of Italians reject the referendums to curtail television advertising and to reduce Berlusconi's main television channels from three to one (June). A special law extends franchises to local radio and television (Nov.). Leading newspapers compete with one another by giving out books, videos and encyclopedias by instalments.

1996

First ever strike by professional footballers (Sunday 17 March). Over 110,000 applications for 1,400 vacancies as *carabinieri* (June). Huge outcry follows the military court's ruling that the former Nazi SS officer Erich Priebke is guilty of participating in mass murder of Italian civilians in 1944 but unpunishable because time-barred by the statute of limitations; the government steps in and Priebke is rearrested to be tried again (Aug.). Racist comments follow the election of a dark-skinned 'Miss Italy' (Sept.). Fernanda Contri joins the Constitutional Court as its first woman judge (Sept.). The same court declares that blasphemy is no longer a punishable crime (Sept.). A confidential telephone hot-line is set up to encourage people to inform on tax evaders (Dec.). The last psychiatric hospitals are closed down, to be replaced by appropriate hostels (Dec.). Nearly 6 million Italians possess a mobile phone. Almost 90 per cent of young people aged twenty to twenty-four – especially males – live with their parents. Debate rages over whether state-controlled brothels should be re-established (they were closed nearly thirty years earlier). Government and Church are opposed to them.

An inferno destroys the renowned La Fenice theatre in Venice (Jan.). The roof of the baroque cathedral of Noto, Sicily, collapses (March). Fininvest discontinues the use of party political broadcasts (March). Eugenio Scalfari retires as editor of *La Repubblica*, which he founded in 1976; he is replaced by Ezio Mauro (Apr.). Partial privatisation of Cinecittà (June). Public share offering of part of Berlusconi's television empire, Mediaset (July). RAI's new five-member board of directors appoints the heads of the three state-owned channels' news services (Aug.). ANSA and Reuter's sign an agreement to set up a common data bank (Aug.). First 'soap opera' series, *Un posto al sole* (A Place in the Sun), is produced by RAI (Oct.). The satirical weekly *Cuore* closes down (Nov.). The construction magnate Franco Caltagirone purchases *Il Messaggero* – he already owns the other major Roman daily, *Il Tempo*. Rosi's *La tregua* (The Truce), based on Primo Levi's book, is released. Marcello Mastroianni dies.

1997 Franco Marini is the new leader of the PPI (Jan.). Former Health Minister Francesco De Lorenzo is condemned to more than eight years' imprisonment: it is the first time that an ex-Minister has been found guilty of criminal association (March). The Albanian crisis and the arrival of many Albanians in Italy prompt the government to send troops to head an international military mission there, to provide humanitarian aid; on Good Friday an Albanian patrol boat loaded with refugees collides with Italian naval ship: some ninety people, mainly women and children, are drowned (March–Apr.). At local elections across the country both the Olive Tree government coalition and the Polo opposition perform well; the loser is the Lega Nord (Apr.). Government repeals the clause of the constitution prohibiting male descendants of the Savoy dynasty from settling in, or even entering, Italy (May). Stronger powers for the President are the main recommendation of the *Bicamerale*, the parliamentary commission entrusted with the revision of the constitution. (June–Nov.). Failure to attain the quorum (50 per cent of the electorate) invalidates seven referendums on various issues proposed by the Partito Radicale (15 June). Toni Negri returns from his Paris exile, begun in 1983, to complete his gaol sentence (July). Italy enters the Schengen agreement (no passport controls) in October, but is soon criticised because of its inability to prevent the landing of (mainly) Kurdish refugees on southern coasts. First general election in 'Padania' to draw up a constitution for independence (Oct.). Rifondazione Comunista forces Prodi's government into resignation over welfare cuts, but reaction from various quarters (including trade unions) makes the party reverse its decision – though, in return, Prodi is forced to agree in principle to the introduction of the thirty-five-hour week (Oct.). Di Pietro wins senatorial by-election as the candidate for the Olive Tree coalition (Nov.); new round of local elections give resounding victory to centre-left mayors in some main cities, including Rome (16 and 30 Nov.).

Mini-budget to raise further 15·5 trillion lire to meet the 'no more than 3 per cent of GDP' deficit required by the rules of EMU (Apr.); the target will be fully met by the end of the year (2·7 per cent). The Lega Nord's trade union, Sin.Pa., launches a campaign against the three big confederations (CGIL, CISL and UIL) and claims to have 50,000 members (Aug.). Telecom Italia is privatised through its merger with STET, already detached from IRI (Nov.). Changes in taxation system: fewer income-tax bands, new tax for companies and the self-employed to incorporate several old levies (Dec.). Official bank rate down to 5·5 per cent, the lowest for twenty-five years. Italy's membership of the EMU is virtually certain, although the ratio between gross public debt and GDP remains sky-high (over 120 per cent) and unemployment (over 12 per cent) is unrelenting.

1997

A million copies of St Mark's Gospel are distributed free to all Roman households, after it was revealed that only 10 per cent of the Romans go to Mass (Jan.). Bill is introduced to enable women to enlist in the army as volunteers (Jan.). National lottery to be drawn twice a week, after 126 years of Saturday-only draws (March). Eight self-styled 'fighters for the independence of Venice' seize the bell tower in St Mark's Square, but are soon dislodged and arrested (May). A law is passed to protect privacy (May). Gianni Versace is murdered in Miami (July). Five hundred troops are stationed in Naples to fight the Camorra (July). Erich Priebke is sentenced to fifteen years at his retrial; ten years are condoned in what is mainly a symbolic sentence (July). Court of Cassation ruling: sexual harassment is not a crime if there is love (Aug.). For the first time the number of registered non-EU immigrants is above 1 million (Aug.). Earthquake in mountain districts of central Italy: eleven dead, thousands homeless; extensive damage to the Church of St Francis in Assisi (Sept.); tremors continue for months. Bob Dylan sings in front of the Pope and 300,000 youths in Bologna (Sept.). Padre Pio close to canonisation. Controversy over a cancer treatment created by an elderly medical researcher, Luigi Di Bella: the authorities are sceptical but people support Di Bella in a bitter anti-establishment attitude (Dec.).

La Padania, the first daily of the Lega Nord, is launched and distributed as far 'south' as Tuscany (Jan.). Almost 90 per cent of television sets are tuned to the final evening of the San Remo song festival (Feb.). The Milan daily *Il Giorno* is purchased by the same industrial group which owns Florence's *La Nazione* and Bologna's *Il Resto del Carlino* (Feb.). The weekly *L'Espresso* and the daily *La Repubblica*, both belonging to De Benedetti's publishing group, are combined under the same editorial board (March). The Socialist daily *Avanti!* is resurrected (March). Palermo's Teatro Massimo reopens after twenty-three years (May). The main political parties launch their web sites on the Internet, while the Vatican decides to broadcast through satellite television (Aug.). A maxi-screen is set up at Rome's Olympic Stadium in a live broadcast of the Fiorentina–Roma football match, played in Florence: 50,000 spectators attend in Rome against 40,000 in Florence (a disappointing result: 0–0) (Oct.). RAI-TV (RAISAT) starts Open University-style degree course (Oct.). The eighth and last volume of Renzo De Felice's biography of Mussolini appears posthumously and incomplete. Nobel prize for literature is awarded to playright Dario Fo.

1998 Anti-American outrage when a US aeroplane brings down a cable car in the Dolomites, apparently as a result of recklessness by the crew, killing twenty people (Feb.). 'Bassanini decree' is introduced to reduce red tape and to set civil service on a private-contract footing, making transfers and sackings easier (Feb.). PDS congress in Florence: the party is renamed Democratici di Sinistra (DS, left-wing Democrats) and the hammer-and-sickle motif disappears altogether from the party logo (Feb.). Irene Pivetti joins the small centre party led by Foreign Secretary Lamberto Dini, Rinnovamento Italiano (March). Animated discussion in Parliament, with scuffles, after controversial football match (Juventus–Inter-Milan, 1–0) (Apr.). Mario Segni leads a cross-party group to campaign for a referendum on a straight first-past-the-post election system (April). Public dismay at the virtually unanimous vote in Parliament to introduce a semi-automatic form of party financing out of voters' income tax (Apr.). Success of the centre-right in local elections (May–June). *Bicamerale* commission collapses because of Berlusconi's *volte-face* (June). Bill to grant Italians abroad the right to vote in parliamentary elections where they live fails again because of MPs' absenteeism (July). Ex-President Cossiga sets up a moderate party, Unione Democratica per la Repubblica (UDR), which attracts members of CCD and CDU – the latter disbands (July). Berlusconi is convicted – for the third time in twelve months – of bribery, but he is spared gaol; he claims to be the victim of a plot by 'red judges' (July). Prodi government resigns after losing parliamentary confidence by a single vote, following Rifondazione Comunista's withdrawal of support; this brings about a split of Rifondazione Comunista, enabling Massimo D'Alema to resurrect a centre-left coalition, supported also by UDR. D'Alema is the first ex-PCI leader to become Prime Minister: six of the twenty-five Ministries, including the Home Office, are handed over to women (Oct.). Wrangling between Italy and Turkey over the refused extradition of Abdullah Ocalan, the head of Turkey's outlawed Kurdish Workers' Party, who had been arrested in Rome (Nov.). At local elections the turn-out is, for the first time, only around 50 per cent (Nov.–Dec.).

Law on part-time and temporary employment enables international agencies (including Manpower and Kelly) to open offices in Italy (Jan.). Two new companies are allowed to enter the telephone market, thus breaking the monopoly of Telecom Italia (Feb.). Shopkeeping regulations thoroughly simplified, with more freedom on opening hours and abolition of highly differentiated licences, which are to be replaced by two general licences, for food and non-food shops (March). Under pressure from Europe's looming single currency, Istituto Bancario San Paolo, a retail bank, and Istituto Mobiliare Italiano, a financial conglomerate, merge and become, as San Paolo-IMI, the largest Italian bank (Apr.). Great achievement is claimed when Italy is admitted to Europe's single-currency club, EMU (May). First tranche of state holding company and energy conglomerate, ENI, offered to private investors (June). The last of the big state-owned commercial banks, Banca Nazionale del Lavoro, is privatised (Nov.). New 'social pact' between government, unions and employers, setting up a framework for a differentiated wage system aiming at increasing employment – especially in the South (Dec.). Official bank rate down to 3 per cent, in line with other EMU countries (Dec.). Inflation in 1998 down to 1·8 per cent, but unemployment up to near 13 per cent – although 37 per cent of work force are reckoned to be active in 'black economy'.

1998

Pope John Paul II's journey to Castro's Cuba is hailed as yet another victory of Catholicism over Communism (Jan.). Di Bella's saga continues, with heated debates eagerly followed on television (Jan.) – official tests will later prove that his 'cure' is ineffective. First multi-million-pound jackpot prize win with *SuperEnalotto* (a new lottery established in December 1997) (Jan.) 1998 will be punctuated by bigger and bigger wins, inducing more and more people to try their luck, but also calling upon various saints (St Anthony is their favourite) to give them a hand. New law to regulate immigration, with quotas decided year by year and more severe rules on illegal immigrants (March), but throughout the year illegal immigration continues unabated. AC Lazio is the first Italian football team to be quoted on the stock exchange; players are involved in television commercials to induce their supporters to purchase shares (Apr.). First killing in the Vatican City: a young Swiss guard shoots dead his newly appointed commander and the latter's wife, and commits suicide; it is officially explained as a case of insanity (May). Law on conscientious objection is approved, with twenty years' delay on the first proposal (June). Climber cyclist Marco Pantani wins both the *Giro d'Italia* and the *Tour de France* (June–July). Pope's apostolic letter stamps out any dissent and reiterates the Church's opposition to women priests (July). Fines on streetwalkers and/or kerb-crawlers are introduced in many northern cities in an attempt to 'clean pavements' of prostitution (Aug.). Cardinal Michele Giordano of Naples is investigated for crimes which include conspiracy in loan sharking, extortion, embezzlement, and aiding and abetting money laundering (Aug.). Pope's encyclical *Fides et Ratio* (Faith and Reason) calls on Catholics to be open to insights coming from outside Christianity (Oct.). Student demonstrations against government proposal to give financial aid to private – i.e. Catholic – schools (Nov.). Patrizia Reggiani is sentenced to twenty-nine years in prison for orchestrating the killing of her ex-husband and one-time fashion tycoon Maurizio Gucci (Nov.). There are more mobile phones in Italy than in any other European country. Italians aged over sixty-four are more numerous than those aged under sixteen and the gap is increasing as the birth rate is, allegedly, the lowest in the world.

The newspapers' marketing battle continues: the *Corriere della Sera* offers 'Visual Guides to Europe'; *La Repubblica* responds with instalments of E. H. Gombrich's *Story of Art* and an encyclopedia (Jan.). New Vatican satellite broadcasting station, SAT 2000, prepares the world for the Jubilee in 2000 (Feb.). Following the latest changes of PDS, *L'Unità* becomes an independent daily (Feb.). Fifteen million people watch San Remo festival on television (Feb.). An eight-member authority is established to watch over television programmes; members are nominated by Parliament (March). Preventive censorship of films is abolished, following protests at the censoring for blasphemy of *Totò che visse due volte* (Totò Who Lived Twice), by Daniele Ciprì and Franco Maresco (March). Pope preaches via Internet on the Vatican web site (Aug.). Nineteen-seventies pop singer and icon Lucio Battisti dies; main television evening news devoted to the event, while news of an earthquake in Calabria (two dead) comes second (Sept.). News Corp Europe is set up by Rupert Murdoch, to co-ordinate his interests on the Continent: it is to be based in Milan, chaired by Letizia Moratti (a former head of RAI) (Nov.). *La vita è bella* (Life is Beautiful), a romantic comedy about the Holocaust by the maverick actor-director Roberto Benigni, is showered with prizes, including two at the Cannes and Jerusalem Film Festivals. Danilo Dolci, the now forgotten 'Gandhi of Sicily' (*The Economist*) dies.

Bibliography

General

Anania, F., and G. Tosatti, *L'amico americano. Politiche e strutture per la propaganda in Italia nella prima metà del Novecento* (Rome, Biblink, 2000).

Arduini, L. (ed.), *Guida agli archivi audiovisivi in Italia* (Rome, Presidenza del Consiglio dei Ministri, Dipartimento per l'Informazione e l'Editoria, 1995).

Arnold, W. V., *The Illusion of Victory. Fascist Propaganda and the Second World War* (Berne, Peter Lang, 1998).

Ballini, P. L. (ed.), *1946–1948. Repubblica, Costituente, Costituzione* (Florence, Polistampa, 1998).

Ballini, P. L., and M. Ridolfi (eds), *Le compagne elettorali nella storia d'Italia* (Milan, Bruno Mondadori, 2001).

Benedetti, A., *Gli archivi delle immagini. Fototeche, cineteche e videoteche in Italia* (Genoa, Erga, 2000).

Bogani, L., and C. Maffei, *Comunicare un partito politico* (Milan, IPSOA, 1990).

Bosworth, R. B., and P. Dogliani (eds), *Italian Fascism. History, Memory, Representation* (Basingstoke, Macmillan, 1999).

Bussolati, S., and A. Perin, *Piccolo manuale di comunicazione ad uso dell'elettore e del politico* (Milan, Zelig, 1999).

Calvi, G., and G. Minoia, *Gli scomunicanti. La pubblicità politica com'è e come potrebbe essere* (Milan, Lupetti, 1990).

Cannistraro, V., *La fabbrica del consenso. Fascismo e mass media*, preface by R. De Felice (Bari and Rome, Laterza, 1975).

Cazzullo, A., *I ragazzi che volevano fare la rivoluzione, 1968–78. Storia di Lotta Continua* (Milan, Mondadori, 1998), chapters 3 and 4.

Ceci, S., *Produrre comunicazione politica*, preface by Rosy Bindi (Modena, M & B Publishing, 1996).

Cole, R. (ed.), *Propaganda in Twentieth Century War and Politics. An Annotated Bibliography* (Lanham, MD, Scarecrow, 1997).

Cole, R. (ed.), *International Encyclopedia of Propaganda* (London, Fitzroy Dearborn, 1998).

Costantino, S., and S. Scimeca, *Visibilità e democrazia. La comunicazione politica nell'Italia degli anni Novanta* (Palermo, Promopress, 1994).

De Rosa, A., *Fare politica in Internet* (Milan, Apogeo, 2000).

Echaurren, P., and C. Salaris, *Controcultura in Italia, 1967–77. Viaggio nell'underground* (Turin, Bollati Boringhieri, 1999).

Ellwood, D. W., 'The Limits of Americanisation and the Emergence of an Alternative Model: the Marshall Plan in Emilia-Romagna', in M. Kipping and O. Bjarnar (eds), *The Americanisation of European Business* (London, Routledge, 1998), pp. 149–69.

Falabrino, G., *I comunisti mangiano i bambini. La storia dello slogan politico* (Milan, Vallardi, 1994).
Flores, M. (ed.), *Il 'Quaderno dell'attivista'. Ideologia, organizzazione e propaganda nel PCI degli Anni Cinquanta* (Milan, Mazzotta, 1976).
Gobbo, M., *Propaganda politica nell'ordinamento costituzionale. Esperienza italiana e profili comparatistici* (Padua, CEDAM, 1997).
Gourevitch, J. P., *L'Image en politique. De Luther à Internet et de l'affiche au clip* (Paris, Hachette, 1998).
Gruber, K., *L'avanguardia inaudita. Comunicazione e strategia nei movimenti degli anni Settanta* (Genoa, Costa & Nolan, 1997).
Gundle, S., 'Italy', in D. Butler and A. Ranney (eds), *Electioneering. A Comparative Study of Continuity and Change* (Oxford, Clarendon Press, 1992), pp. 173–201.
Gundle, S., *Between Hollywood and Moscow. The Italian Communists and the Challenge of Mass Culture, 1943–1991* (Durham, NC, Duke University Press, 2000).
Gundle, S., and L. Riall (eds), *Charisma and the Cult of Personality in Modern Italy*, special issue of *Modern Italy*, 3:2 (1998).
Hixson, W. L., *Parting the Curtain. Propaganda, Culture and the Cold War, 1945–61* (Basingstoke, Macmillan, 1997).
Jackall, R. (ed.), *Propaganda* (Basingstoke, Macmillan, 1995).
Jacobelli, J. (ed.), *La comunicazione politica in Italia* (Bari and Rome, Laterza, 1989).
Jowett, G. S., and V. O'Donnell, *Propaganda and Persuasion* (London, Sage, 1999, 3rd edn).
Lanchester, F., 'Propaganda', in F. Santoro-Passarelli (ed.), *Enciclopedia del diritto* (Milan, Giuffrè), vol. XXXVII (1988), pp. 126–47.
Leone, P. A., 'Per una filosofia dei linguaggi della politica' (degree thesis, University of Rome – La Sapienza, 1983–84).
Leone, P. A., *Lo spettacolo della politica*, foreword by T. De Mauro (Cosenza, Bios, 1987). Shortened and revised version of the thesis.
Leso, E., 'Alle origini della parola "propaganda"', *Quaderni costituzionali*, 16:3 (1996), pp. 337–43.
Lutzemberger, M. G., and S. Bernardi, *Cultura, comunicazioni di massa, lotta di classe* (Rome, Savelli, 1976).
Masi, D. M., with F. Maffioli, *Come 'vendere' un partito. Ovvero la teoria della comunicazione politica* (Milan, Lupetti, 1989).
Michie, D., *The Invisible Persuaders* (London, Bantam, 1998).
Mignemi, A. (ed.), *Propaganda politica e mezzi di comunicazione di massa tra Fascismo e democrazia* (Novara, Istituto Storico della Resistenza, and Turin, Gruppo Abele, 1995).
Pozzi, E., and S. Rattazzi, *Farsi eleggere. La campagna elettorale nella Seconda Repubblica* (Milan, Il Sole–24 Ore, 1994).
Pozzo, N., and P. Russo, 'Berlusconi and Other Matters: the Era of "Football Politics"', *Journal of Modern Italian Studies*, 5:3 (2000), pp. 348–70.
Pratkanis, A. R., and E. Aronson, *Age of Propaganda. The Everyday Use and Abuse of Persuasion* (Basingstoke, Freeman, 1999, 2nd edn).
Propaganda (periodical of the Press and Propaganda Department of the PCI, published from 1947 to 1977 to provide information and directives to activists).
Pujas, V., 'The Funding of Political Parties and Control of the Media: Another Italian Anomaly?', in M. F. Gilbert and G. Pasquino (eds), *Italian Politics. The Faltering Transition* (Oxford, Berghahn, 2000), pp. 139–52.
Pustetto, M. B., *Il manuale del candidato politico* (Milan, Bridge, 1991).
Rawnsley, G. D. (ed.), *Cold War Propaganda in the 1950s* (Basingstoke, Macmillan, 1998).
Romano, A. A., 'Propaganda elettorale', in B. Paradisi (ed.), *Enciclopedia giuridica* (Rome, Istituto della Enciclopedia Italiana), vol. XXIV (1991), pp. 1–4.
Shaw, T., *Propaganda and the Cold War* (London, Addison Wesley Longman, forthcoming).
Spagnolo, C., *La stabilizzazione incompiuta. Il Piano Marshall in Italia (1947–1952)* (Rome, Carocci, 2001).

Taithe, B., and T. Thornton (eds), *Propaganda, Political Rhetoric and Identity, 1300–2000* (Stroud, Sutton, 1999).
Taylor, P. M., *Munitions of the Mind. A History of Propaganda from the Ancient World to the Present Era* (Manchester University Press, 1995).
Teodori, M., *Soldi e partiti. Quanto costa la democrazia in Italia?* (Florence, Ponte alle Grazie, 1999).
Thomson, O., *Easily Led. A History of Propaganda* (Stroud, Sutton, 1999).
Tinacci Mannelli, G., and E. Cheli, *L'immagine del potere. Comportamenti, atteggiamenti e strategie d'immagine dei leader politici italiani* (Milan, Franco Angeli, 1986).
Various authors, *Gli archivi dei partiti politici* (Rome, Ministero per i beni culturali e ambientali, 1996).

Official information

Arena, G. (ed.), *La comunicazione di interesse generale* (Bologna, Il Mulino, 1995).
Associazione Comunicazione Pubblica, *La comunicazione pubblica in Italia* (Milan, Editrice Bibliografica, 1995).
Bentivegna, S. (ed.), *Comunicare politica nel sistema dei media* (Genoa, Costa & Nolan, 1996).
Cortesi Gay, A., *L'informazione, un diritto del cittadino* (Milan, Franco Angeli, 1994).
Faccioli, F., 'Diritto all'informazione e comunicazione pubblica. Come parlano le istituzioni', *Sociologia e ricerca sociale*, 44 (1994), pp. 8–24.
Ferrarotti, F., *La perfezione del nulla* (Bari and Rome, Laterza, 1997).
Fiorentini, G., *Il marketing dello Stato* (Milan, Editrice Bibliografica, 1995).
Fioritto, A., *Manuale di stile. Strumenti per semplificare il linguaggio delle amministrazioni pubbliche* (Bologna, Il Mulino, 1997).
Frabotta, M. A., 'Numero verde e dintorni. Lo sportello al cittadino', in Various authors, *Gli sviluppi della comunicazione istituzionale nel 1992–93* (Rome, Presidenza del Consiglio dei Ministri, Dipartimento Informazione ed Editoria, 1994), pp. 175–7.
Frabotta, M. A., 'Una ricerca sulla storia dell'informazione istituzionale. Il Centro Documentazione della Presidenza del Consiglio, 1951–57', *Le carte e la storia*, 1:2 (1995), pp. 110–12.
Frabotta, M. A., *Il governo filma l'Italia* (Rome, Bulzoni, 2001).
Gadotti, G., *Pubblicità sociale* (Milan, Franco Angeli, 1993).
Ghidiglia, A., 'Molti ciak all'Archivio di Stato', *Idee e sistemi*, 10–11 (1955), pp. 16–19.
Mancini, P., *Manuale di comunicazione pubblica* (Bari and Rome, Laterza, 1996).
Ortoleva, P., *Mediastorie* (Parma, Pratiche, 1995).
Paolone, F., 'Il cinema come strumento pubblicistico', *Saggi e studi di pubblicistica* (1955), pp. 113–30.
Rolando, S., *Il principe e la parola. Dalla propaganda di Stato alla comunicazione istituzionale* (Milan, Comunità, 1987).
Rolando, S., *Lo stato della pubblicità di Stato* (Milan, Il Sole–24 Ore, 1990).
Rolando, S., *Comunicazione pubblica* (Milan, Il Sole–24 Ore, 1992).
Rolando, S., *Un paese spiegabile. La comunicazione pubblica negli anni del cambiamento, delle autonomie territoriali, e delle reti* (Milan, Etas Libri, 1998).
Rovinetti, A., *Comunicazione pubblica. Istruzioni per l'uso* (Bologna, Calderini, 1994).
Sainati, A. (ed.), *La Settimana INCOM. Cinegiornali e informazione regli anni '50* (Turin, Lindau, 2001).
Spantigati, F., *La comunicazione nella Seconda Repubblica* (Rome, Bulzoni, 1995).
Various authors, *La promozione della cultura italiana all'estero* (Rome, Presidenza del Consiglio dei Ministri, Dipartimento Informazione ed Editoria, 1992).
Various authors, *Professione comunicatore* (Milan, Etas Libri, 1991).
Various authors, *Gli sviluppi della comunicazione istituzionale nel 1990* (Rome, Presidenza del Consiglio dei Ministri, Dipartimento Informazione ed Editoria, 1991).

Various authors, *Gli sviluppi della comunicazione istituzionale nel 1991* (Rome, Presidenza del Consiglio dei Ministri, Dipartimento Informazione ed Editoria, 1992).
Various authors, *Gli sviluppi della comunicazione istituzionale nel 1992–93* (Rome, Presidenza del Consiglio dei Ministri, Dipartimento Informazione ed Editoria, 1994).
Vignudelli, A. (ed.), *La comunicazione pubblica* (Rimini, Maggioli, 1992).
Visani, P., *Forze armate, mass media ed opinione pubblica nell'Italia attuale* (Rome, Edizioni Stato Maggiore Marina Militare, 1994).
Zuanelli, E. (ed.), *Il diritto all'informazione in Italia* (Rome, Presidenza del Consiglio dei Ministri, Dipartimento Informazione ed Editoria, n.d. [1990]).
See also 'Cinema', below.

Italian immigration into Britain

Bernabei, A., *Esuli ed emigrati nel Regno Unito, 1920–40* (Milan, Mursia, 1997).
Bottignolo, B., *Without a Bell Tower. A Study of Italian Immigrants in South West England* (Rome, Centro Studi Emigrazione, 1985).
Carigue, P., and R. W. Firth, 'Kinship organisation of Italianates in London', in R. W. Firth (ed.), *Two Studies of Kinship in London* (London, Athlone Press, 1956), pp. 67–93.
Cavallaro, R., *Storie senza storia. Indagine sull'emigrazione calabrese in Gran Bretagna* (Rome, Centro Studi Emigrazione, 1981).
Chistolini, S., *Donne italo-scozzesi. Tradizione e cambiamento* (Rome, Centro Studi Emigrazione, 1986).
Colpi, T., *The Italian Factor. The Italian Community in Great Britain* (Edinburgh and London, Mainstream, 1991).
Colpi, T., *Italians Forward. A Visual History of the Italian Community in Great Britain* (Edinburgh and London, Mainstream, 1991).
Dutto, M. (ed.), *The Italians in Scotland. Their Language and Culture* (Edinburgh, Consolato Generale d'Italia, 1986).
Gillman, P., and L. Gillman, *'Collar the Lot!' How Britain Interned and Expelled its Wartime Refugees* (London, Melbourne and New York, Quartet, 1980).
Holmes, C., *John Bull's Island. Immigration and British Society, 1871–1971* (Basingstoke, Macmillan, 1988).
Hughes, C., *Lime, Lemon and Sarsaparilla. The Italian Community in South Wales, 1881–1945* (Bridgend, Seren Books, 1991).
King, R., 'Work and Residence Patterns of Italian Immigrants in Great Britain', *International Migration*, 16:2 (1978), pp. 74–82.
Macdonald, J. S., and L. D. Macdonald, *The Invisible Immigrants* (London, Runnymede Industrial Unit, 1972).
Marin, U., *Italiani in Gran Bretagna* (Rome, Centro Studi Emigrazione, 1975).
Palmer, R., 'The Italians: Patterns of Migration to London', in J. Watson (ed.), *Between Two Cultures. Migrants and Minorities in Britain* (Oxford, Blackwell, 1978), pp. 242–68.
Sponza, L., *Italian Immigrants in Nineteenth Century Britain. Realities and Images* (Leicester University Press, 1988).
Sponza, L., 'La présence italienne en Grande Bretagne à travers ses journaux (1890–1990)', in M. Dreyfus and P. Milza (eds), *L'intégration italienne en France* (Brussels, Complexe, 1995), pp. 389–97.
Sponza, L., *Divided Loyalties. Italians in Britain during the Second World War* (Berne, Peter Lang, 2000).
Sponza, L., and A. Tosi (eds), *A Century of Italian Emigration to Britain, 1880–1980s. Five Essays*, supplement to *The Italianist*, 13 (1993).
Tassello, G., 'Esiste una politica italiana verso gli italiani all'estero?' *Studi Emigrazione*, 34 (1997), pp. 487–99.
Tosi, A., *Immigration and Bilingual Education* (Oxford, Pergamon Press, 1984).

Cinema

Argentieri, M., *La censura nel cinema italiano* (Rome, Editori Riuniti, 1974).

Argentieri, M., *L'occhio del regime. Informazione e propagada nel cinema del Fascismo* (Florence, Vallecchi, 1979).

Argentieri, M., *Il cinema in guerra. Arte, comunicazione e propaganda in Italia, 1940–44* (Rome, Editori Riuniti, 1998).

Aristarco, G., *Sciolti dal giuramento. Il dibattito critico-ideologico sul cinema negli anni Cinquanta* (Bari, Dedalo, 1981).

Aristarco, G., *Il cinema fascista. Il prima e il dopo* (Bari, Dedalo, 1996).

Armes, R., *Patterns of Realism* (New York, Garland, 1986).

Bernagozzi, G. (ed.), *Il cinema corto. Il documentario nella vita italiana, dagli anni Quaranta agli anni Ottanta* (Florence, La Casa Usher, 1980).

Bernagozzi, G., *Il mito dell'immagine. L'immagine del mito* (Bologna, CLUEB, 1983).

Bernagozzi, G. (ed.), *Dentro la storia. Cinema, Resistenza, pace* (Bologna, Patron, 1984).

Bignardi, I., *Memorie estorte a uno smemorato. Vita di Gillo Pontecorvo* (Milan, Feltrinelli, 1999).

Brunetta, G. P., *Storia del cinema italiano* (Rome, Editori Riuniti, 1993, 2nd edn), 4 vols.

Brunetta, G. P., 'Divismo, misticismo e spettacolo della politica', in G. P. Brunetta, *Storia del cinema mondiale*. Vol. 1/1. *L'Europa. Miti, luoghi, divi* (Turin, Einaudi, 1999), pp. 527–59.

Brunetta, G. P., *et al.*, *La cinepresa e la storia. Fascismo, antifascismo, guerra e Resistenza nel cinema italiano* (Milan, Bruno Mondadori, 1985).

Brunetta, G. P., *et al.*, *Cinema, storia e Resistenza, 1944–85* (Milan, Franco Angeli, 1987).

Cardillo, M., *Il Duce in moviola. Politica e divismo nei cinegiornali LUCE* (Bari, Dedalo, 1983).

Cigognetti, L., L. Servetti and P. Sorlin (eds), *La storia con le immagini* (Bologna, Istituto Regionale 'Ferruccio Parri' per la Storia del Movimento di Liberazione e dell'Età Contemporanea, 1999).

Ciusa, F., *Memoria presente. Fascismo, antifascismo e Resistenza nel documentario italiano* (Comune di Reggio Emilia – Istituto per la Storia della Resistenza, 1994).

Cocchi, F., 'Il tempo dei cinegiornali annullato dalla televisione', *Problemi dell'informazione*, 18:3 (1993), pp. 341–50.

Ellwood, D. W., 'The 1948 Elections: a Cold War Propaganda Battle', *Historical Journal of Film, Radio and Television*, 13:1 (1993), pp. 19–34.

Ellwood, D. W., 'The USIS–Trieste collection at the Archivio centrale dello Stato, Rome', *Historical Journal of Film, Radio and Television*, 19:3 (1999), pp. 399–404.

Forgacs, D., 'The Making and Unmaking of Neorealism in Italy', in N. Hewitt (ed.), *The Culture of the Reconstruction. European Literature, Thought and Film, 1945–50* (London, Macmillan, 1989), pp. 51–87.

Frabotta, M. A., 'Il cammino dei cinegiornali', *Cinema & cinema*, 67 (1993), pp. 53–74.

Gili, J. A., *Fascisme et Résistance dans le cinéma italien, 1922–68* (Paris, Lettres Modernes, 1970).

Gili, J. A., *Stato fascista e cinematografia* (Rome, Bulzoni, 1981).

Gili, J. A., *Le cinéma italien à l'ombre des faisceaux, 1922–45* (Perpignan, Institut Jean Vigo, 1990).

Gobetti, P. (ed.), *Memoria, mito, storia. La parola ai registi. 37 interviste* (Turin, Archivio Nazionale Cinematografico della Resistenza, 1994).

Gori, G. M., *Patria diva. La storia d'Italia nei film del Ventennio* (Florence, La Casa Usher, 1988).

Iaccio, P., *Cinema e storia. Percorsi, immagini, testimonianze* (Naples, Liguori, 1998).

Lasi, P., 'Cinema e politica culturale del PCI, 1945–84' (degree thesis, University of Bologna, 1983–84). Copy lodged at the Biblioteca del Cinema 'Umberto Barbaro', Rome.

Levi, P., 'Contestazione, politica cinematografica e sinistra storica', *Cinemasessanta*, 181–2 (1988), pp. 22–36.

Liggeri, D., *Mani di forbice. La censura cinematografica in Italia* (Alessandria, Falsopiano, 1997).

Lizzani, C., *Attraverso il Novecento* (Turin, Lindau, 1998).

Marcus, M., *Italian Film in the Light of Neorealism* (Princeton University Press, 1986).

Micciché, L. (ed.), *Studi su dodici sguardi d'autore in cortometraggio* (Turin, Lindau–Associazione Philip Morris, 1995).

Michalczyk, J. J., *The Italian Political Film-makers* (London and Toronto, Associated University Presses, 1986).
Mignemi, A., 'La lanterna magica: le filmine elettorali del PCI', in A. Mignemi (ed.), *Propaganda politica e mezzi di comunicazione di massa tra Fascismo e democrazia* (Turin, Gruppo Abele, and Novara, Istituto Storico della Resistenza, 1995), pp. 385–9.
Morbidelli, M., 'Il PCI e la cinematografia, 1944–56' (degree thesis, University of Rome – La Sapienza, 1992–93), copy lodged at the Biblioteca del Cinema 'Umberto Barbaro', Rome.
Moscati, I. (ed.), *1969: un anno bomba. Quando il cinema scese in piazza* (Venice, Marsilio, 1998).
Olivetti, P. (ed.), *Cinema e Resistenza in Italia e in Europa* (Rome, Archivio Nazionale Cinematografico della Resistenza, 1997).
Overbey, D. (ed.), *Springtime in Italy. A Reader on Neorealism* (London, Talisman, 1978).
Reeves, N., *The Power of Film Propaganda. Myth or Reality?* (London, Cassell, 1999).
Renzi, R. (ed.), *Il cinema dei dittatori. Mussolini, Stalin, Hitler* (Bologna, Grafis, 1992).
Ricci, R. (foreword), *La Resistenza nel cinema italiano, 1945–95* (Vercelli, Istituto Storico per la Resistenza, 1995).
Scarfò, G., *Cinema e Mezzogiorno* (Cosenza, Periferia, 1999).
Sorlin, P., *Italian National Cinema, 1896–1996* (London, Routledge, 1996).
Sorlin, P., 'Guerra e Resistenza', in G. P. Brunetta (ed.), *Storia del cinema mondiale.* Vol. 1/1. *L'Europa. Miti, luoghi, divi* (Turin, Einaudi, 1999), pp. 699–720.
Stewart, J., *Italian Film. A Who's Who* (Jefferson, NC, MacFarland, 1994).
Tinazzi, G. (ed.), *Il cinema italiano degli anni Cinquanta* (Venice, Marsilio, 1979).
Tranfaglia, N. (ed.), *Il 1948 in Italia. La storia e i film* (Florence, La Nuova Italia, 1991), with videocassette.
Vitti, A., *Giuseppe De Santis and Postwar Italian Cinema* (Toronto University Press, 1996).
Wagstaff, C., 'Il cinema europeo e la Resistenza', in L. Cigognetti, L. Servetti and P. Sorlin (eds), *L'immagine della Resistenza in Europa, 1945–1960. Letteratura, cinema, arti figurative* (Bologna, Il Nove, 1996), pp. 39–61.

Myths, symbols and rituals

Achten, U., M. Reichelt and R. Schultz, *Mein Vaterland ist International. Internationale Illustrierte Geschichte des 1. Mai, 1886 bis Heute* (Oberhausen, Asso Verlag, 1986).
Agulhon, M., *Marianne into Battle. Republican Imagery and Symbolism in France, 1789–1880* (Cambridge University Press, 1981).
Amendola, E. P., and M. Ferrara, *È la festa. Quarant'anni con 'L'Unità'* (Rome, Editori Riuniti, 1984).
Arvidsson, C., and L. R. Blomqvist (eds), *Symbols of Power. The Aesthetics of Political Legitimation in the Soviet Union and Eastern Europe* (Stockholm, Almqvist & Wiksell, 1987).
Belardelli, G., *et al.*, *Miti e storia dell'Italia unita* (Bologna, Il Mulino, 1999).
Berezin, M., *Making the Fascist Self. Culture, Politics and Identity in Fascist Italy* (Ithaca, NY, Cornell University Press, 1997).
Cannadine, D. (ed.), *Rituals of Royalty* (Cambridge University Press, 1987).
Capomazza, T., and M. Ombra, *Otto Marzo. Storie, miti, riti della giornata internazionale della donna* (Rome, Cooperativa Utopia, 1987).
Corbin, A., N. Gérome and D. Tartakowsky, *Les Usages politiques des fêtes au XIX–XX siècles* (Paris, Publications de la Sorbonne, 1994).
Donno, G. C. (ed.), *Storie e immagini del Primo Maggio. Problemi di storiografia italiana ed internazionale* (Manduria, Bari, and Rome, Lacaita, 1990).
Drescher, S., D. Sabean and A. Sharlin (eds), *Political Symbolism in Modern Europe. Essays in Honor of George L. Mosse* (New Brunswick, NJ, Transaction Books, 1982).
Falasca-Zamponi, S., *Fascist Spectacle. The Aesthetics of Power in Mussolini's Italy* (Berkeley and Los Angeles, CA, University of California Press, 1996).
Favre, P., *La Manifestation* (Paris, Presses de Sciences Politiques, 1990).

Ferrara, F., 'The Feste dell'Unità', in Various authors, *Formations of Nations and People* (London, Routledge, 1984), pp. 122–30.
Figes, O., and B. Kolonitskii, *Interpreting the Russian Revolution. The Language and Symbols of 1917* (New Haven, CT, Yale University Press, 1999).
Gavelli, M., *Colorare la Patria. Tricolore e formazione della coscienza nazionale, 1797–1914* (Florence, Vallecchi, 1996).
Gentile, E., *The Sacralization of Politics in Fascist Italy* (Cambridge, MA, Harvard University Press, 1996).
Ghirardo, D., *Building New Communities. New Deal America and Fascist Italy* (Princeton University Press, 1989).
Gianaria, F., and A. Mittone, *Giudici e telecamere. Il processo come spettacolo* (Turin, Einaudi, 1994).
Hobsbawm, E., and T. Ranger (eds), *The Invention of Tradition* (Cambridge University Press, 1983).
Isnenghi, M. (ed.), *I luoghi della memoria.* 3 vols: *Simboli e miti dell'Italia unita; Strutture ed eventi dell'Italia unita; Personaggi e date dell'Italia unita* (Bari and Rome, Laterza, 1996–97).
Kertzer, D. I., 'Politics and Ritual. The Communist "Festa" in Italy', *Anthropological Quarterly*, 47 (1974), pp. 374–89.
Kertzer, D. I., *Ritual, Politics and Power* (New Haven, CT, Yale University Press, 1988).
Kertzer, D. I., *Comrades and Christians. Religion and Political Struggle in Communist Italy* (Prospect Heights, IL, Waveland Press, 1990, 2nd edn).
Kertzer, D. I., *Politics and Symbols. The Italian Communist Party and the Fall of Communism* (New Haven, CT, Yale University Press, 1996).
Kubik, J., *The Power of Symbols against the Symbols of Power. The Rise of Solidarity and the Fall of State Socialism in Poland* (University Park, PA, Pennsylvania State University Press, 1994).
Leonesi, L., *Così cominciò la Festa dell'Unità* (Milan, Synergon, 1992).
Mach, Z., *Symbols, Conflict and Identity. Essays in Political Anthropology* (Albany, NY, State University of New York Press, 1993).
Marchetti, A., 'Un teatro troppo serio. Appunti di analisi del corteo operaio e dello slogan politico di strada', *Classe*, 21 (1982), pp. 235–63.
Mosse, G. L., *The Nationalization of the Masses. Political Symbolism and Mass Movements in Germany from the Napoleonic Wars through the Third Reich* (New York, Howard Fertig, 1975).
Mosse, G. L., *Masses and Man. Nationalist and Fascist Perceptions of Reality* (New York, Howard Fertig, 1980).
Mosse, G. L., *Fallen Soldiers. Reshaping the Memory of the World Wars* (Oxford University Press, 1991).
Ozouf, M., *Festivals and the French Revolution* (Cambridge, MA, Harvard University Press, 1988).
Pivato, S., *Il nome e la storia. Onomastica e religioni politiche nell'Italia contemporanea* (Bologna, Il Mulino, 1999).
Pratt, J. C., *A Study of Social Change and Conservative Ideologies in Tuscany* (Göttingen, Herodot, 1986).
Quazza, G., *et al.*, *Un'altra Italia nelle bandiere dei lavoratori. Simboli e cultura dall'Unità d'Italia all'avvento del Fascismo* (Turin, Centro Studi Piero Gobetti and Istituto Storico della Resistenza in Piemonte, 1982).
Quinn, M., *The Swastika. Constructing the Symbol* (London, Routledge, 1994).
Regalia, I., *Lotte operaie e sindacato. Il ciclo 1968–72 in Italia* (Bologna, Il Mulino, 1978), pp. 179–236. On workers' meetings.
Rivière, C., *Les liturgies politiques* (Paris, Presses Universitaires de France, 1988).
Straniero, M., *I comunisti. Una religione dell'aldiquà* (Milan, Mondadori, 1997).
Strong, R., *Art and Power. Renaissance Festivals, 1450–1650* (Woodbridge, Boydell, 1984).
Tarozzi, F., and G. Vecchio (eds), *Gli italiani e il tricolore* (Bologna, Il Mulino, 1999).
Tobia, B., *Una patria per gli italiani. Spazi, itinerari, monumenti nell'Italia unita, 1870–1990* (Bari and Rome, Laterza, 1991).

Tobia, B., *L'altare della Patria* (Bologna, Il Mulino, 1998).
Vaudagna, M. (ed.), *L'estetica della politica. Europa e America negli Anni Trenta* (Bari and Rome, Laterza, 1989).
Ventrone, A., *La cittadinanza repubblicana. Forma-partito e identità nazionale alle origini della democrazia italiana (1943–48)* (Bologna, Il Mulino, 1996).
Wilentz, S. (ed.), *Rites of Power. Symbolism, Ritual and Politics Since the Middle Ages* (Philadelphia, PA, University of Pennsylvania Press, 1985).

The press

Albertini, L., *I giorni di un liberale. Diari 1907–1923*, ed. L. Monzali (Bologna, Il Mulino, 2000).
Arfé, G., *Storia dell'"Avanti!'* (Rome and Milan, Mondo Operaio–Edizioni dell'Avanti!, 1977).
Bechelloni, G., 'The Journalist as a Political Client in Italy', in A. Smith (ed.), *Newspapers and Democracy* (Cambridge, MA, MIT Press, 1980), pp. 228–43.
Bechelloni, G., and M. Buonanno, 'Un quotidiano di partito sui generis: *L'Unità, Problemi dell'informazione*, 6:2 (1981), pp. 219–42.
Bechelloni, G., and P. Murialdi, 'Autoritratto del "Manifesto". Conversazione con Rossanda e Pintor', *Problemi dell'informazione*, 6:1 (1981), pp. 9–43.
Bettiza, E., *Via Solferino* (Milan, Mondadori, 1999). On the *Corriere della Sera.*
Buonanno, M., L. Griffo, M. Mafai and F. Nirenstein, 'Le giornaliste in Italia: molta visibilità, poco potere', *Problemi dell'informazione*, 18:3 (1993), pp. 271–95.
Cardini, A., *Tempi di ferro. 'Il Mondo' e l'Italia del dopoguerra* (Bologna, Il Mulino, 1992).
Carocci, G. (ed.), *'Il Mondo'. Antologia di una rivista scomoda* (Rome, Editori Riuniti, 1997).
Casella, M., *Giornali studenteschi in Italia prima del '68. Il Centro Italiano Stampa Studentesca, 1954–68* (Lecce, Argo, 1999).
Castronovo, V., and N. Tranfaglia (eds), *Storia della stampa italiana* (Bari and Rome, Laterza, 1976–94), 7 vols.
Ceccarini, L., 'Chiesa, comunicazione e politica nella realtà locale. I settimanali delle diocesi italiane' (doctoral thesis, University of Urbino, 1998).
Ceccarini, L., 'Comunicazione, "opinion leader" e chiesa locale. I settimanali diocesani e i loro direttori nella transizione politica italiana', *Polis*, 13:2 (1999), pp. 273–94.
Di Meglio, U., 'Il ruolo della stampa nella nascita del MSI', *Rivista di studi corporativi*, 11:5–6 (1981), pp. 219–36.
Emiliani, V., *Gli anni del 'Giorno'. Il quotidiano del Signor Mattei* (Milan, Baldini & Castoldi, 1998).
Ferrigolo, A., 'L'avventura editoriale del "Manifesto"', *Problemi dell'informazione*, 6:1 (1981), pp. 45–69.
Grandinetti, M., *I quotidiani in Italia, 1943–91* (Milan, Franco Angeli, 1992).
Isnenghi, M., 'Il grande opinionista da Albertini a Bocca', in S. Soldani and G. Turi (eds), *Fare gli italiani. Scuola e cultura nell'Italia contemporanea*. Vol. 2. *Una società di massa* (Bologna, Il Mulino, 1993), pp. 251–85.
Lumley, R., *Italian Journalism. A Critical Anthology* (Manchester University Press, 1996).
Mancini, P., 'The Public Sphere and the Use of News in a "Coalition" System of Government', in P. Dahlgren and C. Sparks (eds), *Communication and Citizenship. Journalism and the Public Sphere in the New Media Age* (London, Routledge, 1991), pp. 137–54.
Mangano, A., *Le riviste degli anni settanta. Gruppi, movimenti e conflitti sociali* (Bolsena [Viterbo], Massari, with Centro di documentazione di Pistoia, 1998).
Mangano, A., and A. Schina, *Le culture del Sessantotto. Gli anni sessanta, le riviste, il movimento* (Bolsena [Viterbo], Massari, with Centro di documentazione di Pistoia, 1998).
Mazzanti, A., *L'obiettività giornalistica: un ideale maltrattato* (Naples, Liguori, 1991).
Melega, G., *L'anima m'hai venduto* (Milan, Feltrinelli, 1998). On *Il Giorno.*
Murialdi, P., *La stampa italiana dalla Liberazione alla crisi di fine secolo* (Bari and Rome, Laterza, 1998).
Murialdi, P., *Storia del giornalismo italiano* (Bologna, Il Mulino, 2000).

Ottone, P., *Preghiera o bordello. Storia del giornalismo italiano. I protagonisti, i fatti e i retroscena, gli scandali e i segreti* (Milan, Longanesi, 1996).
Paolozzi, L., and A. Leiss, *Voci dal quotidiano. 'L'Unità' da Ingrao a Veltroni* (Milan, Baldini & Castoldi, 1996).
Paolozzi, L., and A. Leiss, *Il giornale in rosso. Chi la incastrato 'L'Unità?* (Rome, Editore Riuniti, 2001).
Parnell, A., 'The Press in Post-war Italy', in A. M. Brassloff and W. Brassloff (eds), *European Insights. Post-war Politics, Society, Culture* (Amsterdam, North-Holland, 1991), pp. 197–213.
Parpaglioni, E., *C'era una volta 'Paese Sera'*, preface by P. Ottone (Rome, Editori Riuniti, 1998).
Pinelli, F., and M. Mariano, *Europa e Stati Uniti secondo il 'New York Times'. La corrispondenza estera di Anne O'Hare McCormick, 1920–1954* (Turin, Otto, 2000).
Porter, W. E., *The Italian Journalist* (Ann Arbor, MI, University of Michigan Press, 1983).
Ridolfi, M., 'L'Avanti!', in M. Isnenghi (ed.), *I luoghi della memoria. Simboli e miti dell'Italia unita* (Bari and Rome, Laterza, 1996), pp. 317–28.
Ruffolo, S., *Vestire i giornali* (Turin, Gutemberg, 1987).
Salvetti, P., *La stampa comunista. Da Gramsci a Togliatti* (Milan, Guanda, 1975).
Scalfari, E., *La sera andavamo in via Veneto. Storia di un gruppo, dal 'Mondo' alla 'Repubblica'* (Milan, Mondadori, 1986).
Various authors, *Storia del giornalismo italiano. Dalle origini ai giorni nostri* (Turin, UTET, 1998).

Graphics

'Anonymous from Romagna', *Amarcord del PCI. Le tessere del Partito dal 1921 al 1991* (Ravenna, Il Monogramma, 1991).
Audino, D. G., and G. Vittori (eds), *Via il regime della forchetta. Autobiografia del PCI nei primi anni '50 attraverso i manifesti elettorali* (Rome, Savelli, 1976).
Baeri, E., and A. Buttafuoco (eds), *Riguardarsi. Manifesti del movimento politico delle donne in Italia* (Siena, Protagon Editori Toscani, 1997).
Bonnell, V. E., *Iconography of Power. Soviet Political Posters under Lenin and Stalin* (Berkeley, CA, California University Press, 1998).
Branzaglia, C., and G. Sinni (eds), *Partiti! Guida alla grafica politica della Seconda Repubblica* (Florence, Tosca, 1994).
Buton, P., and L. Gervereau, *Le Couteau entre les dents. Soixante ans d'affiches communistes et anticommunistes* (Paris, Chêne, 1989).
Camuffo, G. (ed.), *Grafici italiani* (Venice, Canal & Stamperia, 1997).
Carucci, P., F. Dolci and M. Missori (eds), *Volantini antifascisti nelle carte della Pubblica Sicurezza, 1926–43* (Rome, Ministero per i Beni culturali e ambientali, 1995).
Cheles, L., '"Dolce stil nero"? Images of Women in the Graphic Propaganda of the Italian Neo-Fascist Party', in Z. G. Barański and S. W. Vinall (eds), *Women and Italy. Essays on Gender, Culture and History* (Basingstoke, Macmillan, 1991), pp. 64–94.
Cheles, L., '"Nostalgia dell'Avvenire". The Propaganda of the Italian Far Right between Tradition and Innovation', in L. Cheles, R. G. Ferguson and M. Vaughan (eds), *The Far Right in Western and Eastern Europe* (London, Longman, 1995), pp. 64–94.
Cheles, L., *Grafica Utile. L'affiche d'utilité publique en Italie, 1975–1996* (Université de Lyon, 1997).
Codareschi, S., *Tutti tesserati!* (Milan, Triangulus, 1984).
Colonnetti, A., and A. Rauch (eds), *Epoca! 1945–1999. Manifesti in Italia tra vecchio secolo e nuovo millennio* (Siena, Protagon Editori Toscani, 1999).
Dané, C. (ed.), *Parole e immagini della Democrazia Cristiana in quarant'anni di manifesti della SPES* (Rome, Broadcasting & Background, 1985).
Di Nallo, E., *Indiani in città* (Bologna, Cappelli, 1977).
Donadei, M., *L'Italia delle cartoline, 1945–74* (Cuneo, L'Arciere, 1979).
Echaurren, P., *Volantini italiani. Frammenti storici del XX secolo* (Bertiolo [Udine], AAA Edizioni, 1997).
Echaurren, P., *Parole ribelli. I fogli del Movimento del '77* (Rome, Stampa Alternativa, 1997).

Einandi, L., 'La simbologia dei partiti politici italiani dal 1919 al 1994', *Mezzosecolo*, II (1994–96), pp. 254–306.
Ellenius, A. (ed.), *Iconography, Propaganda and Legitimation* (Oxford University Press, 1998).
Fagone, V., G. Ginex and T. Sparagni, *Muri ai pittori. Pittura murale e decorazione in Italia, 1930–50* (Milan, Mazzotta, 1999).
Fioravanti, F., L. Passarelli and S. Sfligiotti (eds), *La grafica in Italia* (Milan, Leonardo Arte, 1998).
Fresnault-Deruelle, P., *L'image placardée. Pragmatique et rhétorique de l'affiche* (Paris, Nathan, 1997).
Ganapini, L., and G. Ginex (eds), *Cipputi Communication. Immagini, forme, voci per i lavoratori* (Milan, Mazzotta, 1997).
Garelli, C., *Il linguaggio murale* (Milan, Garzanti, 1978).
Gervereau, L., *Terroriser, manipuler, convaincre! Histoire mondiale de l'affiche politique* (Paris, Somogy, 1996).
Guillemin, A., *La Politique s'affiche. Les affiches de la politique* (Paris, Didier Erudition, 1991).
Kampfer, F., *Der rote Keil. Das politische Plakat. Theorie und Geschichte* (Berlin, Gebr. Mann, 1985).
Kunzle, D., *Che Guevara. Icon, Myth and Message* (Los Angeles, UCLA Fowler Museum of Cultural History, with the Center for the Study of Political Graphics, 1997).
Mancini, P., *Il manifesto politico. Per una semiologia del consenso* (Turin, ERI, 1980).
McQuiston, L., *Graphic Agitation. Social and Political Graphics since the Sixties* (London, Phaidon, 1993).
McQuiston, L., *Suffragettes to She-devils. Women's Liberation and Beyond*, foreword by G. Greer (London, Phaidon, 1997).
Memmi, D., *Du Récit en politique. L'affiche électorale italienne* (Paris, Presses de la Fondation Nationale des Sciences Politiques, 1986).
Novelli, E., *C'era una volta il PCI. Autobiografia di un partito attraverso le immagini della sua propaganda* (Rome, Editori Riuniti, 2000).
Ottaviano, C., and P. Soddu (eds), *La politica sui muri. I manifesti politici dell'Italia Repubblicana, 1946–1992* (Turin, Rosenberg & Sellier, 2000).
Philippe, R., *Political Graphics. Art as a Weapon* (Oxford, Phaidon, 1982).
Piazzo, S., and C. Malaguti, *La Lega Nord attraverso i manifesti* (Milan, Editoriale Nord, 1996).
Quintavalle, A. C., and G. Bianchino, *L'immagine UIL dalla Costituzione al 10° congresso nazionale* (Rome, Edizioni Lavoro Italiano, n.d. [1990]).
Romano, L., and P. Scabello (eds), *C'era una volta la DC. Breve storia del periodo degasperiano attraverso i manifesti elettorali della Democrazia Cristiana* (Rome, Savelli, 1975).
Rubanu, P., and G. Fistrale, *Murales politici della Sardegna* (Bolsena [Viterbo], Massari, 1998).
Sartogo, A., *Le donne al muro. L'immagine femminile nel manifesto politico italiano, 1945–77*, introduction by U. Eco (Rome, Savelli, 1977).
Spadolini, G., *Tessere repubblicane. Un percorso in immagini* (Ravenna, Circolo Culturale C. Cattaneo, 1981).
Steiner, A., *Il manifesto politico*, ed. L. Steiner (Rome, Editori Riuniti, 1978).
Sturani, E., *Otto milioni di cartoline per il Duce* (Turin, Centro Scientifico Editore, 1995).
Timmer, M. (ed.), *The Power of the Poster* (London, Victoria and Albert Museum, 1998).
Various authors, *Le immagini del Socialismo. Comunicazione politica e propaganda del PSI dalle origini agli anni Ottanta*, preface by B. Craxi (Rome, PSI, n.d. [1983]).
Veltroni, W., *et al.*, *Bruno Magno. Dal PCI al PDS. I manifesti e altre immagini 1971–91* (Rome, Salemi and Editori Riuniti, 1991).
Zeri, F., *I francobolli italiani. Grafica e ideologia dalle origini al 1948* (Genoa, Il Melangolo, 1993).

Radio and television

Bentivegna, S., *Comunicare politica nel sistema dei media* (Genoa, Costa & Nolan, 1996).
Bentivegna, S., *Al voto con i media. Le campagne elettorali nell'età della TV* (Rome, Nuova Italia Scientifica, 1997).

Bettinelli, E., *Par condicio. Regole, opinioni, fatti* (Turin, Einaudi, 1995).

Calabrese, O., *Come nella boxe. Lo spettacolo della politica in TV* (Bari and Rome, Laterza, 1998).

Dorfles, P., *Carosello* (Bologna, Il Mulino, 1998).

Eco, U., 'Independent Radio in Italy', in *Apocalypse Postponed*, ed. R. Lumley (London, British Film Institute, 1994), pp. 167–76. Essay originally published in 1978, in Italian.

Ferretti, C., U. Broccoli and B. Scaramucci, *Mamma RAI. Storia e storie del servizio pubblico radiotelevisivo* (Florence, Le Monnier, 1997).

Grasso, A., *Storia della televisione italiana* (Milan, Garzanti, 2000).

Gundle, S., 'RAI and Fininvest in the Year of Berlusconi', in R. S. Katz and P. Ignazi (eds), *Italian Politics. The Year of the Tycoon* (London, Westview Press, 1995), pp. 195–218.

Gundle, S., and N. O'Sullivan, 'The Mass Media and the Political Crisis', in S. Gundle and S. Parker (eds), *The New Italian Republic. From the Fall of the Berlin Wall to Berlusconi* (London, Routledge, 1996), pp. 206–20.

Isola, G., *L'ha scritto la radio. Storia e testi della radio durante il Fascismo, 1924–44* (Milan, Bruno Mondadori, 1998).

Livolsi, M., and U. Volli (eds), *La comunicazione politica tra la Prima e Seconda Repubblica* (Milan, Franco Angeli, 1995).

Livolsi, M., and U. Volli (eds), *Il televoto. La campagna elettorale [1996] in televisione* (Milan, Franco Angeli, 1997).

Mancini, P. (ed.), *Persone sulla scena. La campagna elettorale 1992 in televisione* (Turin, Nuova ERI, 1993).

Mancini, P., and G. Mazzoleni (eds), *I media scendono in campo. Le elezioni politiche del 1994 in televisione* (Turin, Nuova ERI, 1995).

Marletti, C., 'Parties and Mass Communication: the RAI Controversy', in R. Nanetti, R. Leonardi, and P. Corbetta (eds), *Italian Politics: a Review* (London, Pinter, 1988), pp. 167–78.

Mazzoleni, G., 'The Role of Private TV Stations in Italian Elections', in D. L. Paletz (ed.), *Political Communication Research* (Norwood, NJ, Ablex, 1987), pp. 75–87.

Mazzoleni, G., 'Media Logic and Party Logic in Campaign Coverage: the Italian General Election of 1983', *European Journal of Communication*, 2:2 (1987), pp. 81–103.

Mazzoleni, G., 'Emergence of the Candidate and Political Marketing: Television and Election Campaigns in Italy in the 1980s', *Political Communication and Persuasion*, 8 (1991), pp. 201–12.

Mazzoleni, G., *Comunicazione e potere. Mass media e politica in Italia* (Naples, Liguori, 1992).

Mazzoleni, G., 'Italy', in J. Mitchell and J. G. Blumler (eds), *Television and the Viewer Interest* (London, Libbey, 1994), pp. 123–34.

Mazzoleni, G., 'The RAI: Restructuring and Reform', in C. Mershon and G. Pasquino (eds), *Italian Politics. Ending of the First Republic* (Oxford, Westview Press, 1995), pp. 151–63.

Mazzoleni, G., 'Towards a "Videocracy"? Italian Political Communication at a Turning Point', *European Journal of Communication*, 10:3 (1995), pp. 291–319.

Mazzoleni, G., 'The Italian Broadcasting System between Politics and the Market', *Journal of Modern Italian Studies* 5:2 (2000), pp. 157–68.

Mazzoleni, G., and C. S. Roper, 'The Representation of Italian Candidates and Parties in Television Advertising', in L. Lee Kaid and C. Holtz-Bacha (eds), *Political Advertising in Western Democracies* (London, Sage, 1995), pp. 89–108.

Monteleone, F., *Storia della radio e della televisione in Italia* (Venice, Marsilio, 1999), 2nd edn.

Monticone, A., *Il Fascismo al microfono* (Rome, Studium, 1978).

Morcellini, M. (ed.), *Elezioni di TV. Televisione e pubblico nella campagna elettorale '94* (Genoa, Costa & Nolan, 1995).

Novelli, E., *Dalla TV di partito al partito della TV. Televisione e politica in Italia, 1960–95* (Florence, La Nuova Italia, 1995).

Ortoleva, P., *Televisione privata e società in Italia, 1975–95* (Florence, Giunti, 1995).

Papa, A., *Storia politica della radio in Italia* (Naples, Guida, 1978), 2 vols.

Pezzini, I., *Lo spot elettorale. La vicenda italiana di una forma comunicazione politica* (with an essay by P. Guarino) (Rome, Meltemi, 2001).

Ricolfi, L., 'Politics and the Mass Media in Italy', *West European Politics*, 20:1 (1997), special isue on *Crisis and Transition in Italian Politics*, pp. 135–56.

Sani, G., and P. Segatti, 'Programmi, media e opinione pubblica', in S. Bartolini and R. D'Alimonte (eds), *Maggioritario per caso. Le elezioni politiche del 1996* (Bologna, Il Mulino, 1997), pp. 11–34.

Savarese, R., *L'americanizzazione della politica in Italia. TV ed elezioni negli anni Novanta* (Milan, Franco Angeli, 1996).

Segatti, P., 'I programmi elettorali e il ruolo dei mass media', in S. Bartolini and R. D'Alimonte (eds), *Maggioritario ma non troppo. Le elezioni politiche del 1994* (Bologna, Il Mulino, 1995), pp. 147–73.

Statham, P., 'Berlusconi, the Media and the New Right in Italy', *Harvard International Journal of Press/Politics*, 1 (1996), pp. 87–105.

Statham, P., 'Television News and the Public Sphere in Italy. Conflicts at the Media/Politics Interface', *European Journal of Communication*, 11 (1996), pp. 511–56.

Tinacci Mannelli, G., *Il telecomizio. Aspetti semiologici e sociologici del messaggio politico televisivo* (Urbino, Montefeltro, 1971).

Torchia, F., *La videopolitica nelle campagne elettorali* (Vibo Valentia, Mapograf, 1997).

Language

Alfieri, G., and A. Cassola (eds), *La lingua d'Italia. Usi pubblici e istituzionali* (Rome, Bulzoni, 1998).

Baldelli, I., 'Il linguaggio neologico politico', in M. Medici and D. Proietti (eds), *Il linguaggio del giornalismo* (Milan, Mursia, 1992), pp. 9–24.

Bonsaver, G., 'Dialect, Culture and Politics: the Northern League(s)', *Journal of the Institute of Romance Studies. Supplement 1* (1996), special issue on *Italian Dialects and Literature*, eds E. Tandello and D. Zancani, pp. 97–107.

Cianflone, G., and D. Scafoglio, *Fascismo sui muri. Le scritte murali neofasciste di Napoli* (Naples, Guida, 1976).

Cortelazzo, M. A., 'Note sulla lingua dei volantini', *Versus*, 10 (1975), pp. 57–77.

Cortelazzo, M. A., 'Il guitto Marco. Appunti per un ritratto linguistico di Pannella', *Belfagor*, 36 (1981), pp. 711–20.

Dardano, M., 'Il sottocodice politico', in *id.*, *Il linguaggio dei giornali italiani* (Bari and Rome, Laterza, 1981), pp. 141–84.

De Mauro, T., 'Il glotto-kit di Berlusconi', *La Repubblica*, 17 May 1994.

Desideri, P., *Il potere della parola. Il linguaggio politico di Bettino Craxi* (Venice, Marsilio, 1987).

Desideri, P., 'Il discorso politico. Profilo linguistico di Moro, Craxi, Pannella', *Italia contemporanea*, No. 174 (1989), pp. 5–15.

Desideri, P., 'L'italiano della Lega', *Italiano e oltre*, 8 (1993), pp. 281–95; 9 (1994), pp. 22–8.

Eco, U., 'Il laboratorio in piazza', in *id.*, *Sette anni di desiderio* (Milan, Bompiani, 1983), pp. 64–7. On the language of the Movimento del '77.

Eco, U., 'Political Language: the Use and Abuse of Rhetoric', in *Apocalypse Postponed*, ed. R. Lumley (London, British Film Institute, 1994), pp. 103–18. Article originally published in 1973, in Italian.

Euchner, W., F. Rigotti and P. Schiera (eds), *Il potere delle immagini. La metafora politica in prospettiva storica. Die Macht der Vorstellungen. Die politische Metapher in historischer Perspektive* (Bologna, Il Mulino, and Berlin, Duncker & Humblot, 1993).

Feldman, O., and C. De Landtsheer (eds), *Politically Speaking. A Worldwide Examination of Language Used in the Public Sphere* (New York, Praeger, 1998).

Flores d'Arcais, P., and G. Mughini, *Il piccolo sinistrese illustrato*, with preface by G. Bocca and cartoons by Altan (Milan, SugarCo, 1977).

Forconi, A., 'Tutte le parole del Presidente [Cossiga]', *Italiano e oltre*, 7 (1992), pp. 97–104.

Forconi, A., *Parola da Cavaliere. Il linguaggio di Berlusconi dal tempo del potere al tempo dell'opposizione* (Rome, Editori Riuniti, 1997).

Gualdo, R., 'Osservazioni sul linguaggio dei Verdi', in *S[ocietà] L[inguistica] I[taliana]*, 11 (1985), pp. 258–72.
Leso, E., 'Momenti di storia del linguaggio politico', in L. Serianni and P. Trifone (eds), *Storia della lingua italiana*. Vol. II. *Scritto e parlato* (Turin, Einaudi, 1994), pp. 703–49.
Malaspina, T., 'Sono nevrile, non difficoltatemi. Nuovi linguaggi: il Berlusconese', *L'Espresso*, 11 March 1994, pp. 54–6.
McCarthy, P., 'Silvio Berlusconi': la parola crea l'Uomo Politico', *Europa Europe*, 3:3 (1994), pp. 241–56.
McCarthy, P., 'Italy: a New Language for a New Politics?', *Journal of Modern Italian Studies*, 2:3 (1997), pp. 337–57.
Novelli, S., and G. Urbani, *Il dizionario italiano. Parole nuove della Seconda e Terza Repubblica* (Rome, Datanews, 1995).
Novelli, S., and G. Urbani, *Dizionario della Seconda Repubblica. Le parole nuove della politica* (Rome, Editori Riuniti, 1997).
Paccagnella, I., 'Retorica politica: gli interventi di Togliatti all'Internazionale nel 1926', in Various authors, *Attualità della retorica*, with preface by G. Folena (Padua, Liviana, 1975), pp. 169–86.
Pallotta, G., *Dizionario del politichese* (Milan, SugarCo, 1991).
Paradisi, E., 'Il discorso comunista del secondo dopoguerra', in Various authors, *La lingua italiana in movimento* (Florence, Accademia della Crusca, 1982), pp. 195–213.
Pedemonte, E., 'Neolinguaggi: Sparlare verdese', *L'Espresso*, 22 September 1991, pp. 78–84.
Reboul, O., *Le Slogan* (Brussels, Complexe, 1975).
Rigotti, F., *Metafore della politica* (Bologna, Il Mulino, 1989).
Rigotti, F., *Il potere e le sue metafore* (Milan, Feltrinelli, 1992).
Rosiello, L., *et al.*, *La lingua italiana e il Fascismo* (Bologna, Consorzio provinciale di pubblica lettura, 1977).
Salaris, C., *Il Movimento del Settantasette. Linguaggi e scritture dell'ala creativa* (Bertiolo [Udine], AAA Edizioni, 1997).
Semino, E., and M. Masci, 'Politics is Football: Metaphor in the Discourse of Silvio Berlusconi in Italy', *Discourse and Society*, 7:2 (1996), pp. 243–69.
Sensini, A., *Caro Silvio, caro Massimo. La neolingua della politica* (Rome, RTM, 1997). On the language of Berlusconi and D'Alema.
Sobrero, A. A., 'Lingue speciali', in A. A. Sobrero (ed.), *Introduzione all'italiano contemporaneo*. Vol. II. *La variazione e gli usi* (Bari and Rome, Laterza, 1993), pp. 237–77.
Squarcione, M., 'Occhetto e Berlusconi. Percorsi linguistici e strategie argomentative', in M. Morcellini (ed.), *Elezioni di TV. Televisione e pubblico nella campagna elettorale '94* (Genoa, Costa & Nolan, 1995), pp. 163–90.
Violi, P., *I giornali dell'estrema sinistra* (Milan, Garzanti, 1977).

Terrorism

Apter, D. E., 'Political Violence in Analytical Perspective', in D. E. Apter, (ed.), *The Legitimization of Violence* (Basingstoke, Macmillan, and Rome, UNSDRI, 1997), pp. 1–32.
Battaglini, M., and V. Boraccetti (eds), *Eversione di destra, terrorismo, stragi* (Milan, Franco Angeli, 1986).
Bianconi, G., *A mano armata. Vita violenta di Giusva Fioravanti terrorista neofascista quasi per caso* (Milan, Baldini & Castoldi, 1996).
Boatti, G., *Piazza Fontana. 12 dicembre 1969: il giorno dell'innocenza perduta* (Turin, Einaudi, 1999).
Braghetti, A. L., *Il prigioniero* (Milan, Mondadori, 1998). On Moro's captivity.
Calvi, F., and F. Laurent, *Piazza Fontana. La verità su una strage* (Milan, Mondadori, 1997).
Catanzaro, R. (ed.), *La politica della violenza* (Bologna, Il Mulino, 1990).
Catanzaro, R. (ed.), *The Red Brigades and Left-wing Terrorism in Italy* (London, Pinter, 1991).
Corsini, P., and L. Novati (eds), *L'eversione nera. Cronache di un decennio, 1974–84* (Milan, Franco Angeli, 1985).

De Lutiis, G., *Il lato oscuro del potere. Associazioni politiche e strutture paramilitari segrete dal 1946 ad oggi* (Rome, Editori Riuniti, 1996).
Della Porta, D., *Il terrorismo di sinistra* (Bologna, Il Mulino, 1990).
Della Porta, D., *Social Movements. Political Violence and the State* (Cambridge University Press, 1995).
Dianese, M., and G. Bettin, *La strage. Piazza Fontana: verità e memoria* (Milan, Feltrinelli, 1999).
Dini, V., and L. Marconi, *Il discorso delle armi. L'ideologia terroristica nel linguaggio delle Brigate Rosse e di Prima Linea* (Rome, Savelli, 1981).
Drake, R., *The Revolutionary Mystique and Terrorism in Contemporary Italy* (Bloomington, IN, Indiana University Press, 1989).
Ferraresi, F., *Threats to Democracy. The Radical Right in Italy after the War* (Princeton University Press, 1996).
Flamigni, S., *Convergenze parallele. Le Brigate Rosse, i servizi segreti e il delitto Moro* (Milan, KAOS, 1998).
Franceschini, A., *Mara, Renato e io. Storia dei fondatori delle BR* (Milan, Mondadori, 1988).
Lumley, R., *States of Emergency. Cultures of Revolt in Italy from 1968 to 1978* (London, Verso, 1990).
Medici, M., 'Nel ventre del mostro. Le caratteristiche stilistiche e le fonti di ispirazione dei volantini prodotti dal terrorismo italiano', *Italiano e oltre*, 5:1 (1990), pp. 17–30.
Merkl, P. H. (ed.), *Political Violence and Terror. Motifs and Motivations* (Berkeley, CA, and London, University of California Press, 1986).
Moss, D., *The Politics of Left-wing Violence in Italy, 1969–85* (Basingstoke, Macmillan, 1989).
Moss, D., 'Politics, Violence, Writing. Rituals of Armed Struggle in Italy', in D. E. Apter (ed.), *The Legitimization of Violence* (Basingstoke, Macmillan, and Rome, UNSDRI, 1997), pp. 83–127.
Novelli, D., and N. Tranfaglia (eds), *Vite sospese. Le generazioni del terrorismo* (Milan, Garzanti, 1988).
Rossanda, R., 'Sequestro e uccisione di Aldo Moro', in M. Isnenghi (ed.), *I luoghi della memoria. Strutture ed eventi dell'Italia unita* (Bari and Rome, Laterza, 1997), pp. 495–513.
Schmid, A., and R. Crelinsten (eds), *Western Responses to Terrorism* (London, Frank Cass, 1993).
Stajano, C., *L'Italia nichilista. Il caso Donat-Cattin, la rivolta, il potere* (Milan, Mondadori, 1982).
Tarrow, S., *Democracy and Disorder. Protest and Politics in Italy, 1969–75* (Oxford, Clarendon Press, 1989).
Tessandori, V., *BR. Imputazione: banda armata* (Milan, Baldini & Castoldi, 2000).
Tranfaglia, N., 'Un capitolo del "doppio stato". La stagione delle stragi e dei terrorismi, 1969–84', *Storia dell'Italia repubblicana*. Vol. 3/2. *L'Italia nella crisi mondiale. L'ultimo ventennio. Istituzioni, politiche, culture*, ed. F. Barbagallo (Turin, Einaudi, 1997), pp. 5–80.
Violante, L. (ed.), *Storia d'Italia. Annali 12. La criminalità* (Turin, Einaudi, 1997), especially: I. Pezzini, 'La figura del criminale nella letteratura, nel cinema e in televisione', pp. 65–120; D. Della Porta, 'Il terrorismo', pp. 371–420; G. De Lutiis, 'L'omicidio politico e la sua protezione (1945–95)', pp. 493–522; F. Ferraresi, 'La strage di Piazza Fontana', pp. 619–81.
Wagner-Pacifici, R., *The Moro Morality Play. Terrorism as Social Drama* (University of Chicago Press, 1986).
Weinberg, L., and W. L. Eubank, *The Rise and Fall of Italian Terrorism* (London, Westview Press, 1987).
Willan, P., *Puppetmasters. The Political Use of Terrorism in Italy* (London, Constable, 1991).

Satire

Altan, F., *Animo, Cipputi*, introduction by L. Tornabuoni (Milan, Bompiani, 1977).
Anon., 'La satira razzista', in D. Bidussa *et al.*, *La menzogna della razza. Documenti e immagini del razzismo e dell'antisemitismo fascista* (Bologna, Grafis, 1994), pp. 147–61.
Bergamasco, F., *L'Italia in caricatura* (Rome, Newton & Compton, 1995).

Brilli, A., *Dalla satira alla caricatura* (Bari, Dedalo, 1985).
Bucchi, M., *Storie di pazzi* (Milan, Mondadori, 1991).
Chiappori, A., *Padroni e padrini* (Milan, Feltrinelli, 1974).
Chiesa, A., *La satira politica in Italia*, introduction by T. Pericoli (Bari and Rome, Laterza, 1990).
Chiesa, A., 'La stampa satirica e i vignettisti', in V. Castronovo and N. Tranfaglia (eds), *La stampa italiana nell'età della TV, 1975–94* (Bari and Rome, Laterza, 1994).
Davidson, S., *The Penguin Book of Political Comics* (Harmondsworth, Penguin, 1982).
Di Castro, F., *et al.*, *Satira e attualità politica. 41 disegnatori dal 1914 al 1981* (Milan, Electa, 1981).
Del Buono, O., and L. Tornabuoni (eds), *Il Becco Giallo, 1924–31* (Milan, Feltrinelli, 1972).
Fossati, F., *Guida al fumetto satirico e politico* (Milan, Gammalibri, 1979).
Franchi, S., *'Tango' e il PCI. Comunisti e satira nell' Italia del dopoguerra* (Soviera Mannelli [Cosenza], Rubbettino, 2000).
Gianeri, E., and A. Rauch, *Cento anni di satira politica in Italia, 1876–1976* (Florence, Guaraldi, 1976).
Gombrich, E. H., 'The Cartoonist's Armoury', in *Meditations on a Hobby Horse* (London, Phaidon, 1971), pp. 120–42.
Gombrich, E. H., 'The Experiment of Caricature', in *Art and Illusion* (Oxford, Phaidon, 1977), pp. 279–303.
Hillier, B., *Cartoons and Caricatures* (London, Studio Vista, 1970).
Leparulo, W. E., 'La caricatura come critica del costume: radice umoristica essenziale dei racconti di Giovannino Guareschi', in A. Franceschetti (ed.), *Letteratura italiana e arti figurative* (Florence, Olschki, 1988), pp. 1185–91.
Lepre, A., *La guerra delle matite. La satira in Italia dal 1940 al 1943* (Naples, Liguori, 1990).
Lopez Nunes, S., *Abbasso il fassio. La satira politica nel Ventennio* (Milan, Baldini & Castoldi, 1999).
Mojetta, A. M. (ed.), *Cento anni di satira anticlericale* (Milan, SugarCo, 1975).
Pericoli, T., *Cronache dal Palazzo*, introduction by C. Cederna (Milan, Mondadori, 1979).
Ratano, F., *La satira italiana nel dopoguerra* (Messina and Florence, D'Anna, 1976).
Venè, G. F., *La satira politica* (Milan, SugarCo, 1976).

Music

Accademia degli Scrausi, *Versi rock. La lingua della canzone italiana negli anni '80 e '90* (Milan, Rizzoli, 1996).
Baldazzi, G., *La canzone italiana del Novecento* (Rome, Newton & Compton, 1989).
Bermani, C., *Una storia cantata, 1962–97. Trentacinque anni di attività del Nuovo Canzoniere Italiano* (Milan, Istituto Ernesto De Martino/Jaca Book, 1997).
Berselli, E., 'Politics and Karaoke', in R. S. Katz and P. Ignazi (eds), *Italian Politics. The Year of the Tycoon* (Oxford, Westview Press, 1996), pp. 183–94.
Berselli, E., *Canzoni. Storia dell'Italia leggera* (Bologna, Il Mulino, 1999).
Borgna, G., *Storia della canzone italiana*, preface by T. De Mauro (Bari and Rome, Laterza, 1985).
Borgna, G., *L'Italia di Sanremo. Cinquant'anni di canzoni, cinquant' anni della nostra storia* (Milan, Mondadori, 1998).
Borgna, G., and S. Dessì, *C'era una volta una gatta. I cantautori degli anni '60* (Rome, Savelli, 1977).
Branzaglia, C., *et al.*, *Posse italiane, centri sociali, underground musicale e cultura giovanile in Italia* (Florence, Tosca, 1992).
Carrera, A., *Musica e pubblico giovanile. L'evoluzione del gusto musicale dagli anni Sessanta ad oggi* (Milan, Feltrinelli, 1980).
Castaldo, G. (ed.), *Il dizionario della canzone italiana*, foreword by R. Arbore and musical annexes by P. Prato (Rome, Curcio, 1990).
Castaldo, G., *La terra promessa. Quarant'anni di cultura rock, 1954–94* (Milan, Feltrinelli, 1994).

Cavallo, P., and P. Iaccio, *Vincere! Vincere! Vincere! Fascismo e società italiana nelle canzoni e nelle riviste di varietà, 1935–43* (Rome, Ianua, 1981).
Currà, A., G. Vettori and R. Vinci, *Canti della protesta femminile* (Rome, Newton & Compton, 1977).
Dazieri, S., *Italia overground. Mappe e reti della cultura alternativa* (Rome, Castelvecchi, 1996).
De Grassi, G., *Mille papaveri rossi. Storia d'Italia attraverso la canzone politica* (Bologna, Fuori Thema, 1991).
Dessì, S., and G. Pintor (eds), *La chitarra e il potere. Gli autori della canzone politica contemporanea* (Rome, Savelli, 1976).
Ferretti, G. L., M. Zamboni and A. Campo, *Fedeli alla linea. Dai CCCP ai CSI* (Florence, Giunti, 1997).
Filippa, M., 'Popular Songs and Musical Cultures', in D. Forgacs and R. Lumley (eds), *Italian Cultural Studies. An Introduction* (Oxford University Press, 1996), pp. 327–43.
Finardi, E., *Canzoni d'amore e di rabbia* (Milan, Lombardi, 1992).
Franzina, E., 'Inni e canzoni', in M. Isnenghi (ed.), *I luoghi della memoria. Simboli e miti dell'Italia unita* (Bari and Rome, Laterza, 1996), pp. 117–62.
Giannotti, M., *Sanremo: fermate quel Festival! Dietro le quinte del più popolare evento musicale italiano* (Florence, Tarab, 1998).
Guichard, J., *La chanson dans la culture italienne. Des origines populaires aux débuts du rock* (Paris, Champion, 1999).
Guichard, J. (ed.), *Regards sur la chanson italienne contemporaine*, special issue of *Franco-Italica* (University of Chambéry/University of Turin), 12 (1997). Published in 1999.
Jachia, P., *La canzone d'autore italiana, 1958–97* (Milan, Feltrinelli, 1998).
Jona, E., and M. L. Straniero, *Cantacronache. Un'avventura politico-musicale degli anni Cinquanta* (Turin, Scriptorium/Paravia, 1995); with CD.
Leydi, R., *Canti sociali italiani* (Milan, Edizioni Avanti!, 1963).
Leydi, R., 'La canzone popolare'. 1. 'La possibile storia di una canzone (Bella Ciao!)', in R. Romano and C. Vivanti (eds), *Storia d'Italia.* Vol. 5/2. *I documenti* (Turin, Einaudi, 1973), pp. 1183–97.
Luperi, F., *Storia della canzone italiana* (Rome, RAI–ERI, 1999).
Madera, R. (ed.), *Ma non è una malattia. Canzoni e movimento giovanile* (Rome, Savelli, 1970).
Marchi, V., *Nazi-Rock. Pop music e Destra radicale* (Rome, Castelvecchi, 1997).
Mimma, G., *L'industria della canzone* (Rome, Editori Riuniti, 1981).
Mingati, F., 'Jukebox Boys: Postwar Italian Music and the Culture of Covering', in H. Fehrenbach and V. G. Poiger (eds), *Transactions, Trangressions, Transformations, American Culture in Western Europe and Japan* (Oxford, Berghahn, 2000), pp. 148–65.
Pacoda, P. (ed.), *Potere alla parola. Antologia del rap italiano* (Milan, Feltrinelli, 1996).
Perris, A., *Music as Propaganda. Art to Persuade, Art to Control* (Norwich, CT, Greenwood, 1986).
Piccinini, A., *Fratellini d'Italia. Mappe, stili, parole dell'ultima generazione* (Rome, Theoria, 1994).
Rauti, I., L. Romagnoli and M. L. Veca, *L'arpa e la spada. Inni e canzoni di rivolta nazionale e popolare*, foreword by Pino Rauti (Rome, Movimento Sociale Fiamma Tricolore, n.d. [1997]).
Saffioti, T., *Enciclopedia della canzone popolare e della nuova canzone politica*, foreword by M. L. Straniero (Milan, Teti, 1978).
Savona, V., and M. L. Straniero, *I canti dell'Italia fascista, 1919–45* (Milan, Garzanti, 1978).
Straniero, M. L., *et al.*, *Le canzoni della cattiva coscienza. La musica leggera in Italia*, preface by U. Eco (Milan, Bompiani, 1964).
Straniero, M. L., *Cento canti politici e sociali da 'Addio Lugano bella' a 'Contessa'* (Milan, Gammalibri, 1984).
Straniero, M. L., *Mira il tuo Pop. Origini e peripezie del canto cristiano* (Milan, Mondadori, 1988).
Various authors, *Canzoniere della protesta* (Milan, Edizioni Bella Ciao, 1972–77), 6 vols.
Various authors, *Il Nuovo Canzoniere italiano dal 1962 al 1968*, preface by C. Bermani (Milan, Mazzotta, 1978).
Vettori, G. (ed.), *Canzoni italiane di protesta, 1794–1974* (Rome, Newton & Compton, 1976).

Dress

Amendola, E. P., *Storia fotografica del PCI* (Rome, Editori Riuniti, 1981), vol. 2.

Barthes, R., *The Fashion System* (London, Cape, 1985).

Bevilacqua, E., *Guida alla Beat Generation* (Rome, Theoria, 1994).

Bonami, F., M. L. Frisa, and S. Tonchi (eds), *Uniforme. Ordine e disordine, 1950–2000* (Milan, Charta, 2001).

Bottero, A., *Il potere e la moda* (Milan, Il Pungolo, 1990).

Brusatin, M., *Storia dei colori* (Turin, Einaudi, 1993).

Butazzi, G., and A. Mottola Molfino, *L'uniforme borghese* (Novara, De Agostini, 1991).

Calefato, P., *Moda, corpo, mito. Storia, mitologia e ossessione del corpo vestito* (Rome, Castelvecchi, 1999).

Calefato, P., G. Ceriani and M. P. Pozzato, *La moda. Analisi semiotiche* (Urbino, Documenti e pre-pubblicazioni dell'Università di Urbino, 1993).

D'Amico, T., *Storia fotografica della società italiana. Gli anni ribelli, 1968–80* (Rome, Editori Riuniti, 1998).

Davis, F., *Fashion, Culture, Identity* (University of Chicago Press, 1992).

Descamps, M. A., *Psicologia della moda* (Rome, Editori Riuniti, 1979).

Donadio, F., and M. Giannotti, *Teddy-boys, rockettari e cyberpunk* (Rome, Editori Riuniti, 1996).

El Guindi, F., *Veil. Modesty, Privacy and Resistance* (Oxford, Berg, 1999).

Filkestein, J., *The Fashioned Self* (Oxford, Polity Press, 1991).

Giorgetti, C., 'La contromoda', in *Manuale di storia del costume e della moda* (Florence, Cantini, 1992), pp. 420–39.

Giorgetti, C., and E. Colarullo, *La moda maschile dal 1600 al 1990* (Florence, Octavo, 1994).

Grandi, R., and G. Ceriani (eds), *Moda. Regole e rappresentazioni* (Milan, Franco Angeli, 1995).

Grandi, S., A. Vaccari and S. Zannier, *La moda del secondo dopoguerra* (Bologna, CLUEB, 1993).

Harvey, J. R., *Men in Black* (London, Reaktion, 1997).

Hollander, A., *Seeing through Clothes* (Berkeley, CA, University of California Press, 1993).

Joseph, N., *Uniforms and Non-uniforms. Communication through Clothing* (New York, Greenwood Press, 1996).

Kaiser, S., 'La politica e l'estetica dello stile delle apparenze', in P. Calefato (ed.), *Moda e mondanità* (Bari, Palomar, 1992), pp. 165–84.

Köning, R., *Il potere della moda* (Naples, Liguori, 1992).

Lakoff, R. T., and R. Scherr, *Face Value: the Politics of Beauty* (London, Routledge, 1984).

Lambin, R. A., *Le voile des femmes. Un inventaire historique, social et psychologique* (Berne, Peter Lang, 1999).

Lurie, A., *The Language of Clothing* (London, Bloomsbury, 1992).

Mambri, S., *Cosmesi. Un'arte per la bellezza* (Florence, Loggia De' Lanzi, 1995).

Morace, F., *Controtendenze. Una nuova cultura del consumo* (Milan, Domus Academy, 1990).

O'Hara, G., *Dizionario della moda. I protagonisti, i movimenti, i segni, le parole: tutto ciò che fa moda dal 1840 ai giorni nostri*, eds R. Panuzzo and J. Valli (Bologna, Zanichelli, 1990).

Polhemus, T., *Bodystyles* (Luton, Lennard, 1988).

Polhemus, T., 'Il vestito postmoderno', in M. P. Pozzato (ed.), *Estetica e vita quotidiana* (Milan, Lupetti, 1995), pp. 123–9.

Squicciarino, N., *Il vestito parla. Considerazioni psicosociologiche sull'abbigliamento* (Rome, Armando, 1986).

Tarlo, E., *Clothing Matters. Dress and Identity in India* (London, Hurst, 1996).

Various authors, *La moda italiana* (Milan, Electa, 1987), 2 vols.

Zaleto, L. (ed.), *L'abito della Rivoluzione* (Venice, Marsilio, 1987).

Index

Note: 'n.' after page reference indicates a note number on that page.